Excursion, as ... I have been wholly unable to carry out my intention of visiting schools; — there could not even have been time to make the preliminary arrangements. The schools I have visited were most interesting & will supply copy for a long series of articles in the Claidheamh. Some of the large city schools are like large hotels — only finer & more spacious than any hotel in Dublin, or for that matter in London, Paris, or Brussels. The rural schools are more like our own at home.

I write to you rather than to Seosamh Ua Muantain, in order I make sure of catching you in good time, as Fionan may not call at the office on Thursday morning, when this is due.

Tá . mé agam go bfuil mé ag fás go maić, 7 raċ ráṡfaiḋ mé ḋín ar néo leo oiḋçe to cup ofaił.

Miṡe, 7 ḋeifip an ṡiaḃul opm,
to éupa go buan,
Pádpaic Mac Piapar.

P.S. — ... az oḃaip ap fuaś an lae óṅ óċ a ḋloż ap maiṡin go uṫ a ṫé ṫé a ḟaiċ tpáṫóna.

THE LETTERS OF P. H. PEARSE

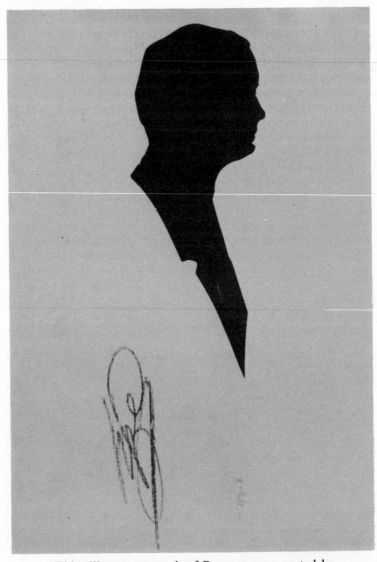

This silhouette portrait of Pearse was executed by
a lightning artist on the top of the Woolworth
Skyscraper, New York, in April 1914.

THE LETTERS

OF

P. H. PEARSE

edited

Séamas Ó Buachalla

with a foreword by

F. S. L. Lyons
Provost, Trinity College, Dublin

COLIN SMYTHE
Gerrards Cross, 1980

Copyright © 1980 Séamas Ó Buachalla

First published in 1980 by Colin Smythe Ltd.,
P.O. Box 6, Gerrards Cross, Buckinghamshire

British Library Cataloguing in Publication Data

Pearse, Patrick Henry
   The letters of P. H. Pearse, 1897–1916.
   1. Pearse, Patrick Henry
   2. Revolutionists—Ireland—Correspondence
   I. Ó Buachalla, Séamas
   941.7082′1′0924   DA965.P4

ISBN 0–901072–87–7

Printed in Great Britain
Set, printed and bound by Billing & Sons Limited,
Guildford, London and Worcester

Contents

Foreword

In this centenary year of the birth of Patrick Pearse there is certain to be much reassessment of the man and of his contribution to Irish history. This reassessment will doubtless involve some recoil from the romantic view of Pearse which dominated most writing about him for fifty years after his death, but the recoil will be as misleading as the myth it replaces if it does not take account of Pearse as he was rather than as his heirs and exploiters would wish to present him to us.

Pearse "as he was" has been hard to get at chiefly because the biographical information about him has been deficient and unsatisfactory. Séamas Ó Buachalla has therefore rendered an outstanding service by collecting from the most diverse sources Pearse's letters, which run from 1897 to within a few moments of his execution before a firing-squad in May 1916. It is a larger correspondence than we could have dared to hope for and it is peculiarly valuable because it deals not only with each phase of his career but with each facet of a life which was dedicated with an almost monastic austerity to the cause of Irish freedom.

Mr. Ó Buachalla in his introduction explains very clearly the nature and variety of the letters. Here it is enough to point to their most outstanding feature and the one which will surprise many readers – the rigorous exclusion of the poet and dreamer from a scene dominated by the able organiser and the devoted, if sometimes also distraught, headmaster.

The letters are for the most part extremely down-to-earth and as such they are bound to change the popular view of Pearse. In doing so, however, they will not diminish his reputation; rather will they place it on a firmer and more credible basis. These are the letters of a man who knew exactly where he was going and what he was doing, a characteristic in itself sufficient to set him apart from the great majority of his Irish contemporaries. He was, in short, a natural leader who had not many illusions about his fellow-workers but yet knew how to manipulate men and circumstances for his own ends.

The ends were not personal in any obvious or ordinary sense. Whether he was writing about the Gaelic League, or manoeuvring to become editor of the League's paper, *An Claidheamh Soluis,* or running his two famous schools, St. Enda's and St. Ita's, he is always a man with a mission transcending self. He is also a mercifully clear and crisp correspondent, seldom writing lengthy letters unless driven to extremity. His particular extremity was always financial and right up to the outbreak of the Easter Rising he was fighting like a tiger to keep St. Enda's solvent, though he had been unable to avoid closing St. Ita's several years earlier.

The view of him as a brilliant and forward-looking headmaster can only be enhanced by the publication of the letters which bring out repeatedly his attention to detail, his meticulousness in money matters, and above all his personal knowledge of and affection for the boys under his care.

Affection, by his own account, was something he did not readily extend to adults. In a letter to himself written under a pseudonym he published a singularly disenchanted view of his own character and although this was partly in jest we are left with an uneasy feeling that he was cutting very close to the bone. "I am undecided," he says, "as to whether I like you or not. I wonder does anyone like you. I do know many that dislike you. I never heard anyone say 'I like Pearse' ... Pearse, you are a reserved person! You do not associate with Gaels. You shun their company. On the occasions when you join them, a black cloud accompanies you which as it were settles over them. Those who were talkative before your arrival grow silent and those who were merry become gloomy. I wonder if it is the English blood in you which is responsible for that?"

Even within the family, though it was a close-knit family, this reserve was evident, haunting him until the last hours of his life. In one of the poems written for his mother – it is called "To My Mother" – just before his execution, he says:

> O mother (for you know me)
> You must have known, when I was silent,
> That some strange thing within me kept me dumb,
> Some strange, deep thing, when I should shout my love,
> I have sobbed in secret
> For that reserve which yet I could not master.

It was different with crowds, as well he knew, and different also with revolutionary conspiracy where his voice and influence were so persuasive. Naturally enough, this part of his life did not produce many letters. Very little was put on paper for his immediate colleagues with whom he was in daily contact. Of the relatively few political letters in this collection some of the most important are addressed to Irish–American sympathisers, especially his friend and benefactor, Joseph McGarrity. They are severely practical, being concerned mostly with requests for arms and money. Only once do we catch a glimpse of Pearse the platform-orator whose apocalyptic vision did so much to create the atmosphere of the Easter Rising. When the Howth gun-running of 1914 was followed immediately by the killing of civilians by the troops at Bachelor's Walk in Dublin, Pearse at once saw the significance of the incident which, he wrote to McGarrity, had given public sentiment "just that turn that was desirable ... The whole movement, the whole country, has been rebaptised by blood shed for Ireland".

Yet the very fact that this is an untypical letter is perhaps the most important thing about it. Future biographers will have to weigh this pragmatic correspondence against the flamboyance, sometimes even the barely suppressed hysteria of Pearse's published writings from 1914 onwards. In doing so perhaps they will come at last to a balanced view about a man whose letters no less than his actions stamp him as one of the most remarkable creators of the Irish revolution.

F. S. L. Lyons

1979

TO
EILÍS
NIAMH and SINÉAD

Introduction

The letters presented in this volume, over four hundred in number, cover the period in Pearse's life from the year after he left school, 1897, literally to the eve of his execution in May 1916. They cover all aspects of his public life in turn, the Gaelic League, his editorship of *An Claidheamh Soluis*, his eight demanding years at St. Enda's and his political activity from 1912 to the Rising; there are also some letters, though not many, of a personal nature. The letters reveal the earnest, sensitive student and the dedicated committee member, the hard-pressed editor and the crusading leader writer, the headmaster with a remarkable innovative concept of the educative process and the demented school manager seeking funds to ensure the continuity of his school. In the political field, the complex web of intrigue and allegiance which characterised the period from 1912 onwards, is conveyed by the letters and the quickened pulse of his own political life is clearly evident in the letters written during and after the American tour of 1914.

Those letters written before 1908 refer mainly to various aspects of the work of the Gaelic League; its publishing work with which he was involved, the weekly bilingual journal, its educational policy in the formation of which he participated and a number of projects concerning the social economy of the Irish-speaking districts. One is made keenly aware in the letters of the internal politics of the League and of the various personality clashes; Pearse's letters in 1903 in connection with his campaign for the editorship of *An Claidheamh Soluis*, reveal an appreciation of the political reality and a capacity to operate that reality to his advantage. As secretary of the Publications Committee of the League, he was regularly in correspondence with J. J. Doyle, and Enri Ó Muirgheasa (H. Morris), two authors whose work the Committee published and who were also local leaders of the League; Archbishop Walsh of Dublin was also a regular correspondent at that time, in his dual capacity of Commissioner of National Education and League supporter. Besides this trio who were the principal recipients he also corresponded with Edward Martyn, Dr. S. O'Kelly who was later medical consultant to St. Enda's, Fr. John Myles O'Reilly of Clare Island and Colonel Maurice Moore in relation to League affairs.

His letters to Pádraig Ó Domhnalláin in 1903 show a sensitivity to others in his practical approach to the plight of Colm de Bhailís, the poet, who was then in the workhouse.

On becoming editor of *An Claidheamh Soluis* in 1903 the range of his correspondence widened considerably; his editorial office brought him into touch with members of the Gaelic League and others from all parts of the country and involved him in issues which hitherto had not arisen in his work on the Publications Committee. His correspondents include in addition to authors and League members, friends in Belfast, where he had many contacts, contributors to *An Claidheamh* in each of the provinces and in London, the editor of a national daily newspaper, teachers and school managers and younger writers whom he was encouraging to develop their writing skills and contribute to the paper. When away from Dublin in this period, either in Ireland or in Belgium, he wrote regularly to Séan T. Ó Ceallaigh, the paper's capable manager, ensuring that copy and proofs are handled with dispatch and on one occasion, seeking to keep an edition of the paper from certain named Dublin artists lest they be offended by a review of their exhibition! In one of his letters to the exiled poet and writer, Tomás Ó Flannghaile, he answers a query from the latter concerning the ecclesiastical status of the lexicographer, Fr. Dineen, with an answer which is the essence of prudence and tact. One can sense in the letters of this period the widening of his social horizons which accompanied his enhanced position within the League. In a remarkable letter to Dr. Séamas O'Kelly, written on St. Stephen's Day 1904, he recounts the topics of conversation from the dinner table in Belfast to which he had been invited to meet Cardinal Logue; in doing so he shows a distinct capacity for interpreting social situations and for the analysis of the political stances being adopted. One of the interesting minor topics in his letters concerns his wish to launch an Irish based trade union for journalists; he floated this proposal to some experienced journalists in 1905. He utilised the combined resources of his own correspondents around the country and the columns of *An Claidheamh* to operate an employment bureau for girls from the Irish-speaking areas; in 1907 he and some of his correspondents formed a committee under the chairmanship of Dr. Michael F. Cox to organise a health education programme on tuberculosis in Connemara.

The letters of a more personal kind, are mainly written to people whom he met through his Gaelic League activities; frequently these personal letters deal with matters tangentially related to language or educational issues. He is frequently consulted on the correct forms of Irish names for children or houses; one such letter to Miss

xii

Brownrigg, a Church of Ireland teacher, is unusually chatty and is accompanied by a gift copy of his book *Three Lectures on Gaelic Topics*. That same tone of easy friendliness is consistently present in his letters to Mrs. Margaret Hutton, the Belfast Celtic scholar and translator of the *Táin*, who later came to live in Dublin and whom he invited to take charge of Sgoil Íde. As his status in the educational world grew, he was in demand as a referee especially among Gaelic League teachers desiring positions in the giving of the Commissioners. Máire Níc Shíthigh of Clonakilty was one such teacher whom he also encouraged to write for *An Claidheamh*. The letters contain only a few references to the business or to stone cutting possibly because the family were now about to part with the firm established by James Pearse. Two of the earliest letters concern a stone tablet which the firm designed and inscribed for Liosdúnáin National School near Carrickmacross, where his friend Enri Ó Muirgheasa presided. Sculpture figures also in some later letters to Margaret Hutton when his opinion was asked on the Irish form of the inscription for a bust of Cardinal Logue which was exhibited at the Royal Academy. When his friend and League colleague, Stiofán Bairéad, asked him to be godfather to his daughter Sighle, he was evidently pleased and regular letters accompanying appropriate gifts are full of a joyful seriousness.

There are some surprising aspects to the correspondence for this period before the opening of St. Enda's; very few letters to his family survive. Given the frequency with which he was away from home one would have expected him to have written to his mother, Margaret or Willie; there are no such letters surviving. There are other lacunae too in the surviving correspondence. Mary Hayden, the historian, was a close friend of his from his early League days – they went on holidays together. We know that she wrote to him frequently when away from Dublin, yet there are no letters from him to her which survive. Peadar Mac Fhionnlaoigh (Cú Uladh) was a senior member of the Gaelic League who was a collaborator with Pearse in many activities before 1908; there are no surviving letters from Pearse to him except in relation to the school.

Early in 1908 the school begins to emerge in his correspondence as he discloses his plan and seeks guarantees of support from friends and from parents of potential pupils. In this period prior to the opening of St. Enda's, he carried a very heavy work load and he also faced some important decisions involving financial and occupational consequences for himself. While still editing *An Claidheamh Soluis*, which he continued to do until autumn 1909, he was busy supervising the publication of Eoghan Ó Neachtain's *Euclid* and Enri Ó Muirgheasa's *Sean-Fhocla Uladh* and *Greann na Gaeilge.* He finds time however to express his sympathy to a friend on the death of an infant and says that he has some awareness of the sorrow and heartbreak involved though he is not himself a parent.

In canvassing support for his Irish high school, Pearse outlined in detail his educational philosophy and his reasons for seeking to establish St. Enda's and he enclosed with these letters a memorandum on the school organisation he proposed; the letter to Patrick McManus in March 1908 is typical of these letters. His earlier approaches in February to the wealthy Catholic landlord Edward Martyn, brought sympathy but no explicit support despite Pearse's offer of generous collateral security involving his house, his cottage in Connemara and an insurance policy on his own life. Judging by the correspondence that has survived, Pearse had very little concrete guarantee of support when he decided to establish the school; he was dependent on his own meagre resources and the proceeds derived from the closure of his father's firm. His plans, which involved the printing of an impressive bilingual prospectus, must have been adequately advanced by mid-August when he left Dublin for a holiday in the west.

Once the school opened in September 1908 at Cullenswood House, Pearse's correspondence took on a new pattern in which the affairs of the school in all its aspects predominated and in which Gaelic League business declined gradually. The two main categories are those concerned with the financial affairs of the school and letters to the parents of pupils embodying in some cases formal and informal reports. In the first year there was a sustained correspondence with Archbishop Walsh, by which Pearse sought to clarify the situation of the school chaplain, and in which he kept the Archbishop informed on the progress of the school. The letters show that his financial difficulties began to appear early in 1909; the slender capital base on which he opened and the renovations and extensions which he carried out during the Christmas vacation caused a crisis in January which prompted him to write to Joseph Dolan of Ardee who, as he did on other occasions, came to his aid with a generous loan. During the following year, the transfer of the school to the Hermitage, Rathfarnham in August, colours most of his correspondence. The letters and circulars which he sent to his friends seeking support for the move, show that he had set his heart on the fifty-acre estate and mansion. The response to his appeal permitted him to lease the property and to proceed with the essential building required. Most of his contributors gave small amounts; few were as generous as the sisters of The O'Rahilly who between them contributed a third of the rent and insisted on

xiv

anonymity. Towards the end of 1910 he wishes to hold a meeting of those who contributed, possibly with a view to forming a limited company, which was indeed set up in 1911 and later liquidated. Throughout the entire correspondence, Pearse conveys in his letters on financial affairs a devastating frankness and a simple persuasiveness which combine to enable his correspondents to share in his own conviction of the importance of his educational work at St. Enda's. Idealist he certainly was, but when he came to deal with the harsh reality of finance he was a practical realist. His financial arrangements became extremely complicated, yet his letters and records show a clear grasp of the situation; the financial statement which he prepared in 1914 as part of his testamentary papers, shows that he was by no means naïve in matters financial.

The letters concerning the non-financial aspects of the school reflect in their variety the extensive range of the school's activities and the fullness of the educational ethos which informed it. There are items relating to school fees, acknowledgements for same and some beseeching letters sent to reluctant or tardy parents; there are also the mundane domestic items concerned with ordering books, hurleys or replacement cylinders of the patent gas which illuminated the premises. On a higher aesthetic level there are the points of contact with Yeats and the theatrical movement, which brought the plays of Sgoil Éanna on to the stage of the Abbey Theatre and attracted the attention of critics like Pádraig Colum who wrote a play for one of the school productions. The Commissioners of Intermediate Education were the recipients of some interesting letters; he threatened law on them because the ambiguity of their rules almost cost Pearse's brilliant student, Denis Gwynn, his exhibition in 1910. Later he begged to differ with their examiners in English as to the marks accorded to some of his pupils and requested a review.

The letters to parents which include comments on the pupils, offer a very valuable picture of Pearse the headmaster and provide some indicators of his priorities as to educational outcomes. To him the academic performance is only one aspect of the educational process; consequently he gives as much prominence to the student's personal development and his social behaviour as to his academic record when reporting on him to parents. These reports and letters to parents are refreshingly varied in their terminology and in their personal style they would support his own assertion that he both knew and catered for each pupil in the school, as an individual.

There are two sets of letters which deserve some specific comment, the letters from *An Barr Buadh*, the short-lived weekly of 1912, and the letters which he wrote while in America in 1914.

Under the pseudonym of "Laegh Mac Riangabhra", Pearse wrote a series of letters to public figures and politicians and published them in the paper as "a bunch of letters which had been mislaid"! Each letter provides a frank analysis of the public life of the individual concerned and offers some salutary advice; the fact that he included a letter to himself in which he was equally frank, may have helped to raise the tolerance level among his correspondents. During his three months' absence in the United States to raise funds for St. Enda's in 1914, he maintained a regular correspondence with his brother Willie who was acting headmaster and with his mother. The familiar tone of these letters from America does not hide the serious purpose of his tour, to raise funds for the school; very few of the letters on either side of the correspondence fail to mention the financial situation. His great involvement with his pupils and his commitment to their welfare is expressed in the hortatory communique, entitled *To Sgoil Éanna*, which he addressed to the pupils from America in late March and which Willie read to the assembled pupils after the Easter vacation. His sojourn in America was made worthwhile by its financial success and was made memorable by the generous hospitality of Joe Mc Garrity of Philadelphia and by his meeting with relatives of his mother's family. The political situation at home was forcibly brought home to him in Celtic Park, New York, when a group of Redmondite Volunteers assaulted him on the platform; a letter in April expresses his gratitude to the Major Nolan who rescued him. There are however more lighthearted aspects to the American tour; he went to the top of the Woolworth skyscraper where he had his portrait taken, he was fascinated by Mc Garrity's automobiles and one of his students sent him shamrock across the Atlantic for St. Patrick's Day. Above all else when he sailed for home in May he had secured three American pupils for the school, one of whom accompanied him on the R.M.S. *Baltic.*

After the American tour, the political issues and the preparations for the Rising begin to dominate his correspondence. Already on the return journey he had written a letter to Devoy with a list of the Volunteer executive, which he mailed on landing at Cobh. He remained in regular contact with Clann na Gael in America, with Mc Garrity, Devoy and with Reidy; his mail at this time was being intercepted by the police and he tended to use a courier whenever possible – one such courier was Fr. Mc Garrity. At home, his correspondents now include Volunteer officers around the country, political associations wishing to engage him as a speaker at functions and, decreasingly, parents of pupils at the school.

His letters from the period immediately prior to the Rising

confirm the impression already created that Pearse was meticulous and systematic and that his growing political involvement did not diminish his systematic approach. In 1914 he had drawn up two testamentary statements, one financial, the other literary; these he had deposited with his former school friend and solicitor, Dan Maher. In the week before the Rising he wrote to the lady who had leased Cullenswood House instructing her to make the quarterly rent payable to his mother in his own absence from home as she was acting as his agent. He also corresponded with the publisher of his last political pamphlets, the series which he wrote between Christmas 1915 and the Rising, *The Separatist Idea, The Spiritual Nation* and *The Sovereign People*; he wished that they would be published and for sale by April 17th as a prelude to the Rising. On Easter Sunday evening, he found time, amidst the confusion caused by the MacNeill coutermand, to write a note enclosing a payment of five pounds to one of his creditors.

The letters and communiqués emanating from the G.P.O. during the Rising and the letters which Pearse wrote after the surrender are of special significance not because they are different from the rest of his correspondence but because they are so similar. They carry many of the same hallmarks which characterised his other letters except that the circumstances in which they were written heighten their poignancy. The letters written from Kilmainham on the eve of his execution display the same composure and balance which was evident in most of his letters. His final letters to his mother and his note to Willie are marked by a spontaneity which has triumphed over the approach of death, a spontaneity which spills over into the poems he composed for them.

In general, the letters which survive from Pearse's correspondence may not enable us to unravel fully his complex personality and character. They may however help to throw further light on many aspects of his career which heretofore were occluded by a simplified image, an image compounded of the pious poet, the militant visionary and "the crazy insolvent schoolmaster". The letters may not of themselves dispel all the elements of the stereotype; they may however show the man's life in a larger matrix where the Gaelic League's struggle for "the intellectual independence of Ireland", St. Enda's search for educational liberation and the desire for political separatism which inspired the Rising, all find a common point of convergence.

Editorial Note

This collection of the letters of Pearse is drawn from all the accessible sources, both institutional and private, which are known to the editor. Most of the transcription has been done from holographic materials or from authenticated photographic copies; a small number of letters were transcribed from published sources, where the holograph or copies were not available.

During the academic year 1911/12 and perhaps for most of 1912, Pearse drafted his correspondence in a large desk diary which has survived among his papers; it contains over two hundred items, very few of which are dated and the majority of which comprise routine letters and school reports to parents. Individual items from the desk diary which have been considered of significance, have been incorporated in this volume.

Of the letters collected, about one hundred were written totally in Irish and a further smaller number were bilingual. Those written in Irish have been collected separately and are presented in Appendix I, while a translation of each is inserted in the main body of the letters. Where bilingual letters occur, the Irish portions are translated in the accompanying headnotes. Both letters in Irish and bilingual items are identified as such in the text by the letters G and B respectively.

The annotational convention followed is based upon comprehensive headnotes; these contain relevant contextual comment and biographical material on those figures mentioned who do not merit individual biographical notes. The biographical notes in Appendix II cover not only the major personalities who figure in Pearse's correspondence but also those of his contemporaries who are significant in the cultural and political milieu of his period.

Each letter is identified and preceded by a three-element code, which includes the serial number allocated to the item in this collection, the archival source and where relevant a symbol to indicate that the letter was written in Irish; thus L. 151/NLI/G. Where postcards or telegrams occur this is indicated by bracketing the abbreviations pc. or tel. after the L and before the serial number.

The archival sources are indicated as follows:

(i)	N.L.I.	National Library of Ireland.
(ii)	N.M.I.	National Museum of Ireland.
(iii)	D.D.A.	Dublin Diocesan Archives.
(iv)	M.P.C.	Museum Poiblí Chorcaí.
(v)	S.C.M.	Sligo County Museum.
(vi)	O.C.S.	O'Connell School Museum.
(vii)	T.C.M.	Tipperary County Museum (Clonmel).
(viii)	P.R.O.	Public Record Office, Dublin.
(ix)	E.M.	Enniscorthy Museum.
(x)	P.Ms.	Manuscript in private ownership.
(xi)	D.D.	Pearse's Desk Diary.
(xii)	B.B.	An Barr Buadh.
(xiii)	P.S.	Published Sources.

The open letters which Pearse wrote to prominent figures in 1912 and which he published in *An Barr Buadh* as *Beart Litreach do Chuaidh Amugha* are included as offering a valuable perspective on his relationship with those figures at that critical time.

In some cases other documents were included with the original letters; where these have been traced and located, they have been included with the appropriate letter.

In arranging the letters in chronological order, some problems arose from a small number of undated items and from the letters selected from the Desk Diary which bore no date. It was possible in all such cases to arrive at a probable date from interal evidence and by reference to relevant dated items. Items which were undated but whose approximate date has been established, are located according to the established date in the chronological sequence: such approximate dates are enclosed in square brackets.

Pearse made frequent use of abbreviations in both his English and Irish manuscripts and he devised a personal shorthand scheme which he sometimes used in drafting his letters. Where any such abbreviations occur in the letters, they have been rectified; with this one exception the letters have been reproduced as written.

Acknowledgements

In locating, collecting and examining the letters in this volume, a project which has extended over a decade, I have been assisted and facilitated by many individuals and by the staffs of the libraries, archives and museums which have custody of relevant manuscript material. To all who were so generously co-operative and obliging, I am deeply grateful.

I wish to express my appreciation and gratitude to the Provost of Trinity College, Dr. F. S. L. Lyons, for finding time amidst a very heavy schedule to write the foreword to this volume.

I wish to record my special indebtedness to Éamonn de Barra and John Maher, Solr., joint trustees of the Pearse estate, to the Trustees of the National Library of Ireland, to Most Rev. Dr. D. Ryan, Archbishop of Dublin, to Phyllis Bean Uí Cheallaigh, to Síghle Bean Uí Dhonnchadha, to Rev. Br. W. P. Allen, O'Connell Schools, Dublin, to Mr. W. B. Bolger, to Mrs. Eibhlín Tierney, to Laisiríon agus Maedhbh Ní Mhuirgheasa, to Máirín Iníon Uí Dhomhnalláin, to A Shoillse, An Cairdinéal Tomás Ó Fiach, Ard-Easbog Ard Mhaca, to the late Cearbhall Ó Dálaigh, to the Rev. Mother, Sr. M. Kevin and Community, Convent of Mercy, Clonakilty and to Mr. C. Griffith of the Office of Public Works, Dublin.

In a work of this kind, one is critically dependent on the services of institutional archives; in this context I wish to pay special tribute to the efficiency, courtesy and co-operation of the staff of the National Library of Ireland and in particular to the Director, Alf. Mac Lochlainn and to the Keeper of Manuscripts, Mr. Dónal Ó Luanaigh. I wish also to express my gratitude to the Librarian and staff of the Library of Trinity College, to Pádraig Ó Snodaigh of the National Museum, to Breandán Mac Giolla Choille, Director of the Public Records Office, to Miss Ann Barry, Archivist of the Cork Archives Council, to Pádraig Ó Maidín of Cork City Library, to Aodh Ó Tuama of Museum Poiblí Chorcaí, to Mr. Séamas Fennessy, County Secretary, Tipperary S.R., to Mr. L. Walsh, Curator, Limerick Museum and to Sligo County Museum. I am especially grateful to Mr. C. Ó Túinléigh, Librarian, University

College, Galway for enabling me to include letters which came to light recently.

Numerous individuals and institutions responded to a public appeal for letters and documents; to each of the following I wish to express my appreciation and my thanks; Mr. A. McAleer (Omagh), Brian Mac Aonghusa, Cáit Bean Mhic Aonghusa, Síghle Bairéad, Mr. and Mrs. Sean Brooks (Howth), Mrs. Ian Bloomer (Killiney), Peadar Ó Casaide (Carrickmacross), Mr. J. Clarke (Ballina), Professor Cormac Ó Ceallaigh, An Br. Oirm. A.P. Caomhánach, Senator Séamas Dolan, Peadar Ó Donnabháin, Greagóir Ó Dúill, Mr. T. F. Figgis, Major R. G. Gregory, Mr. Aidan Heavey, Mr. J. Horgan (Tralee), Rev. Dr. K. Kennedy, Rev. Professor F. X. Martin O.S.A., Miss O'Meara (Limerick), Mrs. Kathleen O'Neill (Ballineen), Éamonn Ó Meachair (Cill Fiontain, Áth Cliath), An Br. Oirmh. S.P. Ó Nualáin, An Dr. Tarlach Ó Raifeartaigh, Mrs. K. Riordan (Dublin) Donnchadha Ó Súilleabháin, Mr. George Waters (R.T.É.), Mr. Pádraig Buckley (R.T.É. Cork), Rev. Fr. S. Farragher, C.S.Sp., Blackrock College, Dublin and Mrs. M. Cronin.

I am especially grateful for their advice and assistance to Professor G. Quinn, Trinity College, Eámonn Ó hÓgáin M.A., Riobard Mac Goraín and Uaitéar Ó Ciaruáin.

Professor Augustine Martin intended collaborating with me on this volume; however, pressing academic duties prevented him from doing so. I am very grateful to him for his participation in the early stages and for his advice.

In the research work, associated with Scoil Éanna and Pearse's educational work, it has been my pleasure to meet and interview most of the surviving past pupils; I wish to record my deep indebtedness over a number of years to Feargus de Búrca, to Brian Seoighe, to Seán Ó Dúnlaing, to General Joe Sweeney, to Fred O'Doherty and to Aodán Mac Fhionlaoigh – their admiration and regard for their headmaster was matched only by their willingness to share their recollections and their memories of their school – fad saoil agus sláinte dóibh uilig!

The editor will welcome information on any other Pearse letters which are not included in this volume and on other aspects of the work which readers may wish to bring to his attention.

May 1979

Séamas Ó Buachalla
Trinity College,
Dublin

Chronology

1879.　Born at 27 Gt. Brunswick Street, Dublin.

1887.　Attended a junior school at Wentworth Place (now Fenian Street).

1891.　Enrolled at the Christian Brothers' School, Westland Row, where he graduated in the Senior Grade in 1896.

1898.　His first book *Three Lectures on Gaelic Topics* was published; elected to the Executive Committee of the Gaelic League and began his university studies at the Royal University.

1899.　Represented the Gaelic League at the Welsh Eisteddfod, and the Scottish Mod. Began teaching in the League classes.

1900.　Elected secretary of the Publications Committee of the League.

1901.　Was awarded the degrees B.A., B.L.

1903.　Appointed as editor of *An Claidheamh Soluis.* Taught Irish at Alexandra College, at C.B.S. Westland Row and at University College.

1905.　Visited Belgium and other European centres to study educational systems and especially bilingualism.

1908.　Founded Sgoil Éanna, a secondary school for boys, at Cullenswood House, Ranelagh, Dublin.

1910.　Moved Sgoil Éanna to Rathfarnham and established Sgoil Íde, a school for girls at Ranelagh.

1912.　Founded and edited *An Barr Buadh*, a weekly political journal in Irish.

1913.　Involved in the founding of the Irish Volunteers and became a member of the Irish Republican Brotherhood.
　　　　His play *An Ri* was produced in the Abbey Theatre, as was his Passion Play of 1911, both acted in by the boys and masters of Sgoil Éanna.

1914.　Spent three months in America lecturing and collecting funds for his educational work.

1915.　Appointed a member of the Military Council and of the Supreme Council of the I.R.B.

1916. Published several political pamphlets, *Ghosts, The Separatist Idea, The Spiritual Nation* and *The Sovereign People.*
Military leader of the Rising and President of the Provisional Government of the Republic.
Executed by firing squad, on May 3rd, at Kilmainham and buried in a quicklime grave at Arbour Hill.

LETTERS
1897–1916

To Eoin Mac Neill.

In the period between taking his Senior Grade examination in 1896 and enrolling as a student of the Royal University at University College in 1898, Pearse founded the New Ireland Literary Society of which he and Éamonn Ó Néill, his school companion, were the principal founding members. At the Society's weekly meetings its members and invited guests presented papers; the three addresses which Pearse delivered to the Society in 1897 were published as *Three Lectures on Gaelic Topics* (1898).

Eoin Mac Neill was among the invited guests who spoke to the Society early in 1898; the arrangements for that occasion are the subject matter of the two letters written by Pearse to him in December 1897. Mac Neill's lecture on Ossianic Gaelic Poetry was delivered in January in the Molesworth Hall to an audience which included Dr. George Sigerson.

Pearse had been a member of the League since 1896 and was beginning to attract notice as an enthusiastic member of the prestigious Central Branch. He was possibly already, though a much younger man, on friendly terms with Eoin Mac Neill, who besides his academic duties as first Professor of Irish in St. Patrick's Training College, Drumcondra, was editor of the League's *Gaelic Journal* and Irish editor of the popular newspaper *Fáinne an Lae* and secretary of the League. At the January meeting of the New Ireland Literary Society, MacNeill appealed to Pearse and his fellow members to affiliate their society to the League; they responded by disbanding the society, and most of the members followed Pearse into the League.

L. 1/NLI

20.12.1897.   27 Gt. Brunswick St.
                               Dublin.

Dear Mr. MacNeill,
    You will recollect that on Friday evening, I, as part of the New Ireland Literary Society requested you to deliver a lecture before us, towards the middle or end of January. I now enclose you a copy of the Rules of the Society.
    When the idea of organising a public lecture was started, your name was the first that suggested itself to us; for we knew that a lecture by you on some phase of the Irish language movement, or, better still on some phase of Gaelic Literature, would not only be the most delightful of events to us members but would also attract a larger number of strangers than any other available person.

I know of course, that you are simply overwhelmed with other business, *Gaelic Journal* work, general League work, conducting of classes and other pressing duties. Of this I was aware before I approached you, and I was consequently far from anxious, personally to make a further demand on your time and labour. I really think however that to one like you, the time necessary for writing a lecture on a subject in which you are quite at home, will not be very great, particularly considering that the New Ireland Literary Society is neither a very large nor a very important body.

I hope and believe, then, that if it is at all possible you will see your way to comply. If you consent, it would be well for you to fix in your reply, the *subject* and the date, the latter we leave entirely to yourself. We can have the Molesworth Hall any night in the week except Monday. It would be advisable, of course, in forming the date, to select if possible, a night on which there would be no important meeting of the Gaelic League, in order to secure a good attendance of League members. For this reason, a Tuesday or a Thursday night, would perhaps be the best. Immediately on receiving a favourable reply, we shall set about getting the tickets printed.

Again expressing the hope that you will see your way to consent, I remain, dear Mr. Mac Neill, Yours very sincerely, P. H. Pearse.

To Eoin Mac Neill.

In most of his early letters Pearse underlined his signature heavily; in later years this was replaced by a flourish.

L. 2/NLI

30.12.1897   27 Gt. Brunswick St.,
                                        Dublin.

Dear Mr. Mac Neill,
    Needless to say, I was delighted on receiving your letter of the 27th., and I thank you very sincerely, both on my own part and on that of the Society, for so kindly consenting to deliver a lecture before us. The subject you have chosen is a splendid one and in your hands it is certain to prove most entertaining.

    We find that the Molesworth Hall will be occupied on Tuesday Jan 25th. We have accordingly fixed on Tuesday 18th and as the time is thus rather short we are getting the tickets printed immediately. If it happens that this date would not suit you, it would be well for you to let me know at once; but if we receive no communication from you in a day or two, I suppose we can go on with the printing. We are anxious to have the tickets ready by Saturday evening or at the very latest by Monday.

Our Secretary will let you have all final arrangements, as soon as possible. With renewed thanks, I remain, dear Mr. Mac Neill, Sincerely yours, P. H. Pearse.

To Eoin Mac Neill.

At this time, Pearse was teaching, as a monitor or tutor, in his alma mater at Westland Row Christian Brothers' School. Through the Superior there, Brother Kenny, he received a request from a Brother Kilkelly in Westport to assist in having a poem or fragment by Raftery, published in the *Gaelic Journal* edited by Eoin Mac Neill. Brother Kilkelly, a fluent Irish scholar, was familiar with the strong Raftery tradition of east Galway and had received the poem as a cutting from the American bilingual monthly newspaper *An Gaodhal* founded by Mícheál Ó Laocháin, for the Brooklyn Philo-Celtic Society in 1881.

With this letter in the Mac Neill papers there is a single page containing the following note in Pearse's hand:

Rev. Br. Kilkelly of Westport is very anxious to have the enclosed published in the *Gaelic Journal*. The author was the celebrated Raftery – one of Dr. Hyde's favourite poets. In forwarding it, Br. Kilkelly says "Be sure to keep it safe, and return it to me when you are done with it. If you could get it into the *Gaelic Journal*, it would be better type than this; and some priest or Gaelic scholar in East Galway might give a biographical sketch of Raftery (the author). As well as I can remember what I heard of him in my early days, he died some time between 1830 and 1840."

Raftery I believe, was blind and could neither read nor write, but that he was a true poet is beyond all doubt. I heard Br. Kilkelly, who is a good Irish scholar, repeat some of his extempore verses. It would be well if the facts of the lives of such lesser known Gaelic poets as Raftery could be gathered up before it is too late and printed in the *Gaelic Journal* in the form of short biographical notices – in Irish preferably.

11.1.1898.   27 Gt. Brunswick St.,
                                      Dublin.

Dear Mr. Mac Neill,
   Rev. Br. Kenny, Superior of Christian Brothers Schools,
Westland Row, has asked me to send you the enclosed. He received
it from Br. Kilkelly of Westport, who asked him if possible to get it
inserted in the Gaelic Journal. Br. Kilkelly requests that the cutting
be returned to him, as he received it from a very valued friend in
America. I am, dear Mr. Mac Neill, Yours sincerely, P. H. Pearse.

To Eoin Mac Neill.

Dr. Hyde's *Amhráin Diadha Chúige Chonnacht*, was part of his
multi-volume *Amhráin Chúige Chonnacht* which he began
publishing in 1890. It would appear that Mac Neill did not publish
the Raftery fragment in the *Gaelic Journal.*

10.5.1898.   27 Gt. Brunswick St.
                                      Dublin.

Dear Mr. Mac Neill,
   You will recollect that in January last I sent you at the request of
Rev. Br. Kilkenny (sic) of Westport, a cutting from the *Gaodhal*,
containing portion of a poem by the Galway poet, Raftery. I was
aware, that you rarely reprint matter already published, but Br.
Kilkenny, considered the piece worthy of insertion in the *Gaelic
Journal.* I have since read the poem in Dr. Hyde's *Amhráin
Diadha*, where if I recollect, it is considerably longer.
   Br. Kilkenny (sic) has become anxious about the fate of the
cutting which he received, as I think I told you, from a very valued
friend in America. He would on this account be very much put
about if it were lost and he requests me to see if I can get it for him.
If you have no use for it, you might kindly return it to me and I
shall send it on to him. I remain, dear Mr. Mac Neill, Sincerely
yours, P. H. Pearse.

To Eoin Mac Neill.

This undated letter from Pearse to Mac Neill was possibly written in 1898 or 1899, in relation to a competition for the League members of Inis Meadhon in the Aran Islands for which Pearse was acting as adjudicator.

The postcript refers to a lecture which Pearse gave to the Bray branch of the League.

L. 5/NLI

n.d.

Dear Mr. Mac Neill,

I leave for you the letters sent for adjudication by the Inish-meadhon Branch. If you possibly can send them by this evening's mail to Galway as Mr. Coonan N.T. says they are most anxiously awaited. Kindly incorporate in your letter to him the remarks in English re spelling etc. which I have made on the accompanying slip of notepaper. The winning letters are nos. 4 and 5. Sincerely yours, P. H. Pearse.

P.S. I have received letter from Bray, asking me to go out this evening. Shall do so.

To Eoin Mac Neill.

Questions of dialect differences, spelling and regional variations in the spoken language were prominent issues in the early days of the Gaelic League. Pearse was possibly referring in this letter to a League publication intended for Ulster and in the preparation of which he was assisting Mac Neill; it seems that he was proofing a portion of the volume.

L. 6/NLI

15.1.1899.

Dear Mac Neill,

I am sending you all that I have completed of the booklet. In that I have written words as they are now spelled, I have not rejected the dialect effect altogether. Since the book is intended for Ulster, it were better for us that we provide for the dialect difference; consequently I thought I should write "annsin" "annseo", "damh", "le" and other forms rather than "annsain", "annso" "dom" etc.

Certainly, I regret that I have not completed more. This section contains only twenty five pages. Pádraig Mac Piarais.

To the Editor, An Claidheamh Soluis.

At Coole in 1897, Lady Gregory and Yeats discussed the establishment of an Irish Literary Theatre; they succeeded in doing so in May 1899 and the first production offered Edward Martyn's *Heather Field* and Yeat's first poetic play, *Countess Cathleen* which he had written in 1892. The Yeats play had been the focus of controversy arising from alleged blasphemy; in this letter to the Editor of *An Claidheamh Soluis*, Pearse is not concerned with the issue of blasphemy but raises the more general question of the propriety of categorising literature written in English as Irish literature.

The reference to literary societies was very likely aimed at The Irish Literary Society, founded by Yeats in London in 1891 and The National Literary Society which John O'Leary and Yeats founded in Dublin in 1892. The association of such orthodox figures as O'Leary and Douglas Hyde with the Dublin Society did not diminish Pearse's mistrust; subsequent letters indicate that the twenty year old student substantially modified his views on this question.

Lord Salisbury (1830–1903) was the Prime Minister of Britain 1895–1902, and was associated with policies of high conservatism.

L. 7/P.S.

May 13th 1899   27 Gt. Brunswick St.,
                                  Dublin.

Dear Sir,
    Ireland is notoriously a land of contradictions and of shams, and of Irish contradictions and shams, Dublin is assuredly the hot bed. We have in the capital of Ireland "Irish" national newspapers whose only claim to nationality is that they run down – whilst they imitate – everything English; we have "Irish" nationalist politicians who in heart and soul are as un-Irish as Professor Mahaffy; we have a "national" literary society which is anti-national without being so out-spoken as Trinity College. Apparently the only thing necessary to make a man or an institution Irish is a little dab of green displayed now and again to relieve the monotony, a little eloquent twaddle about the *"children of the Gael"* or a little

meaningless vapouring about some unknown quantity termed "Celtic Glamour". Take away the dab of green, strip off the leafy luxury of words and what have you? The man or the institution is as English as Lord Salisbury. Newspapers, politicians, literary societies are all but forms of one gigantic heresy, that like a poison has eaten its way into the vitals of Irish nationality, that has paralysed the nation's energy and intellect. That heresy is the idea that there can be an Ireland, that there can be an Irish literature, an Irish social life whilst the language of Ireland is English.

And lo! just at the country is beginning to see through the newspapers and the literary societies, here we have the Anglo-Irish heresy springing up in new form, the "Irish" Literary Theatre. Save the mark! Much ink has been spilled in our newspaper offices over this same "Irish" Literary Theatre, but I note that not a single "national" daily impeaches it on the only ground, on which details apart, it is impeachable namely, that literature written in English cannot be Irish. Why waste time in criticising stray expressions when the whole thing is an imposture, a fraud, a heresy? Had Mr. Yeats and their friends called their venture, the "English Literary Theatre" or simply "The Literary Theatre" I would have been the last in the world to object to it. But in the name of common sense, why dub it "Irish"? Why not select Hindoo, Chinese, Hottentot or Eskimo? None of these would be true, for a play in English, if it is a play at all, must be English literature; but any one of them would be quite as appropriate as "Irish". What claim have these two English plays to be called "Irish" literature? None in the world, save that the scene in each is laid in Ireland. Is, then, *Timon of Athens* Greek literature? Is *Romeo and Juliet* Italian literature? Is *Quentin Durward* French Literature? Is the *Vision of Don Roderick* Spanish literature? When Greece, Italy, France and Spain claim these works as their respective properties, then may Ireland claim *The Countess Cathleen* and *The Heather Field* as her own.

The "Irish Literary Theatre", is in my opinion, more dangerous, because glaringly anti-national, than Trinity College. If we once admit the Irish literature in English idea, then the language movement is a mistake. Mr. Yeat's precious "Irish" literary Theatre may if it develops, give the Gaelic League more trouble than the Atkinson-Mahaffy combination. Let us strangle it at its birth. Against Mr. Yeats personally we have nothing to object. He is a mere English poet of the third or fourth rank, and as such he is harmless. But when he attempts to run an "Irish Literary Theatre", it is time for him to be crushed. Very sincerely yours. P. H. Pearse.

9

To Henry Morris.

This letter and that of 1–9–1899 refer to a stone tablet which had been commissioned by Morris from the firm of James Pearse for the National School at Lisdoonan, Co. Monaghan, where Morris was a teacher from 1888 to 1901. Pearse had apparently consulted Lloyd as to the correct version of the place-name. A similar stone tablet was ordered from the Pearse firm in 1900 for the National School at Donaghmore. Patrick Morris (1879–1946) a brother of Henry's taught at Donaghmore N.S., was an active Gaelic Leaguer with whom Pearse also corresponded (c.f. letter of 12.1.1901).

L. 8/NLI

30.8.1899

Dear Sir,
   Your tablet will be ready for forwarding tomorrow (Tuesday). I have received no communication from Mr. Lloyd, the reason probably being that he is out of town. You need however have no fear as to the correctness of the spelling "Liosdúnáin", which I think is unimpeachable. "Naisiuntach" should be "Náisiúnta" – there is no guttural at the end and the 'u' should have síneadh fada. The inscription as it appears on the tablet is therefore:

> Sgoil Náisiúnta,
> Liosdúnáin.

The letters which are 2″ long look fine and bold. As the tablet is for the exterior of a building the letters are not painted as in the open air, the paint would wear off in a few months.
   Trusting that this tablet will please you and that you will be able to put others of the kind in my way. I remain, faithfully yours. James Pearse. PHP.

To Henry Morris.

This letter, like that of August 30th, while formally from James Pearse, is written by P. H. Pearse. The brother of H. Morris referred to, is probably Eoin Morris who worked in Dublin from 1892 as a draper's assistant in the employment of a Mr. Howe, a merchant draper.

L. 9/NLI

1.9.1899.   Ecclesiastical & Architectural
                                                                Sculptor.
                                          27 Gt. Brunswick St.
                                          Dublin.

Dear Sir,
   Your brother called on me today and I arranged with him to
forward tablet to his Dublin address tomorrow. I am having letters
painted in order to give the inscription a bolder and more striking
effect. Faithfully yours, James Pearse. P.H.P.

To The Press.

This letter to the Press was part of the Gaelic League campaign of
February 1900 on Irish in the national schools and the reform of
elementary education. The other writers in the campaign were Mr.
Eoin Mac Neill, Rev. Dr. M. O'Hickey and Miss Norma Borthwick. The four letters which appeared in sequence in the national
dailies during the month, were collected and published by the
League under the title *Irish in the Schools* as No. 3 in the Penny
Pamphlet series.
   The two-fold demand put forward by the Gaelic League,
mentioned in the first paragraph was the policy enunciated by the
Executive Committee of the League and presented by Dr. O'Hickey
in his letter. The policy demanded
i)   that where Irish is the home language, pupils shall be taught to
     read and write Irish and their education shall be through the
     medium of their home language.
ii) that where Irish is not the home language, it shall be lawful to
     teach Irish as a remunerated subject within school hours at the
     earliest stage at which pupils are capable of learning it.
At that time, Irish could be taught only outside school hours, its
teaching was remunerated only in the fifth and sixth standards, and
it was classed like Latin or French as an "extra subject" – it was
treated as a foreign language.

11

February 1900   Sandymount,
                          Co. Dublin.

Dear Sir,

Now that the air is rife with talk of reform in our primary system, the trumpet call of Rev. Dr. O'Hickey comes with singular appropriateness. I am convinced that if we succeed in bringing home clearly to the Irish public (i) the present state of education in the Irish-speaking parts of Ireland (ii) the two-fold demand put forward by the Gaelic League, the country will not be slow in making up its mind to support strenuously and whole-heartedly that demand. The second point has, I think, been made sufficiently clear by Dr. O'Hickey, and the object of this letter is to set forth as lucidly as may be a few concrete facts which will show the condition of affairs actually existing in the Irish-speaking area at the present moment. This is not a matter which demands fine writing or indignant declamation. Let us regard the facts of the case calmly, sanely. Naked facts speak with an eloquence more moving than the rhetoric of orators.

For the present I confine myself to those districts where Irish is the language of the children's homes. Let us take the case of the child who, on entering for the first time the door of a national school, knows only Irish. Irish is the language which he has imbibed with his mother's milk; Irish is the language of his home, of his companions, of his prayers, of his pastimes, the language in which he thinks and lives. From the very hour in which he enters the National school he is set to learn a foreign and unfamiliar speech; and worse still, he is set to learn this foreign and unfamiliar speech through the medium of itself – the unknown through the medium of the unknown.

To realise what this means let us take a parallel case. Suppose that I wish to learn French and that I have not, at present the most elementary knowledge of that language. Suppose that I get a Frenchman, who knows no English and that we seat ourselves at a table. How long should I take to learn French? Should I ever succeed in mastering it? Pick up a few words, a few phrases, I might – a parrot could do that much – but as to mastering the language, as to assimilating its idioms, as to making it part and parcel of my intellectual being, as to learning to think in it, to read in it with intelligence, to write it – the feat would be impossible. Why? Because between me and the Frenchman there is no bond, no means by which we can communicate one with the other, no common medium through which he can impart his knowledge to me. This is exactly the condition of affairs in scores of schools in the north-west, west and south of Ireland at this moment. I have been in schools where the children did not understand one word the master uttered and the master did not understand one word the children uttered.

"But", it will be said, "can any Board calling itself a Board of Education tolerate, much less sanction, such a system? Do the Commissioners make no provision for purely Irish-speaking children?" Yes, the Commissioners do make a provision; they actually concede that, where a child fails to grasp the meaning of a lesson, the master – if he happens to be able – may explain the subject-matter in Irish. This permission, as officially interpreted, means nothing more than that the teacher is at liberty – always provided that he is able – to explain an English word or phrase by the corresponding Irish expression. Even this limited power is to a large extend a dead letter, as most of the teachers do not know Irish.

And, of this system, ignoring as it does the only language with which the child is familiar, or at least, the language with which he is most familiar, and which in the normal course of events should form the basis of his education, what, as a matter of practical working, are the results? It is found that either one or other of two things happens, according as the system is applied in an exclusively or almost exclusively, Irish-speaking district, or in a district already partially Anglicised. In the former case, whatever smattering of English and other subjects the child, parrot-like and by mere imitation, happens to acquire at school, is within a year or two after leaving school completely forgotten; it has been mere memory work, the reasoning faculties have not come into play at all, and hearing nothing but Irish in the home, the child soon forgets whatever little he has learned in school. In other words the net result is that he lapses into absolute illiteracy. I have seen in the West of Ireland young men and women, who after six years spent at a National School could neither read nor write, and did not know the meaning of the English word "man". I have met boys who could tell me that the c-o-w spelt "cow", "cow" was a common noun, third singular, feminine gender; but who were profoundly ignorant of what the word "cow" meant, and, of course, had not the faintest conception of the signification of the terms "noun", "common," "singular", "feminine" or "gender". I remember on one occasion meeting in a remote district in Connacht a little fellow of twelve, who was absolutely the most intelligent child I have ever met. I happened to be collecting the names of wild flowers in Irish, and the boy went out of his way to show me all sorts of wild plants, telling me their

13

names and properties with an ease and accuracy which to me was amazing. I asked him, out of curiosity, did he know any English? No, not a word. Had he ever been to school? Yes, for four years. How was it, then, that he had no English? "He could never make out what the mistress used to be saying'. This is "education" in the West of Ireland.

In the partially Anglicised districts the results of the National School system are even more appalling. There the product of the National Schools is that worst of human monstrosities – the being who has a smattering of two languages, but knows neither sufficiently well to be able adequately to express himself in it. Surely it is not an exaggeration to say that the system which allows all of this is an abnormity – that the whole thing from top to bottom, is at once a colossal blunder and a colossal crime? The impression which an examination of it at close quarters leaves on the observer is that no other civilised country in the world would stand it for a single hour. Ireland has stood it for over half a century.

One other incident, and I have done. Some three or four years ago two Intermediate students, alumni of a certain well-known college in the West of Ireland, were passengers on the steamer which plies between Galway and Aran. They were discussing the difficulty of the Senior Grade Trigonometry paper which had been set at the late exam. Beside them sat a peasant lad who had no English and did not, of course, understand a word of the conversation. Suddenly he caught the word "Trigonometry" and his face lit up. He asked one of the students, who happened to be Irish-speaking, what they were saying about Trigonometry. The case was explained to him, and having asked for the paper, he worked out all the problems with absolute accuracy. He had, it transpired, learned the science during the winter evenings from an old Irish-speaking schoolmaster.

What does this incident show? It is not, perhaps, a very brilliant achievement to tackle successfully a Senior Grade Trigonometry paper. No, but the moral of the story is this: six years at a National School had failed to teach that boy English, whilst a few evenings by the fireside had given him a respectable knowledge of a difficult branch of mathematics, because he had been taught through the medium of the language he understood.

Educate on rational lines the mountaineers and glensmen and islemen of Irish-speaking Ireland and in these even the children of the Pale will admit that we have the bone and sinew – ay, and the brain – of Ireland; teach them to read and write their own language first, teach them English or any other useful subject you choose through the medium of that language and watch the results.

Perpetuate the present system, and you perpetuate illiteracy – and worse.

Let the people, the parents, the school managers of Ireland speak; let them fearlessly voice their demands through their representatives in Parliament, through their elective bodies, through the Press; let them take action, action determined strenuous, persevering; above all let them move now – it is the psychological moment. I am, dear sir, faithfully yours, P. H. Pearse.

To J. J. Doyle.

This and other letters following, are addressed in English and Irish to J. J. Doyle (Seosamh Ua Dubhghaill) a native of Kerry who was an Excise Revenue official in Derry at the turn of the century. He was one of those who were encouraged by Pearse to write for the various Gaelic League publications. He wrote extensively in Irish under the pen-name "Beirt Fhear", the title of his first story. His other works include *Leabhar Cainte* (1901), *Tadhg Gabha* (1901) and *Cathair Contraí* (1901). He lived in Belfast later and was active in the Gaelic League there and served on some of its central committees. "Aodh agus Diarmuid" were two characters from Doyle's *Beirt Fhear ón dTuaith*, a typical dialogue or conversational piece, very popular as learning material in the Gaelic League. He also wrote under the pen-name "Tadhg Méith". After twelve years as Superintendant of the Derry Excise Revenue District he was transferred on promotion to the Manchester District in 1908.

L. 11/NLI

2nd July 1900.   Connradh na Gaedhilge,
                                 Áth Cliath.

Dear Mr Doyle,

We are now re-organising our Publications Comtee. after the Oireachtas, and it occurs to me that you may be free to do some work for us. The object of the Comtee. is to place in the hands of students, both of schools and colleges and in League classes, a series of carefully edited and carefully selected modern Irish texts, with introductions (where necessary), full vocabularies and no translations. The idea is to give students a scientifically edited and up-to-date series of texts, similar in style and matter to those used in the study of French, German etc. The series will comprise

15

modern classics, prose & poetry, such as the works of Keating, Ó Bruadair, etc., the best of the later Ossianic prose tales, etc., and also original modern Irish work. Do you think you could manage to get anything ready for us? – a volume of stories or sketches, a book of dialogues in the style of 'Aodh agus Diarmuid' or anything else that suggests itself to you? A book of the kind by the writer of Beirt Fhear would sell like wildfire. I shall be glad to hear from you at your convenience as to whether you are inclined to undertake anything on the lines indicated. I remain, dear Mr. Doyle, Yours sincerely. P. H. Pearse. *Hon. Sec. Publications Comtee.*

To J. J. Doyle.

Pearse having encouraged J. J. Doyle to write for the League, promised to place his proposals before the Publications Committee. The education issue referred to concerned the depressed status of Irish in the new curriculum introduced in the National schools in 1900 following upon the findings of the Belmore Commission.

L. 12/NLI/G

12.7.1900   The Gaelic League,
                                             Dublin.

Dear Mr Doyle,
   I am in receipt of your letter and am very pleased to learn that you are prepared to write for us. I will place your letter before the next meeting of the directors of the Publishing Company and I can assure you that I shall not make delay nor dallying (as the old stories say) until I send you word of their decision. Thanking you for your letter, I remain your friend, Pádraig Mac Piarais.

P.S.   As regards the education question do your level best by hook or crook to get up an agitation on the subject of the language. Leave no stone unturned. Bring pressure to bear from all quarters. The rumour re Bill is quite true. This is the crisis in the history of the movement. Make use of that public meeting for all it is worth. P. H. Pearse.

To J. J. Doyle

The fluid situation on educational policy following on the Belmore Commission (1898) on primary education and the Palles Commission on Intermediate Education (1899) prompted a cautious policy on textbook publication by the Gaelic League at the turn of the century. In primary schools its counter strategy involved a bilingual programme which provided differentially for the teaching of the language in Irish-speaking and English-speaking communities. The League expected that the Revised Programme of 1900 would reflect a reformed attitude on the part of the National Board towards the Irish language and its place in the national school curriculum. The League conducted a vigorous campaign in the press and published a series of pamphlets to attract public support for its policy. It sought a bilingual programme, for which it received support from managers, teachers and a wide sector of political opinion. Despite these allies however, the New Code published in July 1900 was a disappointment to the League; it allowed Irish to be taught only as an extra-subject out of regular school hours and in Irish-speaking districts it could only be used as an aid to the teaching of English.

To express their opposition to the New Code, the League organised a mass meeting at the Rotunda, Dublin on July 19th at which messages of support were received from W. B. Yeats, Cardinal Logue, A.E., and Lady Gregory. During the meeting Douglas Hyde read a letter from one of the Commissioners of the National Board, Professor Fitzgerald of Trinity College; in the letter the Commissioner stated "I will use all my influence, as in the past, to ensure that Irish as a spoken language shall die out as quickly as possible". A parliamentary debate shortly afterwards resulted in a modification from which some improvement is observable; of the 8,684 national schools in 1900, Irish was taught in 88, whereas by 1903 the number had risen to over 2,000. This dramatic improvement should be interpreted cautiously, bearing in mind the political significance increasingly attaching to the language question and the variable quality and quantity of the teaching.

25th July 1900.   Connradh na Gaedhilge,
                                   Áth Cliath.

Dear Mr. Doyle,
    The Publication Comtee. at its meeting last night was very glad indeed of your offer, and will bear it in mind when making arrangements for new books. We have received however a piece of news which causes us to modify somewhat our plan of pushing on at once a costly series of texts. It is to the effect that the days of Intermediate exams by specified text-books are all but numbered. This, coupled with the changes of the National Board programme, has made us decide not to undertake any new books immediately – as the only means of making them pay is to get them on the programme of some board – and to turn our attention for the present to such things as primers etc., for the new Board programme ... Four or five books which are already in the printer's hands will be proceeded with, but for the present we think it well not to undertake anything new. You will thus for the present be relieved of the necessity of starting to work for us, and will be able to concentrate yourself on your inimitable Claidheamh Soluis work.
    As regards bilingual fight, I am sure you are doing your best up north. The Commissioners are plainly wavering and a fierce agitation now may win the fight. Special public meetings held locally to follow up our splendid Dublin meeting would mean much. Could such a meeting be got together in Derry? Mise do chara, Pádraig Mac Piarais.

To Eoin Mac Neill.

Pearse became Secretary of the League's Publications Committee in June 1900; the following is a notice of a meeting of the Committee in August which also contains the order of business for the meeting. The Primer mentioned in the notice was *Primh Leabhar Gaedhilge le hAghaidh na Naoidheanán* published later in 1900; the Song Book was *Ceol-Sidhe* a collection by Norma Borthwick published in 1900. The Keating reference in the Agenda possibly denotes discussion of the volume, published in 1900, of poetry by Keating, *Dánta, Amhráin's Caointe Sheathrúin Céitinn*, under the editorship of Fr. E. C. Mc Erlean S.J.

3.8.1900   Connradh na Gaedhilge,
                                24 Upper O'Connell St.,
                                Dublin.

Publications Committee,
Meeting, Tuesday, 7th inst, at 8 sharp.
  Business.
        Correspondence.   Rev. P. S. Dineen. S.J.
        Primer: estimate for.
        Song Book: estimate for.
        Keating: arrangements re cover etc, fixing price.
        Pamphlets,
        Leaflets.
                        Pádraig Mac Piarais.

To Eoin Mac Neill.

The League published in 1900 *Outlines of the Grammar of Old Irish* by Rev. Edmond Hogan S.J. of University College; this is the Grammar whose proofs are mentioned in the first sentence of the letter.

Pearse shows an early appreciation of the importance of adequate aids in language learning by his suggested approach to providing reading books readily by the stereotyping of materials already published in *An Claidheamh Soluis.*

Dr. W. J. Walsh, Archbishop of Dublin, was a Commissioner of National Education and was a strong supporter of the League; following the publication of the Revised Programme of 1900, he expressed his own and the League's dissatisfaction with the continuing neglect of the Irish language in the national schools. He threatened to resign as Commissioner on a number of occasions and failing to get any satisfaction, he did so in June 1901.

L. 15/NLI

2.9.1900.   Connradh na Gaedhilge,
                                Áth Cliath.

A Eoin Uasail,
    I forward the first proofs of the Grammar which have just come to hand.
    It has been suggested that the *Reading Lessons in Irish* (Pádraig

and Seaghan) in the last two numbers of *An Claidheamh Soluis* would form an excellent reading book to be used in conjunction with the *Simple Lessons.* They supply what has been so long asked for – "something to follow O'Growney". If the lessons are to be continued from week to week as I presume they are, why not have the successive instalments stereotyped? We should thus in a very few weeks have the makings of a first-rate penny or twopenny book of reading lessons, or rather we should have the book ready-made.

You will doubtless have heard by this that the Archbishop has resigned his seat on both the Intermediate and the National Education Boards. The fact is not to be published yet but there is no harm in disseminating it quietly.

I owe you an apology for inflicting on you a business letter during your well-earned holiday. Yours very sincerely. P. H. Pearse.

To Edward Martyn.

Edward Martyn's pamphlet *Ireland's Battle for her Language* (1900) was No. 4 of the Gaelic League series published through its Publications Committee of which Pearse was Honorary Secretary. Dr. W. J. Walsh, Archbishop of Dublin, one of the Commissioners of National Education, strongly supported the League in its opposition to the Revised Code of 1900 and contributed a pamphlet on Bilingual Education to the League's series.

From 1900 to 1922, the English Monarchy was represented in Ireland by the Lord Lieutenant who was responsible for Irish affairs in the British government assisted by a Chief Secretary who was an elected politician. Lord Cadogan was Lord Lieutenant from 1895–1902. The three Boards of Education Commissioners were appointed by and reported to the Lord Lieutenant. The election referred to was the General Election of late September 1900 which returned a Conservative majority. Pearse's father, James, died on 5th September 1900 at 185 Gt. Russell St., Birmingham.

L. 16/P.Ms.

24.9.1900.   Connradh na Gaedhilge,
                                  Áth Cliath.

Dear Mr. Martyn,
    Many thanks for ms. of pamphlet. I will send you the proofs as soon as possible. In view of some recent developments, not yet

generally known, some passages might need a little modification or softening down. This can of course be done when correcting proofs.

The true state of affairs at the National Board is this. The Archbishop sent in his resignation but the Lord Lieutenant did not accept it. The Archbishop then consented to re-consider his resignation until November when, if the bilingual reforms are not granted, he will resign and publish his reasons for doing so. All this is known only in confidence, and as a matter of courtesy to the Archbishop, it should not just now be publicly referred to. Meanwhile there is every reason to hope that before November the reforms will be granted. In view of all this, it will be well to avoid too strong language, or too furious a denunciation of the Board. It will thus be necessary in view of the facts to slightly modify references to the Archbishop.

Your suggestion that the book should be out in time for the elections is an excellent one, and I trust that we shall be able to manage it.

Thanking you for your kindly words of sympathy on my father's death. Sincerely yours, P. H. Pearse.

To Edward Martyn.

In 1900 the League published Martyn's *Ireland's Battle for her Language*, one of the early series on Education. This pamphlet appeared during the general election in September, which gave a Conservative victory under Robert Gascoyne-Cecil, the Marquis of Salisbury.

L. 17/NMI

4.10.1900.   Connradh na Gaedhilge,
                                    Áth Cliath.

Dear Mr. Martyn,

I told the office staff of the League to send two or three dozen copies of the pamphlet to you at Kildare Street Club, and trust you received them as also my letter on Monday. I enclose half-a-dozen additional copies. Should you require any more I can, of course, let you have them. The pamphlet was duly published on Tuesday and was widely distributed through the country and city branches on that evening.

I handed your cheque to the Treasurer, Mr. Barrett, who will by this time have sent you a receipt.

The Publication Comtee., which met on Tuesday, was very well pleased with the pamphlet, and congratulates you on so effectively keeping the language to the front during the elections. A stirring call of the kind was badly needed, and yours, I trust will not have been made in vain.

Thanking you, on behalf of the Comtee. for your ... in writing the pamphlet. Sincerely yours, P. H. Pearse.

To J. O'Kelly (Séamas Ó Ceallaigh).

This lengthy letter, which includes a sketch by Pearse of the trews described, was obviously in reply to a query from O'Kelly, a prominent Gaelic Leaguer, as to the appropriate national constume for a Feis (cultural festival) organised by the League.

William Robert Wilde (1815–1876), physician, travel writer and antiquarian, father of Oscar Wilde, published in 1858 his *Catalogue of the Contents of the Museum of the Royal Academy* in three volumes. Collier's *History of Ireland* was published in Belfast in 1884.

L. 18/NLI

26.10.1900   5 George's Villa,
                              Sandymount.

My dear O'Kelly,

I have been away from home for a few days and until this morning could not get an opportunity of looking at the pair of trews in the Royal Irish Academy Collection in the National Museum. As the collection is being re-arranged and catalogued, they are not on exhibition now but Mr. Coffey very kindly unearthed them for me and gave me an opportunity of examining and handling them.

They really resemble nothing so much as a modern pair of drawers of the kind usually worn by men. In fact one would at first sight take them for a rather clumsily made and ill-treated pair of modern gentlemen's drawers. They are tight fitting and reach down to the foot, the extremities being pointed at each side. There is no opening in front and the wearer must hence have found considerable difficulty in putting them on. The material is a thick strong woollen stuff. There is a seam on the inside of each leg. As for the colour, the legs are plaid or cross-barred with black and yellow stripes all the way down, the upper portion back and front in plain yellow.

There is absolutely no means of judging of the age of the garment. Probably it is not older than the 16th century. It must have been worn by some farmer or labouring man and was probably made by his wife. At least I cannot imagine an Irish gentleman of three or four centuries ago wearing so clumsy an article or dress. Frankly, I should much prefer to see you arrayed in a kilt, although it may be less authentic, than in a pair of these trews. You would if you appeared in the latter, run the risk of leading the spectators to imagine that you had forgotten to don your trousers and had sallied forth in your drawers. This would be fatal to the dignity of the Feis. If you adopt a costume, let it, at all events, have some elements of picturesqueness.

The accompanying rough outline will give you a very fair idea of what the trews are like. Numerous pictures of them have however been published. I think you will find one in Wilde's Catalogue and in Collier's History of Ireland. The trews worn by a peasant or soldier shown there correspond exactly to the pair in the R.I.A. collection. With the trews were worn a pair of shoes identical with the "pampooties" now worn in Aran, a tight fitting jerkin or vest and a large heavy woollen cloak. Of all these I have seen specimens. It is quite certain that these were the ordinary dress of the lower class in Ireland in the 16th centruy. But then I cannot see that they are entitled to the dignity of being called a "national" costume. Are they not the hose, jerkin and cloak worn universally throughout Europe during the Middle Ages and down to the end of the 18th century? Very sincerely yours. P. H. Pearse.

To Eoin Mac Neill.

Eoin Mac Neill lived at this time at 14 Trafalgar Square, Monkstown and would consequently pass along Gt. Brunswick St. on his way to Drumcondra each morning.

L. 19/NLI

10.11.1900.   24 Upper O'Connell St.,
                                             Dublin.

A Chara,
    I enclose final proof of Primer, which you might kindly glance over, especially the last page, containing suggested names of letters. I am anxious to give the order to print off early on Monday, so you

might kindly post me the proof tomorrow night or hand it in at Gt. Brunswick St. on Monday morning. Mise, Pádraig Mac Piarais.

To Most Rev. Dr. Walsh D.D., Archbishop of Dublin.

The many letters which Pearse as Secretary of the League's Publications Committee, addressed to Dr. Walsh are characterised by an elaborate courtesy and a pronounced deference. It was essential for the League and for Pearse to secure the total support of the clergy in seeking to have the bilingual policy accepted by the Commissioners of National Education and implemented in the schools. The support of Dr. Walsh as a Commissioner and as the leading educational spokesman for the Catholic hierarchy was essential to the League's strategy. Pearse consulted him on many minor issues, such as the Primer for infants, the topic of this letter, which the League published in 1900.

L. 20/DDA

22nd Nov. 1900   Connradh na Gaedhilge,
                                  Áth Cliath.

May it please Your Grace,
   I have to thank Your Grace for having so kindly looked through the proof of the Irish Primer, which Rev. Dr. Hogan, at my request, sent to Your Grace. As Father Hogan will already have informed you, Your Grace's suggestions on most points have been adopted, whilst the remaining suggestions will be considered when the second edition of the book is being printed. For the present a comparatively small edition (1000 copies) has been ordered, so as to afford an early opportunity of making such alterations as experience of the book in practical use may show to be necessary.
   I have the honour to enclose two copies of the Primer and shall be glad if Your Grace can make any further suggestions. I also enclose proofs of two circulars which the League proposes to address to managers and teachers, respectively, of National Schools with regard to the use of the Primer, and to the whole subject of the teaching of Irish under the New Rules. I should be glad to have Your Grace's opinion on these circulars before getting them printed off, and to hear Your Grace's suggestions not only as regards the circulars – or circular, as the wording of both is the same – as a whole, but as regards any of the points touched on, in some of which I know Your Grace takes a keen personal interest. I refer to

such points as the names of the letters, the system of teaching for Irish-speaking and non-Irish-speaking children, respectively, etc., etc.

With many thanks on my own and on the Committee's part for the interest which Your Grace has taken in the project, I have the honour to be, Your Grace, Your Grace's obedient servant, P. H. Pearse.

To Eoin Mac Neill.

Mac Neill and Pearse were members of both the Executive and of the Publications Committee at this time.

L(p.c.) 21/NLI

15.12.1900.   24 Upper O'Connell St.
                                                          Dublin.

There will be a special meeting of the Publications Committee on Tuesday next, 18th inst at 7.45 p.m. As a meeting of the Executive has been summoned for 9 p.m. on that evening, members of the Publications Committee are requested to attend punctually at 7.45 p.m. Pádraig Mac Piarais.

To Eoin Mac Neill.

The heavy nature of Pearse's workload in connection with the League is evidenced in this letter written when he was in his final year at University. It would appear that he spent the weekend attending to his League secretarial duties; this letter was written on Sunday. He has also begun in this letter to use abbreviations such as "wd.", "cd.", for "would" and "could" which later became a feature of his regular correspondence.

The proofs referred to as dialogues from Neilson are probably those of the volume *Ráiteachas an Chead Chuid* (1901), a collection of illustrative material from the Grammar of William Neilson.

Cormac Ua Chonaill was a short novel by Father P. Dineen based upon the exploits of the Earl of Desmond in the Munster Rebellion of 1579.

L. 22/NLI

16.12.1900.   24 Upper O'Connell St.,
                               Dublin.

My dear Mac Neill,
   I enclose proofs of first portion of the dialogues from Neilson.
You might kindly insert a preliminary note which should be in Irish
and English, explaining what they are and so on, and mentioning
that they will be published as instalments as penny booklets until
the whole is reprinted. If you could bring me in the proofs on
Tuesday night, it would be so much the better.
   You might kindly let me have back the proofs of "Cormac Ua
Conaill" as the printer is now working on them. Please bring them
on Tuesday night or better still have them at my office when
passing on tomorrow or Tuesday. Yours very sincerely, P. H.
Pearse.

To Dr. Walsh.

Dr. Walsh delivered a lecture on Bilingual Education, to the
students of Our Lady of Mercy Teacher Training College, at
Baggot St., Dublin, on December 7th 1900. The Archbishop's
lecture was published in 1901 as *Bilingual Education* by the
League, the costs of publication being borne by Dr. Walsh.

L. 23/DDA

19th Dec. 1900   Connradh na Gaedhilge,
                               Áth Cliath.

May it please Your Grace,
   I have the honour to acknowledge Your Grace's favour of
yesterday, together with copy of pamphlet. I have handed the latter
to the printers, and will forward the proofs to Your Grace as soon
as possible. I am ordering a first edition of 10,000 copies. The
pamphlet will, of course, be stereotyped, and further editions can be
printed off as they may be called for. It is the intention of the
Publication Committee to send a copy of the pamphlet to every
manager and teacher in Ireland, and also to circulate it, broadcast
through the medium of the Branches, and the other usual channels.
   With reference to type, the Committee decided to adopt a
somewhat larger size than any that has hitherto been used in our
26

pamphlets. This will improve the appearance of the pamphlet, and render it more readable and attractive.

As regards the title, the Committee would suggest – "*Bilingual Education* By the Most Rev. Dr. Walsh, Archbishop of Dublin". This would get over the difficulty to which Your Grace refers, and would also be a short and convenient title. Pending Your Grace's opinion, I have not made any change in the title given in the Ms.

I have to sincerely thank Your Grace, on behalf of the Publications Committee, for so kindly placing the address at our disposal and for the great trouble to which Your Grace has gone in preparing it for the press. The publication and wide circulation of the pamphlet will do more to show managers and teachers their powers under the New Rules, and to induce them to put a scheme of bilingual education into actual practice than any other means that could possibly be adopted and the Committee recognizes that, in placing this pamphlet at its disposal, Your Grace is adding immensely to the debt of gratitude due you by every one concerned for the progress of the Irish language and Irish education. I have also to thank Your Grace for the generous offer to be responsible for the cost of bringing out the pamphlet. I have the honour to be, Your Grace, Your Grace's obedient servant, P. H. Pearse. Hon. Sec. Publications Comtee.

To Dr. Walsh.

Under the aegis of the League, many managers of national schools signed a memorial to the National Board seeking to have a programme of bilingual education introduced. The memorial and the list of managers were included in Dr. Walsh's pamphlet. Pamphlet No. 5, in the League Series, *Parliament and the Teaching of Irish* contains the debate, as reported in the London *Times*, on The Irish Language which took place in the House of Commons on July 21st. 1900. Mary E. L. Butler was a prominent member of the League, whose pamphlet outlined the role of the home and women in the language revival. Mr. Charles McNeill was a member of the League and a brother of Eoin Mac Neill.

L. 24/DDA

22.12.1900.   Connradh na Gaedhilge,
                                     Áth Cliath.

May it please Your Grace,
   I have the honour to enclose proof of Your Grace's pamphlet,
which has just reached me.
   Mr. Charles MacNeill has suggested that it might be advisable
to add, as a second appendix, the list of signatures to the Managers'
Memorial. This would have the effect of bringing home to the
managers who signed, the fact that they now stand committed to
introduce a bilingual system into their schools. I compute that the
pamphlet, as it stands at present, will run to about 22 pages. The
inclusion of the list of signatures will bring it up to 24 pages.
   I enclose a copy of our latest pamphlet, *Parliament and the
Teaching of Irish*. It forms No. 5. of the series, but No. 6. Miss
Butler's pamphlet on *Irishwomen and the Home Language*,
which Your Grace had doubtless seen, appeared before it. The paper
employed in this pamphlet – No. 5 – is that which we propose to
use in Your Grace's. It is of Irish manufacture, and compares very
favourably with the foreign paper hitherto used. We intend, as far
as possible, to use Irish-made paper in all our future publications.
   I shall be glad to learn whether Your Grace will require to see a
proof of the pamphlet in page form. I have the honour to be, Your
Grace, Your Grace's obedient servant, P. H. Pearse. Hon. Sec.
Publications Comtee.

To Eoin Mac Neill.

This letter is written to Mac Neill as editor of *An Claidheamh
Soluis* by Pearse as secretary of the Publications Committee, the
annual report of which he enclosed.
   An tAithriseoir was the collection of prose and poetry jointly
edited by Pearse and Tadhg Ó Donnchadha and published in 1900;
its popularity was such that a second edition was published in 1903.

L. 25/NLI

22.12.1900. The Gaelic League,
24 Upper O'Connell St.

Dear Sirs,

Kindly notice enclosed pamphlet in next issue of *An Claidheamh Soluis*. The fact that the Archbishop is bringing out his Baggot St. address as a League pamphlet, mentioned in the report of the Publications Committee, herewith, should be commented on in the editorial notes.

An tAithriseoir, a penny Irish Recitation Book, forming No. 1. of the League's series of penny popular booklets, in Irish is due on Friday or Saturday next as mentioned in the Report and this fact might be announced editorially. Yours etc, P. H. Pearse. Public. Comtee.

To Henry Morris.

This letter initiates the project by which Henry Morris wrote a seven part series of popular stories under the title of *Greann na Gaeilge* (I–VII). The series appeared as separate books from 1901–1907 and constitute an important part of the League's "*Leabhairíní Gaeilge le haghaidh an tSluaigh*" (Penny popular booklets in Irish). The O'Growney books referred to are the Rev. Eugene O'Growney's *Simple Lessons in Irish*, in five parts, published between 1897 and 1900; parts IV and V were completed by Eoin Mac Neill due to O'Growney's ill-health. *An tAithriseoir* (I, II,) published 1900–1902 was a miscellany of prose and poetry compiled and edited by Pearse and Tadhg Ó Donnchadha (Tórna). The request in the letter by Pearse to modify the dialectal emphasis reflects the current friction in the language movement, which Pearse sought to counter by giving equal editorial exposure to all the main dialects.

L. 26/NLI

9.1.1901. Connradh na Gaeilge,
Áth Cliath.

Dear Mr. Morris,

Mr Lloyd has handed me as Hon Sec. of the Publications Committee your letter to him dated 15th December and your Ms of short stories. Such a book, light and popular in character, containing simple Irish and suitable to follow the O'Growney books as a first reader, is urgently needed just now and would form a valuable addition to our series of penny popular booklets, No. 1 of which *An tAthriseoir* has just issued. I think the Publications Comtee would be willing to accept your selections and publish it at their own expense.

It would be necessary however to somewhat modify the dialectic peculiarities. I do not mean to destroy altogether its Ulster flavour, quite the contrary. I wish merely to *tone down* somewhat the purely local forms, leaving the Ulster *blas* intact. I would not thus interfere with such characteristic forms as *chan* any more than I would object to writing the Munster "Ná fuil". Any changes made would be under the supervision of Mr. Lloyd and you could confidently trust to his sympathetic editorship to see that nothing like the vandalism or wholesale boycotting of Ulster forms would be attempted. I shall be glad to hear from you on the subject and trust that we may be able to bring out the collection as a League booklet. With best wishes, Sincerely yours, P. H. Pearse.

To Dr. Walsh.

L. 27/DDA

12.1.1901   Connradh na Gaedhilge,
                                    Áth Cliath.

May it please Your Grace,

I have the honour to acknowledge Your Grace's of yesterday. I am very glad indeed that the pamphlet is on the eve of publication. I look for great results from it. I quite agree that it would not be desirable to extend the pamphlet beyond the convenient limit of 24 pages for the sake of including extra matter in the appendix. I thought at first, after a rough computation, that in its present form the pamphlet would not quite extend to 24 pages.

I have the honour to enclose a copy of the Committee's latest publication, being part 1 of a Recitation Book in Irish, the first of a new series of penny popular booklets. I have the honour to be, Your Grace's obedient servant, P. H. Pearse. Hon. Sec. Publication Comtee.

To Pádraig Ó Muirgheasa.

Pádraig Ó Muirgheasa, a teacher at Donaghmore N.S. Co Monaghan, was a younger brother of Enri Ó Muirgheasa and like Enri was active in the Gaelic League, of which he was the local secretary. In this capacity he had written to Pearse inviting him to lecture at their local branch.

The brother's book referred to in the postscript is *Greann na Gaeilge* ; Part II of *An tAithriseoir* edited by Pearse and Torna was published in 1902.

L. 28/P.Ms.

12.1.1901.   Connradh na Gaedhilge,
                                                  Áth Cliath.

A Mhic Ui Mhuirgheasa, A Chara,

I duly received yours yesterday morning, but had not time to reply till this evening. Any date in February would suit me, but I should prefer if possible a Monday evening to any other, as I am anxious not to be absent from town on either a Wednesday or a Friday, having an Irish class at University College on those days.

As for the subject, having regard to what you say, perhaps "The Gaelic League and its Work", would do. This will give wide scope and will enable me to touch briefly on all the more important phases of the movement. I should be glad to hear your views on the point.

Trusting to hear from you again after you have brought the matter before your Committee, Sincerely yours, P. H. Pearse.

P.S.   I am in communication with your brother as to a book of stories which he has collected. I trust we may be able to bring it out as a number of the new series of penny booklets in Irish. Simple popular matter of the kind is exactly what is required. By the way, could you put me on the track of some Ulster poem, narrative if possible, with plenty of action and fire in it, suitable for inclusion in Part II of *An tAithriseoir?* Pádraig MacPiarais.

To Dr. Walsh.

Dr Walsh's lecture at Baggot St. Training College in December 1900, was published by the Gaelic League in January 1901 as No. 8

of its special series of pamphlets on Education, of which thirty four in all were issued between 1898 and 1910.

L. 29/DDA

19.1.1901.   Connradh na Gaedhilge,
                                    Áth Cliath.

May it please Your Grace,
   I have the honour to enclose some copies of Your Grace's pamphlet, the first delivery of which was made on yesterday evening. I will instruct the office staff to send Your Grace a further supply of copies. I hope to be able to make arrangements for the circulation of this pamphlet on a wholesale scale, and, in addition to distributing it through the ordinary channels will see that a copy is sent to every manager and every National Teacher in Ireland.
   I have, both on my own part and on that of the Publications Committee, to thank Your Grace. for the kindness with which you have placed this pamphlet at our disposal. I hope and believe that it will be the means of inducing a number of managers to forthwith put a bilingual system into practice. I have the honour to be, Your Grace's obedient servant. P. H. Pearse.

To H. Morris.

The book by Henry Morris, the printing details of which are discussed here was *Greann na Gaeilge.*

L. 30/NLI

21.1.1901.   Connradh na Gaeilge,
                                    Áth Cliath.

Dear Mr. Morris,
   I duly received yours of the 12th. which I had not time to acknowledge sooner. I am very glad that we have received your collection as a penny booklet. It will fill a long felt want. I note what you say re toning down and you may rest quite satisfied that your wishes shall be duly observed.
   As regards the vocabulary, by far the best thing will be to wait until the book is set up and paged. You will want to know the pages, lines etc. in order to give references. Moreover I have an idea that the whole collection will not fit in a 16 page booklet. What I propose to do is to hand the book to the printer as it stands, get it

set up and paged and send the paged proof to you to prepare the
vocabulary. Of course you will not include the words in
O'Growney? It would be a great waste of space ... the words not
given in O'Growney – or at least Parts I, II and III of O'Growney
and should devote special attention to the explanation of the
Western forms that occur.

I will endeavour to push the book through as quickly as possible
but our printers are elephantine in their slowness and assinine in
their stupidity, whilst we on whose unhappy shoulders the reading
of proofs fall have so many things on hand that delay is inevitable.
Do not therefore be surprised if the work proceeds more slowly than
you would wish. With best wishes, Sincerely yours. P. H. Pearse.

P.S.   What do you propose to call the book? An attractive and
pithy title will mean much. *Ceol Sidhe*, *Sgéilíní*, *An tAithriseoir*
and *Ráiteacheas* all owe much to their short and catching titles.

To J. J. Doyle.

Mr. Hayes was a Gaelic League musician. Doyle's story *Tadhg
Gabha* which won an Oireachtas literary prize in 1900 appeared in
serial form in the national daily *The Independent* and was issued by
the League as one of its popular penny booklets in 1901.

L. 31/NLI

8th Feb. 1901.   Conradh na Gaedhilge,
                                    Áth Cliath.

Dear Mr. Doyle,
   Yours of the 6th. to hand this morning. I am writing Mr. Hayes,
asking him would he be available for your concert. Failing him, I
will try to make out someone else. You might perhaps write him
yourself also; his address is 48 Cabra Park, Phibsboro'.
   The Publications Comtee have decided to publish your *Tadhg
Gabha* as a penny booklet. Many thanks for so kindly placing it at
our disposal. The *Independent* people have consented to our
republishing it. Kindly do not lose patience if the booklet is an
unconscionable time in making its appearance, as it almost
certainly will be. Our printers are as slow as possible, and we
unfortunates, on whose shoulders the odious task of proof-reading
falls, have already so much more to do than we can manage, that

we are often constrained to keep proofs some weeks in hands before we can find time to read them. I will, of course, send you proofs.

By the way, a letter addressed to me at 5 George's Villa, Sandymount will always find me sooner than one addressed to the League Offices. Yours sincerely, P. H. Pearse.

To J. J. Doyle.

Pearse and J. J. Doyle exchanged opinions in their letters as to the usage and terminology employed in the League publications. *Ráiteachas* was the title of |volume II of "Leabhairíní Gaeilge le haghaidh an tSluaigh", the League's popular penny series.

L. 32/NLI

10.3.1901.   Connradh na Gaeilge,
                                           Áth Cliath.

Dear Mr. Doyle,
Yours of the 7th to hand. You should not have gone to the trouble of sending the stamps. As a compromise, I will apply them to Gaelic League purposes.

I am glad to hear that you are thinking of the Phrase Book competition at the Oireachtas. I recollect that you asked me in a former letter what kind of French and German phrase books were meant in the syllabus. I had not time to reply at the moment, but inserted a description of such a phrase book in the Oireachtas notes which I send to *An Claidheamh* every week. I suppose this caught your eye. The book I referred to – Bosent's – may be had for 1/ = from Gill, I presume. I hope you will try some other competitions also, for instance, the dramatic sketch.

I return you *Tadhg Gabha* and the other pieces. I have not yet been able to get *Tadhg* into the printers hands but hope to be able to do so shortly.

I am glad you like *Ráiteachas*. As regards "Le haghaidh an tSluaigh", I think it fairly common throughout north and south. I first heard it from Fr. O'Leary. "Sluagh" is the common word in Scotland for "the people". You must have heard, also, the Ulster proverb, "Síleann gadaidhe na gcruach gur sladardhe an sluagh". "ar n-a bhaint", is of course, archaic, but I can think of nothing to supply its place. "Bainte" appears to me to be a béarlachas, what would you suggest yourself?

I agree with you that the question of putting *An Claidheamh*

34

on a new footing financially and otherwise, must shortly be tackled. It will probably come up at the next congress. I should be sorry, however, to see the "Irisleabhar" disappear. Mise do chara, Pádraig Mac Piarais.

To Eoin Mac Neill.

I dTaobh na hOibre by Eoghan Ó Neachtain, was one of the popular booklet series published by the League in 1901.

L. 33/NLI

18.3.1901.   Connradh na Gaedhilge,
                                         24 O'Connell St. Upper,
                                         Dublin.

My dear Mac Neill,
    If coming to the Executive meeting tomorrow night, kindly do not forget proofs of *I dTaobh na hOibre*. If unable to come, please leave them for me at Brunswick St., or post them to me at your earliest convenience. I am anxious to get the booklet out at once, as it has now been in hands for some months. Yours very sincerely, P. H. Pearse.

To Eoin Mac Neill.

The conclusion to this letter reads "I remain in haste". The opening greeting "My dear MacNeill" suggests that Pearse was now on more familiar terms with his senior colleague in the League.

L. 34/NLI

22.3.1901.   The Gaelic League,
                                         24 Upper O'Connell St.,
                                         Dublin.

My dear Mac Neill,
    I send you the concluding galleys of *Cormac Ua Conaill*. I should be much obliged of you would let me have them back by Tuesday, as I wish to push the book through as rapidly as possible. You may have read some of those sheets before.

I trust you have by this time shaken off your severe cold. Mise agus deabhadh orm, Pádraig Mac Piarais.

To Dr. Walsh.

Arising from the written and oral evidence presented to the Commission on Intermediate Eduction which reported in 1899, the League resolved to publish in pamphlet form the evidence tendered in regard to the position of the Irish language in the Intermediate curriculum. Those pamphlets of which there were ten in all (two were published later in 1901), contain the evidence of Mahaffy, Bernard, Atkinson, Gwynn and Purser of Trinity College in favour of "expunging" or lowering the status of Irish and the counter evidence of Hyde, MacNeill, O'Hickey, W. B. Yeats, supported by the professional opinions of some foreign scholars, who collectively argued that Irish should be accorded equal prominence as French and German. It is most probable that Pearse did most of the editorial work for these pamphlets.

L. 35/DDA

25.4.1901.   Connradh na Gaedhilge,
                                      Áth Cliath.

May it please Your Grace,
   I have the honour to enclose, as requested by Dr. O'Hickey, advance copies of the eight pamphlets dealing with Irish in the Intermediate system. I trust they will reach Your Grace in due time. I have but just got them from the printers. Three of them are as yet only in proof, one being still in galley form. The whole series will be published tomorrow, and will be immediately circulated to the Commissioners, the Bishops, M.P's, Heads of Intermediate Schools and the Press. I shall give orders at the League Office that copies be sent to Your Grace as soon as they are published. I have the honour to remain, Your Grace, Your Grace's obedient servant. P. H. Pearse.

To Dr. Walsh.

Dr. Walsh sponsored a competition for the best bilingual teaching schemes for National schools in 1901; the winners were M. Coonan,

J. J. Doyle and M. O'Malley. The prize-winning schemes were published by the League in 1901 as *Bilingual Instruction in National Schools.*

L. 36/DDA

4.5.1901.   Connradh na Gaedhilge,
                                             Áth Cliath.

May it please Your Grace,
   The Committee understand from Rev. Dr. O'Hickey that Your Grace is now ready to announce the result of the competition for the best scheme of Bilingual Education, and that, at Dr. O'Hickey's suggestion, Your Grace is willing that the prize schemes should appear as a Gaelic League pamphlet, or series of pamphlets.
   I am directed to inform Your Grace that the Committee will have much pleasure in publishing the schemes, and feel that their publication in that form will be a fitting sequel to the issue of Your Grace's pamphlet on *Bilingual Education.* The Committee would suggest that the four schemes be published in one pamphlet – a course which would render comparison and reference more easy.
   I shall be happy to receive the mss. at Your Grace's convenience. I have the honour to be, Your Grace, Your Grace's obedient servant, P. H. Pearse.

To J. J. Doyle.

The congress referred to, the annual Ard Fheis of the Gaelic League was held in the Gresham Hotel, Dublin on 31st. May. The Pearse family had moved from St. George's Villa to Liosán in March 1901.

L. 37/NLI

27.6.1901.   Connradh na Gaedhilge,
                                             Áth Cliath.

Dear Mr. Doyle,
   Yours to hand. My reason for delaying *Tadhg Gabha* is that there is another booklet due before it, which has met unavoidable delay in going through the press. I am now getting this through, and will then push on *Tadhg* as rapidly as possible. I will send you proofs, and will also, as you suggested, send them to Mr. Comyn. I went to the League Offices the day after the congress, in order to

find out where you were staying, as I wished to ask you to spend an evening with me. I found, however, that you had just left for your train. The next time you are in Dublin you must pay me a visit. By the way, my address henceforth is "Liosán, Sandymount", I left my previous address some three months ago.

Please give my kind regards to Mrs. Doyle, I am, dear Mr. Doyle, Sincerely yours, Patrick H. Pearse.

To Dr. Walsh.

A paper on the philosophy of the language movement by Rev. Patrick Forde, B.D. was presented at Maynooth in December 1899; it was subsequently published in *An Claidheamh Soluis* and issued by the League as *The Irish Language Movement; its Philosophy* in 1901.

L. 38/DDA

17.7.1901.   Connradh na Gaedhilge,
                                      Áth Cliath.

My Lord Archbishop,
    I have the honour to acknowledge receipt of the ms. sent by Your Grace to the League Offices on Monday last. I have handed it to the printer, and hope to let Your Grace have the first proofs by the end of the week.

With regard to one of the points referred to by Your Grace on Saturday, viz – as to whether the schemes should appear in one single pamphlet, or should be divided between two, – the Committee is of the opinion, pending final instructions from Your Grace, that the former plan is the better. We shall, however, be in a better position to judge when the matter is set up in type.

I have to thank Your Grace for so kindly placing these schemes at our disposal. Their publication will supply the need of the hour in the schools in the Irish-speaking localities.

We are formally announcing the forthcoming appearance of the prize schemes as a League pamphlet, – without, of course, mentioning the names of the winners. I presume Your Grace will make the award public previous to the appearance of the pamphlet.

I have the honour to enclose a copy of our latest pamphlet, Father Forde's paper on the philosophy of the Language movement. I have the honour to remain, Your Grace's obedient servant, Patrick H. Pearse. Hon. Sec. Publications Comtee.

To H. Morris.

Mr. Naughton (Eoin Ó Neachtain) was an active member of the League as was Una ni Fhaircheallaigh; her novelette was published in 1901 as was his popular instructional pamphlet. Mr. Naughton was editor of *An Claidheamh Soluis* before Pearse.

L. 39/P.Ms.

19.7.1901.   Connradh na Gaedhilge,
                                          Áth Cliath.

Dear Mr. Morris,

Yours to hand. I have handed back proofs to printer and the booklet should be issued by the end of next week. I note what you say re cover. By the way, there are several ways of spelling "Henry" in Irish, – Hanraoi, Eanraoi, Enri, etc., Which do you prefer? Again, in what form would you wish to announce your authorship on the cover? "E. Ua Muirgheasa do sgriobh" or "do bhailigh" or "do ghléas"? Kindly let me have your wishes on these points as soon as possible.

Of course, the printers are not wholly to blame for the delay in the publication of your booklet. That delay was intentional on the part of the Committee. It would never do to hurl Irish books at the head of the public in too rapid succession. Time must be allowed for each book to be advertised, to get known, to sell. As it is, many believe we are forcing the pace too hard. We are anxious to give Mr. Naughton's *I dTaoibh na hOibre* and Miss O'Farrelly's *Gradh agus Cradh* a chance of selling before launching your book. I have some six or eight mss. for booklets in hands at present, but am withholding them in order to allow a little breathing time. We have at present some *36* books in preparation or in the press, and each must take its turn. I can easily understand your impatience, however, to see the collection of stories on sale.

I must apologize for not answering your last two letters. It was a physical impossibility for me to do so. Moreover, it did not occur to me that an answer was necessary, as I presumed you would make the changes suggested when reading the final proofs. I am, dear Mr. Morris, Yours very faithfuly, Patrick H Pearse.

To H. Morris.

Sean-fhocail na Mumhan was published as Volume VI in the Popular Penny Pamphlets in 1902.

L. 40/P.Ms.

24.7.1901.   Connradh na Gaedhilge,
                              Áth Cliath.

Dear Mr. Morris,
  Yours of the 22nd to hand. I note your wishes re your name, etc., on cover of *Greann na Gaedhilge.*
  The Publications Committee meets only once a month – on the first Tuesday in each month; there has hence been no opportunity of formally obtaining its sanction for a second booklet of stories. I think, however, you may safely proceed with the work, and I venture to promise you that the Committee will accept it. We have already decided on publishing a series of penny collections of proverbs, classified according to provinces. The ms. of the first of these – *Sean-fhocail na Mumhan* – collected by Tadhg O'Donoghue has been ready for the press for some time. If you could get together a similar collection of Ulster proverbs, you may take it for granted that we will publish it. Mr O'Donoghue's collection contains some 750 proverbs. They are arranged in alphabetical order. Half a dozen such booklets could be compiled with little trouble. I am, dear Mr. Morris, Yours very faithfully. Patrick H. Pearse.

To Dr. Walsh.

L. 41/DDA

27.7.1901.   Connradh na Gaedhilge,
                              Áth Cliath.

May it please Your Grace,
  I have the honour to enclose proofs of the prize bilingual schemes. I hoped to have them quite a week ago, – indeed, the printers promised them by Saturday last, – yet they came to hand only to-day.
  I note that the pamphlet will run to 24 pp. I did not give the pamphlet any title, nor do I recollect that Your Grace suggested any. The present title seems to have been given by the printers.

The great object of publishing these schemes being, as I take it, to induce managers and teachers to form schemes for their own schools and to show them how to go about it, it occurs to me that it would be advisable to include in the introduction a note recommending managers and teachers in Irish speaking districts to draw up programmes for their schools on the lines of the models given, making such modifications as the needs of their respective localities may require, and then to forward these programmes for approval to the National Board. This would, I hope, have the effect of inducing a certain number of managers to introduce a bilingual programme at once, – and this is the need of the hour. We shall take care that the pamphlet is brought prominently under the notice of the proper parties, by forwarding a copy to every manager and teacher in the Irish speaking area. I have the honour to be, Your Grace's obedient servant, Patrick H. Pearse, Hon. Sec. Publications Comtee.

To Dr. Walsh.

Dr. M. O'Hickey was a native of Carrickbeg, that part of the Tipperary town on the Suir which lies in Co. Waterford.

L. 42/DDA

29.7.1901.   Connradh na Gaedhilge,
                                      Áth Cliath.

May it please Your Grace,
   I have the honour to acknowledge Your Grace's of yesterday. I am glad Your Grace has returned the proofs direct to Browne and Nolan, as it will save time. It is most desirable that these model schemes should be in the hands of the public as early as possible. Everyday the necessity for something of the kind is brought home to members of the League Executive. At the last meeting for instance, letters were read from two teachers asking us to draw up programmes for them. We replied that Your Grace's prize schemes would shortly be published, and that teachers should draw up programmes for themselves on the lines of these.
   I think Dr. O'Hickey is at present at Carrickbeg, Carrick-on-Suir. I had a letter from him from that address on the 25th inst. I have the honour to be, Your Grace's obedient servant, Patrick Pearse. Hon. Sec. Publication Committee.

To J. J. Doyle.

L. 43/NLI

3.8.1901.   Connradh na Gaedhilge,
                             Áth Cliath.

Dear Mr. Doyle,
    At long last I send you the first galley of "Tadhg". It reached me
from printer only to-night. I am sending proof also, as you
requested, to Mr. Comyn. I will let you have balance by Thursday.
I will see that the booklet is on sale before the date of the Munster
Feis. Please let me have proof back by return. Mise agus deabhadh
orm, Pádraig Mac Piarais.

P.S.   As you are doubtless aware, we are printing as a League
pamphlet the four best of the Bilingual schemes sent in to the
Archbishop. Yours is one of them, as I think the Archbishop has
told you. They will be published in a week or ten days.

To H. Morris.

L. 44/P.Ms.

7.8.1901.   Connradh na Gaedhilge,
                             Áth Cliath.

Dear Mr. Morris,
    I enclose you a few copies of *Greann na Gaedhilge* which has
just been published. If you let me know how many copies you would
wish for your own use, I will have them forwarded to you. You
might also say if there are any local or other papers to which you
would wish copies to be sent for review. The booklet will be sent in
the ordinary course to the chief Dublin and provincial papers but
there may be some local journals which you might wish to get
copies.
    As regards Part II, the committee think it best to wait some little
while. We shall then be able to see how Part I is going. Moreover I
have the mss of several booklets in hand, which must be worked off
gradually.
    With reference to the collection of proverbs, you may proceed
with it, and let me have the ms. when completed, for submission to

the Committee. I think you ought to confine yourself to Ulster proverbs, as Munster is being dealt with by Mr. O'Donoghue, and I am looking out for someone to take up Connacht. Mise do chara, Pádraig Mac Piarais.

To J. J. Doyle.

The serialised version of *Tadhg Gabha* in *The Independent* was used as manuscript to publish the story in booklet form. The Phrase Book was an attempt by Doyle to provide a work in Irish comparable to Bosent's French Phrase Book already referred to in the letter of 10.3.1901. It was published by the League in 1902 under the title *Leabhar Cainte.*

L. 45/NLI

8.8.1901.   Connradh na Gaedhilge,
                                    Áth Cliath.

Dear Mr. Doyle,
   I duly received yours with corrected proof, which I have returned to printer. I have no objection to the few changes you suggest, – "chun a d'iarraidh", "nár tháinig", etc. My own idea is that so long as substantive uniformity and consistency in spelling are secured, a reasonable latitude may be given to individual tastes, especially in professedly colloquial works like *Tadhg Gabha.*
   I return the *Independent* copy, as you requested. I also send you the balance of proofs, which please return to me as early as possible. To save time, you might address them to me at Liosán, Sandymount. I suppose you will not require to see the second proofs.
   By the way, what is your rendering in Irish of "Republished by permission of the proprietors of the daily *Independent & Nation?*" It will be necessary to prefix something to that effect to the story, that being the condition on which the *Independent* people gave it to us.
   We are publishing the Phrase Book. The editing, which has been undertaken by Mr. Barrett, will be tedious as it will be necessary to amalgamate the four books. We have not yet decided whether to issue the work in one volume or in parts. Mise do chara, Pádraig Mac Piarais.

43

To J. J. Doyle.

The address and date are missing from this letter; from internal evidence and from earlier and later letters to Doyle, it would seem to have been written in mid-August 1901.

Tadhg Gabha was published by the League according to its own catalogue in 1901. The concluding greeting reads: "I remain in great haste etc."

L. 46/NLI

[August 1901.]

Dear Mr. Doyle,

I enclose a few copies of *Tadhg Gabha* which was published on Monday. If you let me know how many copies you would like for your own use, I will have them sent on. You might mention also if there are any particular local papers to which you would wish copies to be sent for review. They will be sent in the ordinary course to the dailies, and chief Dublin and provincial weeklies. Mise agus deifir an domhain orm. Pádraig Mac Piarais.

To H. Morris.

Cormac Ua Conaill was a story by Fr. Dineen of the Desmond Rebellion in Munster, published by the League in 1901. Morris was collecting and editing the Ulster proverbs.

L. 47/P.Ms.

18.8.1901.   Connradh na Gaedhilge,
                                     Áth Cliath.

Dear Mr. Morris,

Yours of the 12th to hand. I have given directions at the League Offices for a dozen copies of *Greann na Gaedhilge* to be forwarded to you. Of course, if you require additional copies at any time, they are at your disposal. I am sending copies for review to the papers you mention.

It is wonderful how misprints escape one in reading proofs. *Cormac Ua Conaill,* for instance, was read three times by our most accurate proof-readers, yet misprints are numerous. Dr. O'Hickey read the proofs of the Pastoral *thirteen* times, detecting

44

new misprints each time, and yet, when it appeared, there were several mistakes.

As regards the proverbs, I would prefer to see no translations except in the case of obscure or difficult ones. Mr. O'Donoghue's collection has no translations. I think from 600 to 700 proverbs without translations could be fitted into a 16-page booklet. As you say, it would be well to have the various collections uniform. Mise do chara, Pádraig Mac Piarais.

To J. J. Doyle.

The League was divided as to its appropriate involvement with those other Celtic movements which collectively were known as the Pan Celts. Professor Heinrich Zimmer was Professor of Sanskrit and Celtic Languages in the University of Greifswald; Kuno Meyer held the Chair of Celtic Languages at Liverpool University.
The postscript translates as "I am going to the Munster Feis on Monday, I hope to enjoy my visit".

L. 48/NLI

31.8.1901.   Connradh na Gaedhilge,
                                        Áth Cliath.

My dear Mr. Doyle,
    I have given orders at the League Offices for the number of copies of "Tadhg" and of the Bilingual Programmes which you require to be sent on to you. You will probably have received them by now. You are welcome to as many further copies of each as you may require.
    By the way, I send copies of all our publications to the *Derry Journal*, but do not know whether they are reviewed or not. It might be in your line to see that they are, or, if necessary, to write notices yourself. It is desirable that all our books and pamphlets should be reviewed prominently by the local papers.
    I am sending "Tadhg" for review to the papers you mention, as well as to about twenty-five others. I sent *Greann na Gaedhilge* to a number of Northern papers, and will send it to one to two others.
    I agree with you as to our proper attitude towards the Pan-Celts. The fact is that the League made a gigantic blunder two years ago in deciding to have nothing to do with the affair. The result is that the foreign visitors and delegates, seeing nothing of the real

language movement, have gone away with the impression that the Gaelic League is a fraud, and that there is no language movement in Ireland. One of the Highlanders publicly stated as much. Some may say, of course, that it does not matter after all what foreigners think. Still it is regrettable that the leaders of kindred movements, as well as such men as Zimmer, Kuno Meyer and Robinson, should leave Ireland with the impression that no effort is being made to save the language. That they have this impression is not the fault of the Pan-Celts here, who did the best they could, but of the Gaelic League. Mise do chara, Pádraig Mac Piarais.

P.S.   Táim ag dul go Feis na Mumhan Dia Luain. Tá súil agam le haimsir aoibhinn a chaitheamh ann.

To Dr. Walsh.

L. 49/DDA

12.10.1901.   Connradh na Gaedhilge,
                                     Áth Cliath.

May it please Your Grace,
    Knowing that Your Grace was away from home, I did not forward you copies of the pamphlet containing the prize bilingual schemes on its publication. I now have the honour to enclose some copies and will have a further supply forwarded on Monday next.
    I take this opportunity of thanking Your Grace on behalf of the Publications Committee for so kindly placing these schemes at our disposal. I trust their publication will have the desired effect. Copies have been forwarded, or are being forwarded, to every manager and teacher in the country.
    I hope shortly to send Your Grace a proof of the First Irish Reading Book (to follow the Primer), and trust, as in the case of the Primer, to have the benefit of Your Grace's suggestions and criticisms on it. I have the honour to be, Your Grace, Your Grace's obedient servant, Patrick H. Pearse.

To Mr. Morris.

Blátha Bealtaine, written by Máire de Buitléir and translated by

Tomás Ó Conceanainn, was published in 1902; the biography *Dubhaltach Firbhisigh* was written by Eoin Ó Neachtain and published in the same year.

L. 50/P.Ms.

22.10.1901.   Connradh na Gaedhilge.
                               Áth Cliath.

Dear Mr. Morris,
    Yours to hand. I see no objection to your proceeding with *Greann na Gaedhilge*, Part II, first. There are, however, three booklets due before it, – *Blátha Bealtaine, Sean-fhocail na Mumhan* and *Beatha Dubhaltaigh Mhic Firbhísigh*. These three should, if not all published, at least be all in type within three weeks or a month, and by that time we should be able to push on *Greann na Gaedhilge*. We intend in future to illustrate any booklets that lend themselves to illustration so you might mention one or two of the stories which you think most adaptable for illustration.
    I have not yet seen the returns as to the sale of Part I of *Greann na Gaedhilge*, but as soon as they come to hand I will let you know. Mise do chara, Pádraig Mac Piarais.

To Fr. J. M. O'Reilly.

The pamphlet *The Threatening Metempsychosis of a Nation*, published by the League in 1901, was based on a paper delivered by Fr. O'Reilly before the Maynooth Union in June 1900.
    This letter was written by Pearse on one side of a double sheet of Gaelic League notepaper. In replying Fr. O'Reilly, used the three remaining sides of the original notepaper; he explains that he is forced to use "this unmannerly" procedure because his own supply of notepaper was weather-bound. He was at that time curate on Clare Island off the Mayo coast.

L. 51/NLI

1.1.1902.   Connradh na Gaedhilge,
                               Áth Cliath.

Dear Father O'Reilly,
    I enclose you a dozen copies of your pamphlet. If you let me

47

know how many more you would like for your own use, I will have them forwarded to you.

I hope shortly to send you further proofs of the First Reading Book.

Again thanking you for placing your paper at our disposal. I am, dear Father O'Reilly, Yours sincerely, Patrick H. Pearse.

To H. Morris.

L. 52/P.Ms./G

13.1.1902.   The Gaelic League,
                                     Dublin.

Dear Friend,

I received your letter and the copy for *Greann na Gaeilge* enclosed. I have sent the manuscript to the printer. I will forward the proofs to you as soon as I receive them from him. I remain, your friend, Patrick Pearse.

To J. J. Doyle.

During his extended visit to the Aran Islands in 1897, Pearse developed a keen interest in the Irish names of birds, flowers and wild animals. He checked the names he collected in Inis Meadhon with various friends and compared the Ulster and Munster versions with those from Connacht. He published his Aran Collection in *Irisleabhar na Gaeilge* in 1899.

L. 53/NLI/G

17.1.1902.   The Gaelic League,
                                     Dublin.

Dear Friend,

I received your letter. We will willingly send you as many copies of the Phrase Book as you require. A batch will be dispatched to you tomorrow. Should you require further supplies, you may have them.

There is a brisk demand for the book according to what I have
heard. Your friend, P. Mac Piarais.

P.S. I have collected around the country the names of birds,
which I intend to submit to *Irisleabhar na Gaeilge*. Could you
kindly supply me with any unusual names which you have heard in
Kerry or Donegal? I should be very grateful to you. Which Irish
names have you got for magpie, falcon, owl, linnet, redwing,
redpole? I have Irish versions for these but I am interested in the
Kerry versions.

To Mr. Morris.

L. 54/P.Ms.

22.1.1902.   Connradh na Gaedhilge,
                              Áth Cliath.

A Charaid,
  Here is the ms. of that story after all. It was under my hand
when I last wrote to you, yet, I did not see it!
  I intend – with your permission – to propose at the next meeting
of the Publications Comtee, that the Comtee. recommend the
Coisde Gnotha to place you on that Comtee. I hope you will have
no objection, as I imagine the work of the Comtee. will have an
interest for you, and the northern element wants strengthening.
Mise do charaid, Pádraig Mac Piarais.

To J. J. Doyle.

Following on his queries of 17th January, Pearse in this letter is
checking on specific forms of bird names from different districts
some of which Doyle had sent to him. *Beirt Fhear* was the serial
which Doyle was writing for *An Claidheamh Soluis*.

L. 55/NLI/G

7.2.1902.   The Gaelic League,
                                       Dublin.

Dear Friend,
   Many thanks for the bird names which you sent. Here are some
queries concerning them: Is "Conchubhairín a' chaipín" the same
as "Conchbhairín a' charabhat"? Are "Máire Fhada" and "Nóra
na bportaithe" the same? What kind is "Diarmín riabhach"? Is it
the hedge sparrow?
   I think it would be appropriate to publish *Beirt Fhear* as a
book – I will raise the question with the Publications Committee. I
remain, in great haste, Pádraig Mac Piarais

To Miss Brownrigg.

Miss Brownrigg was a national teacher in a Church of Ireland
school in Dublin who was a member of the Gaelic League. She
seems from this letter to have been friendly with Pearse for a
considerable time; the book which he described as "long-promised"
was *Four Lectures on Gaelic Topics* which he published in 1898.
Looking back four years later he sees his first excursion into print
as being rash and somewhat of a boyish exploit.
   Seemingly Miss Brownrigg requested Pearse to propose a
suitable Irish form for the house of a friend "Hillside".

L.56/P.Ms.

7.2.1902.   Liosán,
                                       Sandymount.

Dear Miss Brownrigg,
   I owe you an apology for my delay in answering yours of the 2nd.
My excuse must be that I am afflicted with the chronic complaint
of Gaelic Leaguers – overwork, so much so indeed, that I sometimes
find it hard to get time to even say my prayers.
   I think the best name for the house would be "Taobh na Coille"!
"Taobh" (literally "side") is used in place-names to denote the side
of a hill; "coill" of course is "wood", so that the name means "The
hill-side of the wood". The pronunciation as far as it can be
represented in English letters is "Thaev na Cullia". In the northern
half of Ireland the first word would be pronounced "Theev".
   By the way the description you sent me of the situation of the

house was so delightful that I am quite envious of the fortunate possessor.

I send you by this post the long-promised copy of the little book I rashly published four years ago. Kindly recollect that its publication was, in every sense what an Irish romanticist would call a "mac-gníomh" or "boyish exploit".

I have never heard any direct Irish equivalent of "I wish you a happy birthday." An Irish speaker would probably say something like "Go mbadh slán bhéas tú bliadhain ó inniu"! "May you be well this day twelvemonth"! I am, dear Miss Brownrigg, Yours sincerely, Patrick H. Pearse.

To J. J. Doyle.

Pearse is still sorting out the bird names and in the process shows that he has a sound knowledge of ornithology.

He frequently discussed forms and idioms with informed authorities like Doyle and here he illustrates how closely he had studied the spoken language of the Connacht Gaeltacht. He was serialising "Lá fá'n Tuaith" in *An Claidheamh Soluis* in 1902 and requests critical comment from Doyle. He stresses his intention to reflect only the expressions and vocabulary which he had heard in Connemara by underlining the sentence which begins "In writing ...... speaker".

Obviously Doyle had questioned him as to the identity of the writer who used the pseudonym "Cnoc na Reidh". *Cill Airne* by Fr. Dineen and *An Leabhar Cainte* by Doyle were recent League publications. Stephen Barrett was treasurer of the League. The sentence in Irish translates: "The amount you request will be gladly paid".

Pearse advises Doyle to include a plot into the dialogue serial which he was writing for *An Claidheamh Soluis*.

L. 57/NLI

10.2.1902.   Connradh na Gaedhilge,
                                          Áth Cliath.

A Chara,

Yours of the 8th to hand. From your description "Conchubhairín a' Charabhat" appears to be either the Blackcap or the Stonechat. I have heard "Donnchadh a' Chaipín" and "Máire a' Truis" applied to the former, but it is a rare bird, and your description seems to

51

suit the latter better. Could you describe "Diarmín Riabhach" for me?

"Teana uait" is very common in Connacht in the sense of "Come along". "Siubhail *uait*" is also used. It is just possible that "teana uait" is a corruption of "teanamuid", but I am inclined to think that "uait" is the prepositional pronoun.

I have frequently heard "Fáinne" used by good native speakers of a ring of persons, animals, etc; "Chruinnigh siad thart timcheall orm 'na bhfáinne"; "Asail ag sodarnaighil thart 'na bhfáinne". How would you express "they gathered round me in a ring"? "Tar éis 'Merioca" is very common in Connacht in the sense of "back from America"; "Raibh se thar éis 'Merioca an uair sin"? "Bhí Tomás thar éis 'Merioca". The man or woman "thar éis 'Merioca" is one of the regular types in Connacht village life.

I should be delighted to hear your remarks on any points of idiom, etc., that strike you in the future instalments of "La fá'n Tuaith". In writing it my aim was *not to introduce a single expression which I had not heard from a native Connacht speaker.* I have managed to include in it a lot of rare words and idioms common in the spoken language but which rarely find their way into print.

Ni feasach me cia hé "Cnoc na Reidh".

Both *Cill Áirne* and *An Leabhar Cainte* were sent to the *Derry Journal.* Could you not engineer reviews of them?

I will see Barrett to-morrow, and arrange with him about sending you copies of the second issue of "Leabhar Cainte". Beidh an méid d'iarrais orainn agat, agus fáilte.

I think you would do well to work a plot through *Beirt Fhear.* It would keep up the interest, which purposeless dialogues might lack. I will write you on the subject after next meeting of Committee. Mise do chara, Pádraig Mac Piarais.

To Dr. Walsh.

L. 58/DDA

3.3.1902.   Connradh na Gaedhilge,
                                                        Áth Cliath.

May it please Your Grace,
    I have the honour to enclose proof of *An Chead Leightheoir*

Gaedhilge or *First Irish Reader* intended to be taken up by pupils of National Schools in Irish speaking districts as soon as they have mastered the Primer published twelve months ago.

Your Grace was so kind as to let us have the benefits of your suggestions on the Primer and the Committee now ventures to trespass on your kindness a second time. I should be grateful if Your Grace would kindly glance over the proof enclosed and note any points that strike you as standing in need of improvement. Needless to say, Your Grace's criticisms and suggestions shall be welcomed by the Committee. Thanking you in anticipation, I have the honour to be, Your Grace, Your Grace's obedient servant, Patrick H. Pearse.

To Dr. Walsh.

L. 59/DDA

12.3.1902.   Connradh na Gaedhilge,
                             Áth Cliath.

May it please Your Grace,

I must thank Your Grace very sincerely for so kindly reading the proof of *An Chéad Leightheoir Gaedhilge* and letting us have the benefit of your suggestions thereon.

Iu and ae on p. 64 are undoubtedly out of place. I have transferred them to a column where they seem to fit in better.

I expect that the pictures will, as Your Grace observes, be much improved in appearance when finally printed off. We have discarded one or two of the pictures for better ones. Amongst those discarded is the "School-House" on p. 39, for which one without a shingle sign-board has been substituted.

I find that Your Grace's subscription to the Language fund for 1900–01 was £10, which was sent about September 1900. I am sure the Executive would be grateful if Your Grace, in forwarding subscription for the current year, would kindly send a letter for publication, dealing with the Fund or with some other question of interest in the Gaelic League world.

Again thanking Your Grace for so kindly looking over the "Reader", I have the honour to be, Your Grace, Your Grace's obedient servant, Patrick H. Pearse.

To Mr. Morris.

L. 60/P.Ms.

23.4.1902.   Connradh na Gaedhilge,
                                               Áth Cliath.

Dear Mr. Morris,
    Yours of the 21st. duly to hand.
    I quite agree with you that *Sean-Fhocail na Mumhan* would have
been much the better of a short vocabulary, or at any rate of
occasional explanatory notes. Indeed a collection of proverbs is to a
large extent, no better than a collection of words, without some sort
of commentary. The issue of *Sean-Fhocail* without vocabulary or
notes was due not so much to set design of the Publications
Committee, as to the taste of the individual editor. The Committee
therefore, will be rather glad than the contrary of the inclusion of a
short vocab. and notes in your book of Ulster proverbs.
    What you say of *Cill Áirne* is very true, but both Father Dineen
and the Committee prefer to make a distinction between the mode
of dealing with original literary work in Irish on the one hand, and
professed students' textbooks on the other. *Cill Áirne* is intended
rather for readers of Irish than for students. At the same time, I
believe personally, that even the most accomplished reader of Irish
would be glad of a vocabulary of the more difficult words. Mise do
chara, Pádraig Mac Piarais.

To Mr. Morris.

L. 61/P.Ms.

17.7.1902.   Connradh na Gaedhilge,
                                               Áth Cliath.

A Chara,
    Yours enclosing ms. of Part II of *Greann na Gaedhilge* duly to
hand. I will send you proofs when I get them from the printers. The
booklet will be formally submitted to the Editorial Sub-Committee
at its next meeting on 29th inst.
    Many thanks for the booklets, which I had not seen before. They
seem admirably adapted for the purpose you have in view. I shall

have pleasure in bringing your views as to books and teaching methods before the Committee. Mise do chara, Pádraig Mac Piarais.

To Eoin Mac Neill.

During the holiday referred to in this letter, which he spent in Galway and Connemara, Pearse visited the Connacht Feis and wrote an article on it for the issue of *An Claidheamh Soluis* of 30th August. He had by now established the practice of retreating to the West for short holidays and when possible, devoting his time there to writing; earlier in 1902 he had spent some time at Easter in Rosmuc where he had written the article *Cois na Siúire* which appeared in *An Claidheamh Soluis* of the 5th April describing his visit to Carrick-on-Suir in March of that year. The opening and closing salutations of the letter read as follows: "Dear Mac Neill", and "I am your friend".

L. 62/NLI

14.8.1902.   The Gaelic League,
                                   24 Upper O'Connell St.,
                                   Dublin.

A Niallaigh, a chara,
   I hope you will be able to let me have back the Ms I sent you for report in time for submission to a second Reader before the next meeting of the Pub. Comtee. As I am leaving home for some days on Tuesday next, it would be necessary for me to have them before then to enable me to post them in time, as I do not expect to return till just before the meeting. Mise do charaid, Pádraig Mac Piarais.

To J. H. Lloyd.

L. 63/NLI/G

18.8.1902.   The Gaelic League,
                                   Dublin.

Dear Lloyd,
   Would you kindly proof this pamphlet and return it to me as soon as possible.

Enclosed please find the account of the discussion at the Ard Fheis. Do you endorse it? I remain, in great haste, (as I am about to depart for Galway), Your friend, Pádraig Mac Piarais.

To Mr. Morris.

L. 64/P.Ms.

16.9.1902.   Connradh na Gaedhilge,
                                              Áth Cliath.

Dear Mr. Morris,

By a rule recently adopted by the Publications Comtee, all books submitted to the Comtee must be read and approved by at least two of the Comtee's Readers before being accepted. When I brought your ms. before the July meeting of the Comtee. it was decided that this rule should apply to it. I then sent it to two Readers, and have only just got it back from the second. In order to save time, I will now hand it to the printer, without waiting for the formal sanction of the Comtee.

As regards the proverbs, there would scarcely be time to have them read and reported on in time for this month's Comtee. meeting. The earliest date at which the Comtee. could consider them would therefore be the October meeting, which will be held in the last week of the month. The printing could then be gone on with at once. Mise do charaid. Pádraig Mac Piarais.

To H. Morris.

The missing story is part of the copy for Part III of *Greann na Gaeilge*; Morris was elected to the Coisde Gnótha or Executive Committee of the League at the 1902 Congress.

L. 65/P.Ms.

20.9.1902.   Connradh na Gaedhilge,
                                    Áth Cliath.

A Charaid,

I owe you an apology for having lost sight of the query in yours
of the 9th inst. The fact is I jotted down some Irish phrases on the
back of your letter, and inserted it in a book with a view to copying
out the phrases at my leisure. This evening I took up the book and
discovered your letter with its unanswered query about the ms. of
the last story you sent me.

I cannot lay my hand on the story at present, but I have it
somewhere. Some of my papers are in my own place, some at the
League Office, and at the moment, I can't say where your story is.
You need not go to the trouble of writing it out again, as it will
certainly turn up, and I will hand it to the printers with the rest of
Part III.

Part II has been well received and favourably reviewed, – except
in one quarter where it has been handled rather roughly.

My congratulations on your joining the Coisde Gnótha, to whose
ranks, I am sure you will prove a valuable addition. Mise do
charaid. Pádraig Mac Piarais.

To Mr. Morris.
L. 66/P.Ms.

2.10.1902.   Connradh na Gaedhilge,
                                    Áth Cliath.

A Charaid,

I enclose proof of *Greann na Gaedhilge* Part II. The whole of it,
together with vocab. should fit into the 16 pages.

At its last meeting, the Publications Committee formally
accepted the book for publication. The Commitee offers you £4 for
the copyright, this being the standard remuneration decided on for
16 page booklets. It is small, but the low price at which the booklets
are sold does not permit the Committee to offer a larger sum. Mise
do charaid, Pádraig Mac Piarais.

To J. J. Doyle.

The last sentence of first paragraph reads: "If so, let me have it, as the Munstermen say" *Ar Lorg Poitin* was a Doyle story, being serialised in *An Claidheamh Soluis.* The last sentence of the letter translates as: "I trust that you and your family are well. Your friend," ...

L. 67/NLI/B

2.12.1902.   Connradh na Gaedhilge,
                                          Áth Cliath.

A Charaid,
  The Publication Committee decided last night to publish *Beirt Fhear.* It is in favour of publishing it all in one book, rather than in penny instalments. As a single book, it will be handier and more useful to students. Do you propose to add any more to what you have already sent me? If so, sgaoil chugham é, mar adeir na Muimhnigh.
  With regard to the other books, as they are largely the same in character as *Beirt Fhear,* the Committee thinks it wiser to defer their publication till we see how *Beirt Fhear* gets on.
  An Claidheamh may republish *Ar Lorg Poitin* for its own benefit when completed.
  Tá súil agam go bhfuil tú féin agus do mhuinntir i sláinte mhaith. Mise do charaid, Pádraig Mac Piarais.

To Mr. Morris.

L. 68/P.Ms.

6.12.1902.   Connradh na Gaedhilge,
                                          Áth Cliath.

A Charaid,
  Yours to hand. You had better send on the other story, as the text is not yet printed, I think. In any case, it will be possible to insert another story.
  The cover on the last proof was set up by the printer on his own hook – hence the omission of your name, and of the number of the

booklets in the series. You may also have noticed that the title was from type and not a block, as it should be.

I think you must be mistaken in your recollection as to the place where *Greann na Gaedhilge, Part I*, was mentioned in the Publication Comtee's report to Congress. I have not a copy of the report by me at the moment but I am quite certain that *Greann na Gaedhilge* was referred to under the head of "Popular Booklets" and under that head only. Mise agus deifir orm, Do charaid, Pádraig Mac Piarais.

To J. J. Doyle.

When Doyle's Phrase Book *Leabhar Cainte* won a prize at the Oireachtas, and its copyright passed to the League, he sought further remuneration following its successful publication. Pearse manages here to mollify an irate author who is also a friend of his, by praising his reviewing activities in the local Derry newspaper. The Reading Charts and the associated Picture Book were instructional aids published by the League, which were pedagogically advanced in concept and design.

L. 69/NLI

9.12.1902.   Connradh na Gaedhilge,
                                               Áth Cliath.

A Charaid,
    Yours of yesterday to hand. The Coisde Gnótha has referred the whole matter back to the Publications Comtee, so that we shall discuss it again at our next meeting, when, I hope, we will come to a more satisfactory decision.

    Lest you might think there was an animus of any sort behind the Comtee's decision, I had better let you know the exact ground of the decision. The Minutes, as Minutes always are on such points, are rather unsatisfactory.

    It was urged that the *Leabhar Cainte*, was sent to the League on certain definite conditions, – viz., that if successful, a certain sum was to be paid as prize, and the book would henceforth become the property of the League. The fact of the book's subsequently proving a valuable property to the League did not affect the bargain; all that was weighed when the book was sent in as an Oireachtas competition. These are not my own views, – I merely report them as the opinions which were given expression to at the meeting. The

59

Comtee, rightly or wrongly, approached the question from a strictly shop-keeper standpoint.

As a matter of fact, however, I believe exaggerated notions are entertained of the success, in a *commercial* sense, of the book. That it will pay *ultimately*, I have no doubt, but up to the present it has not paid, or anything like it. I have not the figures before me, but I believe I am well within the mark in saying that the receipts on the sale of the book up to the present have not done much more than pay a quarter of the cost of its production. I mention this not, of course, as justifying, but in a certain sense as explaining the Comtee's apparent niggardliness.

However, we will thrash out the whole matter again, and shall be able, I trust, to make you a proposal which you can consider.

I suppose you are working away at *Beirt Fhear*, the remainder of which you can let me have at your convenience. Beir Buaidh agus beannacht, Do charaid, Pádraig Mac Piarais.

P.S. Many thanks for your valuable little notices of our new books in the *Derry People* and elsewhere. We are publishing two important new works this week – the Reading Charts and the Picture Book – which I hope you will boom. It is a pity that more Leaguers do not follow your example in contributing pars. on new books to the local press.

To H. Morris.

Pearse was anxious to confine all the League's Penny pamphlet series to a uniform length of 16 pages; in his earlier letter of 20th September to Morris, that may have been the real issue in the case of the "missing" story, which the author wished to incorporate in Part II. The reference here to *An tAithriseoir* Part II, of which Pearse was a co-author, may indicate that Morris had pointed out an exception to the 16-page rule.

The Report furnished by Pearse, as Secretary of the Publications Committee, to the Ard Fheis of the League, may have displeased Morris as to its accuracy in defining his authorship of *Greann na Gaeilge*. Pearse promises amends and clarification before publication of the report.

13.12.1902. Connradh na Gaedhilge,
Áth Cliath.

Dear Mr. Morris,

I duly received additional story and vocabulary for *Greann na Gaedhilge.* On looking into the matter, however, I found that the material already in type made exactly 16 pages. It was a mistake of the printer's to spread it into 20 pages, by inserting a title-page and leaving 2½ pages blank. It was, of course, a 16-page booklet that we contemplated all along. We shall, therefore, hold the additional story over for Part III, which, I suppose, will be forthcoming sometime. These 16-page booklets are phenomenal value, and we could not well afford to increase them in size without an increase in price. Part II of *An tAithriseoir* has 20 pages because the matter could not possibly have been crowded into 16.

I told the printers to print and deliver at once, as, now, that no new matter is going in, I suppose you will not require to see a further proof. There is no time to be lost, if the book is to be out before Xmas. Printers are always exceptionally busy at this time, and it is well to give them no excuse for disappointing us. Mr. Lloyd read the last proofs and made a few slight orthographical changes.

If you let me know how many copies you would like for your own use, I will direct that they be forwarded to you as soon as delivered. Cheque will be passed at the next meeting of the Finance Comtee.

As regards the reference in the Report, I really think that the obvious meaning of "a collection of humorous short stories by Mr. H. Morris" is that the stories are *by* you i.e. written by you. In the case where such words as "folktales", "proverbs", etc., are used, that obvious meaning is, of course, negatived. I admit that the word "edited" used further on is scarcely accurate in the circumstances, and will delete it before the Report is published in pamphlet form. Mise do charaid, Pádraig Mac Piarais.

To Eoin Mac Neill.

This undated postcard to MacNeill may possibly have been an internal item of correspondence at the League headquarters; it is unstamped and has no sign of having been mailed. It probably refers to a date earlier than 1903; its tone and general content would suggest that it was written before Pearse became editor of *An Claidheamh Soluis.* Mr O'Donoghue (Tórna) was asked to prepare the copy for *The Nation* and the *Independent* newspapers which had no facilities for publishing material in Irish type-script.

L.(p.c.) 71/NLI

n.d.   The Gaelic League.

Dear Mr. Mac Neill,
    The *Freeman* wants Fr. Conny's speech tonight or at the very latest on tomorrow morning. If they do not get it early tomorrow they cannot have it set up on Thursday. Could you manage to let them have it in time? You might also send the original copy to Mr. O'Donoghue, asking him to write copies in Roman type for *the Nation* and the *Independent.* Sincerely yours. P. H. Pearse.

To H. Morris.

Early in 1902 (c.f. letter of 22nd January), Pearse had suggested to Morris that he would be a valuable member of the Publications Committee and offered to propose him for co-option.
    Celtia was the official monthly journal of the *Pan-Celtic* movement and was published by the Celtic Association at 97 St. Stephen's Green, Dublin. It ran from 1901 to 1908. The issue of January 1903 (Vol. III, I, p. 15) contained the short and unfavourable notice of the book of stories by Morris referred to in Pearse's letter. The reviewer criticises the choice of stories and finds only one *An Dara Torramh*, passable; the rest he regards as old chestnuts.

L. 72/P.Ms.

26.1.1903.   Connradh na Gaedhilge,
                                        Áth Cliath.

A Charaid,
    Yours of 24th to hand. The quarter in which *Greann na Gaedhilge* was roughly handled was *Celtia* – which honoured you with a short but unfavourable notice in its January number.
    Thanks for permission to propose your co-option. It is not at all necessary that you should attend the meetings, if inconvenient. Several of the non-resident members of the Coisde Gnótha are on the Publications Comtee. and are accustomed to send their views by post. Mise do charaid, Pádraig Mac Piarais.

To J. J. Doyle.

The request from Doyle for additional remuneration for his *Leabhar Cainte* has elicited a generous increase from the Publications Committee. An Cló-Chumann was the printing house of the League. *Imeachtaí an Oireachtais 1901* contained the proceedings of the annual cultural festival of the League and *Miondrámanna* by McGinley (otherwise Peadar Mac Fhionlaoigh) was a collection of dramatic pieces published as Vol. XI of the Popular Booklets.

The last sentence reads "Will you be in Dublin next Saturday?"

L. 73/NLI

2.2.1903.   Connradh na Gaedhilge,
                                                      Áth Cliath.

A Charaid,

I should have written you sooner to say that the Publications Comtee, a propos of *Leabhar Cainte*, had decided to make the new rule as to doubling the prize retrospectively, and to accordingly offer you £10 for *Leabhar Cainte* in addition to the £10 prize already paid. If you assent to this, I will have cheque passed at next meeting of Finance Comtee.

Beirt Fhear is now in the hands of An Cló-Chumann. I told Mr. Lloyd to send you proofs, which I suppose he is doing. Mr. Concannon's, Phrase Book is also in the hands of the printers. So, too, are your *Sgéalta Gearra*, Sealy, Bryers & Walker being the printers. We are getting illustrations for this, – perhaps you would like to see proofs of these as well as of the text. A man named Donnelly who does rather clever work, is the artist.

I am overwhelmed with work just now, – am trying to work off the pile of correspondence entailed by the recent meeting of the Publications Comtee. Besides, I have to think out and write a lecture which I am to deliver in Enniscorthy on Wednesday evening.

I have just sent *Treoir an Pháisde* to the Editor of the *Derry People* at his request. I hope our book people are keeping you supplied with our new publications for review purposes. There are two new ones just out, *Imtheachtaí an Oireachtais 1901* and MacGinley's *Miondrámanna*. Now that the General Editor is in harness the pace in the publishing line will become tremendous.

An mbeidh tú i mBaile Átha Cliath an Satharn so chugainn? Mise do Charaid, Pádraig Mac Piarais.

To J. J. Doyle.

The last sentence reads: "I am about to depart for County Wexford. I have not time for further comment."

L. 74/NLI

4.2.1903.   Connradh na Gaedhilge
                                        Áth Cliath.

A Charaid,
   Yours to hand, I will have the £13 passed at the next meeting of the Finance Comtee, – sorry for the mistake. I will tell Lloyd to send you on proofs of *Beirt Fhear, Sgéalta Gearra*, and pictures for same as soon as he gets them. I will see about those pictures you mention for *Sgéalta Gearra*. If photos are not available, who would be the nearest photographer?
   Táim ar tí imtheacht go Condae Loch Garmain. Ní'l faill agam le n-a thuilleadh a radh. Do charaid, Pádraig Mac Piarais.

To Eoin Mac Neill.

Pádraig Ó Dálaigh was the first full-time General Secretary of the Gaelic League.

L. 75/NLI

20.2.1903.   The Gaelic League,
                                        24 Upper O'Connell St.,
                                        Dublin.

A Charaid,
   The Publications Committee is considering the publication of some short propagandist leaflets in Irish. Pádraig Ó Dálaigh tells me that you have done something in that direction. Could you let me have your views or anything in that line you may have written, for the Committee's meeting on Tuesday next. Mise agus fuadar fúm, do charaid, Pádraig Mac Piarais.

To H. Morris.

This letter and that of the following day to J. J. Doyle contain similar arguments and claims by Pearse in support of his application. The tone of this one to Morris is pitched at a level likely to appeal to Morris of whose support he seems to be fairly confident. The "unexpected quarters" referred to, from which he was being opposed, may have included, Hyde, MacNeill and Fr. O'Hickey, all of whom supported other candidates.

The postscript reads: The paper you read the other evening was superb; as for Andrias Ó Marcaigh he surpasses anything I have seen.

L. 76/P.Ms.

24.2.1903.   Connradh na Gaedhilge,
                                        Áth Cliath.

A Charaid,
I am applying for the vacant editorship of *An Claidheamh Soluis* as advertised in the current issue of the paper.

I don't know what your views may be with regard to the names (of which mine is one) which have already been informally before the Coisde Gnótha. I find, however, that I am being actively and determinedly canvassed against, and am obliged in self-defence to put my position before one or two members who, I believe, if placed squarely in possession of the facts, would be favourable to me.

My qualifications both in Irish and English; my long and close connection with the details of League work both in the country and at headquarters; my personal acquaintance with nearly all the Irish-speaking districts; all these are well known to you. My training on the Executive for the past five or six years and as hon. sec. of the Publications Comtee for the past three years, has been, as it were, an apprenticeship for such a post, whilst my work on the Publications Comtee. has brought me into close personal touch with all the leading Irish writers and workers.

Though circumstances and associations have made me a Connachtman linguistically and in sympathy, I think I can fairly claim to be above all petty provincial jealousies, and to be in a position to see the movement steadily as a whole. At the same time, I would devote special attention to the development of Ulster and Connacht, as Munster – at least in the matter of literature – can very well look after itself.

It seems to me essential that whilst, of course, our editor must be a capable writer of Irish and English, he must also bring to the management of the paper a steady level and a strong hand; clear sane notions of things; a grasp of facts and issues; the faculty to see and create opportunities and to gather round him a loyal staff of

65

competent writers; above all, he must be able to give a lead to the country, and inspire its confidence. With all this he must combine the requisite amount of Irish scholarship.

If you are in favour of me, I frankly ask for your vote (if present at the meeting) and in any case for your influence. I do so with the less reserve inasmuch as I have reason to believe that I am being fought unfairly, and that too in unexpected quarters. Your own good sense will prompt you as to what is best to be done in the circumstances.

Of course, you will please keep this letter and its contents private. Mise do charaid go buan, Pádraig Mac Piarais.

P.S. Bhí do pháipear a léigheadh an oidhche cheana thar chinn. Agus maidir le Aindrias Ó Marcaigh, bhuail sé a bhfaca me riamh.

To J. J. Doyle.

The financial arrangements in the first paragraph conclude the earlier negotiations concerning Doyle's Phrase Book. The General Editor, recently appointed was J. H. Lloyd.

The Gaelic League was preoccupied in the early months of 1903 with finding an editor for *An Claidheamh Soluis* as successor to Eoin Ó Neachtain. The tensions already operating within the League were apparent in the controversies surrounding this appointment as to the superiority of native speakers and as to the dominance of one province or another. Many believed that only a native speaker could write satisfactory idiomatic Irish. Doyle, in his "prompt and honest reply" to Pearse's letter claimed that whereas Miss Borthwick and Pearse were nearest to acquiring that skill, MacNeill did not and Lloyd never would acquire it, while Father Dineen had lost it in imitating an older style! The various candidates were also assessed as to their likely success in maintaining a strict impartiality as between the provinces; their ability to withstand "the Munster clique" of Fr. Dineen and his friends in Craobh an Chéitinnigh (the Keating Branch) was a major criterion. Pearse in support of his candidature conducted a coordinated campaign during February, writing to Doyle, Morris, Dr. S. MacEnrí (London), T. P. Mac Fhionlaoigh (London) and securing the active support of prominent League officials such as J. H. Lloyd, George Moonan and Stephen Barrett who canvassed on his behalf. In his letters Pearse put forward his qualifications for the post with an air of quiet confidence and a conviction that, if the

66

rules of fair play were observed, he should secure the appointment. This confidence in face of overt opposition, was due mainly to a letter to Pearse dated 30th January 1903 from Fr. M. O'Hickey. As a member of the Special sub-committee of the Coisde Gnótha, O'Hickey was deputed to write to Pearse asking him whether he would accept the editorship if offered it, at £200 p.a. and requesting him to set down his own views on *An Claidheamh Soluis* for the Coisde Gnótha. With his letters he enclosed a four page memorandum (included here with the Doyle letter of 28.2.1903) in which he outlined in detail the editorial role, the functions of the League paper and the plans he proposed for the improvement of its content and layout.

The appointment was made at the Coisde Gnótha meeting of March 2nd; those mentioned as candidates in early February included Pearse, W. P. Ryan of London, Fr. P. Dineen and Pádraig Mac Suibhne of Munster. Ryan however did not formally apply and his strong London support transferred to Pearse, while Fr. Dineen secured the entry of another candidate in the person of J. J. Kelly ("Sgeilg"). The result was a decisive victory for Pearse, gaining nineteen of the twenty six votes cast. The first issue of *An Claidheamh Soluis* which Pearse edited was that of March 14th 1903.

L. 77/NLI

25.2.1903.   Connradh na Gaedhilge,
                                                  Áth Cliath.

A Charaid,

At last night's meeting of the Publications Committee we rectified our blunder and decided to give you £13 more for *Leabhar Cainte*, making £20 in all. The cheque will be passed at the next meeting of the Finance Committee.

We are referring *Ar Lorg Poitín* for the opinions of two of our Readers. We have left the other matters over for the present, as we are at present glutted with mss. and the General Editor has fully twelve months' work before him in the books already accepted. Of course, we will not lose sight of your pieces.

And now for another matter. I am applying for the editorship of *An Claidheamh Soluis* as advertised in the current issue. I don't know what your views may be with regard to the names (of which mine is one) which have already been informally before the Coisde. I find, however, that I am being actively and determinedly canvassed against, and am obliged in self-defence to put my

67

position before one or two members whom I believe, if placed squarely in possession of the facts, would be in my favour.

My qualifications both in Irish and English, my long and close connection with the details of League work, both in the country and at headquarters; my personal acquaintance with practically all the Irish speaking districts; all these are well known to you. My position for the past five or six years on the Executive, and for the past three years as hon. sec. of the Publications Committee, has been, as it were, an apprenticeship for such a post, whilst my work on the Publications Committee has brought me into close touch with all the leading Irish writers and workers. I think too, I may fairly claim to be above all petty provincial jealousies, and to be in a position to steadily regard the movement as a whole.

It seems to me that whilst, of course, our editor must be a capable writer of Irish and English, he must also bring to the management of the paper a steady level head and a strong hand; clear sane notions of things, the faculty of grasping issues and facts, and being able to gather round him a loyal band of competent writers; he must be able to give a lead to the country, and inspire the country's confidence.

If you are in favour of me, I frankly ask your vote (if present at the meeting) and in any case your influence. I do so with the less reserve in as much as I have reason to believe that I am being fought unfairly. Your own good sense will prompt you as to what is best to be done in the circumstances. More may depend on this appointment than any of us yet see.

Of course, you will kindly keep this letter and its contents private. Mise do charaid go buan. Pádraig Mac Piarais.

To J. J. Doyle.

Doyle had replied on the 26th to Pearse's letter of the 25th intimating his interest in the editorship; his letter indicated quite firmly that he favoured a native speaker.

L. 78/NLI

27.2.1903.   Connradh na Gaedhilge,
                                                      Áth Cliath.

A Charaid,
    Many thanks for your prompt and honest reply. Of course, I see that a native speaker should get the preference, other things being

equal – that, however, is the rub. It would be fatal to thrust an untried man into the position simply because he is, or is alleged to be, a native speaker. I am, of course, an interested party, but for the sake of the League, as well as my own, I hope the Coisde will not be guilty of the folly of taking on trust a man with no experience save that of a country town, and about whose general qualifications we have only the word of his own personal friends. We did that on the last occasion, and with disastrous results.

It seems to me that whilst a vernacular knowledge of Irish is important, it is by no means the most essential thing. After all, it is not the business of an editor to write his paper, but rather to get it written, – to organize a staff of representative writers in whom he inspires confidence. Naughton writes practically none of *An Claidheamh*. It is neither necessary nor desirable that the editor should, as a rule, write even his own leading articles; the same style, however good, would pall ultimately. On the contrary he should command the services of the best writers in the country. His own duty should be to keep things going, to organise his forces, to keep in touch with all the workers and centres, to arrange and set in order.

We want a man who will make the best use of the writers at his command, and give the country a lead. That, I think, is far more important than a native knowledge. If we can combine the two, well and good, but can we? In haste, Mise do charaid, Pádraig Mac Piarais.

To J. J. Doyle.

This is the formal letter to Doyle concerning his candidature for the editorship with which the memorandum was enclosed.

L. 79/NLI

28.2.1903.   Liosán,
                                         Sandymount,
                                           Co. Dublin.

A Charaid,
I have applied for the vacant editorship of *An Claidheamh Soluis* as advertised in the current issue.

I enclose you a brief statement of my views as to the future conduct of the paper with special reference to make-up, etc. Mise do charaid, Pádraig Mac Piarais.

I have thought out the internal arrangement and literary contents of *An Claidheamh Soluis* in considerable detail. Below I give only the main points.

A. IRISH DEPARTMENT

1) Everyone is agreed that increased prominence should be given to current news in Irish. I would go further and make news the great outstanding feature of the Irish department. Our ideal should be an Irish newspaper from which the Irish Speaker who does not read the English papers may get a connected and adequate idea of the events of the week, home and foreign. I would devote fully three pages to news pure and simple. I would re-introduce the division into home and foreign news. The great outstanding events should be dealt with at some length, and headings should be introduced. The news columns should be modelled rather on the French than the English lines. The French are the best journalists in the world, and hints might be taken from them not only as to style but as to make up and appearance. The news should be written by competent writers representing the various provinces. The writers should be allowed certain amount of scope, but the main topics to be dealt with each week should be sketched out by the editor.

2) There should be a leading article in Irish each week. This would not necessarily deal with the language movement itself, but would rather treat from an Irish–Ireland point of view the countless vital problems which confront the country, – such as the land question, emigration, industries, agricultural organisation, railway reform, the drink question, technical education, etc. Political and even foreign events of first class magnitude might also be judiciously dealt with. The object of these leading articles should be to lead the thought of the Irish speaking districts, and educate it on the pressing Irish problems of the day. It is neither necessary nor desirable that the leaders should always be written by the same hand; on the contrary the best Irish writers of the day should be pressed into service. This, besides giving all the provinces a fair show, would ensure freshness and new points of view each week.

3) There should be a students section in fact as well as in name. I have thought out this section in great detail. Its leading feature should be a series of reading lessons which could be taken up by any student who has mastered O'Growney, Part III. There should also be exercises for translation into Irish. A department for answering students' queries might also be added.

4) Each issue should contain one or more short bright stories or sketches all the better if of a humorous nature; ponderous pro-

pagandist or other such articles in Irish should be tabooed. We want something attractive and vivid, having thought as well as imagination, to put into the hands of our growing hosts of readers, young and old.

5) There might be a column of humorous paragraphs in Irish. Every Irish speaker has scores of racy anecdotes well worthy of printing.

6) There should be at least one illustration in each issue, – it might be placed in the centre of the first page, and should have a connection with one of the leading Irish Ireland events of the week.

B. ENGLISH DEPARTMENT

1) There should be a leader in English each week. This should have the immediate object of giving the country a lead as to the policy to be adopted with regard to the events of the hour. Such a lead has never been given by the League since the Fáinne days.

2) In the English notes freshness and variety should be aimed at. Countless topics might be touched on apart from the more immediate problems of the language movement. The local and personal note should be struck as much as possible. The local centres and workers should be directly appealed to, and encouraged when they are doing well. A staff of local correspondents should be organized, whose communications might be embodied in the editorial notes or otherwise utilized.

3) The Cork, Belfast, Mayo, etc. notes, which appear at erratic intervals should be discontinued, the services of the writers as local correspondents being retained. The London notes might be retained, but under a different heading. The points specially affecting London could be dealt with elsewhere, and the writer would have more scope for dealing with literary and other subjects.

4) An important feature of the English department should be the adequate and prompt reviewing of new books, whether published by the League or not.

5) Space would be economised by bringing together under a single head, all record matter, such as coming events, the work of the Organisers, the reports of the Coisde and its committee etc. The Branch Reports, in their present form, should be discontinued. Under some such heading as "Amongst the Branches" the striking points in the work of each Branch should be sympathetically dealt with.

6) Each issue would contain at least one literary article in English, dealing with some phase of Irish Ireland. These should be written by the best English writers at the disposal of the League.

Such names as Lady Gregory, Stephen Gwynn, W. P. Ryan, Edward Martyn, W. B. Yeats, F. A. Fahy, Miss Hull and hosts of others occur to one – occasional articles on literary and linguistic points by our best scholars would also be welcome.

C. GENERAL

The increasing of the size of the paper, and possibly the alteration of its shape, should also be considered. Much depends on form, and the general attractiveness of the paper might be considerably increased by due regard to arrangement, spacing, use of headings, etc.

The editor should attend all the more important local Feiseanna and other celebrations. Facilities could of course be got from the Railway Cos. They should deal with such local events not by way of a formal report, but rather in a bright chatty article, or series of notes. Whilst *An Claidheamh* should be more fully utilized as a medium of communication between the Coisde and the branches, its columns should never be allowed to degenerate into the *Dublin Gazette* style.

The editor should, of course, attend the meetings of the Coisde and also those of the Organisation, Publication, Education and Oireachtas.

To H. Morris.

The "brief statement of his views" refers to the memorandum which he circulated with his canvassing letters and which is included here with the previous letter to Doyle of this same date.

L. 80/P.Ms.

28.2.1903   Liosán,
                             Sandymount.

A Charaid,
    I have applied for the vacant editorship of *An Claidheamh Soluis* as advertised in the current issue.
    I enclose you a brief statement of my views as to the future conduct of the paper, with special reference to make-up, etc. Mise do charaid, Pádraig Mac Piarais.

72

To J. J. Doyle.

This letter exemplifies the frequent correspondence among Gaelic League literary people concerning the most appropriate usage and dialectal variants. Tórna (T. Ó. Donnchadha) and P. Ó. Dálaigh were at League headquarters and were authorities whom Pearse could consult on such questions.

An tAthair Peadar Ó Laoghaire conducted lengthy controversies on points of grammar; he is probably the object of the reference here to "spilled ink" and the "Autonomous Verb".

The last sentence reads: "Send me ... Claidheamh and it will be welcome. I will insert the other piece in the students' section".

L. 81/NLI/B

25.3.1903.   "An Claidheamh Soluis.
                                                  agus
                                          Fáinne an Lae"
                                          Áth Cliath.

Dear Friend,

I shall show your letter to Tórna and to Daly. I agree that "chuimil sé deathnach" is an English form etc., but that story was edited by Eoghan and I did not wish to interfere with it. The phrase "amachadh sé leis", is a Galway one and is not faulty.

Neither "casadh dhom" nor "dearbhrathair liom" can be faulted. "Máthair na Clainne" could not possibly write a word or a turn of phrase which was not in use in Co. Galway. The phrases, "casadh dhom", "casadh orm" and "casadh liom" are to be found in Connacht and all have the same meaning. "Casadh dhom" is the most frequent version.

The other phrase "dearbrathair liom" is also correct. It is the ordinary form in Connacht, its meaning, of course, being "a brother of mine", just as "bó liom" means "a cow of mine". Tá beirt liom i nAmerioca" = *not* "There are two with me in America" *but* "There are two children of mine in America".

I agree with you about "Bean Uí Dhinnagain".

I don't think *An Claidheamh* is the place to discuss grammar, idiom, etc. Look at all the ink that has been spilled and paper wasted over the "Autonomous Verb" or "Monotonous Verb" as it is now called in Dublin. It is to be regretted that, owing to the change in the scope of *Irisleabhar na Gaeilge* we have now no journal devoted to Irish grammar and linguistics.

Send me on a short humorous story or something for *An Claidheamh* agus beidh fáilte roimhe. Sgaoilfidh mé isteach an

73

písín ud i gcomhair na mac leighinn. Mise do chara, Pádraig Mac Piarais.

To P. Ó Domhnalláin.

In the midst of the campaign for the *Claidheamh* editorship, Pearse demonstrated an imaginative and practical charity in the case of the personal welfare of Colum Wallace (Colm de Bhailís), the poet from Gorumna Island in Connemara. He had heard that Colum was an inmate of the Uachtar Ard Workhouse, and he inquired of the authorities if the story were correct. The Master, Mr. T. D'Arcy replied that Wallace was there and that though 70 he claimed to be 107!

Pearse opened a fund in *An Claidheamh Soluis* with a view to enabling the old man to spend the evening of his days in Gorumna. His collaborator in this admirable scheme was Pádraig Ó Domhnalláin of Uachtar Ard who found a hospitable house for Wallace in Uachtar Ard. Pearse collected the poems of Wallace, wrote a commentary and published them in 1903 with separate prefaces by Douglas Hyde and J. H. Lloyd. The proceeds from this booklet were devoted to the Wallace fund. This letter and those of July 8th and 29th. to Ó Domhnalláin refer to the Wallace project.

L. 82/P.Ms.

10.6.1903.   An Claidheamh Soluis,
                                                        24 Sráid Uí Chonaill.

A Chara,
    As you will have seen I have opened a fund in *An Claidheamh Soluis* for the purpose of enabling Colum Wallace to leave Oughterard Workhouse, and return to spend the evening of his days in Gorumna. The London Gaelic League has opened a fund in aid, and the Camberwell (London) Irish class is organising a Céilidh. I hope, too, that a concert or Aeridheacht will be organised in Dublin. I have at present about £10 in hands, having received £5 this morning from London, too late for acknowledgment in this week's *Claidheamh Soluis*. I do not know how much we shall be able to collect, but I have hopes that it will be something decent.
    My object in writing to you is this. Could you make it your business to see Colum and tell him what we are doing? Our present idea is to get someone in Gorumna to take the old man as a lodger so to speak, we to pay the party taking him a small sum weekly. We

74

are communicating with the clergy in Gorumna on the point. You could sound Colum as to how he would like this idea. I do not know whether he would have any delicacy in accepting our offer. You could mention to him that similar collections have been got up for such men as Parnell and T. D. Sullivan. Tell him that the members of the Gaelic League are determined that the author of *Cúirt an tSrutháin Bhuidhe* shall not die in a workhouse if they can help it. At your convenience, you might let me know his views on the whole matter. I write you because you are the only Gael in Oughterard I am in touch with, and because your article in Irish was the immediate cause of my starting the fund just now, though I had the idea in mind for a long time previously. Mise, le meas mór, Do chara, Pádraig Mac Piarais.

Eagarthóir, *An Claidheamh Soluis.*

To P. Ó Domhnalláin.

The photograph sent by Ó Domhnalláin was published by Pearse in *An Claidheamh Soluis* and his review article is in the issue of August 8th 1903.

L. 83/P.Ms.

8.7.1903.   An Claidheamh Soluis,
                                             Áth Cliath.

A Chara Chroidhe,
   I am so pressed that I did not get time to send you a receipt for the generous donation of your Craobh to the Colum Wallace Fund, but you no doubt saw the acknowledgment in *An Claidheamh.*
   We have failed so far to get anyone in Gorumna or in Carrowroe to take Colum so Father Brett C.C. has been making inquiries. Would it be too much to ask you to make inquiries as to whether someone could be got in or near Oughterard, or indeed anywhere. Time is passing and the old man may die any minute. We have now enough money to take him out of the Workhouse, if there was only some place for him to go. Please do your best. What do you think he would say to being placed in some Home for Aged People, in Galway or elsewhere? He would, of course, be sure of good care and food there. No doubt he needs to some extent, invalid treatment.
   Many thanks for photo which I hope to make use of. I am thinking of writing a short article in English on Colum, to appear

75

along with the photo. I can lay my hands on "Cúirt an tSrutháin Bhuidhe" and on "Amhrán an Tae". Another poem of his is "An Bás", which I think has never been printed. Could you get me a copy of this? Indeed, I should be grateful if you could send me copies of any poems, long or short by him that you can get, also any short rhymes, anecdotes, epigrams, etc., as well as any incident in his life that has not yet been published. Now is the time to collect all this. In a few months it may be too late. I am sure an interesting article could be written giving quotations from his poems etc. Afterwards we might bring out the poems in a little book.

Please let me know as soon as possible how you are getting along with inquiries about a house. In great haste, Mise do chara, Pádraig Mac Piarais.

To Col. M. Moore.

Col. Moore was the manager of a national school on his estate, Moore Hall in Co. Mayo, in which he had organised an evening school for the adults of the area. Despite the National Board's official policy of promoting such evening schools, the Moore Hall programme was not recognised by the Board. Col. Moore by means of a public controversy, was successful in overcoming the opposition of the Board. There is further correspondence on this issue in *An Claidheamh Soluis* of 27.7.1903.

L. 84/NLI

10.7.1903.   An Claidheamh Soluis,
                                         Áth Cliath.

A Chara,
    Congratulations on your victory over the National Board. Is there any history, beyond that is already published, attached to their capitulation? Please let me know, in order that, when referring to the matter in next week's *Claidheamh* I may have more than the bare fact, – if there is more to be known. In haste, Yours sincerely. P. H. Pearse. Editor.

To P. Ó Domhnalláin.

Pearse shows in this letter his capacity for organisation and an orderly systematic approach to financial arrangements.

L. 85/P.Ms.

29.7.1903.   An Claidheamh Soluis,
                                    Áth Cliath.

A Chara Chroidhe,
   I am very glad indeed that you have been able to close with Mrs.
Toole as regards terms. It relieves me of a great deal of anxiety. I
enclose you cheque for £3, which I think should be sufficient to fit
Colum out respectably and keep him in pocket money for some
time. In order to keep everything square I intend to make all
payments by cheque. The present cheque I make payable to you
and you can change it, and give the £3 to Colum. Try, if possible to
complete everything to-morrow and next day, so that Colum may
take up his residence with Mrs. Toole on Saturday 1st. I will send
you cheque £2 for Mrs. Toole on Friday evening. I am anxious to be
able to announce in next week's *Claidheamh* that everything is
complete and that Colum is now comfortably housed *outside* the
workhouse.
   Many thanks for "An Bás" and "Cúirt an tSrutháin" I will only
quote from them in the Article. Would it be too much to ask you to
let me know before Monday in what year (approximately)
"Amhrán an Tae", "An Bás" and "Cúirt" etc. were composed and
also where the "Cúirt" was, and whether it is still standing?
   You will hear from me again by Saturday morning.
   I need scarcely say that I am most grateful to you for the way
you have helped me throughout. But for you, it would have been
quite impossible for me to carry the matter through. Mise do chara
go buan. Pádraig Mac Piarais.

To Mrs. Mgt. Hutton.

Mrs. Hutton was a friend of Pearse and an active member of the
League in Belfast and was anxious to employ an Irish-speaking
maid in her home. Pearse through *An Claidheamh Soluis* organised
an employment agency for boys and girls of the Gaeltacht.

L. 86/NLI

9.9.1903.   An Claidheamh Soluis,
                                           Áth Cliath.

A Chara,

I fear the two girls referred to are no longer available, but I have
forwarded your letter to Father Considine, Galway, who may be
able to secure a suitable girl for you. I have not yet heard from him.

I wonder whether you could find time to contribute an English
article to *An Claidheamh*? I am anxious to make the English side
of the paper as attractive as possible, and aim at covering the whole
ground, – literary, linguistic, critical, historical, propagandist,
educational, industrial, etc. I am sure an article from your pen
would be very welcome to the readers of the paper.

I leave home for a month on Friday next. If Father Considine
can get a girl to suit you he will write to you direct. Mise do chara,
Pádraig Mac Piarais.

To H. Morris.

L. 87/P.Ms.

17.10.1903   An Claidheamh Soluis,
                                           Áth Cliath.

A Chara Chroidhe,

You know the "Sgéala ó na Chúig Cúigí" section in *An
Claidheamh Soluis*? I propose, in future, to divide it into separate
sections, one for each of the provinces. Could you possibly
undertake to supply me with three or four paragraphs of Ulster
news each week? From time to time I receive numerous contributions from Donegal writers, hence I am anxious to give Ulster
proper a chance on the present occasion.

What I want is three or four paragraphs written by an Ulster-
man, dealing with Ulster affairs, – important proceedings of public
bodies in the north, big political and other meetings, the more
important Gaelic League functions, the state of the weather, crops,
markets, etc., – in short everything of specific interest to Ulster-
men. You can put in as many Ulster words and idioms as you like –
the more the better – but I would like a reasonable uniformity of
spelling to be aimed at. The contribution would require to reach me

on Monday morning each week. If you can see your way to undertake this, could you let me have the first instalment by Monday morning, or if pressed for time by Tuesday morning? *I am most anxious* to start the new feature next week. Mise do chara go buan, Pádraig Mac Piarais.

To S. Bairéad.

The infant in question was Síle Bairéad, who followed in her father's footsteps as a dedicated member of the Gaelic League. Pearse presented her with an Irish-made robe for her christening as the following letter indicates. The robe and other later birthday gifts from Pearse, are still treasured by Miss Bairéad.

L. 88/P.Ms./G

25.11.1903.   39 Marlboro Road,
                                                    Donnybrook.

A Chara Chroidhe,
    I send my congratulations to yourself and to your good wife. May God grant the young Gael a long life – may she see a hundred.
    I shall be very pleased to be Godfather to her. Being a Godfather, is no small honour especially to one, who will be, as your daughter will, an Irish speaker from the cradle. I trust that mother and baby are well.
    I am sure that I will see you tomorrow in your office. If not, perhaps you would send word to me concerning arrangements and when I should go to you on Friday. I am, your friend for ever, P. Mac Piarais.

To S. Bairéad.

L. 89/P.Ms./G

26.11.1903.   39 Marlboro Road,
                                                    Donnybrook.

A Chara Chroidhe,
    Enclosed is a small gift for the baby. Since you are having a real

79

Irish christening – a real Irish robe was appropriate, I thought. Perhaps you have one already – however a pair is useful. It is of Irish manufacture. I am, your constant friend, Pádraig Mac Piarais.

To J. J. Doyle.

After six months as Editor, Pearse was concerned with the finances of the paper and his letters show a sensitivity to increasing costs caused by encroaching on advertising space. Seán T. Ó Ceallaigh as manager was eager to increase advertising revenue and the circulation of the paper.

On the vertical margin of the first page of this letter there is a postscript which reads: "I will search for *Ar Lorg Poitín* – everything is confused here". This is a reference to Doyle's story which according to his letter of 23.11.1903 to Pearse, he had forwarded with a view to having it accepted for publication by the League in booklet form.

The "Giotaí" (literally Pieces) section was a column in *An Claidheamh Soluis* which contained miscellaneous items. The last sentence of the letter is a New Year Greeting which reads: "May God grant you and yours every joy and good fortune in the coming year.

L. 90/NLI/B

31.12.1903. An Claidheamh Soluis,
Áth Cliath.

A Chara,
I would have written you sooner about the publication of a vocabulary to *Leabhar Cainte* in *An Claidheamh*, only I had not made up my mind on the matter. The chief obstacle was the difficulty of finding room; at the time you first broached the matter pressure on our space was enormous and there were no signs of its decreasing. It would not do to discontinue the "Business Directory", as the manager finds it very useful as an inducement to advertisers.

I have now come to the conclusion, however, that the vocabulary would form a useful feature of the new "Students' Page" announced this week. If, therefore, you send it along, I will make use of it as opportunity offers. Some weeks the pressure on space is very great, and other weeks I find difficulty in filling the paper, (this is due mainly to the fluctuation in the advts.) Accordingly, I may be able to give a fairly large instalment some weeks and be compelled

80

to give a very small one other weeks, and occasionally to hold it over altogether for a week or two. You might send me as much as you can at a time, so that the printers may be working at it when they are not busy. Will the words be in alphabetical order? You might write a few lines of introduction for the first instalment.

You ought to write to the Publication Committee as to whether they would think of afterwards publishing the vocabulary as a booklet. If so, the type could be kept standing, – but this would cost money and could not be undertaken without sanction of Publication and Finance Committees. I will keep the first few instalments standing pending an arrangement.

You are not sending me much literary matter nowadays. What I want most is short original stories in Irish, humorous if possible, – in the vein of *Tadhg Gabha* only shorter. Could you do something in this line for me? Short scraps of prose or verse for the "Giotaí" section would also be very welcome.

Could anything be done to get advts. from public bodies, etc., in your part of the world, or to improve the circulation? The financial position of *An Claidheamh* is very serious, mainly on account of the paucity of advertising and the low rates. It is costing a great deal to produce, – so much so that the more copies sold the greater the loss! It is all – or nearly all – a question of advts.

"Éireannach" of the *Derry People* is obviously Father Mullen of Killygordon; he has a grievance against me because some letters which he got some friends of his to write for the purpose of boosting his *Key to Ulster Irish* were (unavoidably) held back for a week or two. A personal grievance is almost always at the bottom of such outbreaks. His charges are utterly unfounded – except of course the changes in spelling, which I deal with in this week's *Claidheamh.*

Rath agus séan go gcuirfidh Dia ort agus ar go chomhluadar san ath-bhliadhain, Mise agat, Pádraig Mac Piarais.

To Seán T. Ó Ceallaigh.

Seán T. Ó Ceallaigh was business manager of *An Claidheamh Soluis* and was responsible for advertising space. If the League wished to draw attention to some item in *An Claidheamh* of special interest to some group (e.g. schools or clergy), the practice was to mark the copies indicating the relevant page. Dr. Henry (Seán Mac Einrí) was the author of the multiple volume *A Handbook of Modern Irish* which was very popular in schools and League classes.

L. 91/OCS

7.1.1904.   An Claidheamh Soluis,
                                                      Áth Cliath.

A Chara,
   I enclose list for "marked copies", which please have sent out
to-morrow without fail.
   I hope you will be able to fill up page 7 with advts. It is quite
impossible to get sufficient literary matters to fill it without using
up so much as to threaten the succeeding week's supply. Mise do
chara go buan, Pádraig Mac Piarais.

P.S. *Important*
I had not time to get out that circular I thought of sending to the
Intermediate schools re Dr. Henry's "Handbook", but I refer to the
point in editorial notes, p. 5. I think it would be well to send a
marked copy to the head of every *Catholic* Intermediate school and
college in Ireland marking both the "Handbook" p. 3. and the notes
referring to it p. 5. Some, at least, would be pretty sure to adopt the
suggestion. If necessary, omit sending the copies to the Bishops
(except the three especially named) rather than omit sending them
to as many Intermediate schools as possible.

To H. Morris.

Pearse was accustomed to give advance notice and publicity in *An
Claidheamh Soluis* to the Gaelic League events around the country.
This postcard refers to such a Feis, possibly at Dundalk where
Morris was now teaching.

L. (p.c.) 92/P.Ms./G

18.2.1904   An Claidheamh Soluis.

Dear Friend,
   I will mention your Feis in next week's issue. I had no space this
time. Best wishes and fortune, Your friend, Pádraig Mac Piarais.

To J. J. Doyle.

This letter in response to Doyle's request to publish the index or foclóir (glossary) for his Phrase Book in *An Claidheamh Soluis*, reveals the editorial pressure which the financial position of the paper exerted on Pearse. He is anxious to utilise all existing articles which are in typeset according to the old format.

L. 93/NLI

27.2.1904.   An Claidheamh Soluis,
                                                          Áth Cliath.

A Chara Chroidhe,
I will insert your "Giotaí" and note re Scots–Gaelic this week.

As regards index to *Leabhar Cainte*, as I explained to you when in town, the demands on space have been enormous for some weeks past. We have, as you know, decided to change the form of *An Claidheamh* and the next issue will be the last in the present form. This means that every scrap of matter already in type must be used up in the forthcoming issue. There are a lot of "Ceist Agus Freagra", branch reports, English articles etc., in type for a few weeks past and these *must* be packed into the next issue, or they will have to be re-set. When this congestion is got rid of, I will have room for the Foclóir and will insert it at the very earliest opportunity, – probably the week after next. Beir buaidh agus beannacht, Mise agat, Pádraig Mac Piarais.

To H. Morris.

This is the Feis at Sráid, Dundalk referred to in the letter of 18.2.1904. Pearse would appear to be working under great pressure at this time.

L. 94/P.Ms./G

18.5.1904

Dear Friend,
I shall be with you for the Feis, if I live. Best wishes and fortune, I remain, your true friend, Pádraig Mac Piarais.

To Colm Ó Gaora.

This letter has been presented as having been written by Pearse to various people in different parts of the country; from internal evidence in relation to his writings, it is easily established as a letter to Colm Ó Gaora of Rosmuc, whom Pearse encouraged to write for *An Claidheamh Soluis*. Ó Gaora was among the group of young men who were examined by Pearse for certification as Gaelic League teachers in Rosmuc on his visit there in 1903. Ó Gaora related the incident in his autobiography "Mise", in the first edition of which he published a holograph copy of this letter. The multiple copies of the letter and their dispersal over time were responsible for confusion as to the identity of the recipient. The abbreviated form in Irish which Pearse devised for "etc." appears in this letter as "agus c".

L. 95/MPC/G

19.10.1904.   An Claidheamh Soluis,
                                         Áth Cliath.

Dear Friend,
    I should have written to you long ago to acknowledge that I had received *Sgolbglas Mac Riogh 'n Éirinn* and to assure you that I will publish it as soon as I have space for it. I am afraid that it may be some time before I can include it as I have an adequate supply of Connacht Irish at the moment (Cnoc na nGabha – etc) and the Munstermen and Ulstermen would complain if I put more in. As regards the other old stories, continue writing them, but there is no need to send them to me until *Sgolbglas* is published and finished. I hope that you and your family are well, Best wishes and good fortune, Pádraig Mac Piarais.

To T. Flannery (T. Ó Flanghaile).

Tomás Ó Flanghaile (1846–1916) a native of Co. Mayo, who spent all his adult life in London, exercised an early influence on Pearse especially through his book, *For the Tongue of the Gael*, which Pearse choose as a bookprize on the results of his Senior Grade examination in 1896. Ó Flanghaile contributed extensively to *An Claidheamh Soluis*. "Giolla Sitric" and "Sil East" were pseudonyms of correspondents.

L. 96/NLI

26.10.1904.   An Claidheamh Soluis
                                       Áth Cliath.

Dear Mr. Flannery,
    Proof reached me in good time and the article has gone in this
week. So has the first portion of your letter re 1st. Singular
Imperative. It was necessary, to divide the latter in two, owing to
exigencies of space. It does not, I think suffer by being divided as
the remaining portion deals with an entirely different aspect of the
position from the portion printed.
    You must have misunderstood my last letter or I must have
written in such a way as to give an impression exactly opposite to
what I intended to give. My remarks re my desire that grammatical
discussion should not encroach too much on the Irish literary
columns were in explanation of my delay in publishing your letter
but certainly were not intended to imply that such contributions as
yours were not welcome. I have rejected several contributions to the
discussion because some of them were by people who really were
not competent to discuss the question and who put forward all sorts
of wild notions and because others consisted chiefly or entirely of
abuse – such as "Giolla Sitric's" reply to "Sil East's" contribution.
But I have no desire to closure helpful discussion or to discourage
writers of your authority and position from debating this or other
points to the full. I think your present contribution pretty well
settles the question – unless "Giolla Sitric" takes up your challenge
which is doubtful.
    The Finance Comtee. meets tomorrow when your cheque will be
passed. Since we agreed as to terms there has been only one
meeting and at that meeting no *Claidheamh* business was tran-
sacted owing to the unavoidable absence of the manager. I much
regret delay. Yours very sincerely, P. H. Pearse.

To Dr. W. J. Walsh.

The Tawin school fund was one of the projects organised by the
League through *An Claidheamh Soluis* to assist the maintenance of
small national schools in the Gaeltacht areas. Pearse attracted wide
support for the Tawin school, receiving donations from Kuno Meyer
in Liverpool, from a number of Welsh supporters as well as from
Archbishop Walsh and Roger Casement. This school in south
Galway was developed under its manager Fr. Keane and with the

assistance of the League was later the centre for inservice courses for teachers, at some of which Éamonn de Valera was a teacher.

L. 97/DDA

19.11.1904.   An Claidheamh Soluis,
                                                     Áth Cliath.

May it please Your Grace,
    I have the honour to acknowledge Your Grace's letter of yesterday's date, and beg most sincerely to thank Your Grace for your generous subscription towards the Tawin School Fund. That subscription practically completes the sum required, and I hope that in a week or so Dr. Hyde, to whom I am sending all the moneys received, will be able to send Father Keane a cheque which will enable him to commence the building work at once. It is very encouraging to find that *An Claidheamh* has been able to raise the sum required so quickly. We should have been much slower but for the great generosity of Your Grace and Mr. Casement.
    With Your Grace's permission, I will publish your letter in the next issue of *An Claidheamh*. Its publication will be a great help to the Fund and to the movement generally. With renewed thanks, I have the honour to be, Your Grace's obedient servant, P. H. Pearse.

To Mrs. Mgt. Hutton.

A number of letters written by Pearse during December 1904 are concerned with his visit to Belfast in the middle of the month to address a public meeting of the League. The meeting which was held at St. Mary's Hall was attended by a large representative audience and the speakers included Eoin Mac Neill, Pearse, Cardinal Logue and Dr. Henry, Bishop of Down and Conor. Dr. Henry had invited Pearse to dinner on the evening of the meeting to meet the Cardinal and Mrs. Margaret Hutton had invited him to stay with her at Deramore Park, Malone Road.
    The public meeting was politically significant as is evident from the tone and content of Pearse's letter to Seamas Ó Ceallaigh of the 26th December.

14.12.1904.   39 Marlboro' Road,
                               Donnybrook,
                               Co. Dublin.

A Chara,

It is very kind of you to offer me hospitality during my stay in Belfast. I have accepted the invitation of Dr. Henry, the Bishop, to dine with him before the meeting, but after the meeting I shall be free, and as I have not made any other arrangement it will be a great pleasure and honour to me to accept your hospitality for one night, – I must get away early on Friday. You will doubtless be at the meeting, where I shall see you. I do not arrive in Belfast till after 3, and go straight from the station to the Bishop's.

With many thanks for your kindness in thinking of me, Mise agus meas mór agam ort, Do Chara, Pádraic Mac Piarais.

To Mrs. Mgt. Hutton.

Pearse obviously had a heavy schedule during his short visit to Belfast. The Gaelic League in Belfast embraced a wide social and political range in its membership and was active in the economic and industrial as well as in the more usual cultural spheres. The Miss Mac Neill whose school Pearse visited, was a friend of Casement's, was a native of the Glens of Antrim and was an active member of the League. She was not a relation of Eoin Mac Neill.

19.12.1904.   39 Marlboro Road,
                               Donnybrook.

Dear Friend,

I wish to thank you and your noble husband for your kindness to me during my stay in Belfast. I am undoubtedly under a great compliment to you both. I shall not easily forget the generous welcome extended to me by you.

I had unfortunately no opportunity to visit the Industrial Society you mentioned. I spent so much time in Miss Mac Neill's school that I had to run as fast as I could to catch the train.

Best wishes and good fortune! Every blessing and happiness on you and yours in this holy season, I remain yours truly, Pádraig Mac Piarais.

To Séamas Ó Ceallaigh.

Pearse, in giving an account of what transpired at Dr. Henry's dinner table during his Belfast visit, is answering queries from Ó Ceallaigh who was keenly interested in divining the Bishop's stance vis-a-vis the League and the language movement as well as the general political network which linked the United Irish League, the Catholic Association and the Catholic bishops. The United Irish League was founded in 1898 by William O'Brien in Co. Mayo as a land reform movement dedicated to achieving the distribution of large estates by political action and agitation. The last sentence translates: "Christmas Greetings to you. Yours as ever".

L.100/NLI

26.12.1904.   An Claidheamh Soluis,
                                          Áth Cliath.

A Shéamuis na gCarad,

Many thanks for your letter. First let me say what I had not time properly to say when I saw you – how sorry I was to hear of your recent illness and how sincerely I hope you are now quite recovered. Your stay in the country will, I trust, build you up again.

Now, as to your queries. At the Bishop's, the most notable feature of the conversation was several good-natured passages-at-arms betwen the Cardinal and Mgr. O'Laverty, – the Cardinal telling stories at the Monsignor's expense, and the latter retorting by stories at the expense of a former Primate. For the rest, diocesan history, relics, miracles, and the price of wine were discussed. Very little was said about the movement. Some toasts were drunk, and in replying to one Eoin Mac Neill got in some useful remarks on the lines of his reference to politics at the public meeting. I gather from my observations that the Bishop is quite sincere in his support of the movement, but he does not understand it very well. He is a Churchman, not merely above and beyond all else, but to the exclusion of everything else. I don't imagine he is *consciously* trying to make use of the League as a prop for the Catholic Association but yet in a sort of subconscious way his support of the Gaelic League may spring from his dislike of the U.I.L. He wants to show that he is as good an Irishman as any in the U.I.L. Mac Neill, who is an old pupil of Dr. Henry's and knows him very well, agrees with this estimate, as far as I know, – I have not discussed the matter with him very definitely.

Personally, I think the support of the Bishop a much more valuable asset than the support of the local U.I.L., and, whilst making it perfectly clear that the League is no mere appendage to the Catholic Association or to the Bishop, I would use the latter for all he is worth, especially as regards the schools, etc. The U.I.L. cannot well stand out against you, in view of the attitude of Dillon, Redmond, etc.

This brings me to the point referred to in your last paragraph. Don't you think *I have* been perfectly frank with Redmond and Dillon? I have told them that whilst the League itself is precluded from "sympathising" with them, individual members are free to sympathise as much as they like. Eadrainn féin, the U.I.L. is making a determined effort to capture the League in Dublin. The leaders of the Parliamentary Party see clearly that the majority of Leaguers are sympathetic towards the Hungarian Policy. They fear, and justly – that in a few years Parliamentarianism as a policy may have to fight for its existence. Hence their anxiety to capture the young men of the metropolis for their policy. In a short time every Dublin craobh may become a cockpit for Parliamentarianism and Abstention. At such a moment it is essential, even at the risk of hurting people, that the Gaelic League should make it absolutely clear that it, as a corporate body, is to be captured by neither one political party nor the other. Dr. Hyde, by the way, has written me warmly approving of the matter and tone of my notes of last week.

Thanks for your hints re Belfast. I will endeavour to work in references to those you name next week or the week after.

Beannachta na Nodlag chugat. Mise do chara go buan, Pádraig Mac Piarais.

To Tomás Ó Flanghaile.

This is the same correspondent as the T. Flannery of the letter of 26.10.1904. It would appear that Ó Flanghaile had questioned Pearse in his previous letter as to the clerical status of Fr. Dineen who had been a Jesuit. The paragraphs in Pearse's reply containing the reference to Dineen are written in Irish and translate as follows:

"As to the question you put to me in your last letter, Fr. Padraig Ua Duinín was a member of the Society of Jesus (S.J.) but he left the society three or four years ago. He has no position in the church now; he lives on his own in Dublin and makes his living writing Irish and editing Irish books. It is in order for me to tell you this since you questioned me."

L. 101/NLI/B

13.1.1905.   An Claidheamh Soluis,
                                                     Áth Cliath.

A Chara,

I had intended to publish the enclosed in this week's *Claidheamh* but the printers did not let me have proof in time to send it to you, so I held it over.

Maidir leis an gceist chuir tú orm, sa litir deiridh a scríobh tú, ba de Chumann Íosa (S.J.) an tAthair Pádraig Ua Duinnín, acht d'eirigh sé as, tá a trí' nó a cheathair de bhliantaibh ó shoin ann. Níl aon phosta aige san Eaglais anois, acht é in a chomhnaí leis fhéin i mBaile Átha Cliath ag saothrughadh a bheatha ag scriobhadh Gaeilge agus ag cur leabhair Gaeilge in eagar. Ní miste dom an méid sin 'innseacht duit ó tharla gur chuir tú an cheist orm.

Beir buaidh agus beannacht, Mise do chara go buan, Pádraig Mac Piarais.

To Tomás Ó Flanghaile.

Recalling that Ó Flanghaile had included an article on "Irish Dictionaries" in his book *For the Tongue of the Gael*, Pearse requests him to write a review or article on Fr. Dineen's Irish–English Dictionary, the first edition of which was published in 1904.

The O'Reilly Dictionary referred to is that of Edward O'Reilly of Co. Cavan, who having learned Irish in Dublin, published there in 1817 his Irish–English Dictionary, John O'Donovan added a supplement to the edition of O'Reilly published in 1864.

The article by Dr. O'Hickey which according to Pearse was critical of Dineen's dictionary, appeared in the *Irish Ecclesiastical Record.*

L. 102/NLI

20.1.1905.   An Claidheamh Soluis,
                                                     Áth Cliath.

A Chara,

Very many thanks for your article just to hand. I enclose your cheque £1 . . 0 . . 0 in payment for it and for the article (No. IV) published in this week's *Claidheamh.*

I have two articles in type for next week, so that I shall have to keep yours over. I shall therefore be able to send you a proof.

I think some papers from you on Fr. Dineen's Dictionary would be very desirable. I had meant to return to it myself in *An Claidheamh* but other things intervened. You will do it much better. My first notice on the subject of Irish Dictionaries were, I recollect, taken from the paper on the subject in your *For the Tongue of the Gael*, which I selected as a prize in school in 1896. If you write as interestingly now as you did then, your papers will be very valuable indeed.

Dr. O'Hickey in his article in the *Irish Ecclesiastical Record* is very severe on the Dictionary. His conclusion is that, on the whole, it is not much of an advance on O'Reilly. It would perhaps, be well for you to see the Record before writing. I have not a copy or I would send it to you. I saw it in the National Library. Dr. O'Hickey is to return to the subject. Mise do chara go buan, Pádraig Mac Piarais.

P.S.   What is the Irish of McPhail and Kiernan? I am perpetually being bothered with requests to Irishise surnames. I wish we had a good book on the subject. P. Mac P.

To W. J. Ryan.

W. J. Ryan, editor of the new *Irish Independent*, was favourably disposed towards the Coisde Gnótha of the League whereas the *Freeman's Journal* supported the members of the Keating Branch and offered space generously to its leading members especially to Fr. Dineen. Pearse seems to be seeking support for the concept of an Irish Union of Journalists among the editorial staffs of the main dailies; he may have been the instigator of the opening letter in the campaign, which appeared in *An Claidheam Soluis* under the name of Liam Ó Flannagáin.

L. 103/NLI/G

1.2.1905.   An Claidheamh Soluis,
                                         Áth Cliath.

A Chara,
   First, congratulations on the new *Independent*. There are, of course, things in it which I do not care for, but it is an immense way beyond any other daily in Ireland.

91

I see that a column of Irish language notes in English appears to-day. With reference to this may I make a suggestion intended of course, solely for your own ears? For reasons which you know, the *Freeman* gives prominence only to the doings of a *section* of the Gaelic League. The *Independent* appears to be starting out on sounder and more patriotic lines. My suggestion is that in the Irish Language notes and otherwise you will be able to give the public a conspectus of the activities of the whole Gaelic League – in other words, that good speeches which happen to be delivered by, say, John Mac Neill and good articles which happen to appear in *An Claidheamh* will not be boycotted. To-day I see the writer quotes with approval an article from last week's *Claidheamh*. This is one of the very best ways not merely of helping *An Claidheamh*, but of strengthening the hands of the governing body and benefiting the movement as a whole. Rank-and-file Leaguers will not be slow in recognising that the *Independent*, if it follows such a course, will be the truest friend of the movement.

What do you think of "Liam Ua Flannagáin's" letter in *An Claidheamh* a fortnight ago, urging the formation of an *Irish* Union of Journalists? Would you think of sending me a short letter on the subject over your name? It would be a great pity if the proposal should fall flat.

Beir buaidh agus beannacht Mise do chara go buan, Pádraig Mac Piarais.

To W. J. Ryan.

L. 104/NLI/B

2.2.1905.   An Claidheamh Soluis
                                       Áth Cliath.

Dear Friend,

Many thanks for your letter. I am very grateful to you for taking so much trouble. I know that you will do your best in the case.

I understand your position re the Institute of Journalists and see your reason for preferring not to be prominent at this early stage of the discussion re an Irish institute.

With greetings and best wishes. Your friend for ever, Pádraig Mac Piarais.

To H. Morris.

In the internal politics of the League, Moran's *Leader* was a strong supporter of that group mainly from Munster and led by Fr. Dineen, which found editorial support in the *Freeman's Journal* in their opposition to *An Claidheamh Soluis* and the officials and establishment of the League.

The 'Democrat' was the *Dundalk Democrat*, to which Morris who taught in the town, was a regular contributor. Obviously those who opposed the election of Pearse to the editorship of *An Claidheamh*, continued in active opposition to him for a number of years. The charge against his managerial capacity implied in the letter to the *Democrat* and occasionally repeated since overlooks the evident reality that from early 1904 *An Claidheamh* was making a profit and further that from the summer of 1903, the management of the paper was in the hands of Seán T. Ó Ceallaigh.

L. 105/P.Ms.

20.2.1905.   An Claidheamh Soluis,
                                      Áth Cliath.

A Chara,
   I am still convinced that the best policy for the League *as a body* (and consequently for *An Claidheamh*) is to steadily ignore the *Leader*. Of course, it is a good thing to utilise the outside press against it, as you are doing in the *Democrat*. Do you know the author of the letter signed by "A Gaelic Leaguer" in this week's *Democrat*? I believe it was written in Dublin, and strongly suspect that the writer is a certain personal friend of Moran's, who was largely instrumental in importing him to Ireland, and who, shortly after the *Leader* started, vowed the desire that it should be made the mouthpiece of the League, *An Claidheamh* being discontinued. This desire he evidently still cherishes. If you reply to this correspondent you might hint at this. You might also state definitely that *An Claidheamh* is *not* now subsidised by the Coisde, that (as anounced in the statement of Income and Expenditure now issued in connection with Seachtmhain na Gaedhilge) it has been paying its own way since April last and that there is a clear profit on each month's working. You might quote with effect from a leading article in the *Church of Ireland Gazette* for Feb. 10, which comparing *An Claidheamh*, the *United Irishman* and the *Leader* speaks of the last named as *"intellectually the least influential of the three"*. In great haste, Mise do chara go buan, Pádraig Mac Piarais.

93

To Lady Gregory.

In *An Claidheamh Soluis* of 22.4.1905 Pearse reports and comments on a meeting held at University College during the previous week at which W. B. Yeats and George Russell (AE) spoke on "Nationality in Literature". Pearse endorses and praises the opinions expressed by Yeats but stoutly rejects the obsessive support which Russell gives to the notion that "art is cosmopolitan".

L. 106/P.Ms.

29.4.1905.   An Claidheamh Soluis,
                                                  24 Upper O'Connell St.
                                                  Dublin.

A Chara,

I should have written you before now to thank you for your letter and to say how glad I was that my note in *An Claidheamh* had not vexed you. When I saw the first note in print it occurred to me that (quite unintentionally) it appeared a little carping in tone, and so on my own motion I wrote the correcting note in the following issue. I really think *Kincora* a beautiful play and (though Mr. Yeats dislikes the word) an excellent piece of *propagandism*.

I know that "your own share of trouble" is said – it is quite common all over the country – but I have never heard such expressions as "my share of talk", "my share of songs", etc. I don't think the idiom in "share of trouble" is quite the same as in "share of talk" etc. However I ought not to be dogmatic, as I know that both in Irish and English expressions are current in one district which are unheard of in the next barony.

I have been trying in *An Claidheamh* to promote a closer comradeship between the Gaelic League and the Irish National Theatre and Anglo–Irish writers generally. After all we are all allies. Plays like Mr.Synge's however, discourage me.

May I beg you, whenever you can find time to send me an article for *An Claidheamh*? It would be very welcome both to me and to my readers.

Beir buaidh agus beannacht. Mise agus meas mór agam ort,
Pádraig Mac Piarais. (P. H. Pearse)

To Seán T. Ó Ceallaigh.

Pearse's visit to Belgium in June 1905 lasted longer than he had expected and consequently the internal editorial arrangements in the *Claidheamh* office had to be extended. Seán T. Ó Ceallaigh and Seoirse Ó Muanáin (George Moonan) were responsible for the English section while Tadhg Ó Donnchadha (Tórna) edited the Irish material.

The Fontenoy Excursion, organised and led by Major John Mac Bride and John O'Leary sought to commemorate the Irish Brigade which fought under Patrick Sarsfield at Fontenoy in 1745 in the War of Austrian Succession.

Pearse's educational visits which were organised with the official support of the Ministry of Public Instruction, afforded him an opportunity to visit thirty institutions at different levels and under different forms of management. These visits provided material for two series of articles in *An Claidheamh Soluis* which ran from August 1905 to March 1907. A valuable contribution to studies in comparative education, they form a significant element in Pearse's educational writings.

The last sentences in the letter read: "I trust that you are all well and that you will bear with me for thrusting this extra work on you.

"I remain in hellish haste etc."

The postscript reads: "I work each day from eight in the morning until six or seven in the evening".

L. 107/NLI

4.7.1905.   Hotel Cour du Mexique,
                                46, Rue de Brabant,
                                Bruxelles.

A Chara Chroidhe,

I find that it will be impossible for me to get home before Thursday week next, July 13th. It took several days to get permission to visit the schools. There were endless formalities to be gone through, and an amount of red tape to be used. I will not finish my programme here till Thursday next, and then I go on to Malines, Antwerp, Ghent and Bruges. Can I count on Seoirse Ua Muanáin and yourself to manage the English part of *An Claidheamh*, and on Tadgh to manage the Irish part, for a week longer? If Seoirse is not available – I hope he will be – you will be able to make some other arrangement. Tell An Muanánach that I am sorry to thrust an additional week's work on him but I cannot help it. I did not at all foresee the delays that I have experienced. It

95

is well that I did not come on the Fontenoy Excursion, as in that case I should have been wholly unable to carry out my intention of visiting schools, – there would not have even have been time to make the preliminary arrangements. The schools I have visited were most interesting and will supply copy for a long series of articles in *An Claidheamh*. Some of the large city schools are like huge hotels – only finer and more spacious than any hotel in Dublin, or for that matter in London, Paris or Brussels. The rural schools are more like our own at home.

I write to you rather than to Seoirse Ua Muanáin, in order to make sure of catching you in good-time, as Moonan may not call at the office on Thursday morning, when this is due.

Tá súil agam go bhfuil sibh ar fad go maith agus nach dtógfaidh sibh orm an méid seo oibre do chur oraibh.

Mise, agus deifir an diabhail orm, Do chara go buan, Pádraig Mac Piarais.

P.S.   Bím ag obair ar feadh an lae ó'n ocht a chlog ar maidin go dtí a sé nó a seacht tráthnóna.

To T. Ó Flanghaile.

The Oireachtas was the annual cultural and literary festival of the League and the Ard Fheis was its annual delegate general meeting. There is one word missing in the penultimate sentence; it refers to the number of the paragraph which is duplicated in the proofs.

L. 108/NLI

17.8.1905.   An Claidheamh Soluis,
                                       Áth Cliath.

A Chara,
    I owe you many apologies for the long delay in writing to you. After my return from Belgium, I was away again to the West for a few days and since my return have been kept busy by the Oireachtas and Ard Fheis arrangements. You will be able to gather from last week's and this week's *Claidheamh* all that has to be done by the officials here during these few weeks. The competitions are going on at present and the Ard Fheis is in session. I have just left the hall in order to write this.

    I enclose your cheque for the four articles also proofs of last article. Those of the (?) paragraph seem to be duplicated. Do you wish the new matter to be substituted for the matter already sent?

Mise agus meas mór agam ort, Do chara, Pádraig Mac Piarais.

To Seán T. Ó Ceallaigh.

L.(p.c.) 109/NLI/G

24.8.1905.   Kerin's Royal Hotel,
                                            Galway.

Send the proofs of his article on the Dictionary to Tomás Ó Flanghaile and ask him to return them by Tuesday. They may be required for *An Claidheamh* next week.

I am in great haste as the post is about to depart. The Feis was very Irish in spirit. P. Mac P.

To Eoin Mac Neill.

The book mentioned here, *Aids to the Pronunciation of Irish*, published in the autumn of 1905, was written by an Irish Christian Brother, Br. S. I. Mac Giolla Phádraig (J. J. Fitzpatrick) who in the early years of the century contributed significantly to improving the teaching of Irish in primary and secondary schools by the various texts on grammar, composition and pronunciation which he wrote and published. He collaborated with Dr. Hyde, an tAthair Peadar Ó Laoghaire, Pearse, Eoin Mac Neill and other Gaelic League writers in his campaign to provide suitable learning aids for the schools which were teaching Irish.

L. 110/NLI/G

16.9.1905.

Dear Mac Neill,

Enclosed please find a letter which I received from the author of *Aids to the Pronunciation of Irish*. I would be very grateful, if you could give me the review for the issue of next week. I would not wish to irritate this Brother. Greetings and best wishes, Yours ever, Pádraig Mac Piarais.

To T. Ó Flanghaile.

This letter is of special significance as in its last sentence it contains clear proof that Pearse was the author of all the unsigned material in *An Claidheamh* during the period of his editorship.

Ó Flanghaile was obviously interested in the identity of "An Gruagach Bán" who was contributing to the paper following Pearse's encouraging letter to him of 19.10.1904.

Colm Ó Géaraigh's surname frequently appeared as Ó Gaora.

L. 111/NLI

30.9.1905.   An Claidheamh Soluis,
                                                    Áth Cliath.

A Chara,
  I will let you have proofs of Article V as early as possible.
  The name and address of "An Gruagach Bán" are
        Colm Ó Géaraigh,
            Inbhear,
                Rosmuc. Co. na Gaillimhe.
He is a young lad of sixteen or seventeen, one of several in that exclusively Irish-speaking parish who are now commencing to write Irish for publication. He was referred to in my recent review of *The Songs of Two Country Boys.*

  I quite agree with you as to the advisability of pseudonyms except in special cases, but the fashion seems to have caught on in Irish. Of course such names as "Conán Maol", "Feargus Finnbhéil", "Tórna", "Beirt Fhear", "An Dairbhreach Dána" "Gruagach an Tobair", "Diarmuid Donn", "Cois Fhairrge", "An tUltach Beadaidhe" etc. are now no longer mere pseudonyms, so generally is the identity of the writers known. But on the whole, it would be better for people to write over their names, and I have more than once tried to get some of my contributors to see this. Of course all *unsigned* reviews and articles are written by me. Mise do chara go buan, Pádraig Mac Piarais.

To Hon. Sec. Catholic Graduates' Association.

The subject of the Mac Neill lecture at the Catholic Commercial Club in O'Connell St., at which Pearse presided was "Method in Teaching Irish". The text of the lecture was later published in *An Claidheamh Soluis* of 9.12.1905. In the period prior to the establishment of the National University in 1908, associations such as the Catholic Graduates' Association were frequently divided on issues relating to government policy on the university question.

L. 112/P.Ms.

23.11.1905.   An Coiste Gnótha,
                                                    Áth Cliath.

A Chara,

I regret very much that, inasmuch as I have to take the chair at Eoin Mac Neill's lecture in the Catholic Commercial Club to-night, it will be impossible for me to attend the adjourned meeting of the Catholic Graduates' Association.

Allow me to protest in *absentia* against the action of the member or members of the Association who supplied the garbled account of last Thursday's meeting which appeared in Friday's *Independent.* I thought that everyone understood that the proceedings were confidential. Apart from the fact that to publish any account of the proceedings was a breach of confidence, the account actually published was most partial and unfair. Of course its publication involved the publication of the subsequent report of the hon. secs. who took the only course open to them in the circumstances. It almost appears as if the author of the garbled report of Friday had no other object in view than to make mischief. I hope the society will take steps to discover the identity of the disloyal member, and will deal with his action in the strongest manner.

I am in favour of the publication of a judiciously-edited summary of the report read by the hon. sec. last Thursday. Mise do chara go buan, Pádraig Mac Piarais.

To W. J. Ryan.

Pearse had been in correspondence with Ryan earlier in 1905 (February) and had obviously interested him in attending the course on History and Language in University College in which Pearse was lecturing. Perhaps Ryan wished to publish some of the lectures in the *Independent.*

4.12.1905.   An Claidheamh Soluis,
                                    Áth Cliath.

A Chara Chroidhe,
   Apologies for my delay in answering your note. The classes (both
History and Language) at University College are open to the public
at following rates:- History 5/- for course; Elementary Language,
7/6 for course; Advanced language, 10/- for course. I fancy the
advanced language class (Mondays and Fridays at 4 p.m., with
lecture on literature on Wednesday same hour) would suit your
standard. Oral, grammatical and literary instruction combined.
Reporters are not invited, but history and literature lectures may be
published later on. Mise do chara go buan, Pádraig Mac Piarais.

To Mrs. Mgt. Hutton.

A sculptor friend of the Huttons, Miss Kathleen Shaw had made a
bust of Cardinal Logue in 1904 which was exhibited at the Royal
Academy in London the following year. In preparing to exhibit it at
the Royal Hibernian Academy in Dublin in 1906 she wished to
have the catalogue entry and description in Irish. She had asked
Mrs. Hutton to translate for her: "Michael Cardinal Logue,
Archbishop of Armagh, 1904". Being unsure of the correct form of
Logue, she had consulted Pearse who obliged with the translation in
this letter.
   Dail Uladh was the Ulster executive of the Gaelic League which
was attempting to establish an Ulster Summer Training College for
Teachers on the lines of the Connacht College at Tuar Mhic Éide
and the Dublin College, Coláiste Laighean.
   The last sentence reads: "Greetings from self and from my
family to you and yours". The two families had become acquainted
when the Huttons visited the Pearse family as indicated in the
Hutton letter of 13.2.1906. which prompted this reply by Pearse.

L. 114/NLI

17.2.1906.   39 Marlboro' Road,
                                    Domhnach Broc,
                                    Áth Cliath.

A Chara,
   I owe you an apology for my delay in answering your letter.

Extreme pressure of work must be my excuse. I hope the delay has not inconvenienced your friend.

The inscription, I think, might run:-

Micheál, Cairdinéal Ó Maolmhaodhóg,
Ard-Easbog Ard Mhaca,
1904.

It is usual nowadays to leave such names as Ard Mhaca unaffected in the genitive. Instead of "Ard-Easbog Ard Mhaca" one might introduce the old Gaelic title, still in use, "Comharba Phádraig".

I am very glad to hear about Dáil Uladh. Before the next meeting I must send you the information I promised you about the Connacht College. You will have seen the details of the Dublin scheme.

Beannacht uaim féin agus óm' mhuinntir chugat féin agus chuig do mhuinntir-se! Mise agus meas mór agam ort, Pádraig Mac Piarais.

To H. Morris.

L.(p.c.) 115/P.Ms./G

2.3.1906.   Connradh na Gaedhilge,
                                           Áth Cliath.

Dear Friend,
I received the manuscript, for which many thanks. Your friend for ever, Pádraig Mac Piarais.

To Mrs. Mgt. Hutton.

L. 116/NLI/G

7.3.1906.   39 Bóthar Marlboro',
                                           Domhnach Broc.

Dear Friend,
I enclose with this letter the account of the Connacht College which I promised you. I trust that it reaches you in time. It is some time since I received it but lost it and only discovered it yesterday.

I send greetings to you and to your noble husband, I remain with kind regards, Pádraig Mac Piarais.

To Mrs. Mgt. Hutton.

L. 117/NLI/G

17.3.1906.   39 Marlboro' Road,
                                              Donnybrook.

Dear Friend,

I received your letter and have written to Miss Naughton. I am expecting her tomorrow evening (Sunday) and I shall be very pleased to see herself and her sister.

I send greetings and the blessings of God and Patrick to you. Your friend for ever, Pádraig Mac Piarais.

To Seán T. Ó Ceallaigh.

The subject matter of this letter is probably some articles or proofs for *An Claidheamh* which Pearse had worked on while on holidays in Ros Muc. The enclosed letter was for Tadhg Ó Donnchadha (Tórna) who assisted editorially with the paper.

L. 118/NLI/G

21.8.1906.   Post Office,
                                              Ros Muc,
                                              Co. Galway.

Dear Seán,

I had intended sending these to you before now, but I could not as due to inclement weather I was forced to stay in a place which had no post office nearby. I trust all is going well. Please give the enclosed to Tadhg; I am asking him to give any assistance he can to *An Claidheamh*. I am, your friend for ever, Pádraig Mac Piarais.

To Seán T. Ó Ceallaigh.

L. 119/OCS/G

29.8.1906   Carlisle Arms Hotel,
                                                      Cong.

Dear Seán,
    I trust all is going well with you.
    If there is a meeting of the Finance Committee before I return
home, I would be grateful if you would deposit my salary cheque in
my bank to my account. I left very little money in the account when
I left home. Yours ever, Pádraig Mac Piarais.

To H. Morris.

L. 120/P.Ms./G

15.11.1906.   An Claidheamh Soluis,
                                                      Áth Cliath.

Dear Friend,
    I regret that I shall be unable to go to Dundalk on Monday
night, although I should like to go if it were possible. You know
that I am always busy working on the *Claidheamh* on that night.
    I trust that the lecture will be a success. Your friend for ever,
Pádraig Mac Piarais.

To S. Bairéad.

The Christmas gift to his godchild was a miniature china teaset in
the blue willow pattern which Pearse is said to have favoured
himself. The set is still intact in the possession of the recipient.

24.12.1906. Cúil Crannach,
Leeson Park,
Dublin.

Dear Friend,
I enclose a gift for Sighle. It is unlikely that she will have an interest in them now but she may as she grows up.
With Christmas Greetings, Your friend for ever, Pádraig Mac Piarais.

To H. Morris.

The subject or object of the review by Morris, *Ceachta agus Comhrá* was not published by the League and hence Pearse's concern lest an unsigned notice which was strongly critical should be taken as coming from him.
The last sentence reads: "How are the proverbs progressing?" This refers to the volume on the Ulster proverbs which Morris was preparing.

L. 122/P.Ms.

3.1.1907. Connradh na Gaedhilge,
Áth Cliath.

A Chara,
Your review of *Ceachta agus Comhradh* duly to hand. A notice of the book (contributed) has already appeared in *An Claidheamh*. I see no objection, however, to publishing yours provided you sign it. I have not read the book, and I would not like your fairly strong strictures to appear as editorial. May I put in your signature?
Cia an chaoi bhfuil na sean-fhocail ag dul ar aghaidh? Mise do chara go buan, Pádraig Mac Piarais.

To Máire Nic Shíthigh.

Máire Nic Shíthigh, a teacher in the Convent of Mercy, Clonakilty, was an active member of the Gaelic League and wrote for *An Claidheamh Soluis*. She was born at Lackandubh near Clonakilty where she learned Irish from her parents; she was a very successful and popular teacher in the local classes of the Gaelic League. She translated Molière's *Le Bourgeois Gentilhomme* into Irish as *An Geogach Duine Uasal;* it was produced in the Damer, Dublin in 1958 as *Ag Sodar in Diaidh na nUasal.*

These letters from Pearse to Máire Nic Shíthigh, all written during 1907, were found in 1971 during reconstruction at the Convent of Mercy School at Clonakilty. Máire Nic Shíthigh died in 1955 and is buried in Timoleague Abbey.

L. 123/NLI/G

21.2.1907.   The Gaelic League,
                                              Dublin.

Dear Friend,
    Your letter and manuscript reached me today and I am sending the manuscript to the Committee's readers. Their judgement will be placed before the Committee when it convenes and I will communicate with you shortly after that.
    I do hope that the Committee will accept your play but we must leave that to the judgement of the readers. Yours with regards, Pádraig Mac Piarais. Secretary of the Publications Committee.

To Seán T. Ó Ceallaigh.

Fr. Kennedy was a Wexford priest who had been executed in 1798. P. J. Gregory was a local political figure with League associations. The object of the letter was to secure favourable considerations for Willie Pearse as the sculptor of the memorial.

L. 124/NLI

4.3.1907.   Connradh na Gaedhilge,
                                              Áth Cliath.

A Sheaghain na gCarad,
    I see that a Comtee has been formed in Wexford to erect a memorial to Fr. Kennedy. P. J. Gregory is a member. Would it be too much to ask you to drop him a line putting before him the claim of my brother to at least a chance of the order? You might point out that he is a Gaelic Leaguer (mentioning his connection with me), has advertised in *An Claidheamh* since the first number and so on. As for merit he has exhibited at the Royal Hibernian

105

Academy and the Oireachtas and the firm has done a good deal of work in Co. Wexford, including the Communion Rail in Wexford Cathedral and nearly all the work in the new Ross Church. If you know Father Cloney, C.C. or any other prominent person likely to have influence perhaps you could also drop them a line?

Of course the earlier we are in the field the better. Mise do bhuan-chara, Pádraig Mac Piarais.

To Máire Nic Shíthigh.

L. 125/NLI/G

14.3.1907.   The Gaelic League,
                                                  Dublin.

Dear Friend,

Your play *Seoinín* has been praised by the readers, but they think that you should read it through with the assistance of some Gaeilgeoir such as "Seandún" in Cork, because there are some idiomatic intricacies in it which they do not like. I suppose that you would be prepared to do that?

Now as regards publishing it, I suppose that you would require some money from the Committee. How much would you expect? I do hope that you will not be too hard on us!

As you already know, the Oireachtas Committee were planning to produce the play during the Oireachtas, but the Finance Committee, who met the same day said that it would cost too much. (We lost money on last year's play). The whole question will be placed before the Coistre Gnótha; i) whether there will be a drama at the Oireachtas this year and if so, if it will be *Seoinín*, ii) if the Coiste Gnótha does not agree to produce *Seoinín* at the Oireachtas, then I fear that the Finance Committee will not permit its publication. That is the position.

As regards *An Stór*, the readers think that it should not be published just now. I remain your friend, Pádraig Mac Piarais.

P.S. I should be grateful if you would send me an article or a short story for *An Claidheamh* now and again.

To Dr. W. J. Walsh.

The leading article which Dr. Walsh commented upon in his letter to Pearse, was that entitled *The Work of the Schools* which appeared in *An Claidheamh Soluis* of April 20th 1907. In it Pearse criticised the total reliance on "pen and ink" examinations by the Board for Intermediate Education and especially the system of examination for modern languages i.e. by paper questions alone without oral examination by inspectors. He quoted Douglas Hyde who had described the modern language system as "the ne plus ultra of stupidity" and attributed the position in the schools to the parsimony of the British Treasury which countered every educational initiative with "I forbid".

L. 126/DDA

25.4.1907.   An Claidheamh Soluis,
                              Áth Cliath.

My Lord Archbishop,
    I was very glad to receive Your Grace's letter supplementing my leading article about the Intermediate Board and correcting the mistake into which I had fallen. I would have wished to comment upon it at greater length, but as it did not reach me until we were practically "closing up" for press, I had merely time to insert it with a few lines of introduction. I am very glad to find that *An Claidheamh's* statement (that the fault for the unsatisfactory state of affairs with regard to modern language examination did not rest with the Intermediate Board) was read with pleasure by Your Grace. The whole discussion has I think, been useful in bringing out this fact so clearly. I am posting Your Grace the extra copies of this week's paper.
    I am, My Lord Archbishop. Your Lordship's servant, Pádraig Mac Piarais (P. H. Pearse)

To Máire Nic Shíthigh.

L. 127/NLI/G

16.5.1907.   An Claidheamh Soluis,
                              Dublin.

Dear Friend,
I would be grateful to you if you could send some stories, verses, acrostics or riddles and jokes in Irish to me from week to week. The stories which you sent to me a month ago were much appreciated by the readers of *An Claidheamh*. Success and blessings, Your friend, Pádraig Mac Piarais.

To Pádraig Ó Domhnalláin.

Pádraig Ó Domhnalláin was Pearse's friend in Uachtar Ard with whom he organised the scheme in 1903 to rescue Colm de Bhailís from the workhouse.

This letter concerns the scheme which Pearse evolved for four provincial correspondents who would contribute regional news to *An Claidheamh*.

The opening sentence reads: "I am proposing to make *An Claidheamh* a real newspaper and to appoint correspondents in each province".

The bilingual sentence reads: "For the present, I can only offer you £1 a month by way of remuneration but perhaps I may have more money to spare within a short time".

The concluding sentence reads: "Will you do this much for me and could you begin next week"?

L. 128/P.Ms./B

17.5.1907. Connradh na Gaedhilge,
An Coisde Gnótha,
Áth Cliath.

A Chara,
Táim ag brath ar páipear nuaidheachta amach 's amach 'a dheanamh de'n *Claidheamh Soluis* feasta, agus "correspondent" a cheapadh i ngach cúige. Will you become my Connacht correspondent? I would want from you *without fail every Monday morning*, say 3/4 column of short notes, putting the point of view of a Connacht Gael on the local and general happenings of the week, Irish–Ireland, political, industrial etc. They should chiefly deal with events in Connacht, but might also give Connacht views on general events. For the present, I can only offer you £1 a month by way of remuneration acht b'fhéidir go mbéadh níos mó airgid le sparáil agam i gceann tamaill.

108

An ndéanfaidh tú an méid seo dhom, agus an bhféadfá tosnughadh an tseachtmhain seo chugainn?

Beir bhuaidh agus beannacht, Mise do chara go buan, Pádraig Mac Piarais.

To M. Nic Shíthigh.

It would appear that Máire Nic Shíthigh was applying for some office under the Board of Commissioners of Intermediate Education, for which she sought the support of Pearse. It could have been as examiner (in the Intermediate grades) or as superintendent in the annual Intermediate examinations – both of which were in the giving of the Resident Commissioner, W. J. M. Starkie.

L. 129/NLI/G

20.6.1907   The Gaelic League,
                                                      Dublin.

Dear Friend,

Your letter reached me the day before yesterday. Be assured that your other letter did not perturb or anger me – why should it? My skin is not that sensitive after four years as editor! I do not think you are correct in relation to the spelling of your name, although I admit that you may spell it as you wish. It's certain that Mac Síthigh is the correct form and if so, that you would use Nic Shíthigh in relation to a woman.

You have my full permission to make any use you wish of any material concerning you in *An Claidheamh.* I do hope you are successful. There are many people applying for those positions. I will write a reference for you, if you deem it of advantage to you. Perhaps you should write to Úna Ní Fhearcheallaigh (65A Upper Leeson St. Dublin is her residence), as she is a good friend of Starkie's.

As you may have observed, I am publishing gradually those later pieces which you sent me. Any other similar pieces will be very welcome. Best wishes and greetings, Your friend, Pádraig Mac Piarais.

To H. Morris.

The son of Enrí Ó Muirgheasa whose birth is mentioned in this postcard was Colm, whose death is mentioned in a later letter of April 1908.

L.(p.c.) 130/NLI/G

24.6.1907.   Áth Cliath.

Dear Friend,
   I must congratulate you on the birth of your son – may he enjoy a long life. With regard to the Sráid Bhaile Feis, I regret that I will not be able to attend as by that time I shall be in the heart of Connacht on my holidays. Were it not for that I would certainly attend the Feis.
   Greetings and blessings, Your friend for ever, Pádraig Mac Piarais.

To F. J. Bigger.

This letter refers to the journey which Pearse, Dr. P. Mac Henry, Tomás Ó Concheanainn and F. J. Bigger made in the latter's open touring car in the Gaeltacht and which is refered to in *An Claidheamh* as "the Gaelic League motor party". Pearse contributed a detailed account of the trip to *An Claidheamh* under the title of "Ar Siubhal sa Ghaeltacht" (ACS July–August 1907). They visited Donegal, Sligo, Leitrim, Mayo and Galway, and spoke at Gaelic League meetings and summer colleges. When after completing the tour of Donegal, Bigger and his car left them at Sligo, the others continued on into Erris and Connemara.
   Tommy was the driver of Bigger's car. The Ulster League organised its summer college at Cloch an Fhaoilligh, Co. Donegal, where it held its courses for teachers.
   The little boy referred to in the postscript may have been Colm Mac Donnell, a nephew of Úna Ní Fhearchallaigh; he was later a pupil at Sgoil Éanna and became an eminent Dublin physician.

L. 131/NLI

31.7.1907.   Cúil Crannach,
                                    Cill Mhuire Chairrgín,
                                    Áth Cliath.

A Chara,
   Since I got back to town early last week I have been chasing a

110

moment to write to you in, to thank you for the pleasant time we spent on the gluaisteán in Tirconnell and Sligo. I for one enjoyed myself thoroughly; and, what is more important, I think we did a deal of really valuable work which is bound to tell and which, in fact is already bearing fruit in more places than one. The people at headquarters here feel that they owe you more than they can repay. I think we owe a good deal to Tommy also who under such trying circumstances, stuck so gallantly to his post. I hope he is now quite himself again. Will you remember me to him?

We did good work in Erris after parting from you though, of course, we should have done more if we had had the motor. Connacht and especially Erris and Connemara, stands in much more need of a rousing than Donegal. Next year the League must do something for the West.

Your photos of the Cloughaneely meeting reached me today. Thanks very much for them. They are admirable. Both the snapshots of myself are really capital – the best I have seen, I think. They will be very interesting mementoes of our trip. I did not know that you photographed the meeting at all.

If you are coming to the Oireachtas, perhaps some evening during the week I shall have the pleasure of seeing you here, with some kindred spirits?

By the way, the *Freeman* badly mutilated the report of the Sligo part of our work. They left out *all* that you had written about Grange and Inishmurray and some of my own stuff. Your matter duly reached me and I embodied it and sent it along. The *Freeman* will only print journalese. With kind regards, Mise do chara go buan, Pádraig Mac Piarais (P. H. Pearse)

P.S. Are you at the bottom of the police mutiny? If it is not asking too much, I should be grateful if you could send me another copy of the photo in which I am standing. I have a gradh for the little boy in the forefront of the group on my right and I should like to send him a copy.

To Seán T. Ó Ceallaigh.

This undated pencilled note which carries no address but the cryptic "Maidin Diardaoin" (Thursday morning) conveys an urgent appeal to Ó Ceallaigh who was manager of the paper to divert a few hundred copies of An Claidheamh Soluis away from Dublin.

The exhibition in question was the Oireachtas Art Exhibition, organised by the League and held during the first week of August at the Hibernian Academy in Lower Abbey Street. *An Claidheamh Soluis* of August 10th contains a review of the exhibition, the main portion of which was written by Pearse. He praises the general standard of the works and mentions in particular the names of Beatrice Elvery and her sister, Hone, Purser and other artists.

It seems that in the early copies of the paper, some artists' names were misprinted or confused; these were the copies of the paper that Pearse wished to be diverted from the critical gaze of Dublin's artistic circles. Since Thursday morning was dispatch morning at the Claidheamh office, it would seem that this note was written on August 10th. and delivered to Ó Ceallaigh's office before dispatch began.

The exhibition in question was an historic one in that it contained the life-size statue of Parnell which now crowns the monument in O'Connell Street, by the Dublin-born, Irish–American sculptor, Augustus St. Gaudens. Pearse, in his review, praised the work and added this interesting comment: "The face has not the wild and haggard look of the hunted weary man who is the Parnell of our personal recollections, the Parnell of 1890 and 1891".

L 132/NLI

n.d.   Maidin Diardaoin.

A Sheaghain, a Chara,

A few hundred copies of *Claidheamh* have been printed off containing some serious errors in second form. These are those first folded this morning. Could you arrange to have these sent out to country places and *not circulated in Dublin, above all not sent to Miss O'Brien or anyone connected with the Art Exhibition*?

Some artists' names got mixed up. P. Mac P.

To H. Morris.

This letter covers the printing and publication details of *Sean-Fhocla Uladh* by Morris, which was printed by Tempest at the Dundealgan Press, Dundalk, and published as one volume in 1907. Tempest and Pearse had some common interests through the Castle Bellingham Feis and also the archaelogy of Co. Louth; it was Tempest and the Dundealgan Press which published the second volume of Pearse's short stories, *An Mháthair agus Scéalta Eile* in January 1916.

L. 133/P.Ms./G

28.9.1907   The Gaelic League,
                             Executive Committee,
                             Dublin.

Dear Friend,
   Greetings and blessings. I must congratulate you on your election
to the board. The elected six will do great work.
   Concerning *Sean-Fhocla Uladh.* Which would you prefer to
publish it as one volume initially or in two separate volumes? And
how many pages in each volume? I suppose that we must put a
price of 2s. 6d. at least on the book. Would you please ask Tempest
to send in his account so that we can cost the book. We would need
that information before settling the price.
   I will place the question of *Greann na Gaeilge* before the next
meeting of the Publications Committee. I will be going to Connacht
on my holidays next week and I will not return for a fortnight or
three weeks. It appears that the Publications Committee will not
hold a meeting until the end of October or the beginning of
November.
   The reason I did not reply to your postcard on that occasion was
that I did not know the date of the meeting which had not then
been decided. As soon as it was arranged you were notified. My
renewed congratulations, Yours ever, Pádraig Mac Piarais.

To H. Morris

There seems to have been some confusion and mutual recrimination
in the Pearse–Morris relationship at this stage concerning the rate
of progress in the publication of *Sean-Fhoclá Uladh.* It is most likely
that the unbound pages were with Tempest in Dundalk whom each
expected the other to contact.

L. 134/NLI/G

8.11.1907   The Gaelic League,
                             Dublin.

Dear Friend,
   Be sensible! If everyone in the League worked as hard as the
officers of the Publications Committee, our situation would be
fortunate.
   Who has the proverbs now? I cannot arrange to have them

bound and covered until I discover where they are. Yours ever, Pádraig Mac Piarais.

A Chara (member of a League Committee).

This Committee, of which Pearse was the secretary, was responsible for a very unusual Gaelic League activity – a public health education programme in the Connemara Gaeltacht beginning in January 1908, directed against tuberculosis. At the beginning of the century, tuberculosis was a major problem over large areas of the country; one out of six deaths in 1907 were due to it and in the western Atlantic regions the rate was even higher.

The Committee was established following a symposium on the disease given by Dr. Seán O'Beirne and other experts at the College of Surgeons, Dublin in December 1907, to which representatives of the League were invited. Pearse initiated a fund through *An Claidheamh Soluis* to support the campaign; the committee was thus enabled to finance the release of Dr. O'Beirne from his position as medical officer at Leenane, Co. Galway with a view to conducting the health education programme in the Connemara Gaeltacht.

The committee, in addition to Dr. O'Beirne and Pearse, included as members Dr. Seán Mac Einrí and Dr. Michael F. Cox, in whose Merrion Square house they met.

L. 135/NLI/G

December 1907.   An Claidheamh Soluis,
                                            Áth Cliath.

Dear Friend,

The Education Committee has nominated you as one of the group which will direct the campaign of Dr. O'Beirne against tuberculosis. Could you come to the house of Dr. Cox, 26 Merrion Square, at 8.30 p.m. this evening (Friday) to plan the launching of the project? Yours, Pádraig Mac Piarais.

To H. Morris.

This letter represents the nodal points in the differences between Pearse and Morris concerning the proverbs book. The letter also

114

provides some evidence as to the workload carried by Pearse as an official of the League, a load which required him to devote Christmas Eve to this type of detailed routine correspondence.

L. 136/P.Ms./G

24.12.1907.   The Gaelic League,
                      The Executive Committee.

Dear Friend,
  You yourself are responsible for whatever delay surrounded *Sean-Fhocla Uladh* and for any related consequences. You did not explain to me fully your intentions and I did not know whether it was to be bound and covered in Dundalk or in Dublin. When I failed to secure any information from you, I had to write to Tempest and after a few days I heard from him that he would prefer that it be bound in Dublin. I sent for the books then and they arrived after a week. We could not get an estimate on the binding until we had the books. There was no time to consult with you if we were to have the books out for Christmas, as we wished. What we did then was to issue some copies in haste for Christmas; they are merely a "temporary edition".
  Now I wish to consult you regarding the remainder. What we propose to do is as follows: i) to issue copies at two shillings bound in linen, similar to the book enclosed, ii) to issue copies bound in good cloth at half-a-crown, iii) to issue the book in four parts, in paper covers at sixpence a part.
  What do you think of this arrangement? Write to me as soon as you have time.
  Christmas greetings to self and family, Yours ever, Pádraig Mac Piarais.

To S. Bairéad.

The Christmas gift to Sighle Bairéad, his godchild, was a doll's house with miniature furniture.

L. 137/P.Ms./G

2.1.1908   Cúil Chrannach,
                                  Leeson Park.
                                  Dublin.

Dear Friend,
   Enclosed is a small gift which I am sending for Sighle. It should
have arrived for Christmas but I could not secure it in time. It was
made in the Glens of Antrim, both the house and the furniture. The
furniture may be a little too big to place in the house, but it is not
possible to get smaller furniture of Irish manufacture.
   I wish you all every happiness in the New Year, Yours, ever,
Pádraig Mac Piarais.

To H. Morris.

Greann na Gaeilge was the seven-part collection of stories by
Morris, which the League published between 1901 and 1907;
Morris was obviously anxious to continue the series but the
Publications Committee due to financial constraints was not willing
to do so.
   The reference to O'Grady's *Silva Gadelica*, a collection of stories
from ancient Irish manuscript sources, published in 1892, may
indicate that Morris had proposed to edit a modern version of the
story *An Ceithearnach Caoilriabhach* which is contained in the
O'Grady work. The League later published in 1910 a Munster
version of this story under the editorship of Pádraig Ó Siochfhradha
(An Seabhach).
   Pearse's collection of short stories, *Íosagán agus Sgéalta Eile* was
published in 1907 under the League imprint; these stories had
appeared in *An Claidheamh Soluis* during the previous two years.
The 1907 edition contains an introduction by Pearse detailing the
location of each of the stories in the environs of Ros Muc in
Connemara and the background to each story. The collection was
illustrated by Beatrice Elvery (later Lady Glenavy) who figured in
the 1907 Oireachtas Art Exhibition and who executed some of the
artistic decoration in Sgoil Éanna.

L. 138/P.Ms./G

15.1.1908.   The Gaelic League,
                                         The Executive Committee.

Dear Friend,

I received your letter today. I was waiting until the copies bound in good cloth were ready as I regarded these as the most suitable to send to those who helped you. They are not ready yet and will not be for a while because the Finance Committee did not accept our recommendations; they have postponed a decision on the matter. Send me a postcard indicating whether I should send you the copies bound in light cloth or wait until I have these bound in heavy cloth.

The advertisement in the newspapers will be changed next week. Copies of *Sean-Fhocla Uladh* were sent to the *Freeman*, the *Independent* and to all the papers.

I submitted the question of *Greann na Gaeilge* to the Publications Committee but no decision was reached yet.

An Ceithearnach Caoilriabhach is a good story. There is a version of it in print in Standish Hayes O'Grady's *Silva Gadelica*. I do not think that the Gaelic League will accept any new book for some time, because they have not the money to spend on it, but you could send it to me nevertheless.

I enclose for you a copy of my own book, *Íosagán*. Perhaps you would recommend it to schoolmasters for their students or you may wish to write something about it in one of the papers. Yours ever, Pádraig Mac Piarais.

To Eoghan Ó Neachtain.

Eoghan Ó Neachtain was one of the most industrious of the League's authors. The work in question here was his translation of Euclid I published in 1908; volume II followed in 1913. Sealy, Bryers and Walkers were the Dublin publishing firm.

L. 139/OCS/G

31.1.1908   The Gaelic League,
                                         Dublin.

Dear Eoghan,

That question is fixed. Sealy Bryers are willing to do the

inaccurate diagrams again and are already working on them. What about the title page?

The cover is ready, Yours, Pádraig Mac Piarais.

To H. Morris.

L. 140/P.Ms./G

31.1.1908.   The Gaelic League,
                                        Dublin.

Dear Friend,

At a meeting of the Publications Committee last Friday, it was proposed that a few hundred volumes of the seven parts of *Greann na Gaeilge* be bound together, without however reprinting the work or writing a new dictionary for the joint volume. The method proposed involves removing the paper covers from the single volumes and binding them together seven by seven. I assume that you will be happy with this arrangement.

The Committee has asked me to request you to forward *An Ceithearnach Caoilriabhach* so that we can submit it to the judgement of our readers.

I am awaiting permission from the Finance Committee to issue the extra copies of *Sean-Fhocla Uladh*. They will have a meeting next week.

Greetings and best wishes, Your friend, Pádraig Mac Piarais.

To H. Morris.

L.(p.c.) 141/P.Ms./G

19.2.1908.   The Gaelic League,
                                        Dublin.

Dear Friend,

The other copies of *Sean-Fhocla Uladh* arrived today, and I have instructed the shop staff to send you a half dozen of each type (light and heavy binding). I trust that you are happy with them. Yours as ever. Pádraig Mac Piarais.

To Eoin Mac Neill.

Early in 1908, Pearse again took up the question of opening an Irish "High School", a project which he had already tentatively examined in 1906, in conjunction with Eoin Mac Neill and Thomas P. O'Nowlan of Roscrea Cistercian College. In late February and early March, he wrote in turn to Mac Neill, Edward Martyn and Patrick Mac Manus outlining his school plans and seeking their approval and financial support; later in July he approached Dr. W. J. Walsh, Archbishop of Dublin. Unfortunately not all the items from this critical correspondence are available; the missing items include other letters to Mac Neill written on the 29th February and 3rd March, and his initial letter to Martyn, the reply to which prompted Pearse's letter of February 27th.

The initial letters to all are similar in their contents and emphasis; the variations are related to the degree of familiarity which he enjoyed with the correspondents and to their relative potential for assisting the scheme financially. In this letter to Mac Neill, Pearse is more concerned with securing his personal support and approval, secure in the knowledge that such would be critical in gaining a wider support for the school, from ecclesiastical and secular friends. It is clear also that apart from financial support or a promise of sending his sons, Pearse is seeking the views of one whose judgement he respects, on an enterprise to which he himself is strongly drawn.

Mac Neill replied to this and to another letter from Pearse on 4th March and his letter gives a clear indication of his position vis-a-vis Pearse's proposed school. He criticises those who have crusaded against the clerical influence in education, mentioning the *Peasant* in particular, and points out that reform in Irish education would come only by the aid of the clergy. Consequently, he advises Pearse to avoid in his school, anything savouring of Clergy v. Laity, to secure the active approval of Archbishop Walsh, who could be counted on as a friend of such an undertaking. Mac Neill put forward in his letter a most imaginative alternative scheme based on the League's Leinster College – "a rudimentary school" starting with a moderate number of pupils and utilising the premises and facilities of the college. Such a solution would certainly have obtained the automatic support of Dr. Walsh, who was among the original committee of the Leinster College and a member of its Board of Trustees. Mac Neill's letter also questions the efficacy of day schools in imparting fluency in Irish, which he contends requires a domestic situation or its school equivalent; the language taught in a day-school "Will never be more than a simulacrum of the living thing". The opening sentence explains that he is writing the letter in English so as to express his thoughts more clearly.

L. 142/NLI

24.2.1908.   Connradh na Gaedhilge,

A Niallaigh na gCarad,

Sgriobhfaidh mé an litir seo i mBéarla mar is doigh gur i mBéarla is fearr d'fhéadfainn mo smaointe a nochtadh ar an gceist áirithe seo.

I wonder whether I can interest you in a project which, as I think you know, I have had at the back of my head for the past two or three years and which, if I can see my way clear, I am now more than ever anxious to proceed with? It is the project of a High School for boys in Dublin on purely Irish Ireland lines. The arguments in favour of the establishment of such a school are irresistible. There is no *Irish* High School in Ireland. There is no High School for Catholic boys conducted by laymen in Ireland. My idea is, if possible to fill this two-fold need.

There are a number of Gaelic Leaguers in Dublin and throughout the country who have brought up their children more or less Irish speaking and who are now anxiously looking round for a school which would provide these children with a genuine *Irish* education, while at the same time of a high standard generally. Already I have received one or two definite promises from parents to send me their boys in the event of my starting and I have hopes of definite promises from others. You know that I have had considerable experience as a secondary and as a university teacher and that for the past six or seven years my chief hobby has been the study of education in most of its phases. In a word, I feel that I have ideas on the subject of the education of boys which are worth putting into practice. Among the features of my scheme would be:— (1) An *Irish* standpoint and "atmosphere" (2) *bilingual teaching* as far as possible, (3) all language teaching on the *Direct Method* (4) special attention to science and "modern" subjects generally, while not neglecting the classical side (5) association of the pupils with the shaping of the curriculum, cultivation of observation and reasoning, "nature Study" and several other points to which I have devoted a good deal of thought (6) physical culture, Irish games etc, (7) above all formation of character.

Mr. O'Nowlan, was, as I think you will remember, originally associated with me in the project, but I don't know that since his marriage he would be able to take the prominent part originally intended. However, I have no doubt, that I should be able to secure first-class teaching capacity in the various departments. The school would of course be a Catholic one. I think the Archbishop and some prominent Catholic laymen might be got as patrons or visitors and there would be a priest as chaplain. The professors would be laymen and I would propose to take both boarders and day-boys and the terms would be reasonable as possible. My association with the scheme would of course involve my resigning the editorship of *An Claidheamh Soluis*.

Now all this means capital and here I come to my difficulty. I feel confident that this scheme would pay ultimately but we should have to be prepared to face a loss on the first two or three years working. I am running over in my mind the people who would be likely to invest money in such an undertaking. My object in writing to you is to ask (1) whether you would be willing to join in and subscribe some of the capital and (2) whether in the event of my starting you would send me your boys and use your influence with other parents of your acquaintance to do the same? In any case I should be grateful for your views in the whole matter.

I believe that the successful establishment of such a school as I outline would be one of the most important and far reaching things that have yet grown out of the language movement.

For the present, you might kindly observe absolute secrecy about the matter. It may come to nothing as yet. It would not do to have it talked about and then collapse. Yours very sincerely, Pádraig Mac Piarais.

To Edward Martyn.

Arising from the work of the Committee established by the Gaelic League to deal with the high incidence of tuberculosis in Connemara, Dr. Seán O'Beirne launched a campaign of public health education. Pearse who was secretary of this Committee, gave the campaign vital support in *An Claidheamh Soluis* and launched a fund with Dr. O'Beirne to run a Home Improvement Scheme for which *An Claidheamh* offered prizes. Edward Martyn had contributed towards this fund.

This letter shows that Pearse had already begun early in 1908 to gauge the support available to him for his "High School on Irish lines". It would appear that he had approached Martyn before this letter and that he had raised such points as the likely pupil numbers, the adoption or rejection of the Intermediate Programme and the central question of the financial backing which the project

121

required. Pearse's suggestion of the possibility of opening the school at his home is of interest in view of the kindergarten and junior school which Miss Margaret Pearse conducted there. His attitude to the Intermediate Programme and its examinations, despite his broad denunciation of both in his later educational writings, is far from doctrinaire; his opinion expressed here, that one could adopt the intermediate courses without materially diminishing the Irish character of the school, was later put into practice successfully in Sgoil Éanna when parents requested it.

Pearse had written similar letters to others of his immediate acquaintances and it was essential that the matter remain confidential until announced at the appropriate moment. His ability to conduct such preliminary confidential negotiations with discretion and prudence is demonstrated throughout his correspondence with many friends and supporters of Sgoil Éanna.

L. 143/P.Ms.

27.2.1908.   Connradh na Gaedhilge,
                                        An Coisde Gnótha,
                                        Áth Cliath.

A Chara,

Many thanks, in the first place, for your cheque towards the Home Improvement Scheme in connection with Dr. O'Beirne's work in Connemara, I have acknowledged it, with some others in the current issue of *An Claidheamh.*

Thanks, in the second place, for your sympathy and encouragement with regard to my project of a High School on Irish lines. I am very glad to know that you are in accord with my ideas. I have broached the matter to one or two other friends likely to be interested and on whose discretion I can rely and they have all encouraged me to go on if I can see a way. Already I have received one or two definite promises from parents to send me their boys, and I feel that once the thing gets fairly started there will be little difficulty on the score of pupils.

The question of the adoption of the Intermediate Programme would be one for consideration. Some think (and I am inclined to agree) that it could be taken up without materially interfering with the Irish character of the school. But I expect that in the beginning the majority of the pupils would be below the Intermediate age.

To come to the financial question, what I am anxious to get is three or four persons who would each put a few hundred pounds into the scheme or else one who would put a thousand. I calculate that £1,000 would be ample for equipment and also to provide against a possible loss on the first year or two. Forty pupils would ensure the *absolute* financial success of the school, but I think we should start if we were sure of twenty for the first year. It would be well to commence modestly and feel our way very carefully. At the present stage it is difficult to give a detailed financial estimate but I shall go carefully into the matter with two or three friends and give you such an estimate as soon as I can. I have to make inquiries about building classrooms, a small laboratory, etc. The house where I live (a large detached one adjoining Leeson Park) would be suitable if two class-rooms were built in the garden, where there is ample room. I could buy my landlord's interest for £210. I think £300 would build and equip classrooms and laboratory, (the Department would go halfway towards providing funds for the latter), and granting that we had £1,000 to start with, this would leave £500 to our credit in the bank to meet emergencies and carry out future developments.

I should be very grateful if you would let me know in a general way how far you would be prepared to go. In the meantime, I should be getting together my detailed figures, and trying to get promises from parents within my immediate acquaintances. We can, of course, say nothing, publicly or semi-publicly until we have made up our minds to go ahead.

With many thanks, and trusting to hear from you, Mise do chara, Pádraig Mac Piarais.

To Edward Martyn.

In this, the third letter seeking support for the school from Martyn, Pearse is at pains to set aside Martyn's doubts as to the school's viability; he counters the latter's lack of enthusiasm by his own confidence, the confidence of a man who has found his life's vocation and is determined to follow it.

It is possible that Martyn and Eoin Mac Neill had been in touch, since both had been approached; each used the Cló-Chumann of the League as an example of an Irish–Ireland project which had been unsuccessful. Mac Neill had also been the intermediary whom the Archbishop (Dr. W. J. Walsh) had used later to answer Pearse's letter on the school.

Martyn was generous in his philanthropy and given Pearse's offer of securities it seems strange that Martyn was unwilling to invest in a project which was at once Catholic and national, unless

123

he had some fundamental objection to a school conducted by a layman.

Pearse's expression of fear that some people in the Gaelic League might try to wreck his scheme is surprising; one would have expected that the "fiach bunaidh" or original feud which developed around his appointment to the editorship of *An Claidheamh Soluis* would have lost its meaning by 1908.

L. 144/P.Ms.

29.2.1908.   Cúil Chrannach,
                                          Cill Mhuire Chairrgín,
                                          Baile Átha Cliath.

A Chara,
    Many thanks for your letter. I can easily realise that the demands on you are numerous and I know that there have been many unsuccessful Irish–Ireland undertakings. But I think mine stands in a different category from such things as say, An Cló-Chumann. I would ask you not to decide until I am in a position to put a full estimate before you. In my former letters I contemplated the possibility of a loss on the first few years working. On going into the matter with friends who are interested in it, I began to see that by commencing very modestly and by avoiding heavy responsibilities in the matter of large salaries etc, I shall be able to make the scheme pay from the very start. I assume that if I can convince you of this you will be willing to invest? At present I am quietly endeavouring to get guarantees from parents to send me their boys in the event of my starting. Suppose that in a month's or six weeks time I am in a position to go to you and say: "I have received definite promises of so many boys; that would represent a net revenue of so much; the corresponding expense on rent, teaching power, and general working would be so much, leaving clear profit of so much on the year's work? – would you not then be able to consider the whole question of investment with full data before you? I would ask you to keep your mind open until I can submit to you such an estimate, based on the actual promises of parents and the money value represented.

    In the event I hope for and anticipate that there would be a moral certainty, humanly speaking, of a profit on each year's working. In the meantime, you might turn over in your mind two alternatives:—

(i) That you should join with me and some friends in each putting say, £300 or (in my case) its equivalent in premises etc., into the scheme; or

(2) That you should put say £1,000 into the scheme on the security
  (a) of the house with the added class-rooms, worth at least £500 or £600 and
  (b) of some additional security which I might devise means of giving you; for instance, I have a small cottage and a plot of land in Connemara, or I could get an additional policy of insurance on my life, and so on.

You see, I am so confident of the ultimate success of the project that I am willing to give up my position in the League (worth as you know, £230 a year) and practically stake my whole worldly future on it. I feel that I am cut out for this particular work and granted a fair start, it seems to me that failure is impossible to a determined man engaged at the work for which, above all others, he feels a natural aptitude and to which he can give all his enthusiasm.

I will write you further as soon as I have completed my enquiries, and got a sufficient number of guarantees. Meantime please observe strict secrecy, because there are people in the Gaelic League – you can guess to whom I am referring – who for sheer malice would do their best to wreck the scheme before it got started. Mise do chara, Pádraig Mac Piarais.

To Patrick Mac Manus.

This letter to Patrick Mac Manus, a brother of Séumas Mac Manus and a friend of Tomás Bán Ó Concheanainn, seeking a financial commitment to the support of the proposed school, is of singular importance. It identifies the context in which St. Enda's was conceived by Pearse and the basic specifications which he had written for his educational venture. With this letter, as with similar requests to his other supporters, he enclosed a two-page document outlining the object and scope of the proposed school. His initial intention was to call the school Sgoil Lorcáin (St. Lorcan's) in honour of the patron saint of the Catholic Archdiocese of Dublin. In changing the name to Sgoil Éanna, Pearse may have wished to commemorate the educational nature of the monastic settlements on the Aran Islands founded by Éanna, and perhaps at the same time to signal the degree of support for his school which he had received from his friend, Dr. W. J. Walsh, the Archbishop of Dublin.

Dr. Walsh had been approached in 1906 by a teacher in Mount Mellery Cistercian College (Co. Waterford), a Mr. Thomas P. O'Nowlan, who sought his "paternal advice" on the opening of a "secondary school for Catholic boys in Dublin of which he (O'Nowlan) would be Principal, Manager and Proprietor". In his letter to Dr. Walsh O'Nowlan proposed that Dr. Walsh, with Mr. John Mac Neill, Mr. Edward Martyn and Dr. Douglas Hyde would act as Visitors and that Mr. Patrick Pearse, B.A., B.L., would be Vice-President of the school. There is no documentary indication available as to why this educational proposal did not materialise, although the fact that O'Nowlan had been a Jesuit for fifteen years may have diminished his prospects of securing ecclesiastical approval. Lay initiative in education, especially managerial initiative, could hardly expect enthusiastic support from the Catholic bishops in an era when their spokesman on education Dr. Dwyer of Limerick, had declared unequivocally, that "no laymen had the right to teach". Pearse may possibly have learned some valuable lessons from his peripheral involvement in the O'Nowlan scheme; his letters to Dr. Walsh in connection with Sgoil Éanna, display a tentative and sensitive approach which is absent from the letter of O'Nowlan of two years earlier.

It is of significance that Pearse states in this letter that his chief hobby over the previous six or seven years had been "education in all its phases". His establishment of Sgoil Éanna, therefore is not to be regarded as some escapist plagiarisation of the ideas of others; it is rather the working out in practice of educational concepts and principles which he had elaborated and internalised during ten years of reading, analysis, reflection, writing and comparative fieldwork. The logical outcome of his pre-1908 educational writings would have demanded some practical effort to reform the system he so totally rejected and a commitment to an alternative system. St. Enda's epitomised that personal commitment and the practical effort to reform.

Tomás Bán Ó Concheanainn, was prophetically accurate in his assessment of the scheme as likely to make history. Pearse's expectation, contained in the last paragraph, that the school would be "one of the most important and far-reaching things" to emerge from the language movement, may not have been realised in the literal sense of survival and widespread reform; the pedagogical impact of the school and of Pearse's educational writings may yet await their full realisation.

Patrick Mac Manus was in favour of establishing the school and promised financial support to Pearse; yet three years later, it would appear that he had not honoured his promise. In a letter to Tomás Bán of September 1911, Pearse is speculating whether Mac Manus is back in Ireland from the States and whether he would invest the money he had promised in 1908, if he saw the progress the school was making.

The document accompanying this letter gives an accurate picture of the school as it functioned from 1908 to 1916; all its major innovative features and organisational details are outlined as being essential elements in the proposed school.

L. 145/NLI

4.3.1908. Connradh na Gaedhilge,
An Coisde Gnótha.
Áth Cliath.

A Chara,

I wonder whether I can interest you in an important educational project in which, with one or two friends, I am about to embark, provided I can see my way quite clear? It is the project of an Irish High School for boys in Dublin. Your brother Séumas will, I think, join in with me and so will Thomas Concannon, Edward Martyn, John Mac Neill and others. Some of these would take part in the actual working of the school and others, like your brother, would simply supply some of the capital.

The arguments in favour of the establishment of such a school are irresistible. There is no *Irish* High School in Ireland. There is no High School for Catholic boys conducted by laymen in Ireland. My idea is to supply this two-fold need.

There are quite a number of Gaelic Leaguers in Dublin and throughout the country who have brought up their children more or less Irish-speaking and who are now anxiously on the lookout for a school which would provide these children with an education genuinely Irish while at the same time, up to a high standard generally. Already I have received two or three definite guarantees from parents to send me their boys in the event of my starting and I have quite a long list of Irish–Ireland parents whom I still have to approach.

I have had considerable experience as a secondary and as a university teacher, and during the past six or seven years, as you will perhaps have gathered from the editorial columns of *An Claidheamh Soluis*, my chief hobby has been the study of education in most of its phases. In a word, I feel that I have ideas on the subject of the education of Irish boys which are well worth putting into practice. I give you (very roughly) on a separate sheet the main points which would be embodied in my scheme. Later on I will, of course, submit a detailed prospectus and programme to all who are interesting themselves in the matter. Just at present, I am

127

endeavouring privately to ascertain, in a general way, how much moral and financial support I may expect.

The school would, of course, be a Catholic one, but the professors would be laymen. I expect that the Archbishop and some prominent lay Catholics would be willing to act as Visitors or Patrons and there would be a priest as chaplain. I shall have no difficulty in securing first-class teaching power in the various departments, and such eminent specialists as John Mac Neill, Dr. J. P. Henry, Dr. Sigerson etc., will be available as extern lecturers. I would take both boarders and day-boys and the terms would necessarily have to be reasonable.

The governing note of the school would be its *Irish* character. It would be a school for Irish-speaking boys and for boys whose parents are anxious that they should be educated on bilingual lines. Thus, it would not actively compete with the existing great ecclesiastical schools and colleges which, catering as they do for all Ireland and for the more anglicised classes in particular, must for many years to come remain predominantly English speaking. Our school would be designed to meet a special need which has sprung up within the past few years, – the need for high-class education in and through Irish for a limited but important and growing section of the Youth of the country.

My connection with the scheme will, of course, involve my resigning the editorship of *An Claidheamh Soluis*.

Now I come to one of our difficulties, – the question of capital. We all feel sure that the school will pay its way ultimately, but we require a certain sum to build class-rooms, provide equipment and lay up against a possible loss on the first year's working. We want two or three more Gaels who would each put a few hundred pounds into the scheme, – or else one who would put a thousand. My object in writing you is to ask whether *you* would be willing to join in and provide this sum or any part of it? All you could give me at present, I suppose, is a general assurance of your willingness pending further details; but by the time I hear from you I hope to have my detailed scheme ready to forward you. We should have to open our doors in *September* if we commence this year at all.

Can you help in any way? I feel confident that you will be making a sound investment from the business point of view, but over and above that you will be enabling us to go ahead with a scheme which, as T. Concannon says, will *make history*. Certain it is that such a school as we project – Irish of the Irish will be one of the most important and far reaching things that have yet grown out of the language movement.

128

Beir buaidh agus beannacht, Pádraig Mac Piarais. (P. H. Pearse)

Please observe strict secrecy for the present. It will not do to let the project be talked about until we are quite sure that we are going ahead.

Rough notes as to object and scope
>   Sgoil Lorcáin,
>   (St Lorcan's School)
> An Irish School For Catholic Boys.

Object To provide an elementary and secondary education of a high type for Irish-speaking boys and for boys not yet Irish-speaking whose parents are desirous that they should be educated on bilingual lines.

Chief Points
 (a) An *Irish* standpoint and "atmosphere".
 (b) *Bilingual teaching* – as far as possible,
 (c) All language teaching on *Direct Method.*
 (d) Special attention to science and "modern" subjects generally, while not neglecting the classical side.
 (e) Association of pupils with shaping of curriculum, cultivation of observation and reasoning, "nature study" etc., etc.
 (f) Physical culture; Irish games, etc.
 (g) Systematic inculcation of patriotism and training in the duties of citizenship.
 (h) Above all, *formation of character*

School Catholic in tone; religious training under superintendence of duly-approved chaplain; professors, laymen; eminent specialists (such as Dr. Sigerson, Dr Henry, John Mac Neill, etc.) as extern lecturers.

School Library and School Museum to be established. Feature to be made of "Friday Afternoon Lectures" – talks on Irish History etc, illustrated by Magic Lantern; visits to city museums, picture galleries, botanical gardens, and so on, or country rambles for purpose of studying nature or visiting spots of antiquarian interest.

School garden to be cultivated by pupils. Gymnasium; physical culture, Irish Dancing, Irish Music (harp, pipes, violin, piano, vocal).

Terms to be moderate (say from seven to ten guineas per term for day boys and from thirty to thirty two guineas for boarders, according to age). Reduction for brothers and for boys coming long distances. Clothes and outfits of boys to be of Irish manufacture.

Building to be decorated and furnished artistically and as far as possible on Celtic lines. Boys to be taught to value moral and physical beauty. Manliness, earnestness and self-sacrifice to be inculcated.

One or two scholarships to be established (1) to give promising boys from Irish-speaking districts a secondary education at the school and (2) to give these boys later on a University education if they are found deserving. P. H. Pearse.

To H. Morris.

Colm, the infant son referred to died at the age of nine months, and his mother died within a few months.

The comments by Pearse in this letter relating to the version by Morris of the story *An Ceithearnach Caoilriabhach*, are significant in the context of a later letter to Morris of 12.12.1909. The Publications Committee had apparently sanctioned another writer, Pádraig Ó Siochfhradha, to edit this story for publication and did not inform Morris accordingly. Pearse was not a member of the Committee at that stage and thus was unaware of the situation obtaining.

From the summer of 1908, when he founded Sgoil Éanna, Pearse was forced to reduce drastically his involvement with the Gaelic League; he relinquished his official positions except the editorship of *An Claidheamh Soluis* which he retained until the late autumn of 1909.

The group associated with Fr. Dineen, to which Pearse refers in the penultimate paragraph, were mainly a Munster group based in Dublin, who were opposed to the alleged strong influence of Connacht and its dialect within the League. They were closely identified with the Keating Branch and found ready journalistic support in the pages of the *Leader* and the *Freeman's Journal*. While the overt basis for these League factions related to linguistic and provincial loyalties, it is quite probable that much of the internal feuding arose more from personality clashes, personal ambition and power politics as well as from ability differentials in spoken and written Irish.

L. 146/P.Ms./G

11.4.1908.   The Gaelic League,
                                    The Executive Committee
                                    Dublin

Dear Friend,

My heart is heavy on hearing of the death of your infant. I suppose that I or anyone else who is not a parent cannot fully understand the sorrow and heartbreak suffered by parents whose infant is snatched from them; yet I have some awareness of it, I think. May God console you both. I heard that your good wife was not well and this was another reason why I did not write to you sooner on business matters. I trust that she has improved by now.

I sent the manuscript of *An Ceithearnach Caoilriabhach* back to you yesterday. The readers say that the story is worth publishing but they think that it would require re-editing and that you would need to compare your text closely with that of O'Grady and with some of the versions in the Academy here. I do not think that the Publications Committee will accept any new books for some time to come. I will write to you again concerning the whole question.

It is not the Publications Committee which is responsible for the money due to you but the Finance Committee, or should I say the new company (Clodhanna Teo.) which the Executive Committee has established to direct the book business in future. The Registrar of Joint Stock Companies in London has refused to register the company in Irish and the matter is under discussion between the League and the Registrar since. Until this is resolved no monies can be disbursed, as funds are in the care of two trustees neither of whom may sign a cheque in the present impasse. I will send in your bill to the Directors of the company and it will be paid at the first meeting after the question of registration is finalised. That situation, I understand, is near at hand.

I am glad to hear that you share my view concerning Fr. Dineen. I believe that there are one or two in that group whose one objective is to break the League. The majority of them are pleasant but they are led by those one or two others.

A question to you! Would you have time to write a short notice in English on *Íosagán* for *An Claidheamh.* Since it is my own book, I cannot promote it in the same manner as I would the books of others. Pádraig Ó Domhnalláin wrote something in Irish on it but it is necessary to introduce the book to English speakers also. I would be very grateful to you if you would write a short article as a review "from the literary point of view" as it were. Yours ever, Pádraig Mac Piarais.

To Seán T. Ó Ceallaigh

There seems to have been a standing arrangement whereby Seán Mac Einrí assisted editorially on *An Claidheamh Soluis* whenever Pearse was absent. Following his proposal of May 1907 (cf. letter 17.5.1907) Pearse had appointed a number of provincial correspondents to supply regular copy to the paper; Ó Donnchadha, Ó Searcaigh and Ó Domhnalláin were the principal correspondents. An Dálach, (Pádraig Ó Dálaigh) was the General Secretary of the League. Pearse's comment about Seán T. knowing everybody worth knowing in Dublin was not an empty flattery; as a politician and an active member of various cultural-political groups Seán T. had an extensive network of friends and contacts.

L. 147/NLI/G

19.6.1908   Connradh na Gaeilge.
                                   Áth Cliath.

Dear Seán,

I suppose that Seán Mac Einrí the League organiser, will come from Galway to look after *An Claidheamh*. I shall be leaving on the first train tomorrow morning (Saturday) and since Seán Mac Einrí is unlikely to be here until Monday morning, I would be grateful to you if you would open tomorrow's post and give any material for next week's *Claidheamh* to the printers. I am expecting the news from Éamonn Ó Donnchadha, Séamus Ó Searcaigh and perhaps from Pádraig Ó Domhnalláin. Ó Dálaigh said that he would look through these scripts and correct them. Please give them to him and then send them directly to the printers. In the event of Seán Mac Einrí not arriving early on Monday morning, you should open the post and any copy for the printers contained should be dispatched to them.

Here enclosed is some copy to be given to the printers tomorrow. Should any important letter arrive during the week you may send it to me; Ros Muc, Co. Galway will reach me.

I was hoping to have an opportunity to converse with you both yesterday and today but I did not succeed. I thought that I should tell you first that I am undertaking other work which will mean my resignation from the editorship of *An Claidheamh*. The work in question is the headmastership of a secondary Bilingual School for boys which I and a few others are founding in Dublin. I will speak to you about it when I return from the country. Perhaps you could find some students for me as I think that you know anyone worth knowing in Dublin! There will be a letter before the Executive

Committee tomorrow night. Do not discuss this with anyone until the letter is read. I suppose there will be a major controversy in choosing another editor!

I am very grateful to you for the reduced ticket, Yours ever, Pádraig Mac Piarais.

P.S.   I enclose some letters for yourself.

To Séamas Hampton P.E.

Very few schools included gymnastics in the curriculum at this time and fewer still would be prepared to count the teacher of physical education as a regular member of staff. Pearse, included the subject as a regular curricular element in Sgoil Éanna and Sgoil Íde; in the girls' school he organised classes in Swedish Drill on Saturdays for pupils and outsiders in conjunction with the Swedish Institute, which were attended by Sighle Humphreys among others. During the school years 1908–1910 at Sgoil Éanna Gymnastics and Drill were taught by William Carroll.

L. 148/OCS/G

10.7.1908.   Cúil Chrannach,
                                  Cill Mhuire Chairrgín,
                                       Áth Cliath.

A Chara,

I wonder if you heard of the school which I am establishing – a bilingual secondary school for boys? It will be located at Cullenswood House in Rathmines. I will require a teacher of gymnastics and as I understand that there is nobody in Dublin to surpass you in this field, I would like to know if you would be willing to come once a week to conduct a class. Please state your terms. I would place your name on the Prospectus among the other teachers. Please write to me as soon as you can as there is urgency in publishing the Prospectus.

I do hope that you can do this for me; otherwise I do not know what I will do. The person would need to be a Gael and have some knowledge of Irish. Your friend, Pádraig Mac Piarais.

To Dr. W. J. Walsh.

We do not know if the two intermediaries mentioned here, Fr. Curran and Eoin Mac Neill had acted on behalf of Pearse in seeking Dr. Walsh's support for Sgoil Éanna or whether they merely conveyed his reaction back to Pearse. In view of Pearse's friendship with the Archbishop, it is highly unlikely, that he would entrust such a task to another. Fr. Curran, Dr. Walsh's secretary, may not have known Pearse but would have known Mac Neill who was on the staff of St. Patrick's Training College, Drumcondra. Having ascertained through Mac Neill, that Dr. Walsh, while sympathetic, could not publicly associate with a project which had not a high probability of success, Pearse seeks in this letter to take the delicate issue one stage further by submitting his School Prospectus (at proof stage) to the Archbishop. The approach is sensitive with a decided and detectable note of autonomy on Pearse's part; he is not seeking permission but ensuring that there is nothing in his plans to which his Grace could object.

Pearse is also anxious to secure a regular chaplain and had approached the parish priest of Rathmines before seeking a permanent appointee from the Archbishop, preferably a bilingual priest. This question of a permanent chaplain for the school proved a difficult question and, as subsequent letters to the Archbishop show, a question that was never satisfactorily solved. Pearse had approached the Augustinian Fathers at their Orlagh House of Studies seeking a bilingual chaplain and later was in correspondence with the Jesuit Fathers at Rathfarnham Castle who supplied priests on an informal basis but were reluctant to formalise the arrangement in the absence of an agreement negotiated with the Archbishop.

Among the potential chaplains mentioned by Pearse was Fr. Myles Ronan, the noted scholar and historian of the Archdiocese.

L. 149/DDA

15th July 1908.   Cúil Chrannach,
                                                      Cill Mhuire Chairrgín,
                                                            Áth Cliath

May it please Your Grace,

I have the honour to enclose a proof of the Prospectus which I propose to issue in connection with my project of a Boarding and Day School on bilingual lines for Catholic boys in Dublin. Of this project Your Grace has already heard, through Father Curran, from Mr. Mac Neill. It seems to me that, as a Catholic, attempting an important educational work amongst Catholic boys, I ought not to send out my statement of what I propose to do without first submitting it for Your Grace's observations. I do not, of course, expect that you could in any public way associate yourself with the project. I gather from Mr Mac Neill that, while sympathetic, Your Grace cannot see your way to recommend support of a scheme, of the chances of success of which you are more than doubtful. I see, of course, the entire reasonableness of this, and my sole desire is to make sure that there is nothing in any part of my plans to which, as Archbishop, Your Grace would *object.*

The School is to be thoroughly Catholic in tone. Canon Frisker, in whose parish it will be situated, has very kindly said that one of the parochial clergy will visit it from time to time to test the boys in religious knowledge etc. I have not yet settled with him as to the form of words in which this fact is to be stated in the Prospectus, and indeed he would seem to prefer that it should not be stated at all. I am anxious, however, that there should be something in the Prospectus to mark definitely the Catholic character of the School, and to give parents an assurance that the religious education of their boys will be in proper hands.

It has occurred to me that it might be possible for Your Grace to name some priest in the city who has been prominently identified with the language movement and who would come to the School from time to time and give religious instruction both in Irish and in English. His name might appear on the Prospectus under some title as "Spiritual Director" or "Chaplain". The School would very willingly pay an honorarium to compensate for trouble and expense in coming. The work would not, of course, be sufficiently great to require the whole time of a priest, or anything like it. What I am thinking of, rather, is a weekly visit by some such priest as Fr. Mac Enerney, Father Joseph O'Callaghan, Father Moriarty, Father Ronan, Father Flanagan, etc., or amongst comparatively near neighbours Father Farrell of Donnybrook or Father Deane of Milltown. If this arrangement were possible it would have the great advantage of allowing us to apply the bilingual principle in the fullest sense to the teaching of the Catechism. The school, I should add, will comprise pupils whose *only* language, on first coming to school, will be Irish.

Trusting to hear that Your Grace has been able to give favourable consideration to this suggestion, I have the honour to be, Your Grace's obedient servant. P. H. Pearse.

To Seán T. Ó Ceallaigh.

It appears that Pearse took a short vacation in Ros Muc after the hectic summer months of preparation and before the opening of Sgoil Éanna on September 8th. This letter refers to the travel arrangements for this vacation.

L. 150/NLI/G

24.8.1908.   An Claidheamh Soluis,
                                                      Áth Cliath.

Dear Seán,
   Did you get those tickets? I will not be departing until tomorrow morning (Tuesday). The tickets would be in time if I had them tonight. I fear that I am unduly troubling you, Your friend as ever, Pádraig Mac Piarais.

To Seán Mac Giollarnath.

When Pearse opened Sgoil Éanna, he continued as editor of *An Claidheamh Soluis* for over a year and consequently he needed editorial assistance during that period. This letter the recipient of which was Seán Mac Giollarnath outlines the details of the arrangements made regarding the position of assistant editor. Mac Giollarnath succeeded Pearse as editor in late 1909.

L. 151/NLI/G

22.10.1908   Cullenswood House,
                                                      Rathmines,
                                                      Dublin.

Dear Friend,
   I received your letter which you sent me from the Connacht College a few months ago, but I could not answer since I had not made any definite decision on the question. If you are prepared to do the work for £100 p.a. I will give you the assistant editorship. Please write to me by return of post, indicating whether you will accept and if so when you can come. The sooner you can come the better. ... Sean Mac Henry wishes to leave and I cannot manage the work all on my own. I would appreciate if you could commence next week, if such is possible. Hoping for word from you, Yours ever, Pádraig Mac Piarais.

To Seán Mac Giollarnath.

This letter to Mac Giollarnath implies that he had accepted Pearse's offer of the post of assistant-editor; he was to begin his duties at the end of October.

Micheál Breathnach, the writer and principal of Coláiste Chonnacht, died of tuberculosis in Dublin on 28.10.1908.

L. 152/NLI/G

26.10.1908.   Sgoil Éanna,
                               Cullenswood House.

Dear Friend,
    Very well then, I will be expecting you on the 31st. You would need to see Seán Mac Einrí and then come out here. I have no time for travelling into the city.
    I am looking forward to seeing you. Yours ever, Pádraig Mac Piarais.

P.S.   Poor Micheál Breathnach is very weak. It is said that he will hardly survive another few weeks. P.Mac P.

To Dr. W. J. Walsh.

This letter is in effect a reply to a letter from Archbishop Walsh which Pearse never received, but of whose existence and contents he learned by means of a letter from Fr. Curran, the Archbishop's secretary, to his brother and friend of Pearse's, Mr. Con. Curran. The vicarious mode of communication between Dr. Walsh and Pearse seems strange as does the degree of detail included by Fr. Curran in the letter to his brother – detail which concerned a confidential request to the Archbishop by a third party. This suggests that it was known at Archbishop's House that the letter to Pearse had never reached him; if so, the rational next step would have been to send a second or duplicate unless it was deemed inappropriate to communicate directly with Pearse at all on the issue. Later, however, in December Dr. Walsh is replying directly to Pearse. It is significant that in the last pararaph of this letter Pearse seeks written confirmation of the version of the missing letter conveyed to him via the Currans.

    Fr. Landers visited the school in its first week and later became its first chaplain.

The R.U.I. or Royal University of Ireland, (est. 1878) was a non-teaching university which was superseded by the National University of Ireland in 1908, referred to here as "the new University". C. P. Curran, as a contemporary of Pearse at the Royal University.

L. 153/DDA.

17.11.1908.   Sgoil Éanna.
                               Cullenswood House,
                               Rathmines.

May it please Your Grace,

I have just seen a letter written by Father Curran to his brother, from which I learn that Your Grace wrote to me some time ago with reference to my request that you would kindly appoint some Irish-speaking priest as chaplain or spiritual director to St. Enda's School. This letter never reached me, but it is a great pleasure to me to know now that it was written, as, while I was reluctant to write to you again, I was at a loss to account for Your Grace's apparent silence. I am very grateful for what I gather to have been the kindly and sympathetic tone of Your Grace's communication, and am more pleased than I can say that we have your good wishes for the success of our great and somewhat perilous undertaking.

I understand that what Your Grace said in the missing letter was that I might select any of the priests I mentioned, after signifying my desire for an Irish-speaking priest to the parochial clergy of Rathmines. Father Curran adds that Your Grace also explained why you could not become patron of the School, but that you wished it all success and expressed pleasure at hearing of its success so far.

I am glad to say that our success has been maintained. We have now seventy-five pupils, forty-three being pupils of the Senior boys' school (St. Enda's School proper) and the rest, including girls and little boys, pupils of the Preparatory School in connection. In the senior school we are teaching all the subjects of a secondary school course, from Greek to Shorthand, all the instruction being more or less bilingual, and Irish being the ordinary medium of intercourse throughout the day. Our highest class is of Senior Grade standard; we do not propose, however, to send our pupils forward for the Intermediate Examinations, but are working rather on the lines of the Matriculation Examination of the R.U.I., – our intention being, if possible to send forward our best pupils for matriculation at the new University.

Our boarders attend daily mass and the Catechism is taught

each day from 12–12.30. The Rathmines and Cullenswood priests frequently look in, but we have felt the want of a regular chaplain. I am not sure whether the name of Father Landers, C.C. of St. Andrew's Westland Row, was amongst those I mentioned in my previous letter, but, at any rate, if the matter were entirely in my own hands it is he I should like to choose. May I beg Your Grace to write me authorising me to approach him, or, failing him, any other Irish-speaking priest whose duties would allow him to visit us once a week? At present we have a class of boys preparing for First Holy Communion on the Feast of the Immaculate Conception and it would be a great matter if we had our Irish-speaking chaplain appointed in time to give them a few half-hours instructions and to pass them for the Sacraments.

Now that we are in full working order we see more clearly than ever the possibilities before us and the usefulness of what we are attempting. We hardly know which side of our work is the more fascinating – the educating for the first time in their own language of Irish-speaking boys (of whom we have some fifteen or sixteen) or the giving a knowledge of living Irish and a genuine love for Ireland to boys from English-speaking homes. We calculate that at the present rate of progress the quicker of the purely English-speaking boys who came to us last September will be Irish speakers within twelve months.

Thanking Your Grace for your kindness and awaiting the favour of a reply confirming the contents of the missing letter and authorising me to approach Father Landers. I have the honour to be, Your Grace's obedient servant, P. H. Pearse.

To Dr. Walsh.

This letter is a reply to what is the Archbishop's first letter to Pearse on the topic of the school, a letter which would seem to have conveyed the sentiments of approval and best wishes for the success of Sgoil Éanna.

L. 154/DDA.

16.12.1908.

Sgoil Éanna,
            Teach Fheadha Chuilinn,
                Rath Ó Maine.

May it please Your Grace,
    I am very much obliged for Your Grace's kind letter of the 13th

inst., and am delighted to know that we can have Father Landers as our chaplain or spiritual director. I have heard of his regrettable illness, but was not aware of it when writing to Your Grace. We adjourn for the Christmas Holidays on Friday, the 18th inst., and I trust that by the time we re-assemble on Jan. 11th he will be again strong enough to commence work, but if not we must, of course, wait until his recovery is complete.

We are all much encouraged by Your Grace's kindness, and glad to know that we have your best wishes for our success. I think I may say that our success is now almost assured. With many thanks, I remain, Your Grace's obedient servant. P. H. Pearse.

To J. T. Dolan.

Joseph Dolan of Ardee was one of Pearse's staunchest supporters in maintaining Sgoil Éanna financially. The crisis referred to here arose from the building works carried out in Cullenswood House during the Christmas Vacation of 1908.

The new boarder referred to who arrived on 2nd February was a nephew of Tomás Bán Ó Concheanainn, Brian Seoighe, from Inis Oirr in the Aran Islands. He attended the University from Sgoil Éanna, participated in the Rising with the Rathfarnham Company and returned to the school as a teacher with Frank Burke until its closure in 1935. Both are happily with us to this day. The postcript refers to the campaign by the League to have Irish made an essential subject in the National University.

L. 155/P.Ms.

1.2.1909.   Teach Fheadha Chuilinn,
                                         Rath Ó Maine,
                                         Áth Cliath.

A Chara,
    There is no sign of Padraig Mac Manus' money, though a reply to Tomás Ó Concheanainn's letter is now due. The bank bill of which I spoke to you will be presented for payment in a few weeks and some of the contractors who carried out the additions and improvements here are also pressing for a settlement. In the circumstances, it becomes necessary for me to avail of your own most generous and welcome offer. If you can advance me £300 at 5%, I will give you a bill or promissory note for that amount plus the amount already advanced by you, – i.e. £300 in all, or, with

140

interest on that sum for one year, £367..10s. This is to be re-payable in a year, but if I am unable to re-pay it in full in a year you would, as I understand be willing to renew the bill at interest. This will relieve me from the possible pressure of unfriendly creditors, while your money will be safe, for the house and premises will always be to the good, and the prospects of the school are looking brighter and brighter. Since I last wrote to you we have got two or three new day-boys, and a new boarder arrives to-morrow. This makes 54 pupils in the Senior School, with about 35 in the Junior.

As one of the contractors is becoming threatening it would be the greatest boon if you could let me have the £300 this week. I would let you have the promissory note, duly perfected, by return.

With a thousand thanks for your confidence in me and in the future of my effort, Mise do chara go buan, Pádraig Mac Piarais.

P.S. The University prospects are not, I think so gloomy as they were a few days ago. I know for a fact that the Archbishop of Dublin is not definitely against us. His mind is still open.

To Mrs. Mgt. Hutton.

Pearse's cottage was built for him on a plot of land which he had bought in 1905, overlooking Loch Eileabhrach. He succeeded in finishing it by summer 1909 when he occupied it with some of his students from Sgoil Éanna. It was primarily as a Gaeltacht summer centre for his pupils and other students that he built the cottage at Rosmuc. From 1909 to 1916 he used it as a retreat holiday home; it was partially destroyed and its interior wrecked by the Black and Tans in 1920. A local committee renovated it in the forties and it is now in the keeping of the Commissioners of Public Works.

The schoolmaster at Gortmore was Proinsias Ó Conghaile whose son, Proinsias with two others from Rosmuc, Pádraig Óg Ó Conaire and Colm Ó Neachtain enrolled at Sgoil Éanna on its opening day. Proinsias, later attended the University from Sgoil Éanna, taught for a while in the school and later became Professor of Veterinary Science in Dublin.

L. 156/NLI.

10.4.1909.   Sgoil Éanna,
                                        Teach Fheadha Chuilinn.
                                        Rath Ó Maine.

A Chara,

I am sorry to say that my cottage is not yet habitable. The building has been complete for more than twelve months past, but some flooring and plastering remain to be done and there is no furniture in it. The fact is that I have spent on St. Enda's the money I meant to devote to completing and beautifying this cottage. I intend to make an effort to have finished this summer, but I do not expect that it will be habitable till towards the end of June, when I hope to go down myself to spend the rest of the summer there. Even then it will hardly be in a condition in which I would like to offer it to a friend even for a short residence. It would have given me great pleasure to let you have the cottage, and I am sure you would have liked the district, which, as well as being wildly beautiful, is absolutely the most Irish-speaking in Ireland. Perhaps next year or in some future year you will again be on the lookout for a retreat in the Gaedhealtacht, and I shall be only too delighted to let you have my eyrie.

There is a cottage in which I occasionally stay in Rosmuc in which you could get a clean room and good attendance. It is not so picturesquely situated as mine, and has the drawback of being opposite the only public house in the district. Also it is the one spot in the parish where English is frequently heard. The schoolmaster and schoolmistress at Gortmore, who are great friends of mine, might also put you up. Their children are Irish-speaking, the younger ones almost exclusively so. I should be only too glad to use my good offices to have you made comfortable in either place, but I suppose neither would quite meet your ideal of a cottage retreat, as mine if ready, would have done.

I am sorry to hear you are run down, and trust that your holiday which I hope you will be able to arrange, will give you back all your old strength. Mise do chara go fíor-bhuan, Pádraig Mac Piarais.

To Mrs. Mgt. Hutton.

This letter obviously is in reply to one from Mrs. Hutton seeking practical information on Ros Muc as a holiday centre. The Miss Young referred to may have been the Belfast artist Mabel Young.

142

L. 157/NLI.

15.5.1909   Sgoil Éanna,
                                   Teach Fheadha Chuilinn.
                                   Rath Ó Maine.

A Chara,

I am writing you to Brokley Park, as Miss Young told me you would be there next week, and I fear you may have left Belfast.

I hardly know how to apologise for my delay in giving you the information you asked about Rosmuck. My only excuse must be that amid a multiplicity of pressing and worrying affairs I kept putting it off until "the next post", with the result that I am afraid you must now have made your plans without my information.

Rosmuck is about ten miles from Maam Cross, the fourth station from Galway on the Clifden line. The comfortable house I recommend (though opposite the public house) is that of "Mrs D. Walsh, Turloughbeg, Rosmuck, Co. Galway". Failing her, you might try "P. Walsh, P.O., Kilbricken, Rosmuck, Co. Galway", and "T. O'Malley, Post Office, Rosmuck, Co. Galway". The teachers, who will give you every help are Mr. and Mrs. P. Connelly, Gortmore N.S. (Rosmuck parish), Maam Cross, Co. Galway. Unfortunately, my dear friend Father Mc Hugh, the parish priest of Rosmuck for the past eight years has just been transferred to another parish; if there, he would have been delighted to meet you and help you for my sake.

Please excuse this hurried note, and above all its lateness. Mise do chara go buan, Pádraig Mac Piarais.

To J. Holloway.

This bilingual card, is significantly inscribed from "the Masters and the pupils" in keeping with the spirit of pupil participation which Pearse advocated and encouraged in Sgoil Éanna. Holloway was Pearse's architect, was a keen theatre goer, and kept a detailed diary of Dublin social and cultural life.

L.(p.c.) 158/NLI/B.

June 1909.   St Enda's School,
                                  Cullenswood House.
                                  Rathmines.

The Masters and Pupils of St. Enda's School request
the pleasure of the Company of
Mr. Holloway

On Tuesday, June 22nd, at 3.30 p.m. when the Pupils will perform
the Pageant, "Mac-ghíomhartha Chúchulainn" ("The Boy-Deeds
of Cúchulainn"), after which the First Annual Distribution of
Prizes will take place.

If the weather on the 22nd inst, be unsuitable the Pageant and
Distribution will be postponed till the following day. R.S.V.P.

To Wm. Bulfin.

One of the first pupils at Sgoil Éanna was Éamonn Bulfin, whose
father William, author of *Rambles in Eirinn* was editor of *The
Southern Cross* in Buenos Aires. Éamonn was prominent among the
senior pupils and distinguished himself on both stage and playing
field. His sister Mary was among the students at Sgoil Íde
1910–1912; she later married Mr. Seán Mac Bride S.C. international jurist and Nobel and Lenin prize winner.
"Che Buenos" was the name by which Bulfin was affectionately
known in Argentina.

L. 159/NLI.

1.7.1909   Sgoil Éanna,
                                  Rath Ó Maine.

A Chara,
    I am enclosing Report on Eamonn's work during the year, and
also a/c for some extras. In the report I shall speak all too coldly of
the fineness of his character and his desire to please. He is a
splendid boy – a worthy son of "Che Buenos".
    I had not time to check our list of books, etc. with Éamonn. If
there are any inaccuracies we can adjust them later on.
    A thousand thanks for your brilliant but too flattering article in
An Claidheamh. Mise do chara go buan. Pádraig Mac Piarais.

To Col. Maurice Moore.

Col. Maurice Moore, whose son Ulick was a pupil at Sgoil Éanna was an active member of the Gaelic League. The books referred to by Pearse, were probably manuscripts or volumes of essays on the folklore and oral traditions of Co. Mayo. Moore consulted Pearse as to their value. Molloy was likely to have been the owner, author or collector of the manuscripts, though in view of Pearse's comments as to his ability he probably had some direct part in their compilation. Col. Moore was a brother of George Moore, the novelist.

L. 160/NLI.

18.8.1909.   Sgoil Éanna,
                              Teach Fheadha Chuilinn,
                                 Rath Ó Maine.

A Chara,
    These books reached me just before the vacation, but as I went away immediately after I had not time to look through them. Since my return, too, I have been so busy that not till this morning did I find an opportunity of going through them.
    They are exceedingly interesting, and show astonishing learning, industry and patience. The penmanship is beautiful, quite as good as that in any of the old mss. It is wonderful how the old art of the scribes survives. The books, however, have no scientific value. The philological learning displayed is half a century behind the time, many of the theories fantastic, and the whole characterised by eccentricity. Who is Molloy and how does he earn his living? He would be a splendid cataloguer of mss. or compiler of an index.
    Give my kind regards to Ulick. He will find great changes here. The new buildings double our space. Mise do chara go buan, Pádraig Mac Piarais.

To Wm. Bulfin.

This is an interesting letter in so much as it illustrates the detailed care which Pearse exercised in regard to the educational development and prospects of each of his pupils. It also indicates his fine grasp of financial reality in his costing of the extra teaching provided.
    It appears that Bulfin may have been surprised that Pearse had

decided to compete for the Intermediate examinations; where the examination methods coincide with his teaching methods then he sees no objection to using the Intermediate examinations, whose courses he finds it possible to praise. The appointment of some Intermediate inspectors in 1909 gave Pearse hope for improvement; Joseph O'Neill from Aran, was one of those inspectors. O'Neill, a man of wide learning and experience, a novelist, was among the three inspectors who examined Sgoil Éanna in May 1910.

L. 161/NLI

14.9.1909. Sgoil Éanna,
Teach Fheadha Chuilinn,
Rath Ó Maine.

A Chara,
Very many thanks for letter and for cheque £20, for which I enclose receipt. Yes, the Spanish fee may well stand over till later. We had great difficulty last year in getting a Spanish teacher. Finally we got an excellent one, and Éamonn got on very well under him for some weeks. Unfortunately, his health broke down, and we did not care to look for another teacher, hoping from day to day that he would be able to resume the lessons. In the end he had to return to South America, of which he was a native. It was then so near the end of the school year and we were so busy with the pageant, etc. that we thought it best to let the matter stand over to this year. We have now a good Spanish teacher available, and he will start work as soon as we have our time-table fixed. For the lessons Éamonn received last year I paid £2 . . 2s., the amount actually charged in last year's a/c. I think the charge of £3 . . 3s. in this half-year's a/c is moderate. What they charge in other schools for a "special grind" of this sort is 4/- an hour, the teacher receiving 3/6 an hour. Éamonn's lessons in Spanish for the coming year will cost me £5 or £10.

I think you are right about Éamonn going for a science course. His tastes certainly lead that way. Unfortunately, he is weak in Mathematics, which enter largely into the science course – he is much stronger in Irish, French and English than in Mathematics. It was this latter fact that made me think for a moment of a Modern Literary course for him.

As for the Intermediate, it is for you and Éamonn to decide. I feel sure that we are right in introducing it into the School. We meant to have it from the start (and announced so in our original Prospectus) but held back last year because there was no oral inspection and we knew we should not get credit for our viva voce

146

teaching. Now all that is changed. Inspection by such competent men as O'Neill and the others means due credit for sane teaching methods. Really it is the *abuse* of the Intermediate system and not the *use* of it that has worked havoc. The Programme itself is a magnificent one – wider and better than Matric. or 1st Arts – and I believe that we here at Sgoil Éanna are strong enough and competent enough to make use of it without being led away into a scramble for honours or into "cramming" our boys. Question Éamonn when you see him as to whether it has made any change in our methods and I think he will answer "no". Mise do chara go buan, Pádraig Mac Piarais.

P.S. Excuse omission to send receipt for last year's extras. I was in the wilds of Connemara and not in business harness. I enclose it now.

To Miss C. M. Doyle.

The identity of Miss Doyle is difficult to establish; she certainly seems to have been a member of the language movement, and in view of her reference to her mother's death, Pearse must have been acquainted with her family. There is no indication that her collection of national newspapers was actually given to the school.

Miss Doyle's address on the letter is given as 39 Shelbourne Rd. but on the envelope there appears, overwritten by the Post Office the following address 7 Mt. Pleasant Ave., Mt. Pleasant Sq. Ranelagh.

L. 162/NLI

24.10.1909.   Sgoil Éanna.
                                        Rath Ó Maine.
                                        Áth Cliath

A Chara Dhilis,
    Pray excuse my long delay in replying to your letter. I have been exceedingly busy. No, I had not heard of your mother's death. Accept my sincere condolence in your great sorrow. I sometimes think that the greatest sorrow of my own life is still before me, and will come in the death of my mother, and familiarity with that thought makes it easy for me to sympathise with you. Ar dheis-láimh De go raibh anam do mháthar.
    It is very kind of you to think of us in connection with the

disposal of your collection of national newspapers. Yes, they would be a most valuable and valued addition to our library, and I gratefully accept your offer. If you have in particular a set of *An Claidheamh* since I undertook the editorship in March 1903 it will be specially welcome, for, strange as it may seem, there is no complete set at the office, – a few numbers are missing.

It is only now, on re-reading your letter, that I see you asked me to write by return. I hope I have not inconvenienced you by my long delay. Perhaps I am now too late to avail of your generous offer, but this does not lessen my gratitude to you. Sincerely yours. P. H. Pearse.

To H. Morris.

This apologetic letter from Pearse to Morris concerns the manuscript (An Ceitheranach Caoilriabhach) which was the subject of earlier correspondence between them in April of 1908. It is difficult to disentangle the circumstances and establish whether Pearse, overwhelmed with the cares of Sgoil Eanna, mislaid the manuscript or was aware of the Committee's decision to publish the version by Ó Siochfhradha, and attempted to soften the blow for his friend by delaying sending it in or informing Morris of the situation. Whatever the truth, his apology and regret carry conviction.

L. 163/P.Ms./G

12.12.1909.   Sgoil Éanna.
                                            Rath Ó Maine.

Dear Friend,
    When the manuscript of *An Ceithearnach Caoilriabhach* reached me the second time from you, I had already resigned the secretaryship of the Publications Committee and I had no connection with the Committee or with the work of the League in any way except that I was nominally the editor of *An Claidheamh Soluis*. What I should have done was to send the manuscript to the Secretary of the Committee but I knew that they did not intend issuing any more books due to lack of money, and I thought that it would be sufficient to give them the manuscript when they resumed publication. Consequently I put the manuscript safely away but alas did not think of it until I received your letter a few weeks ago. The only excuse I can offer is that I was so busy with the affairs of

the school that I never thought of the *Ceithearnach*. I am sorry for that and beg your pardon.

I did not know that a Munster version of the *Ceithearnach* was to appear until I received your letter and even yet I do not know who is preparing it. I am not, as you would say, in touch with the language movement for almost a year and a half, except that I am devoting all my attention to my business in Sgoil Éanna and neglecting most other things. I hardly open or read any letters which do not bear on the work of the school. You were always very kind to me and I am extremely sorry that I neglected a matter which concerned your affairs. Will I return the *Ceithearnach* to you or should I send it to the Secretary of the Publications Committee? Yours ever, Pádraig Mac Piarais.

To H. Morris.

The saga of the *Ceithearnach* is still unfolding with Pearse assuring Morris that now, as a member of the Publications Committee, he will speak out strongly against those of "the Dublin people" whose integrity Morris doubts. *Bruidhean Chaorthainn* (literally the Rowan-tree fort) was one of the stories of valour from the Fiannaíocht or Fenian Cycle. The League had already published Pearse's rendering of this story in 1908.

L. 164/P.Ms./G

23.2.1910.   Sgoil Éanna,
                                         Rath Ó Maine.

Dear Friend,

Here is the *Ceithearnach*. I am again a member of the Publications Committee and I will speak strongly at the next meeting concerning the shameful trick which they played on you. They all should have known that you were working on the *Ceithearnach*. It was reported in the minutes that you were requested by the Committee to compare your version with the copies in the Academy. It is certain that Lloyd knew that you were working on the story. It is not possible that he could forget that.

It is no wonder that you are angry sometimes with "the Dublin people". I do not agree with you that they are dishonest, but they are not very good as businessmen – some of them at least, of which I may be the worst offender!

I am very pleased to learn that *Bruidhean Chaorthainn* is still in

the popular folk memory. Would Dáil Uladh publish your version?
If not, the League should do so. What do you think of having it
appear in serial form in *An Claidheamh Soluis?* Yours ever,
Pádraig Mac Piarais.

To H. Morris.

L. 165/P.Ms./G

16.4.1910.   Sgoil Éanna,
                               Cullenswood House,
                               Rathmines.

Dear Friend,
I will readily do what you request. There will be a meeting of the
Committee next Wednesday and I will raise the question. I will say
that it behoves the Committee to publish the *Bruidhean* as
recompense for the injury sustained by you in relation to *An
Ceithearnach.* There was no meeting of the Committee since. Yours
ever, Pádraig Mac Piarais.

To Mr. Whelan.

Whelan was a bookseller and also a retailer of hurleys.

L. 166/OCS

18.4.1910.   Sgoil Éanna,
                               Cullenswood House.
                               Rathmines.

Dear Mr. Whelan,
I have mislaid your a/c. If you let me know the amount of it I
will send you cheque by return.
Could you supply us at the earliest possible moment with 2 doz.
good hurleys at about 2/- each? Let me know immediately. We
require them for a match on Sunday, without fail, but would like
them sooner for practice. Your Sincerely. P. H. Pearse.

To Mr. Whelan.

L. 167/OCS

20.4.1910.   Sgoil Éanna,
                              Cullenswood House,
                              Rathmines.

A Chara,

I enclose cheque £3 .. 6 .. 8. in settlement of a/c. Yes the 2/3 hurleys will do. Please let us have them at the earliest possible moment.

Mise do chara, Pádraig Mac Piarais.

To Mrs. Humphreys.

This four page printed circular letter was sent accompanied by a returnable subscription form to a number of friends and supporters of Sgoil Éanna with the direct purpose of convincing them of the validity of Pearse's educational philosophy and of the need to support him in his proposal to move Sgoil Éanna to Rathfarnham. While the contents of the letter are based mainly on the articles which Pearse contributed to *An Macaomh* (June 1909 and December 1909 issues) under the title of "By Way of Comment", the letter nevertheless constitutes a coherent basic statement of his educational principles which find echoes in his later writings and are eventually crystallised in *The Murder Machine (1916)*.

In the last analysis the intellectual appeal contained in this circular provoked little response among those of his friends and League associates who saw education merely in its private and personal dimension as a social escalator and did not perceive of it as having a national socio-cultural dimension. Consequently when it came to finding the £300 to purchase the lease on the Hermitage, it was not the former who rallied to his support, but those whose conviction ran deeper. Pearse had hoped to raise up to £10,000 by means of this appeal; when he signed the contract for the lease of the Hermitage property on 1st July 1910, he was dependent for the completion of the rental of £300 on the £100 which he received that morning from two sisters who requested that their donation remain anonymous.

While many of his League and Irish-Ireland friends admired

151

what Pearse was doing at Sgoil Éanna, they did not share his concern with the need to reform Irish education qualitatively and hence did not see the need to support financially Pearse's practical efforts towards that end. A total of sixty-five responded to his appeal and contributed £2194 for the new Sgoil Éanna.

L. 168/P.Ms.

10.5.1910.   St. Enda's School,
                                                   Cullenswood House,
                                                   Rathmines.

Dear Madam

St. Enda's School was founded in the autumn of 1908 with the object of providing a secondary education distinctively Irish in complexion, bilingual in method, and of a high modern type generally, for Irish Catholic boys. The aim and scope of the School are explained in the following extracts from the editorial notes contributed by me to the first two issues of *An Macaomh*.

"I interested a few friends in the project of a school which should aim at the making of good men rather than of learned men, but of men truly learned rather than of persons merely qualified to pass examinations; and as my definition of a good man, as applied to an Irishman, includes the being a good Irishman (for you cannot make an Irish boy a good Englishman or a good Frenchman), and as my definition of learning, as applied to an Irishman includes Irish learning as its basis and fundament, it followed that my school should be an Irish school in a sense not known or dreamt of in Ireland since the Flight of the Earls. ... "

"The value of the national factor in education would appear to rest chiefly in this, that it addresses itself to the most generous side of the child's nature, urging him to live up to his finest self. I think that the true work of the teacher may be said to be to induce the child to realise himself at his best and worthiest. And if this be so the fact of nationality is of prime importance apart from any ulterior propagandist views the teacher may cherish. ... "

"What I mean by an Irish school is a school that takes Ireland for granted. You need not praise the Irish language – simply speak it; you need not denounce English games – play Irish ones; you need not ignore foreign history, foreign literatures – deal with them from the Irish point of view. An Irish school need no more be a purely Irish-speaking school than an Irish nation need be a purely Irish-speaking nation; but an Irish school like an Irish nation, must be permeated through and through by Irish culture, the repository of which is the Irish language. I do not think that a purely Irish speaking school is a thing to be desired; at all events a purely Irish-speaking secondary or higher school is a thing that is no longer possible. Secondary education in these days surely implies the adding of some new culture, that is of some new language with its literature, to the culture enshrined in the mother-tongue; and the proper teaching of a new language always involves a certain amount of bilingualism – unless, indeed, we are to be content with construing from the new language into our own, a very poor accomplishment. The new language ought to become in some sense a second vernacular; so that it is not sufficient to speak it merely during the limited portion of the school day, that can be devoted to its teaching as a specific subject; it must be introduced during the ordinary work of the school as a teaching medium, side by side with the original vernacular. ..."

"Bilingualism in practice implies the teaching of the vernacular of the pupils; the teaching in addition, of a second language and the gradual introduction of that second language into the ordinary curriculum with the proviso, however, that any further language taught, be taught always on the direct method. ..."

"We constantly speak and write as if a philosophy of education were first formulated in our time. But all the wise peoples of old faced and solved that problem for themselves, and most of their solutions were better than ours. Professor Culverwell thinks that the Jews gave it the best solution. For my part, I take off my hat to the old Irish. The philosophy of education is preached now, but it was practised by the founders of the Gaelic system two thousand years ago. Their very names for 'education' and 'teacher' and 'pupil' show that they had gripped the heart of the problem. The word for 'education' among the old Gaels was the same as the word for 'fostering'; the teacher was a 'fosterer' and the pupil was a 'foster-child'. Now, to 'foster' is exactly the function of the teacher; not primarily to 'lead up', to 'guide', to 'conduct through a course of studies' and still less to 'indoctrinate' to 'inform', to 'prepare for exams' but primarily to 'foster' the elements of character already present. ... The true teacher will recognise in each of his pupils an individual human soul, distinct and different from every other human soul that has ever been fashioned by God, miles and miles apart from the soul that is nearest and most akin to it, craving, indeed, comradeship and sympathy and pity, needing also, it may be, discipline and guidance and a restraining hand, but imperiously demanding to be allowed to live its own life, to be allowed to bring itself to its own perfection; because for every soul there is a perfection meant for it alone and which it alone is capable of attaining. So the primary office of the teacher is to 'foster' that of

153

good which is native to the soul of his pupil, striving to bring its inborn excellences to ripeness, rather than to implant in it excellences exotic to its nature. It comes to this, then, that the education of a child is greatly a matter, in the first place, of congenial environment and next to this, of a wise and loving watchfulness whose chief appeal will be to the finest instincts of the child itself."

During the two years that the School has been at work the ideals in aim and method thus enunciated have been faithfully kept in view. The central purpose of the School has been not so much the mere imparting of knowledge (and not at all the "cramming" of boys with a view to success at examinations) as the formation of its pupils' characters, the eliciting and development of the individual bents and traits of each, the kindling of their imaginations, the placing before them of a high standard of conduct and duty; in a word, the training up of those entrusted to its care to be strong and noble and useful men. While a wide and generous culture has been aimed at, and classical studies have been assigned a prominent place in the curriculum, the education provided by the School has been on the whole "modern" in type. The course enters at every point into relations with actual life and is framed with particular reference to the needs and conditions which prevail in our own country today.

Believing that the function of education is to prepare for life and that the most important part of life is that which centres round the profession and practice of religion, our first care at St. Enda's has been to provide a proper religious and moral training for our pupils. The religious instruction is under the superintendence of a chaplain approved by His Grace the Archbishop of Dublin. In the general curriculum the first place is given to the Irish Language, which is taught as a spoken and literary tongue to every pupil. The teaching of Irish and of all modern languages is on the direct method, the most attractive devices of continental teachers being freely adopted. To boys who are Irish-speaking to start with, English is taught on the direct method; to boys who are English-speaking to start (these of course being the great majority) Irish is taught on the direct method. Foreign languages other than English (French, German, Italian and Spanish) are taught on the same lines. Under this system every pupil who passes through St. Enda's will, at the end of his course, have obtained a good oral and literary knowledge of at least three modern languages. Latin is taught to all boys in the upper forms and Greek and Old Irish to such as exhibit an aptitude for classical studies. All teaching, other than language teaching, is as far as possible bilingual – that is to say, each subject is taught both in Irish and English. This applies in greater or less degree to

154

Christian Doctrine, History, Geography, Nature-Study, Experimental Science (Chemistry and Physics) Mathematics (Arithmetic, Algebra, Euclid and Trigonometry), Handwriting, Drawing, Manual Instruction, Hygiene and First Aid, Book-keeping, Shorthand, Typewriting, Elocution, Vocal and Instrumental Music, Dancing and Physical Drill.

From the foregoing subjects a suitable course is selected for each pupil. In making this selection, not only the wishes of the parents or guardians, but also, to a certain extent, the wishes and inclinations of the pupil himself are consulted. No pupil of St. Enda's is forced into a groove of study for which he evinces no special talent or native inclination. Where parents so desire pupils are prepared and sent forward for the examinations of the Board of Intermediate Education. In the higher forms the courses are co-ordinated with those of the Universities, and this year a class is being prepared for the Matriculation Examination of the National University of Ireland. Pupils are also prepared for the various professional preliminary examinations.

Nature-Study forms an essential part of the work at St. Enda's. The instruction does not take the form of a mere dry-as-dust teaching of the rudiments of zoology, botany and geology, but consists rather in an attempt to inspire a real interest in and love for beautiful living things. Practical Gardening and elementary Agriculture are taught as part of this scheme. In connection with this side of the programme there has been established a School Museum containing zoological, botanical and geological specimens, together with some illustrations of industrial processes and a few objects of historical and antiquarian interest. There is also a School Library of 2,000 volumes which is open to all the pupils.

A feature of the work at St. Enda's is the series of weekly "Half-holiday Lectures" on Irish and general History by the Magic Lantern. These Lectures are sometimes given by members of the School Staff and sometimes by distinguished outsiders. Among those who have already addressed the boys or have promised to do so in the near future are Dr. Douglas Hyde, Professor Eoin Mac Neill, Mr. W. B. Yeats, Mr. Standish O'Grady, the late Senor William Bulfin, Mr. Séumas Mac Manus Miss Mary Hayden, Mr. Shane Leslie, Miss Agnes O'Farrelly, the Hon. William Gibson, Mr. Charles Dawson, Miss Helen Laird, Professor T. M. Kettle M.P., the Lord Abbot of Mount Mellery, Dr. John P. Henry, Professor David Houston, Mr. Arthur Darley, the Rev. Dr. O'Daly, Professor John Cooke, Mrs. Dryhurst, and Mr. Jos. T. Dolan. The lectures are frequently replaced by social or musical reunions of the pupils, by visits to the city Museums, Art Galleries, and Zoological and Botanical Gardens, or by excursions to places of scenic, historic or antiquarian interest near Dublin.

By their performances of Irish and Anglo-Irish plays in their School Theatre and more recently in the Abbey Theatre the pupils of St. Enda's have attracted the attention and won the sympathy of every student of dramatic art in Ireland. Irish music and dancing are of course cultivated. A review under the title of *An Macaomh* has been established as a medium for the publication of work done in the School. In the domain of athletics, our boys signalised their entry into the Gaelic Athletic Association by several notable victories and now stand in the foremost rank of minor football and hurling in Dublin. Recently we have taken the initiative in organising a schools League in Hurling and Gaelic Football for Leinster. Chess is encouraged as an indoor game.

The organisation of the School embodies some new and important principles. With a view to encourage a sense of responsibility among the boys, and establishing between them and the masters a bond of fellowship and esprit-de-corps, the pupils are as far as possible actively associated with the administration (though not with the teaching work) of the School. They are consulted with regard to any proposed departures in the curriculum or system of organisation, and are frequently called on for suggestions as to schemes of work or play. At the beginning of each school term they are asked to elect from their own ranks a School Captain, a Vice-Captain, a Secretary, a Librarian, a Keeper of the Museum, Captains of Hurling and Football, a Master of Games, and a House Committee. An "Éire Óg" Club, or juvenile branch of the Gaelic League, was established in the School during the first term.

The original programme of St. Enda's, foreshadowing as it did all these phases of activity, immediately attracted attention. Whether judged by the number of pupils who have come to it, by the satisfaction expressed by their parents with the results of its system or by the wide and growing reputation which it has established, the School has achieved an astonishing success. Thirty boys assembled on the opening day, of whom ten were boarders; by the end of the first year the boarders had swelled to twenty and the day-boys to fifty. At present, as the second school year nears its close, we have forty boarders and sixty-five day-boys, – a hundred and five pupils in all. The most valuable feature of the growth has been that it is largely due to the enthusiasm of the pupils themselves and of their parents and friends. Each boy has become a sort of recruiting sergeant for the School. For instance, last year we had one pupil from a district in Co. Kildare; this year we have four. Last year we had one pupil from the Castlerea district; this year we have seven. The surest guarantee that St. Enda's will continue to grow and flourish is the fact that it inspires the love and loyalty of all its pupils.

Fortunate in the numbers of our supporters, we have been still more fortunate in their character. A large proportion of our pupils are the sons or near relatives of men and women who are forces in the new movements in contemporary Ireland. Among the well-known Irishmen whose sons are being educated in St. Enda's are Mr. Stephen Gwynn, M.P., Professor Eoin Mac Neill, the late Senor William Bulfin, Mr. W. P. Ryan (Editor of the *Irish Nation*), Colonel Maurice Moore, Mr. P. J. O'Shea ("Conán Maol"), Mr. P. T. Mac Ginley, Mr. W. L. Cole, Mr. H. Connell Mangan, and Dr. Conn Murphy; while we have the nephews or other relatives of such prominent Gaels as Miss Mary Hayden, Miss Agnes O'Farrelly, the Rev. Dr. O'Hickey, Mr. S. J. Barrett (treasurer of the Gaelic League). A further gratifying fact is that a large number of our pupils are the near relatives of or have been recommended to us by Irish-Ireland priests.

So remarkable has been the growth of the School that we are now in sight of the time when Cullenswood House, spacious as it is, will no longer be large enough for our requirements. Partly with a view to securing a permanent and entirely worthy centre for the great educational work we are attempting, and partly in order that we may be free to develop certain sides of our programme in a way that is not feasible in suburban surroundings, it has been decided to remove the School to a new locale, a mansion with a beautiful demesne of 50 acres in South County Dublin which is now available, and the acquisition of which will place St. Enda's in a position to carry out its programme to its logical conclusion, and in particular will enable it to develop still further as a boarding school. The effect on the whole future of Irish education of an Irish-Ireland College, housed and equipped as St. Enda's will be under these new conditions, will be incalculable. It is hoped that the Irish-Ireland public has sufficient faith in the possibility of regenerating Ireland through her schools to endow this great undertaking in such a manner as shall ensure its permanent success.

The house and lands can be had subject to a small rent for £6,000, or can be rented on lease at £300 a year. The balance of the £10,000 is required for the necessary additions and the equipment of the place.

It is believed that all friends of education in Ireland who recognise the importance of placing St. Enda's in the position of a permanent national institution will be prepared to subscribe for that purpose.

157

If the total subscribed should amount, as is hoped, to £10,000, it is intended to purchase. If it should not amount to that sum, the place will be leased with the option of purchasing later on.

The repayment of the sum will be secured either by Debentures in a company which would be formed, or else by a charge to trustees on behalf of the subscribers and which would be a first claim upon the property as acquired with all additions made to it, and to bear interest at £4 per cent per annum.

In whatever arrangements may take place, it will be secured that the existing academic control shall be continued without any interference whatever, but provision will be made to appoint a Board of Governors for other administrative departments, such as finance, etc. The following are prepared to act as such a Board:-

Joseph T. Dolan, M.A.	Mrs. Stephen Gwynn.
Miss Mary Hayden, M.A.	Shane Leslie, B.A.
John P. Henry, M.A., M.D.	Séumas Mac Manus.

I should add that a movement is on foot for establishing a girls' school on similar lines to St. Enda's at Cullenswood House as soon as we vacate it. The very young day-pupils of St. Enda's can thus remain undisturbed; the older day-pupils will, it is hoped, follow us to our new home.

As one known to be a friend of Irish education, and interested in the well-being of St. Enda's these points are submitted to you. Should you be prepared to undertake to subscribe, please fill up, sign and return the annexed form. I should be glad to have your reply at your earliest convenience. There is no time to be lost if the premises referred to are to be secured and made ready by the commencement of the next school year.

When the extent of the financial support can be determined from the replies, a further communication will be made to intending subscribers.

I am, dear Madam. Yours truly, P. H. Pearse.

To Dr. W. J. Walsh.

The rapid growth in the enrolment at Sgoil Éanna and the limited potential for expansion at Cullenswood House prompted Pearse to seek a more extensive location for the school which would allow his educational philosophy a fuller scope for expression. In May 1910 he found such a property, "The Hermitage", situated between the Loreto Convent and St. Columba's College in Rathfarnham – a mansion and fifty acres of land – which was owned by the

Woodbyrne family. It had been built in the eighteenth century, by Edward Hudson, whose son William Elliot Hudson (1796–1857) was a friend of Davis and a supporter of the Young Irelanders. William Hudson also befriended the early language revival societies and endowed the Royal Irish Academy for the preparation and publication of an Irish dictionary.

The additional house which Pearse rented to accommodate the increased members at Cullenswood was Sunnyside – a two-story residence directly opposite Cullenswood House on Oakley Road. This was occupied by the senior boarders and by William Pearse in 1910.

Rockwell College near Cashel was founded by the Holy Ghost Fathers on a large estate and the farm buildings were converted into classrooms. Pearse would have learned of this from Thomas Mac Donagh who had been a teacher at Rockwell. He carried out a similar plan at the Hermitage locating the various general and specialist classrooms around the farmyard and constructing a covered ambulatorium around the yard. Fr. Landers was appointed chaplain to Sgoil Éanna in December 1908, while acting as curate in St. Andrew's Westland Row.

L. 169/DDA

15.5.1910.   Sgoil Éanna,
                                                      Cullenswood House.
                                                      Rathmines.

My Lord Archbishop,
Your Grace showed such kindly interest in St. Enda's School when I first projected it some two years ago, that I feel sure you will be interested in the larger development outlined in the circular which I enclose. Cullenswood House, large as it is, is not large enough for the forty boarders which we now muster; and as everything points to the fact that the School will continue to grow, a change has become inevitable. As a change has to be made, I think it better to make it at once rather than to continue for another year or two here with makeshift arrangements, such as the renting of an additional house etc. The place that offers is singularly suitable. It is known as "The Hermitage" and is about half a mile beyond Rathfarnham, past the Convent towards St. Columba's College. The lands include large gardens, pretty woodlands, a little lake, over 20 acres of pasturage etc., etc. An old hermitage or church, in which a hermit is said to have lived, a cromlech or druid's altar, and ogham stone, and other objects of antiquarian interest give the place a special attraction from our immediate point of view. There

159

is a fine range of farm buildings which, as was done at Rockwell College, can be converted into splendid classrooms.

Father Landers, our Chaplain, wrote to me a month or two ago saying that owing to pressure of parochial work, he would be unable to continue to visit us. It is so near the end of the year now that I suppose it is hardly worth while to appoint a new chaplain, especially in view of the approaching change. There is a pretty little chapel already at the "Hermitage" and I would like next year, if possible, to have a resident chaplain who should also be a member of the teaching staff. When matters are in a more forward stage I will again communicate with Your Grace on this subject.

I am enclosing a copy of No. 2 of *An Macaomh* which Your Grace may not have seen. I have the honour to be, Your Grace's obedient servant, P. H. Pearse.

To Mrs. Mgt. Hutton.

Mrs Hutton responded to Pearse's appeal with characteristic generosity and alacrity; she was perturbed possibly by the phrase in the subscription form which accompanied the appeal.

This phrase read "... and to sign any further application which may be necessary. ..."
Pearse in the second paragraph here clarifies the meaning of this phrase and outlines the legal basis of his proposals.

L. 170/NLI

15.5.1910   Sgoil Éanna,
                                              Cullenswood House,
                                              Rathmines.

A Chara Dhil,
    A thousand thanks for your generous promise of £50 towards the development of Sgoil Éanna. I am proud of this proof of your confidence and approbation. I hope the new scheme will go forward – I am almost sure, with God's blessing, that it will – and it shall be my endeavour to make the new St. Enda's worthy of the generous friends who are helping me to create it. The place I have in mind, and about which I am negotiating, is about half a mile beyond Rathfarnham; it is singularly beautiful and from many points of view singularly suitable.

    Those words in the application form only mean that you will sign the formal application when it is ready. The subscribers will incur no financial responsibility, – they will be like debenture-holders and not like ordinary share-holders. The School will be legally mine, but I shall be responsible to the subscribers for the sums they advance. This arrangement will secure them in the (I hope impossible) event of a failure.

I will write you further about the project of the girls' school when it is further advanced. With many thanks and kindest regards, Mise do chara, Pádraig Mac Piarais.

To Miss O'Rahilly.

Miss O'Rahilly and Mrs. Ellen Humphreys were sisters of The O'Rahilly (Michael O'Rahilly) who was prominent in the Gaelic League, the Volunteers and in the Rising in which he was shot dead in a final sortie on Moore St. from the Post Office.

Mrs. Humphrey's son, Dick, was a student at Sgoil Éanna from September 1909 and her other son, Emmet was there later. Dick showed extraordinary allegiance to Pearse and though he had left Sgoil Éanna by 1916, he used his uncle's open touring car to ferry food supplies to the Post Office and returned, despite Pearse's remonstrations, to join actively in the fighting for the rest of the week.

This letter and those of 13th June, 29th June and 1st July are concerned with the generous gift of £100 which Miss O'Rahilly and Mrs. Humphreys made to Pearse at a critical stage in his negotiations for the leasing of the Hermitage. Their generosity and support for his move to Rathfarnham were enhanced by their request to him (c.f. letter 1.7.1910) not to disclose their names and donations. Theirs was the £100 which enabled him to pay the required £300 on July 15th when he signed the lease.

L. 171/P.Ms.

18.5.1910   Sgoil Éanna,
                                   Cullenswood House,

Dear Miss O'Rahilly,

A thousand thanks for your generous promise of support for our new scheme. Please thank Mrs. Humphreys on my behalf for her similar promise. I am proud of this mark of approval and confidence, and in our new surroundings must work harder and harder to be worthy of the good opinion of you and other generous friends.

I think there is hope for Ireland yet through her schools, and am delighted to see that that opinion is shared by you and others.

The new place – it is just beyond Rathfarnham – is singularly beautiful and in many ways singularly suitable. To live in such a place will in itself be an inspiration to boys and masters. I missed Dick from school yesterday, but was relieved to see him turn up brightly this morning and to hear that he had had only a passing indisposition.

I will send you a formal acknowledgement in a day or two. In the meantime accept my sincere and grateful thanks, With kindest regards, sincerely yours, P. H. Pearse.

To Mrs. Mgt. Hutton.

This was a printed circular to be sent to those who promised financial support; there was provision for inserting the individual sums promised.

L. 172/NLI/G

24.5.1910.   Sgoil Éanna,
                                          Cullenswood House.

Dear Friend,
I have received your letter promising £50 for the support of the work of the school and I am very grateful to you for it. I will communicate with you shortly. Your friend, Pádraig Mac Piarais.

To Owen Clarke.

Owen Clarke was a son of Mrs. Emily Clarke of Frankfort, Blackrock, who was a close friend of Pearse, acted as guarantor for him and generously supported Sgoil Éanna. Owen Clarke did occupy Pearse's cottage in 1910 and became a close friend of his. He lived at Knock Oulart, Shankill, Co. Dublin and died in 1947.

3.6.1910.   Sgoil Éanna,
                                   Cullenswood House.

A Chara,
   The most intensely Irish-speaking part of Co. Galway (indeed of
Ireland) is Iar-Connacht, and the most Irish-speaking part of
Iar-Connacht is the parish of Rosmuck. It is out of the tourist
track, but the scenery is wild and glorious. There is good fishing,
the best of it belongs to Lord Dudley who has a lodge at Inver, and
is preserved, but there is fair fishing in the unpreserved loughs and
streams, and in many cases people are not very strict. Besides you
are only 8 miles from Cashel, where O'Loughlin of the Hotel has
fishing. The district is purely Irish-speaking, apart from the few
outsiders settled in the place, and perhaps the families who
regarded themselves as important.
   I have a cottage in the parish furnished comfortably enough
although the goods and chattels are scant. I could let it to you for
the month of June, if you would care to cater for yourself, and
could take down bed clothes and some table utensils. There is a
woman who minds the place, and would cook and wash for you. It
is picturesquely situated on a lake. Should you think it too much
trouble to housekeep yourself, then I would recommend the house
of Miss Sarah Walsh, Turloughbeg, Rosmuck, Co. Galway (this is
the full address). I have often stayed there and have always been
comfortable. If she has not room, then try Mr. P. Walsh, P.O.
Kilbricken, Rosmuck or Mr. T. O'Malley, Post Office Rosmuck. I
have stayed in both places and like the people in both – but they are
fond of speaking English. My own cottage is really the ideal place if
you are not afraid of the trouble. My cottage is at Gortmore, 8
miles from Maam Cross Station. Rosmuck is two miles further on.
Mise do chara, Pádraig Mac Piarais.

To Mrs. Mgt. Hutton.

L. 174/NLI

9.6.1910   Sgoil Éanna,
                                   Cullenswood House.

A Chara,
   You will be glad to hear that I have now completed

arrangements for the leasing of our new home at Rathfarnham, and that the arrangements for the girls' school here are also practically complete. I must deposit £300 early next week as security for the rent of the "Hermitage" (this is the name of the new place), and must also have a sum in hand to proceed with the building scheme. I should therefore be very grateful if you could let me have the amount you so kindly promised. As soon as matters are perfected (which will not be for some time yet) I will communicate with you as to the steps to be taken to safeguard your and the other subscribers' interests. The plan I propose is a charge to trustees in your favour. Mise do chara go buan, Pádraig Mac Piarais.

To Mr. J. Holloway.

This second appeal to Holloway, a month after the first, indicates the pressure on Pearse to secure funding for the move to Rathfarnham. Attached to this letter there was a returnable subscription form.

L. 175/NLI

9.6.1910.   St. Enda's School,
                                                Cullenswood House.

Dear Sir (or Madam),
   Referring to my letter of May 10th last with regard to the development of St. Enda's School, you will, I am sure, be glad to hear that matters have now reached a much more forward stage. I have decided to lease the house and grounds referred to in my former letter, and to transfer Sgoil Eanna thither, while arrangements are almost complete for the establishment of a girls' school on similar lines at Cullenswood House. The sum of £1,200, in addition to the amount already promised, will enable me to transform the new premises into the most perfectly planned and equipped school in Ireland. It is important that the greater part of the building scheme should be completed by the beginning of September. May I, therefore, beg you to let me have a reply indicating the amount of support you are able to give by, at latest, the 21st. inst? I should add that, if it suits your convenience, only half the sum guaranteed will be called in immediately, the other moiety to be called in in six months' time. Trusting to hear from you, I am, dear Sir (or Madam), Yours very truly, P. H. Pearse.

To H. Morris.

L. 176/NLI/G

11.6.1910.   Sgoil Éanna,
                                           Cullenswood House.

Dear Friend,
  I am very grateful to you for the support which you have
promised for Sgoil Éanna. I have decided to take the new place on
rent. It is a very beautiful place. The lease will be signed next
Monday and I shall have to pay £300 immediately as a warranty
for the rent. I shall also need some money in hand to start on the
new rooms.
  On these grounds I am calling in the monies promised by my
friends and I would be grateful if you would forward the amount
you have promised. I will write to you soon with details of the legal
contract which I shall have with those subscribing. Yours ever,
Pádraig Mac Piarais.

To Miss O'Rahilly.

L. 177/P.Ms.

13.6.1910.   Sgoil Éanna,
                                           Cullenswood House.

Dear Miss O'Rahilly,
  You will, I feel sure, be interested to know that I have decided to
lease the "Hermitage", Rathfarnham, as the new home of St.
Enda's and that arrangements are practically completed for a girls
school to succeed us here. The lease of the "Hermitage" is to be
signed this week and it is necessary for me to deposit a sum of £300
as security for the rent. I also require some money in hands to
proceed with the building scheme – a scheme which will transform
the "Hermitage" into the most perfectly planned and equipped
school in Ireland. For this reason I am calling in the sums promised
by those who are subscribing to the scheme, and should be very
grateful if you could send me the amounts promised by Mrs.
Humphreys and you. I shall, shortly communicate with you as to
the way in which I propose to secure the subscribers' interests. Mr.

Henry Dixon is working out this part of the plan for me, and I am leaving it in his hands. I am, dear Miss O'Rahilly, Yours very sincerely. P. H. Pearse.

To Mrs. Mgt. Hutton.

This letter acknowledging Mrs. Hutton's donation of £50 is receipted below with a penny stamp over which Pearse has appended his signature.

L. 178/NLI

16.6.1910.   Sgoil Éanna,
                              Cullenswood House.

A Chara,
    Very many thanks for your cheque, £50, to be applied towards the development of Sgoil Éanna. My solicitors, (Messrs Gerrard) are working out a plan for securing the interests of the subscribers, while leaving them free from all financial responsibility. They propose a charge to trustees for the benefit of the subscribers, as the simplest way of securing their capital and at the same time freeing them from liability in the (I hope) unlikely event of a financial smash. Mise agus mor-mheas agam ort, Do chara, Pádraig Mac Piarais.

To Gaelic League, Limerick.

The original of this letter contains the following written in pencil diagonally across the top left-hand corner: "Do labhras le P.M.P. tríd an gléas gotha. T.Ó. R. 25.6.10" (Trans: I spoke to P.M.P. (P. Mac Piarais) on the telephone. T.Ó R. 25.6.10)
    It also contains the following written over Ó Catháin's name in pencil, "C. na G. Luimneach" (trans: The Gaelic League, Limerick).
    This letter was probably written to a prominent friend in Limerick seeking the whereabouts of Ó Catháin and Ó Ceallacháin with a view to offering them teaching posts in Sgoil Éanna.

L. 179/NLI/G

21.6.1910   Sgoil Éanna,
                                    Cullenswood House.

Dear Friend,
   Could you send me the present addresses of the following (i)
Giollabhríde Ó Catháin and (2) Proinnsias Ó Ceallacháin M.A.,
the man who wrote those Bilingual Science lessons. I need the
addresses urgently, Your friend. Pádraig Mac Piarais.

To Mrs. Mgt. Hutton.

As will be seen in his letter of June 16th., Pearse had already
acknowledged and receipted the £50 sent to him by Mrs. Hutton,
who having left Belfast on the death of her husband Arthur, was
now living at 17 Appian Way, Dublin. Pearse was overworked and
overworried during this period due to the financial and other cares
associated with the move from Rathmines to Rathfarnham.

L. 180/NLI

22.6.1910.   Sgoil Éanna,
                                    Cullenswood House.

A Chara,
   I owe you an apology for an oversight in excuse for which I can
only allege the fact that I have been overworked and overworried
during the past week than I have ever been before and (I hope)
shall ever be again. I received your cheque so generously and
promptly sent in due course, and drafted the enclosed receipt to
send you, and then being called away to attend to something
connected with the Intermediate Exams., then (and still) in
progress, completely forgot to enclose the receipt in a covering
letter and to send it to you. This is only one of several acts of
omission for which I have had to take myself to task this week. I
know you will forgive me, ungracious and unbusiness-like though it
must seem.
   Thanks to you and others, I have now enough money in to make
the necessary deposit, though not yet enough to warrant me in
going on with the building scheme. But I feel that that will come.
   I am still extraordinarily busy, but I must find time to avail of
your invitation to speak to you about the girls' school and other

167

matters. I may call to-morrow (Thursday) evening at 8.30. With kind regards, Sincerely and gratefully yours, P. H. Pearse.

To Brian Ó hUigín

L. 181/OCS

26.6.1910.   Sgoil Éanna,
                                            Cullenswood House.

A Chara,

Many thanks for your promise of support. I hope the new St. Enda's will be worthy of you and of the other generous friends who have made it a possibility. The new place is singularly beautiful and in many ways singularly suitable, – a noble house and some 50 acres of delightful woodland and pasturage. My tenancy commences on July 1st. and the lease is to be signed early this week. I must lodge £300 immediately for the rent, and I must also have in hands a sum of money to enable me to proceed with my building scheme. For these reasons I am calling in the amounts subscribed and should be grateful if you could let me have the sum so kindly promised by you. I will communicate with you shortly as to the way in which it is proposed to safeguard the interests of the subscribers. Mise do chara go buan. Pádraig Mac Piarais.

To Miss O'Rahilly.

The negotiations for the leasing of the Hermitage were complicated by a number of factors, not least that the property had been leased tentatively for the summer. At one stage, his estate agents, North and Co. advised Pearse to consider the adjoining property of Marley Grange, rather than await the conclusion of negotiations on the Hermitage.

Part of the second paragraph of this letter is indecipherable, and refers to a rumour which Dr. Henry had heard that Pearse was going to purchase or lease a property of the Carmelites (a Catholic order of priests). There was then no Carmelite establishment near the Hermitage; it is highly unlikely that Terenure College was the subject of the rumour. If so, it is most probable that Dr. Henry was joking with Pearse.

L. 182/PMs.

29.6.1910 Sgoil Éanna,
Cullenswood House.

Dear Miss O'Rahilly,
   No, there is no truth in the report that I have not been able to get the place in Rathfarnham. The place *had* been let for the summer to a lady, but on the understanding that if a permanent letting was effected the letting to her was to lapse. As soon as I came to terms with Mr. Woodbyrne (the vendor) three or four weeks ago, he communicated with this lady's agents and their agreement, as arranged, came to an end. The solicitors on each side have been perfecting the legal formalities, and my tenancy is to commence on Friday next, July 1st. I have put back the signing of the lease till Friday, chiefly because of your letter saying that you would be able to let me have your and Mrs. Humphreys' subscription on that day. Counting your subscription I have been able to get in just enough to pay the deposit of £300 (which is to be done on Friday) and to have something in hand to go on with the essential part of the building. Other things not so necessary must be left over till next year.
   It is funny how rumours spread. Dr Henry told me last night that he had heard I was taking the Carmelites ... No, as soon as I saw the "Hermitage" I set my heart on it, and it would take a great deal to keep me from it. In beauty of site and suitability of surroundings the new St. Enda's will be the finest school in Ireland; I only hope that in all other respects it will be worthy of you and of the other generous friends who have made it a possibility.
   I am gratefully counting on your cheque on Friday when, if all goes well, the lease will be signed and I enter into possession.
   Kind regards to Dick and his mother, Believe me, dear Miss Rahilly, Yours sincerely. P. H. Pearse.

To Miss O'Rahilly.

Pearse in his published statements as to the sources of his financial support for Sgoil Éanna respected the expressed wish of Miss O'Rahilly and Mrs. Humphreys for anonymity. However in the audited accounts for the 1910 appeal their subscriptions are

169

credited to them by name with the sixty or so others who between them subscribed £2,194 for the new Sgoil Éanna.

L. 183/P.Ms.

1.7.1910.   Sgoil Éanna,
                                                        Cullenswood House.

My dear Miss O'Rahilly,
   A thousand thanks for cheque, which reached me in good time. Everything is now straight, and if God blesses our undertaking, as I feel sure He will, I believe that we are about to do glorious work for Ireland in the Boys' school at Rathfarnham and in the girls' and little boys' school here. I have undertaken a great responsibility, and I only hope I shall prove worthy of it and equal to it. Such good will as you and Mrs. Humphreys, have shown gives me confidence.
   I will of course respect your wish that your names and the amounts of our subscriptions be kept strictly private. This makes your generosity all the greater. With kind regards, Yours very sincerely, P. H. Pearse.

On reverse of the original the following appears:

   "cheque £100 sent June 30th 1910 to assist Sgoil Éanna,
                 Anna O'Rahilly & Mrs. Humphreys,
                            36 Ailesbury Rd.,
                                 Dublin".

To Brian Ó hUigín.

L. 184/OCS/G

1.7.1910   Sgoil Éanna,
                                                        Cullenswood House,

Dear Friend,
   Many thanks to you. I am very grateful to you for sending me your book. It is a marvellous thing to have young Irish poets coming forward. Yours ever, Pádraig Mac Piarais.

To H. Morris.

Henry Morris in sending a subscription in answer to Pearse's St. Enda's appeal, signed the cheque in the Irish form of his name. The bank would not accept the cheque and returned it to Pearse.

L. 185/NLI/G

4.7.1910.   Sgoil Éanna,
                              Cullenswood House.

Dear Friend,
   This cheque was returned to me with the enclosed letter. What should we do? I suppose that "Enri Ua Muirgheasa" will not be accepted when the legal forms are signed as "Henry Morris". Yours ever, Pádraig Mac Piarais.

To Dr. W. J. Walsh.

The essential part of the building scheme involved the classrooms around the quadrangle and a refectory.
   The oratory had been erected by previous owners of the Hermitage. Fr. Michael Burke became Chaplain to Sgoil Éanna in 1910.

L. 186/DDA

16.7.1910.   Sgoil Éanna,
                          Cullenswood House,
                               Rathmines.

My dear Lord Archbishop,
   I have finally closed with Mr. Woodbyrne, the owner of the Hermitage, Rathfarnham, and am to enter into possession of it on August 1st. I am taking it on lease at the somewhat stiff rent of £300 a year, with the option of purchasing within ten years at £6,250. I have just enough money to set my building scheme going, and hope to have the essential part of it completed before Christmas. A building debt will remain which I must devise means of paying off later on. Sgoil Éanna opens at the Hermitage about September 11th; while Cullenswood House will become a girls' school with a department for little boys. I feel that in our two centres of activity we shall, with God's blessing, accomplish a great national and educational work.

171

There is, as I think I mentioned in a previous letter to Your Grace, a little oratory at the Hermitage which we intend to make our School Chapel, and where we hoped ultimately to have the privilege of daily mass celebrated by our own Chaplain. For the present we must content ourselves with repeating the arrangement that has subsisted here – viz. our boys to attend mass at the local Church, while religious instruction in the school shall be looked after by a visiting Chaplain. I was speaking to Canon O'Keeffe to-day, and he said that he thought Father Burke, who is Chaplain to Rathfarnham Abbey, would be glad to visit us once a week and give catechetical instruction as was done by Father Landers here. I presume that Your Grace will have no objection to my selecting Father Burke in place of Father Landers? He knows a little Irish, though not of course anything like Father Landers; but it would be too much to expect Father Landers or any other priest to come out from town once a week. I have arranged with Canon O'Keeffe that our boys are to form a guild of the Sodality of the Sacred Heart in Rathfarnham as they did here at Beechwood, where Father Hogan and his curates have been very kind to us.

I felt it right to let Your Grace know all this and to consult you about the chaplaincy before issuing my Prospectus. I am, dear Lord Archbishop. Your Grace's obedient servant, P. H. Pearse.

To Miss Margaret Pearse.

"Wow-Wow" was the nickname by which Margaret Pearse was known within the family. The Dowling brothers and Milo Mc Garry who were pupils went to Rosmuc that summer. John Dowling recalls Pearse swimming in Loch Eileabhrach with the aid of a rubber tyre and also that the overflow of guests camped in the area behind the cottage. Frank Dowling played Cúchulainn in the 1909 Pageant and John, Milo Mc Garry and Fred O'Doherty were the Three Red Pipers, whose chanting in *The Destruction of Da Dearga's Hostel*, Pearse described as possessing "a vast solemnity and a remote mysteriousness". This play written by Pádraig Colum especially for Sgoil Éanna, based on an old Irish tragedy, was performed with Pearse's *Íosagán* in the School in February and in The Abbey Theatre in April.

L. 187/P.Ms.

18.7.1910.   Sgoil Éanna,
                                        Cullenswood House.

My dear Wow-Wow,
   I enclose postal order of 15/-. I am just leaving for Connemara,
as I see that if I don't get away now I shall not be able to get away
at all. John and Frank Dowling and Milo Mc Garry may be coming
down, so if you are inviting anyone down this or next week there
will not be much room for them. There is really no news except that
the lease for the Hermitage is signed and we are to get possession
on Aug. 1st. but the building is not commenced yet. Best love, Pat.

To Mr. J. Holloway.

Farmer Bros., were the builders who undertook the conversion of
the stables and courtyard at the Hermitage into the classroom
quadrangle and the covered ambulatorium.

L.(tel.) 188/NLI

27.7.1910.   Rosmuc.

To Holloway, 21 Northumberland Road,
          Accept Farmers' tender.
                    Pearse.

To Mrs. Gwynn.

Denis Gwynn was the son of Stephen Lucius Gwynn (1864–1950),
who was M.P. for Galway 1906–1919. He was among the first
students at Sgoil Éanna and carried the academic banner of the
school proudly into the National University by winning the first
Entrance Classical Scholarship in Greek, Latin and Irish. Having
served in the British army in the first World War he returned to
become Research Professor of History at University College Cork.
   It is quite possible that Pearse was so preoccupied with the move
to the Hermitage during the summer that he was unable to
supervise the examinations as closely as he normally would. Or
perhaps, Gwynn may have been advised by some of the assistant
masters. In the event, his achievement in matriculating at the

National University in autumn overshadowed any exhibition he might have gained in the Intermediate Senior grade.

L. 189/NLI

17.8.1910   Sgoil Éanna,
                             Cullenswood House.

Dear Mrs. Gwynn,

Owing to some misunderstanding which I cannot at present explain, Denis does not appear to have sat for the Geometry paper at the recent examination, though duly entered for the subject. He must somehow have got the impression that one mathematical subject was sufficient in Senior Grade, and so have dropped Geometry in order to concentrate on his special subjects. This is only a surmise – in the absence of Denis and my assistant masters (whom he may have consulted) I cannot tell how the thing took place. I cannot remember that he or anyone else consulted me. As Denis was not taking Trigonometry, Geometry *was* necessary, – two mathematical subjects are necessary for a pass in mathematics. The result of this disastrous blunder is that poor Denis loses his whole examination. It is a new and strict rule that, in the case of a student who does not take all the necessary subjects the marks scored by him cannot be divulged. Accordingly I do not know how Denis may have done in classics and modern languages, but Mr. Johnston, the Assistant Commissioner gave me to understand that his answering would at any rate have entitled him to an exhibition – to what other distinctions and prizes we shall never know. This is a terrible calamity for the School, for a high exhibition in Senior Grade in our first year would have made our reputation as an Intermediate School. But I am still more concerned for the disappointment to Denis. Nothing can be done. I am of course asking the Board to give the case special consideration, and am seeing and writing to various Commissioners, but I have no hope that the rule can be waived. If you and Mr. Gwynn have influence with any of the Commissioners you should not hesitate to use it – but there is really little chance of remedy.

In order to be able to compete for the Scholarships in the National University in October next, Denis will now have to pass the approaching Matriculation, Its date is Sept. 27th, and the last day for entering on the ordinary fee (£1) is Aug. 23rd. I therefore enclose form of notice of intention to present, which must be filled up by Denis himself and lodged with the Registrar on or before August 23rd accompanied by a fee of £1 and evidence of age which I can get from Intermediate office and send you. I am sending it on to you as the quickest way of reaching Denis, who I understand, is still abroad.

Need I tell you how the mishap about the Intermediate grieves me? I have not slept since, I received the first inkling of it two days ago. Since then I have been trying to discover whether there is not some mistake on the Board's part, but there is none. It seems quite clear, that, under what impression I know not, Denis did not sit for Geometry. He and we must bear the disappointment as best we can. Believe me, dear Mrs. Gwynn, Sincerely yours, P. H. Pearse.

To Somhairle Mac Garvey.

Somhairle Mac Garvey was a student at Sgoil Éanna who completed Senior Grade in 1910; it appears that being ill during the examinations he was not optimistic of being successful. Pearse encouraged him and in this letter he is congratulating him and indicating to him the role of will-power in overcoming adversity.

The sister who is mentioned is most probably Margaret who had responsibility for the domestic affairs of the school. Mac Garvey was one of the principal actors in *The Destruction of Da Dearga's Hostel* in 1910 and was honourably mentioned by Pearse in *An Macaomh*.

The school had already transferred to Rathfarnham when this letter was written yet the letter carries the Cullenswood House address.

L. 190/NLI

29.8.1910   Sgoil Éanna,
                                                Cullenswood House.

My dear Somhairle,
Congratulations on your success at the Intermediate. You have passed in Senior Grade despite all your prognostications and depression on the eve of the exam. I told you to keep your head up and to hope for the best and you see I was right. You have passed in the six subjects necessary, English, Irish, French, two Mathematical subjects and science; a splendid achievement considering the circumstances. Now take this success as a good omen; keep up your heart and get well as quickly as you can. One can do a lot, even in overcoming illness by *will power*. You have a fighter's soul and must not give way.

My sister is sending you some books to read – cheap and trashy

175

novels which I picked up, but one does not want anything very heavy or intellectual when on a convalescent's couch.

I am quite frightfully busy or I should have written to you sooner. Will write again, Beir buadh agus beannacht, Mise do chara go buan, Pádraig Mac Piarais.

To Mrs. Humphreys

Pearse's younger sister Mary Brigid assisted Vincent O'Brien and Owen Lloyd in teaching music from 1910 onwards.

Canon O'Keeffe was Parish Priest of Rathfarnham; his family who owned the animal skin processing plant in Thomas St., lived in Ballsbridge adjacent to the Humphreys.

L. 191/P.Ms.

24.9.1910   Sgoil Éanna,
                                   Rathfarnham.

Dear Mrs. Humphreys,
    Very many thanks for cheque, receipt for which I have pleasure in enclosing.

Dick has started his music, and his teacher likes him; a high compliment, for this younger sister of mine is a person very hard to please.

The £3 . . 3s pays for music for the year, so that there will be nothing under this head in the next a/c. Mr. O'Brien's fees would have amounted to £6 . . 6s for the year.

I was talking to Canon O'Keeffe about Dick this evening. I did not know you were friends. He thinks Dick very quiet; but he should see him here sometimes! With kindest regards, Sincerely yours. P. H. Pearse.

To Dr. Walsh.

The Irish Catechism referred to by Dr. Walsh was *An Teagasc Críostaighe* by Archbishop John Mac Hale of Tuam which was published in Dublin in 1839 and was the basic religious textbook used in the Gaeltacht. Archbishop Mac Hale was born in 1791 and died in Tuam in 1881, was the dominant ecclesiastical figure in the West in the middle of the century and provided political leadership as well which was frequently at variance with the toryism of Cardinal Cullen in Dublin.

L. 192/DDA

23.8.1910.   Sgoil Éanna,
                                       Cullenswood House,

My Lord Archbishop,
    I am very grateful for Your Grace's letter of the 21st inst. Canon O'Keeffe, who is taking a very kindly interest in the school, has suggested Father Burke's name as Chaplain, and, as Your Grace says that any arrangement I may make with Canon O'Keeffe has your sanction I am adopting his suggestion. I don't know yet how far Father Burke will be able to give Religious Instruction in Irish, but our masters will of course teach the Catechism in the two languages as hithertofore. What Your Grace says about the Irish Catechism is very true; I think the best instructed lay Catholics I have ever known are to be found among the old men and women of the West of Ireland who learned Mac Hale's Irish Catechism forty or fifty years ago. I mean the best instructed in the *essentials* of Catholic faith and practice; they may not know as much about Church History etc., etc., as many others whose opportunities have been greater. With many thanks, I have the honour to be, Your Grace's obedient servant, P. H. Pearse.

To Denis Gwynn.

This letter to his former student, is a sequel to the letter written to Gwynn's mother a month earlier, concerning the consequences of Denis not having taken a second mathematics subject (geometry) in the Senior Grade examinations in June. Pearse had appealed to the Board of Commissioners of Intermediate Education the chairman of which was Chief Baron Palles. Upon the Board rejecting the appeal, Pearse is proposing a legal action to compel the Board to grant Gwynn the results and distinctions which despite the missing paper he had obtained. The school was also at a loss as annual income from the Board was based on the examination results of the students. There is no evidence that this legal action was proceeded with.
    Owen was Denis Gwynn's younger brother. The Language Procession was the annual public demonstration organised by the

Gaelic League to publicise its demands on language and educational policy.

L. 193/NLI

17.9.1910.   Sgoil Éanna,
                                              Rathfarnham.

A Dhonnchadh na gCarad,

I should have written to you sooner but I wanted to have something definite to report. Unfortunately there is nothing. The Chief Baron pronounced against us at the meeting and the majority was swayed by him. But the Chief Baron's answer to our point is of the flimsiest description. Rather, he does not answer it at all. He admits that the rules are faulty, and this admission in my opinion gives away his case. I believe that the battle is not yet lost, and that if we press it on we may carry off our due glory and renown, if not the evening's spoil. The Board are seeking to impose a condition which, whatever they may have *meant*, is not clearly set forth in their rules. You cannot have been expected to be able to read their minds; you had only their printed rules to go by, and you took a meaning out of those rules which is certainly a possible one. You are therefore entitled to your exhibition and rewards. I propose to commence an action against the Board to compel them to publish your marks and distinctions and to hand you your exhibition and us our result fees. Even if we do not win the action we shall right ourselves before the public and show up the Board and its disgracefully drawn rules. The action would be taken by me as Head Master and by you suing through your next friend, who is your father. I hope your father will consent. Could you drop me a postcard to say whether he is still in London and at the same address.

Thanks for your good wishes. We have a great many new boys, so many that it seems hardly the same school. I hope you will come out and spend a long evening with us when you have time. I am looking forward to the coming of Owen.

Could you join us at the Language Procession to-morrow? The Educational Section musters at the corner of Leeson St. at 1 p.m. and we shall be somewhere about there. Some of last year's boarders have not yet returned, so we shall not make so large a show as we should. Mise do chara go buan, Pádraig Mac Piarais.

Mr. S. Hampton.

Mr. Carroll, an international gymnast, had been the teacher of gymnastics and drill in Sgoil Éanna from 1908. Where drill was taught in school, it was frequently taken by serving army sergeants who were encouraged by official army policy to undertake this work in their official time. Carroll and Hampton would have been among the few teachers available in Dublin who were not either soldiers or ex-soldiers of the British Army.

L. 194/OCS

26.10.1910.   Sgoil Éanna,
                               Rathfarnham.

A Chara,
    Would it be possible for you to undertake to teach our boys here drill and gymnastics? Mr. Carroll is unable to find time, and he has suggested your name. I don't want a soldier or ex-soldier, and it seems the number of competent instructors in Dublin who are not or have not been in the British army is very limited. If you could come it would relieve us of a great difficulty, and it would be a splendid thing to have a prominent Gael for this department as we have for all other departments. I hope it will be possible. If so, please say what your terms would be. I suppose one lesson a week would be sufficient? I should be grateful for a reply at your earliest convenience, as the session is now nearly half over and drill has not yet started. I had been counting on Mr. Carroll. Mise do chara, Pádraig Mac Piarais.

To Seán T. Ó Ceallaigh.

The confidential nature of the financial affairs outlined in this letter would indicate that it was written to a very close friend. Seán T. Ó Ceallaigh was manager of *An Claidheamh Soluis* up to 1910 and may have worked later in Dollard House.

14.11.1910   Sgoil Éanna,
                              Rathfarnham.

Dear Seán,
   You were so good as to promise me, some time ago, that you
would put your name to a bill for £20 and that you would pay £5
each quarter on the bill until it was cleared. I need money badly at
the moment and I would be deeply indebted to you if you could do
that for me now.
   We could visit the bank together and I am sure that the manager
would arrange the matter for us. We would need to be there before
three o'clock. I cannot be in town before three o'clock on any day
except Wednesday. I know that you are always busy on Wednesday; but I could call into Dollard House and we could call to the
bank when you are going for your lunch. You would not waste
much time that way. Please send a postcard to me, telling me if I
am to call on you next Wednesday. I could not be in town before
two o'clock. Yours ever, Pádraig Mac Piarais.

To Mr. G. Berkeley.

George F. H. Berkeley, of Harwell Castle, near Banbury, England
was a wealthy stockbroker who had contributed £25 to the school
fund in answer to Pearse's appeal. In reply to the May letter from
Pearse, Berkeley had said that "all his Irish funds are invested" and
that he could not do more than the £25 he was subscribing.

L. 196/NLI

23.11.1910.   Sgoil Éanna,
                              Rathfarnham.

A Chara,
   A meeting of those who, in response to my letter of May 10th
last have subscribed or promised to subscribe to a fund for the
development of St. Enda's School, will be held at the School on
Saturday Dec. 3rd next at 2 p.m. The business of the meeting will
be (a) to consider a proposal for regulating the relations between
the subscribers and myself so as to leave the former free from
financial liability and (b) to discuss means of raising funds for the
completion of an absolutely necessary building scheme and, if
possible, for the purchase of the freehold of the Hermitage. I hope

it will be convenient for you to attend; if not perhaps you could favour me with your views in writing? Believe me, Sincerely yours, P. H. Pearse.

To Mrs. Mgt. Hutton.

This letter to Mrs. Hutton is identical with that to Berkeley and to the other subscribers.

L. 197/NLI

23.11.1910.   Sgoil Éanna,
                                       Rathfarnham.

A Chara,

A meeting of those who, in response to my letter of May 10th last have subscribed or promise to subscribe to a fund for the development of St. Enda's School will be held at the school on Saturday Dec. 3rd next at 2 p.m. The business of the meeting will be (a) to consider a proposal for regulating the relations between the subscribers and myself so as to leave the former free from all financial liability and (b) to discuss means of raising funds for the completion of an absolutely necessary building scheme and if possible, for the purchase of the freehold of the Hermitage. I hope it will be convenient for you to attend; if not perhaps you could favour me with your views in writing. Believe me, Sincerely yours. P. H. Pearse.

To Bolger & Doyle Ltd.

Bolger & Doyle were the builders who carried out some construction work at Sgoil Éanna, including the erection of a wooden-floored handball alley and a swing in the field on the left of the drive approaching the house.

181

30.11.1910. Sgoil Éanna,
Rathfarnham.

Dear Sirs,

I regret that I am not in a position to let you have cheque on a/c this week. There are a great many calls on me, and I must try to keep everything going. In a few weeks I hope to be able to let you have a substantial cheque. I hope the delay will not inconvenience you. Yours v. truly, P. H. Pearse.

To Mr. J. Dolan.

Mr. Dolan was one of the most generous of Pearse's friends in the establishment and maintenance of Sgoil Éanna. According to the document drawn up by Pearse of the 25th November 1914 Mr. Joseph Dolan had advanced £1,000 in all to him.

Clause (2) in this letter showed that Pearse was anxious to ensure the continuity of the school by enabling its goodwill to fall to Dolan who would have been willing to continue it.

Vol. 2, No. 1 of *An Macaomh* was published at Christmas 1910. The builders in question were Farmer Bros. who constructed the classroom block at the Hermitage.

L. 199/P.Ms.

16.12.1910. Sgoil Éanna,
Rathfarnham.

A Chara,

As I wired you to-day, I have been kept so busy with School exams, with getting the boys off on their holidays, and in the afternoons with seeing *An Macaomh* through the press, that I found it impossible to write you sooner, especially as I wanted to see my solicitor before writing. I was set free this afternoon and was able to talk the whole matter over with my solicitor, and can now give you the assurances you want. My solicitor says it is better and safer to give you a mortgage, – the total cost, including duty, registry, etc. will be £8. This will put you in an unassailable position, and will be much better than an amateur deed drawn by me. I therefore undertake:-

(1) In respect of this £500, to assign my interest in the Hermitage to you by way of mortgage. This will be the *first* claim on the

property. The £500 to be repaid in 6 months with interest at 5% and interest on the existing loan.

(2) To execute an agreement assigning the goodwill of the School to you so that in case you are compelled to foreclose the mortgage, or in case of my death, etc., you may be able to take over the school, if you wish, and carry it on as a going concern.

(3) As to your former advances, with regard to these, you and Séumas Mac Manus stand on the same footing, except that your amount is larger than his. I propose therefore to execute immediately one *second* mortgage to both of you to secure the amounts due to the two of you. Do you approve of this? Séumas Mac Manus' amount is £350.

Matters will thus stand: (i) Your claim for £500 comes first of all; (2) you have right of entering and taking control in case of failure; (3) with regard to the rest, you and Séumas Mac Manus stand on the same footing pro rata and before all others.

If you wish, I will get an insurance on my life effected and send it on to you.

I will proceed immediately with the drawing up of these three agreements. Meantime, I hope, if you have been successful at the bank, you will send me the £500. It is important I should have it before the builders who are threatening, strike a sudden blow. That might jeopardise everything. I need not labour my gratitude to you for coming in this way to the rescue of Sgoil Éanna. It is one of the generous noble things which make great movements possible, and which great movements always call forth. I hope and believe that God will prosper and bless this undertaking, for your sake, and for Ireland's sake. Mise do chara go buan, Pádraig Mac Piarais.

To Bolger & Doyle Ltd.

L. 200/P.Ms.

7.1.1911.   Sgoil Éanna,
                                              Rathfarnham.

Dear Sirs,

I did not expect my acceptance would be due till Monday. I have written to the Bank asking them to hold it over till Monday or Tuesday. I am not, as I explained to you, able to take it up in full, but will reduce it each time it falls due and renew for the balance.

If I send you cheque for £20 on Monday or Tuesday, and an acceptance for the balance, will you not be able to lodge them in the Bank against the acceptance now falling due? Yours v. truly, P. H. Pearse.

To Bolger & Doyle Ltd.

L. 201/P.Ms.

11.1.1911.   Sgoil Éanna,
                                    Rathfarnham.

Dear Sirs,
    I enclose cheque £10 in reduction of bill. I regret that I cannot conveniently reduce it by a larger sum this time. If you send me renewal for balance I shall be very glad to accept it and return it to you without delay. I am, dear Sirs, Yours v. truly. P. H. Pearse.

To Bolger & Doyle Ltd.

L. 202/P.Ms.

14.1.1911.   Sgoil Éanna,
                                    Rathfarnham.

Dear Sirs,
    I enclose renewal bill duly completed. I hope to reduce it further next month. Yours v. truly, P. H. Pearse.

To Mrs. Mgt. Hutton.

This circular was sent to all those who had subscribed to the May 1910 appeal; it contains the proposals which emerged from the meeting held at Sgoil Éanna on 3rd. December 1910. Canon Ryan, was a very prominent Gaelic League member who had been among the first managers to introduce the bilingual programme into the national schools of his parish in north Tipperary.

Mr. Bertram Windle, a distinguished scientist, had been dean of the Medical faculty at Birmingham University until 1904 when he came to Queen's College, Cork. Appointed President of University College, Cork in 1908 he later went to Canada.

L. 203/NLI

21.1.1911.   St. Enda's College,
                                    Rathfarnham.

A Chara,

As the outcome of a meeting held here on the 3rd ultimo, and of subsequent correspondence, we have agreed on the following as a basis for the organisation of a body of patrons and governors in connection with St. Enda's and St. Ita's Colleges. The points we have borne in mind in coming to an agreement are chiefly three:-

(a) The supreme importance of maintaining and developing the noble work on behalf of Irish education which has been inaugurated in the founding of St. Enda's College for boys and the sister College of St. Ita's for girls. In the two Colleges a hundred and fifty boys and girls, seventy of them boarders, are already being educated on Irish lines.

(b) The importance, with this end, of leaving the founder of the Colleges, who is the Headmaster of St. Enda's and the Director of St. Ita's, in effective executive control, especially as he bears, and is willing to bear, the sole financial liability.

(c) The desirability of officially associating with the Colleges those who have subscribed, or may in the future subscribe, towards a fund for their development, while keeping these subscribers (in accordance with the expressed wish of the majority of them) free from all financial liability in connection with the Colleges.

We believe that these ends will be secured by the adoption of the following scheme:-

(1) Subscribers of £1 or upwards shall form a body of Patrons, who shall meet at least once a year.

(2) The Patrons at their Annual Meeting shall elect a Consultative Committee for membership of which only subscribers of £20 or upwards in one sum, or of £5 a year or upwards for five years shall be eligible.

(3) The Consultative Committee shall meet at least once a quarter. Its duties shall be (a) to audit the accounts of the Colleges; (b) to "visit" the Colleges, at such times as it may find convenient; (c) to receive each quarter a report from the Head Master, and to offer, if it thinks fit suggestions as to the working of the Colleges, these, however, not to override the supreme executive

185

control of the Head Master; (d) to submit a report on the working of the Colleges during the year to each annual meeting of the Patrons; (e) to organise further financial support for the Colleges and to issue public or private appeals or take such other steps as it may think desirable for this end.

(4) Membership of the body of Patrons or of the Consultative Committee shall imply no financial liability in connection with the Colleges, the sole financial liability, with the supreme executive control, remaining with the Head Master.

The undersigned, who have been acting as a temporary Consultative Committee since May last, propose to call the first annual meeting of subscribers for Saturday, February 25th, 1911, when this scheme of organisation will be submitted and, if approved of, come into force, and the election of a Consultative Committee for 1911–1912 be proceeded with.

Meantime it is most important that further financial support for the Colleges should be forthcoming. St. Ita's has ample accommodation for many years to come, and is practically free from debt, having inherited the classrooms, etc., originally erected for St. Enda's and already paid for, or virtually so. For the wiping out of a debt on its splendid new classrooms and the provision of a new dormitory, the necessity for which will shortly become urgent, St. Enda's stands in need of a further endowment of £1,500. It has been suggested that many of those who have already subscribed will be willing to double their subscriptions, and that all will be able to interest new friends; and it is hoped that many who have not hitherto subscribed will gladly do so now that the position of subscribers in connection with the scheme, and their freedom from financial liability has been clearly defined.

We beg that you will fill up the annexed form and post it to the Head Master before Saturday, February 18.1911. We remain, Yours very truly. Consultative Committee (pro tem): Joseph T. Dolan, Mary Hayden, John P. Henry, Shane Leslie, Séumas Mac Manus, Arthur (Canon) Ryan P.P.V.G., Bertram C. A. Windle.

P. H. Pearse, Head Master.

To P. H. Pearse, Esq.,

Head Master,
St. Enda's School Rathfarnham.

I have read the circular letter dated January 21st 1911, of the Consultative (pro tem) of St. Enda's College, and am willing to become a subscriber to the College under the scheme there outlined. I have already forwarded a subscription of .... I enclose .... value .... being amount of my subscription.
I undertake to send a subscription of .... on ....
every year for .... years.

    Signed..............................
    Address..................................
    Date.......................

(Please delete any portion of the above which you do not wish to sign).

To Bolger & Doyle. Ltd.

L. 204/P.Ms.

10.2.1911.   Sgoil Éanna,
                       Rathfarnham.

Dear Sirs,
   I enclose cheque £15 in reduction of your bill due to-morrow and shall be glad to accept renewal for the balance if you kindly forward it to me. I am, dear Sirs, Yours, P. H. Pearse.

To Bolger & Doyle Ltd.

L. 205/P.Ms.

11.2.1911.   Sgoil Éanna,
                       Rathfarnham.

Dear Sirs,
   I enclose bill initialled as desired.
   Half of one of the sides of the Handball Court was knocked down last night by the wind, and lies in a state of wreckage. Please send out and have it repaired at the earliest possible moment, as it

will be very inconvenient for us not to have the use of the court. I am afraid the props were very weak. Yours, P. H. Pearse.

To J. Holloway.

Pearse's "man", Mr. Rodgers, was more widely known as Micheál Mac Ruadhrai, the head gardener and supervisor of the grounds of the Hermitage, who lived in the lodge at the main gate. He was an accomplished storyteller and had won numerous gold medals at the Oireachtas and had also written extensively in Irish. He taught horticulture and practical gardening to the pupils.

L. 206/NLI

17.2.1911.   Sgoil Éanna,
                                      Rathfarnham.

Dear Mr. Holloway,
    Yours to hand. I have also received the certificate and a/c from Messrs Farmer, and will attend to it in due course in accordance with the arrangement agreed on between us through our respective solicitors.
    The W.C's are still most unsatisfactory, and I should be glad if you could look at them again and see that they are set right. When you call, if I am not in, ask for my man, Mr. Rodgers, as he knows more about these things than I do. Sincerely yours, P. H. Pearse.

To J. Holloway.

The study hall was located in the flat-roofed wing which ran eastwards from the main building to which it was added at a later date.
    The rain water was pumped to the house and farmyard from the lake. The Rathmines water was supplied by the Rathmines local authority which charged a water rate for its provision.

11.3.1911.   Sgoil Éanna,
                              Rathfarnham.

Dear Mr. Holloway.

My landlord, Mr. Woodbyrne, has complained of the removal of
the gravel from the roof of the study hall, the old billiard room by
Messrs Farmer, and requires me to have it replaced immediately.
He says that in the absence of this gravel the roof is liable to crack
and serious injury will accrue to the building. He adds that if I do
not get it done at once he will do so himself at my expense. I don't
think Messrs Farmer ought to have removed this gravel at all. You
might kindly see that they replace it immediately. It will be a
serious matter for me if injury is done to the building, or even if
Mr. Woodbyrne fancies injury is done to it, as he has power under
the lease to close on a deposit of £300 I made and to re-enter into
possession if I do not keep my covenants.

The defective W.C.'s are still as bad as they were before Messrs
Farmer repaired them. They have not restored the rain water to the
tap in the yard, this must be done, as it is very wasteful to have the
Rathmines water, for every gallon of which I have to pay, running
there. They have painted some of the railings reddish and some
white; they have also left some woodwork unprimed. Yours v. truly.
P. H. Pearse.

To Countess Markievicz.

This postcard is not dated. The meeting with Yeats accompanied by
the Countess and Mrs. Reddin most likely concerned a production
by the school players at the Abbey; they performed there on three
occasions, May 1910, April 1911 and May 1913. Since the Reddin
boys did not come to Sgoil Éanna until September 1910, this
postcard may refer to one of the later occasions in 1911 or 1913. In
May 1913 Yeats produced Pearse's *An Ri* and Tagore's *Post Office*
as a benefit for Sgoil Éanna.

L.(p.c.) 208/OCS

April 1911 or May 1913.

Countess Markievicz,
Surrey House,
Leinster Road,
Dublin.
I have made an appointment with Mr. Yeats at the Abbey Theatre
for to-morrow (Friday) morning at 10.45. Mrs. Reddin said that
you would be glad to come with us. I hope this hour will suit you?
Gratefully, P. H. Pearse.

To J. Holloway.

This post card contains the direction to Holloway regarding the
building work on one side and the notice of the Sgoil Éanna Passion
Play at the Abbey on the other.
    The Passion Play combined some traditional Irish songs and
liturgical music with a dramatic presentation in Irish of the Gospel
narrative. It was presented on Good Friday and Holy Saturday,
involved pupils and teachers of both schools and was enthusiastically reviewed by, among others, Pádraig Colum in the *Irish
Review.*

L.(p.c.) 209/NLI

10.4.1911.   St. Enda's College,
                                        Rathfarnham.

Dear Mr. Holloway, – please tell Messrs Farmer to proceed with
the restoration of gravel and repair of crack *at once* at their
estimate of £6. P. H. Pearse.

Front of P.C.
        On Friday and Saturday 7th and 8th April 1911 at 8.15 the
        Pupils of St. Enda's College, Rathfarnham and of St. Ita's
        College, Rathmines, will perform a *Passion Play* in Irish
        arranged by P. H. Pearse, in the Abbey Theatre Dublin.
        Tickets 3s, 2s, 1s, and 6d.   Booking at Cramer's.

To Mrs. Bloomer.

Miss Maura Canning, a pupil of Sgoil Íde, won the gold medal for solo singing at the Dublin Feis Ceoil, the annual spring music festival.

L. 210/NLI

11.5.1911.   Sgoil Éanna,
                                    Rathfarnham.

Dear Mrs. Bloomer,
    Congratulations to you, to Miss Canning, and to St. Ita's on her success at the Feis Ceoil. It is a splendid achievement, and will be a splendid advertisement for the College. I saw her picture in the *Independent* to-day. It is fine to think that we can do something worthy in every phase of education we take up. The boys all join in congratulations. Sincerely yours, P. H. Pearse.

P.S.   I am going to Belfast to-morrow to speak at a meeting, but I hope to be back in time for the Prizewinners' Concert on Saturday at which I suppose Maura will sing.

To Dr. W. J. Walsh.

William Woodbyrne, who died in 1913, inherited the Hermitage from his father, Henry Woodbyrne (1798–1889), who had an extensive medical and dental practice at 24 St. Stephen's Green and who also owned Glenville estate in Co. Cork.
    The Augustinian Friars had a house of studies at Orlagh a few miles from Sgoil Éanna. Pearse was a friend of Fr. Philip Doyle O.S.A., a member of the Orlagh community at the time, through whom he probably discussed the question of a chaplain being supplied from Orlagh.

L. 211/DDA

13.5.1911.   Sgoil Éanna,
                                    Rathfarnham.

My dear Lord Archbishop,
    I am anxious, if at all possible, to have a regular Chaplain attached to St. Enda's next year, so that we may have the great privilege of daily mass in the College. At Cullenswood our boys

were able to go out to mass every morning, but this has not been possible since we came to Rathfarnham. We are a mile or more from the Church, and, even apart from the question of weather in the winter, there would be difficulties in the way of going down to mass every morning, – for instance, it would push on the beginning of lessons too late. Moreover, I feel that a Catholic College is not complete without its Chapel and the presence of the Blessed Sacrament. I think we should interweave religion into our daily lives at every point and that the truest education is that which best combines the spiritual with the heroic inspiration. We have now some sixty boarders and I expect that we shall have a good many more next year; adding masters, servants and day-boys, we are a little Community of about a hundred, and quite large enough to have our own little Chapel.

Fortunately there is a room built for a Chapel by a former proprietor, which only needs to be decorated and furnished. I propose committing the designing of a scheme of decoration etc., and the making of an altar to my brother.

My idea is that the Chaplain should say mass every day and give Benediction of the Blessed Sacrament on Sunday. He should also hear the boys' confessions, have charge of religious instruction and prepare them for First Communion etc. I think he might also take charge of these latter matters in St. Ita's also, and St. Ita's could contribute something towards his salary.

I need hardly say that we should like an Irish speaker so that prayers etc. might be in Irish and the religious instruction bilingual. I don't know whether some young priest fresh from Maynooth and waiting for a mission, or a member of an order, would be better. Orlagh is not very far, and the Augustinians might be able to cooperate with us. I am not quite sure whether we shall be able to provide rooms or not, and on the whole I think it better that the Chaplain should live outside the College. I should be grateful if Your Grace could let me know whether you could appoint such a chaplain as I suggest, and what salary we should be expected to provide. I have already told Canon O'Keeffe of my intention to get a Chaplain of our own, if possible. I remain, my dear Lord Archbishop, Sincerely yours, P. H. Pearse.

To Mr. Johnston.

Dr. Patrick Doody (1883–1917) from Ballinaboly, Kilmacow, Co. Kilkenny had been a teacher in St. Colman's College, Fermoy before he came in 1909 to Sgoil Éanna. He taught Latin, Greek and Mathematics and also was responsible for organising the hurling and football teams which captured many of the Dublin inter-school trophies. Dr. Doody was an accomplished violinist and played at many of the school concerts and informal gatherings.

Dr. Doody, with Pearse, initiated in 1910 the Leinster Inter-Colleges Championship of which he was secretary, until he left Sgoil Éanna in 1914. In Sgoil Éanna, Dr. Doody was in charge of the stocking and ordering of textbooks and was regarded as a very efficient teacher who favoured a disciplined approach to learning. He left Sgoil Éanna to go to St. Joseph's College, Roscrea and he died at the early age of 34 in 1917.

Mr. Johnston was Assistant Commissioner of Intermediate Education at 1 Hume St., Dublin.

L. 212/P.Ms.

20.5.1911.   Sgoil Éanna,
                                       Rathfarnham.

Dear Mr. Johnston,

Dr. P. Doody is one of the Senior members of our Staff. He applied for the Intermediate Superintendentship earlier in the year but has not so far been appointed. He thinks that perhaps there may be one or two vacancies arising now and that he may have a chance of one of them. I don't think the Board could make a more useful addition to its staff. Dr. Doody is a teacher of long experience. He is an admirable disciplinarian and exceedingly methodical and businesslike in his work. Indeed we regard him as the business man of the College and for this reason we entrust to him the ordering and distributing of books, stationery etc. required by the boys. He has long experience in conducting examinations and presiding at study. If you have a vacancy now I think you will have reason to congratulate yourself if you appoint Dr. Doody. Yours faithfully. P. H. Pearse.

To Bolger & Doyle

L. 213/P.Ms.

20.5.1911.   Sgoil Éanna,
                                                            Rathfarnham.

Dear Sirs,
   I enclose cheque £5 in reduction of Bill due to-morrow. I regret
that I cannot send a larger cheque this time. If you kindly renew for
balance I shall be happy to complete bill and return it to you. You
can charge stamp interest etc. to me. Yours, P. H. Pearse.

To S. Ó hAodha.

Séamas Ó hAodha was a music teacher and a member of the Gaelic
League. He later became an Inspector of Music in the Department
of Education.
   The reverse side of this postcard carries the photograph of the
Sgoil Éanna hurling team of 1910/1911.

L.(p.c.) 214/NLI/G

28.5.1911.   Sgoil Éanna.

Many thanks. Please send me the names of the songs you will do
and name the evenings that suit you best. We will have a musical
gathering each evening at 7.30. The more often you come, the
better. P. Mac P.

To Mrs. Mgt. Hutton.

The subject of this letter is the organisation of past and present
masters and pupils, which was entitled Ord Éanna (or the Order of
Enda). The dinner for which external caterers were employed was
held on 6.6.1911 at the school; Mrs. Hutton was not able to attend
but the guests included Dr. Douglas Hyde, President of the League.
   The printed menu for the occasion was entirely in Irish; the
toasts included, Sláinte na hÉireann, Sgoil Éanna and Sgoil Íde
and the newly established Ord Éanna.

L. 215/NLI

30.5.1911.   Sgoil Éanna,
                              Rathfarnham.

Dear Mrs. Hutton,
   We are asking a few friends to dinner on Whit Tuesday in
connection with the foundation of a League of Past and Present
masters and pupils of St. Enda's, and should be very glad if you
could join us. Dinner at 7 p.m.; some music and a toast or two.
Hoping to have the pleasure of your company, Sincerely yours,
P. H. Pearse.

To Mrs. Mgt. Hutton.

L. 216/NLI

12.6.1911.   Sgoil Éanna,
                              Rathfarnham.

A Chara,
   An unwarrantable action on the part of one of the firms with
which we deal has produced a temporary crisis in the financial
affairs of Sgoil Éanna. There was an understanding that they would
give us long credit, but, nettled at a fancied grievance, they
demanded last week instant payment of their a/c. I was unable to
pay at the moment, and was so busy with our reunion and the
approaching exams, that I could not even take steps to get in
money. They immediately served a writ and now they threaten to
mark judgement unless the amount is instantly paid. It will take me
some weeks to get in the sums owing to me – small amounts for
books, extras, etc., – and in the meantime I must provide cash to
settle with these people. If they mark judgement the fact will
become public property, others will come down on us, and firms will
refuse to give us credit. In the circumstances my only resource is to
appeal to those who have generously interested themselves in Sgoil
Éanna. Not to beat about the bush, would it be possible for you to
place at my disposal till September next the sum of £100? I hate to
have to ask you this, but the need is urgent, and it would be terrible
if the prestige of the College were to suffer or its work be
threatened. If what I ask is impossible you have only to say so, but I

am hoping it may be possible. As soon as the pupils' fees come in in September I will repay you.

I am very sorry you were unable to be with us last week. We had a most successful gathering; Dr. Hyde's presence gave it great importance. Yours very sincerely. P. H. Pearse.

To Bolger & Doyle.

L. 217/P.Ms.

23.6.1911.   Sgoil Éanna,
                                        Rathfarnham.

Dear Sirs,

I enclose cheque £5 in reduction of your bill and acceptance for the balance. I cannot do better this time. I don't see that your bank has any reason to complain seeing that the bill is being steadily reduced month by month. I am the only loser, as I have to pay interest. Yours v. truly, P. H. Pearse.

To J. Dolan.

It would appear that Joseph Dolan had to undertake an overdraft in his own bank to enable him to support Sgoil Éanna with his generous subscriptions.

Gerrards was a firm of solicitors who were acting for Pearse.

L. 218/P.Ms.

29.6.1911.   Sgoil Éanna,
                                        Rathfarnham.

A Chara,

I am sorry to say that I am not in a position to let you have back any of your advance this month, as I had hoped. Sources on which I was counting have not yet materialised, though they will, I hope, do so in the near future. I must ask you to have confidence in me a little longer. I sincerely hope this disappointment will not injure you with your bank. If you can get them to allow the overdraft to stand a little longer, as I hope and trust you will, you will find that at the earliest possible moment I will keep my word with you. At the very worst I can let you have something substantial in September, but I think it will be sooner. Meantime I have asked Gerrard's to push on the agreement, and I will also get a new insurance on my life and hand it over to you. I hate to think that you are inconvenienced by your generous support of my venture, but this is a thing that will not and cannot fail and the inconvenience for both of us will only be temporary. Mise do chara go buan. Pádraig Mac Piarais.

To Dr. W. J. Walsh.

The question of having a school oratory at Sgoil Éanna involved both permission from Rome and securing a chaplain to officiate daily. At this stage of negotiations it would appear that neither of these factors, permission or a chaplain, was the major constraint; from this letter it seems that his perilous financial situation forced Pearse to weigh even this development with caution despite the willingness of Fr. Philip Doyle and the Augustinian Orlagh Community to assist by supplying a daily chaplain.

L. 219/DDA

29.6.1911.   Sgoil Éanna,
                                        Rathfarnham.

My dear Lord Archbishop,
   I owe you an apology for my delay in replying to Your Grace's letter, and in thanking you for your approval by way of experiment and for one year of my proposal as to the appointment of a special chaplain for St. Enda's College. I have had so much extra work and worry in connection with various things of which the examinations (not yet concluded) are only one, that I have had to turn aside from all correspondence, even the most important.
   While thanking Your Grace for your approval, I have to ask your guidance as to my further procedure. I do not know whether it is through Your Grace, or directly, I am to apply to Rome for permission to establish the oratory; and if the latter, to what official of the Holy See, and in what form, I should address myself. I am furthermore anxious as to whether it might be looked on as discourteous if, having got permission from the Holy See, I should not find it possible to proceed this year? I mean if I could not come to an arrangement with the Orlagh priests, or if I could not set free enough funds to be sure of having the oratory completed and the

chaplain honorarium guaranteed? I am trying to do a great deal on a very small capital, and there are moments when I have grave anxiety as to how exactly I am to make ends meet, – though they generally *do* meet in the long run. I should like if possible, to have permission from Rome to go ahead if possible; in a few weeks it will be more clear to me whether I can safely go ahead in September or had better wait till Christmas or even till next year.

I shall be very grateful for a line from Your Grace as to the form in which I should approach Rome. In the meantime, perhaps I may venture to inquire whether in the event of permission being given the Orlagh Community would be able to supply a priest – or had this better be held over till authorisation comes from Rome, as all will depend on that? Believe me, My dear Lord Archbishop, Sincerely and respectfully yours. P. H. Pearse.

To Dr. W. J. Walsh.

L. 220/DDA

7.7.1911.   Sgoil Éanna,
                                  Rathfarnham.

My dear Lord Archbishop,
    I am very much obliged for Your Grace's letter of 1st inst. which I find on returning from a short excursion.

I will make the application to the Holy See, and on learning favourably from H.E. the Cardinal Prefect of the Sacred Congregation *de Sacramentis* will enter into communication with the Orlagh Community.

With many thanks for Your Grace's advice in the matter, I remain, My dear Lord Archbishop, Sincerely yours, P. H. Pearse.

To Mr. J. Holloway.

When Pearse entered into the leasing contract with the Woodbyrne estate in July 1910, very strict conditions were attached to his occupation of the Hermitage. The students were not to enter the house proper from the beginning of school in the morning until evening. These constraining conditions forced Pearse into providing external classroom and refectory accommodation almost immediately and raised the question of whether he should be required to build a dormitory also. He built the refectory and converted the farmyard buildings into a fine set of classrooms; as indicated in this letter he proposed to build the dormitory in 1912.

It would appear that Wrenn, the architect for the Woodbyrne estate, was satisfied with Pearse's approach; O'Connell, the Woodbyrne solicitor was of a different mind and interpreted the architect's report in a different light. Holloway and Wrenn met and sorted out the question to Pearse's satisfaction.

When William Woodbyrne died in 1913, Sir John Robert O'Connell, LL.D. Solr., with offices at 84 Kildare St., Dublin, was appointed joint trustee of the estate with Mr. John Redmond Colfer. He had been Henry Woodbyrne's legal guardian from 1899 and during Pearse's tenancy it was he who conducted all legal and financial negotiations.

L. 221/NLI

22.7.1911.   Sgoil Éanna,
                              Rathfarnham.

Dear Mr. Holloway,

Very many thanks for your letter and for the promptness with which you attended to the matter. These seems to be some confusion between Wrenn and O'Connell, for whereas Wrenn, as you say, (and it is my own impression also from his report) does not seem to think that very much, if anything, is required, provided I proceed with the building next year, O'Connell appears to be of the opinion that Wrenn wants something done now, and keeps sending me urgent letters of which I enclose the latest. I am now writing O'Connell reporting the result of your interview with Wrenn, and asking him to communicate with the latter.

It is my intention to proceed with the new building next June. If, pending this Wrenn would consent to let things stand as they are, it would, I need hardly say, be a great matter for me.

When I hear from O'Connell I will again communicate with you. I feel very much that I have not yet been able to let you have any of your fees. You know the great struggle I have to carry through my tremendous undertaking and to make it a success. Just now I have to provide for the half-year's rent and for a further payment to Messrs Farmer. As soon as I can I must let you have at least something on account. Meantime I appreciate very much your great consideration in not even asking for a payment, as well as your great care for my interests. Believe me, dear Mr. Holloway. Yours sincerely, P. H. Pearse.

P.S. I enclose copy of Mr. Wrenn's report, which you might kindly return when you are next writing.

Bolger & Doyle.

L. 222/P.Ms.

31.7.1911.   Sgoil Éanna,
                                        Rathfarnham.

Dear Sir,
   I enclose cheque and renewal bill as arranged. In haste, Yours truly, P. H. Pearse.

To Bolger & Doyle.

L. 223/P.Ms.

14.8.1911.   Sgoil Éanna,
                                       Rathfarnham.

Dear Sirs,
   You might kindly have rings of swing replaced at your earliest by a pair of proper strength. One of the present rings wore through after being a few days at work. Thoroughly strong rings are required so as to avoid danger. There are a few planks loose in the ball alley too which you might kindly set right at the same time. I should be grateful if you would attend to this at your earliest, as I want everything to be shipshape before the return of the boys. Yours truly. P. H. Pearse.

To Bolger & Doyle.

The firm of Bolger and Doyle were very accommodating in dealing with Pearse which he in turn appreciated; he expressed himself accordingly in this series of letters. However in seeking to have the

swing repaired he displays a spirit of independence which is not
normally found in supplicant debtors.

L. 224/P.Ms.

2.9.1911.   Sgoil Éanna,
                                             Rathfarnham.

Dear Sirs,
    I enclose new acceptance for amount of bill and discount, with
thanks for the courtesy of renewal, and apologies for my delay in
forwarding.
    I have had the swing fixed temporarily, but I find that one of the
iron hooks in the crossbar is also considerably worn by the friction
and will not last much longer. There is something wrong about your
mode of fixing the swing; the iron you use is too soft, or else there
must be some other way of attaching the ropes. We had none of this
trouble with our swing at Cullenswood House which has now stood
three years without repairs, though in more constant use than this.
As it stands, the swing here is exceedingly dangerous and I doubt if
I can let the boys use it. I will let you have cheque during week.
Yours, P. H. Pearse.

To Tomás Bán Ó Concheanainn.

This report to Tomás Bán on his nephew, Brian Seoighe, covers the
Junior Grade examinations of 1911 and Brian's remarkable
achievement in Sgoil Éanna from February 1909 when he arrived
from Inis Oirr in the Aran Islands.
    Patrick Mac Manus, a brother of Séumas Mac Manus and a
good friend of Tómas Bán, had been one of those who promised
support for Sgoil Éanna in 1908. Pearse had written to him in
March 1908 outlining his ideas on the proposed school and seeking
his support (c.f. letter of 4.3.1908.)

L. 225/P.Ms./G

4.9.1911

Dear Tomás,
    Enclosed please find Brian's account for the half-year. He
returned on Monday in enthusiastic mood for the year's work.
    He succeeded in the examination in Irish, English, Arithmetic
and Algebra, in Geometry, Nature Study, Drawing, in History and

in Geology. He failed in French. But of course half the country failed in French, this year and this "failure" proves nothing except that the examiner does not know his business. Brian knows more French than I did when I secured the third or fourth place in the country in that grade.

I am very pleased with Brian's performance generally. Very few would have expected a year and a half ago, that he would succeed as he has in Arithmetic, Algebra and Geometry. We propose to enter him for honours next year (he was in for honours Irish this year and received 399 "honours mark"). In addition to the Intermediate course, he will do commercial arithmetic and other items relating to commerce etc.

Is it true that Patrick Mac Manus is back in Ireland? If so, do you think that you might persuade him to subscribe the money to us which he promised three and a half years ago? If he saw the place, I am certain that he would like it. Yours ever, Pádraig Mac Piarais.

To Bolger & Doyle.

This letter is one of the earliest in the Desk Diary and occurs immediately after the letter to the same firm of August 14th 1911; we can assume that Pearse began using the Desk Diary to draft his letters before the opening of the school year and continued doing so until the spring of 1912. Subsequently he used end pages to draft pupil reports covering the whole school year.

L. 226/DD

[September 1911]

Dear Sirs,

I am obliged for yours of 31st ult. I find that you have not yet made the lean-to roof of the last classrooms erected at Cullenswood House watertight. It is proposed now to convert it into a library, but this is impossible as long as water comes down between the roof and the wall whenever there is a shower. You might kindly have this attended to at once.

I am looking up the tarpaulins I thought these had been returned to you. I am dear Sirs, Yours very truly, P. H. Pearse.

To Kernan & Sons Ltd.

This letter, to the photographic firm which had photographed the school teams and the Passion Play of 1911, requests them to send prints to the printing firm of Hely's who produced the school postcards using these illustrations.

L. 227/DD

[September 1911]

Dear Sirs,
   Please send immediately to Messrs Hely, Acme Works, Dame St. prints of the photos of the hurling and football teams, you did for us recently and also a print of the Virgin in our Passion Play – the position with hands raised and joined. These need not be mounted.
   Please send me one copy of the following mounted: Hurling team; Pilate (front position); Virgin (both positions); Christ (standing not kneeling); High Priest; Roman Soldier (arms folded not sword drawn). I think that these had better be done in brown but on unglazed paper so ...

incomplete.

To A Chara,

"Feargus Finnbhéil" was the pseudonym of Diarmuid Ó Foghludha a Limerick friend of Pearse who was an active member of the League. His son was competing in the W. E. Yudson scholarship and for which Pearse was examiner. Ó Foghludha was a regular contributor to *An Claidheamh Soluis*, translated Arabian tales into Irish and composed the League anthem, "Go mairidh ár nGaeilge slán". A native of Castlemaine, Co. Kerry, he was a member of the staff of Coláiste na Mumhan at Ballingeary; he died in 1934.

L. 228/DD

[September 1911]

A Chara,
   "Feargus Finnbhéil" tells me that you have kindly agreed to superintend the examination of his boy for the W. E. Yudson scholarship. I am very grateful to you for stepping into the gap. I learn that the League rooms in Limerick are available. If you could

be there at 1.30 to-morrow, give the exam. papers and return the answer books to me by to-morrow evening's post, you would place me under a great obligation. There is no candidate from Limerick but "Feargus Finnbhéil's" boy; you can give him the Irish and English at one sitting say 1.30 to 3.30; and the History and Arithmetic at another, say 4 to 6. This is the time-table we have arranged for the Dublin centre. Sincerely and gratefully yours, P. H. Pearse.

To Madam.

This letter in reply to an enquiry from the mother of a prospective pupil, presents Pearse's educational philosophy at Sgoil Éanna, his combination of scholarship and character formation, secured by securing the comfort and happiness of each boy and then providing for each according to his own particular needs.

It is possible to detect a note of determination in this letter to secure every possible student for the school.

L. 229/DD

[September 1911]

Dear Madam,
Many thanks for your postcard of yesterday, in reply to which I have the pleasure in enclosing our Prospectus. I need hardly say that we should be very glad to receive any pupil you may be in a position to send us. I can promise him a happy school life at St. Enda's and a careful education in healthy and beautiful surroundings and with very suitable and congenial companions. Our first care is to make each of our pupils comfortable, our next to give each such teaching and training as suit him and his own particular needs. As an outcome we reap the best possible results in character and in scholarship.

I shall be happy to give you any further information and to meet your views in every way possible. Trusting to hear from you, I am, dear Madam, Yours very truly. P. H. Pearse.

To Mr. Reddin.

The Language Procession organised by the Gaelic League in early

September was a spectacular demonstration by schools and other bodies on behalf of better policies on Irish. Kenneth and Norman Reddin were students of Sgoil Éanna from September 1910.

The establishment of the National University in 1908 which replaced the Royal University of Ireland introduced a new Matriculation system, which in Pearse's view, demanded a higher standard than the older system.

L. 230/DD

[September 1911]

Dear Mr. Reddin,

I am enclosing a/c for the boys' schooling for the half-year.

I should be grateful if you could arrange with them to stop with us next Saturday afternoon and night. We want to make as good a display as possible at the Language Procession on Sunday, and we have arranged to have a sort of practice march in the grounds on Saturday evening. I should like Kenneth and Norman to be present at this, as well of course as at Sunday's procession, and it will be much more convenient for them to stay with us over Saturday night than going out to you late and returning first thing on Sunday. If they wish they can of course go home on Sunday after the procession.

I think they ought to do Middle Grade in 1912 and not go for Matriculation till 1913. They are really not yet up to standard, nor could they be expected to be. A year ago they were weak Junior Grade students, and in June they said they felt too weak (though in this I disagreed with them) to stand for Middle Grade. I consented to their not going on for Middle in June on the understanding that in fairness to us they should go on for it next June. Kenneth said it would be a "rotten thing" to fail; you may be perfectly certain that (without a miracle) they will fail in Matriculation at the end of this year, and equally certain that they will pass in Middle. Is it not better to do the feasible thing, and to "make haste slowly"? Sincerely Yours, P. H. Pearse.

P.S. You must remember that Matriculation is no longer what it was. The Matric. of the R.U.I. was easier to get through than Middle Grade, the Matric. of the National is harder to get through than the Senior. It is folly for the boys who thought themselves too weak for Middle this year to think of going for an examination harder than Senior next year.

To T. F. O'Connell & Sons, Solrs.

Sir John Robert O'Connell was the principal of the legal firm of T. F. O'Connell & Sons of Kildare St., Dublin and was one of the Trustees of the Woodbyrne Estate.

L. 231/DD

[September 1911]

Dear Sirs,

I beg to enclose cheque £144 in payment of half-year's rent, minus interest on deposit.

Am I not entitled to be allowed in respect of the Income Tax demand and receipt for which I enclose? If so, the amount can be deducted from the half-year's rent.

The repairs on roof required by Mr. Wrenn have been carried out, and I am advised that the roof is now quite water-tight. Yours faithfully, P. H. Pearse.

To Bolger & Doyle Ltd.

L. 232/DD

[September 1911]

Dear Sirs,

I enclose cheque £5, and regret I cannot make it larger. The demands on me at present are very numerous and I must try to keep everyone going.

The new metal rings for the swings are again worn through; in fact they lasted only two days. As I have told you so often these are not the proper rings for a swing; not the proper sort of ring and not the proper sort of metal. The soft metal you use will not stand the friction for more than a few hours. One of the hooks in the timber crossbar is also worn through. I would ask you kindly to supply the proper fastenings for a swing and have them fixed at once. We had to take down the swing two days after the boys' return, and as it is one of the chief amusements of the smaller boys it is very awkward to be without it. Since it was originally erected we have not got 3 weeks use out of it altogether.

Would you undertake the erection of a ladder arrangement for swinging from rung to rung? I don't know what they are called but

they are common in some schools and gymnasiums. Yours truly,
P. H. Pearse.

To Solicitors for the Swift Estate.

L. 233/DD

[September 1911]

Dear Sirs,
   I enclose cheque £48 .. 17 .. 11 being half-year's rent for
Cullenswood House, as promised. Should there have been any
deductions for taxes this time? Yours truly, P. H. Pearse.

To Mrs. Burke.

Frank Burke, a pupil at Sgoil Éanna from September 1909,
completed his education there, excelled at games and attended the
National University from Sgoil Éanna and fought in the Easter
Rising with the Rathfarnham Company. He was Headmaster of
Sgoil Éanna from 1925–1935.

L. 234/DD

[September 1911]
Dear Mrs. Burke,
   Very many thanks for cheque for which I have much pleasure in
enclosing receipt.
   Frank is well, in excellent spirits and working steadily. He is
anxious to do Matriculation this year, and I think he might be
allowed. I will write you at length when I have had an opportunity
of talking things over with him in detail. With kindest regards,
Sincerely yours, P. H. Pearse.

To Mr. Reddin.

Further to his earlier letter, it would appear that the Reddins were allowed to stay in school on the Saturday night prior to the Language Procession which was held on Sunday September 17th.

L. 235/DD

[September 1911]

Dear Mr. Reddin,
I find that the Procession starts from Rutland Square at 1.30 p.m. Sunday. The Education Section (in which we shall be) assembles on the West side. I expect it will be about 3 p.m. when Smithfield is reached, and the meeting will take at least two hours. That would leave it 5 p.m. or after when you start for home – that is if you wait for the whole meeting. Kenneth and Norman will be free as far as we are concerned when we reach Smithfield. I am very much obliged to you for falling in with my suggestion that they should remain with us over Saturday night.

I spoke to them about their exams to-day and they agreed on my putting the case before them to work for a Middle Honours course in 1912 as a stepping stone to Matriculation in 1913. I am convinced more and more that this is the proper thing. With kind regards, Sincerely yours, P. H. Pearse.

To W. J. Shannon, Solr.

These are possibly the local authority rates on Cullenswood House.

L. 236/DD

[September 1911]

Dear Sir,
Herewith find cheque £14 . . 5 . . 7 in payment of rates as demanded on enclosed. Yours truly, P. H. Pearse.

To Mr. O'Doherty.

Vincent and Fred O'Doherty of Co. Mayo were students at Sgoil Eanna from September 1909; Vincent matriculated in 1911 and began his university course at Queen's College, Galway. Pearse had begun the practice of having former students of Sgoil Eanna remain in residence while pursuing their university courses.

L. 237/DD

[September 1911]

Dear Mr. O'Doherty,

I am enclosing a/c for Fred's schooling for the half-year.

We are putting him on for Middle Grade next year. He has asked to be allowed to drop French and as he seems positively to dislike the language there is no use in keeping him at it. He will devote the time saved to Latin. He did very well at his exam in everything except in French, and the Middle Grade course will be no trouble to him. He does not yet know much Latin but in a year, with all the time we will give him at it, should make good headway.

I am sorry Vincent will not be with us this year. No doubt it will be pleasant for him to be in Galway with his sister, but it would have been a great advantage to commence his University career in Dublin; and he would have the society of the boys, the games etc. Is it not possible still to arrange for him to come to us? With kindest regards, Sincerely yours, P. H. Pearse.

To Mr. O'Connor.

The account in question in this letter from internal evidence, would seem to have been with a firm which supplied both schools regularly on a large scale. It seems most likely to have been Magees the grocery and provision firm in Rathmines, of which the O'Connor family were the proprietors.

L. 238/DD

[September 1911]

Dear Mr. O'Connor,

I enclose cheque £50 on a/c. I will let you have a further cheque on a/c of St. Enda's as soon as possible, and will also see that you get a cheque in a/c of St. Ita's at the earliest possible moment. I am sorry I can't wipe out the whole balance just now, but will do my best to work it down, and will at any rate let you have a cheque covering the quarter's a/c every quarter as promised. With thanks for your consideration in the matter, Yours sincerely, P. H. Pearse.

To Tutorial School

This letter was written to a commercial or secretarial school of which there were many in Dublin; they specialised in preparing students for secretarial positions and for junior administrative and civil service posts.

L. 239/DD

[September 1911]

Dear Sirs,
   I should be much obliged if you would let me know whether you could supply us with a teacher to give an hour or two's instruction per week to some of our boys in handwriting, correspondence, English spelling, etc., and at what terms. I am not satisfied with the handwriting, spelling etc., of several of our boys, and I feel that I and the members of my staff – specialists in classics, modern languages, science and so on are not the people to correct these defects, – at least that a trained commercial or civil service tutor will correct them much more easily and efficiently than we could. For this reason I am anxious to supplement our teaching of English by a course under one of your teachers, could such a course be arranged. Please let me hear from you at your earliest.
   Perhaps one or two of our boys will take up Shorthand too. Yours v. truly, P. H. Pearse.

To Secretary D.A.T.I.

The Department of Agriculture and Technical Instruction, under establishing legislation of 1899, was responsible for education in agriculture and technical subjects; it provided grants to secondary schools for science teaching and for courses in art and drawing. It was under the aegis of this Department that Mr. Richard Feely A.R.C.Sc.I. taught science at Sgoil Éanna.

L. 240/DD

[September 1911]

Sir,
   I beg to enclose Form of Application for the Renewal of Recognition of classes in Experimental Science and Drawing at St. Enda's College.

I should be obliged if you would let me know whether it would be possible for a few pupils in our Girls' College of St. Ita's Cullenswood House, who have worked through Preliminary Courses in other schools to take up a special course in Drawing even though there is no Preliminary course in operation in St. Ita's.

To Pádraig ...

The recipient of this letter may have been Pádraig Ó Conaire or Patrick Tuohy, or Patrick Campbell, the only "Patricks" among the pupils of the first few years. There is no indication as to the nature of the position in question; it may have been in the Gaelic League.

L. 241/DD/G

September.

Dear Pádraig,
    Greetings and best wishes!
If someone is to be elected in place of Micheal O'Brien do not worry – I will speak on your behalf. Sgoil Éanna people must stand together. With every best wish, Yours. P. Mac Piarais.

To Pádraig Ó Conghaile.

Frank Connolly was a student at Sgoil Éanna from September 1908, arriving on the first day with two other Connemara students, Pádraig Óg Ó Conaire and Colm Ó Neachtain. He graduated in science and later became Professor in the Veterinary College, Ballsbridge. His parents lived at Maam Cross and were the teachers of the Gortmore National School in the parish of Rosmuc. They were friends of Pearse and he had frequently stayed with them and recommended their house to others like Mrs. Hutton who wished to holiday in Connemara.

L. 242/DD/G

[September 1911]

Dear Friend,

Enclosed please find the half-yearly account for Proinsias. I am obliged to pay £500 before the end of this month and consequently I need to collect all the premiums.

If I owe you anything, please deduct it from this account. I regret very much that I could not manage to go down this year – perhaps I may manage to make a Christmas visit.

Eilís certainly excelled in the examination. Trusting that You all are well, Yours ever, P. H. Pearse.

To Mr. Houston.

Professor David Houston F.L.S. of the College of Surgeons and Trinity College, who lived at Mt. Eden near the Hermitage was a friend of Pearse and of Mac Donagh. He advised Pearse on the courses in Nature Study, Biology and Horticulture which were provided in Sgoil Éanna and as this letter shows he had procured a teacher to undertake the class in the academic year 1911/1912.

Michael Mac Ruadhraí (Rodgers), the gardener, had previously conducted classes in horticulture in Cullenswood House. Pearse allowed Houston to bring his students on regular field trips to the Hermitage grounds; his descriptive terminology on these ecological outings earned him the nickname "Crawling Out" from the boys of Sgoil Éanna.

L. 243/DD

[September 1911]

Dear Mr. Houston,

We have had the bench fitted up in the greenhouse – just roughly by the gardeners – but we have not yet put down the gravel beds for the potting. The gardener, Rodgers has ideas on this latter subject and would like to talk over the matter with you. Meanwhile perhaps the class could be getting organised. I suppose there will be a lot of preliminary work in the laboratory before anything is done in the open air. What sort of pots, jars, etc., do we require for the laboratory? Could you get Miss Alderton to drop me a line saying if she could undertake this class, whatever would suit her, and what

her terms would be? I am very sorry you are leaving Rathfarnham,
With kindest regards, Sincerely yours. P. H. Pearse.

A Chara.

The recipient of this letter is not identifiable but was most likely
one of the teachers funded by the Department of Agriculture and
Technical Instruction under its Manual Instruction Scheme who
taught classes outside regular school hours.

L. 244/DD

[September 1911]

A Chara,
   Could you possibly undertake a Class in manual instruction for
us? I think one hour a week would be sufficient. We have two
rough benches but no other apparatus. I can't afford to spend much
money in equipment; I just want the simplest things so as to teach
boys to be useful in their own homes. Sincerely yours, P. H. Pearse.

To Mrs. Dowling.

Frank and John Dowling were pupils at Sgoil Éanna from 1908 and
1909 respectively; Frank was a number of years junior to John.
Frank figured prominently in the first pageant *Mac Ghníomhartha
Chúchulainn* in June 1909 playing the lead part with distinction
and John (or Eoin as Pearse called him) figured in the dramatic
rendering by Colum of *Da Dearga's Hostel* in Spring 1910. In the
same year John distinguished himself in the Junior Grade
examination winning an exhibition in modern Literature and prizes
in Science and Irish.
   This informal report by Pearse on the two Dowling boys is
typical of his approach to evaluating and reporting on student
performance; it is candid, detailed and balanced; while seeking to
give the parents an objective picture it offers the pupils a basis for
commendation and motivation for renewed effort.

L. 245/DD

[September 1911]

Dear Mrs. Dowling,

Very many thanks for note £8 to hand, for which I have pleasure in enclosing receipt.

John should certainly do well this year. He has had a splendid chance. We have carefully arranged the classes so as to be able to give him full attention, and if he does not get on it will not be our fault. Later in the year I will give him special grinding myself as I did the year before last.

Frank is certainly weak in handwriting, spelling and so on, and seems to improve very slowly. He is not clever, and seems to find it very hard to concentrate his attention. At the same time he certainly makes efforts. I think he is doing better during the last few weeks than before. I am asking the masters to pay special attention to his weak points, and for the benefit of him and one or two others I am arranging for a special course of lessons in writing, spelling and what may be called "civil service" subjects generally, under an expert in these things, and I hope for good results from this. With kindest regards to all, Sincerely yours, P. H. Pearse.

To A. J. Nicholls Esq.

A. J. Nicholls was an official of the Gaelic League at Mount Argus to which the Sgoil Éanna branch was affiliated.

L. 246/DD

[September 1911]

My dear Mr. Nicholls,

We have started our Language Collection and shall be very glad to send on the proceeds through you. We have of course our own "Éire Óg" Branch of the Gaelic League in the College, but as you have charge of the district the collection may properly be sent on through you and acknowledged "per Craobh Éanna per Craobh S. Arguis". We will also send on through you the St. Ita's collection. With kindest regards, Always yours sincerely, P. H. Pearse.

To Morton's School of Typewriting.

This is very similar to the earlier letter to the secretarial college and may suggest that Pearse had failed to get a suitable teacher from the first source.

L. 247/DD

[September 1911]

Dear Sir,
 Could you supply or recommend us a teacher who would give some of our boys a course of lessons in handwriting, spelling, and dictation etc. I feel that some of them do not write or spell as well as they might, and I and the members of my staff (specialists in classics, modern languages, science, etc.) feel somewhat at sea in the matter, and recognise that a specialist in "civil service" or "commercial" subjects would be much more likely to improve them than we. For this reason I am anxious to supplement our English lessons by some lessons on the civil service or commercial style. Please say if you can help us and what the terms would be.

To Mr. T. O'Toole.

This letter in answer to an application by Mr. O'Toole of the Rathfarnham Gaelic Football Club reveals a generous offer on Pearse's part to accommodate the locals while safeguarding the interests of his pupils and of the property.

L. 248/DD

[September 1911]

Dear Mr. O'Toole,
 I duly received yours of 19th inst, and am very glad to hear that there is a prospect of the establishment of a Wolfe Tone Club in Rathfarnham. I am glad to hear too that Gaelic games are commencing to flourish again; I hope that the Rathfarnham Dwyers will soon regain their old fame.
 Need I say that I consider it a duty to help you in every way I can? Unfortunately, there are difficulties about giving you the use of the field, and it is only by coming to a very definite understanding, and strict adherence to it, that the difficulties can be overcome. The boys are free on Sundays up to 5.30 p.m. and require

215

the use of the field and after 5.30 it would of course be too dark for you to play in winter. I called a few of the boys together yesterday and we talked the matter over; they are willing to withdraw from the field and give you the use of it from 3 to 4.30 p.m. on Sundays. I hope the hour will suit you; it is absolutely the only hour that will suit us. I should like the following conditions to be strictly observed. (1) only members of the club to be admitted; (2) the players to have access to the playfield only and not to the woods or walks, (3) steps to be taken to prevent boys and others from crossing the walls or injuring the place in any way. Mr. Rodgers will discuss details with you; and (4) none of your members to come before 3 p.m. or to remain after 4.30.

I do not fear that your members will do any damage, but I fear the depredations of followers and hangers on, and I know that you and all the members will co-operate with me, in trying to reduce these to a minimum. If the privilege of using the place were in any way abused, or if damage was incurred, it would of course have to be withdrawn.

On Sunday next there will be other visitors here, but on any succeeding Sunday you can commence if you give me due notice. Sincerely Yours, P. H. Pearse.

To Mrs. Mac Neill.

Eoin Mac Neill's two sons Niall and Brian were students at Sgoil Éanna from September 1908 and attended the junior section until 1911 when they were students in the Preparatory Grade. Niall became a very keen scientist and in adult life as Director of the Ordnance Survey and colonel in the army, he devoted much time to the conservation and ecological work of the Dublin Naturalists Field Club.

L. 249/DD

[September 1911]

Dear Mrs. Mac Neill,

I am enclosing a/c for the boys' schooling for the half-year, amounting with the balance due from last year to £15 odd. I have to provide £500 by the last day of this month in addition to current expenses (about £200 a month) so that I have to scrape in every penny possible, and I hope you will be able to get Mr. Mac Neill to send me a cheque.

216

We have put Niall and Brian in the Preparatory Grade class, though the latter will be too young for examination. We are anxious that Niall should go on for the First Year's Course in Experimental Science under the Department, but the classes will be held in the afternoons from 5.30 to 7.30; could he stay with us twice a week for dinner and the Science class? He could be home about 8.15, and would not of course have any further study to do on those evenings. The course is most useful and interesting and it would be a very great pity for Niall not to have the advantage of it. With kind regards, Sincerely yours. P. H. Pearse.

To A Chara.

This letter to the parent of a young student Fergus, answers points raised by the parent concerning games and religious instruction.

L. 250/DD

[September 1911]

A Chara,

Very many thanks for cheque for which I have much pleasure in enclosing receipt.

Fergus has opportunities of playing games at playtime each day and on the half-holidays but we have not got our "juventissimus" team properly organised yet. This will be done in a few days, and I hope Feargus will join it and play. He is not very keen on hurling and football, and seems to prefer simply to "play about" with the very little boys but we must try to get him to take part in the organised games.

The religious instruction is under the superintendence of our Chaplain, Father Bourke, who is also Chaplain to the Convent. He visits us at least once a week and gives half an hour's instruction. When classes are preparing for the sacraments or the whole school for the annual Diocesan Examination he visits us more frequently. In addition the smaller boys have half-an-hour's catechism every day, as well as frequent spells at the Irish prayers; the bigger boys half-an-hour's Catechism, Bible History, or Religious Instruction four times a week. We devote more time to Religious Instruction than any secondary school for boys I know. At last year's Diocesan Examination we got 99% in Catechism and were very highly praised by the Diocesan Inspectors to the great delight of the local clergy. I give frequent "sermons" myself and my discourses, while

most orthodox, are so framed as to interest and attract boys.
Sincerely yours, P. H. Pearse.

To Hely's Ltd.

This refers to the proofs of postcards which the printing firm
produced based on photographs of the school activities; they were
the subject of an earlier letter to the photographers.

L. 251/DD

[September 1911]

Dear Sir,
    I return postcard of Passion Play duly revised and also copy of
postcard of Pageant with shorter wording.
    You have not yet delivered the Hurling Team, Yours, P. H.
Pearse.

To Secretarial College.

This letter continues the search for a teacher who would undertake
classes in Book-keeping and related subjects.

L. 252/DD

[September 1911]

Dear Sir,
    Many thanks for yours of 26th inst. Before deciding I should be
glad to know whether Mr. McCarthy could give lessons in Book-
keeping and Commercial Arithmetic to one or two boys and what
the charge for this would be. Yours truly, P. H. Pearse.

To Mr. T. O'Connor.

Joseph O'Connor was a pupil at Sgoil Éanna from September 1910
and in this letter Pearse is persuading his father to allow Joseph to
complete the academic year at the school rather than employ him in
the family business.

L. 253/DD

[September 1911]

My dear Mr. O'Connor,

I am very much obliged for cheque, for which I have much pleasure in enclosing receipt. We are arranging a course in commercial correspondence, book-keeping, and commercial arithmetic for Joe which will prove very useful. I suppose he will hardly want shorthand?

I think you are wise in deciding to put him to your own business. I would make a strong appeal to you, however, to leave him with us till the end of the school year, i.e. till June. It would be a very great pity to take him away in the middle of the year. He promises to do a splendid year's work, and in justice to himself and us he ought to be allowed to finish it. The 2nd Year's Course under the Department that he has entered on is most valuable, – it gives a splendid training, in neatness and accuracy which will be of the utmost benefit to him. I should be sorry to lose the credit (and the results fees) attending the success he is bound to achieve if he finishes the year's course, but this is not what I am chiefly thinking of. I am thinking of Joe himself and of the pity it would be if he were not allowed to carry the course of study – general and commercial – I have mapped out for him. I was counting on having him till June and was laying my plans accordingly. It would be a pity to cut short his school days so suddenly; he will have to face the world soon enough. Let him then finish the present school year. I do not think you will have cause to regret it.

His violin teacher says he is very promising, but in order to derive full benefit from her instructions he wants a little theory teaching. I presume you would approve of his taking a session's lessons in theory? It will make progress at the violin ever so much quicker, Believe me, Sincerely yours, P. H. Pearse.

Mr. O'Doherty.

In a previous letter Pearse had appealed to Mr. O'Doherty to allow Vincent to attend University College Dublin from Sgoil Éanna; this letter is a reply to the arguments put forward in favour of Galway by Mr. O'Doherty. Fred was Vincent's younger brother who was still at Sgoil Éanna.

L. 254/DD

[September 1911]

My dear Mr. O'Doherty,

Many thanks for cheque, for which I have much pleasure in enclosing receipt.

I am sorry Vincent will not be with us this year. I see your reasons, but I think the arguments on the other side are stronger. As regards the extra cost in Dublin. I would willingly make very special terms with you so as to secure Vincent the advantages of a Dublin course from the first and ourselves the advantage of his presence.

Fred is working away at Latin. We will prepare him for Matric. and send him forward at the earliest possible moment. Sincerely yours, P. H. Pearse.

To Mr. J. Burchill.

This letter although written on behalf of Pearse, is drafted in his own hand in the Desk Diary. He was in constant demand by Gaelic League branches around the counry for lectures and feis openings. On this occasion, the London invitation for October 7th, took precedence over the Abbeyleix meeting. The probable date of dispatch of this letter is October 1st 1911.

L. 255/DD

[1.10.1911.]

A Chara,

Mr. Pearse has asked me to acknowledge your letter and to say that he is very sorry that he cannot go to Abbeyleix on Sunday 8th. He promised to go to London on the 7th to give the inaugural address of the session for the London Gaelic League, and will not be back till Monday 9th. Perhaps some other time he will be able to help you. Beir buaidh agus beannacht. Mise. P. H. Pearse.

To Hon. Sec. Gaelic League. London.

This letter draft is also in Pearse's hand though written on his behalf. He travelled to London and delivered the inaugural address in Fleet St. on Saturday October 7th. While there he had discussions with George Gavan Duffy and other advisors and friends concerning solutions to the financial problems of Sgoil Éanna.

L. 256/DD

[October 1911]

A Chara,
Re meeting in London on Saturday, Mr. Pearse would be grateful for a note by return confirming arrangement and giving particulars as to time and place. Also, if there is any particular phase of the movement on which you would like him to touch, and for how long should he hold forth? He has no information about meeting except your wire. Beir Buaidh agus beannacht. Mise, P. H. Pearse.

To Mr. Carney

Desmond Carney was a student at Sgoil Éanna from September 1910; in 1912 he was prominent as "Giolla na Naomh" in Pearse's play *An Ri*. His father was seriously ill during his time at Sgoil Éanna and Pearse's concern for both Desmond and his father is evident here and in other letters. He was a particularly brilliant student.

L. 257/DD

[October 1911]

Dear Mr. Carney,
Very many thanks for money order £12 .. 10s to hand, for which I have pleasure in enclosing receipt.

I will pay strict regard to your wishes about Desmond. I don't think he has ever been punished and I will see that he is not kept in to finish work undone. Indeed he has instructions from me never to do more than he feels able and never to spend more than the ordinary study time at work. Sometimes I even tell him to omit a particular exercise so as to get off to bed, before second study concludes. I know how willing he is and that he might out tax himself if allowed, and I take every opportunity of lightening his programme. He has plenty of time before him, and as you say, has both ability and application. Hoping you are getting stronger. Sincerely yours. P. H. Pearse.

To Dr. Bradley.

Liam Bradley was at Sgoil Éanna from Easter 1910; his father who lived in Drogheda was a faithful supporter of Pearse's efforts by repeated financial contributions to the school funds.

L. 258/DD

[October 1911]

Dear Dr. Bradley,
   I am very grateful for your renewed generous support of St. Enda's. I will assign you fifteen £1 shares in the Limited Liability Co. in respect of this and your former contributions. With renewed thanks and kindest regards. Sincerely yours. P. H. Pearse.

To W. Gibson. (Lord Ashbourne)

L. 259/DD/G

[October 1911]

Dear Friend,
   Greetings and good health. I am very grateful to you for your promise of support. I have decided to establish a Limited Company to undertake the management of the two schools under my direction as Headmaster. Thirty shares, at £1 each, will be assigned to you. With every best wish, Yours ever, P. H. Pearse.

To Mr. T. O'Toole.

This letter was obviously written after the 20th October. Further to the earlier letter to O'Toole, the local Gaelic Athletic club is given permission to have the use of the sportsfield for League games.

L. 260/DD

[October 1911]

Dear Mr. O'Toole,

Yours of 20th inst to hand. I very gladly agree to give the use of our field for some of the League matches, half the proceeds to go to us and half to the League. I imagine that the "gate" will be rather small, the distance from town being so great. I hope you will see that the stewarding is carefully done and that the public are confined strictly to the playing field. Yours very truly. P. H. Pearse.

To Mr. F. F. Armstrong.

"Glanmire" was the property adjoining Cullenswood House which Pearse had leased in 1909 and which he subsequently subleased to Armstrong.

L. 261/DD

[October 1911]

Dear Mr. Armstrong,

Very many thanks for cheque for which I have much pleasure in enclosing receipt.

Thanks also for your congratulations and good wishes. I hope Mrs. Armstrong is better and that your own health is keeping satisfactory. With kindest regards. Sincerely yours. P. H. Pearse.

To Mrs. Burke.

Mrs. Burke whose son Frank was in Sgoil Éanna, had responded to Pearse's appeal and had contributed to the school fund.

Pearse's comments on the prospects of the secondary teachers were very accurate; in 1914 Augustine Birrell, Chief Secretary for Ireland, introduced a scheme which improved the salary and tenure conditions for lay teachers in Irish secondary schools. Pearse's promise of a position on the staff of Sgoil Éanna to Frank Burke was indicative of the confidence he placed in him from an early age; he later was headmaster of the school from 1925 to its closure in 1935.

L. 262/DD

[October 1911]

My dear Mrs. Burke,

Very many thanks for your money order for which I have pleasure in enclosing receipt. I will assign you three shares in the Company in respect of it. When the Prospectus is ready I will send you copies of it, and if you are able to induce friends to become shareholders I will be very grateful indeed.

Frank is in excellent health, and is working with even more than his usual earnestness. I am glad to say he was elected Vice-Captain of the college the other day, as well as Captain of the Senior Hurling Team. If he remains here after Bulfin he will almost certainly succeed him as College Captain.

He seems to have made up his mind to adopt secondary teaching as his profession. The prospects of secondary teachers are bound to improve in the next few years and I think it is a very good decision. If St. Enda's is in existence when he is qualified he will not want a position. With kindest regards and thanks, Sincerely yours. P. H. Pearse.

To Mrs O'Toole.

The O'Tooles were cousins of Frank Burke; Brendan and Vincent were at Sgoil Éanna from January 1910 and Joseph joined them in September 1911. They lived in Edenderry, Co. Offaly.

L. 263/DD

[October 1911]

Dear Mrs. O'Toole,

I am very grateful for your generous promise of support. I will send you Prospectus and formal application for shares as soon as they are ready. Yes, I shall still be in command as heretofore and no one will come between me and the boys. The Company will leave me free in everything, the big difference being that it will relieve me of some of the financial anxiety.

I will tell the boys to meet you on Saturday. They are all three well and busy. With thanks and kindest regards. Sincerely yours. P. H. Pearse.

To Mr. M. Murphy.

Mr. Murphy supplied the boys with hurleys and other sports equipment. To avoid any unnecessary demands on the school finances, the boys undertook the management of their own orders for hurleys.

L. 264/DD

[October 1911]

Dear Sir,

I will bring your a/c before the meeting of the College Council next month and have the cheque passed. I regret that it has been overlooked so long. The master who had charge of it was not present at the last meeting. Our boys are now ordering from you direct (as I have placed the games in their own hands) and will always send you p.o. for amount of order. I hope it will not inconvenience you to wait till the middle of the month. Yours very truly, P. H. Pearse.

To W. Gibson (later Lord Ashbourne)

L. 265/DD/G

[October 1911]

Dear Friend,

Greetings and best wishes.

I am very grateful to you for your most generous help. Long may you prosper! Shares will be assigned to you for this £30 and for the subscription which you made eighteen months ago. They will be sent to you as soon as the Company is legally established. With every best wish, Yours, P. H. Pearse.

To Mr. J. J. Reddin.

L. 266/DD

[October 1911]

Dear Mr. Reddin,

I should have written sooner to thank you for your promise to take shares in our Company. I will assign you shares also in respect of your former subscription. The Prospectus and Forms of Application will not be ready for a week or two yet. With kind regards. P. H. Pearse.

To Joseph T. Dolan.

The appeal of May 1910 and the scheme of patrons and governors which evolved from the meeting of Dec. 3rd. 1910, were not adequate to guarantee the financial viability of Sgoil Eanna. The Consultative Committee which was to have emerged from the meeting called by the temporary Consultative Committee on February 25th 1911, does not seem to have ever become a reality in terms of influencing the schools' financial or administrative fortunes. Consequently, on the advice of legal and financial experts, especially Gavan Duffy in London and Alex Wilson in Belfast, Pearse is moving slowly towards the conviction that he should establish a limited company to run the two schools. Armed with the imaginative proposal of Gavan Duffy to utilise commissioned collectors to gather subscribers, he is busy in late 1911 securing directors for the company.

Pearse at this stage was endeavouring to attract as wide a spectrum of support as possible for the school. Seán Forde (Seán Mac Giollarnath) editor of *An Claidheamh Soluis* 1909–1916, and Cathal Brugha, a prominent Gaelic Leaguer and Dublin businessman, were organising a Gaelic games tournament in support of the school. Mrs. Alice Stopford Green (1847–1929) an eminent historian and a friend of Roger Casement, had promised support to Pearse.

L. 267/P.Ms.

12.10.1911. Sgoil Éanna,
Rathfarnham.

A Chara,

I have just returned from London where I spent a few days seeing people interested in Sgoil Éanna. The plan I have decided to adopt (and it is recommended to me by people who are prepared to back it) not only as promising the most immediate relief but also possibly as affording the best final settlement, is to promote a limited liability company to take over the financial control of the two schools, leaving the entire academic and the working executive control in my hands as Head Master of St. Enda's and Managing Director of the Company. I have talked over the matter in great detail with George Gavan Duffy who, as I suppose you know, is a London solicitor and was able to give me a great deal of useful advice. We agree that the Company ought to be formed on the widest possible basis so as to secure the support of everyone in the country who is able to take a £1 share. Gavan Duffy proposes in addition to the usual ways, one method of securing shareholders which has not hitherto been tried in these countries, but is common in France. It is to send round an organiser to call on people and get them to take shares, paying him a percentage; moreover to set local people at work in the same way and to pay them a percentage similarly. Thus a priest, a teacher, or a Gaelic Leaguer might collect £10 in shares in his district, and would be authorised to keep say £1 of it. I believe that this plan may be very productive if we only get the right man to work it; I am consulting Concannon, – if *he* would undertake the organising secretaryship we might collect thousands. I am going ahead with this scheme at once. As you, next to myself, have a larger interest in St. Enda's than anyone, I think it right to ask you first of all whether you would join the Board of Directors. I think in your own interests that you should; it will keep you in touch with the way our finances are going, give you a control over expenditure, and enable you to safeguard your interests in various ways. On the other hand, your advice would be very valuable to us, and your name would inspire confidence. I hope therefore that you will agree to become a Director. I understand that a Board of Directors is formed in the first instance by a series of co-options; the first two co-opt a third, these three a fourth, and so on. You and I would seem to be the obvious first two, as *I* am practically Sgoil Éanna and so much of *your* money is involved. If you agree we might co-opt first Michael Smidic as a good sound business man who would share the hard work with me, and other

227

names that we might consider would be Alex Wilson of Belfast (who will back us financially) Miss Hayden, John Mac Neill, Dr. Hyde, Dr. Windle, Dr. Henry, and Shane Leslie. Please let me hear from you as to this at your earliest; your own interests no less than mine and the Schools' require us to push the thing through with all possible speed.

I assume that you would be willing to allow the early part of your advances to Sgoil Éanna to remain in the Company and to accept shares in respect of them? As regards the later advance of £500 the Articles of Association should authorise its repayment out of the capital at the earliest moment funds would become available.

While I am pushing ahead this scheme for all I am worth, Forde and C. Brugha will go on with the organising of the Tournament; and Mrs. Green's help will be available as soon as we have a permanent and satisfactory business basis with a body of business men at the head of affairs. Thus, provided no unsympathetic creditor precipitates a catastrophe before we have got things organised, your money is reasonably safe. There is one plan by which I might be able to repay you sooner. I could raise £1000 on an Endowment Policy in the Norwich Insurance Co. provided I had two sureties to guarantee the payment of the annual premiums of £100 for ten years. Would it suit you better to exchange your present position for that of one of my guarantors, provided I can get another? I mean, supposing I had you and another as sureties, I could raise £1000 which I would immediately pay to you and you would have the use of your cash and would only be liable to the Insurance Co. in the unlikely event of my default. Perhaps this position would be more irksome to you than your present one; I suggest it only as a means of giving you again immediate command of the cash you so generously advanced, should that be of great importance to you. And of course I am not sure that I could get a second surety. It is a thing which we could best discuss orally, as there is so much to be said for and against.

I enclose you the financial statements I spoke about. You will see that the Balance Sheet is serious enough, so large a part of the assets (though most valuable to us) not being realisable. But on the other hand the Revenue a/c for 1910–1911 and the Estimates for 1911–1912 are most encouraging, and show that we have actually reached the paying point. And the work we are doing among our boys (and girls) becomes daily more valuable. More than ever, despite so much anxiety, I am convinced of the greatness of our work, of the fact that it is worth while, and of the solemn duty devolving on me and on us all to keep the flag flying. Sincerely yours, P. H. Pearse.

P.S. I shall be anxious to hear from you so as to get on with the Prospectus. Please return the Balance Sheet, etc. P. H. P.

To Mrs. G. Bloomer.

The financial crisis caused by demanding creditors and the partial failure of the schemes of 1910 and early 1911, prompted Pearse to undertake a thorough examination of the finances of Sgoil Íde. This he did in conjunction with his auditor, Mr. Alex Wilson of Belfast, who was also a generous contributor to his plans.

Pearse was the Director of Sgoil Íde, so all cheques in relation to the school were signed by him. Magee's were the grocery firm in Rathmines who supplied both schools; the firm was owned by the O'Connor family, one of whose sons was a student in Sgoil Éanna. The boys and girls of the Holden family were pupils in the two schools.

L. 268/NLI

13.10.1911   Sgoil Éanna,
                                             Rathfarnham.

My dear Mrs. Bloomer,

I was very sorry on returning from London to hear of your illness. I am glad to hear you are better and hope you will soon be quite yourself. I should have called only that I have been very busy and much worried trying to stave off a crisis in our finances here.

As the result of advice from friends whom I saw in London I have decided to promote a Limited Liability Co. to take over the financial control of the two Colleges, leaving me the responsible executive control as Head Master of St. Enda's and Managing Director of the Company. If we can attract a sufficient amount of capital to float the Company properly it will relieve both you and me of the load of financial worry that at present presses on us. Our idea is to accept the help of every Gaelic Leaguer or friend of education in the country who can afford to take a £1 share. So far as I see this is the one hope of placing the financial affairs of the College on a sound financial basis. I am pushing on the Prospectus as rapidly as possible. It will be necessary as a preliminary to get through a rough balance sheet and Profit and Loss a/c of St. Ita's and an estimate of income and expenditure for the coming year. When do you think you will be strong enough (and will have the time) for the auditor and me to call? I imagine that the three of us together will be able to do it in a few hours.

Am sorry funds come in so slowly. I return the cheques signed. Magee's have written to me about their St. Ita's a/c. They are owed nearly £100 up to 30th Sept., and have got only £1 . . 15 or so since the a/c was opened. At all hazards we must give them a cheque soon. Try to get in the money. It would be disastrous if Magee's got uneasy.

Our arrangement with Mr. Holden was £30 for Divenna inclusive of laundry but not of any other extras, this, however subject to 5% discount in respect of the 4 children; music extra. You ought to send this a/c if you have not already done so. He pays promptly.

I am full of anxiety as to the immediate future but of hope as to the ultimate result if we can tide over present difficulties. Very sincerely yours, P. H. Pearse.

To Mrs. Mgt. Hutton.

The intense financial pressure on Pearse at this time is clearly evident from this letter to Mrs. Hutton, to whom he instinctively turned in times of crisis. His claim that both schools were then paying concerns was borne out by the audited accounts prepared by Alex Wilson, the Belfast accountant. The classrooms and their furniture constituted a major new debt which swallowed up the money subscribed to cover the move to the Hermitage.

L. 269/NLI

13.10.1911   Sgoil Éanna,
                              Rathfarnham,

A Chara,

I have decided (on the advice of several friends who are willing to back the scheme) to form a Limited Liability Company to take over the financial control of St. Enda's and St. Ita's Colleges, leaving me in responsible executive control of the teaching work of the two schools, and in more immediate control as heretofore of St. Enda's itself. Our intention is to form a Company on the widest possible basis, so as to give everyone in the country that is interested in the ideal for which St. Enda's and St. Ita's stand a chance of associating him or herself with our work. The capital will be divided into shares of £1 each, and every Gaelic Leaguer and every friend of true education in Ireland will be asked to take one or more shares. The Prospectus is at present being drafted and will be issued to the public as soon as possible.

Apart from the desirability of ensuring a permanent future for the great work on behalf of Irish education to which St. Enda's and St. Ita's have so successfully addressed themselves, the new step is made imperative at present by the need of further capital (a) to pay off the existing building debt and (b) to complete the new wing so as to provide accommodation for the growing number of boarders at St. Enda's. As portion of the debt is at present due for repayment, and urgently presses, I am venturing to ask a few friends who have identified themselves with St. Enda's either by sending their children to it or otherwise, and on whose support for the new Company I have reason to count, to anticipate the formal application for shares by a few weeks. For any sum you are able to send me in response to this appeal I will assign you shares out of those which will be allotted to me in the Company as soon as it is floated, which will be as soon as the legal preliminaries are complete. I should add that both St. Enda's and St. Ita's are now paying concerns, and that our sole anxiety proceeds from the existence of a burdensome debt for building and equipment, portion of it due to very unsympathetic Creditors. A preliminary meeting is to be held on the 28th inst., and I should therefore be grateful for a reply at your earliest convenience, but not later than the 25th inst. Sincerely yours. P. H. Pearse.

To Dr. Coffey.

Dr. Coffey, a physiologist, was a graduate of the Medical School of Newman's Catholic University, who having studied on the continent, was appointed dean of the medical school. In 1909 he was appointed President of University College, Dublin under the Act of 1908 and governed University College until 1941. It is possible that the main objective of this specific lunch appointment was the question of Irish in the National University which was about to become a very live issue.

231

9.11.1911   Sgoil Éanna,
                                       Rathfarnham.

Dear Dr. Coffey,
   I have much pleasure in accepting your invitation to luncheon on
Sunday next to meet His Grace, the Archbishop. Sincerely yours,
P. H. Pearse.

To Fr. Meehan.

Fr. Meehan was the headmaster of a secondary school who had
written to Pearse asking if he knew of any teacher who was free.
Mr. Frank O'Nolan, M.A. had been teaching with Pearse for a
year; previously he had taught classics at Loreto College, Stephens
Green – possibly part-time while doing some University work at
University College. Nolan's name appears on the published
prospectus of Sgoil Éanna for the academic year 1911–12; he
obviously left Sgoil Éanna during the first term. The salary
mentioned £120 p.a. was the recognised total salary for a male
graduate in secondary schools; female graduates earned £80 p.a.
Birrell's campaign of 1911–1914 sought to improve the salary and
conditions of lay secondary teachers.

L. 271/DD

[November 1911]

Dear Father Meehan,
   Mr. F. P. O'Nolan MA, until lately a member of the staff of St.
Enda's, is now free. He is an Irish speaker, a ripe scholar, a close
student of educational science (a course which he has been
following under the Professor of Education in the National
University). He would be a most valuable man to have, if you could
afford such a salary as he would expect – £120 a year or so. I know
no one else who is free at present. Sincerely yours, P. H. Pearse.

To A Chara.

From internal evidence and by comparison with the list of Council
members published in the school Prospectus, this letter may have

232

been written to Canon Maguire, P. P. Trillick, Co. Tyrone or to
Miss Una Farrelly M.A. both of whom were good friends and
devoted Gaelic Leaguers. Canon Arthur Ryan, had been President
of St. Patrick's College, Thurles and was then Parish Priest in Co.
Tipperary. There are similar letters to Edward Martyn, Miss
Hayden and U. Mac Giolla Bríde (in Irish). This letter would
obviously have been sent later than those to Martyn and Mary
Hayden since they are both referred to in it as having agreed to join
the Council. Canon Maguire joined the Academic Council, Miss
Farrelly did not.

L. 272/DD

[November 1911]

A Chara,
   Would you be willing to become a member of the Academic
Council of St. Enda's and St. Ita's Colleges? It will involve no
financial or other responsibility, beyond attending an occasional
meeting and being consulted as to academic matters. The business
and financial responsibility will be in the hands of the Boards of
Directors, but it is felt that it would be well to have as well a purely
academic body of representative people who would inspire confidence as to the educational programme of the Colleges. The
following have already consented to join the Academic Council:
V. Rev. Canon A. Ryan, P.P., Dr. J. P. Henry, Miss M. Hayden,
M.A., Dr. B. C. G. Windle, Mr. Shane Leslie, Mr. Jos. T. Dolan,
M.A. and Mr. Séumas Mac Manus. We felt that your name would
strengthen it very much. I should be grateful for a reply at your
earliest, as the Prospectus will very shortly be issued to the public.
Sincerely yours. P. H. Pearse.

To Edward Martyn.

L. 273/DD

[November 1911]

A Chara,
   Would you be willing to become a member of the Board of
Directors of the Company which is being formed to take over
financial control of St. Enda's and St. Ita's Colleges? The Directors

233

so far as they are at present determined are Jos. T. Dolan, of Ardee, Alex C. Wilson of Belfast, Mr. Smithwick and myself. The being a Director will involve you in no financial liability beyond whatever shares in the Company you take and as for trouble it will only mean about one meeting a month. Mr. T. P. Gill, who is taking great interest in the scheme, is particularly anxious that you should be a Director.

In any event I should be grateful if you would give me your name for the Academic Council, a body which will have no business responsibility at all, but will simply be consulted from time to time on educational matters. Already on it are Canon Arthur Ryan, Dr. Windle, Miss Hayden, Shane Leslie, Jos. T. Dolan, Dr. Henry and Séumas Mac Manus. It is intended as a guarantee to the public that the Colleges are both Catholic and National. Sincerely yours, P. H. Pearse.

To Miss M. Hayden.

L. 274/DD

[November 1911]

A Chara,

Would you be willing to become a member of the Board of Directors of the Company which is being formed to take over the financial control of St. Enda's and St. Ita's Colleges? The Directors as far as they are at present determined are Jos. T. Dolan, of Ardee, Alec C. Wilson of Belfast, M. Smithwick and myself. The being a Director will involve no financial liability beyond the value of the shares which you have already promised to take, and as for trouble it will mean only about one meeting a month. We think it most important, almost essential, that you should be on to represent the girls' interests and to advise and criticise re St. Ita's. Sincerely yours, P. H. Pearse.

To W. Gibson (later Lord Ashbourne)

L. 275/DD/G

[November 1911]

A Chara,

Would you be willing to become a member of the Academic Council of Sgoil Éanna? It will not entail attendance at too many meetings nor involvement in the financial affairs of College. This Council will have as members people in whom the general public can repose confidence as to questions of faith and nationality. They are consulted from time to time as to questions of educational concern. The following have already accepted invitations to join the Council, Miss M. Hayden, Dr. S. Mac Henry, Dr. Windle, Joseph T. Dolan, Shane Leslie, S. Mac Manus and Canon Arthur Ryan.

I am now requesting yourself, Úna Ní Fhaircheallaigh, Edward Martyn and Father M. Maguire to kindly become members of the Council. Kind greetings and best wishes, Yours P. H. Pearse.

To S. Bairéad.

The Hibernian Bank, advanced a loan to Pearse (of which the unpaid portion stood at £619 . . 5 . . 9 in November 1914), on the security of an insurance policy on his own life and the title deeds of Cullenswood House; the remainder of the loan to the value of £275 was secured by the signature of Mr. Stephen Barrett of 55 Blessinton St. to whom this letter is addressed. In a financial statement which he drew up Pearse requested Clann na Gael in America to indemnify Mr. Barrett should he have to pay any of the sum, for which the Bank held his signature.

L. 276/DD/G

[November 1911]

Dear Stiofán,

Would you be willing to become one of the Directors of the Company which we are founding to undertake the management of Sgoil Éanna and Sgoil Íde? The Directors already appointed include Joseph Dolan, M. Smithwick, Alex. Wilson and myself. We would like to have some one like you with the reputation for business acumen, to join with us; further on account of your name being attached to the bill in the bank thereby giving you a stake in the work, it would be wise for you to have a voice in the direction of the work. Yours as ever, P. H. Pearse.

To Maunsel & Co.

Pearse initiated a series of school textbooks written by the masters of Sgoil Éanna, called "Leabhráin Éanna" (The St. Enda Books) for Irish Schools. This, the first in the series was an Irish reader with associated grammatical lessons entitled *An Sgoil* part 1. It contained notes for teachers and students.

L. 277/DD

[November 1911]

Dear Sir,
    I enclose proofs of Lessons at last. They stop about at p. ... so that there are some pages at the end missing. If you look these up and send them to me I will return them immediately. Note that the notes are to go at the foot of each page, so that the whole thing will have to be re-paged. I am prepared now to push on the book as rapidly as you like. What about Geography? Messrs Dollard will send you the College seal. Yours truly. P. H. Pearse.

To E. Martyn.

L. 278/DD

November 1911]

A Chara,
    Many thanks for your letter. I am sorry not to have you as Director, but grateful at any rate to be able to number you among the Academic Council. Yours sincerely. P. H. Pearse.

To Mr. Roberts, Maunsel & Co.

L. 279/DD

[November 1911]

Dear Mr. Roberts,
   I return balance of proofs of Part 1 of *An Sgoil.* I will push it on as fast as I can, but I am strongly of opinion that the Geography should not be held back for my book. I have always maintained that by publishing the two books in rapid succession you only get half the advertisement which can be got by giving a fair interval between them. The tendency will be to review both together instead of giving each a separate review.

To Dr. J. L. Day, M.D.

In 1911 some boys in Sgoil Éanna contracted some illnesses specified under the Health Acts; Dr. Day attended the boy mentioned here and forwarded a bill to the parent who in turn forwarded it to Pearse.

L. 280/DD

[November 1911]

Dear Sir,
   Mr. J. Donnellan of Strokestown has referred the enclosed to me. I do not think he is liable for this charge, as his boy was removed from here under the Public Health Acts by direction of Dr. Croly and without consulting him; indeed Dr. Croly left me no option in the matter either saying that it was necessary in the interest of public health that Master Donnellan should be removed at once, as in the previous case of Master O'Connor. I am, dear sir, Yours truly. P. H. Pearse.

To S. Bairéad.

L. 281/DD/G

[November 1911]

Dear Friend,

I am very grateful to you for your letter. I will arrange that seven shares from those allocated to me will be assigned to you.

I enclose a copy of the draft prospectus; I would appreciate its return as soon as possible. Yours as ever, P. H. Pearse.

To National Telephone Co.

L. 282/DD

[November 1911]

Dear Sirs,

I should be glad to know at your earliest whether we could have the telephone here on the penny-in-the-slot system. I find it does not pay us to have it in the ordinary way. Last year it was used three times by workmen, pupils and others for every once it was used by us, and it is not always easy to make a charge for the use when there is no automatic arrangement. For this reason I did not renew subscription, but I find now that is somewhat inconvenient to be without telephone, so I am anxious to have the penny-in-the-slot arrangement installed as soon as possible. Yours, P. H. Pearse.

To W. J. Holden.

Mr. Holden had sent a pair of boots to his son Fred which were given in error to another Fred – the surname having been erased from the packet.

[November 1911]

Dear Mr. Holden,

Yours of yesterday to hand. I find on inquiry that the parcel was given by mistake to another boy, Fred Fogarty. The name Holden having been torn and only the words "Master Fred" being legible. My sister assumed that the parcel was for Master Fogarty knowing that he dealt at Winstanley's and he assumed that his father had had the boots etc. sent to him on approval. The mistake was discovered on Sunday last when Fred made inquiries and the parcel was then handed over to him by Master Fogarty. I regret the trouble caused you but if anyone is to blame it is the postal or train people who tore the label! With kindest regards, Sincerely yours. P. H. Pearse.

To The Literary and Debating Society, University College, Galway.

This letter, although sent by his sister on his behalf, was drafted *in toto* by Pearse in his desk diary. As part of the public debate surrounding the creation of the National University in 1908, the educational system, its role and function were frequently topics of discussion. The inclusion of Irish as an essential subject for Matriculation became the main issue in the controversy between the Gaelic League and the Senate of the N.U.I., a controversy which culminated in the dismissal of Dr. Michael O'Hickey from the Chair of Irish in Maynooth. It is possible that Pearse used this lecture as part of the campaign in support of "essential Irish".

L. 284/DD

[November 1911]

Dear Sir,

Mr. Pearse has asked me to reply to yours of 21st inst., and to say that he will be very glad to deliver a lecture to your society. The subject he proposes to deal with is "The Function of Education", should that recommend itself to your views. As for date, what date approximately would suit you best, and would you like the lecture to be before or after Christmas? Yours truly.

To Hely's Ltd.

This letter refers to the school postcard which was produced by Hely's and which carried a photograph of Mary Bulfin as the Virgin in the Passion play of 1911.

L. 285/DD

[November 1911]

Dear Sirs,
   I return proof of "Virgin" with wording for type matter. Please send further proof so that I may correct type. Yours truly. P. H. Pearse.

To A Chara.

L. 286/DD/G

[November 1911]

Dear Friend,
   Greetings and best wishes!
I have received your letter. When I got the typewriter from you I expected that I would be in a position to pay cash down. But due to the heavy costs attaching to the erection of the new buildings here, I was left with little ready cash. Consequently I shall have to pay for the typewriter in instalments. I am enclosing £2 with this.
   You will see from this letter that the type is not very clear. What is the matter? Does it require a new ribbon? With every best wish, Yours, P. H. Pearse.

To Pitner Lighting Co.

The main rooms of the house and the Study Hall (or Halla Mór) were illuminated by gas utilising the Pitner system of patent fittings.

L. 287/DD

[November 1911]

Dear Sirs,

We were expecting your man yesterday (Monday) as arranged but he did not come, nor did he come to-day (Tuesday). I would beg you to send him early to-morrow (Wednesday) without fail, as we are suffering the greatest inconvenience from the way in which the gas goes up and down. Work is almost impossible under the present conditions, and it is most trying on the sight. Please do not fail. Yours truly, P. H. Pearse.

To Mr. R. J. Feely.

Mr. Feely was a science teacher under the Department of Agriculture and Technical Instruction under which body science and technical subjects were provided in secondary schools from 1900. Mr. Feely taught his classes in Sgoil Éanna in the evening during the hours of study and outside the regular time-table schedule.

L.(p.c.) 288/OCS

1.12.1911.

No Science class this evening. P. H. P.

To S. Mac Seaghainín.

This letter to a staff member of one of the Dublin newspapers, the *Irish Independent*, was possibly written in December 1911; it appears in the Desk Diary a few pages after an item dated 5th December. The recipient's name may have been Jones, Jennings or Johnston and he was possibly connected with the organisation which organised the occasion on which Pearse delivered the lecture on "Education under Home Rule".

There is a certain ambiguity attaching to the dating of this letter however; Pearse delivered a lecture on "Education under Home Rule" in the Mansion House, Dublin on the 11th December 1912. An account of the lecture with a photograph over the caption P. H. Pearse appears in the *Irish Independent* of December 12th. 1912.

The letter is inserted here in the chronological position in which it appears in Pearse's Desk Diary.

L. 289/DD/G

[December 1911]

Dear Friend,
    Greetings and best wishes.
    I am grateful to you for that booklet. I assume that you have by now received the letter I sent indicating the title I have chosen for the lecture: i.e. "Education under Home Rule". I enclose my photograph since you are anxious to have one. When you are announcing the lecture, I would prefer if you referred to me as "P. H. Pearse" if you are writing in English than as "Pádraig Mac Piarais"; I deem it very strange to have an Irish form of a foreign name in an article or advertisement written in English.
    We are forming a Limited Company to accept control of Sgoil Éanna and Sgoil Íde. Do you know any person in Cork who would provide an introduction to people there who would be willing to take shares in the Company? With every best wish, Yours. P. H. Pearse.

To Assistant Commissioners, Intermediate Education, Hume St. Dublin.

St. Enda's and St. Ita's received grants from the Intermediate Education Board on those students who were pursuing courses leading to the Board's various examinations; the grants were awarded on a "payments-by-results" principle.

L. 290/DD

[December 1911]

Gentlemen,
    I return Form of Claim for Grant in connection with St. Ita's College, with apologies for my oversight in omitting to sign on the inside pages. I am, Gentlemen, Yours obediently.
    P. H. Pearse.

To S. Ó Giobhthan.

This letter to the parent of a prospective pupil is of special interest in that, besides offering the parent the practical information relating to fees and terms, it also contains a succinct statement of Pearse's educational philosophy in the second paragraph and describes the advantages attaching to St. Enda's as a boarding school. The comfort of his pupils is his first concern; their education and training according to individual needs, he sees as the essence of the secret of St. Enda's.

L. 291/DD

[December 1911]

A Chara,

Very many thanks for your letter. I have pleasure in enclosing a copy of our Prospectus, in which you will find the terms set forth on the last page. Our Christmas-Easter session begins on January 8th., and this is a most favourable point in the year for a boy to start. I would agree to take him from Jan. 8th to Midsummer for an inclusive fee of £21, extras as in the Prospectus. I trust that this offer will enable you to send him to us.

Need I say that we can promise him a happy school life at St. Enda's and a careful education in healthy and beautiful surroundings and with very suitable and congenial companions? The best tribute to the success of our work (more important even than our brilliant academic record) is the affection our boys have for the place and the satisfaction expressed by their parents with the results of our system. Our first care is to make each boy comfortable, our next to give each such teaching and training as suit him and his own particular needs. I need hardly say that we make each boy an Irish speaker.

I shall be happy to give you any further information and to meet your views in every way possible. Greetings and best wishes. Yours. P. H. Pearse.

To Dónal Ó Buachalla.

Dónal Ó Buachalla who conducted a general grocery business in Maynooth, was an active Gaelic Leaguer and the leader of the Volunteers of Co. Kildare, whom he led in to join the Rising on Easter Monday. He was later, in the interval before the inauguration of the Republican Constitution in 1937, nominated as Seanascal or Head of State by Mr. de Valera. His son Joseph, was a student at Sgoil Éanna from the opening day in 1908; he died in 1976.

L. 292/DD/G

[December 1911]

Dear Friend,
   Enclosed please find a statement of the books etc. which Joseph received since the beginning of the session. I have deducted from the account the amount you have already sent (5/6). You also paid £1 . . 1 . . 0 for the woodwork and carpentry classes, but no sooner had the classes begun than the teacher left. We shall have a new teacher after Christmas and the classes will re-commence.
   Joseph enjoyed excellent health this year and we are all very pleased with his work. He will be at home with you by Friday. With every best wish, Yours sincerely, P. H. Pearse.

To W. Wilson & Co. Solicitors.

In writing to her solicitors in this vein, Pearse is ensuring a reasonable reaction from Mrs. Swift, from whom he had leased Cullenswood House and to whom he paid a yearly rent of £47 . . 15 . . 10, paid half-yearly. The office of Wilson & Co. was at 36 College Green.

L. 293/DD

[December 1911]

Dear Sirs,
   I am in receipt of yours of yesterday, and am much obliged to Mrs. Swift for meeting me in the matter. I am also very much obliged to you for your invariable courtesy. You may, I think, confidently count on cheque by the 10th prox. I am, dear Sirs, Yours truly. P. H. Pearse.

To Col. Maurice Moore.

Colonel Maurice Moore, a brother of George Moore, of Moore

Hall, Co. Mayo, sent his son Ulick to Sgoil Éanna and then sought Pearse's advice as to a suitable school on the Continent for him. This letter is the reply. Fr. Alfons Tas was a friend and professional colleague of Pearse since 1905 when they met during his visit to the College de St. Pierre at Uccle, of which Tas was a young professor. Tas was present at Cullenswood House on September 8th 1908 when Sgoil Éanna opened.

Ulick Moore enrolled at the Jesuit College in Brussels.

L. 294/DD

[December 1911]

Dear Col. Moore,

A friend of mine, a Belgian priest, who has been my guest several times in Dublin, is a Professor in one of the leading Catholic day and boarding schools near Brussels. His name is M. l'Abbe Tas, and the College is the College de St. Pierre, Uccle, Bruxelles. He is a Fleming, and speaks (in addition to Flemish) French, German, and English. I don't know very much about his College, but I gather from him that it is among the best Catholic schools in Belgium, and if the other professors are as cultured and able as Father Tas it must be a very good school indeed. There are day boys and boarders from Monday to Saturday – none of them stay over the week-end. If this school suits you from other points of view, it might be pleasant for Ulick to have among the staff a friend who knows Ireland and Sgoil Éanna. Uccle is just beyond Ixelles, and a tram takes one there in a short time from the Gare du Nord in Bruxelles. Remember me to Ulick. Sincerely yours. P. H. Pearse.

P.S.   The Jesuits have a large secondary day school in Brussels, and there are numerous state secondary schools.

To Dr. Coffey, University College.

Mr. F. P. Nolan, was on the teaching staff of Sgoil Éanna in 1910/11 and left very early in the 1911/12 academic year, before the middle of October. Perhaps his salary of £120 was beyond the financial means of Sgoil Éanna; in this and the earlier letter to Fr. Meehan, Pearse praises Nolan's ability and scholarship. In the earlier letter (cf. L271) Pearse refers to his former teacher as O'Nolan.

L. 295/DD

[December 1911]

Dear Dr. Coffey,

I understand that there is or is likely to be a vacancy for an assistant classical tutor or lecturer in University College and that Mr. F. P. Nolan, M.A. is among the applicants for it. Mr. Nolan was until a month or two ago one of our masters at St. Enda's. He is a ripe scholar, a genuine student, a man of wide culture and an Irishman of fine character. He is an Irish speaker and has been an earnest worker in the Gaelic League. I sincerely hope that if an appointment is to be made it will go to him; at any rate I bespeak for him your interest and kind offices. Sincerely yours, P. H. Pearse.

To Cathal O'Shannon.

Cathal O'Shannon was centrally active in the Gaelic League and other nationalist organisations in Belfast. The Emmet commemorations were usually held in early March.

L. 296/DD/G

January 1912.

Dear Friend,

Mr. Pearse has asked me to apologise for his failure to reply to your letter sooner – he has been very busy. He will be very pleased to go to Belfast to deliver the Emmet Memorial Lecture this year. As soon as the arrangements are made, please write and inform him of the date. With every best wish. Miss Mgt. Pearse.

To Assistant Commissioner, Intermediate Education.

This letter to the Assistant Commissioner, seeks to have the Science Master at Sgoil Éanna appointed as a superintendent at the annual examinations. Thomas Mac Donagh had occupied such a position in the summer of 1910 when he served in Coleraine. Pearse wrote another reference for R. J. Feely in August 1912, when he was leaving Sgoil Éanna; this reference is included below.

L. 297/DD

22.1.1912.

Dear Sir,

Mr. Richard J. Feely A.R.C.Sc.I., has been Science Master at St. Enda's College for the past two years. He is an efficient disciplinarian and keeps his classes well in control. He is accustomed to the setting and conducting of school examinations, is methodical and businesslike in his habits and has the qualities and experience which should make an efficient Superintendent at examinations under the Intermediate Education Board. (signed) P. H. Pearse. Head Master.

29.8.1912.

Mr. R. J. Feely A.R.C.Sc.I., has for the past three years been Science Master at St. Enda's College. His subjects have included Experimental Science, (Physics and Chemistry), Special Chemistry (Third and Fourth Year courses) under the Department of Agriculture and Technical Instruction, and Mathematics in the Higher Intermediate Grades and Matriculation classes. As a teacher he has been characterised by zeal, ability and firm grip of his subjects. He has received very favourable reports from the Department Inspectors, his work last year and this having been specially commended. All the pupils presented for the honours test both years qualified and were highly commended by the Inspectors. Mr. Feely is an efficient member of our staff, and should be a valuable acquisition to any staff he may join. P. H. Pearse. Head Master.

To Mr. J. Holloway.

As indicated in the following letter to Woodbyrne's solicitor, Sir John Robert O'Connell, the latter was very concerned lest the use of The Hermitage as a school should be detrimental to the upkeep of the residence. Hence he included strict conditions in the lease whereby the boys were excluded from the main building for most of the day. Pearse accordingly planned to erect a dormitory block separate from the main building. In this connection he is arranging to have his architect, Holloway, meet the builder Bridge and the Hermitage owner Woodbyrne.

247

L. 298/DD

22.1.1912.

Dear Mr. Holloway.

Yours of yesterday to hand. I have no idea whether the estimate of Mr. Bridge is a moderate one or not and should like your opinion on it. I am also most anxious for you to fix an hour at which you could meet Mr. Woodbyrne here and point out to him what you propose to have done. He said he would keep any appointment we make. I want him to be assured that we are taking proper measures for the protection of the building pending the erection of the dormitory. Sincerely yours, P. H. Pearse.

To Sir John Robert O'Connell.

Sir John, the principal of the legal firm of T. F. O'Connell, tended to be more demanding of Pearse in his tenancy of the Hermitage than Woodbyrne.

The original of this letter contains the following in Pearse's hand under asterisk; "Building and Decoration £2.066; Furniture and Fittings £350; Laboratory £250". These are the sub totals in the total of £2666 which Pearse expended on the Hermitage. This was mainly in connection with the block of six classrooms which were erected in the farmyard and the sheltered ambulatorium surrounding the quadrangle.

The dormitory block was never erected.

L. 299/DD

22.1.1912.

Dear Sirs,

Referring to yours of 17th inst., which extreme pressure of business prevented my answering sooner, I am of course aware of the condition you draw my attention to, and am observing it except in so far as permission has been given by Mr. Woodbyrne. My original intention was to build the new dormitory first: as my builders found some difficulty in being allowed access to that part of the building before Mr. Woodbyrne gave up possession, they commenced the classrooms first and pushed them on (I was away at the time) and in the end it was found impossible to finish the dormitory in time, so, with Mr. Woodbyrne's consent, I postponed it, and got his express consent to use the bedrooms as boys' bedrooms in the meantime. The classrooms and decoration ran away with more money than I had anticipated and last summer I again asked and got Mr. Woodbyrne's consent to postpone the dormitory for another year. He understood of course that this would involve the use of the bedrooms as boys' dormitories for a further period. I look forward to commencing the dormitory next summer.

I should like however to explain that during the daytime the boys have no access to the dwellinghouse in the way you seem to imagine. Our rules on the point are very strict. The dormitories and dwellinghouse are locked against the boys all day. At 9.30 p.m. they are opened and the boys file up to bed under conduct of a master. At 10 p.m. the boys are in bed and lights out. In the morning as soon as they have risen the house is again closed against them. There is thus absolutely no opportunity for such wear and tear as Mr. Woodbyrne fears. Visitors often find it hard to realise that just sixty boys are housed here, the main house is so free from their presence during the day. We have built a new refectory, and none of the rooms of the house are used as playrooms, studies, classrooms or even as libraries.

I may add that I have already spent £2,666* on building decoration and fitting at the Hermitage and that I have accepted a further estimate of £800 for the dormitory.

The rent, as usual, will be paid early in February. Yours truly, P. H. Pearse.

* Building & decoration £2,066; furniture and fittings £350; Laboratory £250.

To Seán T. Ó Ceallaigh.

This post-card to John T. O'Kelly Esq., T.C. is remarkable; it is undated and whereas the message is entirely in Irish, the name and address are in English. It is a request to Seán T. to meet Pearse with a view to engaging him as the main agent in collecting share subscribers for the limited company. In his letter to Joseph Dolan of 12.10.1911, Pearse expressed the hope of getting Concannon (Tomás Bán) as his organising secretary for the scheme of shares. He obviously failed to get him and is now about to discuss the scheme with Seán T. From the letter of 28th January it would appear that the latter undertook the work; consèquently this postcard was written in the middle of January before the 28th and after the opening of the spring term.

L. 300/OCS/G

[January 1912]

I would like to have a discussion with you concerning a scheme
which I have started. Could you come out here some evening or
would you prefer that I should go in to you? Send me a card, fixing
the time and the place. I am not free until 5.0 p.m. P. Mac P.

Seán Mac Giollarnath.

Although there is no clear indication as to whom this letter is
written all the internal evidence points to the editor of *An
Claidheamh Soluis*, Seán Mac Giollarnath.

The Cox referred to was not Sir Micheal F. Cox of 27 Merrion
Square, the eminent physician who was very active in university
affairs and also in Gaelic League circles; Pearse was on close terms
of acquaintance with him.

Micheál Mac Ruadhraí was the gardener and highly cultured
lodge-keeper of Sgoil Éanna.

L. 301/NLI/G

28.1.1912.   Sgoil Éanna,
                              Rathfarnham.

Dear Friend,
    I am very grateful. I will send that bill in to the bank tomorrow.

    The money is coming in disappointingly slowly. The amount
promised so far barely exceeds £200. The directors met yesterday
and decided not to go ahead until we had £500 at least. I would be
very grateful if you would speak to every Gael you meet and exhort
him/her to take a share or two. I enclose a few copies of the
Prospectus and Application Form. We will continue collecting until
we have adequate funds.

    Could you send me the address of the man Cox again? I lost the
letter which you gave me containing his address.

    You should insert a nice piece in *An Claidheamh Soluis* about
Micheál Mac Ruadhraí's marriage. He brought his wife home a
fortnight ago; he married without telling anyone. Yours ever,
Pádraig Mac Piarais.

To Seán T. Ó Ceallaigh.

L. 302/NLI/G

28.1.1912 Sgoil Éanna,
Rathfarnham.

Dear Seán,

I am delighted to hear that you will be able to undertake that work, beginning this week. We had a meeting yesterday and because we had not half enough money, we decided that we would not divide the shares until we had at least three hundred more. Do your level best for us among Leaguers, public men and business circles in Dublin. We agreed at the meeting that we would pay you according to the money you would bring in, although we are not enpowered to pay a percentage on the money itself; but Alec Wilson and I will see to it that you are paid. You can explain to people that there is no significance in that date "Jan 22nd" and that we will be collecting money for another while.

Enclosed are some copies of the Prospectus. I will send you some more tomorrow. Yours ever, Pádraig Mac Piarais.

To J. Holloway.

Pearse was still in correspondence through Holloway with Woodbyrne in relation to the demands made on him by the owners of the Hermitage arising out of the lease.

L. 303/NLI

29.1.1912. Sgoil Éanna,
Rathfarnham.

Dear Mr. Holloway,

I sent on your letter to Mr. Woodbyrne, asking him if possible to meet you at your office to-day, but I have just had a letter saying that he is ill in hospital and will not be able to see you for some time. He is to communicate with me when better and I will then communicate with you. Yours sincerely, P. H. Pearse.

To Dan. Maher.

There is no list of the shareholders who subscribed in 1912 to Sgoil Éanna Ltd.; the "Dan" in this letter was Dan Maher a former neighbour and school friend of Pearse at Westland Row C.B.S. This generous contribution came from "Dan" and his sister. Mr. Maher was later the Pearse family solicitor.

L. 304/P.Ms.

14.2.1912.   Sgoil Éanna.
                                              Rathfarnham.

My dear Dan,
   Many thanks for your generous letter and its enclosure £9 for shares in Sgoil Éanna, Ltd. I am very glad to have you there among our shareholders. It is a link between my own earliest school days and the present attempt.
   Would you mind filling up one of the enclosed forms each – i.e. signing where I have pencilled the crosses? These formal applications have to be signed before the Bank will lodge the cheque to the credit of Sgoil Eanna, Ltd., or send official receipt. Please thank your sister for me, With kindest regards, Sincerely yours, P. H. Pearse.

To Seán T. Ó Ceallaigh.

The society which Pearse proposed in this letter to some of his close friends and League associates was Cumann na Saoirse (The Freedom Association) which had a short existence during the spring and early summer of 1912. Its formation marks a change in the tempo and alignment of Pearse's political activity, a change which is also signalled by the publication of his weekly political journal *An Barr Buadh*, his oration at the Emmet commemoration in March, the militant speech at the Home Rule rally on the 31st March in O'Connell Street, and the separatism which is clearly evident in his poems of this period such as *Mise Éire* and *Mionn*. His attitude to Home Rule in 1912 was consistent with the approach he adopted to the Irish Council Bill of 1907, which he espoused in association with Terence Mac Swiney; according to him, to remove one manacle from a prisoner enables him to escape. Ultimately to Pearse, the 1907 Bill which gave among other things "control of Irish education to the Irish People" and the Asquith

Home Rule Bill of 1912 were equivalent to the removal of one of Ireland's manacles. In his rally speech in O'Connell Street he expressed a realism and a commitment to separatism which following any possible Home Rule debacle would support militant action as the answer to English betrayal.

Cumann na Saoirse numbered among its members, Éamon Ceannt, Brian O'Higgins, Desmond Ryan, Con Colbert, The O'Rahilly, Cathal Brugha, Tomás Mac Donnell and Seán T. Ó Ceallaigh.

Pearse may have hoped that such an organisation, dedicated to political analysis and discussion in Irish, might prove the ideal vehicle to carry the financial burden of the publication of the weekly *Barr Buadh*. As the Cumann did not prosper, the costs of publication were added to Pearse's already heavy debts.

Unlike most of his correspondence, this letter was typed; the signature is in Pearse's hand.

L. 305/NLI/G

17.2.1912.   Sgoil Éanna.

Dear Friend,
        Greetings and best wishes!
Would you be willing to attend a small gathering of Gaels to discuss the following matter i.e. the possibility of forming an association in which Irish-speakers can analyse and express their political sentiments and initiate political action. It appears to me to be a severe loss to Ireland that those who are active in the language movement are not interested in political matters and that Irish suffers a severe setback in so far as all political discussion is conducted in the foreign tongue. Now is the time to form such an association. If a Home Rule statute is implemented Irish-speaking members will be needed in the Irish parliament and if Home Rule is not introduced a sustained agitation will be needed, in which we must ensure that the battlecry is not sounded in the foreign tongue. Only those who are prepared to defend the rights of Irishmen against all and sundry and who are Irish-speakers will be admitted to the association.

I will expect word from you at your convenience. I am sending a similar letter to six or seven others. Greetings and best wishes, Yours, Pádraig Mac Piarais.

To Mrs. Mgt. Hutton.

External lectures by prominent persons on literature, the arts and the Gaelic League were a regular feature of Sgoil Éanna from its foundation. They were sometimes illustrated by means of Pearse's "magic lantern".

L. 306/NLI

17.2.1912.   Sgoil Éanna,
                                     Rathfarnham.

A Chara,
    Could you find time to address the members of St. Enda's Branch of the Gaelic League in our Study Hall some Friday evening in the near future? The subject of the address need not be immediately concerned with the work of the Gaelic League – any subject likely to appeal to imagination of young Gaels would do; history, literature, science, travel, antiquities, industries, even politics in the wider sense, would all be admissible. Neither need the address be in Irish, for we masters and the elder boys will see to it that sufficient Irish be heard in the other speeches. If you can come, could you name your subject and the most suitable Friday between this and Easter? If Friday does not suit we could perhaps arrange another evening. Sincerely yours. P. H. Pearse.

To Seán Mac Caoilte.

Seán Mac Caoilte, an active member of the Gaelic League, was employed at Sealy, Bryers and Walkers the publishers and printers where some of the League printing was done. In August 1921 he was appointed Honorary Film Censor by Dublin Corporation. He was a member of the mission sent to the United States by the Provisional Government in March 1922, which also included Piaras Béaslaí, Professor Smiddy of U.C.C. and James O'Mara. He died in October 1922.

18.2.1912.   Sgoil Éanna,
                                    Rathfarnham.

Dear Friend,
     Greetings and best wishes,
Would you be willing to attend a small gathering of Gaels to
discuss the following matter i.e. the possibility of forming an
association in which Irish-speakers can analyse and express their
political sentiments and initiate political action? It appears to me to
be a severe loss to Ireland that those who are active in the language
movement are not interested in political matters and that Irish
suffers a severe setback in so far as all political discussion is
conducted in the foreign tongue. Now is the time to form such an
association. If a Home Rule statute is implemented Irish-speaking
members will be needed in the Irish parliament and if Home Rule
is not introduced a sustained agitation will be needed, in which we
must ensure that the battle cry is not sounded in the foreign tongue.
Only those who are prepared to defend the rights of Irishmen
against all and sundry, and who are Irish-speakers will be admitted
to the association.
     I will expect word from you at your convenience. I am sending a
similar letter to six or seven others. Greetings and best wishes,
Yours, Pádraig Mac Piarais.

To Séan Réamonn. (John Redmond M.P.)

Beginning in the first issue of *An Barr Buadh,* Pearse wrote a series
of open letters to public figures under the pseudonym, Laegh
Mac Riangabhra (Cuchulainn's charioteer). In these letters, he
indicated to the political leaders and League personalities where the
path of duty lay for them if they were willing to serve the national
interest. In style they are hortatory and are frequently spiced with
irony and humour. The series contains one letter written to himself
from the pen of Iubhar Mac Riangabhra – the brother of Laegh.
These letters were collectively titled in *An Barr Buadh* as "Beart
litreach do Chuaidh Amugha" ("A Bundle of Stray Letters"). The
letters are written in a style approximating to that of the original
Fiannaíocht stories as befits the work of Cuchulainn's charioteer!

L. 308/BB/G

16.3.1912.

Greetings and best wishes!
On hearing that you are intending to defend the rights of the Gael against the Gall, I decided to send you these small words of praise and exhortation, that they may raise your spirits and stimulate your courage in the fray.

You were, at one period in your career, the idol of the Gaels. Those of us who opposed you, admitted that you had shown unusual courage on that day when you stood on Parnell's right hand when the baying of savaging hounds was loud in his ears. You were a young man then and you are middle-aged now. The aged and the young do not view courage and spirit in the same light. Youth is daring. Age is apprehensive and fearful. But remember that the deed which Parnell set out to do remains undone and its achievement now rests on you. Remember that you were dear to Parnell and that you were dear to the Irish people because you were dear to him. Remember that Parnell's straight steel sword is in your hand and his noble regal cloak is on your shoulders, and that you are hailed as his successor. Remember that there are Irishmen at your back. Remember that there are Englishmen in front of you. Remember that Irishmen are depending on you. Remember that the English are watching you. Remember that which Parnell detested and avoid it at all costs – the laugh of an Englishman.

Take to yourself the strength of the lion, the courage of the wolf and the cunning of the serpent. Meet aggression with aggression. Meet ingenuity with ingenuity. Be a mature alert guide. Be a torch of valour. Be a man. Be a leader. Be a Parnell. Greetings, Yours, Laegh Mac Riangabhra.

To John Dillon.

L. 309/BB/G

23.3.1912.

Greetings and best wishes.
I am told that since you do not like counsel, it ill behoves me to write to you. It is said, if it be true, that you are convinced that all matters affecting Irishmen should be left to the joint discretion of

John Redmond and yourself. I do not believe that you are so vain. If I did so believe, then I would offer you some proverbs that have been transmitted as traditional wisdom; such as, "Do not reject advice that may be to your advantage", and "Advice in season is preferable to criticism out of season". If I were hostile to you, I would remind you of this proverb – "He who does not accept counsel – let him accept conflict"; but since I count you among my friends and our enemy accosts us, I will say only this much; "Counsel before battle is preferable to twelve counsels after".

I am told that you abhor above all else the advice of a young man. I admit to being young. Mea culpa, mea culpa. But I am not so young that I do not remember the time when you were young. If you were told then that advice from you to elders was not appropriate – what would you say? You would say something that would not bear printing.

I have heard in the annals of the Gael of another man called John Dillon. You knew that man, indeed he was your own noble father. He was one of the leaders of that group known as the Young Irelanders. There was an old man in Ireland then who did not like advice, especially from young people. Daniel O'Connell was his name. Daniel O'Connell rejected the advice of your father and the advice of Young Ireland. If he had accepted that advice in time, Ireland would now have been free for fifty years with twenty million people inhabiting the country. Enough said. Greetings and best wishes. Yours, Laegh Mac Riangabhra.

To Seán T. Ó Ceallaigh.

Having sounded out potential support in mid-February for his new society, Pearse was planning the first meeting in mid-March.

L. 310/NLI/G

28.3.1912.   An Barr Buadh,
                                             12 Temple St.

Dear Friend,
    Greetings and best wishes!
    I am inviting some friends to a small gathering in Moy Rath Hotel, Trinity Street, on Tuesday evening next, 2nd April at 8.0.p.m. The purpose of the meeting is to establish a society the function of which will be to enable Irish speakers to promote the freedom of Ireland.

I hope you can answer the clarion call, With best wishes, Yours
Pádraig Mac Piarais.

To Seán Mac Caoilte.

This letter is not in Pearse's hand, the handwriting is like that of
Desmond Ryan who frequently assisted secretarially. The signature
is Pearse's.

L. 311/PRO/G

28.3.1912.   An Barr Buadh.

Dear Friend,
    Greetings and best wishes!
I am inviting some friends to a small gathering in Moy Rath Hotel,
Trinity Street on Tuesday evening next, 2nd April at 8.0.p.m. The
purpose of the meeting is to establish a society, the sole function of
which will be to enable Irish speakers to promote the freedom of
Ireland. I hope you can answer the clarion call. With best wishes,
Yours Pádraig Mac Piarais.

To William O'Brien.

The grandfather to whom Pearse refers in this letter was his
mother's father, Patrick Brady, one of seven children, five boys and
two girls, of Walter Brady and Margaret O'Connor of Knobber,
Co. Meath.

L. 312/BB/G

30.3.1912.

    Greetings and best wishes,
I wrote to your old friend, John Dillon some time ago. When I was
a very young boy you and John Dillon as young men, were active in
the cause of defending the Irish from the tyranny of the foreigner. I
frequently read your exploits aloud for my grandfather. He himself
when he was young did a little for Ireland. In the year of '48 he was
among the followers of your friend's father. In '67 he was a Fenian.
He hoped that you and your companions would complete the work
which he and his colleague left unfinished. I did not fully under-

stand the story as I was young. I thought that Parnell would be King of Ireland if you succeeded. I thought that Ireland would have her own army and navy. I thought a hundred things that only a child would think. But there was one thing that I never thought – one thing I would not believe, even if an angel from heaven had forecast it. I would not believe from any source, dead or alive, that you and John Dillon would be enemies in the end of your lives. It appeared to me that you were like Jonathan and David or like Roland and Oliver or Cúchulainn and Ferdia, in the extent of your affection, loyalty and attachment. And it seemed to me that, should you come to a stage in your lives when some issue separated you, that you would behave like Cúchulainn and Ferdia, exchanging sweet merry drinks and tasty food after battle and sleeping on the one bed each night till daybreak.

But that is not how things are. Cúchulainn and Ferdia though on different sides showed affection and fondness to one another. You though on the one side, show hostility and animosity to one another.

I do not know what is between you. Nobody seems to know what separates you. I am told that you think that John Dillon is a fool, and I am told that John Dillon thinks you are a lunatic. To my mind neither of you is thinking properly. It appears to me that you both suffer from the same fault i.e. excessive confidence in one's own opinion.

Have your own opinion. Take my advice. If you think John Dillon to be a fool you do not need to call him such in front of the English. Say what you will in Munster. Remain silent in Westminster if you cannot refrain from insulting your colleague.

One other thing. Why do you state that it is not possible to enact the Home Rule Bill during this Parliament? Would it not be more correct to assert that it *must* be enacted. Greetings and best wishes. Yours, Laegh Mac Riangabhra.

To Joseph Devlin.

The Home Rule Rally of the 31st March 1912 brought thousands to O'Connell Street to hear Redmond, Devlin, Eoin Mac Neill and Pearse speak from different platforms and propound different political gospels. Devlin organised the rally.

L. 313/BB/G

5.4.1912.

Greetings and best wishes.

Bravo and congratulations if you were responsible for organising and arranging the rally attended by thousands in Dublin on Sunday last – and I am sure it was. The sign of your hand was apparent on the occasion – the hand of a young person. I like young people. The Irish like young people. The Irish like you. You were the idol of the crowds on Sunday and not John Redmond.

You have a young heart, o young man! Be careful that it does not petrify, with so many venerable colleagues around you. An old man with a youthful heart is a joyful sight but woe to the young man whose heart becomes old.

You spoke in a lively fashion on Sunday. Some of your words, I found distasteful. Will you be loyal to the British crown when Dublin has a Home Rule parliament? I do not think that you will. Reflect on this question.

Sufficient for the day. Greetings and best wishes, Yours, Laegh Mac Riangabhra.

To T. P. O'Connor M.P.

From the general election of 1885, Parnell carried an impressive eighty six members under his leadership back to Westminster; T. P. O'Connor, from the Scotland Division of Liverpool, was the only one of the eighty six, who represented an English constituency, a constituency however with a very significant Irish population. O'Connor who was a close friend of John Dillon's is chided in this letter by Pearse for basing his constitutional position on arguments deriving from economic and trading considerations.

The first paragraph may also contain an innuendo aimed at Tim Healey M.P.

L. 314/BB/G

12.4.1912.

Greetings and best wishes.

I have never heard you referred to by any other name except "T.P.". I do not know your first name. But I suppose that you were christened "Tadhg" or Timothy, since that name is common amongst politicians and it seems to suit them if we are to judge from Irish folklore. Recall the evidence from the proverb "Tadhg an Dá Thaobh" ("Tim of the Two sides"). If I am wrong in my supposition, and your first name be Thomas or Terence or Tomaltach or Tormad, please forgive me my lack of information.

Speaking in London lately, you said that the Irish did not wish to separate from England. You said also that the Irish would not ever do so. Perhaps you are right. Perhaps you understand the mind of the Irish people better than I do. But be that as it may. The reason you put forward as the basis of your statement was; *as long as the Irish have pigs to sell and the British wish to buy them that it would not be to the advantage of Ireland to separate from Britain.*

I do not wish to anger you nor do I wish to speak rudely to you. But permit one to say directly to you that such sentiments are nothing but wanton and silly nonsense. It were equally valid for me to assert that as long as England wants to buy the wine which France wants to sell, then the two countries should be united or as long as Russia wishes to sell the wheat which England desires to buy then, Russia and England should be united under the same crown.

I have often heard something or other described as likely to make the cats laugh. Your speech would cause the pigs to laugh. Greetings and best wishes. Laegh Mac Riangabhra.

To A Chara (Mrs. Mgt. Hutton?).

L. 315/P.Ms.

20.4.1912.   Sgoil Éanna,
                                    Rathfarnham.

A Chara,
Could you possibly find time to give our boys a lecture or rather talk some Friday evening during the Easter-midsummer term?

The lecture need not necessarily be in Irish or on an Irish subject. The meetings are held at 8.30 p.m. each Friday. If you can come please indicate what Friday would suit you – or perhaps better say what Fridays would not, as others to whom I am writing might fix on the same Friday as you. And mention the subject too. With kind regards, Sincerely yours. P. H. Pearse.

To T. P. O'Connor M.P.

L.(tel.) 316/BB/G

20.4.1912.

I see that you have been nominated as Speaker of the House of Commons in Ireland under the new statute.
Do you know Irish? Yours, Laegh Mac Riangabhra.

To Tim Healy M.P.

L. 317/BB/G

27.4.1912.

Greetings and best wishes,
Those words you spoke in London a week ago would surprise me if they had come from anybody else but you. Coming from you they did not surprise me. You were always a cause of vexation and anguish to whatever company you were in. You accepted the draft bill but did not admit that it constituted a victory for Ireland. You asserted and boasted that the Irish were vanquished. You said that the Bill would not repeal the Act of Union (which was true). You said further that there was no cure for that issue and so much the better. I fear, that you said that, in order to show your venomous disposition towards your fellow Irishmen.
I wish to say to you that you are wrong. A gap is opening before Irishmen. You are not the man to close the gap! Yours, Laegh Mac Riangabhra.

To Douglas Hyde.

L. 318/BB/G

4.5.1912.

Greetings and best wishes,
I have been intending to write to you for a long time. I wrote some

letters lately to some prominent Irish people and not one of them replied. I presume that they are too busy to pay attention to people like me. Or perhaps it is possible that the letters went astray. I addressed them in Irish and it is usual with the postal authorities to delay any letters which are addressed in Irish. If this letter reaches you I know that you will reply for from your noble lineage you are accustomed to be gentle with the destitute and to listen to the supplication of even the most lowly. Such humility was always a royal trait among the Irish no matter how sternly the enemy was treated.

There is no need for me to tease and exhort you as was necessary when writing to those others to whom I referred. You never faltered in any battle no matter how intense. If you had, your own followers would have exhorted you. That is one virtue of the many virtues possessed especially by Gaelic Leaguers. The lowest member of the League enjoys freedom of speech. They have confidence in you but they do not feel that they have to say "Amen" everytime you speak. They are your followers but not your clerks. Servants and clerks are what is desired by other prominent Irishmen, as far as I can observe. I believe that you prefer friends and followers rather than servants and clerks.

Eoin Mac Neill said, a short time ago, that there was too much of what the English call *red tape* associated with the League. He is quite right. Moreover, I think that the League leadership made a major mistake from the beginning. Seeking to exhort and persuade the Irish people, they instituted a structural model of the political parties of their time in Ireland and proceeded to call it the Gaelic League. The Irish have experienced this phenomenon for a hundred years and do not understand an alternative. But despite the efficiency of a large organisation and its associated branches, area committees, organisers and regulations to promote a political purpose, I do not think that it is the most suitable to prosecute the aims of the Gaelic League. What is the object of the Gaelic League? It is to enable the Irish people to become Irish speaking. Which is the more effective to that end, a large organisation with branches, committees, motions and regulations, expending its energies making and discussing rules or small groups travelling throughout the country, one group making music, another group staging new plays, another group exhorting the Irish against the foreigner and so on and all this work being done through Irish. While they talk little about Irish, you understand, they speak nothing else but Irish.

When the Gaelic League was founded, those who adhered to it should have left the city behind and headed for the rural areas.

263

They should have gone amongst the people who spoke Irish and lived there with them. Each of them would have chosen an enterprise which would both satisfy his needs and ensure a livelihood. The poets, performers and artists should take to the roads, going from house to house, reciting and performing for the people receiving hospitality as their reward. Another group should come together who would go around to Gaeltachtai producing new plays in Irish. Another group should accompany them to highlight and lament the oppression of the Irish and to rouse the courage of the people in their struggle against the foreigner. If we undertook these and other similar activities. I fear that some of us might be poorer than we are, and some of us suffering from hunger and destitution, *but we would have saved the Irish Language.* And was that not our objective?

I fear that it is too late to undertake all that now. But some items could be attempted. That company of travelling players, could be organised and sent to the Gaeltacht. There is no other single deed which would benefit the language more. It would do more to spread the speaking of the language in one year than has been achieved by the branches and organisers of the League in twenty years.

This letter is too long. I must cease. Greetings and best wishes, Yours, Laegh Mac Riangabhra.

To P. Mac Piarais.

This open letter written by Pearse to himself serves an interesting double purpose of self-analysis and public advertisement that certain of his activities were to be abandoned in conjunction with the demise of *An Barr Buadh* in May 1912. The "new society without a name" was *Cumann na Saoirse* founded in February/ March of the same year. The fables which Pearse had already written were those which appeared in *An Barr Buadh* concerning the language and political questions; five of these fables were later published in the volume of his Collected Works, titled *Sgríbhinní.*

L. 319/BB/G

11.5.1912.

Greetings and best wishes!

I notice that my brother i.e. Laegh Mac Riangabhra, has been writing letters to the leaders and personalities of Ireland for some time. I notice that some of those letters went astray and were published in *An Barr Buadh*. I do not know why anyone should wish to print anything written by him for he never had any sense and never will. I am afraid that he is a friend of yours and that you compelled the player of the Trumpet of Victory (editor of *An Barr Buadh*) to print those letters, as I am told that he is under your control. Please understand that I am the only member of the Riangabhra clan whose thoughts are wise and whose utterances are eloquent. My letters are worthy of publication but there is little danger of this letter appearing in *An Barr Buadh*. It matters little to me.

I am undecided as to whether I like you or not. I wonder does anyone like you. I do know that many dislike you. I never heard anyone ever say "I like Pearse". I am told that you are held in great affection by the boys of Sgoil Éanna. I am informed that a lady told another lady that a third lady had told her that Tomás Mac Domhnaill had told somebody that he liked you. Perhaps that story is true – perhaps it is not. Tomás Mac Domhnaill is a strange person.

Pearse, you are a reserved person! You do not associate with Gaels. You shun their company. On the occasions when you join them, a black cloud accompanies you which as it were settles over them. Those who were talkative before your arrival grow silent and those who were merry become gloomy. I wonder if it is the English blood in you which is responsible for that?

You have the gift of eloquence. You have the power to move and arouse audiences when you speak publicly. You can make them cry or laugh as you wish. I imagine that there are two Pearses, one a cheerless, wintry person and the other pleasant, calm and serene. The calm serene person is seen all too seldom. On public platforms and in Sgoil Éanna he is most often seen. The dull cheerless person is frequently to be seen. He is not a pleasant type. I do not like him. I grow chill when I see him. The funny aspect of this is that I am not sure which is the real Pearse, the gloomy or the bright one.

You accomplished a good deed in founding Sgoil Éanna and another equally good deed in establishing Sgoil Íde. Take my advice; devote your attention to Sgoil Éanna and to Sgoil Íde and disregard political affairs. You have more than sufficient cares to occupy you. Cast from you the Trumpet of Victory (*An Barr Buadh*) shoot the trumpeter, disband that new society without a name and do well that which you set out to do four years ago. The sandpiper has never succeeded in attending on two strands and you are attempting to attend on four strands. You will not succeed.

One more thing. I beseech you not to write any more fables. Greetings and best wishes. Yours, Iubhar Mac Riangabhra.

To Arthur Griffith.

In this candid letter to Griffith, Pearse offers a rather frank analysis of the character traits and political leadership of the founder of Sinn Féin. The organisation which Griffith founded in 1905 under the name "Sinn Féin" ("Ourselves") had espoused constitutional separation from the United Kingdom; with the launching of the paper *Sinn Féin* in 1906, edited by Griffith, the organisation and its policy of a "Dual Monarchy" received widespread support. Due to the factors which Pearse outlines in this letter, support for Griffith and Sinn Féin declined rapidly by the time Pearse wrote this letter.

Griffith was not the first to use the slogan "Sinn Féin"; in Oldcastle, Co. Meath, on St. Patrick's Day 1902, a four page Irish-Ireland paper was launched, edited by P. J. Bartley of Mountnugent, entitled *Sinn Féin – The Oldcastle Monthly Review*, and published by the *Anglo-Celt* of Cavan. The Oldcastle paper was launched following a public lecture in the Gilson School, Oldcastle by Pearse on "The Gaelic League and its work". Griffith, as editor of the *United Irishman,* reviewed the first number of *Sinn Féin* in the edition of 14th June 1902.

In 1913, Griffith mounted a sustained attack on the Gaelic League in the pages of *Sinn Féin*; it is possible that he feared the potential threat to Sinn Féin contained in the accelerated politicalisation of the League. His allegations drew a sharp response from Douglas Hyde who expressed his anger in uncharacteristic terms; "I do not know if you understand Irish, but there is an old saying which runs:

> 'Do ghnó féin, déan a dhuine
> Ná bac mo ghnó-sa, nó mise'.

Hyde continued
"If your policy is to prevail, then I think I foresee clearly the discredit and defeat of the Gaelic League. Its defeat and discredit does not mean much to you".

L. 320/BB/G

18.5.1912.

Greetings and Best Wishes!
I notice that Sinn Féin is bestirring itself once more. It was about time. You almost killed your child, your own creation. The last signs of life were quickly deserting it. I had very little affection ever for that same child, but I would not like to witness its destruction at

266

the hand of its father. Give it care and attention in the future and perhaps it may live.

You were too hard, too dour and too obstinate. You were too narrow-minded and too headstrong. You did not have sufficient confidence in your friends and you had an excess of confidence in yourself. You had an undue respect for your own opinion. You displayed suspicion of people who were as loyal as you. You would not endorse any course of action except that proposed by yourself. You avoided action. You preferred to show to the world that somebody else erred in doing a particular deed than to do the right thing yourself. You would not initiate any action, but if another proposed to do something you would prove to him that it was not feasible.

There was no future in store for a society governed by the kind of leadership you displayed. Nobody will remain in membership of a society in which he is not offered freedom of speech. Your friends were deserting you one by one and all would have eventually done so, had you continued as you were.

I am sure that you understand all that by now; it is appropriate that you should. I notice a new urgency about you and your followers of late; such a development is long overdue. You have talents which no other Irishman possesses. It would be a great pity if those talents should be wasted because others find it impossible to work under your leadership.

Sufficient for the moment. Greetings and best wishes, Yours, Laegh Mac Riangabhra.

To Thomas Kettle.

Thomas Kettle (1880–1916), son of Andrew J. Kettle one of the founding members of the Land League, was a contemporary of Pearse who displays in this letter a warm regard for his fellow poet and philosopher. Kettle was called to the Bar in 1905 and in 1908 was appointed to the first Chair of National Economics in University College, Dublin. He was an M.P. for East Tyrone from 1906–1910. In the Irish Volunteers, which he joined on their formation, he gave his allegiance to Redmond and having accepted a commission in the Dublin Fusiliers, actively recruited Irishmen to fight in the British Forces in the Great War. He was killed at Givenchy during the battle of the Somme in September 1916. In 1910 he had published *The Day's Burden,* a collection of essays on politics and literature; in the introduction, he had written:

267

'My only programme for Ireland consists, in equal parts, of Home Rule and the Ten Commandments. My only counsel to Ireland is, that in order to become deeply Irish, she must become European.'

In his letter, Pearse refers by implication to the above quotation; his reference to "the sweet words of the ladies" could possibly refer to Kettle's wife, Mary Sheehy and to her two sisters, Mrs. Sheehy Skeffington and Mrs. Cruise O'Brien who could be taken to support the view that Ireland had a right to the allegiance of Irishmen prior to that of "the small nations" of Europe.

L. 321/BB/G

25.5.1912.

Greetings and Best Wishes!
I was always extremely interested in you from the time long ago when you were a student. I always thought that you showed great promise especially from the occasion on which you refused to bend your knee before the English crown. But woe is me, the world's fancies have captivated you; you have honoured and idolised the false gods of the Gentiles and now you tell us that you have little confidence in the human race.

Beware and be careful O Son of a brave father! If it were here on the natural soil of your native land, you had spent the period in which you reached maturity and heights of valour, you would be a different man now. You would have trust and confidence in your brothers and sisters as the most obscure of us here display. You would understand and sympathise with the slogan "To be European, be Irish and to be Irish, speak Irish". You would realise also that many of the new aspects of modern Europe were old features of ancient Ireland.

But, God be praised, you are not too old yet. There is a solemn obligation which I charge you to meet; that you would so inform, train and educate your students, so inspire and motivate them, that they would utilise their knowledge and apply their skills for the benefit and welfare of our own people, to the glory of God and the honour of Ireland.

Forgive me if, in what I say to you, there appears to be any word of venom. I have never lost the affection and regard which I had for you and the confidence I placed in you has not been diminished. And my reason for both affection and confidence stems from the high regard in which I always held your faithful father.

Obviously you did not like the criticism of those who differed from you when you opted to follow John Redmond rather than listen to the sweet words of the ladies. Let it be; the Nation is more honourable than any select group of its people. Greetings and best wishes. Seanchán Torpéist.

To Proinsias Mac Ionraic.

In the course of this letter of acknowledgement to Mac Ionraic, whose address was at 5 Windsor Villas, Fairview, Dublin, Pearse replies in a humourous fashion to a query from Mac Ionraic about *An Barr Buadh*. In the original Irish version of this letter, Pearse uses the abbreviation d.Luain for Dé Luain.

L. 322/NLI/G

31.5.1912.

Dear Friend,
  Greetings and good health.
I am very grateful for your contribution to Sgoil Éanna; please accept my sincere gratitude.
  I enclose a form which I would appreciate if you would fill and return immediately as the directors of the School meet on Monday to distribute the shares.
  Unfortunately the poor Trumpet of Victory (*An Barr Buadh*) will not be played again for some time! Greetings and best wishes, Yours, Pádraig Mac Piarais.

To Miss M. Maguire.

Miss Mary Maguire, a close friend of Thomas Mac Donagh was a teacher in Sgoil Íde 1911–1912 and later married Pádraig Colum the poet. It is probable that the monetary matters discussed in this letter relate to her teacher's salary. She contributed her recollections of Pearse the Educationalist to *The Irish Rebellion of 1916 and its Martyrs*, published in New York in 1916 and edited by Maurice Joy.
  This letter was published in Comhar 11/1975, with an accompanying article in which it is claimed that Miss Maguire kept students of Sgoil Íde as boarders and that Pearse owed her money in that context.

7.6.1912. Sgoil Éanna.

A Chara,

I am sorry to say that there is not a single penny in the treasury of St. Ita's at present and I daren't draw on the all too scanty revenue of St. Enda's. There are fairly large sums due to St. Ita's but it is very hard to get them in. As soon as anything is set free, you shall have it. At all costs we must keep the food bills paid each week till the girls go home. Sincerely, P. H. Pearse.

To Mrs. Bloomer.

Despite the fact that the schools in their operation for the year 1911/12 returned a net profit, the pressure from creditors grew steadily towards the end of the school year. This pressure came mainly from the food suppliers mentioned in the first paragraph. Mr. Alex Wilson was assisting Pearse in unravelling the financial affairs of the schools and it was he who drew up the balance sheets for 1911/12 which show a surplus of £150 in revenue over expenditure. The scheme which Wilson worked out involved the establishment of the Limited Company and the moratorium by creditors on further demands for the year to July 1913.

13.6.1912. Sgoil Éanna,
Rathfarnham.

A Chara,

The financial affairs of St. Ita's have reached a desperate stage. I have not been able to pay Magees for the past three weeks. Eastman, Lucan Dairy, Ferguson, O'Dwyer, and the landlord are exercising constant pressure. Worst of all, Bolands served a writ on me yesterday for the amount of their a/c – some £37 I think. This is very serious, as if it is not paid in ten days they can mark judgement which means that we shall be in the "black list" and that the credit of St. Enda's and St. Ita's is gone. Indeed it will be a signal for everyone to come down upon us. I see absolutely nothing that we can do except, if you are willing to raise a joint loan on both our names in the Munster and Leinster Bank and pay off the really pressing things. I would not propose this if I saw any other way out of it.

Mr. Wilson is at work on a scheme which if it succeed, may permanently right us. In connection with this he wants a fairly accurate statement of our liabilities and assets to this date. I enclose a list of the Liabilities of St. Ita's last October. Could you note on it how far these have changed since then? I have no note of the payments made before I took over the financial side or of those made by you since. I want also an accurate account of the income and expenditure since January 1st. I have all except a few payments received by you, the payments made by you, and the details of the p.c. All this is wanted at once. We must do our best to facilitate this scheme of Mr. Wilson's as nothing else will save us. Yours, P. H. Pearse.

To Alex. Wilson.

With this letter to Wilson, Pearse enclosed various documents outlining the financial position of the school and also an initialled summary statement by Pearse on the achievements of Sgoil Éanna from 1908–1912.

The financial documents were i) an initialled memo outlining the background to the accounts ii) a statement of the revenue and expediture of St. Enda's for the year 1911/12 iii) a statement of the liabilities of St. Enda's iv) a statement of the liabilities of St. Ita's.

The memo on the accounts and the summary statement by Pearse on the school's achievements are inserted here with this letter; the latter is similar in parts to the Prospectus issued in 1910 and was possibly used as an inclusion in the printed Prospectus issued in 1912 for the establishment of the limited company, Sgoil Éanna Ltd.

As is implied in Pearse's earlier letter to Mrs. Bloomer of June 13th it was not possible to assemble a complete statement of revenue and expenditure for St. Ita's for 1911/12 as there was seemingly no systematic accounting method employed. Miss Gavan Duffy's proposal to lease the Cullenswood property and operate the school seems to have been rejected. She later founded a similar school, Sgoil Bhríde, which was located on Earlsfort Terrace and which now is in new premises standing appropriately in the garden of Cullenswood House.

271

23.6.1912.   Sgoil Éanna,
                                    Rathfarnham.

Dear Mr. Wilson,
   During the examinations (which are not over until tomorrow) I found the utmost difficulty in getting time to work at these accounts and statements. I have been working at them for six hours to-day (Sunday) and have finished them just in time for post. The statement as to aims etc., is not done as well as I should have liked, but there was no time to do better. I must leave all the rest to you.

   The statement of revenue is more favourable than we thought. I had omitted one whose a/c had not been opened in ledger, and also forgotten to charge up medicine against the boys though it was included on the other side. We now come out £149 to the good, which is fairly encouraging.

   I hope in God that this effort of yours will be successful. It looks like our last hope – and yet we have turned the corner. It would be a tragedy if we were to go down now. Sincerely and gratefully, P. H. Pearse.

Memo with letter of 23.6.1912.

I am enclosing

(1) Short statement of aims of St. Enda's and summary of the work already accomplished;
(2) statement of revenue and expenditure for the year 1911–12 (July 1st to June 30th) just complete;
(3) statement of the liabilities of St. Enda's;
(4) statement of the liabilities of St. Ita's.

Re (2), the statement of the revenue and expenditure of St. Enda's is prepared from my books and accounts, though the accounts have not yet been audited (the year still having a few days to run). It will be seen that St. Enda's is now a paying concern, and that the only cause for anxiety is the existence of a large debt, due chiefly to our large expenditure (between £5000 and £6000) on building and equipment. If a fund could be raised to pay off the debt, so far as it need be paid off, it would leave me free to develop the school internally and at the same time to organise a permanent endowment in the shape of shares in Sgoil Éanna Ltd. I propose to devote the summer to this latter task, and, judging from my experience in

Co. Wexford, have every prospect of collecting in time sufficient money to float the College properly. An Athletic Tournament and a series of Aeridheachta in aid of the College are also being organised.

No statement of the revenue and expenditure of St. Ita's is at present available, but Miss Gavan Duffy has offered to relieve the Directors of all anxiety on the score of St. Ita's. Her proposal is to lease St. Ita's as a going concern at £180 a year for a term of years. She (Miss Duffy) to have sole financial responsibility and bear all loss, if any, as long as the agreement lasts. She will pay down two years' rent (£360) in advance, which with the assets outstanding will enable the Directors to clear off all the pressing liabilities of St. Ita's. Thus, if our main scheme re St. Enda's be carried through the future of St. Ita's is assured.

In addition to our interest in the buildings, lands, etc., and the furniture and equipment, the outstanding assets of St. Enda's are £250 due by pupils; £82 due for rent; £250 estimated for year's Intermediate and Department grants. About £75 is due to St. Ita's by pupils.

Now that the future of St. Ita's is secured by Miss Gavan Duffy and that St. Enda's is actually paying its way, nothing is needed but a sum of money, whether by way of endowment or of loan for a period of years, sufficient to meet the outstanding obligations from the early years, in order to ensure the permanent success of the tremendously important work for Irish education undertaken by the two Colleges.

I enclose further:

(5) list of people who have subscribed towards St. Enda's and who are willing to accept shares in the Co. in exchange for their subscriptions; and (6) list of shareholders in the Co., including many who had already subscribed.

All these have freely risked their money without any promise of a dividend. P. H. P.

Memo with letter of 23.6.1912.

St. Enda's College was founded by me at Cullenswood House, Rathmines, in September 1908 with the object of providing for Irish boys a secondary education Irish in complexion, bilingual in method, and of a high modern type generally. We set before ourselves from the outset the ideal of producing good men rather than learned men, but of men truly learned rather than persons

273

merely qualified to pass examinations. And as our definition of a "good" man as applied to an Irishman, included the being a good Irishman, and of "learning" as applied to an Irishman included Irish learning as its very basis and fundament, it followed that our school should be more Irish than any that had been known or dreamt of since the Flight of the Earls. We were not aggressively "patriotic" or "nationalist", but rather took Ireland for granted; spoke Irish as far as possible, but taught English and other modern languages and literature as well; adopted Irish games as our school games but did not take up an intolerant attitude to non-Irish games; did not neglect foreign history but dealt with it from an Irish point of view. We found in the language and history of Ireland an appeal of extraordinary force, addressing itself to the finest and noblest part of a boy's nature and helping to bring out all that was manliest and strongest in him. While we gave classical learning an important part in the curriculum, we sought to bring the school life as far as possible into touch with the actual and the practical, and from the beginning gardening, elementary physics and chemistry have been taught.

From the outset we met with gratifying success. Many of the leaders of the Gaelic League and other prominent Irishmen sent us their sons. At the end of the first year we had 19 boarders; at the end of the second 39; at the end of the third 54; at present, at the end of the fourth 60. In addition we have some day-boys – but we are anxious that the school should be as far as possible a boarding school, and the tendency of our day-boys is to become boarders. At the end of the second year the school had grown so large that we found it necessary to leave Cullenswood House, and to take as a permanent and worthy home a beautiful place, 50 acres in extent, a mile beyond Rathfarnham. Here we have the finest surroundings of any school in Ireland. Apart from considerations of space, our plans for nature-study and physical training could not be properly carried out at Cullenswood, nor was it desirable that a boys' boarding school be so near the city. At Cullenswood however, we founded St. Ita's College, a school on precisely similar lines for girls, and during the past two years it has been repeating St. Enda's successes on a somewhat smaller scale.

As to the actual achievements of St. Enda's (1) all our boys are now Irish speakers, many of them being for practical purposes as good masters of the language as native speakers of a similar age; (2) they have a spirit of generous and informed patriotism unlike and finer than anything of the kind that has been known in Ireland in our time; (3) they are the best athletes in Ireland; (4) in actual learning, more especially in what may be called general culture and information as to affairs, they are equal, if not superior to, the students of any of the unilingual Colleges; and (5) we have been successful even beyond our hopes in fostering truth, self reliance, clean living, and in a word all the manlier virtues.

Among our distinctions I may mention:

1. First Classical Scholarship, National University.
2. First Kildare Co. Council Scholarship,   do.
3. Exhibition in Modern Literature, Intermediate.
4. Special Prize in Science Course,   do.
5. Composition Prize in Irish,   do.
6. Eleven Matriculations, National University.
7. Gold Medal, Feis Ceoil.
8. Silver medal,   do.
9. Dublin School Championship and cup, Hurling.
10.   do.   do.   do.   do,   Football.

(We are leading for Leinster Championship 1912).

A pupil of ours won the Taylor Memorial Art Scholarship this year. Thus we more than held our own in public competitions with other schools and colleges, while doing whole phases of work for which there is no parallel in any other school or college in Ireland.

After four years I am more than ever convinced of the importance of the work we have taken in hand, and have satisfied myself of the absolute feasibility of regenerating Ireland nationally and socially, as well as of saving the Irish language, through the medium of the schools and colleges of the country. P. H. P.

To George Berkeley.

This letter to Berkeley and the following letter to Dr. Walsh reveal the urgency of his financial situation. Despite the crisis however, both letters display a quiet confidence in the worthiness of the schools and a pride in the achievements to date, especially "the triumphant success of St. Enda's". The directors of the company were obviously reluctant to go ahead with the scheme to raise a further £2,000 in addition to Alex Wilson's generous surety offer for £1,000. The resulting fall-back strategy involved the voluntary liquidation of the company and Pearse buying back the properties from the Liquidator, and getting the creditors to accept an interim payment of 2/- in the pound on condition that they would not press for further payment before 31 August 1913. All of this was achieved in July and August and enabled Pearse by early September to re-open Sgoil Éanna; Sgoil Íde failed to open – a victim of

275

the financial crisis and perhaps of tension between Miss L. Gavan Duffy and Mrs. Bloomer.

L. 326/NLI

15.7.1912.   Sgoil Éanna,
                                              Rathfarnham.

A Chara,

You have shown such interest in St. Enda's that I feel justified in placing before you the following facts as to its present position in the hope that you may be able to join with some others in the scheme outlined;

(1)   St. Enda's is now paying its way, the accounts for the school year just closed showing a profit of nearly £150 on the year's working.

(2)   St. Ita's is not yet paying its way, but its future has been guaranteed by Miss Gavan Duffy who has agreed to lease it as a going concern from us and to be responsible for its financing for the next four or five years at least.

(3)   On the two schools there is a debt of some £3,000 representing about half of the total capital expenditure (for building equipment etc.), the rest having been paid off. A number of the creditors to whom this sum is due are now pressing for payment, and their claims are so urgent that a serious situation has arisen. My fellow-directors regard the situation so seriously that they have come to the opinion that unless we can raise £3,000 immediately we cannot go on. They are unwilling to face the future with this burden of debt, especially as the Creditors have become so claimant. They and I therefore are endeavouring to raise £3,000 in order that St. Enda's and St. Ita's may be saved. In view of the facts (1) that St. Enda's has been so triumphant a success educationally and morally, (2) that it is actually paying its way, and (3) that the future of St. Ita's which has been the main source of anxiety, is secured by Miss Gavan Duffy, it would be infinitely tragic if anything were to befall us now, – it would perhaps be the most disastrous blow that the whole Irish movement could sustain.

One man, Mr. Wilson of Belfast, is willing to raise £1,000 if others can be got to provide the rest. It is not necessary that anyone should actually pay down money, Mr. Wilson's idea is rather that what is required should be raised in a Bank on the security of names, and he is willing to give his own name for £1,000 provided others step forward to guarantee the rest. This generous offer of his reduces the sum required to £2,000, and we are hopeful that Irish Ireland will not allow so great a thing as St. Enda's to perish for want of so comparatively small a sum. Can you help? either by doing something yourself, e.g. by becoming one of the guarantors, or by introducing me to someone likely to do so; administration of this (as of all the financial affairs of St. Enda's since April last) will be in the hands of the Board of five Directors – Messrs Wilson, Smithwick, Barrett, Dolan and myself. Sincerely yours. P. H. Pearse.

To Dr. W. J. Walsh.

There is a certain irony in Pearse seeking financial support from Dr. Walsh from funds at his disposal for a Catholic lay school; there were many small religious secondary schools in the Dublin Archdiocese which would have quickly exhausted the financial capacity of such funds, whose authorities would resent diocesan money being devoted to an institution which they would regard as a competitor.

The £100 in the sentence in paragraph 2 which reads: "£100 would be quite sufficient in addition to Mr. Wilson's £1,000" should read £1.000. On the edge of the page is inscribed perhaps in Dr. Walsh's hand: "£100 or £1,000"? It is clear from the next sentence that Pearse had the larger sum in mind.

It does seem from the last sentence that Pearse regarded his educational work as a central activity – the work to which he had devoted his life and his resources.

L. 327/DDA

30.7.1912.   Sgoil Éanna,
                                              Rathfarnham.

My dear Lord Archbishop,
    Although it is not clear to me in what direction you could act, still I feel that I ought to make known to Your Grace the facts of a crisis which has arisen in the affairs of St. Enda's and St. Ita's Colleges. They are as follows:
(1)   St. Enda's is now paying its way, the working of the year just closed showing a credit balance of just £150.
(2)   There has been a serious loss on St. Ita's, but the future of St. Ita's has been guaranted by Miss Gavan Duffy who has offered to lease it from us as a going concern and to run and finance it for the next few years. We are confident that we will make a success of it.
(3)   The two places are burdened by a debt of £3,000, part of it

overdue and the creditors pressing for payment. So acute has the crisis become that our Directors have come to the conclusion that we must close both schools unless we can immediately get command of as much money as would clear the liability or at any rate the pressing part of it. We all feel that the abandoning of St. Enda's and St. Ita's would be a national calamity, and a terrible set-back to the whole Irish movement; and it would be especially tragic occurring just at the moment when St. Enda's has shown itself a paying concern and the future of St. Ita's has been secured by the generous offer of Miss Gavan Duffy.

One of our Directors, Mr. Wilson, has offered to provide £1,000 if we can get any person or persons to provide or guarantee in a bank the remainder. £100 would be quite sufficient in addition to Mr. Wilson's £1,000. The position is that unless we get this second £1,000 (and so far no one has come forward) we cannot avail of Mr. Wilson's offer and must close our doors.

I should add that we have every prospect of raising money during the coming year, only it will not be available in time to avert the present crisis. An athletic tournament, a body of donors of £20 each, and a lecture tour in America are in course of organisation. All this will take time and we have literally only a few days before us. Hence the necessity of getting command *now* of a sum which would avert the crisis, and which could be repaid later out of the proceeds of our various schemes.

I do not know whether Your Grace has at your disposal funds which would enable you to come to the assistance of a Catholic lay school, but I have thought it my duty at least to lay the facts before you, for it would be a matter of reproach to me later if I were to neglect any possible chance of securing friendly succour in the crisis which threatens the work to which I have devoted my life and resources. I am, my dear Lord Archbishop, Yours sincerely and respectfully, P. H. Pearse.

To Mrs. Bloomer.

It would appear that Mrs. Bloomer had resigned her position in Sgoil Íde some time prior to the date of this letter; it is possible that the proposals from Miss Gavan Duffy to undertake the management of Sgoil Íde precipitated Mrs. Bloomer's resignation.

It seems from two references in this letter and the very explicit statement in the last sentence that Mrs. Bloomer had offered to come to Pearse's aid in the manner he requested of her in his letter

278

of 13th June by securing a joint loan from the Munster and Leinster Bank in both their names. The reference to "last May" seems to have been an error by Pearse – it should have been June. There is no indication that she and Pearse secured the joint loan.

L. 328/NLI

1.8.1912.   Sgoil Éanna,
                                  Rathfarnham.

A Chara,

I am sorry to hear that misleading reports are in circulation as to the severance of your connection with St. Ita's. Of course you left it voluntarily. I recollect your telling me verbally of your intention to resign and then you wrote a letter in somewhat similar terms to the Directors; finally you wrote to the Directors formally resigning on the ground (though I do not remember your exact words) that you saw it was impossible for you to remain unless you were prepared to run further risk of financial loss which, in view of the large sum you already stood in danger of losing, you were not (and could not be expected to be), prepared to do.

I think the whole matter may be put as follows without injustice to anyone concerned. St. Ita's was in imminent danger. Both you and Miss Duffy were anxious to save it. Miss Duffy was in a position to make an offer which seemed likely to save it, while you, who had already advanced large sums to the school, were not.

The pleasant feature in the whole business is the loyalty of all parties to St. Ita's and their devotion to its interests. It is a great pity that there should be misunderstanding between people who share so great a devotion to an institution. For my part, I owe much to you and to the staff of St. Ita's. If I have done nothing else I have at least gained the co-operation of friends, most of them strangers to me four years ago, who have shown themselves willing to risk and to suffer much for our common idea. I am grateful to Miss Duffy for the offer which I hope (though of this I am not quite certain yet) will enable us to save St. Ita's; and need I say that I am grateful to you for all you have risked in its interests, and especially for coming forward last May at a moment when, without your help, we might have had to close our doors in the middle of a session. Believe me, Dear Mrs. Bloomer, Yours sincerely, P. H. Pearse.

To Mr. Maurice W. D. O'Connell.

This letter was sent with the accompanying circular of the same date, calling the extraordinary general meeting of the limited company at which a liquidator was appointed and the company was wound up. An identical letter and circular was sent to E. Ó. Muirgheasa also dated 23.8.1912.

L. 329/NLI

23.8.1912.   St. Enda's College,
                                                    Rathfarnham.

A Chara,
    With regard to a letter which you will have received from me as Acting Secretary of Sgoil Éanna Ltd., a word of explanation is due you. The Directors of the Limited Co. which I called into existence some months ago have decided to recommend the voluntary liquidation of the Company, as they are unwilling to undertake the responsibility of reopening St. Enda's. It remains therefore for me, as the only chance of securing the future of the great work for Irish education which we have attempted, to re-acquire the College by buying it in from the liquidator, in which event it will become my absolute property again. I am advised that the liquidator cannot sell to me at less than £600. A friend has generously offered to provide £300, and if I am able to raise £400 (£100 being required for expenses over and above the £600) I shall be able to re-purchase St. Enda's and continue as before. The money must be provided by *Saturday 31st inst.* As I am sure that you will be anxious that St. Enda's should go on, I am asking you to help me in this effort by subscribing towards the required £400 such a sum, large or small, as you are able to afford. If I can succeed in this, St. Enda's will re-open as usual on 9th September. Yours sincerely, P. H. Pearse.

Sgoil Éanna Limited

Notice is hereby given that an extraordinary general meeting of this Company will be held at the Registered Office, St. Enda's College, Rathfarnham, Co. Dublin, on Monday, the 2nd day of September, 1912, at 3 p.m. for the purpose of submitting to the Company, and, if it is thought proper, passing the following resolutions:—
(1) That the Company be wound up voluntarily, it having been proved to the satisfaction of the Company that it cannot, by

reason of its liabilities, continue its business, and that it is advisable to wind up the same.

(2) That Mr. D. O'Connor (D. O'Connor & Co.) Chartered Accountant, of 13 Westmorland Street, Dublin, be, and is hereby appointed Liquidator.

Dated this 23rd day of August 1912. By order of the Directors. Patrick H. Pearse. Acting Secretary.

To Seán T. Ó Ceallaigh.

This letter while essentially carrying the same supplicatory message as those of the previous day, has some additional sentences which stress the national dimension to the work of Sgoil Éanna. The letter to Alex Wilson of the 26th August is identical with this letter.

L. 330/NLI

24.8.1912.   St. Enda's College,
                                          Rathfarnham.

A Chara,

I beg your assistance in a crisis which threatens the continuance of St. Enda's College.

The Directors of the Limited Co. which I called into existence some months ago have decided to recommend the voluntary liquidation of the company, as they are unwilling to undertake the responsibility of re-opening St. Enda's. It remains therefore for me, as the only chance of securing the future of the great work for Irish education which we have attempted, to re-acquire the College by buying it in from the liquidator, in which event it will become my absolute property again. I am advised that the liquidator cannot sell to me at less than £600. A friend has generously offered to provide £300, and if I am able to raise £400 (£100 being required for expenses over and above the £600) I shall be able to re-purchase St. Enda's and continue it as before. The money must be provided by Saturday 31st. inst.

As I am sure that you will be anxious that St. Enda's should go on, I am asking you to help me in this effort by subscribing towards the required £400 such a sum, large or small, as you are able to afford. If I can succeed in this, St. Enda's will re-open as usual on 9th Sept.

It would be a national calamity if the work of St. Enda's were to cease, and a tragedy beyond telling if we were prevented from

281

reaping the fruit of what we have sown during the past four years in capital expenditure and in toil. Yours sincerely. P. H. Pearse.

To Mr. Alex Wilson.

L. 331/NLI

26.8.1912.   St Enda's College,
                                               Rathfarnham.

A Chara,
   I beg your assistance in a crisis which threatens the continuance of St. Enda's College.
   The Directors of the Limited Co. which I called into existence some months ago have decided to recommend the voluntary liquidation of the Company, as they are unwilling to undertake the responsibility of reopening St. Enda's. It remains therefore for me, as the only chance of securing the future of the great work for Irish education which we have attempted, to re-acquire the College by buying it in from the Liquidator, in which event it will become my absolute property again. I am advised that the liquidator cannot sell to me at less than £600. A friend has generously offered to provide £300, and if I am able to raise £400 (£100 being required for expenses over and above the £600) I shall be able to re-purchase St. Enda's and continue it as before. The money must be provided by *Saturday 31st. inst.*
   As I am sure that you will be anxious that St. Enda's should go on, I am asking you to help me in this effort by subscribing towards the required £400 such a sum, large or small, as you are able to afford. If I can succeed in this, St. Enda's will re-open as usual on 9th Sept. It would be a national calamity if we were prevented from reaping the fruit of what we have sown during the past four years in capital expenditure and in toil. Yours sincerely. P. H. Pearse.

To Bolger & Doyle Ltd.

This letter to the liquidator, D. O'Connor, containing a proposal from Pearse to buy the property back, was in turn sent by the liquidator to all the creditors with his own circular letter dated 4th.

September. In his circular, the liquidator gives implicit support to Pearse's proposal and indicates to the creditors the advantages involved. The letter also contained notice of a meeting of creditors called for 6th September at Sgoil Éanna to consider the proposal.

L. 332/P.Ms.   Copy proposal from Mr. Pearse

3.9.1912.
D. O'Connor, Esq., Liquidator,
Sgoil Éanna, Limited,
13 Westmorland Street, Dublin.

Dear sir,
I propose to purchase from you, as Liquidator of Sgoil Éanna, Limited, all the interests of the Company now vested in you as Liquidator in the following:—

(a) The house and lands of Sgoil Éanna, formerly known as the "Hermitage", held under lease dated 15th July 1910. Wm. Woodbyrne and another of the 1st part, John R. O'Connell of the 2nd part, and Patk. H. Pearse of the 3rd part, subject to the yearly rent of £300, and also subject to a mortgage to Joseph T. O'Dolan to secure to him £1150 and to Séumas Mac Manus £350 and also to the good will, if any, attached thereto.

(b) The house and School furniture, Laboratory and effects, Husbandry appliances and all movable property at St. Enda's as enumerated by Messrs T. Dockrell, Sons and Company, Limited.

2.   I agree to purchase all the premises and moveable property aforesaid subject to the amount now due on foot of said mortgages, and also subject to the Rents, Rates, and Taxes thereon, and also subject to all liabilities created by the Company since its formation, and subject also to the amount now due on foot of all liabilities which existed immediately before the formation of the Company, and which the Company agreed to take over.

3.   I agree to pay for the interest in the Company and the Property aforesaid, and subject as aforesaid, the sum of £500, same to be paid immediately upon your acceptance thereof, but subject as in clause 7.

4.   You are to do all things necessary at my expense to define the interest of the Company in such property, and to revest same in me as if the Company had never been formed.

5.   In case you desire, I also agree to accept at any time you wish an Assignment from the Company and from you as Liquidator of the premises known as "Glanmire", all situate in Oakley Road, Ranelagh, or at your request, to join in assigning same to the

283

Hibernian Bank as Mortgagee thereon, or otherwise to join with you or the Bank in disposing or letting same as you direct or in surrendering same or any part thereof. I agree to take same subject to the rents chargeable thereon.

6.   I agree to do all things which you require for the purpose of carrying the foregoing proposal into effect.

7.   In case it should hereafter turn out that proceedings were taken by any Creditor or the acceptance of this proposal by you was inadvisable, I agree to revest the property in you as such Liquidator and you are not to be bound to refund any of the money.

8.   As you are aware the funds enabling me to make this offer are being presented to me by friends of the School, upon condition that I assure them that I will be free during the coming school year from pressure for payment of the balance of the debts due, after payment of the dividends which you will be enabled to pay the Creditors. I am therefore to be at liberty to withdraw proposals if all the Creditors would not agree in trusting me for payment of the balance of the debts incurred before the 1st July, 1912, upon condition of their receiving from you a dividend of not less than 2/- in the £. (Signed) P. H. Pearse. 3/9/'12.

To Cathal Brugha.

This subscription from Cathal Brugha was most likely in response to Pearse's appeal of 23rd August in which he outlined his plan to repurchase.

L. 333/P.Ms./G

4.9.1912.

Dear Friend,

I am very grateful to you. I succeeded in buying back the school again; the transaction is almost completed. A thousand thanks and greetings. Yours, Pádraig Mac Piarais.

To Mrs. Mac Neill.

This postcard is one of the series which Pearse designed, showing the various aspects of the Hermitage grounds and items from the school achievements in drama and sport; this one shows the formal garden viewed from the window of Pearse's study.

On this postcard the address is altered to Omeath, Co. Louth to where the card was forwarded from Herbert Park; Mac Neill was Principal of the Irish Summer College at Omeath and the family may have been there with him.

L.(p.c.) 334/NLI

10.9.1912.

We were expecting Niall and Brian all day yesterday.
We have a fine rally of boys, new and old.

To Mr. Reddin.

Mr. and Mrs. Reddin who lived at Rockfield, Artane, Co. Dublin, had been generous supporters of Pearse; their two sons Kenneth and Norman were pupils at Sgoil Éanna from 1910 to 1912 when they took the Matriculation of the National University. Even with financial affairs as a major concern to him, Pearse seemingly found time to impart some instruction by correspondence to Kenneth Reddin who later qualified in law.

L. 335/P.Ms.

19.9.1912.   Sgoil Éanna,
                                             Rathfarnham.

My dear Mr. Reddin,
You must pardon me for my delay in acknowledging your last kind letter and its contribution towards the St. Enda's fund. Please accept my most grateful thanks. We have pulled through all right, and though I realise that there is an uphill fight before us I am fairly confident as to the future.

We thought the boys would return on 9th. to do a few week's work for Matric. I hope they will do well. I am answering some queries of Kenneth's by this post, but it is not easy to give general directions as to Irish composition in the way he asks. The Irish paper is, however, fairly sure to be easy. The two boys *ought* to pass, but one never can tell. With many thanks and kindest regards, Sincerely yours, P. H. Pearse.

To John O'Callaghan.

Due to the financial crisis the school year began later than usual in September 1912. Sgoil Éanna provided a wide curricular choice of subjects and placed an emphasis on combining practical and academic subjects.

L. 336/OCS

28.9.1912.

Dear Sir,

Referring to yours of 19th ult., I should be glad – to have an interview with you if your services as manual instructor are still available. I shall be here every afternoon next week, except Wednesday and am free after 4.30 each day. I am anxious to get the class going at once, and so should be particularly grateful if you could call early in the week. We could then arrange terms, hours etc. Yours truly, P. H. Pearse.

To Mr. J. F. Murphy.

Fintan and Desmond Murphy from Brixton, London were pupils at Sgoil Éanna from September 1910; Fintan attended University from Sgoil Éanna and was a member of the Rathfarnham company which fought in the G.P.O. in Easter Week 1916.

L.(p.c.) 337/OCS

6.1.1913.

School re-opens after vacation Monday 13th inst., on which evening we shall be looking forward to greeting the boys. Classes resume Tuesday morning 14th. P. H. P.

To Dónal Ó Corcora.

Keimaneigh (Céim an Fhiaidh) is a historic pass in the mountains of West Cork on the road from Guagán Barra to Glengarriff; a military episode of the seventeenth century is commemorated in a traditional poem and ballad "Céim an Fhiaidh". Ó Corcora was a teacher in Cork and was active in the Gaelic League.

25.2.1913. Sgoil Éanna,
Rathfarnham.

A Chara,

I am very grateful for your subscription to St. Enda's, which I regard as generous from one with such calls as you must have on narrow resources. I enclose receipt with many thanks.

Thanks too for the copies of the "Outlook" with your Keimaneigh article. You have given life and human interest to what was to me only a name. If ever I publish that anthology of mine, I hope with your permission, to make use of your information.

I can't remember at the moment where Mac Donagh got that third verse, though I think I remember his saying something to me about it. I will ask him the next time I see him and let you know.

Remember me to your mother and sister and thank them for their hospitality to me and for a very pleasant evening in Cork. Mise do chara go buan, Pádraig Mac Piarais.

To Mr. G. Bourke, B.L.

Donal Bourke was a junior pupil in Sgoil Éanna in the first term of 1912/13; the financial pressure forced Pearse to canvass very intensely for new pupils and to strive to retain those he had. Mr. Bourke lived at Irishtown. Ballindine, Co. Mayo.

L. 339/SM

30.3.1913. Sgoil Éanna,
Rathfarnham.

Dear Mr. Bourke,

May we look forward to greeting Donal this coming week, when we re-open after Easter Vacation? Work is resumed on Tuesday morning next. We were looking forward to seeing him during the Christmas–Easter term, but perhaps you thought it safer to keep him at home during the uncertain Spring weather. We have ten new little boys about his own age as additional companions for him.

Hoping to hear from you, Yours sincerely, P. H. Pearse.

To Seán Mac Giollarnath.

In April 1913 Yeats offered to stage *An Ri* by Pearse and Tagore's *Post Office* at the Abbey as his contribution to Sgoil Éanna's fund. Pearse is seeking advance publicity for the occasion from the editor of *An Claidheamh Soluis*. The meeting in Hobson's office was most likely a political meeting.

L. 340/NLI/G

20.4.1913.   Sgoil Éanna,
                                         Rathfarnham.

Dear Friend,
    Please insert this piece this week. Was it not very good of Yeats to do this for us?
    I trust that you are improved; I was sorry to hear that you had been ill. We will have a meeting in Hobson's office on Wednesday evening at 4.0 p.m. Will you be able to attend? Greetings and best wishes, Yours, Pádraig Mac Piarais.

To Mrs. Bloomer.

Máire Canning and Loie Bloomer from Sgoile Íde with two other students formed the chorus of keening women when *An Ri* was performed at Sgoil Éanna in June 1912. The women, in the closing scene of the play sing a Te Deum as the funeral of the warrior king is borne into the monastery.
    The play, as revised by Pearse for the Abbey, was performed at the Sgoil Eanna Fete in June 1913 and later in Tagore's school in India in 1915.

L. 341/NLI

25.4.1913.   Sgoil Éanna,
                                         Rathfarnham.

Dear Mrs. Bloomer,
    You will have seen or heard of my furious activity with the object of raising funds in order to be able to pay everyone something next July. We have in hands plays at the Abbey on May 17th, a Fete at Jones's Road, June 9th to 14th and a Drawing of Prizes on June 21st. I know that you and your friends will do all you can to help us in all three ventures.

It is about the Abbey performance I write at present. Mr. Yeats has kindly decided to give a special performance for us on May 17th. The plays are to be *The Post Office* by the Indian poet and teacher Tagore on whom Mr. Yeats recently lectured, and my play *An Rí*, which we performed in the open air here last June, and which I have re-written to fit it for indoor performance. Well, the point is the *keen* and the *Te Deum* at the end. Last year we had the St. Ita's girls, but this year? Four keeners would be quite sufficient on the small stage of the Abbey. Is Máire Canning available and could you and she between you organise three others? Of course Loie was one last year, so that leaves only two to be provided. As Miss Canning and Loie know the music it will be so much less trouble for them than it would be if we had to get four strangers; and they did it so beautifully last year that I hate to think of anyone else doing it. Please drop me a line. With kindest regards, Sincerely yours. P. H. Pearse.

To Mrs. Bloomer.

Pearse was very pleased with the performance by the four Sgoil Íde girls in *An Rí* on the 17th May at the Abbey Theatre; Mrs. Bloomer in response to his letter of 25th April had contacted them and organised their involvement. Mr. Larchet was the eminent professor of music who commented on the quality of the *keen* (caoine = lament).

L. 342/NLI

19.5.1913.   Sgoil Éanna,
                                              Rathfarnham.

Dear Mrs. Bloomer,
    Please thank all the girls for me and accept my thanks for your own trouble in the matter of the singing at our play. The girls were admirable. Mr. Larchet came to me after the performance and said he had never heard so beautiful a keen. Máire Canning's voice rang out wonderfully in the "Sanctus". The whole thing seemed to move the audience very much. We had dresses which served splendidly. Sincerely yours. P. H. Pearse.

P.S.   Please give enclosed note to Miss Canning.

To Colm Ó Lochlainn.

The meetings in Hobson's office were most likely of a political nature. Hobson's office was the editorial office of *Irish Freedom* the militant republican journal founded by the I.R.B. in 1910. The reference to Merrion Point or Strand could have a significance in relation to a Sgoil Éanna outing. Colm Ó Lochlainn, a university student, was later a teacher in the school and lived at Beechlawn, Rathgar Road. He founded The Three Candles Press.

L.(p.c.) 343/OCS/G

23.5.1913.

Could you come to a small gathering in Hobson's office to-morrow (Friday) at 5.30? If you are too busy disregard it. I received your letter concerning Merrion Point (Strand). P. Mac P.

To Mr. J. Holloway.

At the end of the school year 1912/1913 Pearse was able to honour his promise of August 1912 to his creditors that, should they refrain from pressing their claims for the year, he would pay an instalment of 2/- in the pound by 1st July 1913. This is the subject of this letter to Holloway. He does not seem to have written similar letters to his other creditors; perhaps Holloway who was given to gossip, was of strategic importance in restoring Pearse's standing among his creditors. Pearse's debt to Holloway arose from his services as architect in the various building extensions from 1908 onwards.

L. 344/NLI

26.6.1913.   St. Enda's College,
                                                    Rathfarnham.

Dear Sir,
    You will be glad to hear that, as the result of the consideration of the creditors of St. Enda's and St. Ita's Colleges last year in giving me a whole school year to pull things together, I am now in a position to make you a definite proposal with regard to settling your claim against me in connection with the Colleges. I have first to thank you, in common with all the other creditors, for the confidence extended to me and sympathy shown in my work and to assure you of my determination to see you paid in full.

290

As the yearly loss on *St. Ita's* (the girls' College) was very heavy, it was decided in the general interests not to re-open it. The great point was to keep *St. Enda's* (the boys' College at Rathfarnham) going, not only in the interests of the momentous work for Irish education which it is accomplishing, but in the interests of the creditors of the two Colleges, as, of course any chance of paying them would disappear if St. Enda's had to be closed. I am glad to be able to say that the result has fully justified my decision to keep St. Enda's open. We have had a very successful year. Educationally it has been the most gratifying since the College was founded; and, as regards finance, notwithstanding the threatened disaster of last summer, we have been able to pay our way from week to week, we have not created any fresh liabilities, and we fully re-established our credit. The prospects for next year are still brighter.

As to paying off the old liabilities, Mr. D. O'Connor, Liquidator of Sgoil Éanna, Ltd., has already paid each of the creditors an instalment of 2/- in the pound. After deducting all fees and costs, he has still in his hands out of the sum I paid him for the goodwill of St. Enda's, a balance which will enable him to pay each of the creditors a further small instalment of 6d in the pound. This instalment will be sent out within the next few days. There will then be left 17/6 in the pound for me to pay. Of this, I propose to pay each of you an instalment of 2/6 in the pound on 30th September next, and further instalment of 2/6 in the pound on 28th February. I expect to be in a position to pay other instalments in the following June and September, and will give you definite assurance with regard to these when paying you the February instalment. I regret that the mode of payment is so slow, but I feel that you will recognise the efforts I am making and that you will willingly extend your confidence to me for a further period, so as to enable me to make good to all. It is of course understood that none of the creditors will get preferential treatment, as this would be unfair to the others, and the aim is, by common forbearance and consideration, to secure, that *all* be paid in full.

May I beg you for a line expressing your assent to this? I am dear Sir, Yours very truly, P. H. Pearse.

To Mr. J. F. Murphy.

This incomplete letter was sent to the parent of Fintan and Desmond Murphy. The letter is incomplete, only one sheet remaining of an original double page; the date on the letter has been established in a letter written by Fintan Murphy in 1966 and by reference to other letters to his father from Pearse.

L. 345/OCS

[5.7.1913.]

... such books as English Histories, Geographies, Latin and French books, etc., at a reduction, and in future when Fintan or Desmond require new books I will ask them to write to you.

The boys are in good health, and working steadily. I do hope you will be able to leave them with us for some years to come. They are boys well worth working for and with, – boys whom it is a pleasure to work for. It is a great pity Fintan did not come to us a year to two earlier; he would have been a fluent Irish speaker by now. As it is, he will have made very creditable progress by Mid-Summer. I like both boys very much; Fintan in particular has the sense of a man with all the charm and freshness of a boy. With kind regards, Sincerely yours. P. H. Pearse.

To Mr. J. Murray.

Mr. Murray was a business representative who wished to sell to Sgoil Éanna.

L.(p.c.) 346/OCS

23.8.1913.

Yes, to-morrow (Saturday) at 3.30 will suit me. St. Enda's is a mile beyond Rathfarnham. Pass the chapel take first turn to right, pass Loreto Abbey, and then ours is the second large gate on right. I shall be delighted to see you. P. H. Pearse.

To Assistant Commissioners of Intermediate Education.

This is a draft in Pearse's hand, of his reply to the Board of Intermediate Education concerning an appeal which he lodged against some of the Sgoil Éanna examination results for 1913. It offers a very clear example of the struggle between the bureaucratic machine and the teacher who believed he had a justifiable case and sought to have it investigated. The Commissioners had recourse to semantic evasions to avoid granting Pearse's request for a re-examination of the scripts.

L. 347/P.Ms.

30.8.1913.   St Enda's College,
                                    Rathfarnham.

Gentlemen,

I am in receipt of yours of 29th inst., for which I am much obliged, but I beg to point out that it is in no sense an answer to mine of 26th inst. and that it does not touch at all upon any of the points raised by me.

(1)   I was aware of the existence of the marked paragraph in the circular enclosed but it is not to the point. I can quite conceive that between the issue of the Provisional Pass Lists and the issue of the final Pass Lists you would have time to carry out such "investigation extending to the answer books"; as you have carried out in these cases – which really only means checking your clerk's work – but that is not the sort of investigation I asked for and that the cases demand. What I asked for and what the cases demand is a *re-examination of the papers.* There was no time for this; no time for any investigation properly called.

(2)   Your reply that "after investigation extending to the answer books" you find that the awards in English with which the candidates in question are credited "are in accordance with the judgement of the examiners" is not a reply to my complaint, but a repetition and an enforcement of it. I quite believe that the awards are in accordance with the judgement of the examiners, and it is precisely of this that I am complaining. In other words, what I challenge is "the judgement of the examiners" upon which you fall back.

I therefore apply again for a re-examination of the papers, and I request you to bring this application before the Board. I should be grateful if in acknowledging this letter, you would let me know the date of the Board's next meeting. I am, Gentlemen, Yours obediently, P. H. Pearse.

To Rev. Mother.

There is no indication as to the identity of the nun or the school over which she presided; it may have been M. Columba of Loreto Convent, Nivan. "An Sagart"was one of the short stories in the collection *Íosagán agus Scéalta Eile* published in 1907. Mary Bulfin, whose part in the Passion Play was featured in one of the Sgoil Éanna school postcards, was a student of Sgoil Ide.

L. 348/P.Ms.

20.10.1913.   Sgoil Éanna,
                                                        Rathfarnham.

Dear Rev. Mother,

It was very good of you to send me the programme of your concert containing the synopsis of your Preparatory's dramatisation of *An Sagart*. I read it with great interest. I am only sorry I was not there to see it performed. Please thank your Preparatory children for me, and tell them I must get *our* Preparatorys to try their hand at dramatisation now, for hitherto *I* have written the plays for them. Boys must not let girls beat them!

The dramatised version of *Íosagán* was published in No. 2 of *An Macaomh*. Unfortunately, it is out of print, all the copies having been bought. I have only one or two copies myself, which I must keep for binding. But if you ever think of staging *Íosagán* I could *lend* you one of these copies. Or perhaps bye and bye, I may be able to give you one, as I think of advertising for some copies and buying them back.

Did I send you No. 4. of *An Macaomh*? It contains the Irish and English of our last play *An Rí* – which however, would not be suitable for performance by girls. I must write a play with a girl heroine. I have an idea for one in my mind, but am too busy to work it out.

Your pupils might be interested in the enclosed photos of our Passion Play. The girl who represented the Blessed Virgin was Mary Bulfin, a daughter of the late William Bulfin. Again thanking you, Believe me, dear Rev. Mother, Yours sincerely, P. H. Pearse.

To Sir. J. R. O'Connell, Solr.

Sir John R. O'Connell, a member of the legal firm of T. F. O'Connell of Kildare St. Dublin, was a trustee of the Woodbyrne estate and as such received the rent on the Hermitage from Pearse. This letter is addressed to him; the Mr. O'Farrell referred to was a member of O'Connell's staff.

Overleaf the following appears:

Half year's rent	£150.
Int. on deposit	£6 .. 0 .. 0
Income tax	£8 .. 18 .. 0
Paid	£100 .. 0 .. 0
	£114 .. 18 .. 8.
Cheq. herewith	£35 .. 1 .. 4

L. 349/NLI

31.10.1913.   Sgoil Éanna,
                                             Rathfarnham.

Dear Sirs,

As arranged with your Mr. O'Farrell, I enclose cheque to cover arrears of rent up to 31st January last, and hope to let you have the half-year's rent now due in instalments before another half year becomes due. I regret not being able to pay more punctually, but my pupil's fees are very slow in coming in and I have a constant struggle to keep going.

Cheque is made up as overleaf, I am dear sirs, Yours truly, P. H. Pearse.

To Mr. Holloway.

The Fusiliers' Memorial Arch crowns the main gate into St. Stephen's Green which faces Grafton Street. The committee to which Pearse refers may have been investigating or planning a memorial to '98 and the United Irishmen.

L. 350/NLI

8.11.1913.   Sgoil Éanna,
                                           Rathfarnham.

Dear Mr. Holloway,

Is there any chance of your being able to tell me the approximate cost of the Dublin Fusiliers' Memorial Arch at the entrance to Stephen's Green. I want the information for a Committee of which I am a member, and I don't know anyone who would be likely to be in the way of knowing except you.

St. Enda's still keeps its flag flying, but we are not out of our difficulties yet. P. H. Pearse.

To Miss G. Doyle.

Following the establishment of the Irish Volunteers at the Rotunda on November 25th 1913 at which Pearse, co-founder, spoke his involvement in the armed movement grew rapidly. He is answering this letter of inquiry as a member of the Committee.

L. 351/NLI

30.11.1913.   St Enda's College,
                                                Rathfarnham.

Dear Madam,
    We have been so busy grappling with the immediate problem of organising and drilling the men – between 3,000 and 4,000 – who have joined the Volunteers that we have not yet had time to consider – in any detail the work of the women. First of all there will be ambulance and Red Cross work for them; and then I think a women's rifle club is desirable. I would not like the idea of women drilling and marching in the ordinary way but there is no reason why they should not learn to shoot.
    The matter will be taken up by the Committee as soon as possible. The address of the Hon. Sec. is 12 D'Olier St. Believe me, Yours sincerely, P. H. Pearse.

To A Chara,

This letter to a friend is written in a tone which indicated a bond of friendship closer than that usually found within the Gaelic League membership. It would appear that the friend had written to Pearse telling him of her (?) forthcoming marriage and advising him to follow her example and advice. Pearse's response should not be interpreted in absolute terms; his declaration in favour of not marrying should be read in the context of his heavy financial burden and of his domestic situation which rendered so many female members of his family and relations financially dependent on him.
    The recipient of this letter may have been one of the ladies of the Dowley family of Carrick-on-Suir, who were very active in the Gaelic League. The original letter is in the custody of the South Tipperary Museum at Clonmel. Pearse visited Carrick-on-Suir and the adjacent Gaeltacht of Rathcormack in 1902 and wrote a detailed account of League activities. Fr. Michael O'Hickey was a

296

native of Carrickbeg – that part of Carrick which is on the Waterford side of the river.

L. 352/TCM/G

29.12.1913.

Dear Friend,
     Many thanks for your letter. I understand from what you have said that you are getting married. If so I praise you. But I do not intend to follow your advice nor your example. If I go to America, I do hope to bring back some money – but should there be a lady associated with the money, I will abandon both the lady and the money.
     Sgoil Éanna lives and that is certainly no small achievement. Greetings and best wishes, Yours, Pádraig Mac Piarais.

To Mrs. M. Pearse.

This letter was written from Cobh as Pearse was preparing to begin his voyage to America on board the S.S. *Campania*, which he boarded on Sunday 8th February. It was customary for most travellers sailing from Cobh (Queenstown) to stay overnight in the town. The hotel keepers of Cobh met the trains at Cork with a view to securing guests and showed placards advertising their hotels, at the Cork railway terminus. Pearse selected Brady's hotel on account of his mother's family name.
     Pearse shows a deep concern for his mother's health and welfare – she had been ill before he left; he implies that she had been worrying about his safety. Miss Byrne was a family relation who lived with the Pearse family.

L. 353/P.Ms.

7.2.1914.   Brady's Hotel,
                                              Queenstown.

Dearest Mother,
     You and Miss Byrne never went to the Pantomime. I meant some Wednesday or Saturday to give you the money for it, but never seemed to have the money at the right time. I am enclosing 6/- in stamps now, and you can go on Wednesday next; or if the Pantomime is over (I am not sure) you can go somewhere else. I could not get a postal order, but the stamps will be as good. Willie

can give you cash for them. I left some stamps on the desk, which I suppose Willie has got.

A lot of hotel people were waiting for the train at Cork, and I came with the proprietor of this on account of his name. It is small but comfortable.

We have to be at the Cunard embarking place at 6.30 to-morrow (Sunday) morning for the tender. *The Campania* is expected to sail about 8, but it is often late. The man here says it is a comfortable boat. This is to be its third last voyage.

You need not worry about me at all. I shall be as safe in America as at home. The only cause for worry is the money question. Tell Willie to write up the people if the money is not coming in. Tell him if he can spare £1 to send it to Meers as soon as possible, and £2 to the National Bank.

We are due in New York on Saturday next. This means that you will not hear from me for nearly 3 weeks. If possible I will send a postcard from the tender to-morrow which will probably reach you as soon as this. Goodbye, P.

P.S. I hope you will mind yourself while I am away and that if necessary you will go to the Doctor. Don't run about too much. What good would it be for me to come back with (or without) money and find you laid up?

To Mrs. M. Pearse.

L.(p.c.) 354/P.Ms.

8.2.1914.

Am on board the tender and will be soon going on board the Campania. Goodbye, P.

To Willie Pearse ("Mister").

According to his own account the Atlantic crossing was not a pleasant experience for Pearse; he was ill, and confined to his cabin for the first week of the journey. The notes to which he refers may be the account of his journey in diary from and entitled "The Voyage of Patrick". The *Gaelic American* was the prominent newspaper of the Irish–Americans, the office of which became Pearse's New York headquarters during his trip.

L. 355/P.Ms.

17.2.1914.   On Board s.s. Campania.
                                          Near New York. 10 a.m.

Mister,

The pilot is taking us up the channel and we land about noon. It has been the longest and roughest passage made by this old tub in her infamous career of 21 years. We were due in New York 3 days ago. I enclose you notes written since I was able to come on deck on Saturday last. I expect that I shall not be able to write long letters once I land.

I am well, I think the voyage has done me good. I should be a first class sailor in future.

Send me a full account of *everything.* I am most anxious for news. Will send you address as soon as possible, but meantime you can write c/o *Gaelic American.*

I hope all are well. Hope mother is better and is not overworking. Send *all* news – of money etc.   P.

To Joe Mc Garrity.

Joe Mc Garrity was a leading figure in the separatist movement and one of the three directors of Clann na nGael, the organisation in America which assisted the Rising financially. He was a generous friend of Pearse and was the principal agent in organising his American tour. When in New York Pearse stayed with Miss Mc Kenna at West 144th St.

L. 356/NLI

2.3.1914.   c/o J. Mc Kenna,
                                          517 W. 144th St. N.Y.

A Chara,

Pray accept my thanks for your generous donation to St. Enda's College, which Hobson duly handed me. I was so busy during the week-end that I could not get a moment to send you this acknowledgment sooner. It is good of you to help us so substantially; I hope St. Enda's will always be worthy of its friends, among whom you must now be numbered.

299

My task here is hard, I have not yet made much progress, but people are working for me in various directions, until I am able to make a detailed tour, perhaps next autumn and winter. Would there be any chance of the Clann running a lecture tour for me, the proceeds to be divided between them and St. Enda's?

I hope to see you in Philadelphia next week. I know you will do what you can to put me in touch with people there. a Mr. Mc Laughlin has been mentioned to me as a comparatively wealthy man who, if properly approached, might do something substantial.

Thanks again for your own help and for your promise to put me on the right track when I get to Philadelphia. Believe me, Sincerely yours, P. H. Pearse.

To Bolger & Doyle.

This letter is typed and the original date of February 20th was altered in Pearse's hand to March 20th. It is one of many similar letters which were sent to his creditors when reducing his debts by twice-yearly payments. Pearse was in America from 8th February to the middle of May and so this letter and the others to his creditors were signed before his departure.

L. 357/P.Ms.

20.3.1914.   St Enda's College,
                                                Rathfarnham.

Dear Sir,

Referring to your claim against me in connection with St. Enda's and St. Ita's Colleges, I have pleasure in enclosing cheque, £5.1.0 – being an instalment of two shillings in the £, in reduction of the debt. I hope to be able to pay you a further instalment of a like amount on 30th Sept. next.

Please accept my thanks for your consideration in the matter and a renewed assurance of my intention to clear off the whole liability as soon as possible. Yours very faithfully, P. H. Pearse.

To Sgoil Éanna.

This open letter from Pearse to the boys of Sgoil Éanna was written towards the end of March 1914 from New York and sent with one of his regular letters to Willie. In a letter of 20th February, Willie had asked him for a message which he could read for the boys, who were taking a great interest in his tour. In a letter of 5th April to America, Willie acknowledges receipt of the manifesto which he promises to read to the students on their return after the Easter vacation. This he did on Tuesday 7th April.

In the original of this document portions of the sentences which begin: "In the meantime ... school year." and "Let every ..." are missing. The letter or message is reproduced in full in the concluding chapter of "The Story of a Success" by Desmond Ryan who describes the letter as illustrating the power which Pearse exercised at Sgoil Éanna.

The phrases or commands in Irish in the third sentence translate as "exit", "about turn", "silence", "what's this?" The concluding valediction reads: "Until I see you – my greetings to you. May you triumph and be victorious, O Sgoil Éanna."

L. 358/NLI

March 1914.

Greetings.

You are all, I have no doubt, re-assembled after the Easter Vacation and working hard. So many invitations poured in upon me to lecture and to tell the Americans what fine fellows you are that I was unable to get home, as I had hoped, in time to be in my place to welcome you back from your holidays. However, I shall be on the sea in a very few days from the time this reaches you, and in a week or so thereafter you will again hear my sonorous voice saying "amach libh", "iompodh timcheall", "in bhur dtost", "céard é seo?" etc., I have already promised to give you a special holiday in commemoration of my safe return and happy escape from sea-sharks and land-sharks. In the meantime, I want to appeal to you, and I do most earnestly, to put all your heart into the work that remains to be done during the short month or six weeks that are left of the school year. Let every boy do his best. Let every boy do his level best at his weak subjects especially. Do a six weeks' work that it will be a pleasure to yourselves to look back upon, whatever the results of the examination may be. Show what Sgoil Éanna can do. Remember you have a great reputation. You have a great reputation now even in America. You must live up to that reputation. It would be disgraceful to have an undeserved reputation.

Let every boy start right now, and not slacken until the word is given for "home" some fine day during the third week in June.

I do hope finally that you are making some effort to speak Irish. Remember that that rifle is still unwon. I want to give it away this summer, but it can only be given on condition that some boy wins it by a genuine effort to speak Irish.

Beannacht chugaibh anois go bhfeicidh mé sibh. Beir buaidh chatha agus cosgartha, a Sgoil Éanna, Mise, Pádraig Mac Piarais.

To L. Martin N.Y.

L. 359/NLI

24.3.1914   P.O. Box 1682.
                                   New York.

A Chara,

Allow me to thank you for your subscription to the St. Enda's Building Fund handed me by M. Harford after you had left the *Gaelic American* office yesterday. It is good of you to help us on. On my own behalf and on behalf of our masters and boys I thank you.

I hope you will enjoy your visit home. When in Dublin you must call out to St. Enda's. If I am not back my brother will be very glad to see you. Believe me, Yours sincerely. P. H. Pearse.

To J. Mc Garrity.

Pearse gave numerous lectures on political, cultural and educational topics during March and April in New York, Philadelphia and other centres with large Irish communities.

During his visit to Philadelphia, Pearse stayed with the Mc Garrity family.

L. 360/NLI

1.4.1914.   P.O. Box 1682.
                                   New York.

A Chara,

I duly reached New York on Sunday and the Lecture went off very successfully. On Monday I was rather unwell again; my

302

stomach has gone wrong somehow. Yesterday and to-day I have been better, but I am not yet quite myself.

I posted you yesterday a bundle of copies of my appeal. I have had a letter from Mr. Lally saying that they will be glad to have a meeting for St. Enda's in Wilmington any evening I select during the week commencing April 13th. I have replied saying that Tuesday 14th. or Wednesday 15th. will suit me. I must be back here by the Thursday, as my Field Day at Celtic Park is Sunday 19th, and there are committee meetings and a thousand things to be attended to.

I hope your Anti-Repeal meeting was a great success. I see Wilson has won the first round.

I want to thank you all for your great kindness to me while in Philadelphia as if it were not enough to inflict myself on you I inflicted my illness on you. I will long remember your great kindness and especially your own generosity and thoughtfulness exhibited in such countless ways, little and big. Believe me, Yours very sincerely. P. H. Pearse.

To Mrs. M. Pearse.

In this letter to his mother Pearse relates how he had contacted the family of a distant cousin of his mother, a Brady from Co. Meath. Brady's son-in-law, a Mr. Garvin, (spelled Garvan in a later letter) contributed generously to Pearse's school fund.

L. 361/P.Ms.

9.4.1914.   c/o J. Mc Kenna,
                                             517 W 144th St.
                                                   N.Y.

Dearest Mother,
    Got your letter with Willie's to-day. This is Holy Thursday. I suppose all tbe boys are gone home, but you will have them back nearly as soon as you get this letter.

As I told you in a letter you must not have got when you wrote the letter I am now answering, Brady is dead but the Mr. Garvin who has promised the £100 (which by the way, I have not yet received) is his son-in-law and one of his heirs.

I am thinking of sending Mary Brigid a pound (£1) for her birthday on April 26th. She might be pleased with it. I will send her a cheque which she can cash at Cook's. Tell Miss Byrne I was asking for her. Tell Rodgers I was asking for him too. Tell him I addressed the Mayomen's Association the other night by special invitation.

There is no use coming back here in summer, as it is too hot and there could be no meetings. But I think I must come back next October or so, and stay till Spring. I have to be guided by the advice they give me here.

I don't think there is anything else for me to say, as I have given Willie all the news. Hope you and all are well. I am all right. Love to all.   P.

To Mrs. M. Pearse.

With the gifts from benefactors like Mr. Garvin secured Pearse turned to other methods of ensuring the future of St. Enda's. He advertised for American pupils to come to the school and sought to lease the Hermitage to Americans as a summer residence. This latter scheme was suggested by his mother. Willie and Mrs. Pearse spent a holiday in Warrenpoint Co. Down during Easter and Margaret was in Belgium. It is possible that some of the students accompanied Margaret on this educational tour.

L. 362/P.Ms.

13.4.1914.   c/o Mc Kenna,
                                            New York.

My dearest Mother,

I am very glad to hear that you and Willie have been able to go to Warrenpoint. I hope you enjoyed yourselves.

Easter is not a big holiday here and Easter Monday is not observed at all. The ceremonies in the Church on Easter Sunday were mangificent. The singing was very fine. It was funny to see six boys dressed as pages in yellow and red satin and plumed hats on their heads walking after the priests.

I have now got Mr. Garvan's £100 which makes £406 so far. In sending it he promised another sum of £100 on September 1st and said that if we are still in need of money next year he hopes we will call on him. It would not do to ask him for any more money for a chapel or anything else, he has been so generous. By all accounts, if Brady had been alive he would not have treated me as well as his son-in-law has done.

I will put in an advertisement and try to get pupils, but very few people will send boys 3,000 miles away from home to school. I don't think there would be much chance of letting the place for the summer; furnished as we have it for a school, it is not luxurious enough for wealthy Americans. The study-hall, classrooms, and dormitories would only be in their way. There is no billiard table, smoke room to lounge in, or anything like what they are used to. I may put in an advertisement but I don't think it will be of much use.

I am rushing for the post, and so shall say no more. Glad you are all well. Give love to all.

You asked me in your last letter whether I was getting fat or thin. I think I have got a bit thin.

Good-bye. Shall see you now in a month or five weeks at furthest.   P.

To J. Mc Garrity.

The office of the *Gaelic American* where Devoy was editor was used as a postal address for Pearse in New York. Mr. Lally of Wilmington had organised a function in aid of St. Enda's on April 15th. This letter is written on special American notepaper which carried the St. Enda's address in the right hand corner and in the left hand corner his name and New York postal address thus:

P. H. Pearse,
President,
P.O. Box 1682.
New York. N.Y.

L. 363/NLI

13.4.1914.   New York.

A Chara,
    I did not get yours of the 10th until I came down to the *Gaelic American* office this afternoon after I had been speaking to you on the 'phone. I had an appointment which kept me up town all the morning.

Confirming our arrangement on the 'phone, I will be with you in Philadelphia on Sunday week next, April 26th for the banquet. Mr. Devoy will be able to come with me on that date. I cannot say how I appreciate your goodness in undertaking this second fixture for me. You and Philadelphia are great.

I am kept *very* busy this week by the organisation work in connection with Sunday's Field Day. Therefore I shall stay here till Wednesday afternoon, and travel down to Wilmington direct – not stopping at Philadelphia unless you want me for any special reason. Remember me to all, Sincerely yours, P. H. Pearse.

To Mrs. M. Pearse.

This letter written the following day contains no mention of the difficulties encountered at the Field Day at Celtic Park on Sunday April 19th; it merely recounts the financial aspects of the venture. The "bill stamp" which Willie had sent was for the regular bills by which Pearse was reducing his debts; on paying each instalment, the bill was stamped, signed and returned to the creditor.

L. 364/P.Ms.

20.4.1914.   c/o J. Mc Kenna.
                                         New York.

Dearest Mother,

I got your letter, etc., just after I had written to Willie on Saturday. He had sent me a bill stamp, so I am keeping the one you sent me until the bill is due again. I was very glad to have the *Weekly Freeman* that you sent.

The Field Day at Celtic Park came off yesterday. The weather was splendid but the crowd was not overwhelmingly large, on account I suppose of the earliness of the season. About £90 was taken in cash at the gate, and the ticket money (or most of it) is still to come in. The expenses were heavy, – the teams alone has to be paid £30 between them. The expenses will be about £60 in all, and the net profit on the affair will be anywhere between £30 and £50.

My expenses for the whole trip apart from the Field Day will be about £100. This includes printing, postage, etc., which has been very heavy.

I suppose work is in full swing now. Are all the boys back? Tell Willie to send all news.

As I said in my last, I sail for home in the "Baltic" on Thursday May 7. As the "Baltic" is an eight-day boat, I may reach home on the following Saturday week, May 16th; but perhaps not till 17th or 18th.

I hope that you and all are well, and that everything is going on as it should. I am very anxious to be home now. I hate to have lost so much out of the school year, but of course the time was well spent. When I reach home there will only be about a month to the summer holidays. My love to all, Good-bye.   P.

To Willie Pearse.

Pearse visited the Woolworth skyscraper in New York where his portrait was done in silhouette.

Hunt had been a senior pupil who was now attending University and was doing some teaching, thus releasing Peter Slattery to concentrate on more senior pupils.

Patrick and Willie signed some of their letters in a jocose fashion which at times seemed as if they were mimicking the speech or conversation of a mutual friend or relative.

The Sweeney mentioned was probably a Clann na nGael member in America.

L. 365/P.Ms.

24.4.1914.   c/o J. Mc Kenna.
                                              New York.

Mister Dog,
    I got to-day yours of Easter Monday and Mother's post card from Warrenpoint, and also the *Weekly Freeman*, and p.c. from Wow-Wow from Belgium.
    I have no fresh news except that the Field Day will probably turn out better than I expected when I was writing my last. The expenses are about £50, leaving a net profit of nearly £60; and there is some ticket money still to come in.
    On Sunday I go to Philadelphia again where there is to be a dinner and they are to hand me the proceeds of lecture and collection there. Next week I have three lectures to small societies in or near New York, and shall be busy making farewell calls. I sail, as you know, on May 7.
    You need not write me again after getting this, and I shall have left before any letter could reach. In fact no letter posted after Monday April 27th will catch me I think.
    The silhouette portrait I enclose was cut out while I was standing for half a minute at the top of the Woolworth Building (the building on the P.C. I sent D. Carney). He cut out three together.
    I suppose we had better let Hunt teach the little boys and so give Slattery a little time to work up special boys. Hunt might also help

on weak boys in certain subjects – Kenny for instance. We could not pay him, but I would not mind keeping him for a few weeks.

Glad you enjoyed the holiday in Warrenpoint. Hope all are back. Love to all. Mounseer.

No truth in rumour about Lord Hindlegs. Show Hobson letter sent on by Sweeney. Do not *post* it.

To Major Nolan.

Major Nolan, Colonel Crowley and Captains Guinan, Meenan and Collins were members of the New York Irish Volunteers who assisted Pearse in organising the Field Day on April 19th. Major Nolan was in addition a member of the Committee and it appears that he was especially involved in protecting Pearse from the Redmondites who physically attacked him at Celtic Park.

In the first sentence, second paragraph in which Pearse names the Volunteers, there is an insertion in a hand other than Pearse's adding the names of Meenan and Collins to that of Captain Guinan.

L. 366/NLI

27.4.1914.   P.O. Box 1682.
                             New York.

Dear Major Nolan,

At a meeting of our Committee on Friday evening last a resolution was unanimously adopted thanking the Irish Volunteers for their generous and efficient services at Celtic Park on the occasion of our Field Day, on April 19th.

In conveying this note of thanks to you, I want to add my own personal thanks and the thanks of my staff and pupils at home, and to ask you to express to Colonel Crowley and the officers of the Volunteers and to the companies under Captain Meenan, Collins and Guinan who turned out and gave us such material help, my deep sense of the ready and generous way in which they tendered their assistance, and of the very material help which they gave us in the difficult circumstances we had to encounter at the Park. One of my happiest memories of my visit to New York will be of my pleasant associations with the New York Irish Volunteers.

With thanks to you personally for your own share in my

Committee's work. I remain, dear Major Nolan, With kindest regards, Sincerely yours. P. H. Pearse.

To Ronan Ceannt.

Ronan Ceannt, a son of Éamon Ceannt was a pupil at Sgoil Éanna. The postcard showed the skyscrapers of New York. The address on the card was Bláth Ghort, Carn an gCloch, Dublin.

L.(p.c.) 367/NLI/G

27.4.1914.   New York.

Dear Ronan,
    Here is a card with my greeting and gratitude for the shamrock which you sent me for St. Patrick's Day. It was kind of you to think of me, I will see you within a few weeks with God's help. I remain, your teacher, Pádraig Mac Piarais.

P.S.   These buildings are wonderfully high.

To J. Mc Garrity.

Writing on the 4th to Mc Garrity, Pearse explains how it may not be possible for him to visit Philadelphia again before he sails on Thursday 7th May as he has so many engagements.
    Pearse published in the *Gaelic American* the lists of subscribers to the Sgoil Eanna fund. He gave a lecture on each of the last three evenings before sailing for home. The copy of *Studies* referred to was *Studies*, 11, 1913. which contained an article by Pearse on "Some Aspects of Irish Literature".

L. 368/NLI

4.5.1914.   New York.

A Chara Chroidhe,
    There has been no chance of my going down to Philadelphia ever since my return last Monday, and I am sorry to say there is no chance now before I sail. At least I do not think so. I have an engagement here to-night, an engagement in Springfield, Mass, to-morrow night and an engagement here again Wednesday night. I

309

sail at noon Thursday. By leaving Springfield *very early* Wednesday morning I *may* (but am not at all sure) be able to go on to Philadelphia that day and then back here again, but I fear this too will be impossible as I have two engagements here for Wednesday afternoon and then a lecture in the evening. It has been the same all the week. I lost two days in Providence, R.I., and every other day was taken up with engagements here and in Brooklyn. Will you explain to Father Coghlan how the case stands, and tell him I hope to see him in the Autumn? There is still just the chance of my turning up in Philadelphia Wednesday morning, in which case I shall only have an hour or so to stay. Things have come with a terrible rush this last week or so.

I hope you have posted me the Philadelphia list of subscribers as to-morrow (Tuesday) will be the last day for handing it to the printers for the coming issue of the *Gaelic American.*

I have your copy of the March 1913 issue of *Studies* which if I cannot go down I will mail you. I have been using it in my lectures.

I do hope I shall have the chance of seeing you again and thanking you again for your wonderful generosity and of saying goodbye to you. If not, I will write you before sailing, Believe me, Yours very sincerely, P. H. Pearse.

To John Devoy.

The Provisional Committee which Pearse details in this letter to Devoy was that which governed the Volunteers before Redmond's demand of June 1914 was acceded to. By a majority vote this Committee granted Redmond power to nominate twenty five members to the controlling body of the Volunteers; Pearse, Mac Diarmada and Ceannt were among the seven who voted contra.

The pupil who travelled back with Pearse was Gerry Cronin of Brooklyn.

L. 369/NLI

12.5.1914.   On board R.M.S. "Baltic".

A Chara Chroidhe,
    I had intended to give you a list of the members of the Provisional Committee of the Irish Volunteers before leaving New York – indeed, I made out such a list the night before sailing – but in the hurry of departure Saturday morning I quite forgot to hand it to you.

I now give you the complete list (at least I think it is complete) overleaf. I add after the name of each member the movement etc. with which he has been identified. I think it would be well to publish the names in the *Gaelic American*. Many people in New York and elsewhere asked me who were at the head of the Volunteers, and the accompanying list gives information and shows clearly how representative a Provisional Committee we have.

Within a week I hope to send you for publication a further list of acknowledgements, in connection with the St. Enda's College Building Fund, and a letter returning thanks to all who helped me. There may be one or two subsequent lists.

We have had a most delightful passage home, the days calm and sunny, the nights still and moonlit. My pupil (for I am bringing a new pupil back from Brooklyn) and I are in excellent form. We hope to reach Queenstown Friday morning, when I will mail this.

Please remember me to all at the *Gaelic American* office. With warmest regards, Yours very sincerely, P. H. Pearse.

Provisional Committee, Irish Volunteers.

	Eoin Mac Neill (Vice-Pres. Gaelic League Professor
Hon. Secs.	of Ancient Irish History, National University)
	Laurence J. Kettle (Chief of Dublin Corporation
	Electricity Works, Pigeonhouse Fort; A.O.H.)
	The O'Rahilly (Gaelic Leaguer and Sin Féiner; hon.
Hon.	circulation manager, *An Claidheamh Soluis*)
Treas.	John Gore (Solicitor; well-known total abstinence
	worker; A.O.H.)

Sir Roger Casement (late of British Consular service; Gaelic Leaguer)

Col Maurice Moore (late commander of Connaught Rangers; Gaelic Leaguer)

Thomas M. Kettle (ex. M.P. Professor of National Economics, National University; A.O.H.)

Patrick H. Pearse (President St. Enda's College; Gaelic Leaguer; late editor *An Claidheamh Soluis*)

Éamonn Ceannt. (*anglice* Kent; Gaelic Leaguer and Sinn Féiner)

John Fitzgibbon (Gaelic Leaguer and Sinn Féiner; Pres. Central Branch Sinn Féin)

Bulmer Hobson (Vice-Pres. Na Fianna Éireann)

Peter P. Macken (ex-alderman; Labour Leader, Gaelic Leaguer, and Sinn Féiner)

Thomas Mc Donagh (formerly Assistant Master in St. Enda's; now lecturer in English, National University)

311

Michael J. Judge (A.O.H.)
John Walsh (A.O.H.)
Lenehan (A.O.H.)
Seán Mac Diarmada (Manager *Irish Freedom*)
Jos. M. Plunkett (son of Count Plunkett; editor *Irish Review*)
Peter White (prominent in old Celtic Literary Society; now in Electric Dept. under Kettle)
Colm O'Loughlin (Assistant Master in St. Enda's; represents students of University College on Committee)
Conor Colbert
Edward Martin   Fianna officers.
Patrick O'Ryan

To James Reidy. New York.

James Reidy was an editorial executive on the staff of the *Gaelic American* and had been a loyal supporter of Pearse's tour. When Pearse returned to Sgoil Éanna on May 15th., he was welcomed home by a remarkable demonstration; the boys lined the avenue and the older students lined the roof of the Hermitage, waving the school banner amidst cheering and the traditional three shouts of welcome accompanied by trumpet and the music of the bagpipes.

In April and May while Pearse was still in America, Redmond had been scheming to gain control of the Volunteers and in the course of discussions with Mac Neill and Maurice Moore had indicated his objections to Pearse and Hobson as members of the Provisional Committee, to which he demanded the right to nominate twenty five members. Redmond's ultimatum was issued two days before this letter; the meeting which accepted it by majority vote took place on the 16th June. On the following day the dissenting minority, among them Pearse, Kent, Mc Dermott, Colbert, Béaslaí and Martin, issued a public statement on June 17th. Pearse in the second paragraph of this letter explains the strategy behind that statement and their vote against Redmond's demands.

Mac Donagh reviewed Pearse's *Suantraidhe agus Goltraidhe* in the *Irish Review*, which journal had published the volume in January 1914. The title (literally Songs of Sleep and Sorrow) refers to the legendary harp of Fionn which had only three strings, one each for laughter, sleep and sorrow. The twelve lyrics in the volume were written between 1906 and 1913 and had been published

312

earlier in various journals; Pearse later translated all the lyrics into English which were included in his *Collected Works* (1917).

It would appear that, within a month of returning home, Pearse had hopes of an early return visit to America.

L. 370/NLI

14.6.1914. Sgoil Éanna,
Rathfarnham.

A Chara Chroidhe,

I have been so busy since my return that it has been impossible for me to write any letters except the urgent ones demanded by each day's work. I had a delightful passage home and the boys gave me a rousing reception when I reached St. Enda's. Unfortunately, I found my mother ill (but she is better now) and also that one of my best pupils had just left to keep an invalid father company; two things which spoiled what would otherwise have been a happy homecoming. Ever since I have been busy with the rush of work for exams (which commence Wednesday) annual sports, play, garden party and reunion, (which came off yesterday) and last but not least – Volunteer work.

There has been nothing like this movement in Ireland in our time. The whole country is organising and drilling and clamouring for arms. We have at least 140,000 men now. You will have seen Redmond's manifestos and our counter-proposal. I believe the Party wants to capture the movement *in order to keep it unarmed*; and that the Liberal Government is behind them. We are trying to keep our tempers so as to avoid a split; but it is very hard. At the moment I do not know exactly what turns affairs are going to take. The vast majority of the volunteers themselves are with the Provisional Committee, but the local politicians are with Redmond. A few weeks will see the movement made or marred. The spirit of the country is splendid and if God only inspires us with the right thing to say and do so as to keep the movement straight, without at the same time breaking openly with Redmond, we shall have made history.

I am glad to see from the papers that a fund has been got going in America. I hear that the Gaelic League had trouble at the Feis at Celtic Park – more even than we had.

You told me to send you on from time to time matter which would serve to keep St. Enda's and myself before the Irish–American public in view of my return visit. I post you a copy of the last number of the *Irish Review* in which there is a notice by Professor Thomas Mc Donagh of my book of verse. If you could

313

transfer this to the *Gaelic American*, it would serve me well, for it would (or might) help to get more lecture engagements when I go out again.

I hope your wife is better. Remember me to Mr. Devoy and to all at the *Gaelic American* office, of which place I have affectionate memories. Your own hard work and kindness I shall never forget. Sincerely yours, P. H. Pearse.

To J. Mc Garrity.

When Pearse returned to Dublin in mid-May, only a few weeks remained of the school year before examinations began.

Mc Garrity was Pearse's main focus of support in Philadelphia and had coordinated the work of others such as Fr. Coghlan in Pennsylvania.

Having been defeated on the Provisional Committee by the group led by Mac Neill, Moore and Hobson, Pearse has begun to realise that it is possible to rescue the Volunteers from Redmond's design by acquiring sufficient arms.

The machines referred to in the concluding sentence are the Mc Garrity automobiles of which Pearse had seen a lot in the States.

L. 371/NLI

19.6.1914.   St. Enda's College,
                                                      Rathfarnham.

A Chara Chroidhe,
   Your letter duly reached me, but I have been so busy since my return that it is only to-day (the last day of the school year) that I am able to find time to write. The boys gave me a rousing reception when I reached home (after a delightful passage) and I have been plunged into work ever since – school work and Volunteer work.

I saw your list of acknowledgements in the *Gaelic American*, from which I gather that Father Coghlan has handed you his subscription I see your list totals $1,161 I had previously acknowledged only $1,000 from Philadelphia. Once more I want to thank you for all your work for me, and your own great generosity alike in giving in hospitality and in time. I shall always think of you as the personification of generosity and of Philadelphia as its home.

Have you heard anything of the Wilmington Collection? Mc Ginn might know about it, being in touch with Lally.

The last *Gaelic American* contains your appeal for funds for the Volunteers. The papers here refer to it, and call it a "striking document". I see you are chairman.

You will have seen that the Provisional Committee has had to swallow Redmond's twenty-five nominees. I voted against surrender and think I was right in so voting, but I do not regard the cause as lost – far from it. We all remain in the movement, and shall be watchful to checkmate any attempt on Redmond's part to prevent us from arming. This is the real danger. The future of the movement depends upon our remaining at our posts to see to it that the Volunteers are a real army, not a stage army.

The movement at present is sweeping through the country like a whirlwind and the one cry is "Give us arms". Birrell in Parliament acknowledged the other day that we are recruiting at the rate of 15,000 a week. Of numbers and enthusiasm there is no lack; discipline is being acquired; but guns? If the Parliamentarians help us to arm it will be well worth while having surrendered to them. Whether they will help or not is still a question.

Do you get *The Irish Volunteer* each week? That and the *Weekly Freeman* would keep you in touch – you would then have both the work and the *talk*.

Remember me to Mrs. Mc Garrity and to all in your home. Any chance of your coming over this summer? I should dearly like to see that yellow machine coming up our drive, or the grey one. Sincerely yours, P. H. Pearse.

To James Reidy.

James Reidy was instrumental in having his friend's son, William Collins, come to Sgoil Éanna in September 1914 from New York, to join Gerry Cronin of Brooklyn and John Kilgallon of Far Rockaway.

Thomas Mac Donagh's article in the *Irish Review* contained a translation by him of one of Pearse's poems in *Suantraidhe agus Goltraidhe*, Lullaby of the Woman of the Mountain, which is also included in Mac Donagh's *Literature in Ireland (1916)*.

315

6.7.1914.   St. Enda's College.
                                   Rathfarnham.

A Chara Chroidhe,
   Yours of the 20th ult. duly to hand. Need I say that it will be a
great pleasure to us to have your friend's son at St. Enda's. Please
assure Mr. Collins of my personal interest in his boy and tell him
that we will see to it that he has a happy school life at St. Enda's
and that he receives careful individual instruction and that his
health etc. will be well looked after by my mother and sister.
   You have doubtless shown Mr. Collins a copy of the Prospectus
of which I left you some. The inclusive fee for board and tuition is
$200 a year. If I say $180 in your friend's case it will, I hope, meet
his views.
   We re-open 7th September and the boy should be with us by that
date.
   Young Cronin of Brooklyn is getting on well. He is quick and
intelligent; I have also got another Irish–American pupil for next
term, – his name is Kilgallon and his father owns real estate at Far
Rockaway. He is quite a young man and will rank as a University
resident.
   You will have noted recent developments re Volunteers. I must
send Mr. Devoy a long letter as soon as I get time. The Provisional
Committee has saved an immediate split by yielding to Redmond
for the present. I voted against the surrender but it may have been
the wisest thing in the long run. We all, dissentient as well as the
rest, remain at our posts to guard against any possible treachery.
Recent information would go to show that Redmond is acting in
good faith and would really like to see us armed. Once we are
armed our position will be impregnable; and the watchword then
must be *never to disband or to surrender our arms* no matter at
whose bidding.
   It is interesting to note that in the election of officers now going
on in Dublin, the companies are for the most part rejecting those
who voted for surrendering to Redmond and electing the dissentients and their supporters. Had there been a split Dublin, Cork
City and County, Limerick and Galway cities and all Co. Kerry
would have adhered to us. I am not sure as to the rest of the
country but there would have been a large minority with us
everywhere.
   By the way if you publish that article of Mac Donagh's from the
Irish Review, please omit his translation of the poem beginning "O
little head of Gold". The *North American Review* has accepted a

translation of the same poem done by myself and it is as well that a previous translation should not appear in America.

A thousand thanks for your good offices re Mr. Collin's son. Sincerely yours, P. H. Pearse.

To J. Mc Garrity.

This is a most important letter as it indicates the position on the Volunteer Provisional Committee, as Pearse saw it, after Redmond had secured numerical control of the movement. It shows that Pearse clearly undestood that Redmond's strategy was to prevent arms from reaching those of the volunteers whom he could not control. Further the purpose which Redmond saw in arming the volunteers was not that of opposing England but to impose Home-Rule on the reluctant Orangemen of Ulster and thus to precipitate the partition of the country. It is implied by Pearse that Redmond in his arms transactions had the conniving assistance of Asquith's government in his anti-Carsonite stance.

The differences of opinion and conviction which two years later are clearly manifest in the Rising are already evident in the body which exercised authority over the Volunteers. It seems quite clear that Pearse was by this a spokesman for those, whom he describes as "the physical force men", whose objective was not the subjection of the northern Unionists but the expulsion of the British. It is of some significance that in describing the nationalists, Pearse distinguishes between the Sinn Féiners and the Separatists; his analysis of the quality of the members of the Standing Committee is equally significant. His evaluation of Hobson is remarkably generous; he presents his motives for voting in favour of Redmond's demands and regrets that the I.R.B. had consequently dismissed him from the editorship of *Irish Freedom.* This dismissal and his loss of the position of Dublin correspondent of the *Gaelic American,* Pearse regards as excessively harsh.

The Meredith who figures on the Provisional Committee, appears later in a different context in Pearse's financial affairs; in September 1915 J. C. Meredith, a Redmondite, offered the legal advice to J. R. O'Connell which prompted him to issue a writ against Pearse, the outcome of which could have been the closure of Sgoil Éanna.

In the period of 1914–16 Pearse used Cullenswood House as the postal address for his political mail to America which he wished to evade the police censor; the Miss Byrne in question was a relative of

317

the family who may have occupied the building after Sgoil Íde closed in 1912.

L. 373/NLI

17.7.1914. St. Enda's College,
Rathfarnham.

A Chara Chroidhe,

I am writing on behalf of the large and important element in the Irish Volunteers represented by the nine dissentients on the Provisional Committee; in other words, on behalf of the men who are still determined to keep the movement straight and to lead it, if they can, to a genuine national purpose. Our appeal is this; we want the American Committee to make arrangements, if possible, to send us *at once* at least as much arms and ammunition as will arm our men in Dublin, – say 1,000 rifles with a fair amount of ammunition for each. We want this request to take precedence of any other request that may have been made by Mac Neill or by anyone else. A friend of mine will be in America before this reaches you, and, though he was not one of the nine dissentients, his *bona fides* is above suspicion, and he will, I think, give you further reasons showing the necessity of doing what I suggest, if the situation is to be saved. The men with whom I am acting more immediately in this are Sean Mac Diarmada, Kent, and Fitzgibbon. Let me, at the risk of writing an unduly long letter, give the facts of the situation as they exist at the present moment.

I give my colleagues who voted for the surrender to Redmond credit for doing what seemed to them absolutely the best thing in the interests of the movement. Most of them expressed distrust of Redmond, but said that a split must be avoided at all hazards at this stage. Hobson made a strong Separatist speech, saying that Redmond was out to smash the movement, and that the best way to prevent him was to accept his terms for the present and to remain in the movement to meet and best him should he try treachery later on. (I think they have been too hard on Hobson on your side, and regret very much to hear that he has been dropped as Dublin correspondent of the *Gaelic American.* He has lost the acting editorship of *Freedom* too, and is left without income of any sort. He may have to leave Dublin, which would be an incalculable loss. Weigh all this.) To resume, I admit the temptation to vote for unity in Ireland was very great (no one foresaw the American difficulty) but I and the eight others resisted mainly on these grounds.

1.   That we were bound to keep faith with those who had come

318

into the movement on our assurance that it was open to all parties; and

2. that we could not be sure that Redmond, so closely allied with Asquith, could or would cooperate with us in arming the Volunteers.

Now, it appears that in the second thing we were wrong; and the danger to be feared from Redmond is of a different and graver sort. He does want to arm the Volunteers, or a portion of them; but he wants *to arm them, not against England, but against the Orangemen*. The Volunteers are to be used to force Home Rule on Ulster, and possibly to enforce the *dismemberment of Ireland*. Some semblance of Home Rule must, at all costs, be placed on the statute books; the Volunteers have been captured in order to secure this, no matter how humiliating the terms. All this has been made plain to us within the last few days. When Gore and Walsh went to London from the Provisional Committee to see Redmond, Redmond told them he had bought 4,000 rifles with ammunition at a cost of £10,000, of which he had paid down a portion so as to secure the rifles, – the balance to be paid when or before del'very could be effected. He looked to the enlarged Volunteer Committee to "run" the guns for him, and hinted (so I understand from Gore) that the Government might relax the precautions so as to convenience us. On Tuesday night last, at the first meeting of the enlarged committee, Devlin stated that he had just "run" enough guns into Belfast to arm his men; and he added afterwards to one of the members that his lot included two machine guns. All this would be excellent if the men were genuine nationalists. But they are only Home Rulers-at-any-price.

Man after man of Redmond's nominees stood up at the meeting and made clear that it is against Ulster the guns are to be used. They spoke of the "massacre" which might break out in the north any minute. They said that all arms reaching us for the present must go to Ulster. It was even suggested that those of us in the south and west who have guns (and guns have just reached Co. Wexford, I know for a fact, and, according to newspapers, Co. Tipperary) should send them north for use by the Catholics there to defend themselves when the "massacre" breaks out. The whole tone of the movement has changed, judging at least from the talk at the Provisional Committee. The men whom Redmond has nominated clearly regard it as a Pro-Asquith and Anti-Carson movement. They speak of the "friendly English government" whose efforts we are to "second".

Now, here is the situation. The Unionists are armed. The Redmondites are rapidly arming. The Nationalists (Sinn Feiners

319

and Separatists) remain unarmed. It will be an irony of ironies if this movement comes and goes and leaves *us* – the physical force men! the only unarmed group in the country. And this is the intention of those at the head of affairs. *Arms are to be prevented from reaching those whom Redmond cannot control.* On Tuesday night (without notice) they carried a resolution appointing a Standing Committee which is practically to take charge of the movement – the full Provisional Committee, is to meet only once a month. The following are the members of the Standing Committee: Burke, Donovan, Fitzgibbon, Hobson, Judge, Meredith, Nugent, Fr. O'Hare, Walsh, Mac Neill, L. Kettle, Gore, O'Rahilly. Of these 13 only Hobson and Fitzgibbon can be absolutely relied on; Judge (though a Hibernian) I believe sound and courageous; Mac Neill and O'Rahilly are honest, but weak and frightfully subject to panic. The rest will do exactly as Redmond tells them. At most we can count on only 5 out of the 13 who now rule the Volunteers; but possibly only 2 or 3.

I think you will see the necessity of our not allowing a crash to come until our men at least are armed. Dublin is with us almost to a man; Cork City and Co., Limerick City, Waterford City, Galway City, Co. Kerry and a large minority everywhere, including all the best men – the young, active men. We owe it to these men to arm them; we shall be stultified forever if we allow the chance to go by. We propose to commence in Dublin, which is the soundest, and where we have most influence.

Now, is it in your power to get 1,000 rifles and ammunition for us? – more if possible, but at least 1,000 to start with. Springfields would do, but better perhaps Mausers, 7 millimetres which is the pattern most easy to get. The great point is to have rifles for which we shall be able to get ammunition easily. Your plan should be, I think, to send someone to Europe to make a purchase and then to come on to Dublin to make arrangements with us. Of course you would not land guns until we had completed all arrangements for receiving and distributing them. If need be, we will stand some of the cost, for, if we know guns are coming, we will see that our Companies retain their Defence of Ireland funds in their own hands instead of forwarding the money to the suspected Provisional Committee or its precious Standing Committee. Now, please act on this at once; disregard other appeals for the present and cooperate with Mac Dermott, Kent, Fitzgibbon and me in seeing the *sound* men are armed at the earliest possible instant. Let us at least reap that much good out of the movement before it degenerates.

You can communicate with me confidentially on this or other matters as follows. All letters addressed to "Miss O'Hara c/o Miss

Byrne, Cullenswood House, Oakley Road, Rathmines, Dublin". will be handed unopened to me. Use plain envelopes. Cables may go to the same address.

Please regard all inside information in this letter as for your private ear or those of colleagues, but not to be used in *Gaelic American* or elsewhere in public. I should not like things said at Provisional Committee to get into the press through me.

I am sending Devoy a letter almost identical with this. The cause is in your hands now. We are here to do our part. God bless you and prosper whatever ·effort you may make. It is up to us and you to *accomplish* something now.

Kindest regards to your family and all Philadelphia friends. Sincerely and fraternally yours, P. H. Pearse.

To J. Mc Garrity.

With the cooperation of generous friends, Roger Casement and Mrs. Erskine Childers organised the funds with which Darrel Figgis purchased arms and ammunition in Hamburg; these were shipped by means of the Childers' yacht, *Asgard* and landed at Howth pier on Sunday July 26th 1914. Other shipments were landed in Bere Island Co. Cork and at Kilcoole, Co. Wicklow during the following week.

The rifles were collected by volunteers of the Dublin Brigade, who marched into Dublin from Howth; at Clontarf they were met by a cordon of police supported by military. Most of the Brigade scattered and only a small amount of the arms was captured by the British. A contingent of the Scottish Borderers returning from Clontarf, passed along Bachelor's Walk, where they were heckled and stoned by the populace. The soldiers opened fire on the civilians, wounding over thirty and killing three. This outrage generated public indignation and secured the first tangible popular support for that section of the Volunteers which disowned the policy of Redmond; the slogan of the Separatist Volunteers henceforth was "Remember Bachelor's Walk". Pearse was correct in his claim in this letter that the events surrounding the Howth gun-running would be to the advantage of the movement.

It seems that Pearse used the address of Miss Mc Kenna at 517 West 144th St., New York, as his main postal route to Mc Garrity and Devoy.

Pearse was in Rosmuc when the gun-running took place.

321

L. 374/NLI

28.7.1914.   Turlough,
                                        Rosmuck,
                                        Co. Galway.

A Chara Chroidhe,

The successful landing of over 2,000 rifles at Howth on Sunday last has to a certain extent changed the situation for the better since I last wrote you. Most of the Dublin Volunteers have now guns; and a large proportion are necessarily in the hands of our friends. There is therefore not quite the same urgent need for haste on your part as there was when I wrote over a week ago. You can do things on a larger scale than I then contemplated, forming your plans carefully, and working to send us as large a consignment as you can of serviceable rifles and ammunition. When our followers in the city are armed we have Dublin County to attend to; and then there is the whole country. The essential thing (and this remains as essential as when I wrote before) is that arms in large quantities should reach *us*, so that *our* men are armed. Strong efforts will be made here to prevent arms from getting into the hands of any men who cannot be relied on to obey Redmond; this is what we have to fight against.

The stirring events of Sunday will rebound enormously to the advantage of the movement. The discipline of the Volunteers was splendid. The soldiers *ran* before them. There has been nothing like it since 1798. The brutal murders of the unarmed crowd by the soldiers who an hour previously had run from the Volunteers have given public sentiment just that turn that was desirable. The army is an object of odium and derision and the Volunteers are the heroes of the hour. The whole movement, the whole country, has been re-baptised by bloodshed for Ireland.

In the meantime, the Redmondites are fastening their grip on the central government. Last Friday's meeting of the Provisional Committee was perfectly disgusting. Two of Redmond's nominees were drunk. We succeeded in getting Sean Mac Diarmada and Col. Moore added to the Standing Committee, but to balance that the aim of the movement was to back up Redmond and the Parliamentary Party. I replied by saying that the aim of the movement was to secure and maintain the freedom of Ireland, and that it must be kept open to all who were willing to work and fight for that end whether followers of Redmond or not. There was a good deal of plain talking and the two parties stand clearly defined. It will be a fight all the way. They have officially decided to send all arms to Ulster – which means to Devlin's followers. We are determined not to acquiesce in this; independently of the Provisional Committee, we must arm our men in every part of Ireland and bid them never to part with their arms. The need, therefore, for you on your side to send arms to *us*, and not to the Provisional Committee, is evident and urgent. I beg of you to see to it that the arms are sent to the right people.

I write in haste. I am sending Devoy a similar letter. My letters go under cover to a friend in New York. Remember the address that gets me if you have anything confidential to say; "Miss O'Hara, c/o Miss Byrne, Cullenswood House, Oakley Road, Rathmines, Dublin". Praying for successful efforts on your side, Sincerely yours, P. H. Pearse.

P.S. I will have a copy of Monday's *Irish Independent* sent to you direct, as it has the best account of Sunday's events. Read the description by a volunteer, and Darrell Figgis's account.

To J. Mc Garrity.

As the European war drew closer and Redmond's commitment to British war needs was more clearly revealed, Pearse became convinced of the urgent need to seek arms in America for those of the Volunteers whose allegiance was to Irish independence alone.

On the same day on which Pearse wrote this letter, it was announced to the House of Commons in London, that the Government had decided to declare war on Germany. Redmond assured the Government of the support of Ireland in the war and suggested that all British forces could with confidence be withdrawn from Ireland as the Irish Volunteers would defend Ireland on behalf of Britain. Those whom Pearse represented on the Volunteer Provisional Committee rejected Redmond's stance and when Asquith declared that Britain was fighting to vindicate the principle "that small nationalities are not to be crushed, by the arbitary will of a stronger and overmastering power", they agreed wholeheartedly with the sentiments of the British Prime Minister. They required however that those lofty sentiments be applied to Ireland first and consequently regarded as the first duty of Irishmen to assert in arms the right of their own country to independence even in opposition to "a stronger and overmastering power".

It seems strange to notice Pearse in this letter exhorting Mc Garrity to take prudent care of his health in matters of sleep and meals. His exhortation to hoard their strength against a possible greater demand would seem to indicate that the inevitability of armed rising was present to Pearse's thinking from after his American tour.

L. 375/NLI

3.8.1914.   Turlough,
                                         Rosmuck,
                                         Co. Galway.

A Chara Chroidhe,

I am here in the country, and yours of the 15th ult has been forwarded to me. Accept my most heartfelt thanks for your remittance of $100 for the St. Enda's College Fund. Please thank Father Coughlan for me; I will write him also myself. To you the main thanks is due and I shall never be able properly to express it. I shall shortly be sending a final list of acknowledgements to the *Gaelic American* and I will pay Philadelphia a special and well-deserved tribute.

You will have received two long letters from me giving you all details of Volunteer affairs for the last few weeks. I need only say here that the need for acting in the direction indicated in those letters is greater than ever. Heaven knows what the future holds if England is drawn into this European war. You will have seen that Carson has stated that his Volunteers will and must take over from the British garrison charge of the whole country. We must fight any move on Redmond's part to offer their services to the English Government but we should be fools if we let slip an opportunity of taking over from the British Army the task of defending the soil of Ireland. History may repeat exactly the same course which it followed in 1779–82. If the British Army is engaged elsewhere, Ireland falls to the Volunteers, and then – well then we must rise to the occasion.

Your committee will be alive to the absolute necessity, in all the circumstances, of pushing on your work of helping us to arm with the utmost rapidity. *Every moment is precious now.* At the funeral of the victims of the military murders the Dublin Volunteers took over for two days practically the whole police and military duty of the city. It was an excellent piece of training.

The wave of Nationalism among the police and among the Irish regiments of the British Army is most significant.

Your situation, with the Ryan Committee on your flanks, is a very trying one. I think you have acted splendidly, and all your pronouncements have been most judicious. Your name within the

324

last few weeks has become well and favourably known among Nationalists here.

You must not work too hard, as you cannot afford – the cause cannot afford – a breakdown of your health. Above all, I would urge you not to neglect sleep and meals. I attribute my own capacity for getting through work to my always taking enough sleep and never neglecting meals. I have seen many break down, and am determined not to break down myself. We must hoard our strength and vitality against a possibly greater demand than even the present one.

The movement is leaping ahead for the past week even faster than before. The one cry is "arms". God bless and prosper your efforts. Believe me, Always sincerely and gratefully yours. P. H. Pearse

To J. Mc Garrity.

Pearse was not in Dublin for the Howth gun-running although there is no evidence in his letters that he was not party to the plan. During his "few busy days" in Dublin he probably attended some meetings of the Volunteer group which realised that they must initiate action outside the Provisional Committee; he certainly is in possession of very detailed intelligence on the arms question when writing this letter. It would seem that the separatist leaders had significant following in the Dublin County Board of the Volunteers; they secured majority support for resolutions of neutrality and attempted to influence the Provisional Committee by parading in front of the headquarters.

Sgoil Éanna was used as a hiding place for the Howth guns and ammunition which Plunkett was stockpiling to avoid their being sent North by Redmond's followers.

L. 376/NLI

12.8.1914.   Turlough,
                                Rosmuck,
                                Co. Galway.

A Chara Chroidhe,

I have come back here after a few busy days in Dublin, and send you the following chronicle of events.

First, to remove some misimpressions which I and others may have given you. I think I told you that the number of guns landed at

325

Howth was 2,500 and Tom Clarke in his cable to "G.A." says 2,000. We have both exaggerated, relying on rumour. The actual number was only 900. The number landed at Kilcoole was only 600. This gives 1,500 in all. They are 11 mm. Mausers of a rather antiquated pattern, without magazines, and are much inferior to the British service rifle and even to those which Carson's men have. Moreover the ammunition landed is useless. It consists of *explosive* bullets, which are against the rules of civilised war and which therefore, we are not serving out to the men. As to these 1500 rifles, the Provisional Committee insists on sending as many as possible to Ulster – which means to Devlin's Hibernians and unheard of efforts will be made to keep guns out of the hands of men not known to be loyal to Redmond. In fact, the last meeting of the Provisional Committee was largely devoted to a squabble as to who is to get the guns. Redmond's men roundly charged us with attempting to steal them and a subcommittee was appointed to ascertain the whereabouts of all the guns and send as many as possible north.

Well, the European crisis finds the Irish Volunteers with 1500 or (allowing for other small quantities landed) 2,000 rifles, and no ammunition. It is obvious that before we can intervene, or even pretend to intervene, in the crisis to any purpose we must have arms. Hence the one great duty of the hour, the duty which overshadows every other duty, is to get guns and ammunition into the country. It is up to the American Committee to act *at once* and on a *large scale*. You are as much alive to the need as I am. Every penny you can command must be expended now and the goods sent to us with as little delay as possible. A supreme moment for Ireland may be at hand. We shall go down to our graves beaten and disgraced men if we are not ready for it.

Publicly, the movement has been committed to loyal support of England; not officially so far, but by implication. To everyone in Ireland that has any brains it seems either madness or treachery on Redmond's part. His followers on the Provisional Committee at its last meeting took no action either way, but simply leave it to Redmond to speak and act for the whole movement in this grave crisis, and squelch any attempt even to discuss his action.

Last week the Dublin Co. Board of the Volunteers made an effort to set things straight. They drew up a resolution for adoption by the battalions expressing readiness to cooperate with Ulster for the defence of Ireland but unwillingness to support the British Government against foreign nations with which Ireland has no quarrel. Three out of five Dublin battalions adopted this unanimously and paraded in front of the Provisional Committee's office

326

during a meeting and sent in spokesmen to convey the resolution to the Committee. The reply of the Provisional Committee was to order the Dublin Co. Board and all concerned to apologize and promise not to adopt resolutions dealing with matters of policy again on pain of suspension. In the meantime companies everywhere are adopting resolutions approving of Redmond's offer of loyal help. In other words, volunteer bodies are not free to pass resolutions or take any action even indirectly dissociating themselves from his offer of loyal help. Redmond's capture of the government of the Volunteers is absolute and complete.

I had hoped that the original members would act together and save the movement from complete capture. That hope has proved vain. All Hibernians and Redmondites (with the honourable exception of Judge) vote with the new members, and steadily vote us down. I personally have ceased to be any use on the Committee. I can never carry a single point. I am now scarcely allowed to speak. The moment I stand up there are cries of "Put the question" etc. – after the last meeting I had half determined to resign, but have decided to stick on a little longer in the hope of being useful at a later stage.

I blame Mac Neill more than anyone. He has the reputation of being "tactful", but his "tact" consists in bowing to the will of the Redmondites every time. He never makes a fight except when they assail his personal honour, when be bridles up at once. Perhaps I am wronging him, as I am smarting under the remembrance of what I regard as very unfair treatment of me personally and of all who agree with me at the last meeting. He is in a very delicate position and he is weak, hopelessly weak. I knew that all along.

Now it is perfectly clear that whatever is to be done for Ireland in this crisis must be done *outside* the Provisional Committee. The men are sound, especially in Dublin. We could at any moment rally the best of them to our support by a *coup d'état*; and rally the whole country if the *coup d'état* were successful. But a *coup d'état* while the men are still unarmed is unthinkable.

The British Government will arm and train us if we come under the War Office and accept the Commander-in-Chief in Ireland as our generalissimo. Detailed plans are already drawn up and have been tentatively submitted. So far, the Provisional Committee is unanimous against it. But if Redmond directs them to submit? Then, I think, the split will come.

I am sending a letter in similar terms to Devoy. Do not use any of this for publication. Sincerely yours, P. H. Pearse.

To Fr. B. Crehan C.C.

Fr. B. Crehan of the Elphin Diocese and curate at Sligo, was a member of the Gaelic League. He was a member of the Committee of Coláiste Chonnacht at Tuar Mhic Éide and in that capacity he invited Pearse to function as extern examiner for the trainee teachers who had taken the course in 1914.

L.(p.c.) 377/SM/G

Autumn 1914.

I was in America when your first letter arrived. I will certainly do the work in question; the £10 will be most useful. I am grateful to you for offering me the post. I am writing to Dr. Henry and to P. Ó. Domhnalláin to ascertain when I am wanted. With best wishes. P. Mac Piarais.

To Joseph Plunkett.

This terse postcard message to Plunkett conveys an urgency and also a secrecy which can only be occasioned by the growing support of Redmond for the British war effort.

Plunkett was one of those concerned in the movement to forge an alliance between the I.R.B. and the militant socialists led by Connolly. A meeting took place on September 9th attended by Clarke, Mc Dermott, Pearse, Plunkett, Connolly, William O'Brien, Major Mac Bride, Ceannt, Mac Donagh and Seán T. Ó Ceallaigh; it was decided to form sub-committees with specific functions in relation to securing German aid and planning an armed insurrection.

L.(p.c.) 378/NLI

24.8.1914.   St. Enda's,
                                   Rathfarnham.

A Chara,
I am anxious to have a talk with you before Wednesday evening. Could you ring me up and make an appointment? Wednesday would suit me better than Tuesday. P. H Pearse.

To J. Mc Garrity.

September 1914 witnessed a rapid deterioration in relations between the Redmondites and the Separatists on the Volunteer Provisional Committee; Pearse was physically assaulted at one meeting and had come to the conclusion that an alternative mechanism was needed. Redmond's Woodenbridge speech of September 20th sealed the fate of the movement and precipitated the final division when he advocated that Young Ireland should voluntarily enlist in the British army to fight "wherever the firing line extends in defence of right, freedom and religion". Those who supported Pearse in the conviction that the aim of the Volunteers was "to secure and maintain the freedom of Ireland", were those whom he describes in this letter as pulling the Volunteers straight. This was done by allowing the vast majority of the 180,000 movement under Redmond's leadership become the National Volunteers while the separatist group, commanding the allegiance of about 10,000 men, retained the original title of Irish Volunteers and their commitment to a policy of separatism.

Joe Mc Garrity's brother was a priest in America; on holiday in Ireland in 1914 he suffered an accident which necessitated hospitalisation and delayed his departure. Pearse was obviously close to him in his convalescence and in return Fr. Mc Garrity acted as courier for conspiratorial mail between Dublin and America.

Pearse in this letter pays a well-deserved tribute to the personal generosity and dedication of Joe Mc Garrity to Sgoil Éanna.

L. 379/NLI

26.9.1914.   St. Enda's College.
                             Rathfarnham.

A Chara Chroidhe,

I had two letters commenced to you, but events were moving so fast that they became out of date. We are now in the midst of so exciting a crisis that I can only delay to tell you the things that are necessary to tell you. A soon as I have time I will write you again at length.

First, the thing about which you will be most anxious. As I cabled you, I saw your brother and found him in excellent general health and spirits. He goes out every day, goes to the theatre twice a week and is now saying Mass again. His accident is serious enough and might have been very serious. He wishes to be the first himself to tell you how it happened. He is wearing a stall over his

329

eye, which is the only outward sign of his injury. He hopes that when all is healed up there will be no permanent blemish. He sails Lusitania, Oct. 24th. There is no need for you to come over for him, as he can quite look after himself.

Next, to thank you for your unparallelled generosity to St. Enda's. I have no words to express what I feel. I heard from your friend that you had to raise the money yourself. Such generosity, such friendship, cannot be appreciated in words. I only hope St. Enda's will prove worthy of it; at any rate, its pupils will repay you in the way you will like best, by work for Ireland in the days to come.

We duly opened on September 7th. I was able to keep things steady until your message came. We have fewer boys than last year. My political opinions are looked upon as too extreme and dangerous and parents are nervous. The war, too, makes everything dearer. It will be an anxious and difficult year; yet, thanks to you, I hope to keep the flag flying till bright days begin, a thousand thanks.

Before this reaches you, *we will have pulled the Volunteers straight.* No matter how badly things look, no matter what accounts you hear of loyalty and recruiting, rely upon the men here to do all that is possible. If at any time we seem to be too quiet, it is because we are awaiting a favourable moment for decisive action as regards the Volunteers.

I know how hard things are with you. They are as hard here. We must all trust in God and hammer away. Believe me, Always affectionately and gratefully yours, P. H. Pearse.

To J. Mc Garrity.

Fr. Mc Garrity sailed for America on October 24th. on the ill-fated *Lusitania*; he carried this letter with him from Pearse. The heightened political tension following the final split in the Volunteers and the decision of the I.R.B. to initiate an insurrection is clearly reflected in this letter. A small committee of three, Pearse, Plunkett and Kent, had been established within the I.R.B. to plan a rising; one of its first objectives was to ensure that American funds were directed to the arming groups who are in their confidence. Pearse here advocates that such funds on the nomination of the donors, be placed at the disposal of the inner group of five who pledged to strike "for the complete thing". The differences of opinion and the divisions in the leadership which beset the Rising are already evident in the autumn of 1914.

The first convention of the Irish Volunteers was originally intended for November 25th, 1914 the anniversary of the foundation meeting, but was brought forward to October 25th. While Redmond's recruitment drive succeeded in luring almost 200,000 to enlist from Ireland, *The Irish Times, The Daily Express* and other papers were enthusiastically encouraging the government to introduce conscription.

L. 380/NLI

19.10.1914.   St. Enda's College,
                               Rathfarnham.

A Chara Chroidhe,
    I take the opportunity of your brother's return to write you at some length. I want to add my personal appeal to appeals which will already have reached you as to the urgent need of making available *now* whatever money you have in America for arming the Volunteers. We do not know the moment when action may be forced upon us. We shall have to act (1) if the Germans land either in Ireland or in England; (2) if the Government enforces the Militia Ballot Act or any other drastic way of securing recruits; (3) if the food supply becomes scarce; (4) if the Government tries to disarm the "disloyal" Volunteers and (5) if the Government commences to arrest our leaders, *who are being pointed out to them* (if they did not know them before) by the Redmondite press. Any one of these things may happen at any moment; any one of them would precipitate a crisis, – *the* crisis; and we are not ready, for we have not arms. If the chance comes and goes, it will in all probability have come and gone forever, certainly for our lifetime. I therefore urge upon you the necessity of sending us *now* whatever sum you have got together. In the last *Gaelic American* to hand the total acknowledged was some $27,000. You had sent us $5,000. That seems to leave $22,000 now available in America for arms for the Volunteers. I ask you to send that sum at once by trustworthy hands. Its coming in time may mean the success of whatever we have to do; it may mean *victory*. Its failure to come may mean either a bloody debacle like '98 or a dreary fizzling out like '48 or '67.
    I would suggest that in sending the money you do not entrust the expenditure of the whole of it to Mac Neill and O'Reilly or any other two men. Not that I doubt their honesty but simply that they are not in or of our counsels and they are not formally pledged to strike, if the chance comes, for the complete thing. I suggest that you name certain sums to be placed at the disposal of certain men

331

whom you know, for the arming of Volunteer companies to be selected by then. This is the only way I can see of securing that the right men are armed. Thus, if T. Clarke, J. Mc Dermott, Hobson, Kent and myself had each $2,500 at his disposal to arm the companies each is in touch with, the arms would be sure to get into the right hands, and the transaction would be perfectly *bona fide* and could be defended before the Provisional Committee as the donors of money are plainly entitled to say who is to have the disbursement of it. This is O'Rahilly's own suggestion and he points out that if the last $5,000 had been earmarked for companies to be selected by named individuals, the rifles bought with it could never have been seized (as they have been seized) by Redmondites. (The greater number of the Howth rifles were stolen by Nugent and others; of the whole 1500 landed at Howth and Kilcoole we have only 600 or 500). Now that the Redmondites have left us, such a thing could not well happen again; still, the only safe plan is to place named sums at the disposal of named individuals. If anyone questions this, the reply is "such is the wish of the donors, and they will give their money on no other conditions".

It is my mature conviction that, given arms, the Volunteers who have adhered to us as against Redmond may be depended upon to act vigorously, courageously, promptly, and unitedly if the opportunity comes. We are at the moment in an immensely stronger position than ever before. The whole body of Volunteers that has supported our stand against recruiting may be looked upon as a separatist body. In other words, the separatist organization has been multiplied by a hundred. In Dublin we have some 2,500 admirably disciplined, drilled, intelligent and partly armed men. Nationalist Ireland, has never before had such an asset. Our main strength is in Dublin, but large minorities support us everywhere, especially in the towns and in the extreme south and west. We expect to have 150 companies, representing 10,000 to 15,000 men represented by delegates at next Sunday's Convention. This small compact, perfectly disciplined, determined *separatist* force is infinitely more valuable than the unwieldy loosely held together mixum-gatherum force we had before the split. The Volunteers we have with us now may be relied upon to the death, and we are daily perfecting their fighting effectiveness and mobilization power.

It seems a big thing to say, but I do honestly believe that, with arms for these men, we shall be ready to *act* with tremendous effect if the war brings us the moment.

The spirit of our Dublin men is wonderful. They would rise tomorrow if we gave the word. A meeting of Dublin officers the other night was as exhilarating as a draught of wine.

332

We gain daily in the country as Redmond's treachery or imbecility becomes more manifest. The recruiting campaign has failed utterly and already he is a discredited politician. The subsidized press of course represents the country as being with him, but it is not. Even those who support his leadership are overtly or covertly against his recruiting efforts. The Government is realizing to its chagrin that Redmond cannot fulfil his bargain. In their fury they are getting their kept papers to threaten the Militia Ballot Act. If *that* comes, the crisis will be upon us, for we must resist at the utmost peril to ourselves.

All of which brings me back to this; let America do its part *now*.

Greetings and kindliest regards to all. Please pass this on to John Devoy. I will write again when I can.

St. Enda's struggles on. Your brother will give you further news. Sincerely and always gratefully yours. P. H. Pearse.

To Miss Mc Kenna.

The postmark on the envelope of this letter (Dublin 1.30 a.m. 14 Dec '14) raises some questions. Did Pearse write it in October and forget to post it until six weeks later in early December? Did he write it much later in November and pre-date it? The reference to "the Convention last Sunday" seems to rule that out; the convention in question was held on October 25th. The most likely explanation is that police censors intercepted the letter and retained it for detailed examination over six weeks.

The three Irish–American pupils were, John Kilgallon, Jerry Cronin and William Collins.

L. 381/P.Ms.

30.10.1914.   St. Enda's College,
                                                      Rathfarnham.

A Chara,

I am sorry to have left you without a leter so long, but you will understand how busy I have been what with exciting political events, developments in the Volunteers and my own worries and cares at St. Enda's. Since I saw you the Volunteers have been bought and sold but – happily – redeemed again, and we are now much stronger and more hopeful than ever, having a compact and disciplined body on which we can absolutely rely. The Convention last Sunday was most inspiring, and we have now got a tiny daily paper (*Eire – Ireland*) in which we shall be able to make our voice heard at any rate until the crisis is over.

How are you all? I am glad to hear that Peter Golden is with you. I hope that John, Paddy, Brigid and yourself are all well. I was very sorry to hear that there has been trouble over the Anne Devlin Entertainment, and that Alice and the Potters were no longer on the old friendly terms with you. I do hope that things have straightened out since. I would not like to think of old friends falling out over an enterprise into which all entered in my interests and with, apparently, such loyal cooperation in the beginning.

Do you see Matt Harford often? Remember me to him and to all the others.

I don't know when I shall have the pleasure of seeing you all again. My projected autumn visit was, of course, made impossible by the Volunteer collection in America as well as by events here which require my presence.

St. Enda's keeps its flag flying, though I have a somewhat smaller school this year. We have three Irish–American pupils.

Remember me to the Fitzgeralds, and to John and Peter Bennett if you see them. With kindest regards, Believe me, Yours sincerely. P. H. Pearse.

To Fr. Brian Ó Criocháin.

This letter of acknowledgement refers to the fee of £10 which Pearse received from the Committee of Coláiste Chonnacht for acting as extern examiner to the Summer Courses for teachers at Spidéal and Tuar Mhic Éide. The letter was accompanied by a signed receipt also dated 30th October 1914.

L. 382/SM/G

30.10.1914.

Dear Father,

I received the £10 for which I am very grateful. I enclose a receipt with my thousand thanks.

I enclose also a short report on the two examinations. I very much appreciate being asked to do this work and am grateful to the Committee. With every best wish, Yours, Pádraig Mac Piarais.

To his legal executors.

This item while technically not an ordinary letter, can be viewed as a communication to his legal representative and is of prime importance in relation to Pearse's complex financial arrangements. The accuracy of expression and the clarity reflect his legal training and also show that he had a very detailed and thorough grasp of his financial affairs. This document would seem to counter the claim frequently advanced that he was careless in book-keeping and feckless in his financial management; his arrangements were certainly complex yet they were coherent and in his own view capable of eventual resolution.

The political developments in the autumn of 1914 and the atmosphere generated by the I.R.B. decision to initiate an insurrection, probably impressed on Pearse the possibility of his early death, execution or lengthy imprisonment. This document was intended to facilitate the continuity of his financial policy in the event of any such occurence so that the interests of his creditors would be formally recorded and provided for.

By July 1920 through the good offices of Michael Collins and the Ministry of the First Dáil, funds from America enabled Mrs. Pearse to purchase the Hermitage and to discharge the outstanding liabilities. Among the last letters sent by Pearse prior to the Rising was one on the 23rd April to Mrs. Gertrude Bloomer enclosing a cheque for £5 as part repayment of the money she had invested in Sgoil Íde. In 1930 Mr. Joseph Dolan wrote to Mrs Pearse in response to her request confirming that he had given £1,100 in all to Pearse and that he would accept in repayment only whatever remained after she had provided for her own and Margaret's future.

L. 383/P.Ms.

25.11.1914.   St. Enda's College,
                                     Rathfarnham.

In view of the possibility of my death or incapacitation before I have fully discharged my liabilities in connection with St. Enda's and St. Ita's Colleges, I desire to make the following statement, which I will intrust to a friend with instructions to hand it to those acting legally for my estate in either of the eventualities referred to. Such persons will make the contents of the document known to the persons mentioned in the following paragraphs, and also to the authorities of the Clann-na-Gael of America.

My total liabilities in connection with the two Colleges amount at this date approximately to £6,000. In addition to trade liabilities, this amount includes the following sums advanced to me by friends.

£1,100	by	Mr. Joseph Dolan, Ardee.
£350	,,	,, Mr. Séumas Mac Manus, New York.
£300	,,	,, Mrs. Clarke, Frankfort, Blackrock.
£100	,,	,, Miss Louise Gavan Duffy, Dublin.
£800	,,	,, Mr. Joseph Mc Garrity, Philadelphia.

A sum of £200 originally advanced as a loan by Mr. Alec Wilson of Belfast was subsequently, at Mr. Wilson's request, regarded as qualifying him for shares in Sgoil Éanna Ltd.; in addition to which Mr. Wilson took a further £100 worth of shares. He subsequently placed a still further sum of £300 at my disposal to enable me to pay each of the trade creditors of the Colleges an instalment at the time the Company was dissolved and I resumed sole control of St. Enda's. These generous donations of Mr. Wilson's are not included in the above-mentioned sum of £6,000.

The following sums are, however, included in the said £6,000; (i) The unpaid portion, amounting at this date (with interest to 31st Dec. next) to £419 .. 17 .. 2, of a sum of £500 advanced to me by the Intermediate Education Board and secured by the signatures of Mrs. Emily Clarke of Blackrock, and Miss Emily Mac Carthy of Arisaig, Shankill; and (2) The unpaid portion, amounting at this date to £619.5.9, of certain advances made to me by the Hibernian Bank, Ltd., and secured by an insurance policy on my life, by the title deeds of Cullenswood House, and, *as to £275 of it*, by the signature of Mr. Stephen Barrett, of 55 Blessington Street, Dublin; also (3) The unpaid portion, amounting to £152 .. 19 .. 5, of certain sums advanced by Mrs Gertrude Bloomer for the upkeep of St. Ita's College, of which she was House-Mistress, on the understanding that she would require repayment only in the event of the financial position of the colleges being sufficiently strong to warrant such repayment.

I hope and believe that, if I live, I shall be able to discharge all these liabilities. If I die, they must remain in great part undischarged. I can only express my sorrow that my attempt to found a system of Irish secondary education in Ireland should have involved financial loss to so many generous friends.

There is one case which I feel bound to place on a different footing from the others. I believe that Mr. Stephen Barrett is not in a position to afford any financial loss. If, therefore, any portion of the sum of £275 for which the Hibernian Bank holds his signature has to be paid by him, I ask my friends in America and especially my friends of the Clann-na-Gael, to raise a fund to indemnify him. I have no right to make such a call upon the Clann-na-Gael, yet I do so because I know them to be the noblest and most generous Irish organisation in the world, because I know them to sympathise with my attempt at St. Enda's College, and because I know that they will be zealous to vindicate the honour and good name of one who shared with them great ideals and mighty hopes. P. H. Pearse.

To Mrs. G. Bloomer.

This apologetic letter of Pearse to the former House-mistress of Sgoil Íde was written in reply to a request from Mrs. Bloomer for the repayment of the advances made by her to the upkeep of the school in 1912. At the date of this letter, the amount unpaid stood at £152.19.5.

It is doubtful if Pearse expected that he could spend six months on an American lecture tour, given the pace of political developments at home.

L. 384/NLI

4.12.1914.   Sgoil Éanna,
                                    Rathfarnham.

Dear Mrs. Bloomer,
    I was engaged in town both yesterday and Wednesday afternoons and evenings, and it is only this evening that I am able to reply to your note.
    I have no money available at present to reduce any of the old liabilities of St. Enda's or St. Ita's and this year, as you will easily imagine, I am having a harder struggle than ever to keep St. Enda's going. My only resource for the reduction of the old debts is the proceeds of lectures, etc., in America, and, owing to the war, I have been obliged to cancel the arrangements I had made for resuming my tour this autumn. I must now wait till my friends there advise me that I can resume with any prospect of success. As soon as they give me the word I will go out again and will then resume the steady, if slow, reduction of the huge debt which still hangs over me.
    I need hardly tell you how I feel the slowness of my progress, and how I feel in particular the non-payment of those later advances of

yours to which you refer. I can only ask you to have patience a little longer and it is a hard thing to ask.

St. Enda's is losing every year, but I dare not let it die, as its continued existence is the sole condition on which I shall be able to pay off the old liabilities for I could not go out and appeal for funds for a defunct institution. The line of least resistance would be to give in, but instinct and honour cry out against that. And it is clear that I have done right in keeping on for the past two and a half years, since everyone has got something, whereas there would have been nothing had I given in in the summer of 1912.

My experience in America last spring convinces me that, given six months there, I could earn and collect enough to clear off the whole thing. It is just a question of trying to keep things going till my friends tell me I may come out again.

I wish I had more definite news for you. Believe me, Sincerely yours, P. H. Pearse.

To Miss Daly.

Miss Daly of Limerick was the sister of Ned Daly who commanded the Four Courts in the Rising and was executed on May 4th; their father had taken part in the Fenian Rising in 1867 and an uncle John Daly had spent twelve years in English prisons. Her sister, Kathleen was married to Tom Clarke, (1857–1916), the veteran Fenian who had served fifteen years penal servitude and was one of the leaders of the Rising.

The nephew referred to was Owen Clarke who came as a pupil to Sgoil Éanna in the Easter term of 1914. The letter is incomplete.

L. 385/P.Ms.

1.3.1915.   St. Enda's College,
                                              Rathfarnham.

Dear Miss Daly,

I have been confined to bed for some days with a bad cold, or I should have answered yours sooner. My brother had written a post card to explain the delay, but I told him not to post it as I should be up in a day or two. I am sorry now I did not let him send it, as you must have been wondering at my silence. I am better, but not quite well yet.

Need I say how glad (and *proud*) we should all be to have your nephew as a boarder at St. Enda's? I can promise care from my mother and sister who look after the boys' health and comfort, and care in his study and mental development from my masters and myself. He would, indeed have a special claim on us all.

I enclose you a copy of our Prospectus. You will see the terms for boarders on the last page. If there is any special way in which I can meet you, please let me know.

After the Easter Vacation will be a very favourable moment for him to join, as school is always most attractive on the approach of summer and the short Easter–Midsummer session will be a good preparation for the longer school year after September.

I enclose you some postcard views of our grounds etc. I do hope you will be able to manage this. It will be good for the boy and good for the cause. Let me know if there is any further ...

To Dr. W. J. Walsh.

Father Lambert Mc Kenna (1870–1953) was a noted Jesuit Celtic scholar who specialised in religious and bardic poetry; he also did valuable work in Irish lexicography – his *Fócloir Béarla agus Gaeilge* appeared in 1935. He had a particular interest in education and chaired the Second National Programme Conference in 1926 which drew up a revised Primary School Curriculum.

L. 386/DDA

9.3.1915.   Sgoil Éanna,
                                          Rathfarnham.

My dear Lord Archbishop,
    We are having a retreat for our boys commencing on Sunday next and lasting for the three days before St. Patrick's Day. It is to be conducted by Father Mc Kenna S.J. We are very anxious to have mass in our school chapel on the four days of the retreat – Sunday, Monday, Tuesday and Wednesday – if we can get the necessary permission. The chapel is properly fitted up with altar, etc., and Father Mc Kenna will be able to bring the altar stone, vestments, and whatever else is necessary.

    We feel that the retreat will hardly be complete unless we have mass each morning and it is rather far to go down to the parish church. We have mentioned the matter to Canon O'Keeffe who says he would be very glad to give us permission, but that it is a matter for the Ordinary or his Vicar General.

May I hope that Your Grace will be able to give us the necessary permission for mass on the four mornings in question? I am, my dear Lord Archbishop, Yours sincerely, P. H. Pearse.

To É. de Valera.

This letter carries no indication of the recipient; Éamonn de Valera however, was the Commandant of the Third Battalion of Dublin Brigade. Pearse as Director of Military Organisation was responsible for training.

L. 387/NLI

11.3.1915.   The Irish Volunteers,
                                            Headquarters,
                                    41 Kildare St. Dublin.

A Chara,
    At last night's meeting of the Executive you were formally appointed Commandant of the 3rd Battalion with Captain Fitzgibbon as Vice Commandant and Capt. Begley as Adjutant. I have mislaid the name of the Quartermaster, but he was also approved of. Could you let me know his name and former rank by return? (to St. Enda's?)
    Could you attend a meeting of the four Battalion Commandants on Saturday evening next after the officers' lecture? There are several important matters which the Headquarters Staff wants to discuss with the Commandants. Sincerely yours, P. H. Pearse.

To Dr. W. J. Walsh.

Due to an epidemic of 'flu at Sgoil Éanna, the retreat was postponed to the following week and held from the 22nd to the 24th. The earlier plans would have included a Sunday on which they would have been expected to go to the parish church at Rathfarnham.

L. 388/DDA

18.3.1915. Sgoil Éanna,
Rathfarnham.

My dear Lord Archbishop,

I have been confined to bed for some days by a bad cold or I should have acknowledged Your Grace's letter of the 11th sooner. I am very grateful for the permission to have mass on the mornings of the Retreat. Owing to my illness and to the fact that a large number of the boys were also victims of the prevailing epidemic of colds, we were obliged to postpone the Retreat, and we now propose to have it on Tuesday Wednesday and Thursday next, those days suiting Father Mc Kenna as well as ourselves. With Your Grace's permission we will have the Holy Sacrifice in our Chapel on each of those mornings. As no Sunday or holiday now intervenes, the difficulty which would have occurred this week is obviated.

With many thanks for the valued privilege which Your Grace's permission confers on us. I remain, My dear Lord Archbishop, Yours sincerely, P. H. Pearse.

To J. Mc Garrity.

This short note by Pearse was delivered to Mc Garrity by Joseph Plunkett, who went to America in the spring of 1915, as an emissary of the Military Committee of the I.R.B., with a view to engaging Clann-na-Gael support in the search for German military help.

L. 389/NLI

12.4.1915. Sgoil Éanna,
Rathfarnham.

A Chara Chroidhe,

My friend Mr. Plunkett will explain to you the situation re St. Enda's. I am trying to hold it until I can go out to America to resume my lecture tour. The need for help to tide me over the crisis is urgent. Indeed, I cannot open in September unless I get help.

You asked me to let you know. With kindest regards to all, Sincerely yours. P. H. Pearse.

To J. Mc Garrity.

Francis Sheehy Skeffington (1878–1916), was a socialist and pacifist who actively supported the feminist cause and contributed widely to periodicals and journals supporting the social and political independence movements. He was imprisoned in 1915 for opposing recruitment to the British Army and after a week on hunger strike, he was released. This letter of introduction by Pearse was used on a trip to the United States to campaign for the independence movement. During the Rising, he was arrested and despite his non-involvement was used as a hostage and shot without any legal formality on April 26th, by Captain Bowen-Cotthurst, who was declared by a court martial to have been of unsound mind. His son, Senator Owen Sheehy Skeffington of Trinity College became an indefatigable advocate of intellectual freedom and of social justice in the period 1945–1970.

Mary Catherine, was the youngest of the Mc Garrity children, who became very attached to Pearse when he stayed with the family during the U.S. tour.

L. 390/NLI

26.7.1915.   St. Enda's College,
                                     Rathfarnham.

A Chara Chroidhe,

This will introduce to you Mr. F. Sheehy Skeffington, with whose name you will be familiar.

He is anxious to get engagements as a lecturer in the United States. His opinions on recent happenings should be welcome to Irish–American audiences.

I hope that you and all my Philadelphia friends are well and flourishing. Remember me to Mrs. Mc Garrity and her mother. I suppose Mary Catherine forgets me? With kindest regards, Yours very sincerely, P. H. Pearse.

To J. Mc Garrity.

The financial crisis, which prompted this letter to Mc Garrity was occasioned by a surprising legal initiative taken by Sir John Robert O'Connell in connection with the rent of the Hermitage. In view of Pearse's regular, if tardy payment over five years, the issue of a writ seemed somewhat unnecessary. It may have been motivated by political considerations, generated by the Lord Chancellor's ambiguous information and the legal advice tendered to O'Connell by J. C. Meredith, a prominent pro-Redmondite who was expelled from the Volunteer Executive. The O'Donovan Rossa speech by Pearse at Glasnevin on August 1st, would have enhanced his value to the Castle and its allies as an object of their machinations.

Pearse gives expression to a deep sense of despondency in this letter at the prospect of these legal proceedings closing Sgoil Éanna and reducing his ability to contribute to the movement for independence at a critical moment. This view was obviously shared by his colleagues in the leadership; Tom Clarke, referred to here as "our friend Tom", sent a cable to America in support of the one sent on the previous day by Pearse, in which he described the appeal for Sgoil Éanna as "urgent and vital". This letter was posted on September 2nd and the letter following, almost identical, was written on the same day but sent by courier. Pearse implies here that his post was being monitored; the fate of his earlier letter to Miss Mc Kenna of New York (30.10.1914) would seem to indicate that the authorities had already begun to intercept his post in October 1914.

To differentiate between these two very similar letters written on September 2nd. to Joe Mc Garrity, the first one which was posted has been coded "mailed" and the second coded as "courier".

L. 391/NLI/(Mailed)

2.9.1915.   St. Enda's College,
                                   Rathfarnham.

A Chara Chroidhe,

I sent you a cable yesterday which I hope has reached you. In it I said that St. Enda's must close unless I have £300 at my disposal by Sept. 8th. Here are the circumstances under which the crisis has arisen.

The Lord Chancellor has stated to Sir John R. O'Connell, Solicitor and Trustee to the estate to which I pay £300 a year rent for the house and grounds of St. End'a, that I am "in a very dangerous position". He must be referring to my political rather than my financial position, of which he can know nothing. O'Connell has taken it to mean that the sooner he realizes the money I owe for rent the better. He has got the legal advice of J. C. Meredith, one of Redmond's expelled nominees, and they have issued a writ against me for £288 plus costs. The second half year is only just entered upon, and in the ordinary course they would be quite content to take a half year's rent and give me ample time –

343

nearly six months – to pay the rest. But they have issued writ for the whole amount, and insist on payment. I have no means of meeting the claim at present, and the situation therefore is that by this day week they will be able to mark judgement against me, put me in the "black list", send in sheriffs to seize the place and sell it up, compel me to close the College and make a bankrupt of me. We are all convinced that it is part of a move to discredit me in the eyes of the public. It is their way of hitting at me. They will represent me as a bankrupt and discredited man who takes refuge in "advanced" politics and hides his failure to meet his creditors by preaching sedition.

Now the effect of this will be not only to smash St. Enda's but to impair most seriously, if not fatally, my public influence and utility. I shall be involved in protracted bankruptcy proceedings, with public examinations by hostile counsel, etc., etc., and it will be impossible for me to give the cause at this supreme moment any useful help. I am down and out.

It can be averted if I have £300 by Sept. 8th. By taking advantage of certain legal proceedings we can stave off the matter for a few days after that, perhaps for a fortnight from now at the furthest. But then it will crash, unless I am helped.

My only resource in this great crisis is my ever generous friends in America. You told me to let you know when St. Enda's was in peril. Well, it and I are in peril now. You said that, if there was no other way, the Clan would put its hand into its pocket. Believe me, it will be worth while. I would not, as such a moment, ask for help if it were a merely personal concern, but much more is involved in this even than the future of St. Enda's. My fall now will – I speak without any exaggerated idea of my importance – be bad for the whole cause, will discredit the whole cause.

If I were free to do so I would go out to America by the first ship and earn and collect the money. But to go to America now would be to desert the danger gap. Whatever the consequences I must stand here as a wreck.

Our friend Tom has backed my cable by one from himself, which I hope has reached. He takes the same view as I do. I am hopeful that you will already have done something. If our friends out there know how really vital this is they will, I am sure, have already come to the rescue. Let me put it to you in one sentence, asking you to take my word, on my honour and truth as a man and as an Irishman, that the matter is so; it is essential that St. Enda's be saved, and if you have not already sent me the remittance I ask for, pray move heaven and earth to send it on receipt of this – we will avail of every legal quibble to hold out till the last moment – and you will save the situation. Ireland will surely repay anyone who makes financial sacrifice. It will be a great thing to defeat all enemies' plots and to hold St. Enda's for a bigger destiny with a clean name and record. Believe me, Yours most sincerely and gratefully, P. H. Pearse.

L. 392/NLI/(Courier)

2.9.1915.   St. Enda's College,
                                              Rathfarnham.

A Chara Chroidhe,
    A cable and a letter which I have sent you will, if they have gone safe, have reached you before this letter can, which I am sending by hand, to be mailed in New York. My fear is that my cables and letters may have been stopped, as the censor may think any communication between you and me dangerous even though, as in this case, on a purely private matter unconnected with politics.
    The crisis I feared with regard to St. Enda's has arisen. It has been precipitated by political opponents, and this is evidently their way of striking at me. I owe a sum of £300 for rent of St. Enda's. Half of it is due for some time, the rest has only just accrued due. In the ordinary course they would be satisfied with half, and give me some months to pay the rest. The solicitor who has charge of the matter, Sir John R. O'Connell, has been informed by the Lord Chancellor that I am "in a very dangerous position" – a broad hint to him to go for me. They have got the legal advice of James C. Meredith, one of Redmond's nominees whom we expelled and they have served a writ for £300 on me (or rather £288, which costs will bring up nearly to £300). This means that in nine days from now they will be able to mark judgement against me unless I can pay the £300. By "entering an appearance" I can stave off the matter for a few days longer, but within a fortnight, at the furthest, they will be able to smash St. Enda's. They can send in sheriff's officers and sell up the place. I shall have to become a bankrupt, and there will be protracted proceedings, with public examination, etc. in the Bankruptcy court. Not only do they hope thus to smash St. Enda's, but they hope to discredit me in the eyes of the public, and to lessen my influence and usefulness. They will be able to point to me as a discredited bankrupt seeking to retrieve his fortune by plunging recklessly into advanced politics. In a word, and without trying to exaggerate my importance, the closing of St. Enda's and the stigma of failure attaching to myself as a result will be a most serious blow for our cause and will render public work on my part next to impossible.

345

I must hold St. Enda's for the sake of the cause. I could bear to see it go down gloriously by my imprisonment for a political offence, but to see it go down squalidly as the result of such a plot will be heart-breaking.

I have no resource in this crisis but to ask my friends in America to come to the rescue. £300 by Sept. 8th or even a few days later, if we can succeed in staving things off, will save the situation. I hate to have to ask you to do anything at such a moment but I cannot help it; much more is involved than my personal fortunes. Were I free I would go right out to America myself and try to earn and collect the money, but this is impossible; my place is here, until the political crisis is over, and if I were to go away it would be a desertion. You told me that, if necessary, the clan would put its hand into its pocket to save St. Enda's. Let that be done, if there is no other way. Even in this letter, which will not pass through the post here, I do not venture to give you all the facts underlying the situation, but you will take it, on my truth and honour as a man and as an Irishman, that my utility to the cause depends largely on my being able to defeat the present attempt to undo my work and public influence, and that I see no way of defeating it except by my ever generous friends of the Clan providing £300 in some way. Ireland some day will, I hope, repay anyone who makes a financial sacrifice now.

I am hoping that, before receiving this, you will have acted on my cable of Sept. 1st. and on my other letters. When this reaches you it will almost be too late for you to do anything and this letter is intended rather as an explanation than as a further appeal. But, by taking advantage of every legal quibble, we may succeed in staving off the crisis even long enough to allow you to act on this if you have not acted already. I need not say more. It would be impossible to give all details, but you will, I know, take my word that the matter is as I tell you and that only such help as I have indicated can save St. Enda's from a squalid end at a moment when it is all-important that it and I should be standing like a rock. Believe me, Sincerely yours. P. H. Pearse.

To Mr. Danaher.

This letter to a parent in London who requested information on Sgoil Éanna, shows that Pearse, despite a heavy burden of political activity and military preparations, was still deeply involved in the school and its pupils. The father seems to have inquired as to the possibility of the boy specialising in the sciences; in answer Pearse quotes the specialist qualifications in science and engineering of one of the masters, Peter Slattery, who also possessed a Ph.D.

Tom Danaher came to Sgoil Éanna in the spring term of 1915 and remained.

L. 393/OCS

4.9.1915.   St. Enda's College,
                                   Rathfarnham.

Dear Sir,

Many thanks for yours of yesterday. I have pleasure in sending you a copy of our Prospectus and I also enclose some postcard views of our place, which will interest you.

Yes, boys of your son's age are just the sort of boys we like to get. It will be a great pleasure to us to have your lad. I can promise him a happy school life at St. Enda's, and careful training and teaching in pleasant and healthy surroundings and with very desirable companions. We always succeed in making our boys feel at home with us, and as we are able to give them individual attention we reap the most gratifying results. We shall be able, while giving your lad a solid general foundation to specialise to a certain extent in the subjects that will be useful in the career you have in view for him. One of our masters is a Bachelor of Engineering as well as a Bachelor of Science, and will take a great interest in directing your boy's study on the right lines. He has done so with success in the case of other pupils.

The terms are mentioned on the last page of the Prospectus. If there is any point in connection with them you would like to discuss with me, I will meet your views in every way. Anything that is necessary on my part to make it possible for you to send us the boy shall be gladly done.

We re-open after vacation on Monday next 6th inst. The sooner the boy joins after the opening the better, as we get into the swing of work at once. We would of course arrange to meet the boy on landing. Hoping to hear from you. I am, dear Sir, Yours very truly, P. H. Pearse.

To Mr. Danaher.

L. 394/OCS

17.9.1915.   St. Enda's College,
                                         Rathfarnham.

Dear Mr. Danaher,

I duly received your kind and very prompt remittance of £41, for which I now enclose receipt. I am sorry to have put you to the trouble of wiring about it, but I was called away from home for a day or two, and since my return have been a little unwell. Allow me to thank you for your great generosity and promptness in the matter.

Tom is in very good spirits and is working satisfactorily. When next writing you, I shall be in a better position to report on him. Again thanking you, Sincerely yours, P. H. Pearse.

To Mr. J. F. Murphy. London.

The recipient of this letter lived in Brixton to whom Pearse had written earlier (5.7.1913) in connection with his two sons at Sgoil Éanna, Fintan and Desmond.

Art O'Briain who was an active member of various Irish groups in London was later to play a prominent role in 1919 as founder-chairman of The Irish Self-Determination League and worked closely with the Irish delegation to the Treaty negotiations in 1921.

L. 395/OCS

29.9.1915.   St. Enda's College,
                                         Rathfarnham.

A Chara,

Please excuse my delay in answering your letter. It would have given me great pleasure to stay with you during my visit to London, but Art O'Brien had previously asked me, and a third friend has asked me since. As Art was first in the field, I have promised to inflict myself on him.

I was not sure until to-day whether I should be free to go at all or not, as an important engagement here turned up, which I have had to get out of as best I could.

I hope at any rate to have the pleasure of seeing you and yours. If I do not see you on Saturday evening I will try to look you up on Sunday. Believe me, With kindest regards, Sincerely yours, P. H. Pearse.

To Arnotts & Co. Dublin.

The London visit occupied the first week of October and Pearse returned to Dublin to find some of his creditors renewing their requests for payment. This letter to the solicitor of Arnotts seeks by rational argument to delay the evil day be pleading the collective good of all as taking precedence over the claims of individual creditors. The sum outstanding, £13 .. 19 .. 9, arose from the Sgoil Íde account of 1912.

L. 396/OCS

7.10.1915.   St. Enda's College,
                                                Rathfarnham.

Dear Sirs,

I have been away from home or I should have replied sooner to yours of 2nd. inst, re Messrs Arnotts' a/c.

The following is the position. Three years ago I found myself personally liable for all the debts of St. Ita's College, Rathmines, in addition to those of my own College, St. Enda's Rathfarnham. There were over a hundred creditors in all, the total amount of liability being above £3,000. I undertook to clear off the whole liability, provided time was given, and all the creditors agreed to give me time on condition that no one of them was treated preferentially. On this understanding, I set to work to reduce the whole debt, earning money for the purpose by lectures, as St. Enda's only barely pays its way, – indeed, in these hard times, it does not even pay its way. Up to the outbreak of the war I had reduced the total liability by 25%, treating all creditors alike. When the war came I had to cancel my arrangements for further lecture tours until the war is over. When the war is over I will resume the lecture tours, and will then recommence the steady reduction of the liability. I am sorry not to be able to make any more definite promise than this; but you will perceive that it is the best I can do in the circumstances. I am not free to make your clients even a payment on a/c, as that would be to break faith with the other creditors, which would not be honourable on my part, and would

349

moreover expose me to the danger that they would all come down on me, in which case I could only call all my creditors together or become bankrupt. The line I am taking is the line which will enable me to make good in the end, and pay everyone to the last farthing. I trust therefore that, in the common interests, your clients will, like all the other creditors, agree to give me the necessary extension of time until the war is over. Yours truly, P. H. Pearse.

To J. Mc Garrity.

This letter records Pearse's gratitude to Mc Garrity, and his friends, John Devoy and Judge Coholan for promptly forwarding the £300 with which to stave off the threatened crisis precipitated by the O'Connell letter of September 2nd. Undoubtedly, Mc Garrity was one of the most generous and steadfast of his supporters in his educational and political work.

In the year before the Rising, contact was frequent between Clan-na-nGael and the Dublin leadership both by open mail and by courier.

L. 397/NLI

15.10.1915.   St. Enda's College,
                                     Rathfarnham.

A Chara Chroidhe,
Just at the critical moment for St. Enda's I was rung up by a city bank and told that £300 had been placed to my credit on instructions from New York. I know that this was the reply of the friends of St. Enda's to the letters I had sent them appraising them of the crisis that had arisen. I did not know, nor do I know yet, the individual or individuals to whose personal generosity I am indebted for this timely and effective help, but I know that your hand was in it, and I want to thank you. I have been enabled to surmount the crisis, and I do not now anticipate any difficulty in finishing yet another school year. We have a bigger school than last year, and on the whole a more promising lot of boys. So I am full of hope.

I don't quite know what to say to you. Your action now and on former occasions had been so prompt and so extraordinarily generous that it leaves me without any adequate words. I wish I could shake you, and all of you, by the hand again. I do not trust myself to write what I feel of the importance of what you have done. To hold St. Enda's for another year means so much.

I am writing to John and to the judge too, for I know that it was they who cooperated with you. I hope these letters will reach you. I waited to send them by hand rather than by mail.

I have just heard that your wife has been very ill and must undergo an operation. I am very sorry to hear this and I pray that she may have a rapid recovery. Please remember me to her. You have had, I fear, much anxiety since I last saw you.

Accept my sincere thanks for your efforts for St. Enda's and all affectionate good wishes, and believe me, Always your sincere friend, P. H. Pearse.

To Miss Maguire.

This letter of acknowledgement concerns a present of an umbrella which the former senior students of Sgoil Íde, led by Máire Maguire and Máire Bulfin, gave Pearse for his 36th birthday. This umbrella is on display in the Pearse collection at the National Museum in Dublin.

L. 398/P.S./G

11.11.1915.   St. Enda's College,
                                              Rathfarnham.

Dear Friend,
I do not know what I should say to you, to Máire Bulfin, and to the other girls, to express my gratitude for your present. Really, you have left me speechless. I was greatly surprised when my mother brought in the present yesterday morning and I could scarcely speak. Please accept my heartfelt appreciation and please convey my gratitude to the other girls.

You are indeed faithful friends, and I shall not forget you for ever, nor indeed the girls and mistresses of Sgoil Íde. It is an elegant present and you could not have chosen a more useful item. Accept my greetings and gratitude, Yours as ever, Pádraig Mac Piarais

To Mr. J. Whelan.

James Whelan was a bookseller who specialised in political literature and the journals of the separatist movement. From June

1913 to February 1914 Pearse had written a column called "From a Hermitage" in the I.R.B. monthly *Irish Freedom*. These were collected and with an introduction, formed the pamphlet which was published in 1915 as *From a Hermitage*.

When in America in 1914 Pearse delivered two Emmet Commemoration addresses, one at the Academy of Music, Brooklyn on March 2nd, 1914 and the other a week later at the Aeolian Hall, New York. The previous summer he had given the oration at the Wolfe Tone Commemoration at Bodenstown Churchyard on June 22nd 1913. These three addresses were similarly collected and together with "An Addendum" written by Pearse on the outbreak of war, they form the pamphlet *How Does She Stand*, published in 1914.

On September 6th 1915 under the guise of an Aeridheacht, a quasi-military display was held at Sgoil Éanna; it involved Volunteer Drill and shooting competitions accompanied by pipe-bands and Cumann na mBan manoeuvres. This is the occasion on which it was not possible to organise a stall for the sale of the pamphlet.

L. 399/NLI

15.11.1915.   St. Enda's College,
                                        Rathfarnham.

Dear Mr. Whelan,

I am having both *How Does She Stand*? and *From a Hermitage* reprinted and will hand the whole edition of both (2,000 copies each) over to you for distribution. *From a Hermitage* will be ready first.

Please include both in all future advertisements and announcements of yours.

If convenient to you, it would perhaps be well to square up our accounts re the first editions, before the second editions are placed on sale. No money has come in to me from any source in respect of the "Hermitage" yet.

By the way, we were not able to place on sale at our Aeridheacht those pamphlets you sent me. Everyone was so busy that we could not get the stall going at all. The parcel is unopened. I will return it to you the next time our man is in town. Yours sincerely, P. H. Pearse.

To Solicitor for Irish Times Ltd.

In the list of unsecured creditors as of 30.6.1912, the sum of £18.10.0 was recorded as due to the *Irish Times, Ltd.* It was on this amount that Pearse paid 2/- in the £ as recorded in this letter; the balance still remained at the time of his execution. The account referred to advertisements inserted in connection with Sgoil Éanna.

L. 400/NLI

1.12.1915.   St. Enda's College,
                                   Rathfarnham.

Dear Sirs,
    Re the a/c of the *Irish Times, Ltd*, it would appear that my brother who sent out the instalments in March 1914 during my absence in America, overlooked them owing to some accident. They are therefore entitled to receive £1.17s., being 2/- in the £, a cheque for which amount I now enclose, thus placing them on the same footing as all the other creditors. For reasons which I have already explained to you, I shall not be in a position to make a further payment to any creditor until after the war, when I will resume the steady reduction of the liability. Yours sincerely, P. H. Pearse.

To Mrs. G. Bloomer.

This letter, in reply to a renewed request from Mrs. Bloomer for payment of the money she had invested in Sgoil Íde, reveals the dire financial straits in which Pearse was. It was on his out-of-school literary activities that he was relying to reduce his debts; he kept a separate bank account for these funds.

L. 401/NLI

3.12.1915.   St. Enda's College,
                                   Rathfarnham.

Dear Mrs. Bloomer,
    I can easily imagine that your position is very difficult in these trying times, and I only wish I could do something substantial towards reducing my debt to you and thus making things easier. The old struggle as regards the finances of St. Enda's goes on

always, or rather the strain increases from month to month and from week to week. I have never enough in the bank to enable me to pay anything off the old liability, and I see no prospect of being able to make a further payment all round until I am able to resume my American Lectures at the end of the war. I can earn or collect at the rate of $100 a week in America, but there is no use in going out again until the war is over. Besides my place is obviously here during the present crisis.

I am almost ashamed to mention the only thing I can do. Out of the infinitesimal private a/c which I keep open in the Royal Bank by lodging in it occasional guineas which I earn for literary or semi-literary work, I think I could manage to send you £5, as I expect to get that sum in a few days from a publisher, and I might be able to follow this up by other small instalments from time to time. Please let me know whether this would be any help to you at all. The small sums I can earn by activities unconnected with the school are the only source on which I can draw for reducing my debt to you, until I am able to send out another instalment to all. Believe me, Always sincerely and gratefully yours, P. H. Pearse.

To Mr. J. A. Lyons.

This letter suggests to the recipient, who was an active member of the Volunteers, that a political information bureau was better than a new political organisation as proposed by Lyons. There is no further information available as to Lyons or the proposals; his name appears in the list of Dublin prisoners taken after the Rising and sent to English jails.

L. 402/P.Ms.

9.12.1915.   St. Enda's College,
                                                  Rathfarnham.

A Chara,
   Am sorry for my delay in answering yours of 29th ult., but have been exceedingly busy.
   I find nothing to object to in your proposals, but I would urge this general consideration, viz., that you will find it extremely difficult to bring a new organisation with branches, etc., into existence at present, and that it would perhaps be better to have merely a small central body in the nature of an information bureau whose duty would be to diffuse information and educate public

opinion by leaflets, pamphlets, press letters, etc. If similar bureaux spring up in other centres, well and good. Sincerely. P. H. Pearse.

To Mr. Danaher.

Tom Danaher was young and his home was in London and consequently his travel plans were more complicated than the average boarding pupil at Sgoil Eanna. The reports sent by Pearse to parents, reveal the remarkable personal knowledge which Pearse had of his students and the convincing analysis which he supplies as to their abilities and endeavours.

L. 403/OCS

14.12.1915.   St. Enda's College,
                                               Rathfarnham.

Dear Mr. Danaher,
    We give Christmas Vacation at 1 p.m. on Friday next, 17th inst., and Tom will be free to go home either on that evening or on Saturday morning. You might kindly let me know what arrangements you would like us to make for his travelling. Vacation lasts three weeks.
    He has been giving satisfaction in his work, and in some branches has made distinct progress. He has, however, a good deal of leeway to make up, and it requires constant watchfulness to get him to concentrate his attention on the task in hand. His conduct is excellent and he has enjoyed good health and been free from the prevalent colds. With kind regards, Sincerely yours. P. H. Pearse.

To Tomás Mac Domhnaill.

Tomás Mac Domhnaill, a teacher at Sgoil Éanna, was an accomplished musician, who composed and arranged music for the school plays and pageants. The two songs mentioned here, "Haidh Didil Dum" and "Mo Churaichín Ó" were among the songs and stories with which Sean-Mhaitias entertained the children in the story *Íosagán.* St. Malachy's College is a diocesan College for boys.

355

L. 404/NLI

12.1.1916.   St. Enda's College,
                                    Rathfarnham.

Dear Tomás,

  The boys of St. Malachy's College, Belfast, propose to produce
Íosagán at the Belfast Feis and Fr. Mac Glennon would like to have
the music of the two songs (i.e. "Haidh Didil Dum" and "Mo
Churaichín Ó"). Would you have time to write out the music and
send it to me? I myself would like to have a copy. With every best
wish, Yours as ever, Pádraig Mac Piarais.

To Séamas Doyle.

Pearse had long-standing links with Co. Wexford, through the
Gaelic League and later through the Volunteers; he was a friend of
Séamas Doyle the recipient of this letter, a prominent member of
the Wexford Volunteers. In September 1915 he had reviewed the
Wexford Brigade of the Volunteers at Enniscorthy and delivered a
significant address on the objectives of the Volunteers and the
political developments associated with the suspension of Home
Rule.

  Séamas Doyle was organising the Emmet Commemoration in
Enniscorthy in March 1916 and wrote to Pearse seeking his
photograph for the Souvenir. The reply by Pearse is prophetic and
witty. He travelled to Enniscorthy to speak at the Commemoration.
Séamas Doyle was prominent in the Rising in Wexford and was
sent to Dublin on Sunday April 30th 1916, to verify the authenticity of the surrender orders issued by Pearse. He was taken to
Arbour Hill where he met Pearse who signed a special surrender
order for Wexford.

L. 405/NLI

17.2.1916.   St. Enda's College,
                                    Rathfarnham.

A Chara,

  On the whole I should prefer not to have my photograph on the
cover. The Souvenir is a very good idea, but I think a portrait of
Emmet would be better (as well as handsomer) on the cover. After
I am hanged my portrait will be interesting, but not before.

  I presume that the 4.30 train (arriving 7.39) will take me down in good time? I shall have to return early on the Thursday morning as I have to be in Belfast on the night of the 2nd. Sincerely yours, P. H. Pearse.

To A Chara.

The surviving letters show that Pearse was extremely busy in the early months of 1916; he travelled to Wexford, Limerick and Belfast where he delivered lectures and attended to Volunteer affairs all within one week in February. This letter came to him from a Volunteer group in the North Dublin area requesting him to lecture to them.

L. 406/P.Ms.

19.2.1916.   St. Enda's College,
                             Rathfarnham.

A Chara,
    Yours dated 13th. February reached here yesterday morning when I was away in Limerick.
    Yes, I can be with you on Sunday night 27th inst., for the lecture you are thinking of. As for title, I suggest "The Nature of Freedom", which would allow me to deal with national and personal freedom, both historically and in reference to present events.
    Let me know as soon as you have made your arrangements definite. Sincerely yours. P. H. Pearse.

To Mr. Mahon.

This letter contains no address and is written on plain blue unheaded notepaper, neither is there any indication as to the identity of the recipient nor of Mr. Mc Garry nor of the geographical location of the Emmet Commemorations referred to.
    We do know that Pearse was the main speaker at the Belfast Emmet Commemoration held on March 1st; his impact on the Volunteer audience is reported in the following issue of *The Workers' Republic* by Cathal O'Shannon.

1.3.1916.

To Mr. Mahon.

I enclose copy of article for Emmet Commemoration Programme which I promised Mr. Mc Garry and which I am sending you direct so as to save time.

The paper cannot appear now on St. Patrick's Day but the scheme is not abandoned. P. H. Pearse.

To a Hatter.

This letter was addressed to a Dublin hatter, seeking samples of different military type hats for the Volunteers, possibly of the broad-rimmed type worn by Pearse himself with one side rim pinned back.

L. 408/NLI

4.3.1916.   St. Enda's College,
                                     Rathfarnham.

Dear Sir,

Could you let me have samples of the three different styles of hat (S. African, Australian and Canadian) by Tuesday evening at H.Q.? How long would it take to deliver 100? What would the cost be, if less than 100 were ordered? And can they be had in grey-green? Yours, P. H. Pearse.

To Mr. J. F. Murphy.

Fintan Murphy, having matriculated, continued to reside at Sgoil Éanna while attending University College; his younger brother Desmond was also a pupil. Fintan was a member of the Rathfarnham Company of the Volunteers and fought in the Rising.

7.3.1916.   St. Enda's College,
                                   Rathfarnham.

A Chara Chroidhe,
   I am very much obliged to you for P.O. for £25, for which I have
pleasure in enclosing receipt.
   The two boys are very well. Desmond is giving great satisfaction
in his school work, and Fintan is regular and punctual in going in to
his university classes. Indeed, we are all as busy as can be. With
kindest regards to you and Mrs. Murphy, Sincerely yours, P. H.
Pearse.

To Mr. J. Whelan.

From Christmas Day 1915 when he completed the pamphlet *Ghosts*
and wrote the preface, to the day he wrote this letter to the
publisher, Pearse wrote and prepared for publication three political
pamphlets, *The Separatist Idea, The Spiritual Nation* and *The
Sovereign People*. In these he claimed that he had examined "the
Irish definition of Freedom"; he concluded the preface which he
wrote to *The Sovereign People* with the words: "For my part, I have
no more to say".
   Pearse wished to have the series on sale by April 17th, a week
before the Rising, so that the people might be prepared for the
event; hence his request to rush publication and the assurance that
the publisher would later appreciate his reason.
   In drawing attention to the misprint in *Ghosts*, Pearse omitted
the number of the page, as if he wrote the letter in haste intending
to check the page number later and forgetting to do so. The
relevant passage occurs on page 230 of the Phoenix edition of his
political writings.
   In the original letter, the second paragraph was underlined in
toto.

31.3.1916.   St. Enda's College,
                                    Rathfarnham.

A Chara,
   I sent you Ms. of *Sovereign People* yesterday (Thursday) with a

hurried note. I had written you a letter, but left it behind me at Headquarters and just scribbled a note in the Post Office.

I want to ask you as a personal favour to me to rush these two last pamphlets through. Please tell printer to send me proof of *Spiritual Nation* at once. I will send it back to him direct, with instructions to print off (which you would confirm), and will not ask to see a revise, so as to save time. In the meantime, put the *Sovereign People* in hands and rush it through, so timing things as to have the *Sovereign People*, the last of the series on sale by Monday April 17th. I ask you to do this for me and you will later appreciate the reason and regard it as sufficient. If any extra cost is involved I will see it paid.

I believe *Ghosts* has sold well. When reprinting, there is one misprint worth correcting. On page ... in the translation of the Irish quatrain, "Thou has" should be "Thou hast". *Separatist Idea* has not been noticed by the papers yet. They are very slow, Yours sincerely, P. H. Pearse.

To Mr. Danaher.

This letter shows Pearse trying to tidy up the school accounts as the planned Rising draws near; his main objective is to gather in any outstanding amounts due. Hence this letter to the parent whose son had joined the school in September.

L. 411/OCS

9.4.1916.   St. Enda's College,
                                         Rathfarnham.

Dear Mr. Danaher,

I am enclosing statement of a/c for the books and sundries with which Tom has been supplied since coming to St. Enda's, giving you credit for the half year's violin lessons which he did not receive. Between the two teachers he will have received a half year's lessons by the end of the school year.

He is very well, and is working satisfactorily. Believe me, Sincerely yours, P. H. Pearse.

To Printers.

This letter concerns the proofs of *The Sovereign People* and *The Spiritual Nation* which Pearse returned directly to the printers so as to avoid delay.

The letter shows signs of great haste; the final valediction is incomplete.

L. 412/NLI

12.4.1916.   St. Enda's College,
                             Rathfarnham.

Dear Sirs,

At Mr. Newman's request I send you back proofs direct, corrected for press. Please have the two tracts printed off at once and delivered in Dublin (to Whelan) by the 17th inst. I have cut out two passages in the *Sovereign People* so as to make it fit into the 20pp.

Please have corrections checked very carefully. There are several "outs", that is, passages where a line or so has been dropped owing to compositor's eye running on from one word to a similar word. Have these checked carefully with Ms. Yours truly, P. H. Pearse.

To Frank Sheridan.

This company mobilisation order was issued by Pearse in the context of the original plans for the Rising according to which it should commence at 4.0 p.m. on Easter Sunday. It was these mobilisation orders issued on Holy Thursday which gave those of the Volunteers who opposed the Rising their first reliable indication that it was imminent. Hobson heard of them late on Thursday evening; he immediately contacted Eoin Mac Neill and having consulted others, they went with Commandant J. J. O'Connell to the Hermitage to confirm what they had heard. Pearse informed them that a Rising was planned; in reply Mac Neill promised to do all in his power short of betraying them to the British to prevent the Rising. They returned to Mac Neill's house where they drafted a series of special orders to the Volunteers. O'Connell was dispatched early on Good Friday to Munster with these orders dated 21st April; effectively they placed O'Connell in complete charge of Munster with authority to countermand any orders issuing from Pearse and power to appoint volunteers to any work he wished.

The resistance of Pearse and the Military Council to the counter-moves of Mac Neill and Hobson was rendered all the more logical by the events of the previous Monday, when a Provisional Revolutionary Government had been constituted and the Proclamation of the Republic drafted; Pearse was chosen to be President and each of the seven members of the Provisional Government signed the Proclamation. On the same day, the famous Castle Document was circulated which indicated that the authorities were planning to order widespread arrests among nationalists and occupy many buildings in an effort to thwart any revolutionary movement. This document had a salutary effect on the Volunteers and impressed on them the urgency of the situation.

The hand-writing on this order is not Pearse's – it is rather like that of Willie who at this date was deeply involved in Volunteer activity.

L. 413/NLI

IRISH VOLUNTEERS   COMPANY MOBILISATION ORDER.
   DUBLIN BRIGADE.

The ...E... Coy ..4th.. Batt., will mobilise Easter Sunday at the hour of 2.45 p.m.

Point of Mobilisation ...... Rathfarnham Castle ......
Full Service Equipment to be worn, including overcoat, haversack, water-bottle, canteen, *full arms and ammunition.*
Rations for .... hours to be carried.
Cycle Scouts to be mounted, and ALL men having cycles or motor cycles to bring them.
             ... P. H. Pearse ...
              Captain or Officer Commanding.
Dated this .. 20th.. day of ... April ... 1916

To Mrs Carey.

After the closure of Sgoil Íde, Cullenswood House was rented to a succession of tenants; Pearse's meticulous approach to financial matters is reflected in this note which seeks to alleviate his mother's financial position in the event of his imprisonment or death.

L. 414/P.Ms.

20.4.1916.   St Enda's College,
                             Rathfarnham.

Dear Mrs. Carey,

In case of my being away from home, you might kindly make cheque for quarter's rent due on 10th May next payable to my mother instead of to me. She is my agent for Cullenswood House and during my absence will have to pay rates, taxes, groundrent, etc. Yours sincerely, P. H. Pearse.

To Seán T. Ó Ceallaigh.

With the confusion surrounding orders and counter-orders increasing hourly and the calamitous news of the *Aud's* failure and Casement's arrest, it was imperative that Pearse be in close contact with Clarke and Connolly, who also spent Saturday night away from home. The oblique tone of the letter was intended more to deceive the bearer than Seán T., who as a member of the I.R.B. would have been party to the plans.

L. 415/OCS

22.4.1916.   St. Enda's College,
                             Rathfarnham.

A Chara,

Could you put my brother and myself up to-night? It is important that we should be in town. If you cannot, can you get some friend to do it? Please let me know by bearer. We should send some traps in the early evening and arrive on bicycles ourselves later. Mise, Pádraig Mac Piarais.

To Mrs G. Bloomer.

In the midst of all the pre-rising activity and the mounting confusion Pearse found time on Easter Sunday to write this note to Mrs. Bloomer enclosing £5.

363

L. 416/NLI

23.4.1916.   St. Enda's College,
                                    Rathfarnham.

Dear Mrs. Bloomer,
   I enclose you cheque £5, as a further small instalment.
   Wishing you a very happy Easter, Sincerely yours. P. H. Pearse.

To Volunteer Leaders.

This cryptic message was composed late on Sunday evening and
dispatched by courier to all parts of the country during the night.

L. 417/P.Ms.

23.4.1916.

We start operations at noon today, Monday.
Carry out your instructions.
                              P. H. Pearse.

To the Dublin Brigade.

The four Dublin battalions were commanded respectively by Ned
Daly, Thomas Mac Donagh, Éamonn de Valera and Éamonn Kent.
Mac Donagh exercised overall Brigade command.
   This order from Mac Donagh was typed on plain paper; the
addendum by Pearse is in ink and in his own hand.

L. 418/NLI

24.4.1916.   Dublin Brigade Orders.
                                    H.Q.

1. The four city battalions will parade for inspection and route
    march at 10.00 a.m. today.
    Commandants will arrange centres.
2. Full arms and equipment and one day's rations.
                                    Thomas Mac Donagh.
                                    Commandant.
Coy E.3 will parade at Beresford Place at 10 a.m. P. H. Pearse.
Comdt.

To All Officers of the Irish Republic.

This was written on a standard memo pad sheet with headings for date, time and place, about two by three inches. It may have been written to cover the passage to the hospital of one of the wounded British soldiers taken prisoner in the Post Office.

L. 419/NMI

24.4.1914.

Give bearer who is wounded safe pass to Jervis St. Hospital, P. H. Pearse.

To Irishmen and Irishwomen.

The Proclamation issued by the Provisional Government of the Irish Republic was composed mainly by Pearse and amended by Connolly and perhaps Mac Donagh. It had been printed on Sunday, 23rd April at Liberty Hall and one of the printers was of the opinion that the manuscript was in Pearse's handwriting. It was read in front of the G.P.O. by Pearse at 12.45 p.m. on Easter Monday and displayed as a poster in public places around the city. It had been signed earlier in the week by the seven members of the Provisional Government.

L. 420/NLI   24 April 1916

PROCLAMATION OF THE REPUBLIC,
THE PROVISIONAL GOVERNMENT OF
THE IRISH REPUBLIC
TO THE PEOPLE OF IRELAND.

IRISHMEN AND IRISHWOMEN: In the name of God and of the dead generations from which she receives her old tradition of nationhood, Ireland, through us, summons her children to her flag and strikes for her freedom.

Having organised her manhood through her secret revolutionary organisation, the Irish Republican Brotherhood, and through her open military organisations, the Irish Volunteers and the Irish Citizen Army, having patiently perfected her discipline, having resolutely waited for the right moment to reveal itself, she now seizes that moment, and supported by her exiled children in

America and by gallant allies in Europe, but relying in the first on her own strength, she strikes in full confidence of victory.

We declare the right of the people of Ireland to the ownership of Ireland and to the unfettered control of Irish destinies, to be sovereign and indefeasible. The long usurpation of that right by a foreign people and government has not extinguished the right, nor can it ever be extinguished except by the destruction of the Irish people. In every generation the Irish people have asserted their right to national freedom and sovereignty; six times during the past three hundred years they have asserted it in arms. Standing on that fundamental right and again asserting it in arms in the face of the world, we hereby proclaim the Irish Republic as a Sovereign Independent State, and we pledge our lives and the lives of our comrades in arms to the cause of its freedom, of its welfare and of its exaltation among the nations.

The Irish Republic is entitled to, and hereby claims, the allegiance of every Irishman and Irishwoman. The Republic guarantees religious and civil liberty; equal rights and equal opportunities to all its citizens, and declares its resolve to pursue the happiness and prosperity of the whole nation and of all its parts, cherishing all the children of the nation equally, and oblivious of the differences carefully fostered by an alien Government, which have divided a minority from the majority in the past.

Until our arms have brought the opportune moment for the establishment of a permanent National Government, representative of the whole people of Ireland and elected by the suffrages of all her men and women, the Provisional Government, hereby constituted, will administer the civil and military affairs of the Republic in trust for the people.

We place the cause of the Irish Republic under the protection of the Most High God, Whose blessing we invoke upon our arms, and we pray that no one who serves that cause will dishonour it by cowardice, inhumanity, or rapine. In this supreme hour the Irish nation must, by its valour and discipline, and by the readiness of its children to sacrifice themselves for the common good, prove itself worthy of the august destiny to which it is called.

Signed on behalf of the Provisional Government: Thomas J. Clarke, Sean Mac Diarmada, P. H. Pearse, James Connolly, Thomas Mac Donagh, Éamonn Ceannt, Joseph Plunkett.

Irish War News – Statement.

The *Irish War News* was issued by the insurgents on Tuesday 25th April priced at one penny; its only edition Vol. 1, No. 1 contained on page 4 a statement by Pearse which was issued at 9.30 a.m. on that day.

L. 421/NLI

25.4.1916.

Statement by P. H. Pearse.

The Irish Republic was proclaimed in Dublin on Easter Monday, 24th April, at 12 noon. Simultaneously with the issue of the proclamation of the Provisional Government the Dublin division of the Army of the Republic, including the Irish Volunteers, Citizen Army, Hibernian Rifles, and other bodies, occupied dominating points in the city. The G.P.O. was seized at 12 noon, the Castle was attacked at the same moment, and shortly afterwards the Four Courts were occupied. The Irish troops hold the City Hall and dominate the Castle. Attacks were immediately commenced by the British forces, and were everywhere repulsed. At the moment of writing this report (9.30 a.m. Tuesday) the Republican forces hold all their positions and the British forces have nowhere broken through. There has been heavy and continuous fighting for nearly 48 hours, the casualties of the enemy being much more numerous than those on the Republican side. The Republican forces everywhere are fighting with splendid gallantry. The populace of Dublin are plainly with the Republic, and the officers and men are everywhere cheered as they march through the street. The whole centre of the city is in the hands of the Republic, whose flag flies from the G.P.O.

Commandant General P. H. Pearse is Commanding in Chief of the Army of the Republic and is President of the Provisional Government. Commandant General James Connolly is commanding the Dublin districts.

Communication with the country is largely cut, but reports to hand show that the country is rising, and bodies of men from Kildare and Fingal have already reported in Dublin.

To Citizens of Dublin.

This manifesto was printed as a small broadside and was read by

367

Pearse to the G.P.O. garrison on Tuesday afternoon. It was intended to acquaint the citizens of Dublin with the events and to boost the morale of the Volunteer forces. The words "Sovereign Independent Irish State" in the opening paragraph are printed in capitals and occupy one line.

L. 422/PS
Manifesto to the Citizens of Dublin.

25.4.1916.

THE PROVISIONAL GOVERNMENT
TO THE
CITIZENS OF DUBLIN

The Provisional Government of the Irish Republic salutes the Citizens of Dublin on the momentous occasion of the proclamation of a

SOVEREIGN INDEPENDENT IRISH STATE,

now in course of being established by Irishmen in arms.

The Republican forces hold the lines taken up at twelve noon on Easter Monday, and nowhere, despite fierce and almost continuous attacks of the British troops, have the lines been broken through. The country is rising in answer to Dublin's call, and the final achievement of Ireland's freedom is now, with God's help, only a matter of days. The valour, self sacrifice and discipline of Irish men and women are about to win for our country a glorious place among the nations.

Ireland's honour has already been redeemed; it remains to vindicate her wisdom and her self-control.

All citizens of Dublin who believe in the right of their country to be free will give their allegiance and their loyal help to the Irish Republic. There is work for everyone; for the men in the fighting line, and for the women in the provision of food and first aid. Every Irishman and Irishwoman worthy of the name will come forward to help their common country in this her supreme hour. Able-bodied citizens can help by building barricades in the streets to oppose the advance of the British troops. The British troops have been firing on our women and on our Red Cross. On the other hand, Irish Regiments in the British Army have refused to act against their fellow-countrymen.

The Provisional Government hopes that its supporters – which means the vast bulk of the people of Dublin – will preserve order and self-restraint. Such looting as has already occurred has been

368

done by hangers-on of the British Army. Ireland must keep her new honour unsmirched.

We have lived to see an Irish Republic proclaimed. May we live to establish it firmly, and may our children and our children's children enjoy the happiness and prosperity which freedom will bring.

Signed on behalf of the Provisional Government. P. H. Pearse, Commanding in Chief of the Forces of the Irish Republic, and President of the Provisional Government.

To Mrs M. Pearse.

This letter to his mother was not delivered to Mrs. Pearse until after Pearse's execution. The St. Enda's boys referred to were the members of the local Rathfarnham Company who were or had been students and were now attending university. A photograph of the St. Enda's group in military uniform, was taken in the school grounds on Easter Sunday evening. To this letter William Pearse added a brief note.

L. 423/PS

26.4.1916.

We are all safe here up to the present (6.30 Wednesday evening). The St. Enda's boys have been on duty on the roof ever since we came in, but have been relieved this evening and will spend tonight on the ground floor with me. They are all in excellent spirits, though very sleepy. We have plenty of the best food, all our meals being as good as if served in a hotel. The dining room here is very comfortable. We sleep on mattresses and some of us have sheets, blankets, pillows and quilts. The men have fought with wonderful courage and gaiety, and whatever happens to us, the name of Dublin will be splendid in history for ever. Willie and I hope you are not fretting, and send you all our love.   P.

WAR BULLETIN

This bulletin was written in the unexpected calm which descended on the Post Office/O'Connell St. area late on Wednesday evening; the calm was a prelude to the offensive being prepared by the re-organised British forces and the augmented garrison in Trinity College.

The bulletin is dated in error; Thursday was the 27th April. Some passages in this document contain echoes of the ebullience which had characterised Pearse's *Claidheamh Soluis* editorials. The military intelligence from the rest of the country seems to have been at variance with the reality; this was obviously for propaganda and purposes of internal morale.

L. 424/NLI

28[27]4.1916.   Irish Republic War Bulletin.

The main positions taken up by the Republican Forces in Dublin at 12 noon on Easter Monday, 24th instant are all still held by us. Our lines are everywhere intact and our positions of great strength.

The Republican Forces have at every point resisted with extraordinary gallantry.

Commandant-General Pearse, Commander-in-Chief, and Commandant-General Connolly, commanding in Dublin, thank their brave soldiers.

Despite furious and almost continuous attacks from the British forces our casualties are few. The British casualties are heavy.

The British troops have repeatedly fired on our Red Cross and even on parties of Red Cross women nurses bearing stretchers. Commandant-General Pearse, commanding in chief for the Republic, has notified Major-General Friend, commanding in chief for the British, that British prisoners held by the Republican forces will be treated as hostages for the observance on the part of the British of the laws of warfare and humanity, especially as regards the Red Cross.

Commandant-General Pearse, as President of the Provisional Government, has issued a proclamation to the citizens of Dublin, in which he salutes them on the momentous occasion of the proclamation of an Irish Republic, and claims for the Republic the allegiance and support of every man and woman of Dublin who believes in Ireland's right to be free. Citizens can help the Republican Forces by building barricades in the streets to impede the advance of the British forces.

Up with the barricades!

The Republican Forces are in a position to supply bread to the civil population within the lines occupied by them.

A committee of citizens known as the Public Service Committee has been formed to assist in the maintenance of public order and in the supply of food to the civil population.

370

The Provisional Government strongly condemns looting and the wanton destruction of property. The looting that has taken place has been done by the hangers-on of the British forces.

Reports to hand from the country show that Dublin's call is being responded to, and that large areas in the West, South and South-East are now in Arms for the Irish Republic. (Signed) P. H. Pearse, Commandant General.

Manifesto.

This manifesto was issued early on Friday morning, having been composed late on Thursday evening; by that time Connolly had been wounded and the Post Office garrison was under heavy pressure.

This document was not printed but was executed in a very fine script on government stationery bearing an embossed offical stamp. The original of this manifesto has not been located; the text was published in the *Sinn Féin Rebellion Handbook*, and the manifesto was reproduced photographically in *The Irish Rebellion of 1916 and its Martyrs* edited by Maurice Joy and published in New York in 1916.

L. 425/PS

28.4.1916.   Headquarters,
                                     Army of the Irish Republic,
                                     General Post Office,
                                     Dublin.

The Forces of the Irish Republic, which was proclaimed in Dublin on Easter Monday, 24th April, have been in possession of the central part of the Capital, since 12 noon on that day. Up to yesterday afternoon Headquarters was in touch with all the main outlying positions, and, despite furious and almost continuous assaults by the British Forces all those positions were then still being held, and the Commandants in charge, were confident of their ability to hold them for a long time.

During the course of yesterday afternoon and evening, the enemy succeeded in cutting our communications with other positions in the City and Headquarters is today isolated.

The enemy has burnt down whole blocks of houses, apparently with the object of giving themselves a clear field for the play of Artillery and Field' guns against us. We have been bombarded during the evening and night, by Shrapnel and Machine Gun fire, but without material damage to our position, which is of great strength.

We are busy completing arrangements for the final defence of Headquarters, and are determined to hold it while the buildings last. I desire now, lest I may not have an opportunity later, to pay homage to the gallantry of the Soldiers of Irish Freedom who have during the past four days, been writing with fire and steel the most glorious chapter in the later history of Ireland. Justice can never be done to their heroism, to their discipline, to their gay and unconquerable spirit, in the midst of peril and death.

Let me, who have led them into this, speak, in my own, and in my fellow-commanders' names and in the name of Ireland present and to come, their praise, and ask those who come after them to remember them.

For four days, they have fought and toiled, almost without cessation, almost without sleep, and in the intervals of fighting, they have sung songs of the freedom of Ireland. No man has complained, no man has asked "why?". Each individual has spent himself happy to pour out his strength for Ireland and for freedom. If they do not win this fight, they will at least have deserved to win it. But win it they will, although they may win it in death. Already they have won a great thing. They have redeemed Dublin from many shames, and made her name splendid among the names of Cities.

If I were to mention names of individuals, my list would be a long one.

I will name only that of Commandant General James Connolly, Commanding the Dublin division. He lies wounded, but is still the guiding brain of our resistance.

If we accomplish no more than we have accomplished, I am satisfied that we have saved Ireland's honour. I am satisfied that we should have accomplished more, and that we should have accomplished the task of enthroning, as well as proclaiming, the Irish Republic as a Sovereign State, had our arrangements for a simultaneous rising of the whole country, with a combined plan as sound as the Dublin plan has been proved to be, been allowed to go through on Easter Sunday. Of the fatal countermanding order which prevented these plans from being carried out, I shall not speak further. Both Eoin Mac Neill and we have acted in the best interests of Ireland.

For my part, as to anything I have done in this, I am not afraid to face either the judgement of God, or the judgement of posterity. (Signed) P. H. Pearse, Commandant General, Commanding-in-

Chief, the Army of the Irish Republic and President of the Provisional Government.

Minute of Provisional Government.

Late on Friday the Post Office was vacated and the leaders gathered in a grocery store in Moore St.; The O'Rahilly while leading a party up Moore St. was caught in machine-gun fire and died almost instantly. On Saturday morning the leaders and the residue of the G.P.O. garrison reached 16 Moore St. where a meeting was held at the bedside of Connolly; Pearse, Clarke, Mac Dermott and Plunkett were present. The decision to open negotiations with the British commander was arrived at by a vote; it has been suggested that Clarke opposed the proposal. The minute was written by Pearse on a rectangular piece of cardboard, possibly the backing of a picture frame. Following this decision, Nurse Elizabeth O'Farrell was sent under a white flag to inform Brigadier-General Lowe of Pearse's wish to negotiate terms. Lowe sent word back offering to treat with him only on the basis of unconditional surrender. In reply to a written message from Pearse, (of which only a fragment has survived) Lowe reiterated his demand for unconditional surrender.

The leaders having held a short meeting, decided to agree to Lowe's terms and at 2.30 p.m. Pearse accompanied by Nurse O'Farrell walked up Moore St. At the corner of Parnell St. he surrendered his sword to General Lowe. He was driven to Headquarters, Irish Command at Parkgate, to meet General Sir John Maxwell, the newly arrived British Commander-in-Chief.

L. 426/NLI

29.4.1916.   H.Q. Moore St.

Believing that the glorious stand which has been made by the soldiers of Irish freedom during the last five days in Dublin has been sufficient to gain recognition of Ireland's national claim at an international peace conference, and desirous of preventing further slaughter of the civil population and to save the lives of as many as possible of our followers, the members of the Provisional Government here present have agreed by a majority to open negotiations with the British Commander. P. H. Pearse, Commandant General, Commanding in Chief. Army of the Irish Republic.

Surrender Orders.

Following his interview with Maxwell, Pearse drafted a surrender document of which some typed copies were made at Parkgate. Pearse signed this order to the Commandants of the various Volunteer units to lay down their arms. On Saturday evening Pearse was transferred to Arbour Hill Detention Barracks. On the following day, he signed further surrender orders.

On the first order signed by Pearse at 3.45 p.m. on Saturday, James Connolly and Thomas Mac Donagh have added, each in his own hand their acceptance of the surrender terms; Mac Donagh indicated that he did so following consultation with Éamonn Kent.

L. 427/NLI

29.4.1916.

In order to prevent the further slaughter of Dublin citizens, and in the hope of saving the lives of our followers now surrounded and hopelessly outnumbered, the members of the Provisional Government present at Headquarters have agreed to an unconditional surrender and the Commandants of the various districts in the City and Country will order their commands to lay down their arms. P. H. Pearse. 29th April, 3.45 p.m. 1916.

Church St.

On Sunday Pearse signed a number of other surrender orders for specific areas or commands; Richard Mulcahy of the 5th Battalion of the Dublin Brigade operating in North County Dublin, came to Pearse to confirm the authenticity of the surrender order which had been brought to them by an R.I.C. Inspector. He met Pearse at Arbour Hill and he was reassured by him that the order to surrender and lay down arms was final and covered the whole country.

When two Capuchin priests from Church Street, Fr. Augustine O.F.M.Cap. and Fr. Aloysius O.F.M.Cap., went to Dublin Castle in search of the surrender document for the Volunteers of the Four Courts/Church Street area, they were taken to see Pearse at Arbour Hill. He wrote the order from memory; this version is slightly shorter than the version issued from Parkgate but contains no substantive change. The original of this order came to light recently and its fate was described in the journal *Comhar*, 1975.

L. 428/PS

30.4.1916.

In order to prevent further slaughter of the civil population and in the hope of saving the lives of our followers the members of the Provisional Government present at Headquarters have decided on an unconditional surrender, and Commandants or Officers commanding districts will order their Commands to lay down arms. P. H. Pearse. 30th April 1916.

Enniscorthy.

A message was brought to the Volunteers who held Enniscorthy on Saturday 29th, that Pearse had ordered an unconditional surrender. They refused to accept the order without written confirmation; to this end two of the leaders, Séamas Doyle and Seán Etchingham were allowed travel to Dublin and were conveyed by the British military authorities to Arbour Hill where they interviewed Pearse. He wrote another order from memory and whispered to them to hide their arms in safe places as they would be needed later. This document is preserved in the Enniscorthy Museum; it shows some slight changes in form from the earlier orders and one major change in substance. The Wexford men are ordered "to lay down their arms or disband".

L. 429/EM

30.4.1916.

In order to prevent the slaughter of unarmed people and in the hope of saving the lives of our followers, the members of the Provisional Government present at Headquarters agreed last night to an unconditional surrender, and Commandants or commanding officers of districts will order their men to lay down arms or disband. P. H. Pearse, 30th April 1916.

To Mrs. Pearse.

Pearse wrote this letter to his mother on Monday describing events since Wednesday when he had written to her from the G.P.O. This letter was never delivered to her; it was given to General Maxwell and used in evidence against Pearse during his Court Martial on the following day. The original is possibly in the records of the Judge Advocate General's Office at the Public Records Office in London; such records are subject to a restriction on examination for a hundred years. A typed carbon-copy of this letter was discovered in the Asquith papers in 1965 by Dr. Leon Ó Broin.

Pearse was mistaken as to where the rest of the G.P.O. and Moore St. group were taken; those who were not wounded were taken to Richmond Barracks, as were the St. Enda's boys. The initials in the last sentence stand for "Wow-Wow" (a pet name for Margaret) and Mary Brigid; Miss Byrne was a family friend or distant relative who lived with the Pearse family.

L. 430/P.Ms.

1.5.1916.   Arbour Hill Barracks,
                            Dublin.

My dear Mother,
    You will I know have been longing to hear from me. I do not know how much you have heard since the last note I sent you from the G.P.O.

On Friday evening the Post Office was set on fire and we had to abandon it. We dashed into Moore Street and remained in the houses in Moore St. on Saturday evening. We then found that we were surrounded by troops and that we had practically no food.

· We decided in order to prevent further slaughter of the civilian population and in the hope of saving the lives of our followers, to ask the General Commanding the British Forces to discuss terms. He replied that he would receive me only if I surrendered unconditionally and this I did.

I was taken to the Headquarters of the British Command in Ireland and there I wrote and signed an order to our men to lay down their arms.

All this I did in accordance with the decision of our Provisional Government who were with us in Moore St. My own opinion was in favour of one more desperate sally before opening negotiations, but I yielded to the majority, and I think now that the majority was right, as the sally would have resulted only in losing the lives of perhaps 50 or 100 or our men, and we should have had to surrender in the long run as we were without food.

I was brought in here on Saturday evening and later all the men with us in Moore St. were brought here. Those in the other parts of the City have, I understand, been taken to other barracks and prisons. All here are safe and well. Willie and all the St. Enda's boys are here. I have not seen them since Saturday, but I believe they are all well and that they are not now in any danger.

Our hope and belief is that the Government will spare the lives of all our followers, but we do not expect that they will spare the lives of the leaders. We are ready to die and we shall die cheerfully and proudly. Personally I do not hope or even desire to live, but I do hope and desire and believe that the lives of all our followers will be saved including the lives dear to you and me (my own excepted) and this will be a great consolation to me when dying.

You must not grieve for all this. We have preserved Ireland's honour and our own. Our deeds of last week are the most splendid in Ireland's history. People will say hard things of us now, but we shall be remembered by posterity and blessed by unborn generations. You too will be blessed because you were my mother.

If you feel you would like to see me, I think you will be allowed to visit me by applying to the Headquarters, Irish Command, near the Park. I shall I hope have another opportunity of writing to you. Love to W.W., M.B., Miss Byrne, ... and your own dear self.   P.

P.S.   I understand that the German expedition which I was counting on actually set sail but was defeated by the British.

To Sir John Maxwell.

Pearse was transferred to Kilmainham Prison on Tuesday evening after his Court-Martial at Richmond Barracks in the morning. From Kilmainham he wrote to Maxwell seeking to ensure that the statements he had drawn up on his financial and literary affairs be safely handed to his mother. He also mentions the poems he had composed while in Arbour Hill on May 1st; these he handed to a soldier on duty before leaving the Arbour Hill Barracks on that morning for the Court Martial. The statements on his financial and literary affairs were delivered to Mrs. Pearse; of the three poems, ("To My Mother", "To My Brother" and "A Mother Speaks") only one was delivered to Mrs. Pearse. On May 3rd Fr. Aloysius O.F.M.Cap., called to the Hermitage and brought three copies of "A Mother Speaks". The originals of the other two poems have not come to light but typed copies were found in the Asquith papers in 1965. The poems were regarded as seditious by Maxwell and included in the prosecution case at the Court Martial.

The mention of Cullenswood House, Oakley Road, as a possible address for Mrs. Pearse and Margaret, may seem strange in view of the fact that the family had lived at the Hermitage since 1910. However Pearse may have expected that the British Army would occupy the Hermitage after the Rising; in this he was correct. Two weeks after the Rising the family left and took up residence at Cullenswood House. Maxwell replied to this letter by a short note in his own hand, dated incorrectly as 1st May; he merely acknowledged receipt of Pearse's letter which he had read. The address on this note is the Royal Hospital, Kilmainham.

L. 431/NLI

2.5.1916.   Kilmainham Prison,
                                         Dublin.

To the General Commanding
the British Forces in Ireland.
Sir,
    I shall be grateful if you see that the three statements on business affairs (two with regard to my financial affairs and one with regard to the publication of some unpublished books of mine) and also the four poems which I handed to one of the soldiers on duty at Arbour Hill Detention Barracks this morning, are duly handed to my mother, Mrs. Pearse, St. Enda's College, Rathfarnham or Cullenswood House, Oakley Road, Ranelagh; or in her absence to my sister, Miss Margaret Pearse, same address.
    I shall also be grateful if you see that the sum of £7 odd (a £5 Bank of England note and two gold sovereigns with some loose change) which were taken from me at Headquarters, Irish Command, on Saturday, be handed to my mother or sister, as also the personal effects taken from me on the same occasion, and the watch and whistle taken from me later at Arbour Hill. I am, sir, Yours, etc, P. H. Pearse.

Court Martial Statement.

On being transferred to Kilmainham after his Court Martial, Pearse wrote a two page statement outlining the substance of his reply to the Court Martial President. He revised and corrected the manuscript and some copies were typed at Kilmainham and stamped as being filed at Kilmainham Detention Barracks on May 3rd.

2.5.1916.

The following is the substance of what I said when asked today by the President of the Court Martial at Richmond Barracks whether I had anything to say in defence:

I desire in the first place to repeat what I have already said in letters to General Sir John Maxwell and to Brigadier General Lowe. My object in agreeing to an unconditional surrender was to prevent the further slaughter of our gallant followers who, having made for six days a stand unparalleled in military history, were now surrounded and (in the case of those under the immediate command of Headquarters) without food. I fully understand now, as then, that my own life is forfeit to British law, and I shall die very cheerfully if I can think that the British Government, as it has already shown itself strong, will now show itself magnanimous enough to accept my single life in forfeiture and give a general amnesty to the brave men and boys who have fought at my bidding.

In the second place I wish it to be understood that any admissions I make here are to be taken as involving myself alone. They do not involve and must not be used against anyone who acted with me, not even those who may have set their names to documents with me. (The Court assented to this).

I admit that I was Commandant General Commanding in Chief the forces of the Irish Republic which have been acting against you for the past week, and that I was President of their Provisional Government. I stand over all my acts and words done or spoken in those capacities.

When I was a child of ten I went down on my bare knees by my bedside one night and promised God that I should devote my life to an effort to free my country. I have kept that promise. As a boy and as a man I have worked for Irish freedom, first among all earthly things. I have helped to organise, to arm, to train, and to discipline my fellow countrymen to the sole end that, when the time came, they might fight for Irish freedom. The time, as it seemed to me, did come, and we went into the fight. I am glad we did. We seem to have lost. We have not lost. To refuse to fight would have been to lose; to fight is to win. We have kept faith with the past, and handed on a tradition to the future.

I repudiate the assertion of the prosecutor that I sought to aid and abet England's enemy. Germany is no more to me than England is. I asked and accepted German aid in the shape of arms and an expeditionary force. We neither asked for not accepted Germany (sic) gold nor had any traffic with Germany but what I

379

state. My aim was to win Irish freedom: we struck the first blow ourselves but should have been glad of an ally's aid.

I assume that I am speaking to Englishmen, who value their freedom and who profess to be fighting for the freedom of Belgium and Serbia. Believe that we, too, love freedom and desire it. To us it is more desirable than anything in the world. If you strike us down now, we shall rise again and renew the fight. You cannot conquer Ireland. You cannot extinguish the Irish passion for freedom. If our deed has not been sufficient to win freedom, then our children will win it by a better deed. P. H. Pearse.
Kilmainham Prison.

To Willie Pearse.

Between midnight on Tuesday 2nd May and 3.30 a.m. on Wednesday when he was executed, Pearse wrote a letter to his mother, one to Willie and he may also have written the poem "The Wayfarer". It seems obvious that Pearse did not expect that Willie would also be executed. These letters were written on official embossed notepaper and typed copies of them were made at Kilmainham. Since the poem "To My Brother" which he wrote at Arbour Hill on May 1st is in essence part of his final message to his brother it is included here with the letter.

L. 433/P.Ms.

3.5.1916.
Dear old Willie,
   Good-bye and God bless you for all your faithful work for me at St. Enda's and elsewhere. No one can ever have had so true a brother as you.   P.

To My Brother.

O faithful!
Moulded in one womb,
We two have stood together all the years
All the glad years and all the sorrowful years,
Own brothers: through good repute and ill,
In direct peril true to me,

380

Leaving all things for me, spending yourself
In the hard service that I taught to you,
Of all the men that I have known on earth,
You only have been my familiar friend,
Nor needed I another.

P. H. Pearse.

To Mrs. Pearse.

Fr. Aloysius O.F.M.Cap. visited Kilmainham at the request of Pearse and Mac Donagh; he administered the sacraments to them and remained with them until shortly before the executions of Pearse, Clarke and Mac Donagh. Fr. Aloysius and the other priests attending the men were forbidden to be present at the executions and were excluded from the prison at about 3.0 a.m. Fr. Aloysius was given a copy of "A Mother Speaks" for Mrs. Pearse which he delivered to the Hermitage that evening.

The 'Micheál' referred to in the first paragraph was Micheál Mac Ruaidhri, the head gardener at St. Enda's; Cousin Maggie was a cousin of his mother's, a Brady, who lived with them.

He wished that the poems, the three written in Arbour Hill and "The Wayfarer", be added to the poems in manuscript which were among his papers in The Hermitage. The two poems "A Mother Speaks" and "To My Mother" are part of his final message to his mother; as such they are included with his last letter.

L. 434/NLI

3.5.1916.   Kilmainham Prison.
                             Dublin.

My Dearest Mother,

I have been hoping up to now that it would be possible to see you again, but it does not seem possible. Good-bye dear, dear Mother. Through you I say good-bye to Wow-Wow, M.B., Willie, Miss Byrne, Micheál, Cousin Maggie, and everyone at St. Enda's. I hope and believe that Willie and the St. Enda's boys will be safe.

I have written two papers about financial affairs and one about my books, which I want you to get. With them are a few poems which I want added to the poems of mine in MS in the large bookcase. You asked me to write a little poem which would seem to be said by you about me. I have written it, and one copy is at

381

Arbour Hill Barracks with the other papers and Father Aloysius is taking charge of another copy of it.

I have just received Holy Communion. I am happy except for the great grief of parting from you. This is the death I should have asked for if God had given me the choice of all deaths, – to die a soldier's death for Ireland and for freedom.

We have done right. People will say hard things of us now, but later on they will praise us. Do not grieve for all this, but think of it as a sacrifice which God asked of me and of you.

Goodbye again, dear, dear Mother. May God bless you for your great love for me and for your great faith, and may He remember all that you have so bravely suffered. I hope soon to see Papa, and in a little while we shall all be together again.

Wow-Wow, Willie, Mary Brigid, and Mother, good-bye. I have not words to tell my love of you and how my heart yearns to you all. I will call to you in my heart at the last moment. Your son, Pat.

To My Mother.

My gift to you hath been the gift of sorrow,
My one return for your rich gifts to me,
Your gift of life, your gift of love and pity,
Your gift of sanity, your gift of faith
(For who hath had such faith as yours
Since the old time, and what were my poor faith
Without your strong belief to found upon?)
For all these precious things my gift to you
Is sorrow, I have seen
Your dear face line, your face soft to my touch,
Familiar to my hands and to my lips
Since I was little:
I have seen
How you have battled with your tears for me,
And with a proud glad look, although your heart
Was breaking. O Mother (for you know me)
You must have known, when I was silent,
That some strange thing within me kept me dumb,
Some strange deep thing, when I should shout my love?
I have sobbed in secret
For that reserve which yet I could not master.
I would have brought royal gifts, and I have brought you
Sorrow and tears: and yet, it may be

That I have brought you something else besides –
The memory of my deed and of my name
A splendid thing which shall not pass away.
When men speak of me, in praise or in dispraise,
You will not heed, but treasure your own memory
Of your first son.

P. H. Pearse.

A MOTHER SPEAKS

Dear Mary, that didst see thy first-born Son
Go forth to die amid the scorn of men
For whom He died,
Receive my first-born into thy arms,
Who also hath gone out to die for men,
And keep him by thee till I come to him.
Dear Mary, I have shared thy sorrow,
And soon shall share thy joy.

P. H. Pearse.

APPENDICES

APPENDIX I

Letters
Written in Irish

L. 6/NLI
15.1.1899.
A Niallaigh, a chara,
   Táim ag cur chugat a bhfuil i gcrích agam do'n leabhairín. Siud is gur chuireas síos na focla do réir mar litrightear anois iad, níor chaitheas amach an chanamhaint ar fad. Ó tharla gur le haghaidh Cúige Uladh seadh an leabhar ní feirrde dhúinn gan chanamhnachas ar bith do ligean isteach agus mar sin de cheapas go mba' chóir dhom "annsin", "annseo" "damh", "le" agus a leithéidí do chur síos inionad "annsin", "annso" "dom" &c. Go deimhin duit, is truagh liom gan bhreis do bheith déanta agam. Nil san méid seo acht cúig leathanaigh is fiche. Pádraig Mac Piarais.

L. 12/NLI

12.7.1900   Connradh na Gaedhilge,
                                   Áth Cliath.

A Mhic Ui Dhubhghaill, a chara,
   Táim thar éis do litir d'fhághail agus ba bhinn liom a chlos go raibh sé ar do chumas rud éigin d'ollmhughadh dúinn. Léighfead do litir ós comhair lucht stiurtha na gClodhann Nua nuair thiocfas siad i gceann a chéile an chéad uair eile, agus geallaim duit nach sosadh ná fad-chomhnuighe dhéanfas mé 'na dhéidh sin (mar adeir lucht innsde na sean-sgéalta) go gcuirfead litir eile ag triall ort ag innsint a dtoile dhuit. Go raibh mile maith agat fá do litir, Mise do chara, Pádraig Mac Piarais.

P.S.   As regards education question do your level best, by hook or crook to get up an agitation on the subject of the language. Leave no stone unturned. Bring pressure to bear from all quarters. The rumour re Bill is quite true. This is the crisis in the history of the

387

movement. Make use of that public meeting for all it is worth. P.H. Pearse.

L. 52/P.Ms.

13.1.1902.   Connradh na Gaedhilge,
                                       Áth Cliath.

A Chara,
    Fuaras do litir agus an choip do *Ghreann na Gaedhilge* do bhi istigh innti. Táim thar éis an leabhairín do chur go dtí an clodóir. Comh luath agus gheobhas mé fromhtha uaidh cuirfead ag triall ort iad. Mise do chara, Pádraig Mac Piarais.

L. 53/NLI

17.1.1902.   Connradh na Gaedhilge,
                                       Áth Cliath.

A Chara,
    Fuaireas do litir. Níor mhór dhúinn an oiread de na leabhair cainte is teastuigheas uait a thabhaird duit, agus mile fáilte. Cuirfear dorn dóibh chugat i mbárach, Má theastuigheann tuilleadh uait, beidh siad agat.
    Tá éileamh an-mhaith ar an leabhar do réir mar chloisim. Do chara, Pádraig Mac Piarais.

P.S.   Ta cnuasach d'ainmneachaibh éan agam do fuaireas annso agus annsúd ar fud na tíre. Táim ag braith ar iad a chur isteach i *nIrisleabhar na Gaedhilge.* B'fhéidir go bhfeádfa-sá ainm neamh-choitcheann ar bith do chuala tú i gCiarraidhe nó i nDún na nGall do chur chugam? Dá gcuirfeá, bhéinn an-bhuidheach dhíot. Cia an Ghaedhilg atá agat ar magpie, falcon, owl, linnet, redwing, redpoll? Tá Gaedhilge agam orra, acht badh mhaith liom a chlos cia an t-ainm atá orra i gCiarraidhe.

L. 55/NLI

7.2.1902.   Connradh na Gaedhilge,
                                       Áth Cliath.

A Chara,
    Go raibh míle maith agat fá na hainmneachaibh do chuiris chugam. Seo ceist nó dhó ort 'na dtaoibh: An ionnann "Con-chubhairín a' chaipín" agus "Conchbhairín a' charabhat"? An

388

ionnann "Máire Fhada" agus "Nóra na bportaithe"? Cia an sórt éin é "Diarmín riabhach"? An é an "hedge sparrow" é?

Sílim gur bhfiú dhúinn "Beirt Fhear" do chur amach 'na leabhar – bhéarfad an cheist ós comhair coisde na leabhar. Mise agus defir an domhain orm, Do chara, Pádraig Mac Piarais.

L. 63/NLI

18.8.1902.   Connradh na Gaedhilge,
                                          Áth Cliath.

A Laoidigh na gCarad,

An gceartócha an leabhrán so, agus é 'chur tha·nais agam chomh luath agus 's féidir leat é?

Seo chugat an cunntas úd ar an diospóireacht do bhí ag an Ard-Fheis. An molann tú é? Mise, agus deifir an diabhail orm, (ó tharla go bhfuilim ar tí imtheacht go Gaillimh), Do charaid, Pádraig Mac Piarais.

L. 81/NLI/B

25.3.1903.   An Claidheamh Soluis,
                                          24 Sráid Ui Chonaill.

A Chara,

Teasbáinfead do litir do Thórna agus do'n Dálach. Leigim leat gur Béarlachas "chuimil se deathnach etc", – acht bhí an sgéal sin in-eagar ag Eoghan agus níor mhaith liom bacadh leis. As Gaillimh seadh an radh "amachadh sé leis", agus níl locht air.

Níl locht ar "casadh dham" no "dearbhrathair liom" acht an oiread. Ni fhéadfadh "Máthair na Clainne" focal ná cor cainnte nach bhfuil i n-úsaid i gCo na Gaillimhe a chur sios. Tá "casadh dham", "casadh orm" agus "casadh liom" le faghail i Connachtaibh agus is ionann ciall dóibh. "Casadh dham" is mó a deirtear.

Ta "dearbhrathair liom" ceart freisin. It is the ordinary form in Connacht, its meaning, of course, being "a brother of mine", just as "bó liom" means "a cow of mine". "Tá beirt liom i nAmerioca" = not "There are two with me in America" but "There are two children of mine in America".

I agree with you about "Bean Uí Dhonnagáin".

I don't think An Claidheamh is the place to discuss grammar, idiom, etc. Look at all the ink that has been spilled and paper wasted over the "Autonomous Verb" or "Monotonous Verb" as it is now called in Dublin. It is to be regretted that, owing to the change in the scope of *Irishleabhar na Gaedhilge* we have now no journal devoted to Irish grammar and linguistics.

Send me on a short humorous story or something for *An Claidheamh* agus beidh fáilte roimhe. Sgaoilfidh mé isteach an pisín úd i gcomhair na mac leighinn. Mise do chara, Pádraig Mac Piarais.

L. 88/P.Ms.

25.11.1903   39 Bóthar Mharlboro'
                                     Domhnach Broc.

A Chara Chroidhe,

Caithfidh mé comhgháirdeachas a dhéanamh leatsa agus led' mhnaoi uasal. Go dtugaidh Dia saol fada séanmhar don Gaedheal óg agus go mairidh sí an céad!

Is mór an t-áthas chuirfeas sé orm bheith im' charas Críost aici. Ní beag an onóir é, dar liom, do dhuine ar bith bheith 'n-a charas Críost ag cailín óg bhéas 'na Gaedhilgeoir ó'n gcliabhán mar bhéas d'ingheansa, bail ó Dhia uirri. Tá súil agam go bhfuil sí féin agus a máthair go maith.

Is doigh liom go bhfeicfidh mé i mbáireach thú i d'oifig. Muna bhfeicim, cuir sgéala chugam ag innseacht dom chuile short i dtaoibh na huaire badh cheart dam dul agaibh Dia hAoine. Mise do chara go buan. Pádraig Mac Piarais.

L. 89/P.Ms.

26.11.1903.   39 Bóthar Mharlboro'
                                     Domhnach Broc.

A Chara Chroidhe,

Seo chugat seachadad beag le haghaidh an pháiste. Ó tharla gur baisteadh fíor-Ghaedhealach bhéas agaibh, shíleas go bhfeilfeadh róba fíor-Ghaedhealach freisin. Is dóigh go bhfuil ceann agaibh cheana, agus ar ndóigh níor mhór péire. Déantús Éireannach ar fad atá ann. Mise do chara go buan. Pádraig Mac Piarais.

390

L.(p.c.) *92/P.Ms.*

18.2.1904.   An Claidheamh Soluis,

A Chara Chroidhe,
  Tráchtfaidh mé ar bhúr bhfeis an tseachtmhain seo chugainn. Ní raibh éin-tslighe agam an bobhta so.
  Beir buaidh agus beannacht. Mise do chara, Pádraic Mac Piarais.

L. *94/P.Ms.*

18.5.1904.   An Claidheamh Soluis,
                                        24 Sráid Uí Chonaill,
                                        Áth Cliath.

A Chara Chroidhe,
  Beidh mé agaibh lá na Feise, má mhairim.
  Beir buaidh agus beannacht, Mise do chara go buan, Pádraig Mac Piarais.

L. *95/MPC*

19.10.1904.   An Claidheamh Soluis,
                                        24 Sráid Uí Chonaill,
                                        Áth Cliath.

A Chara,
  Badh cheart dom scriobhadh chugat fadó, ag innseacht duit go bhfuair mé *Sgolbglas Mac Riogh 'n Éirinn* agus go gcuirfidh mé i gcló é chomh luagh is bhéas áit agam dó. Tá faitchíos orm go mbeidh sé scathamh beag go mbeidh sé ar mo chumas é a chur isteach, mar tá go leor de Ghaeilge Chonnacht agam fá lathair (Cnoc na nGabha, agus c.) agus bhéadh na Muimhnigh agus na hUltaigh ag clamhsán dá gcuirfinn tuilleadh isteach. Maidir leis na sean sgéaltaibh eile, bí ag scriobhadh leat, acht níl aon chall agat iad a chur chugam go gcuirtear *Sgolbglas* i gcló agus go gcriochnuighthear é.
  Tá súil agam go bhfuil tú féin agus do mhuinntir go maith. Beir buaidh agus beannacht, Mise do chara go buan, Pádraig Mac Piarais.

L. *99/NLI*

19.12.1904   39 Bóthar Mharlboro'
                              Domhnach Broc.

A Chara,

Níor mhór dhom sgriobhadh chugat ag gabháil buidheachais leat-sa agus led' fhear uasal as ucht bhur gcarthanais an fhad bhí mé i mBéal Feirste. Ní bréag a radh go bhfuilim fá chomaoin mhór agaibh. Is fada go ndéanfaidh mé dearmad ar an bhfíor-chaoin fáilte chuir sibh romham.

Ní raibh sé d'uain agam, fairíor, cuairt a thabhairt ar an gcumann úd na ndéantús. Chaitheas an oiread sin aimsire i Sgoil Inghine an Niallaigh gurbh éigin dom rith chomh mear is bhi ionnam le breith ar an traen.

Beir buaidh agus beannacht! Sonas agus séan go raibh ort-sa agus ar do chomhluadar an aimsir bheannuighthe seo! Mise agus meas mór agam ort. Do chara, Pádraig Mac Piarais.

L. *104/NLI/B*

2.2.1905.   24 Sráid Uí Chonaill,
                              Áth Cliath.

A Chara,

Go raibh míle maigh agat ar son do litre. Táim an-bhuidheach dhíot as ucht an oiread sin trioblóide a chur ort féin. Tá a fhios agam go ndéanfaidh tú do dhícheall.

I understand your position re Institute of Journalists, and see your reason for preferring not to be prominent at this early stage of the discussion re an *Irish* institute. Beir buaidh agus beannacht! Mise do chara go buan, Pádraig Mac Piarais.

L. *110/NLI*

16.9.1905   24 Sráid Uachtar Uí Chonnaill,
                              Áth Cliath.

A Niallaigh, na gCarad,

Seo litir a fuaireas ó ughdar an leabhair úd, *Aids to the Pronunciation of Irish.*

Dá bhféadfá an cunntas nó an léir-mheas a thabhairt dom i gcomhair na seachtmhaine seo chughainn bhéinn an-bhuidheach dhíot. Níor mhaith liom fearg a chur ar an mBráthair seo. Beir

392

buaidh agus beannacht, Mise, do chara go buan, Pádraig
Mac Piarais.

L. 115/P.Ms.

2.3.1906.   Connradh na Gaedhilge,
                                    Áth Cliath.

A Chara,
  Fuaireas an lámh-sgríbhinn, go raibh maith agat. Mise do chara
go buan. Pádraig Mac Piarais.

L. 116/NLI/G

7.3.1906.   39 Bóthar Mharlboro',
                                    Domhnach Broc.

A Chara,
  Cuirim chugat i dteannta na litre seo an cunntas úd i dtaoibh
Coláiste Chonnacht do gheallas duit. Tá súil agam go sroichfidh sé
i n-am thú. Tá sé tamall beag ó fuaras-sa é, acht chailleas é agus ní
bhfuaras arís é go dtí indé.
  Seolaim mo bheannacht chugat agus chuig d'fear uasal. Mise
agus fíor-mheas agam ort. Pádraig Mac Piarais.

L. 117/NLI

17.3.1906.   39 Bóthar Mharlboro',
                                    Domhnach Broc.

A Chara,
  Fuaireas do litir, agus táim that éis sgriobhtha go dtí Inghean Nic
Neachtain. Táim ag súil lei tráthnóna i mbárach (Dia Domhnaigh)
agus beidh áthas mór órm í féin agus a deirbhshiúr d'fheicsint.
  Seolaim mo bheannacht-sa agus beannacht Dé agus Pádraic
chugat. Mise do chara go buan, Pádraig Mac Piarais.

21.8.1906. Ros Muc,
Co. na Gaillimhe.

A Sheaghain na gCarad,

Bhí fúm iad so do chur chugat roimhe seo, acht níor fhéadas, mar bhí an aimsir chomh dona sin gurbh éigin dom fanacht cúpla lá i n-áit nach raibh aon teach posta 'n-a goire. Tá súil agam go bhfuil gach uile nidh ag eirigh leat go maith. Tabhair an litir seo istigh do Thadhg. Táim ag iarraidh air aon chongnamh 's féidir leis a thabhairt do'n Chlaidheamh. Mise do chara go buan, Pádraig Mac Piarais.

29.8.1906 Carlisle Arms Hotel,
Cong.

A Seaghain na gCarad,

Tá súil agam go bhfuil gach nidh ag eirghe go geal leat.

Má bhíonn cruinniughadh ag Coiste an Airgead sul má dteidhim abhaile bheithinn buidheach dhíot dá ndéanfa mo sheic-se do chur isteach san mBainnc im' chunntas-sa. Níor fhágas mórán airgid ann agus mé ag fágáil an bhaile! Mise do chara go buan, Pádraig Mac Piarais.

15.11.1906. 24 Sráid Uí Chonaill,
Baile Átha Cliath.

A Chara,

Is traugh liom nach mbeidh sé ar mo chumas dul to dtí an tSráid-bhaile san oidhche Dia Luain, cé go mba mhaith liom dul ann, dá mb'fhéidir liom é. Tá a fhios agat go mbim go bruideamhail ag obair ar an gClaidheamh an oidhche sin i gcomhnaidhe, 'ri bruideamhla orm í.

Tá súil agam go n-eireochaidh go geal leis an leictiúir. Mise do chara go buan, Pádraig Mac Piarais.

24.12.1906   Cúil Chrannach,
                                    Cill Mhuire Chairrgín,
                                    Áth Cliath.

A Chara,

Seo chugat féirín beag do Shighle. Ní móide go gcuirfidh sí
spéis ionnta anois, acht b'fhéidir go gcuirfidh nuair fhásfais sí
suas.

Beir beannacht na Nodlag, Mise do chara go buan, Pádraig
Mac Piarais.

21.2.1907.   Connradh na Gaedhilge,
                                    Áth Cliath.

A Chara,

Shroich do lámh-sgríbhinn agus do litir indiu mé, agus tá an
lámh-sgríbhinn dá seoladh agam go dtí "léightheoirí" an Choiste.
Cuirfear a mbreitheamhnas-san ós comhair an Choiste nuair
thiocfas sé i dteannta a chéile, agus cuirfead sgéala chugat go
gairid i na dhiaidh sin.

Tá súil agam go nglacfaidh an Coiste an chluiche uait, acht
caithfimíd é sin fhágáil fá bhreadh na léightheoirí.

Mise agus meas mór agam ort, Pádraig Mac Piarais, Rúnaidhe
Coiste na gClodhann.

14.3.1907.   Connradh na Gaedhilge,
                                    Áth Cliath.

A Chara,

Tá an *Seoínín* molta ag na léightheoiribh, acht ceapann siad nár
mhór dhuit é leigheamh tríd síos uair i bhfochair Gaedhilgeora
éigin mar "Sheandún" i gCorcaigh, mar tá castaí ann nach
dtaithnigheann leo. Is dócha go mbeithea sásta é seo a dhéanamh?

'Seadh, i dtaobh é chur i gcló. Is dócha go mbeitheá ag éileamh
roinnt airgid ar an gCoiste. Cia mhéid a shásóchadh thú? Tá súil
agam nach mbeidh tú ró-chruaidh orainn!

Mar tá a fhios agat cheana, bhí Coiste an Oireachtais ag braith
ar an dráma chur ar an ardán ag an Oireachtas, acht bhí
cruinniughadh ag Coiste an Airgid an lá cheana is dubhradar go

gcosnóchadh sé an iomarcha (Cailleadh airgead ar an dráma bhí againn anuraidh). Cuirfear an cheist ar fad ós comhair an Choiste Ghnótha; i. an mbeidh dráma ag an Oíreachtas i mbliadhan agus má socruightear go mbeidh, an é an *Seoinín* bhéas againn? Muna n aontuigheann an Coiste Gnótha *an Seoinín* 'cur ar an ardán ag an Oireachtas, 's baoghlach liom nach dtiobhraidh Coiste an Airgid cead dúinn é 'cur i gcló. Sin mar tá an sgéal.

Maidir leis *An Stór*, ceapann na leightheoirí gur fearr gan é chur i gcló fá láthair. Mise do chara, Pádraig Mac Piarais.

P.S. Bhéinn buidheach dhíot da gcuirfeá alt nó sgéal gearr chugam le haghaidh an *Claidhimh* anois 's arís.

L. 127/NLI

16.5.1907
An Claidheamh Soluis,

24 Sráid Uí Chonaill,
Áth Cliath.

A Chara,

Bhéinn buidheach dhíot dá bhféadfá roinnt "giotái" – sgéiliní, ranna, tomhaiseanna, "jokes" etc – i nGaedhilge a sheoladh chugam ó sheachtmhain go seachtmhain. Na sgéiliní chuiris chugam mí ó shoin thaithnigheadar go mór le lucht léighte an *Claidheamh*.

Beir Buaidh agus Beannacht! Mise do chara, Pádraig Mac Piarais.

L. 129/NLI

20.6.1907

Connradh na Gaedhilge,
An Coisde Gnótha,
Áth Cliath.

A Chara,

Shroich do litir slán mé athrughadh indé. Go deimhin duit agus níor chuir an litir eile úd aon fhearg ná muisiam orm – cad chuige a gcuirfeadh? Níl an craiceann chomh bog san orm tar éis bheith im' eagarthóir dom le ceithre bliadhna! Ní doigh liom go bhfuil an ceart agat i dtaoibh litrighthe d'ainm, acht admhuighim go bhfuil cead agat é litriughadh ar do rogha slighe. Is cinnte gur Mac Síthigh an ceart agus má seadh nach Nic Shíthigh a déarfaidhe le mnaoi?

Ta lán-chead agat –uaim aon úsáid is maith leat a dhéanamh d'aon bhlúire bhí sa g*Claidheamh* id' thaoibh. Tá súil agam go n-eireochaidh leat. Tá a lán daoine ag cur isteach ar na postaibh úd. Sgríobhfaidh mé teistiméaracht duit, má cheapann tú go ndéanfaidh sé aon mhaitheas duit. B'fhéidir nár mhiste dhuit sgríobhadh chum Úna Ní Fhaircheallaigh (65A Upper Leeson Street, Áth Cliath, a háit comhnaidhthe), mar tá aithne mhaith aici ar Starcai.

Tá na giotaí deireannacha úd do chuiris chugam dá gcur i gcló agam de réir a chéile, mar chonnaicís, is dócha. Beidh Fáilte agam roimh aon nidh de'n tsaghas céadna.

Beir buaidh agus beannacht! Mise do chara, Pádraig Mac Piarais.

L.(p.c.) 130/NLI

24.6.1907.   Áth Cliath.

A Chara,

Níor mhór dhom moladh leat fá mac óg a bheith agat – ó go mairfidh sé i bhfad. I dtaobh Feis an tSráid Bhaile, is truagh liom nach mbeidh sé ar mo chumas dul ann mar beidh mé i gceartlár chúige Chonnacht ar mo laetheanntaibh saoire fán tráth sin. Muna mbéadh sin rachainn chugaibh is fáilte.

Beir buaidh 's beannacht, Mise do chara go buan, Pádraig Mac Piarais.

L. 133/P.Ms.

28.9.1907.   Connradh na Gaedhilge,
                                          Áth Cliath.

A Chara,

Beir buaidh agus beannacht! Níor mhór dhom moladh leat fá bheith toghtha ag an mbórd. Is mór an obair dhéanfas an seisear atá toghtha aca.

I dtaoibh *Sean-Fhocla Uladh.* Cia aca a b'fhearr leat a chur amach i leabhar amháin i dtosach nó é chur amach ar an dá chuma san am chéadna? Agus cia mhéid leathanach bhéas i ngach cuid? Is dóigh go gcaithfimíd 2s . . 6d. ar a laighead a chur ar an leabhar. Iarr ar Tempest, led'thoil, a chunntas a chur isteach ionnus go mbeidh a fhios againn cia mhéid a chosnóchaidh an leabhar. Níor mhór dhúinn an t-eolas sin a bheith againn roimh an luach a shocrughadh.

Cuirfidh mé ceist *Greann na Gaedhilge* ós comhair an chéad chruinnighthe eile do choiste na gClodhann. Beidh mé ag imtheacht go Cúige Chonnacht ar mo laetheannta saoire an tseachtmhain seo

397

chugainn agus ní bheidh mé ar ais go ceann coichighise nó trí seachtmhain. Is cosumhail nach mbeidh cruinniughadh ag Coiste na gClodhann go dti deireadh an Deireadh Fhoghmhar no tús na Samhna.

'Sé an fáth nár fhreagair mé do chárta posta an t-am úd, ní raibh fhios agam cia an uair a mbéadh an cruinniughadh, mar ní raibh an lá socruighthe. Chomh luath 's socruigheadh é cuireadh fuagra chugat.

Ag déanamh chomh-gháirdeachais leat arís. Mise do chara go buan. Pádraig Mac Piarais.

L. 134/NLI

8.11.1907.   Connradh na Gaedhilge,
                                              Áth Cliath.

A Chara,
Bíodh ciall agat! Dá mbéadh gach éinne sa gConnradh ag obair chomh dian is atá oifigigh Coiste na gClodhanna bhéadh an scéal go maith againn.

Cia aige a bhfuil na *Sean-Fhocla* anois? Ní féidir dhom clúdhaigh a chur ortha go mbidh a fhios agam cá bhfuil na leabhra. Mise do chara go buan, Pádraig Mac Piarais.

L. 135/NLI

Nollaig 1907.   An Claidheamh Soluis,
                                              24 Sráid Uí Chonaill,
                                              Áth Cliath.

A Chara,
D'ainmnigh Coiste an Oideachais tusa mar dhuine den chomhaltas so a mbeidh futha obair an Dr. Ó Beirn i dtaobh na heitinne a stiuradh. An bhféadfása teacht go dtí teach an Dr. Mac Coiligh, 26 Cearnóg Mhuirfhthean, ag a 8.30 tráthnóna inniu (Dia hAoine) chun rudaí a leagan amach le dluthas a chur leis an obair? Mise do chara, Pádraig Mac Piarais.

24.12.1907.   Connradh na Gaedhilge,
                               Áth Cliath.

A Chara,
   Tú féin is cionntach le cia ar bith moill a baineadh as *Sean-Fhocla Uladh* agus le cia ar bith mí-adh a lean de. Níor mhínigh tú dhom i gceart tada i dtaoibh an leabhair, agus ní raibh a fhios agam cia aca sa tSráid-bhaile nó i mBaile Átha Cliath a cuirfidhe an clúdach air agus a déanfaidhe é cheangailt. Nuair nár bh'fhéidir liom aon eolas fhághail uait-se, b'éigin dom sgríobhadh go dtí Tempest agus tar éis cúpla lá chuala mé uaidh sin go mb'fhearr leis dá gceangalóchaidhe i mBaile Átha Cliath é. Chuireas fios ar na leabhraibh annsin agus níor thangadar go ceann seachtmhaine. Níorbh' fhéidir meastachán fhághail ar an gceangaltóireacht go dtí go raibh na leabhra againn. Ní raibh am annsin comhairle a ghlacadh leat-sa agus na leabhra a bheith amuigh fá Nodlaig, mar ba mhian linn. 'Séard a rinneamar annsin roinnt cóipeanna a chur amach go deifreach le haghaidh na Nodlag; níl ionnta so mar a déarfa acht "temporary edition".
   Anois badh mhaith liom comhairle a ghlacadh leat i dtaoibh na coda eile de na leabhraibh. Séard táimíd ag braith ar a dhéanamh:–
(1) cóipeanna a chur amach fá líon cloth, mar an leabhar so istigh agus iad a dhíol ar dhá sgilling.
(2) cóipeanna a chur amach fá chlúdach maith éadaigh agus iad a dhiol ar leath-choróin.
(3) An leabhar a chur amach i n-a cheithre codachaibh, fá pháipéar, sé pighne an chuid.
   Cia do mheas ar an socrughadh so? Sgríobh chugam chomh luath is bhéas am agat.
   Beannachta na Nodlag chugat-sa agus chuig do chomhluadar! Mise do chara, Pádraig Mac Piarais.

2.1.1908.   Cúil Chrannach,
                               Cill Mhuire Chairrgín,
                               Áth Cliath.

A Chara,
   Seo bronntanas beag atá mé a chur chugat le tabhairt do Shighle. Fá Nodlaig badh cheart dom é chur chugaibh, acht níorbh' fhéidir liom é fhághail i n-am. I nGleannta Aontruim a rinneadh an teach agus an trosgán. Tá an trosgán ro-mhór le cur

isteach sa teach go héasgaidh, acht ní féidir trosgán de dhéantus Gaedhealach fhághail níos lugha.

Táim ag guidhe séimh oraibh go léir sa mbliain nuaidh. Mise do chara, Pádraig Mac Piarais.

L. 138/P.Ms.

15.1.1908.   Connradh na Gaedhilge,
                                        Áth Cliath.

A Chara,

Fuair mé do litir indiu. Bhíos ag fanacht go dtí go mbéadh na cóipeanna fá éadach maith réidh, mar cheapas gurab iad a b'fheileamhnaighe le cur thart chuig na daoinibh a chuidigh leat. Níl siad réidh fós, agus ní bheidh siad réidh go ceann tamaill, mar níor mhol Coisde an Airgid ár gComhaile-ne fós, – chuir siad an cheist ar fad ar ath-ló. Cuir cárta chugam ag innseacht dom an gcuirfidh mé cóipeanna fá éadach tanaidh chugat nó an bhfanfaidh mé go mbeidh na cinn fá éadach maith agam.

Athróchar an fógra úd ins na páipéaraibh an tseachtmhain seo chugainn. Cuireadh *Sean-Fhocla Uladh* go dtí an *Freeman*, *Independent*, agus na páipéir ar fad.

Chuireas ceist *Ghreann na Gaedhilge* ós comhair Choisde na gClodhann, acht níor shocruigheadar é. Cuirfead ós a gcomhair arís í ag an gcéad chruinniughadh eile.

Is maith an sgéal é *An Ceithearnach Caol-Riabhach*. Tá cóip dhe i gcló ag Standish Hayes O'Grady i *Silva Gadelica*. Ní dóigh liom go nglacfaidh C. na gC. le haon leabhar nuadh go ceann tamaill, mar níl an t-airgead aca le caitheamh air, acht níor mhiste dhuit é chur chugainn.

Seolaim chugat istigh cóip dem' leabhar féin *Íosagán*. B'fhéidir go bhféadfá é mholadh do mhaighistribh sgoile le haghaidh na bpáisti, nó rud éigin a sgríobhadh air i gceann de na páipéaraibh. Mise do chara go buan. Pádraig Mac Piarais.

L. 139/OCS

31.1.1908.   Connradh na Gaedhilge,
                                        Áth Cliath.

A Eoghan na gCarad, – tá an sgéal úd socair. Tá Saoilidh Bradhars rí shásta ar na fighiúiri atá ar cearr a déanamh arís, agus tá siad ag obair ortha anois. Céard mar gheall ar an leathanach teidil? Tá an clúdach réidh. Mise, Pádraig Mac Piarais.

400

31.1.1908.   Connradh na Gaedhilge,
                                    Áth Cliath.

A Chara,
    I dteannta a chéile do choiste na gClodhann Dia Máirt seo ghabh
tharainn, mholadar cúpla céad cóip de na seacht rannaibh de
Ghreann na Gaedhilge a cheangal le chéile, acht gan é chur fá
ath-chló nó gan foclóir nuadh a sgriobhadh le haghaidh an lea –
bhair. 'Séard a dhéanfar na clúdaigh páipéir ata ar na leabhraibh
anois a bhaint dhíbh agus na leabhra a cheangailt le chéile 'n-a
seacht 's 'n-a seacht annsin. Is dóigh go mbeidh tú sásta leis seo.
    Dubhairt an Coiste liom a iarraidh ort *An Ceithearnach Caol-
Riabhach* a sheoladh chúcha ionnus go gcuirtidhe fá bhreitheamhnas
na léightheoirí é.
    Táim ag fanacht le cead ó Choiste an Airgid chun na cóipeanna
eile de *Sean-Fhocla Uladh* a chur amach. Beidh cruinniughadh
aca an tseachtmhain seo cugainn. Beir buaidh agus beannacht. Mise
do chara, Pádraig Mac Piarais.

L.(p.c.) 141/P.Ms.

19.2.1908.   Connradh na Gaedhilge,
                                    Áth Cliath

A Chara, tháinig na cóipeanna eile de *Sean-Fhocla Uladh* indiu,
agus dubhras le muinntir an tsiopa leath-dhuisín de gach sort
(éadach tanaidh agus éadach láidir) a chur chugat anocht.
    Tá súil agam go dtaithneochaidh siad leat. Mise do chara go
buan. Pádraig Mac Piarais.

L. 146/P.Ms.

11.4.1908.   Connradh na Gaedhilge,
                                    An Coisde Gnótha,
                                    Áth Cliath.

A Charaid,
    Is truagh lem' chroidhe a chloisteáil go bhfuair do leanbh bás. Is
dóign nach féidir dom-sa ná d'éinne eile nach bhfuil in-a thuis-
mightheoir tuigsint i gceart goidé an brón agus an briseadh croidhe
bhíos ar athair agus ar mháthair nuair a sgiobtar leanbh uatha,
acht tá tuairim agam dhó, sílim. Dia go dtugaidh solás díbh!
Chuala mé go raibh do bhean uasal go dona in-a sláinte freisin,

401

agus sin fáth de na fáthannaibh fá nár sgríobh mé chugat i dtaoibh cúrsaí gnótha roimhe seo. Tá súil agam go bhfuil biseach uirthi faoi seo.

Chuir mé *An Ceithearnach Caol-Riabhach* ar ais chugat indé. Deir na leightheorí go mb'fhiú an sgéal a chur i gcló, acht is dóigh leo go mb'fhéidir eagar níos fearr a chur air agus nár mhór dhuit do theistimhín-se i.e. do théacs-sa a chur i gcomórtas agus i gcomhmheas le teistimhín Mic Uí Ghrádaigh agus le cóip nó dhó san Acadaimh annso. Ní dóigh liom go nglacfaidh Coisde na gClodhann le haon leabhar nua go ceann tamaill. Sgríobhfaidh mé chugat arís i dtaoibh na ceiste seo ar fad.

Ní ar Choiste na gClodhann atá an t-airgead úd agat acht ar Choiste an Airgid, nó, badh chirte dhom a rádh, ar an gcomhaltas nua, (Clodhanna Teo) atá an Coiste Gnótha thar éis a chur ar bun le obair na leabhar etc. a stiuradh feasta. Dhiultaigh an Registrar of Joint Stock Companies i Lonndain an comhaltas úd a registráil i nGaedhilg, agas ta an cheist dá pleidhe amach idir é fein agus an Connradh ó shoin. Go dtí go socrochar é seo, ní féidir aon airgead a dhíol le héinne, mar tá an t-airgead ar fad ag beirt trustees agus níl cead ag éinne a ainm a chur le seic. Cuirfidh mé do bhille isteach chuig Stiurthóirí an Chomhaltais, agus is dócha go ndíolfar é ag an gcéad chruinniughadh thar éis ceist an registration a shocrughadh. Is gearr sin uaim anois creidim.

Is maith liom a chloisteáil go bhfuil tú ar aon intinn liom i dtaoibh an Athar Uí Dhuinnín. Creidim go bhfuil duine nó beirt ar an dream sin agus gurab é atá uatha an Connradh a bhriseadh. Tá an chuid eile cneasta go leor, acht ta siad meallta ag an duine nó beirt seo.

Ceist agam ort anois. An mbéadh am agat cúpla focal i mBéarla a sgriobhadh i dtaoibh *Íosagán* le haghaidh an *Chlaidheamh?* Ó tharla gurab é mo leabhar féin é ní féidir liom é fhuagairt i gceart mar a dhéanfhainn le leabhraibh eile. Sgríobh P.Ó Domhnalláin rud éigin i nGaedhilg faoi, acht níor mhór é chur i n-aithne do na Béarlóiribh freisin. Bhéinn an-bhuidheach dhíot dá sgríobhfá alt gearr 'ghá léir-mheas, mar a déarfa, ó'n "literary point of view". Mise do chara go buan. Pádraig Mac Piarais.

19.6.1908.   Connradh na Gaedhilge,
                                             Áth Cliath.

A Sheaghain na gCarad,

Is dócha go dtiocfaidh Seaghan Mac Enrí, an timthire,
ó Ghaillimh le breathnughadh i ndiaidh an *Chlaidhimh*. Beidh mé
ag imtheacht ar an gcéad traen maidin i mbárach (Dia Sathairn),
agus ó's dócha nach mbeidh Seaghan Mac Enrí annso go dtí
maidin Dia Luain, bhéinn buidheach dhíot dá n-osglóchtha na
litreacha thiocfas ar maidin (Dia Sathairn) agus aon nidh atá le cur
isteach i g*Claidheamh* na seachtmhaine seo a thabhairt do na
clódóirí. Táim ag súil leis an nuaidheacht ó Éamonn Ó
Donnchadha, ó Shéamus Ó Searcaigh, agus (b'fhéidir) ó Phádraic
Ó Domhnalláin. Dubhairt an Dálach go mbreathnochadh sé tríotha
so agus iad a ceartughadh. Tabhair dhó iad, led' thoil agus annsin
cuir go dtí na clódóirí ar an bpoinnte iad. Má's rud é nach dtagann
Seaghain Mac Enrí go luath maidin Dia Luain níor mhór dhuitse
na litreacha a osgailt agus aon adhbhar cló srl dá bhfuil ionnta a
thabhairt do na clódóirí.

Seo chugat istigh roinnt adhbhar cló le thabhairt do na clódóirí i
mbárach.

Má thagann aon litir tabhachtach i rith na seachtmhaine is féidir
leat í chur chugam; gheobhaidh "Ros Muc, Co. na Gaillimhe"
amach mé.

Bhíos ag súil le comhradh a bheith agam leat indé agus indiu,
acht níor éirigh liom. Cheapas gur cheart dom innseacht duitse ar
dtúis go bhfuilim ag glacadh le obair eile a chuirfeas d'fhiachaibh
orm eirghe as eagarthóireacht an *Chlaidhimh*. 'Sí an obair í seo ná
ardmhaighistreacht sgoile meadhonaìghe dha-theanghaighe le
haghaidh gasúr atá mé féin agus beirt nó triúr eile a' chur ar bun i
mBaile Átha Cliath. Labhróchaidh mé leat 'n-a thaobh nuair
thiocfas mé that nais ó'n tuaith. B'fhéidir go bhféadfa-sa roinnt
gasúr a sholáthar dom mar sílim go bhfuil aithne agat ar gach
éinne i mBaile Átha Cliath ar fiú aithne a bheith air. Beidh litir
uaim ós comhair an Choiste Gnótha san oidhche i mbárach. Ná
labhair 'na thaoibh seo le héinne go leighfear an litir. Beidh troid
mhór ag toghadh eagarthóra eile anois, is dócha!

Táim an-bhuidheach dhíot as ucht an ticéad saoir. Mise do chara
go buan, Pádraig Mac Piarais.

Cuirim chugat roinnt litreacha duit féin freisin.

10.7.1908.   Cúil Chrannach,
                                                  Cill Mhuire Chairrgín,
                                                  Áth Cliath.

A Chara,

Níl a fhois agam an gcualais trácht ar an Sgoil seo atáim á chur
ar bun? – sgoil mheadhonach dhá – theangthach le haghaidh
buachaillí? I n-áit ar a dtugtar Teach Fheadh Chuilinn (Cullenswood House) i gceanntar Rath Ó Maine bhéas sí agam.
Teastóchaidh duine éigin uaim leis an luadaireacht (gymnasium,
etc.) a mhúineadh, agus cloisim nach bhfuil duine ar bith i mBaile
Átha Cliath is oireamhnaighe chun na hoibre sin ná thusa. Badh
mhaith liom fios fhaghail uait an bhféadfá teacht chugainn uair sa
tseachtmhain, abair, chun ceacht luadaireachta a mhúineadh, agus
cia mhéad a bhainféa dhíom? Chuirfinn d'ainm-se ar an gClár, i
measg na n-oidí eile. Sgríobh chugam chomh luath agus is féidir
leat é, led' thoil, mar níor mhór an Clár a chur amach gan mhoill.

Tá súil agam go mbeidh tú i n-ann an méad seo a dhéanamh. Níl
a fhois agam cia eile a dhéanfadh é. Níor mhór Gaedheal maith
agus fear a bhfuil roinnt eolais aige ar an nGaedhilg. Mise do
chara, Pádraig Mac Piarais.

24.8.1908.   An Claidheamh Soluis,
                                                  24 Sráid Uí Chonaill,
                                                  Áth Cliath.

A Sheaghain na gCarad,

An bhfuair tú na ticéidí úd? Ní bheidh mé ag imtheacht go dtí
maidin i mbárach (Dia Máirt). Bhéadh na ticéidí i n-am dá
mbéadh siad agam anocht.

Tá faitchíos orm go bhfuilim ag cur an iomarca trioblóide ort.
Mise do chara go buan, Pádraig Mac Piarais.

22.10.1908.   Sgoil Éanna,
                                                  Rath Ó Máine.

A Chara,

Fuair mé an litir úd a chuir tú chugam ó Coláiste Chonnacht
cúpla mí ó shoin, acht níor fhéad mé freagra a thabhairt uirthí, mar

ní raibh aon nidh socruighthe im'intinn agam. Má tá tú sásta ar an obair a dheanamh ar chéad púnt (£100) sa mbliadhain, tiubhraidh mé an leas-eagarthóireacht duit-se. Sgríobh chugam le filleadh an phosta, led' thoil, ag innseacht dom an dtiocfaidh tú chugam agus, má thagann, cia an uair fhéadfas tú a theacht. Níl, dá luaithe dá dtiochfaidh tú nach amhlaidh is fearr é. Teastuigheann ó Sheaghan Mac Enrí imtheacht, agus ní fhéadaim an obair a dhéanamh liom féin. Badh mhaith liom dá dtosóchtha-sa an tseachtmhain seo chugainn, dá mb'fhéidir é. Ag súil le sgéalaibh go luath, Mise do chara go buan, Pádraig Mac Piarais.

L. 152/NLI

26.10.1908.   Sgoil Éanna,
                               Rath Ó Máine.

A Chara,

Tá go maith. Beidh mé ag súil leat ar an 31adh lá. Níor mhór dhuit Seaghan Mac Einrigh a fheiceál agus annsin a theacht amach annso. Ní bhíonn aon am agamsa chun dul isteach sa gcathair. Mise agus mé ag súil led' fheicéal. Do chara go buan, Pádraig Mac Piarais.

P.S.   Tá Micheál Breathnach bocht go dona. Deirtear nach mairfidh se that cúpla seachtmhain. P. Mac P.

L. 163/P.Ms.

12.12.1909.   Sgoil Éanna,
                               Rath Ó Máine.

A Chara,

Nuair shroich *An Ceithearnach Caol-Riabhach* mé uait an dara huair bhí mé éirighthe as rúnaidheacht Coiste na gClodhann le sgathamh maith, agus ni raibh baint ná pairt agam leis an gCoiste ná le obair an Chonnartha ar aon bhealach acht go raibh mé i n-ainm 's a bheith im'eagarthóir ar an g*Claidheamh Soluis.* 'Séard badh cheart dom a dhéanamh, ar ndóigh, an lámh-sgríbhinn a chur go dtí rúnaidhe C. na gClodhann, acht bhí a fhios agam nach raibh siad le leabhra nua ar bith a chur amach ó tharla nach raibh aon airgead aca, agus cheapas go mbéadh sé luath go leor agam an lámh-sgríbhinn a thabhairt dóibh nuair bhéadh siad ag tosnughadh ar leabhra do chur amach arís. Ar an adhbhar sin, chuireas an lámh-sgríbhinn i dtaisge, acht fairíor! nior chuimhnigh mé uirthi aris go bhfuair me an litir úd uait tá roinnt seachtmhaini ó shoin ann. Níl aon leithsgéal agam acht go raibh mé chomh gnóthach sin le obair na Sgoile, srl, srl, nár chuimhnigh mé ar an gCeithearnach. Tá brón mór orm faoi, agus caithfidh mé do phardún iarraidh. Ní raibh a fhios agam go raibh innsint Mhuimhneach de'n Cheithearnach le teacht amach go bhfuair mé do litir, agus níl a fhios agam anois fein cia tá dá chur amach. Nílim mar adéarfá in touch with obair na Gaedhilge le bliadhain go leith, acht amháin go bhfuilim ag tabhairt aire mhaith dem' ghnó i Sgoil Éanna agus ag déanamh faillighe in gach aon ghnó eile. Ní osglaím ná ní leighim aon litir nach mbaineann le obair na scoile. Bhí tusa an-charthannach liom i gcomhnaidhe agus is truagh lem' chroidhe go ndéarnas faillighe i n-aon nidh a bhain leatsa. An gcuirfidh mé an Ceithearnach chugat nó an gcuirfidh mé go dtí Coiste na gClodhann e? Mise do chara go buan, Pádraig Mac Piarais.

L. 164/P.Ms.

23.2.1910.   Sgoil Éanna,
                                    Rath Ó Máine.

A Chara,

Seo chugat an Ceithearnach. Táim im'bhall dó choiste na gClodhann arís, agus labhróchadh go láidir ag an gcéad chruinniughadh eile i dtaoibh an chleasa mhí-náirigh d'imir siad ort. Badh cheart go mbéadh a fhios aca ar fad go raibh tusa ag obair ar an gCeithearnach. Bhí sé ar na mion-tuairisgibh gur hiarraídh ort an sgéal do chur i gcomórtas leis na cóipeannaibh do bhí san Acadamh. Is cinnte go raibh a fhios ag an Laoideach go raibh tú ag obair ar an sgéal. Ní féidir go n-imtheochadh sé as a chuimhne.

Ní hiongnadh fearg do bheith ort amannta le muinntir Bhaile Átha Cliath. Ní aontuighim leat gur cleasaidhthe iad, acht ní mór le radh iad mar lucht gnótha, cuid aca ar chuma ar bith, agus tá faitchíos orm go bhfuilimse ar an duine is measa aca.

Is maith liom a chlos go bhfuil Bruidhean Chaorthain i mbéal na ndaoine. An gcuirfeadh Dáil Uladh d'insinn-se i gcló dhuit? Muna gcuirfeadh, badh cheart do'n Chonnradh é chur i gcló. Cia do mheas ar é chur amach i n-a chodachaibh san gClaidheamh Soluis? Mise do chara go buan. Pádraig Mac Piarais.

L. 165/P.Ms.

16.4.1910.   Sgoil Éanna,
                              Rath Ó Máine.

A Chara,

Déanfaidh mé an rud iarras tú orm agus fáilte. Beidh cruinniughadh do Choiste na gClodhlann an Céadaoin seo chugainn agus cuirfidh me an cheist ós a gcomhair. Déarfaidh mé leo nach mór an *Bruidhean* do chur amach mar chúitiughadh ar an bhfeall do rinneadar ort i dtaoibh an *Ceithearnaigh*. Ní raibh cruinniughadh ag an gCoiste ó shoin. Mise do chara go buan. Pádraig Mac Piarais.

L. 172/NLI

24.5.1910   Sgoil Éanna,
                              Raith Ó Máine.

A Chara,

Do ghlacas do litir ag geallamhaint ...£50-0-0... le haghaidh oibre na Sgoile seo agus táim fíor-bhuidheach dhíot ar a son. Cuirfead sgéal eile chugat go gairid. Mise do chara, Pádraig Mac Piarais.

L. 176/NLI

11.6.1910.   Sgoil Éanna,
                              Rath Ó Máine.

A Chara,

Táim an – bhuíoch díot as ucht na cabhrach do gheallais le haghaidh Sgoil Éanna.. Tá socraithe agam ar an áit nua úd do thógáil ar chíos. Ait an-álainn is eadh é. Cuirfear ainm leis an léas dé Luain. Agus caithfidh mé £300 d'íoc láithreach mar urradhas go ndíolfar cíos. Caithfidh mé freisin roinnt airgid a bheith ar láimh agam le tosughadh ar na seomraí nua.

Ar na habhraibh seo táim ag glaodhach isteach ar an airgead atá geallta ag mo cháirdibh agus bhéinn fíor bhuíoch díot dá gcuirféa chugam an méid atá geallta agat-sa. Sgríobhfad chugat arís go gairid i dtaobh an "Chumainn" nó an connartha bhéas idir mise agus lucht bronnta an airgid. Mise do chara go buan, Pádraig Mac Piarais.

L. 179/NLI

21.6.1910.   Sgoil Éanna,
                                          Rath Ó Máine.

A Chara,

An bhféadfá seolta (1) Ghiollabríghde Uí Chatháin agus (2) Phroinnsiais Uí Cheallacháin, M.A. .i. an fear do sgríobh na Bilingual Science lessons úd, do chur chugam?

Teastuigheann siad go géar uaim. Mise do chara, Pádraig Mac Piarais.

L. 184/OCS

1.7.1910.   Sgoil Éanna,
                                          Rath Ó Máine.

A Chara,

Go raibh míle maith agat. Agus go raibh céad míle maith agat ar son do leabhráin. Is breagh an rud é go bhfuil Filí Gaedhilge ag éirighe chugainn. Mise do chara go buan. Pádraig Mac Piarais.

L. 185/NLI

4.7.1910.   Sgoil Éanna,
                                          Rath Ó Máine.

A Chara,

Cuireadh an seic seo ar ais chugam agus an litir seo istigh in a theannta. Céard déanfas sinn? Is dócha nach nglacfar le "Enrí Ua Mhuirgheasa" más "Henry Morris" atá thíos agat ar leabhraibh an chonnartha. Mise do chara go buan, Pádraig Mac Piarais.

L. 195/NLI

14.11.1910.   Sgoil Éanna,
                                          Rath Ó Máine.

A Sheaghain na gCarad,

Bhí tú chomh maith agus a gheallamhaint dom, tá tamall ó shoin ann, go gcuirfeá t'ainm le bille £20, agus go n-íocfá £5 gach ráithe ar an mbille sin go mbéadh sé glanta. Teastuigheann airgead go han-ghéar uaim fá láthair, agus chuirfeá fá chomaoin mhór mé dá bhféadfá an méid seo dhéanamh dhom anois. D'fhéadfaimís dul isteach sa mbainnc le chéile agus tá mé 'ceapadh go socróchadh an stiurthóir an gnó dhúinn. Níor mhór bheith ann roimh a trí a chlog. Ní féidir liomsa bheith sa gcathair aon lá roimh a trí a chlog acht amháin Dia Céadaoin. Tá a fhios agam go mbíonn tusa gnóthach Dia Ceádaoin, acht d'fhéadfainn glaodhach isteach ort Tigh Dollard agus d'féadfaimís dul síos go dtí an bainnc le chéile nuair bheithéa ag dul amach le haghaidh do chuid lóin. Ní chaillfeá mórán ama mar sin. Cuir cárta posta chugam, led'thoil ag innseacht dom an nglaochfaidh mé ort an Céadaoin seo chugainn. Níorbh' fhéidir liom bheith sa gcathair roimh a dó a chlog. Mise do chara go buan. Pádraig Mac Piarais.

L.214/NLI

28.5.1911. Sgoil Éanna,

Beir míle buidheachais. Cur chugam led thoil ainmneacha na namhrán déanfas tú agus inis dom na tráthnónta is fearr oirfeas duit. Beidh aeridheacht againn gach oiche ar a 7.30. Dá mhinicí a thiocfas tú ar ndói, is amhlaidh is fearr. P. Mac P.

L. 225/P.Ms.

4.9.1911. Sgoil Éanna,
Rath Fearnáin.
A Thomáis na gCarad,
Seo chugat cúntas Bhriain go ceann na leathbhliadhna.
D'fhill sé Dia Luain agus fonn maith oibre air. D'éirigh leis san sgrúdughadh i nGaedhilg, i mBéarla, i nAireamh, agus i nAilgéabar, i gCéimseatain, i nDúil-Eolas, i dTarraingteoireacht agus i Stair, agus Tlacht-Eolas. Theip air sa bhFrainncis. Acht ar ndóigh theip ar leath na tíre sa bhFrainncis i mbliadhna, agus ní chruthuigheann an "teipeadh" so acht nach dtuigeann an sgruduightheoir a ghnó. Tá níos mó Frainncise ag Brian ná mar bhí agam-sa nuair fuair mé an treas nó an ceathramhadh áit san ngrád.
Táim lán-tsásta leis an gcaoi 'nar chruthaigh Brian tríd is tríd. Is beag a cheapfadh éinne bliadhain go leith ó shoin go n-éireochadh leis chomh maith sin, i nAireamh agus i nAilgéabar agus i gCéimseatain agus d'éirigh. Tá muid le n-a chur isteach ar "onórachaibh" an bliadhain seo chugainn. (bhí sé istigh ar onórachaibh i nGaedhilg an babhta deiridh seo agus fuair sé 399 "honours marks" innti). I dteannta cúrsa an Bhúird déanfaidh sé roinnt commercial arithmetic agus nithe eile a bhaineas le trachtáil srl.
An fíor go bhfuil Pádraig Mac Maghnuis i nÉirinn? Agus má's fíor an meas tú an bhféadfá chur d'iachall air an t-airgead do

gheall sé 3½ bliadhna ó shoin do thabhairt dúinn? Dá bhfeicfeadh sé an áit táim cinnte go dtaithneochadh sé leis. Mise do chara go buan. Pádraig Mac Piarais.

L. 241/DD

[Meán Fomhair 1911]

A Phádraig na gCarad,
   Beatha agus Sláinte,
   Má bhíthear ag toghadh duine i n-áit Mhicíl Uí Bhriain cuirfidh mé focal isteach ar do shon-sa, ná bíodh faitíos ort. Caithfidh muinntir Sgoil Éanna seasamh le chéile. Beir Buaidh agus beannacht. Mise. Pádraig Mac Piarais.

L. 242/DD

[Meán Fomhair 1911]

A Chara,
   Seo chugat cunntas Phroinnsiais go deireadh na leath-bhliadhna. Tá orm £500 d'íoc fá dheireadh na míosa so, agus níor mhór dom bheith ag cruinniughadh isteach na bpighneacha.
   Má tá aon airgead agat orm bain as méid an chunntais seo é. Is truagh liom nar fhéad mé dul síos chugaibh i mbliadhna. B'féidir go ngabhfainn síos fán Nodlaig.
   Nach breagh a chruthuigh Eilís san sgrúdughadh?
   Ag súil go bhfuil sibh uile go maith, Mise do chara go buan,
Pádraig Mac Piarais.

L. 259/DD

A Chara,
   Beatha agus sláinte. Táim fíor-bhuidheach dhíot as ucht do gheallamhaint. Tá ceaptha againn anois Cumann Teoranta do chur ar bun le ceannas an dá Sgoil do ghlacadh agus mise im'stiurthóir agus im' Ard-Mhaighistir. Bhéarfar triocha cuid nó roinn, £1 an ceann, duit ar son do chuid airgid. Beir buaidh agus beannacht. Mise do chara go buan.

410

L. 265/DD

A Chara,

Beatha agus sláinte.

Táim fíor-bhuidheach dhuit as ucht do chongamh fior-fhéile. Go mairidh tú i bhfad! Bronnfar codacha ort ar son an £30 so agus ar son an tsíntiúis do thugais uait bliadhain go leith ó shoin. Cuirfear chugat iad chomh luath is bhéas an Cumann curtha ar bun i gceart. Beir buaidh agus beannacht. Mise, Pádraig Mac Piarais.

L. 275/DD

[Samhain. 1911]

A Chara,

An mbeithéa sásta bheith id'bhall do Chomhairle Acadamhail Sgoil Éanna? Ní bheidh ort freastal ar mhórán cruinniughadh ná aon bhaint do bheith agat le cúrsaí gnótha na Sgoile. 'Sé rud atá sa gComhairle seo roinnt daoine a bhfuuil muinghín ag an bpobal asta i dtaoibh creidimh agus náisiúntachta. Glactar comhairle leo ó am to ham i dtaoibh ceisteanna bhaineas le hoideachas. 'Siad na daoine atá ar an gComhairle cheana – M. Ní Aodáin, An Dr. Mac Enrí, An Dr. Windle, Seosamh O Dóláin, Seaghan Leslie, Séumas Mac Maghnuis agus An Canónach Art Ó Riain. Táim ag iarraidh anois ort-sa, ar Úna Ní Fhaircheallaigh, ar an Máirtíneach, agus ar an Athair M. Mag Uidhir dul uirthi má's é bhur dtoil é. Beir buadh agus beannacht, Mise.

L. 276/DD

Samhain 1911

A Stíopháin na gCarad,

An mbeitheá sásta bheith ar dhuine de na Stiúrthóiribh ar an gCumann atámuid a chur ar bun le ceannus Sgoil Éanna agus Sgoil Íde do ghlachadh? 'Siad na stiúrthóirí atá ceaptha cheana Seosamh Ó Dóláin, M. Smidic, Alasdair Mac Uilis, agus mé féin. Badh mhaith linn fear mar thusa a bhfuil cáil fir gnótha air do bheith i n-ár measg, agus, rud eile, ó tharla go bhfuil t'ainm-se leis an mbille úd san mBainnc agus "stake" agat san obair, mar adéarfa, b'féidir nár mhiste leat féin guth do bheith agat i stiuradh na hoibre. Mise do chara go buan.

411

L. 281/DD

[Samhain 1911]

A Chara,

Táim fíor-bhuidheach dhíot as ucht do litre. Féacfaidh mé le seacht gcuid as an méid bhéas agam féin do chur síos in d'ainm-se. Seo chugat cóip de'n Prospectus, nó an chéad draft de, agus beidh mé an – bhuidheach dhíot má leigheann tú é agus é do chur ar ais chugam chomh luath agus is féidir leat é. Mise do bhuan-chara,

L. 286/DD

[Samhain 1911]

A Chara,
Beatha agus sláinte,
Do gabhas do litir. Nuair fuaireas an cló-sgríbhneoir uait cheapas go mbéadh sé ar mo chumas airgead síos d'íoc, acht b'éigin dom suim mhór airgid do dhíol leis na daoinibh do chuir suas na tighthe nua dhúinn annso, agus d'fhág sé sin ar bheagán airgid mé. Ar an adhbhar sin caithfidh mé íoc ar son an chló-sgríbhneora de réir a chéile. Ta £2 agam dá chur chugat annso istigh. Chífir as so nach bhfuil an cló ró-shoiléir anois. An dteastuigheann ribín nua, nó céard tá air? Beir buaidh agus beannacht. Mise. Pádraig Mac Piarais.

L. 289/DD

A Chara,
Beatha agus slainte.
Táim buidheach dhíot ar son an leabhráin úd. Is dócha go bfhuairis faoi seo an litir do chuireas chugat ag innsint duit an teidil do cheapas le haghaidh na leigheachta .i. "Education under Home Rule". Seo chugat mo pheictiúir, ó's rud go bhfuil sé uaibh. Nuair bhéas sibh ag fógradh na leigheactha b'fearr liom dá luaidhfeadh sibh mé fá'n ainm "P. H. Pearse" má's i mBéarla bhéas sibh ag sgríobhadh 'ná fá'n ainm "Pádraic Mac Piarais", mar sílim gurab aisteach an rud cuma Gaedhealach ar ainm Gallda do chur i n-alt no i bhfógra atá sgríobhtha i mBéarla.

Tá Cumann Teoranta dá chur ar bun againn le ceannus Sgoil Éanna agus Sgoil Íde do ghabháil. An eol duit éinne i gCorcaigh do chuirfead i n-aithne daoine sa gcathair sin, do bhéadh

toilteannach ar codacha do ghlacadh san gCumann? Beir buaidh
agus beannacht, Mise. Pádraig Mac Piarais.

L. 292/DD

Nodlaig 1911.

A Chara,

Seo chugat cunntas ar na leabhraibh, srl, fuair Seosamh ó thús
an tseisiúin. Chuir tú 5/6 chugam cheana, agus tá an méid sin
bainte de'n chunntas, agam. D'íoc tú £1-1-0 freisin ar son na
siúinéireachta, acht is ar éigin bhí tosnuighthe ar an obair ag an
múinteoir nuair d'éirigh sé as. Beidh múinteoir nua againn tar éis
na Nodlag agus rachaidh na buidheanta ar aghaidh.

Fuair Seosamh sláinte an-mhaith i mbliadhna, agus táimíd
lán-tsásta le n-a chuid oibre. Béidh sé abhaile chugaibh Dia
hAoine. Beir buaidh agus beannacht. Pádraig Mac Piarais.

L. 296/DD

A Chara,
Beatha agus sláinte.

D'iarr an Piarsach orm a leithsgéal do ghabháil leat fá nár
fhreagair sé do litir roimhe so, acht bhí sé an-ghnóthach. Beidh sé
lán-tsásta dul go Béal Feirste agus léigheacht chuimhne an
Emmetigh do thabhairt díbh i mbliadhna. Sgríobh chuige chomh
luath is bhéas an dáta socruighthe i n-a cheart agaibh agus innis dó
cad é an dáta atá socruighthe. Beir buaidh agus beannacht. Mise.

L. 300/OCS

[1912]

Badh mhaith liom comhrádh do bheith agam leat i dtaoibh scheme
atá ar bun agam. An bhféadfá teacht amach annso tráthnóna éigin
nó ar b'fhearr leat go rachainn isteach chugat? Cuir cárta
chugam led' thoil ag socrughadh an ama agus na háite. Ní bhím
saor go dtí 5 a clog. P. Mac P.

413

L. 301/NLI

28.1.1912.   Sgoil Éanna,
                                                Rath Fearnáin.

A Chara Chroidhe,
Go raibh míle maith agat. Cuirfidh mé an bille úd isteach chuig an mBannc i mbárach.

Níl an t-airgead ag teacht isteach acht go mall. Níl geallta fós acht beagán ós cionn £200. Bhí cruinniughadh ag na stiurthóiribh indé agus do chinneadar gan dul ar aghaidh go mbeidh £500 ar a laighead againn. Bhéinn fíor-bhuidheach dá labhróchta le gach Gaedheal da gcastar ort agus iad do ghríosadh chun cuid nó cúpla cuid thógáil. Seo chugat cúpla cóip de'n Phrospectus agus de'n Form of Application. Leanfamuíd ag bailiughadh go mbeidh ár ndóthain againn.

An bhféadfá seoladh an fhir úd de mhuinntir Cox do chur chugam aris? Chaill mé an litir thug tú dhom agus a sheoladh air, tá faitíos orm.

Badh cheart duit píosa deas do chur ar an g*Claidheamh* i dtaoibh pósta Mhichíl Mhig Ruaidhrí. Thug sé an bhean abhaile coichighis ó shoin. Phós sé a gan fhios do'n tsaoghal.

Tá súil agam go bhfuil tú go maith id'sláinte arís. Mise do chara go buan, Pádraig Mac Piarais.

L. 302/NLI

28.1.1912.   Sgoil Éanna,
                                                Rath Fearnáin.

A Sheaghain na gCarad,
Is binn liom a chlos go mbeidh tú i n-ann bualadh fá'n obair úd an tseachtmhain seo. Bhí cruinniughadh againn indé agus ní raibh leath ar ndóthain againn, agus shocruigheamar nach roinnfimís na codacha go mbéadh trí chéad eile ar a laighead againn. Déan do dhicheall beathadh agus báis dúinn mar sin i measc connradhóirí, daoine puiblidhe, agus lucht gnótha Baile Átha Cliath. D'aontuigheamar ag an grcuinniughadh go ndíolfaimís thú de réir an airgid do thocfadh insteach, cé nach bhfuil sé de chumhacht againn percentage do thabhairt ar an airgead féin; acht féachfaidh mise agus Alastair Mac Uilis chuige go ndíolfar thú. Is féidir leat a mhíniughadh do na daoinibh nac bhfuil aon bhrídh sa dáta úd .i. "Jan 22nd", agus go mbeimíd ag bailiughadh arigid go ceann tamaill mhaith.

Seo chugat roinnt cóipeanna de'n Prospectus. Cuirfidh mé beart

414

eile chugat i mbárach. Mise do chara go buan, Pádraig Mac Piarais.

L. 305/NLI

17.2.1912. Sgoil Éanna,
Rath Fearnáin.

A Chara,
Beatha agus sláinte.

An mbeitheá toilteannach ar theacht go tionól beag de Ghaedhealaibh chun an ní so síos do chur trí chéile .i. ar bhféidir cumann do chur ar bun tré n-a dtiocfadh le Gaedhilgeoiribh a mbarúla ar cheisteannaibh poilitidheachta do nochtugadh agus do chur i na gniomh? Chítear dhom gurt mór an chaill do chineadh Gaedheal gan spéis dá cur ag lucht na Gaedhilge i gcúrsaibh poilitidheachta agus gur mór a chaill don Ghaedhilg agus cúrsaí poilitidheachta na tíre do bheith dá síorphleidhe san teangaidh iasacta. Anois an t-am a leithéad sin de chumann do chur ar bun. Má chuirtear Reacht Riaghaltais Baile i bhfeidhm beidh gabhadh le buidhin Ghaedhilgeoirí i bhFeis na hÉireann, agus muna gcuirtear Reacht Raighaltais Baile i bhfeidhm beidh gabhadh le dian-troid i nÉirinn, agus beidh orainne féachaint chuige nach san teangaidh iasachta seinnfear an gháir chatha. Ní leigfinn isteach sa gcumann acht daoine do bhéadh toilteannach ar sheasamh amach ar son cirt Gaedheal i n-aghaidh an domhain mhóir, agus iad do bheith n-a nGaedhilgeoiribh.

Bead ag súil le focal uait ar do chaothamhlacht. Tá an litir so dá cur agam chum seisir nó mór-sheisir eile. Beir buaidh agus beannacht. Mise, Pádraig Mac Piarais.

L. 307/PRO

18.2.1912. Sgoil Éanna,
Rath Fearnáin.

A Chara,
Beatha agus sláinte! An mbeitheá toilteannach ar theacht go tionól beag de Ghaedhealaibh chum an ní so do chur tré chéile .i. ar bhféidir cumann do chur ar bun tré n-a dtiochfadh le Gaedhil-geoiribh a mbarúla ar cheisteanna poilitidheachta do nochtudhadh agus do chur i ngíomh? Chítear dhom gur mór an chaill do chineadh Gaedheal gan spéis dá chur ag lucht na Gaedhilge i gcursaíbh poilitidheachta agus gur mór a chaill don Ghaedhilg cúrsaí poilitidheachta na tíre do bheith dá síorphlé sa teanga

iasachta. Anois an tam chun a leithéid sin de chumann do chur ar bun. Má chuirtear Reacht Rialtais Baile i bhfeidhm beidh gabhadh le buidhin Gaedhilgeoirí i bhFeis na hÉireann, agus muna gcuirtear Reacht Rialtais Baile i bhfeidhm beidh gabhadh le dian-troid in Éirinn, agus beidh orainn féachaint chuige nach san teanga iasachta seinnfear an gháir chatha. Ní ligfinn isteach sa chumann acht daoine do bhéadh toilteannach ar sheasamh amach ar son chirt Gaedheal in aghaidh an domhain mhóir agus iad do bheith in a nGaedhealgoiribh.

Bead ag súil le focal uait ar do chaothamhlacht. Tá an litir seo dá chur agam chun seisear nó mór sheisear eile. Beir bua 's beannacht. Mise, Pádraig Mac Piarais.

L. 308/BB

16.3.1912.   An Barr Buadh.

Beatha agus Sláinte,

Ar n-a thuiscint dom go bhfuilir chum cath d'fhearadh i n-aghaidh Ghall ar son cirt Ghaedheal, do ghabhas lem ais na focla beaga molta agus gríosaithe seo do chur chugat go mba méadughadh meanman agus árdughadh aigeanta dhuit i láthair do bhiobhdhadh iad.

Ba gheal le Gaedhealaibh thú tráth ded' shaoghal. An méid dinn abhí id' choinnibh, d'admhuigheamar go raibh misneach agat tar fearaibh Éireann an lá do sheasais ar dheas-láimh Pharnell agus gáir na conairte go garg gáibhtheach ina thimpeall. Do bhís id' fhear óg an tráth sin agus táir id' fhear meán-aosta anois. Ní hionann meanma agus misneach don óige agus do'n aois. Bíonn an óige dána. Bíonn an aois faiteach. Acht cuimhnigh go bhfuil an gníomh do chuir Parnell roimhe chun a dhéanta gan déanamh fós agus gurb ortsa atá a dhéanamh. Cuimhnigh gurb ionmhuin le Parnell tusa agus gurab ionmhuin le Gaedhealaibh tú de bhrigh gurbh' ionmhuin leis-sean tú. Cuimhnigh gurab id' láimh-se atá claidheamh colg-dhíreach cruadh Pharnell agus gurab umat-sa atá brat uasal ríogdha Pharnell, agus gurab dhíot-sa gairmtear comharba Pharnell. Cuimhnigh go bhfuil Gaedhil ar do chúl. Cuimhnigh go bhfuil Gaill ar d'aghaidh. Cuimhnigh go bhfuil Gaedhil ag seasamh ort. Cuimhnigh go bhfuil Gaill ag faire ort. Cuimhnigh ar chlú do chinidh. Cuimhnigh ar ghliochas do namhad. Cuimhnigh ar an ní úd dá dtug Parnell fuath agus – seachain ar d'anam agus ar d'oineach í – i.e. gáire Sasanaigh.

Gabh chugat láidreacht an leomhain agus misneach an mhathghamhna agus gliocas na naithreach nimhe. Bí borb le borb.

416

Bí teann le teann. Bí cruaidh le cruaidh. Bí glic le glic. Bí id'
eolach aibidh. Bí id' choinnill ghaile. Bí id' fhear. Bí id' thaoiseach.
Bí id' Pharnell. Beir buaidh agus beannacht, Mise, Laegh
Mac Riangabhra.

L. 309/BB

23.3.1912.   An Barr Buadh.

Beatha agus Sláinte,
    Deirtear liom gur dána an mhaise dhom scríobhadh chugat, óir
nach dtaithníonn comhairle leat. Deirtear, más fíor, gur dóigh leat
gur fút-sa agus fá'n Réamonnach badh cheart socrughadh gacha
scéal bhaineas le leas Gaedheal d'fhágáil. Ní chreidim go bhfuilir
chomh baoth sin. Dá gcreidfinn, do chuirfinn i n-úil duit roinnt
sean-fhocal tháinig chun Gaedheal le sinnsearacht, mar atá, "Ná
tabhair do chúl ar chomhairle ar mhaithe leat." agus "Is fearr
comhairle i dtráth ioná cáineadh in antráth." Dá mba eascara
dhom thú do chuirfinn an sean-fhocal seo i gcuimhne dhuit i.e. "An
té nach nglacann comhairle glacadh sé comhrac"; acht ós duine
dem' cháirdibh thú agus ár namha ós ár gcomhair ní abróchad leat
acht an méid seo i.e. "Is fearr comhairle roimh chath ioná dhá
chomhairle déag ina dhiaidh."
    Deirtear liom fós gur gráin leat thar aon chomhairle eile
comhairle ó fhear óg. Admhuighim go bhfuilim-se óg. Mea culpa,
mea culpa. Acht nílim chomh óg sin nach cuimhin liom an tráth do
bhís-se óg. Dá n-abróchaidhe leat-sa an uair sin nár oireamhnach
comhairle uait-se do sheanóiribh, cad déarfá? Déarfá rud éigin
narbh' fhéidir a chur i gcló.
    Do léigheas trácht i seanchas Gaedheal ar fhear eile gurbh' ainm
Seán Diolúin. Do bhí aithne agat-sa ar an bhfear sin, óir dob' é
d'athair dílis féin é. Do bhí sé ina dhuine de na taoiseachaibh do
bhí ar an dream dár gairmeadh Éire Óg. Do bhí sean-fhear i
nÉirinn an t-am sin nár thaithnigh comhairle leis, go mór – mhór
comhairle ó dhaoinibh óga. Domhnall Ó Conaill dob' ainm dó. Do
dhiúltaigh Domhnall Ó Conaill do chomhairle d'athar-sa agus do
chomhairle na hÉireann Óige. Dá nglacfadh sé an comhairle sin i
n-am do bhéadh Éire saor le leath-chéad bliadhain agus fiche
milliun duine ag áitreabhadh innti indiu. Ní beag sin. Beir buaidh
agus beannacht. Mise, Laegh Mac Riangabhra.

                                417

L. 310/NLI

28.3.1912.   12 Sráidín an Teampaill,
                               Áth Cliath.

A Chara,
    Beir buaidh agus beannacht.
    Táim ag gairm roinnt carad chum tionóil bhig déanfar i dTigh
Ósta Muighe Ratha i Sráid na Tríonóide Dia Máirt so chugainn 2
Aibreán ar a hocht tráthnóna. Fáth an tionóil chun cumann do
chur ar bun darab aon ghnó lucht labhartha na Gaedhilge do
bhailiughadh do chongnamh Gaedheal ag troid dóibh ar son
saoirse.
    Tá súil agam go bhfreagróchairse an comhghairm. Beir buadh
agus beannacht, Mise, Pádraig Mac Piarais.

L. 311/PRO

28.3.1912.   An Barr Buadh,
                               12 Sráidín an Teampaill,
                               Áth Cliath.

A Chara,
    Beir buaidh agus beannacht!
Táim ag gairm roinnt carad chun tionóil bhig déanfar i dTig Ósta
Muighe Ratha i Sráid na Tríonóide, Dia Máirt seo chugainn, 2
Aibreán ar a hocht trathnóna. Fáth an tionóil chun cumann do chur
ar bun darab aon ghnó lucht labhartha na Gaedhilge do
bhailiughadh do coghnamh Gaedheal ag troid dóibh ar son saoirse.
Tá súil agam go bhfreagróchair-se an chomghairm. Beir buaidh
agus beannacht, Mise, Pádraig Mac Piarais.

L. 312/BB

30.3.1912.   An Barr Buadh.

Beatha agus Sláinte,
    Do scríobhas chum do shean-charad chum Seáin Diolúin tá
tamall ó shoin ann. An uair do bhíos-sa im' mhac bheag do bhís-se
agus Seán Diolúin bhur bhfearaibh óga agus sibh in bhur ndís san
áth ag cosaint Gaedheal ar fhóirneart Gall. Do bhínn-se ag
léigheadh bhúr n-eachtra ós ard dom' shean-athair. Do rinne mo

418

shean-athair beagán ar son na hÉireann an uair do bhí sé féin óg. Do bhí sé ar lucht leanamhna athar do charad i mbliadhain a '48. Do bhí sé ina Fhinín i mbliadhain a '67. Do chreid sé go gcríochnóchadh sibh-se agus bhúr gcompanaigh an obair d'fhág seisean agus a chompánaigh-san gan chríochnughadh. Níor thuigeas-sa an scéal go ró-mhaith óir do bhíos óg. Do cheapas go mbéadh Parnell ina righ ar Éirinn dá n-éireochadh libh. Do cheapas go mbéadh a n-arm agus a gcabhlach féin ag Gaedhealaibh. Do cheapas céad rud nach gceapfadh éinne acht leanbh. Acht do bhi aon rud amháin nar cheapas riamh. Do bhi aon rud amháin nach gcreidfinn dá dtiocfadh aingeal annuas ó na flaitheasaibh agus a réamhfháisnéis dom. Ní chreidfinn ó éinne beo ná marbh go mbeithéa-sa agus Seán Diolúin ag tabhair t fuatha dá chéile i ndeireadh bhur saoghail. Do connachthas dom gur geall le Dáibhíd agus Ionathan nó le Roland agus Oilibhéar nó le Cú Chulainn agus Feirdia sibh ar mhéid bhúr gcarthanacta agus bhúr gcomhbáidhe agus bhúr ndilseachta dá chéile. Agus do shíleas dá dtiochfadh in bhúr saoghal choidhche sibh do bheith i gcoinnibh a chéile gurab é an nós do chleachtfadh sibh nós Con Chulainn agus Feirdia i.e. deocha míne meidhreacha agus biadha so-chaithmhe so-bhlasta do chur chum a chéile tar éis catha gacha lae agus luighe ar aon leabaidh gach oidhche go maidin.

Acht ní mar sin atá. Is amhlaidh do bhí Cú Chulainn agus Feirdia agus duine aca ar thaobh agus an duine eile ar thaoibh eile agus iad ag tabhairt geana dá chéile ina dhiaidh sin. Is amhlaidh atá sibh-se agus bhúr ndís ar aon taoibh amháin acht sibh ag tabhairt fuatha dá chéile ina aimhdheoin sin.

Ní heol dom-sa cad tá eadraibh. Ní heol d'éinne cad tá eadraibh. Ní heol díbh féin cad tá eadraibh. Deirtear liom gur dóigh leat-sa gur amadán Seán Diolúin. Deirtear liom gur dóigh le Seán Diolúin gur gealt tusa. Ní dóigh liom-sa go bhfuil an ceart dá cheapadh ag ceachtar agaibh. Chítear dom gurab é an locht céadna atá ar gach duine agaibh i. an iomarca measa aige ar a bharamhail féin.

Bíodh do bharamhail féin agat. Acht mo chomhairle dhuit. Má's dóigh leat gurab amadán Seán Diolúin ní gabhadh dhuit amadán do ghairm dhe ós comhair Gall. Abair do rogha rud i gCúige Mumhan. Fan id' thost i dTig Feise Lonndan, muna feidir leat labhairt gan do bhráthair do mhasladh.

Rud eile. Cad chuige dhuit aga radh nach féidir dlighe do dhéanamh d'Adhbhar Achta Riaghaltais na hÉireann le linn na Parlaiméide so? Nár chóra dhuit a radh go GCAITHFEAR dlighe do dhéanamh dhe? Beir buaidh agus Beannacht, Mise, Laegh Mac Riangabhra.

5.4.1912.   An Barr Buadh.

Beatha agus Sláinte,

Mo ghoirm thú má's tú do ghairm le chéile agus do riar agus
d'órduigh na slóighte do bhí i mBaile Átha Cliath Dia Domhnaigh,
agus is dócha gur tú. Do bhí rian do láimhe ar an sluaigheadh, rian
láimhe fir óig. Is maith liom fir óga. Is maith le Gaedhealaibh fir
óga. Is maith le Gaedhealaibh tusa. Ba tú ba ghile leis na slóightibh
dia Domhnaigh, agus níorbh'é an Réamonnach.

Tá croidhe na hóige ionnat, a fhir óig. Seachain an gcríonfadh sé
agus a bhfuil de shean-laochraidh id' thimcheall. Mo ghrádh an
sean-fhear a bhfuil croí na hóige ann, acht is mairg an tóg-fhear a
dtiochfadh croidhe seanóra ann.

Is bríoghmhar do labhrais Dia Domhnaigh. Níor thaithnigh
roinn ded' bhriathraibh liom. An mbeir-se dílis do choróin Shasana
an uair bhéas mion-Fheis i mBaile Átha Cliath? Ní chreidim go
mbeir. Déan machtnamh. Ní beag sin den dul so. Beir buadh agus
beannacht, Mise, Laegh Mac Riangabhra.

12.4.1912.   An Barr Buadh.

Beatha agus Sláinte,

Ní chualas d'ainm riamh ort acht "T.P." Ní heol dom t'ainm
dílis. Acht is dócha gur "Tadhg" do baisteadh ort, óir tá an tainm
sin coitcheann i measc feisirí agus is ainm é oireas do lucht
poilitidheachta de réir béal-oidis Gaedheal. Bíodh a fhiadhnuise sin
ar an sean-fhocal .i. "Tadhg an Dá Thaobh." Más rud é nach
bhfuil an ceart agam acht gur "Tomás" nó "Toirdhealbhach" nó
"Tomaltach" nó "Tormad" do baisteadh ort, maith dhom mo
neimheolas.

Ag labhairt duit i Lonndain Shasana an lá cheana a dubhrais
nach mian le Gaedhealaibh scaramhaint ó Shasanaibh. Adubhrais
fós nach scarfaidh Gaedhil ó Shasanaibh go deo. B'fhéidir an ceart
do bheith agat. B'fhéidir gur fearr thuigir-se meon Gaedheal ioná
mar thuigim-sé. Acht ní chuige sin do bhíos acht chuige seo. Is é an
fáth thugais led' bharamhail .i. *an fhaid bhéas muca le díol ag
Gaedhealaibh agus Gaill ag ceannach muc nach n-oirfeadh do
Ghaedhealaibh scaramhaint ó Ghallaibh.*

Níor mhaith liom fearg do chur ort. Níor mhaith liom labhairt
go drochmhúinte leat. Acht tabhair cead dom a rádh leat suas led'
bhéal nach bhfuil sa mhéid sin cainnte acht baois agus dearg-

amadaighe. Do bhéadh sé chomh maith agam-sa a rádh an fhaid
bhéas Franncaigh ag díol fíona agus Sasanaigh ag ceannach fíona
go gcaithfeadh Sasana agus an Fhrainnc bheith ceangailte le chéile,
nó an fhaid bhéas Rúisigh ag díol cruithneachta agus Sasanaigh ag
ceannach cruithneachta go gcaithfidh Sasana agus an Rúis bheith
fá aon choróin amháin.

Is minic do chualas go mbainfeadh a leithéid so nó a leithéid siúd
gáire as na cataibh. Do bhainfeadh do chainnt-se gáire as na
mucaibh. Beir buaidh agus beannacht, Mise, Leagh Mac Riangabhra.

L.(tel.) 316/BB

20.4.1912.   An Barr Buadh.

Chím gur ainmnigheadh thú mar Uachtarán ar Thigh na
gCoitcheann in Éirinn fá'n reacht nua. An bhfuil Gaedhilge agat?
Mise, Laegh Mac Riangabhra.

L. 317/BB

27.4.1912.   An Barr Buadh.
Beatha agus Sláinte,
   Dob' iongnadh liom ó éinne eile na briathra do labhrais i láthair
Feise Gall seachtmhain ó shoin. Níorbh' iongnadh liom uait-se iad.
Ba tú fear mór-bhuaidheartha gacha cuideachtan i gcomhnaidhe.
Do ghlacais leis an Adhbhar Achta. Acht níor admhuighís gur
buaidh do Ghaedhealaibh é. Do mhaoidhis go raibh buaidhte ar
Ghaedhealaibh. Adubhraís nach gcuirfeadh an t-Adhbhar Achta
Reacht na hAondachta ar neimhní (rud dob fhíor duit). Adubhraís
fós nach raibh leigheas ar an scéal sin, agus gurab amhlaidh sin
dob'fhearr. Le olcas ar chomh-Ghaedhealaibh adubhraís an méid
sin is baoghalach.
   Níl agam le radh leat acht nach bhfuil an ceart agat. Tá bearna
dá hoscailt roimh Ghaedhealaibh. Ní tusa an fearr dhúnfas an
bearna sin. Beir buaidh agus beannacht, Mise, Laegh Mac Riangabhra.

4.5.1912   An Barr Buadh.

Beatha agus Sláinte,

Is fada dhom dhá chur romham scríobhadh chugat. Do scríobhas roinnt litreach le deidheannaighe chum deagh-dhaoine de mhaithibh Gaedheal, agus níor ghabhas freagra ó éinne aca. Is dócha go bhfuilid ro-ghnóthach chun áird a thabhairt ar mo leithéid-se. Nó dob' fhéidir gurab' amhlaidh do chuaidh mo litreacha amugha. I nGaedhilg do sheolas iad agus is gnás le muintir an phosta moill do bhaint as litreacha seoltar i nGaedhilg. Má shroicheann an litir seo thú tá a fhios agam go gcuirfir freagra chugam, óir is de mhaithibh líne dhuit bheith séimh leis an duine dealbh agus eisteacht le h-athchuinge gach éinne dhá úirisle. Ba de thréithibh ríoghraidhe Gaedheal an umhlaidheacht sin, dhá bhuirbhe le bíodhbhaibh iad.

Ní gabhadh dhom tusa do ghríosadh ná d'imdheargadh fá má ba ghabhadh dhom ag scríobhadh dhom chum na ndaoine eile dár thagras. Níor staonais-se riamh i gcath dá dhéine. Dá staonfá do dhéanfadh do lucht leanamhna féin tú do ghriosadh. Sin buaidh de na bhuadhaibh atá ag muinntir Chonnartha na Gaedhilge thar fearaibh Éireann. Tá cead cainnte agus cead cáinte ag an té is suaraighe sa Chonnradh. Tá muinighín aca asat-sa acht ní tuigtear dóibh gur gabhadh dhóibh "Amen" do rádh gach uair dá labhrann tusa. Is iad do lucht leanamhna iad acht ní hiad do chléirigh iad. Cléirigh agus giollaí atá ó mhaithibh eile de Ghaedhealaibh de réir mar chítear dhom. Is dóigh liom gur fearr leat-sa cáirde agus lucht leanamhna agat ioná cléirigh agus giollaí.

Adubhairt Eoin Mac Néill, tá seal gearr ó shoin ann, go bhfuil an iomarca de'n ní úd ar a dtugaid Gaill *red tape* ag baint leis an gConnradh. Tá an ceart ar fad aige. Acht ní hé sin é amháin. Is dóigh liom go ndearna lucht ceannais an Chonnartha dearmad mór ó thús. Ag cromadh ar Ghaedhealaibh do ghríosadh dhóibh, is é do rinneadar mac-samhail na gcumann poilitidheachta do bhí i nÉirinn len a linn do chur ar bun agus Connradh na Gaedhilge do ghairm de. Tá taithighe ag Gaedhealaibh ar a leitheidibh le céad bliadhain agus ní thuigid a mhalairt. Acht dá éifeachtaighe mór-chumann agus craobhacha agus coisti ceantair agus timirthí agus rialacha ag baint leis chum cuspóra poilitidheacha do chur ar aghaidh, ní dóigh liom gurab é is oireamhnaighe chum cuspóra Connartha na Gaedhilge do chur ar aghaidh. Cad is cuspóir do Chonnradh na Gaedhilge? Tá, Gaedhil do chur ag labhairt Gaedhilge. Cia aca is éifeachtaighe chuige sin mór-chumann maille le n-a chraobhachaibh agus le n-a choistíbh, le n-a chórughadh agus le n-a riaghlachaibh agus é ag caitheamh a nduthrachta ag déanamh riaghal agus ag diospóireacht fá dtaoibh díobh, nó buidhne beaga do bheith ag suibhal na dúthaighe, buion díobh ag amhránaidheacht, búion díobh ag léiriughadh úrchluichí, buíon eile ag teagasc na ndaoine i dtaoibh talamhaidheachta, buíon eile ag gríosadh Gaedhil in aghaidh Gall, agus mar sin de, agus an obair sin ar fad dá déanamh aca i nGaedhilg? Gan mórán cainnte aca i dtaobh na Gaedhilge, an dtuigeann tú, acht gan dá labhairt aca acht Gaedhealg.

An uair do cuireadh Connradh na Gaedhilge ar bun, badh cheart do gach duine dar lean de a chúl do thabhairt ar an gcathair agus a aghaidh do thabhairt ar an tuaith. Badh cheart dó dul imeasc na ndaoine a raibh an Ghaedhealg aca agus fanamhaint ina measc. Badh cheat dó gnó éigin do tharraing chuige as a saothróchadh sé an oiread agus do choingbheochadh beo é agus bheith sásta leis an méid sin. Badh cheart go rachadh na filí agus an lucht oirfididh ag siubhal na mbóthar agus ag dul ó thigh go tigh ag aithris a gcuid dán nó ag cantain a gcuid ceoil do na daoine agus bheith sásta le hiostas oidhche ina dhíolaidheacht sin. Ba cheart go dtiochfadh buíon le chéile agus dul ar fud na Gaedhealtachta ag léiriughadh úrchluichí i nGaedhilg. Ba cheart go ngeobhadh buíon eile le n-a n-ais le leathtrom Gaedheal do chásughadh i nGaedilg agus misneach Gaedhgeal do mhúscailt agus Gaedhil do ghríosadh i n-aghaidh Gall. Dá ndéanfaidhe an méid sin agus tuilleadh dá shaghas, is baoghalach go mbéadh cuid dínn níos boichte ioná táimíd agus cuid eile dhínn marbh den ocras agus anró, acht *do bhéadh an Ghaedhealg sabháilte againn.* Agus nach é sin do bhí uainn?

Is eagal liom go bhfuil sé ró-dheidheannach chum an méid sin do dhéanamh anois. Acht d'fhéadfaidhe roinnt de do dhéanamh. An buíon cluicheoirí úd, d'fhéadfaidhe í sin do chur síos go dtí an Ghaedhealtacht. Níl ní ar bith is mó do rachadh i dtairbhe do'n Ghaedhilge. Do dhéanfadh sé níos mó chum labhairt na Gaedhilge do leathadh i n-aon bhliadhain amháin ioná mar atá déanta ag craobhachaibh agus ag timthiríbh an Chonnartha le fiche bliadhain. Tá an litir seo ró-fhada. Ní mór dhom stad. Beir buaidh agus beannacht, Mise, Laegh Mac Riangabhra.

11.5.1912.   An Barr Buadh.

Beatha agus Sláinte,

Chím go bhfuil mo dhearbhráthair .i. Laegh Mac Riangabhra ag scríobhadh litreach chum maith agus mór-uasal Éireann le tamall. Chím go ndeachaidh cuid de na litreacha sin amugha agus gur cuireadh cló ortha san mBarr Buadh. Ní thuigim cad é an fáth a gcuirfidhe cló ar aon ní do scríobhfadh an té sin, óir ní raibh ciall riamh aige agus ní bheidh go deo. Is baoghalach liom gur cara ded' chuid-se é, agus gur tusa do chuir d'fhiachaibh ar fhear seannma an Bharr Bhuaidh (óir deirtear liom go bhfuil an fear sin fád' smacht) na litreacha do chur i gcló. Tuig gur mise an t-aon duine amháin d'fhuil Riangabhra a mbíonn gaois ina smaointibh agus snas ar a ráidhtibh. Is fiú mo litreacha-sa do chur i gcló, acht ní baol go bhfeicfear an litir so ar an mBarr Buadh. Is cuma liom.

Ní fheadar an maith liom thú nó nach maith. Ní fheadar an maith le héinne thú. Tá a fhios agam gur gráin le n-a lán thú. Ní chuala éinne riamh dhá radh "Is maith liom an Piarsach." Deirtear liom gurab ionmhuin le macraidh Scoil Éanna thú. Deirtear liom go ndubhairt bean le mnaoi go ndubhairt bean eile le mnaoi eile go ndubhairt Tomás Mac Domhnaill le duine éigin go dtaithnighir leis. B'fhéidir gur fíor an scéal sin agus b'fhéidir nach fíor. Is ait an duine Tomás Mac Domhnaill.

Táir ró-dhorcha ionnat fhéin, a Phiarsaigh. Ní dhéanann tú caidreamh le Gaedhealaibh. Séanann tú a gcomhluadar. An uair thagas tú ina measc tagann mar do bhéadh néall dubh id' fhochair agus luigheann ortha. An té do bhí cainnteach roimh theacht dhuit, bíonn sé ina thost. An té dho bhí geal-gháireach tagann gruaim air. An í an fhuil Shasanach úd ionat is cionntach leis sin, ní fheadar?

Tá buaidh na cainnte agat. Is féidir leat na slóighte do mhúscailt agus do chorraighe an uair labhras tú leo ós ard. Is féidir leat iad do chur ag gol nó iad do chur ag gáire de réir mar is mian leat. Is dóigh liom go bhfuil dhá Phiarsach ann .i. fear gruamdha doineannta agus fear geal soineannta. Ní fheichtear an fear geal soineannta acht go hannamh. Ar ardánaibh puiblidhe agus i Sgoil Éanna is minice chítear e. Bíonn an fear gruamdha doineannta le feiscint go minic. Is olc an saghas é. Ní maith liom é. Tagann fuacht orm an uair a chím é. Agus is í an chuid is greannmhaire den scéal nach eol dom cia aca an fear dorcha nó an fear geal an Piarsach ceart.

Is maith an gníomh do rinnis an uair do chuiris Scoil Éanna ar bun. Is maith an gníomh do rinnis an uair do chuiris Scoil Íde ar bun. Mo chomhairle dhuit: tabhair aire do Scoil Éanna agus do

Scoil Íde agus ná bac a thuilleadh le cúrsaí poilitidheachta. Tá do dhóthain mhór ar d'aire. Caith uait an Barr Buadh, scaoil urchar le n-a fhear seannma cuir deireadh leis an gCumann Nua úd gan ainm, agus déan go maith an rud do chuiris romhat le déanamh ceithre bliadhna ó shoin. Níor éirigh an dá thráigh riamh leis an ngobadán. Táir-se ag iarraidh freastail ar cheithre trághaibh. Ní éireochaidh leat.

Rud eile. Impidhim agus athchuingim ort gan a thuilleadh d' fhabhailscéaltaibh do scríobhadh. Beir buadh agus beannacht. Mise, Iubhar Mac Riangabhra.

L. 320/BB/G

18.5.1912.

Beatha agus Sláinte.
Chím go bhfuil muinntir Sinn Féin ag corruighe arís. Ba mhithid dóibh sin. Is beag nár mharbhuighis do leanbh féin. Do bhí an dé deiridh ag imeacht as. Ní raibh mórán bádha agam-sa leis an leanbh céadna riamh, acht ba thruagh liom a athair féin dá mharbhadh. Tabhair aire mhaith dó feasta agus do b'fhéidir le Dia go mairfeadh an créatúr.

Do bhís ró-cruaidh. Do bhís ró-dhúr. Do bhís ró-chaol-intinneach. Do bhís ró-cheann-dána. Ní raibh do dhóthain muinghíne agat as do cháirdibh. Do bhí an iomarca muinghíne agat asat féin. Do bhí an iomarca measa agat ar do bharúil féin. Do bhí droch-amhras ort fá dhaoinibh do bhí chomh dílis leat féin. Ní mholfá aon chomhairle acht do chomhairle fein. Ni aontócha aon ní acht an ní mholfá féin. Ní dhéanfá aon ghníomh. Do b'fhearr leat a chruthughadh don tsaoghal nach raibh an ceart ag duine eile dhá dhéanamh ná an ní ceart do dhéanamh thú féin. Ní dhéanfá féin aon ghníomh agus dá molfadh éinne eile aon ghníomh le déanamh do chruthóchthá dhó nár ghníomh indéanta é.

Ní raibh aon dul ar aghaidh i ndán do Chumann a raibh a leithéid sin d'fhear ina cheannás. Ní fhanfadh éinne i gcumann muna mbéadh cead cainnte aige ann. Do bhí do cháirde dod' thréigean ina nduine is ina nduine agus do thréigfidís go leír thú dá leanfá mar do bhí agat.

Is dócha go dtuigir an méid sin anois. Ba cheart go dtuigfeá. Chím fuadar nua fút-sa agus fád' bhuidhin le deireannaighe. Má's maith is mithid. Tá buadha agat-sa nach bhfuil ag aon fhear eile d'fhearaibh Éireann. Ba mhór an truagh é dá rachadh tairbhe na mbuadh sin amugha toisc nach bhféadfadh daoine eile oibriughadh fad' cheannas.

Ní beag sin. Beir buaidh agus beannacht. Mise, Laegh Mac Riangabhra.

L. 321/BB/G

25.5.1912.

Beatha agus Sláinte.

Is mór an tsuim do chuireas i gcomhnuidhe ionat ó'n tráth úd fadó, an uair do bhís-se i do mhac-léighinn. Do cheapas riamh gur mianach foghanta do bhí ionat go mór-mhór an t-am úd do dhiultuighís do do ghlúin d'fhaicead roim choróin Shasana, acht mo léan géar is mo chreach chráidhte, rug aer an tsaoghail ort, thugais onóir agus adhradh do dhéithibh bhréige na nGeinteach agus anois adeirir linn gur beag do iontaobh as an gcine daonna.

Faire fút, a mhic an fhir chalma! Dá mbadh gur annso ar fhód nádúrtha do thalmhan dúthchais féin do chaithis an t-achar úd a raibh tú ag teacht i n-aois na fearamhlachta agus na lán-tuigsiona do bhéadh a mhalairt de chruth anois ort. Do bhéadh muinghin agat as do dhearbhráithreachaibh is do dheirbhshiúrachaibh fá mar atá ag an duine is ísle againn annso. Do thuigfeá "nach Eorpach go hÉireannaigh agus nach Éireannach go Gaeilgeoir." Gur iomdha rud nua san Nua-Eoraip gur sean-rudaí iad sa tSean-Éirinn.

Acht a bhuidhe le Dia, nílir id' dhuine ró-aosta go fóill. Tá cúram naomtha uasal ort agus cuirim fá gheasaibh thú do dhualgas do chomhlíonadh. Mar atá, na mic-léighinn dá bhfuil fá do chúram d'oileamhaint agus tabhairt suas iomlán do sholáthar dhóibh, maille leis an spiorad cheart do chur ionnta ar nós go gcuirfidh siad a gcuid eolais chum tairbhe agus go mbainfid feidhm do chum leasa ár ndaoine, do chum glóire Dé agus onóra na hÉireann.

Má chuireas nimh in aon fhocal dár chanas leat maith dhom é. Níor chailleas riamh an cheanamhlacht do bhíodh agam ort agus níor laghduigheadh riamh ar an muinghín do bhí agam asat. Agus is é so an fáth: an meas do bheith riamh agam ar d'athair dílis féin.

Badh chóir go mbadh bheag ort daoine do do cháineadh i dtaobh a ndearnais an uair úd do b'annsa leat claoi le Seán Réamonn ioná éisteacht le binn-briathraibh na mban. Bíodh aca, is uaisle an Náisiún ioná aon dream fá leith dá dhaoinibh. Beir buaidh agus beannacht. Mise, Seanchán Torpéist.

L. 322/NLI
31.5.1912.   Sgoil Éanna,
                                  Rath Fearnáin.

A Chara,
   Beatha agus Sláinte.
   Beir míle buidheachas ar son do 'chonganta do Sgoil Éanna.
Táim buidheach dhíot óm' chroidhe.
   Seo chugat fuirm le lionadh agus dá bhféadfá é do chur chugam
le filleadh an phosta do chuirféa fá chomaoin mhóir mé, mar beidh
tionól ag lucht stiurtha na Scoile Dé Luain agus beitheas ag roinnt
na gcodacha ann.
   Fairíor géar, ní seinnfear *An Barr Buadh* bocht arís go ceann
tamaill. Beir buaidh agus beannacht. Mise, Pádraig Mac Piarais.

L. 333/P.Ms.
4.9.1912.   Sgoil Éanna,
                                  Rath Fearnáin.

A Chara,
   Táim fíor-bhuidheach dhíot. D'éirigh liom an scoil do cheannach
ar ais; tá sé beagnach socruighthe. Beir míle buidheachas is
beannacht. Mise, Pádraig Mac Piarais.

L. 340/NLI
20.4.1913.

A Chara,
   Cuir an dá ghiota so isteach an tseachtmhain so led' thoil. Nach
maith ó'n Yéatsach an rud so do thabhairt dúinn?
   Tá súil agam go bhfuil biseach ort, ba thruagh liom a chlos nach
raibh tú go maith.
   Beidh cruinniughadh againn i n-oifig an Hobsonaigh tráthnóna
Dia Céadaoin ar a ceathair a chlog. An mbeidh sé ar do chumas
bheith ann? Beir buaidh agus beannacht, Mise, Pádraig
Mac Piarais.

L.(p.c.) 343/OCS

23.5.1913

An bhféadfá teacht go dtí tionól beag in n-oifig an Hobsonaigh i mbárach (D. hAoine) ar a 5.30? Ná bac leis má táir ro-ghnóthach. Fuaireas do litir i dtaoibh Rinne Muirbhthean. P. Mac P.

L. 352/TCM

29.12.1913.   Sgoil Éanna,
                                             Rath Fearnáin.

A Chara,

Go raibh míle maith agat fá do litir. Tuigim as a n-abrann tú go bhfuil tú ag dul ag pósadh. Má's fíor sin, molaim thú. Acht ní leanfaidh mé do shompla ná do chomhairle. Má théighim go hAmerioca, tá súil agam go dtiubhraidh mé roinnt airgid abhaile liom, acht má bhíonn bean ceangailte leis an airgead fágfaidh mé an bhean agus an t-airgead im' dhiaidh.

Tá Sgoil Éanna beo agus is mór an ní é sin. Beir buaidh agus beannacht, Mise, Pádraig Mac Piarais.

L. (p.c.) 367/NLI/G

27.4.1914   Nua Eabhrach.

A Ronáin, a Chara,

Seo chugat cárta beag le mo bheannacht do chur chugat agus le buidheachas do ghabháil leat ar son na seamróg do chuir tú chugam fá lá Fhéile Pádraig. Ba dheas uait cuimhneamh orm. Feicfidh tú mé fá cheann cúpla seachtmhain, le congnamh Dé. Mise, do mhaighistir, Pádraig Mac Piarais.

Nach iongantach árd na tighthe iad so?

L. (p.c.) 377/SM

Bhí mé i nAmerioca nuair tháinig do chéad litir. Déanfaidh mé an obair úd agus fáilte. Beidh an £10 an-úsáideach dom. Go raibh míle maith agat mar gheall ar an bposta do thairgsint dom. Táim ag sgríobhadh chum an dochtúra agus chun P. Ui Dhomhnalláin ag fiafruighe dhíobh cia an uair a mbeidh mé ag teastáil. Beir buaidh. Mise, Pádraig Mac Piarais.

L. 382/SM

30.10.1914.

A Athair agus a Chara,
Do fuaireas an £10 úd, agus táim fíor-bhuidheach dhíot ar a shon. Tá admháil agam dá cur chugat annso síos, maille le míle buideachas.

Tá tuarasgbháil gearr ar an dá sgrúdúghadh agam dá cur chugat freisin.

Táim fíor-buidheach dhíot-sa agus de'n Choiste as ucht an obair so do thabhairt dom. Beir míle buaidh agus beannacht, Mise, Pádraig Mac Piarais.

Admhuighim go bhfuaireas ó'n Athair Brian Ó Criocháin seic deich bpúnt (£10) i n-íocaidheacht ar mo chuid oibre mar sgrúduightheoir i gColáiste an Spidéil agus i gColáiste Túir Mhic Eadaigh, 1914. Pádraig Mac Piarais. 30.10.1914. Maille le míle buidheachas.

L. 398/PS

11.11.1915.   Sgoil Éanna,
                                                  Rath Fearnáin.

A Chara,
Níl a fhios agam cad ba cheart dom a radh leatsa agus le Máire Bulfin agus leis na cailínibh eile chun buidheachas do ghabháil ar son bhur mbronntanais. Dar ndóigh, d'fhág sibh gan cainnt mé. Do bhí iongnadh an domhain orm nuair thug mo mháthair an bronntanas isteach maidin inné agus is ar éigin d'fhéadas labhairt. Glac mo bhuidheachas ó bhun mo chroidhe amach agus cuir in iúl do na cailínibh eile é, led' thoil.

Is dílis na cáirde sibh agus ni dhéanfaidh mé dearmad oraibh go deo ná ar chailínibh agus maighistreásaibh Sgoil Íde. Is breagh ar fad an bronntanas thug sibh dom agus ni fhéadfadh sibh cuimhniughadh ar rud do b'úsáidighe.

Beiridh míle buidheachas agus beannacht, Mise do chara go buan, Pádraig Mac Piarais.

12.1.1916.   Sgoil Éanna,
                                        Rath Fearnáin.

A Thomáis na gCarad,

   Tá buachaillí Coláiste Mhaoilsheachlainn chum *Íosagán* do
leiriughadh ag Feis Bhéil Feirste, agus badh mhaith leis an Athair
S. Mac Leanacháin go mbéadh ceol an dá amhrán (.i. "Haidh didil
dum" agus "Mo Churaichín Ó") aige. An mbéadh am agat an ceol
do sgríobhadh agus a chur chugam? Ba mhaith liom é bheith agam
féin freisin. Beir buaidh, Mise do bhuan-chara, Pádraig Mac Piarais.

APPENDIX II

Biographical Notes

ATKINSON, ROBERT (1839–1908), Professor of Sanskrit and Philology in Dublin University (Trinity College), Atkinson, was Mahaffy's chief ally in the campaign against the inclusion of Irish as a subject on the curriculum of Intermediate schools. Before the Commission on Intermediate Education in Ireland (1898), Atkinson objected to the inclusion of Irish on the grounds that its study conferred no mental training and its literature was such "that it was difficult to find a book in which there was not some passage so silly or so indecent as to give you a shock from which you would never recover during the rest of your life". On his death in 1908, Pearse wrote a fair and generous obituary in *An Claidheamh Soluis* (II-I-1908), which while mentioning the Mahaffy–Atkinson campaign also recalled and praised his early scholarly work on Irish texts.

BAIRÉAD, STIOFÁN, was Treasurer of the Gaelic League, an early member of the Executive and a close associate of Pearse from 1898 onwards in many League activities. He had learned Irish in classes conducted in Trinity College by Richard Mulrennan and by Seán Pléimeann, the retired schoolmaster who was editor of *Irisleabhar na Gaeilge.*

Pearse was a close personal friend of Bairéad and was godfather to his daughter Sighle. Bairéad assisted Pearse in securing an advance from the Hibernian Bank for Sgoil Éanna. The advance by the Bank was secured by an insurance policy, by the title-deeds of Cullenswood House and "as to £275 of it, by the signature of Mr. Stephen Barrett of 55 Blessington St.". In his final financial arrangements Pearse arranged that Bairéad should be indemnified, if the Bank required him to pay any of the amount covered by his signature. Stiofán Bairéad died in March 1921.

BLOOMER, GERTRUDE, was the headmistress of Sgoil Íde, the school for girls founded by Pearse at Cullenswood House in 1910.

She was a native of Derry where her family owned The City Hotel; she had studied music in London. She had no involvement with the Gaelic League and it is possible that it was through the artistic circles in which Willie moved, that Pearse came to know her; she was also a friend of Thomas Mac Donagh. On accepting the position in Sgoil Íde, Mrs. Bloomer invested some money in the venture on the understanding that she would require repayment only if the financial position of the school warranted such repayment. The school which closed in 1912 was never in such a fortunate position, yet Pearse sought by regular payments to clear his indebtedness; one of his last letters was one to Mrs. Bloomer written on Easter Sunday.

BREATHNACH, MICHEÁL (1881–1908), writer, teacher and Gaelic Leaguer who never enjoyed good health and spent several periods in the Alps seeking health-giving conditions. Born at Lochán Bheag near Spidéal, he heard no English until he attended the local national school where no Irish was taught. He was seventeen before he had any opportunity to read or write in Irish and he says that at that stage it took him just three months to learn.

Having encountered Tomás Bán Ó Concheanainn, he became an active member of the League; on going to London in 1901, he joined the London branch where his friends, Pádraig Ó Conaire and Dr. Seán Mac Einrí were already active. He laboured energetically in various League activities and was a frequent contributor to *An Claidheamh Soluis* until he fell seriously ill of tuberculosis. In 1905 when he was appointed Principal of Coláiste Chonnacht at Tuar Mhic Éide, he visited Belgium, Germany and France to investigate new language teaching methods. Spending the winter of 1905 in Switzerland he returned to his post in Coláiste Chonnacht in 1906 and was appointed teacher of Irish in Tuam in September 1906. His health however was not improving and he spent the winters of 1906 and 1907 in Switzerland. From there he sent regular contributions to *An Claidheamh Soluis* on current affairs, and literature which later appeared as *Seilg i Measc na nAlp* (1907). His other major work was a translation of Kickam's *Knocknagow* which appeared in serial form in *An Claidheamh Soluis* 1904–05 and in 1907–08. He also wrote a history textbook *Stair na hÉireann* (1911). Having worked in Coláiste Chonnacht in the summer of 1908 he returned to Dublin and died in October of that year.

BULFIN, WILLIAM (1864–1910). Born in Derrinlough, Birr, Co. Offaly, educated locally and at Galway Grammar School, he emigrated at the age of twenty to the Argentine with his brother, Peter. He worked on the pampas and began contributing articles to a Buenos Aires weekly paper, *The Southern Cross,* of which he became sub-editor in 1888 and then editor and owner. Returning to Ireland 1902–04, he travelled the country on a bicycle and wrote extensive descriptions which appeared as *Rambles in Erin* (1907). He was a leading figure in the Irish community of the Argentine and was awarded a papal knighthood for his work on behalf of Irish Catholics.

He was a staunch supporter of Pearse and a frequent visitor to Sgoil Éanna; his son, Éamonn who was one of the leading senior pupils at the school from 1908 to 1911, was a distinguished scholar, actor and athlete. His daughter, Máire (later, Mrs. Seán Mac Bride), was equally prominent as a pupil of Sgoil Íde.

CASEMENT, ROGER (1864–1916). Born at Sandycove, Co. Dublin and educated at Ballymena Academy, he gained an international reputation as an enlightened officer of the British Colonial Service in Africa and South America. In 1904 he reported on the inhuman treatment of native workers in the Belgian Congo and later in Peru; his report on publication in 1912 caused widespread concern. He was knighted for his services and retired in 1912.

By 1912 he was already active in nationalist and Gaelic League circles and was a frequent visitor to Pearse's school where he presented prizes to the pupils. He joined the Irish Volunteers in 1913 and went to Germany in search of military aid for the planned insurrection; the arms ship *Aud* sent by the Germans in April 1916 was captured and scuttled while Casement, who followed by submarine, was captured and dispatched to London for trial. Found guilty of high treason, he was hanged at Pentonville Prison on August 3rd, 1916; his remains were returned to Ireland in 1965 and interred in Glasnevin following a state funeral.

CEANNT, ÉAMONN (Éamonn Kent) (1874–1916). A prominent Gaelic Leaguer, traditional musician and member of Sinn Féin, who was a close associate of Pearse in Gaelic League activities and later in the Volunteers and in the Rising. His son, Ronán, was a student at Sgoil Éanna and Éamonn was frequently involved in the musical occasions and pageants held there because of his membership of the Pipers' Club. He commanded and held the South Dublin Union in the Rising with only forty-two men, was a signatory of the Proclamation and was executed on May 8th, 1916.

CLARKE, THOMAS JAMES (1857–1916). Born in the Isle of Wight of Irish parents, who emigrated to South Africa before settling in Dungannon, Co. Tyrone, when he was ten. On going to America in 1878, he joined Clann na Gael and while on a revolutionary mission in England in 1883 was arrested and sentenced to penal servitude for life; he served fifteen years in the harshest circumstances and on release, returned to America. In 1907 he returned to Dublin, opened two newsagent and tobacco shops (Parnell St. and Amiens St.) which were the centres for renewed I.R.B. activities. He was a member of the inner group with Mac Dermott which planned the Rising during which he served in the Post Office. He was the first to sign the Proclamation and was executed on May 3rd with Pearse and Mac Donagh. He had supported Pearse's educational work and assisted him in gaining American support in 1914.

COLUM, PÁDRAIG (1881–1972). Born in Longford and educated in Co. Cavan, he came to Dublin as a railway clerk when his father became a stationmaster at Sandycove. His early poems and plays were coloured by his early experiences in Longford and Cavan. His first collection *Wild Earth* appeared in 1907. Was a partner with Stephens, Mac Donagh, Plunkett and Houston in the founding of *The Irish Review*. Was an extern lecturer and part-time teacher of English literature in Pearse's school where he was a frequent visitor. He reviewed the school dramatic presentations and publicised their achievements.

In 1912 he married Mary Maguire and in 1914 they emigrated to America where they both lectured at Columbia University. His *Collected Poems* appeared in 1953. Colum's short play, *The Destruction of the Hostel,* was performed at Cullenswood House in February 1910 with Pearse's *Íosagán*; it was written by Colum especially for the students, based on the saga *Bruidhean Da Dearga.*

COMYN, DAVID (Daithí Coimín) (1854–1907). A native of Kilrush, Co. Clare, Comyn spent most of his adult life in Dublin as a bank clerk in the Hibernian Bank; he was editor of *Irisleabhar na Gaeilge* 1882–84. With J. J. Doyle, Fr. T. O'Nolan O.D.C. and others he was responsible for the foundation in 1876 of the Society for the Preservation of the Irish Language and through this organisation achieved significant results along the lines later espoused by the Gaelic League. He divined accurately that the key to the fate of the language was the educational system from which the language had been and was then, assiduously excluded. He

434

succeeded in winning a major concession in 1878 when the Commissioners of National Education sanctioned the teaching of Irish in National Schools on the same basis as that obtaining for Greek, Latin and French. The practical approach of S.P.I.L. is illustrated again in the series of graded textbooks and headline copies in Irish which Comyn planned and wrote for national schools in collaboration with Canon Ulick Burke and Thomas O'Neill Russell. The later sophisticated campaigns of the Gaelic League in regard to education and other issues is already foreshadowed in the objectives and the embryonic work of the S.P.I.L. in the 1870's; they were active in promoting the use of Irish in the newspapers and in advertising and examined the relative merits of using Roman and Irish print. The Society and its off-shoot, The Gaelic Union, were instrumental in having 'Celtic' included as a subject in the secondary schools under the Intermediate Education Act of 1878, a campaign in which David Comyn played a major part.

His published works included *Mac-Ghníomhartha Fhinn* (1881), *Laoi Oisín ar Thír na nÓg* (1880) and *Foras Feasa ar Éirinn* (1902).

CONNOLLY, JAMES (1868–1916). Born of Irish parents in an Edinburgh slum, he came to Ireland first as a British soldier, deserted and returned to marry an Irish girl in Scotland and became active in the emerging socialist cause. He came to Dublin in 1896 as a full-time official of the Dublin Socialist Club and founded the first Irish socialist organ, *The Worker's Republic.* On this base he organised the Irish Socialist Republican Party with the aim of securing "the national and economic freedom of the Irish people".

His forceful and energetic dedication to socialism and his commanding style in speech and written word attracted attention to his work; he toured the United States where he was active in founding the 'Wobblies', the Industrial Workers of the World. Having spent seven years in the States, he returned to Belfast and organised the Transport Workers Union. The 1913 Dublin lock-out and strike brought Connolly to prominence as a political leader; founded the Citizen Army which he later committed to armed insurrection in the Rising. In the preparations for the Rising, he was a member of the inner group with Pearse and Mac Donagh and was appointed Commander of the Dublin forces. He was in command in the G.P.O. and was seriously wounded. A signatory of the Proclamation which he helped to draft, and a member of the Provisional Government, he was sentenced to death; he was taken to

Kilmainham Gaol on a stretcher and, strapped to a chair, was executed by firing squad on May 12th, 1916.

His principal published work is *Labour in Irish History* (1910).

DEVOY, JOHN (1842–1928). Born in Kill, near Naas in Co. Kildare, educated there and in Dublin, to where the family moved in the awful years following the Famine, Devoy had a most colourful career; he epitomised "Ireland in exile" to many and was described by Pearse as "the greatest of the Fenians".

After a brief spell in the French Foreign Legion, he returned to Ireland and coordinated an active Fenian organisation within the British Army; arrested in 1866, he was sentenced to fifteen years penal servitude of which he served five, his release being conditional on exile. Emigrating to America, he worked in journalism, joined Clann na Gael and quickly became a leading figure in the organisation and a central activist in its various projects.

He founded in 1903 a weekly newspaper *The Gaelic American,* of which he was editor and the office of which was the unofficial headquarter of most Irish-American political transactions. Through his leadership, Irish-Americans contributed political and financial support to various Irish projects from Davitt's 'new departure' to the Rising and later his goodwill and that of McGarrity in Philadelphia was regarded as essential to any Irish representative seeking American support.

In 1921, Devoy supported the Treaty and the resulting Free State government; he returned to Ireland in 1924 and was given a warm welcome in the Dáil which he had done so much to make a reality. He died in Atlantic City in 1928 in very reduced circumstances and his remains were brought to Glasnevin. His published works include *Recollections of an Irish Rebel* (1929), *The Irish Land League* (1882). His correspondence was published in 1948 as *Devoy's Postbag,* edited by Desmond Ryan and William O'Brien.

DILLON, JOHN (1851–1927). Son of John Blake Dillon, the friend of Thomas Davis, he was born in Blackrock, Co. Dublin, and qualified as a surgeon but quickly turned to politics, becoming a staunch supporter of Parnell. In the party split of 1891, Dillon became chairman of the anti-Parnellites and when unification appeared possible he stood aside to allow Redmond to lead the party in 1900. Dillon, of all the Parliamentary Party, least deserved the political fate which followed the Rising, the executions and the election of 1918. The party of which he was then leader was decimated and he himself was defeated in East Mayo by Éamonn de Valera. He retired from political life and died in London.

DOLAN, JOSEPH T. (1872–1930), of Ardee, Co. Louth, was a prosperous merchant who devoted his ability and his resources to many aspects of the economic and cultural development associated with the Gaelic League and its activities. An M.A. of the Royal University, he was of a shy and retiring disposition and tended to hide his charitable generosity beneath a cloak of anonymity.

He was a close friend of Pearse and was most generous in assisting Sgoil Éanna financially; in his financial statement of 1914, Pearse indicated that Dolan had loaned him in all £1,100 for which Pearse had offered him various securities, including an insurance policy on his own life. His generosity made possible the continuity of Pearse's school; the extent of his support is indicated in the letter which he wrote to Mrs. Pearse shortly before his death in which he declined the return of the amount loaned except that which was left after her own and her daughter's futures had been provided for.

GAVAN DUFFY, GEORGE (1882–1951). Son of Sir Charles Gavan Duffy, founder of *The Nation* and Prime Minister of Victoria, George Gavan Duffy was educated in England and practised as a solicitor in London until 1917. He acted as envoy to Paris and Rome for the Republican First Dáil 1919–20 and was a member of the Irish Peace Delegation; he was a reluctant signatory of the Treaty and was appointed Minister for Foreign Affairs in the resulting Provisional Government of the Irish Free State. He resigned after six months, abandoned politics the following year and became a notable lawyer and judge.

In his London years, Pearse consulted him in regard to the finances of Sgoil Éanna. His sister, Louise Gavan Duffy supported Sgoil Íde and it would appear that she was anxious to participate in the management of the school. She later founded her own Sgoil Íde which is now located on the Cullenswood House campus on Oakley Road.

GIBSON, WILLIAM (The Honourable) (1868–1942). Son of Lord Ashbourne, an attorney from Tipperary, who had been M.P. for Trinity College and Attorney General for Ireland from 1877 and who was elevated to the peerage and appointed Lord Chancellor for Ireland in 1885. The son attended school at Harrow, and attended Trinity College, Dublin where he first came to have an interest in the Irish language. Later in Oxford where he took a postgraduate degree in philosophy, he began the serious study of

Celtic Languages. In the London branch of the Gaelic League he acquired a proficiency in spoken Irish; in addition he was fluent in German and French. He was a frequent visitor to Gaelic League events, dressed usually in the traditional kilt and was president of London Gaelic League for thirty years. On succeeding to the title, he spoke Irish in his maiden speech in the House of Lords in 1918 and reprimanded the Prime Minister, Lloyd George, for his assertion that "Ireland was not a nation as Wales was, since Wales had a language whereas Ireland had not"; he further showed that the educational system in Ireland had functioned as a denationalising influence, making of each Irish child "A happy English child".

He lived most of his life in France, having married a French aristocrat; he kept in regular touch with Ireland and kept a holiday home at Cloghaneely in Donegal. He was President of the Gaelic League in 1928–33 and was generous in his financial support of the organisation. He died at Compiegne, France in 1942.

GREGORY, ISABELLA AUGUSTA (née Persse) (1852–1932). Born in Roxborough, Co. Galway and educated privately, she married the widower, Sir William Gregory in 1880. He had been Governor of Ceylon 1871–1877 when he retired to his estate at Coole Park, Gort, not far from the Persse property. Following the death of her husband in 1892, Lady Gregory took a more active interest in the arts, literature and the theatre. Was involved with W.B. Yeats and J.M. Synge in the foundation of the Abbey Theatre in 1904; she wrote many comedies based on rural life which were produced at the Abbey. Her home at Coole became a centre of literary activity and cultural fellowship. She learned Irish and produced inspiring translations of the heroic literature in *Cuchulain of Muirthemne* (1902), and *Gods and Fighting Men* (1904) and her *Visions and Beliefs of the West of Ireland* (1920) presents her analysis of local folklore.

Her nephew Hugh Lane was lost aboard the *Lusitania* in 1915, and her only son Robert was killed as an airman in the First World War. She campaigned to have Lane's art collection returned to Dublin; her efforts in this respect are chronicled in *Sir Hugh Lane: His Life and Legacy* (1973) and her *Journals* published in 1978. In 1901 she edited a collection of essays by Yeats, Hyde, Moore, Moran and AE under the title *Ideals in Ireland*.

GWYNN, STEPHEN (1864–1950). Grandson of William Smith O'Brien, educated at St. Columba's College, Rathfarnham, where his father was Warden, and at Oxford. In turn he was a

438

schoolmaster, a journalist and M.P. for Galway City from 1906 to 1918. Was an active member of the Gaelic League and served on its executive. His son, Denis, was one of the first senior pupils in Sgoil Éanna and on his completion in 1910 secured many scholarships and distinctions; Pearse described him as "carrying the banner of Sgoil Éanna proudly into the National University", where he won one of the first Classical Scholarships. When the World War broke out, Stephen Gwynn enlisted with the Connacht Rangers, as did his son Denis. He left public life after the war and devoted his talent to scholarship and writing.

HEALY, TIMOTHY (1855–1931). Born in Bantry, Co. Cork, and educated formally only to the age of thirteen, he became a railway clerk in Newcastle-on-Tyne. In 1878 he moved to London and became parliamentary correspondent of *The Nation* and in 1880 he was returned unopposed as M.P. for Wexford. Called to the Irish Bar in 1884 he built up an extensive practice in land law, aided by the implementation of the Act of 1881, which he had helped to reform in its passage through Parliament.

In the Parnell controversy of 1891, Healy displayed a bitter anti-Parnell capacity and the combined support of Martin Murphy and the Catholic Church ensured his continued parliamentary career despite his expulsion from the party in 1902. A sharp political nose enabled him to detect the coming change in 1916 and by a series of gestures, he obtained a partial acceptance by some sections of victorious Sinn Féin. His nomination as first Governor General of the Irish Free State by Lord Birkenhead and by his cousin Kevin O'Higgins was widely criticised. He retired in 1928.

HOBSON, BULMER (1883–1969). Born at Holywood, Co. Down, of Quaker stock, Hobson was involved in many of the organisations, political and cultural, which combined to create the circumstances leading to the Rising of 1916, in which he himself did not participate but actively opposed. He had collaborated with Countess Markieviecz in 1909 to found Na Fianna Éireann, a youth organisation with a para-military purpose. He was a vice-president of Sinn Féin and was a close friend of Arthur Griffith; yet in 1910 with others he left Sinn Féin and henceforth devoted his energies to separatist policies. He was editor of the I.R.B. paper *Irish Freedom* from 1911 to 1914 when his acquiescence in Redmond's demands to the Volunteers, prompted the I.R.B. to dismiss him and caused Devoy to dismiss him also as the Dublin correspondent of the *Gaelic American*. He was prominent in the Volunteer organisation, yet he was not a party to the planning of the Rising; he joined Eoin

Mac Neill in opposing the Clarke, Pearse, Connolly plans and was arrested by the I.R.B. before the Rising. From 1922 to 1948 he held a position in the Revenue Commissioners and then retired to Roundstone, Co. Galway.

HOLLOWAY, JOSEPH (1861–1944). Born in Dublin and educated at Castleknock and at the School of Art, he was apprenticed to an architect until in 1896 he established his own practice. He had a keen interest in the theatre, attended every Dublin performance, collected theatrical memorabilia and recorded in his journal his comments on theatrical performances and other features of Dublin life.

His professional and theatrical interests combined in bringing him into contact with Pearse and Sgoil Éanna; he was a frequent invitee at the Sgoil Éanna dramatic presentations from the first Cúchulainn pageant in June 1909. From the same period he acted as consulting architect to Pearse in the extensions and innovations which he carried out at Cullenswood and in the Hermitage.

HOUSTON, DAVID, was Professor of Zoology in Trinity College and of Biology in the College of Surgeons and lived in Mount Eden, the property situated south of the Hermitage opposite Marley. He was a friend of Pearse, taught Biology in Sgoil Éanna on modern ecological lines – the nickname he received was "Creeping-out"! His son, Cyril attended the school and Houston senior took a deep interest both in Pearse's educational ideas and in the literary circle of which Pearse, Mac Donagh, Joseph Plunkett formed part. Mac Donagh, while he taught at the Hermitage, lived in the gate lodge of Houston's residence. He was associated with Mac Donagh and Plunkett in the founding of the literary journal *The Irish Review.*

HUTTON, MARGARET, scholar and Gaelic League member, she was the wife of a prominent Belfast business man and their home at Deramore Park, Malone Road, was a centre of cultural and artistic activities. She lectured at Ard-Sgoil Uladh and in 1907 published her *Táin Bo Cuailgne* which received high praise from Irish and foreign scholars; this was the version of the epic which was most popular in Sgoil Éanna.

She was very friendly with Pearse, who stayed with the Huttons on his Belfast visits, and she lectured at Sgoil Éanna on a number of occasions. In order to perfect her oral fluency in Irish, she employed girls from Connemara in her household and through Pearse succeeded in securing other employment outlets for boys and girls from the Gaeltacht. She was a generous supporter of Sgoil

Éanna and when she moved to Dublin in 1912, she attended the artistic and dramatic occasions at the school.

HYDE, DOUGLAS (1860–1949). Born in Frenchpark, Co. Roscommon, son of a Church of Ireland Rector, was a poet and scholar and became first President of Ireland under the new Constitution of 1937. He was educated at Trinity College, Dublin, where he studied Law and adding French and German to the Latin, Greek, Irish and Hebrew he already knew, he obtained a B.A. in 1884 and graduated LL.D in 1887. He spent a year as Professor of Modern Languages in Canada and returned in 1892 to continue his literary work in the Irish language which he had initially learned from the older people of the Roscommon countryside. With Eoin Mac Neill and Fr. Eoghan Ó Gramhnaigh, he founded the Gaelic League in 1893 and for over twenty years was its President and guiding spirit.

In his life and writings he epitomises the campaign of cultural self-realisation which the Gaelic League sponsored and which has been described as "one of the most important events in the history of modern Ireland". Coming from a social milieu which had been traditionally and historically aligned with anti-Irish dispositions, Hyde's espousal of a policy of cultural and political self-determination had an early and wide impact. The League was one of the few organisations which attracted to its membership men and women of all denominations. Between 1879 and 1884, he published over one hundred items of prose and verse compositions under the pseudonym of "An Craoibhín Aoibhinn" – a soubriquet by which he was known in later years. As a young student in Trinity College, he regarded himself as residing in a hostile environment where anti-Irish feeling prevailed. In a poem honouring O'Donovan Rossa, he advised his fellow students to abandon talk and return to the old methods, if they wished for a free Ireland. In a note in his book, *Leabhar Sgéalaigheachta* (1889), he mentions "our long slavery as a nation" and asserts that he did not believe in "resuscitating a great national language by twopenny-halfpenny bounties".

The strategy of national revival which he espoused involved a sustained campaign by the Gaelic League in regard to issues in the realm of educational and cultural policy; in this policy his own role of populariser was of major significance. At the foundation of the League in 1893 he had already published *Leabhar Sgéalaidheachta* (1889), *Beside the Fire* (1990), *An Sgéalaidhe Gaedhealach* (1901) and *The Love Songs of Connacht* (1893). He also contributed many items to journals such as *The Nation* and *The Weekly Freeman*. Perhaps the most significant of his contributions at this phase was

441

his address to The Irish National Literary Society in 1892, on "The Necessity of De-Anglicising Ireland".

The League's earliest concern was the educational sphere and its early policies concentrated on the need to reform the educational system at all three levels. In turn, the League demanded that Irish be given an effective and rational role at the primary, secondary and university levels. In the various government commissions on primary, secondary and university education which sat in the first fifteen years of the League's existence, Hyde played a prominent role. In the 1898 Commission on Intermediate Education, he displayed a courage and strategic ability which effectively countered the assertions made by Mahaffy, Gwynn and Atkinson from Trinity College. His presidency of the League witnessed a rapid spread not only of its branches but of its philosophy in Ireland and abroad; in 1905 he undertook a visit to the United States where he gathered a substantial sum for the League. On his return he was made a freeman of Dublin, Cork and Kilkenny. In 1909 he was appointed to the Professorship of Modern Irish in University College, Dublin which he held until 1932.

If Hyde refrained from participation in the political activities which culminated in the Rising and the War of Independence, his unanimous choice as first President in 1937, indicated that the catalytic role which the League had played was nationally appreciated. He also wrote *A Literary History of Ireland* (1899) *Religious Songs of Connacht* (1906) and some one-act plays, one of which, *Casadh an tSúgáin* when produced in 1901 was the first play in Irish produced on a professional stage.

JOYNT, ERNEST (deSiúnta, Earnán) (1874–1949). Born in Ballina, where his father was the editor of the *Ballina Herald,* he came to Dublin very soon after the foundation of the Gaelic League and became a member. He had heard Irish spoken in and around his native town but did not begin to learn the language systematically until he attended Gaelic League classes in Dublin. A mechanical engineer by profession, he was an employee of the Great Southern Railways at Inchicore and also lectured in the Engineering Department at Bolton St., College of Technology, where he later became Principal. He was a close friend of Douglas Hyde and of the Breton nationalist, Le Roux, who was Pearse's earliest biographer.

He achieved a remarkable fluency and accuracy in Irish and contributed to many of the League journals under the pseudonym of "An Buachaillín Buidhe". His most imaginative contribution to the language movement was *Féilire na Gaelige,* an annual almanac and diary, which provided information on events, publications and personalities in the League, the first number of which appeared in 1904. In connection with Pearse's story, *Poll an Phíobaire* (1906), published by the League under the pseudonym "Colm Ó Conaire", Joynt wrote to Pearse seeking information about the author. In reply, Pearse admitted authorship, said that he did not wish it to be generally known and supplied biographical information for the Féilire which did not directly reveal his identity. This letter from Pearse to Joynt was deposited in Sligo County Museum in the early sixties.

His other published works include *Airgead Beo* (1944) a collection of stories from Greek mythology and *Histoire de l'Irlande des origines á l'Etat Libre* a synoptic history which was published in Rennes in 1935 and which contains portraits of the leaders of the independence movement.

LLOYD, J. H. (Seosamh Laoide). Lloyd, who died in 1939, was one of the Gaelic League's prominent scholars and chief editor of its Publications Committee. Shortly after the establishment of the League he was active in fieldwork in various parts of the country; he gathered stories and other oral material in Irish in Monaghan, under the title *Sgéaluidhe Fearnmhuighe*. More than forty titles were published by the Gaelic League under his editorship.

In an obituary notice, entitled "A Forgotten Patriot", in *The Leader* of October 7th, 1939, Henry Morris attributed his own interest in the oral tradition and local folklore to the example and encouragement of Lloyd. He was employed as an executive with the Great Northern Railways.

MAC EINRÍ, An Dr. S. P. (J. P. Henry), (1862–1930). Born in London and reared in Sligo, he was educated locally before entering Trinity College, Dublin where he graduated in medicine in 1889. Working as a physician in London, he was active in the Gaelic League of which he was Vice-President 1895–1906. He was particularly interested in the methodology of language teaching and produced a new approach to the teaching of Irish in his *Láimhleabhar na Gaeilge* (1904). He was mainly responsible in 1903 for the transition from English to Irish as the administrative language of the League. He was Principal of the League's Coláiste Laighean 1906–10 and later was appointed Professor of Ophthalmology in University College, Galway. From his London days he was a close friend of the writers Pádraig Ó Conaire and Micheál Breathnach; he edited some of the latter's work, *Cnoc na nGabha* and *Seilg i Measc na nAlp* after the author's death in 1908. His

443

own major publication in the period 1905–13 was the authoritative *An Modh Direach* which offered extensive guidance to teachers on the Direct Method of language teaching. He was among the distinguished band of external lecturers who lectured in Sgoil Éanna's half-holiday series.

MAC DIARMADA, SEÁN (1884–1916). Born in Kiltyclogher, Co. Leitrim, he spent most of his adult life in various forms of revolutionary politics, culminating in the Rising of 1916. He worked in Glasgow, Belfast and Dublin and by 1902 was an active Gaelic Leaguer and a fluent speaker of Irish. He joined the I.R.B. in 1906 and within a short time he and Tom Clarke were the controlling forces in the secret organisation. Struck down by polio in 1912, he recovered only to suffer ever after from a painful limp. A member of the Volunteer Provisional Committee, he was one of the minority who refused to surrender control of the movement to Redmond. A signatory of the Proclamation and a member of the Provisional Government, he was a prominent member of the G.P.O. garrison in 1916 and was executed on May 12th, 1916.

MAC DONAGH, THOMAS (1878–1916). Poet, teacher and revolutionary, he was born in Cloughjordan, Co. Tipperary where his parents were teachers. He taught at Kilkenny and St. Colman's, Fermoy before coming to join Pearse in the establishment of Sgoil Éanna in 1908 at Cullenswood House in Ranelagh. Was highly regarded as a teacher both in school and in University College, Dublin to which he was appointed in 1912. Joined the Volunteers in 1913 and was appointed Director of Training. He was a signatory of the Proclamation and commanded Jacob's during the Rising. He was executed with Pearse and Clarke on May 3rd, 1916.

His play *When the Dawn is Come* (1908) offers a strange prophetic picture of later political events.

His works include, *Literature in Ireland* (1916), *Songs of Myself* and *Lyrical Poems.*

MAC FHIONNLAOIGH, PEADAR (T. P. Mc Ginley) (1857–1942), was born in Co. Donegal and was educated locally and in Dublin. He had a lengthy and distinguished career in the British Inland Revenue Service. He was one of the pillars of the Gaelic League and was deeply involved in its various activities and executive committees. He had a special interest in language teaching and also in linking cultural and economic development. His publications include *A Handbook of Irish Teaching* (1903), *An Leightheoir Gaedhealach* (1907), and stories based on historic

444

figures such as *Owen Roe O'Donnell* (1911), *Niall of the Nine Hostages* (1909) and *Conor Mac Neasa* (1914).

He figured in the famous Portarlington controversy of 1905, when the local Gaelic League was attacked from the pulpit for conducting mixed Irish classes for the youth of the town. Mac Fhionnlaoigh and S. B. Roche, both protested in church and answered the allegations of the clergy. The episode, described by W. P. Ryan in *The Pope's Green Island* was a significant incident in the struggle by some clergy to secure control of the League.

Peadar Mac Fhionnlaoigh was one of Pearse's staunchest supporters in establishing and maintaining Sgoil Eanna; he sent each of his ten sons to the school and from the opening day in September 1908 to its closure in June 1935, the roll of Sgoil Éanna contained the name Mac Fhionnlaoigh and sometimes two simultaneously. In his Gaelic League activities he was known as "Cú Uladh", the pseudonym which he used in his Irish writing.

MC GARRITY, JOSEPH (1874–1940). Born in Carrickmore, Co. Tyrone, he was educated at Carrickmore national school; at the age of 16 he emigrated to America and over a period of fifty years in Philadelphia was central to the significant support and commitment which flowed from Irish-American organisations to the cause of Irish political separatism. He became a key figure in Clann-na-Gael and built up an efficient network of contacts between the American organisation and the I.R.B. in Ireland, mainly by means of his friend Dr. Patrick Mc Cartan, also from Carrickmore, who spent five years in Philadelphia before returning to Ireland to study medicine in 1905. Mc Garrity, by the early years of this century was District Officer of the Clann in Philadelphia and was a close confidante of Clarke, Pearse, Mc Dermott, Hobson, Casement and Devoy in the pre-Rising period. Devoy, Keating and he constituted the Directory of Clann na Gael. In the War of Independence 1919–23 he was a major figure in the American support which sustained the First and Second Dáil. He was a faithful supporter of Pearse's efforts in Sgoil Éanna and personally contributed $800 to the school; it was he who planned the American fund-raising tour which Pearse made in the Spring of 1914. He gave Pearse the hospitality of his home, the use of his automobiles, and planned the various lectures, social functions and the Aeridheacht at Celtic Park at which Pearse was physically assaulted by the Redmondites of the A.O.H. Pearse in his numerous letters to Mc Garrity expresses his gratitude and, following the 1914 tour, corresponded with McGarrity on various aspects of the preparations for the Rising.

MAC GIOLLA PHÁDRAIG, SEOSAMH IERÓM (1878–1910).
A Christian Brother, who by his graded textbooks and teaching aids advanced significantly the teaching of Irish in the primary and secondary schools in the early decades of the century. The impact of his Grammar, Aids to Irish Composition and Aids to Pronunciation on generations of students was similar to that exercised on Gaelic League classes by O'Growney's *Simple Lessons*. A man of wide scholarship in modern and classical languages, and of unusual gifts as a teacher, he applied his talents and industry to producing these books while teaching in the Brothers' Secondary School at Synge Street, Dublin.

At the age of twenty three, he published his comprehensive *Graiméar na Gaeilge* (1901) which was followed in 1908 by a simpler Grammar for beginners. His *Aids to Irish Composition* (1907) offered a structured method of learning written and oral command of the language based on the methodology then used to teach English as a second language in European schools. His *Aids to the Pronunciation of Irish* (1905) was followed by a graded text *Irish Composition – Sequel to the Aids* (1907) to which Pearse contributed. For the primary schools, he designed and produced a coloured illustrated Chart and associated pedagogical notes on which conversational lessons could be structured; these later became the main instructional aid for language teaching based on the Direct Method. He corresponded and collaborated with Dr. Hyde, Eoin Mac Neill, An tAthair Peadar Ó Laoghaire and others in many League activities.

MAC GIOLLARNATH, SEÁN (1880–1970). Born in East Galway, his education did not give him what the Gaelic League provided for him in London – an opportunity to learn Irish. As a civil servant and an active League member, he was one of a large group of London exiles who were so creative, active and inventive in cultural and literary fields at the end of the century; this group encompassed on the one hand Stephen Gwynn, Yeats and Robert Lynd and Pádraig Ó Conaire, Tomás Ó Flannghaile, and Micheál Breathnach on the other.

Returning to Galway in 1908, he edited the monthly *An Connachtach* before coming to Dublin in 1909 to succeed Pearse as editor of *An Claidheamh Soluis*. In 1920 he was appointed as the first Judge of the First Dáil Courts in Connemara and continued on the bench in the Western Circuit until 1950.

His literary output included drama translations, folklore from Connemara, books on the natural history of the western Gaeltacht and general volumes for children and on ornithology. His major

works were *Peadar Chois Fhairrge* (1934), *Ríocht na nÉan* (1935)
Saol Éanacha (1925), *Connemara* (1954), *Mo Dhúthaigh Fhiain*
(1949), *Annála Beaga ó Iorrus Aithneach* (1941).

MAC LOCHLAINN, ALFRED. James Pearse, by his first wife,
Emily Fox, had two children, James and Mary (b. 1864); Mary
married Alfred Mc Gloughlin, whose father, John, was a close
friend of her father. They had three children; Alfred, the only boy
and the subject of this note, was a close friend of Willie and Patrick
Pearse. He was artistically skilled and was deeply involved in the
design and fabrication of stage sets and effects for the school
dramatic productions of Sgoil Éanna. He founded his own firm
specialising in ironwork and artistic metalwork.

MC MANUS, SÉUMAS (1869–1960). Born on a small Donegal
farm and educated locally he became a teacher and in 1888
headmaster of his former school at Glencoagh. He had a great
talent for collecting and editing folk stories and traditional lore
which he applied to the rich store still alive in his native county. In
1899 he went to the United States and concentrated on his writing
and extending his metier to include poetry and novels. He married
the poet Eithne Carbery (Anna Johnston) and while they lived
permanently in the United States, they were regular visitors to
Ireland.

When Pearse was launching Sgoil Éanna, Mc Manus featured
the school and its headmaster in a number of American newspapers
to which he contributed. Mc Manus was a close friend of Tomás
Bán Ó Concheanainn in America and was a supporter of the Gaelic
League.

His works include, *The History of the Irish Race* (1903) and an
autobiography *The Rocky Road to Dublin* (1938). He died in New
York.

MAC NEILL, EOIN (1867–1945). Born in Glenarm, Co. Antrim,
educated at St. Malachy's College, Belfast, and later at University
College, Dublin, when he had already taken up employment as a
clerk in the Chancery Division of the Four Courts, Dublin, his
primary field of study was economics, jurisprudence and constitutional law. It was mainly due to his initiative that the Gaelic
League was founded in 1893 following an article by him in
Irisleabhar na Gaeilge of which journal he became editor in 1894.
He was appointed first Professor of Irish in St. Patrick's Teacher
Training College, Drumcondra in 1897 and in 1899 became the
first editor of *An Claidheamh Soluis* – the Gaelic League's own

journal. On the establishment of the National University he was nominated to the Senate and appointed Professor of Early Irish History in U.C.D.

In 1913 an article of his, "The North Began", catalysed the formation of the Irish Volunteers of which he became President. He was not party to the preparation for the Rising and despite his cancellation of the orders issued by Pearse and his associates, Mac Neill was arrested after the Rising and sentenced to life imprisonment. In the First Dáil he was Minister for Finance and was Minister for Education in the first Free State Cabinet 1922–1925. His membership of the Boundary Commission and the premature release of the findings of which prompted widespread criticism, led to his resignation in 1925 and his departure from public life in 1927. He devoted the rest of his life to scholarship and cultural activities.

He was a frequent visitor to Sgoil Eanna and contributed to the series of extern lectures which were a feature of the school programme. His sons, Niall and Brian were students of Sgoil Éanna from its opening day.

His scholarly writings cover a wide range of topics and fields of study in early history, palaeography and archaeology. His major works include, *Phases of Irish History* (1919) and *Celtic Ireland* (1921).

MAC RUADHRAÍ, MICHEÁL (1860–1936), was born in Lacken, Co. Mayo, and claimed that he received more learning from the oral tradition of his locality which was Irish-speaking, than from the formal education system. He published a number of booklets in the Gaelic League series and won seven Oireachtas gold medals for oratory and story-telling. From the foundation of Sgoil Éanna in 1908, he was the school gardener with general responsibility for the grounds. He taught practical gardening and horticulture to the pupils whose ultimate ambition it was to gain access to his prize winning fruit. On festive occasions, the boys frequently persuaded Mac Ruadhraí to recite or dance and his gold medals were a source of constant admiration.

MAGUIRE, MARY (Mrs. P. Colum) (1884–1957). Born in Collooney, Co. Sligo, she was educated locally and in Dublin. She was among the teachers in Sgoil Íde (Pearse's school for girls) 1910–12 where she was very active with Máire Ní Choitir in dramatic and literary achievements and in making the school a mirror image of Sgoil Éanna. She was very friendly with Thomas Mac Donagh. Married Pádraig Colum in 1912 and went with him to America in 1914 where they both taught in Columbia University. Published her autobiography, *Life and the Dream* (1928), *From these Roots* (1938) a book of literary criticism and with her husband *Our Friend James Joyce* (1959). They both had contributed extensively to the *Irish Rebellion of 1916 and its Martyrs* (1916) edited by Maurice Joy and published in New York.

MAHAFFY, JOHN PENTLAND (1839–1919), born in Switzerland of Irish parents, Mahaffy was a noted classical scholar and became Provost of Trinity College in 1914. Before the Commission on Intermediate Education in 1898 he campaigned with the collaboration of Atkinson, Bernard and others to have the status of the Irish language diminished within the educational system; Mahaffy would have wished to exclude the language entirely from the schools. The Gaelic League effectively countered this campaign by calling upon the expert evidence of noted European and Irish scholars who testified to the contrary; the League published a celebrated series of pamphlets in which the proceedings of the Commission were presented to the public. The mutual antagonism between Mahaffy and Pearse and between the Gaelic League and the forces of cultural reaction reached their zenith in November 1914 when Pearse was invited to share a platform with Yeats and Tom Kettle at a Davis Commemoration meeting in Trinity College organised by the College Gaelic Society. Mahaffy used his power as Provost to ban 'a man called Pearse' and the meeting was held outside the college walls after the Gaelic Society had been suspended by the Board.

MARTYN, EDWARD (1859–1923). A wealthy Catholic landowner from Co. Galway, Martyn was a prominent figure in the early part of the century as a patron of the arts and as a creative writer and dramatist. He was educated at Beaumont and Christ Church, Oxford. He was an active supporter of the Gaelic League and wrote one of its popular pamphlets, *Ireland's Battle for her Language* (1900). With W. B. Yeats, George Moore and Lady Gregory he founded the *Irish Literary Theatre* in 1899 which produced his *Heather Field* as one of its first plays. His other plays include *Maeve, The Tale of a Town, Glencolman* and *The Dream Physician*. He was later associated with Joseph Plunkett and Thomas Mac Donagh in founding a short-lived theatre in Hardwicke Street and was also president of Cluicheoirí na hÉireann which had Colum, Pearse and Tom Kettle on its board.

He founded and endowed the Palestrina Choir in Dublin and was a founder of the Feis Ceoil, an annual music festival. His later years were spent in quiet retirement at Tulyra Castle in Co. Galway.

Ó CEALLAIGH, SEÁN T. (1882–1966). Born in Dublin, he was educated at O'Connell Schools and at an early age joined the Gaelic League and the I.R.B. He was among the founder members of Sinn Féin on whose behalf he was elected to Dublin Corporation in 1906. When Pearse was appointed editor of *An Claidheamh Soluis* in 1903, Seán T. was appointed manager and in 1915 he was elected general secretary of the League. He was a close friend and confidant of Pearse and assisted him in the various activities of Sgoil Éanna where his two brothers Micheál and Maitiú were pupils.

He served in the G.P.O. during the Rising, was arrested and interned. On his release he was elected M.P. in the 1918 election and when the First Dáil met in January 1919, he was elected Ceann Comhairle. Later he acted as Envoy for the Republic at Paris, Rome and in the United States. Following the Treaty which he opposed, he participated in the founding of Fianna Fáil and was a senior minister (Local Government, Education, Finance) in each of the de Valera Cabinets from 1932 to 1945 when he was elected President of Ireland in succession to Dr. Douglas Hyde. In all he served two full terms in the Presidency, having been re-elected unanimously in 1952. His autobiography *Seán T.* was published in two volumes (1963, 1972) under the editorship of Pádraig Ó Fiannachta.

O'BRIEN, WILLIAM (1852–1928). Born at Mallow and educated at Queen's College, Cork, he became editor of the Land League journal, *United Ireland* in 1881. His radicalism provoked his arrest which merely assured his election as M.P. on his release. He collaborated with Dillon in initiating the 'plan of campaign' in 1886 and continued this alliance with Dillon in his anti-Parnell stance in 1891. In 1910 he advocated reapproachment between nationalists and unionists in the "All for Ireland" League but the exponential rise of political self-determination demolished his political base and that of many of his party colleagues.

He wrote two novels, *When We Were Boys* (1890) on the Fenians, and *A Queen of Men* (1898) and also published *Recollections* (1906) and *The Irish Revolution* (1928) which offer an account of his political career.

Ó CONCHEANAINN, TOMÁS (1870–1961), scholar, merchant and Gaelic League organiser who was popularly known as "Tomás

Bán", was born on Inis Meadhon in the Aran Islands. He went to America in 1885 where his brothers had a wine business and attended college in California and New York gaining postgraduate degrees in business studies. Founded his own business in Mexico and travelled widely in North and South America, Canada and Cuba. On a visit home in 1898 he met Pearse on Inis Meadhon and was seized by the enthusiasm he witnessed in the League. He was appointed as the League's first Timthire or organiser in 1899 and later its Chief Organiser with responsibility for initiating, promoting and maintaining all the organisation's activities. He accompanied Douglas Hyde on his American trip in 1905 and was responsible for the collection of over $64,000 for the League.

He was a close friend of Pearse and he arranged for his nephew from Inis Oirr, Brian Seoighe to attend Sgoil Éanna; Brian arrived at Cullenswood House in February 1910 and remained a part of the school as senior pupil, master and assistant headmaster until the school closed in 1935.

Tomás Bán was appointed a divisional inspector with the public health Insurance Board in 1911 and lived in Galway where he devoted his talents to writing.

Ó CORCORA, DÓNAL (1878–1964). Born in Cork, educated there and at St. Patrick's College Drumcondra where he trained as a primary teacher. He taught in Cork until 1921 when he resigned and in 1930 was appointed Professor of English at University College, Cork. He was deeply involved in the early years of the Gaelic League in Cork and founded also the Cork Dramatic Society for which he wrote in Irish and English. He was an artist of considerable talent and taught Art and Irish in the vocational schools of Co. Cork from 1921–25. His literary output includes three plays: *The Labour Leader* (1919), *The Yellow Bittern* (1920) and *Resurrection* (1924); his short story collections include *A Munster Twilight* (1916), *The Hounds of Banba* (1920), *The Stormy Hills* (1929) and *Earth out of Earth* (1939); *The Threshold of Quiet* (1917) was his only novel. His works of non-fiction include *The Hidden Ireland* (1924), *Synge and Anglo-Irish Literature* (1931) and. *The Fortunes of the Irish Language* (1954). He exercised a major influence on a generation of Irish writers.

Ó DUBHGHAILL, SÉAMAS (J. J. Doyle) (1855–1929). Born in Kerry he joined the Inland Revenue service and was stationed in England, Scotland, Derry and Belfast. He was an early member of the Gaelic League and wrote extensively for *An Claidheamh Soluis* and for the League; in this connection Pearse and he corresponded frequently in the early years of the century. He derived his pseudonym "Beirt-Fhear" from the work which he serialised in *An Claidheamh Soluis* 1899–1902 and which was published by the League as *Beirt Fhear ón dTuath* (1903). His other works include *Tadhg Gabha* (1901), *Leabhar Cainte* (1901), *Cathair Conroi agus Sgéalta Eile* (1905), *Cainnt na Cathrach* (1910) and *Beartín Luachra* (1927). In his twenties he had been involved in the Gaelic Union and was a close friend of Daithí Pleímonn.

Ó DOMHNALLÁIN, PÁDRAIG (1884–1960). Born in Uachtar Ard, Co. Galway, where he was an active member of the Gaelic League and secretary of the local branch from 1903. Educated locally and at University College, Dublin, he knew Irish from an early age and was a teacher and organiser for the League in Co. Sligo and in Co. Down. He collected the poetry of Colm de Bhailís, the poet of Gorumna; in conjunction with Pearse he organised a fund to remove de Bhailís from the workhouse and settle him in congenial lodgings. He was invited by Pearse in 1908 to become Connacht correspondent for *An Claidheamh Soluis* and he was the Principal of Coláiste Chonnacht 1908–1921 when he moved to Dublin to the editorship of *Misneach* and later of *Fáinne an Lae*. In 1925 he was appointed Professor of Irish and History in Carysfort Training College, Dublin.

His publications include, *Ar Lorg an Riogh agus Sgéalta Eile* (1935) *Na Spiaclóirí agus Sgéalta Eile* (1934), *An t-Iolrach Mór* (1941) and a variety of translations, essays and textbooks.

Ó DONNCHADHA, TADHG (TÓRNA) (1874–1945). Born in Carrignavar, Co. Cork; after secondary education in the North Monastery, Cork, he was trained as a teacher at St. Patrick's, Drumcondra (1892–94) and taught in Dublin. In 1902 he resigned and was appointed editor of *Irisleabhar na Gaeilge* – a post which he held until his appointment as Professor of Irish in St. Patrick's Training College, Drumcondra. In 1916 he was appointed to the Chair of Irish in University College, Cork. He was an active member of various Gaelic League bodies and published extensively. He published his own poetry in Irish, editions of other poets, literary criticism and translations from Old Irish, English, Breton, Welsh, French and German. His early works included *Sean Fhocail na Mumhan* (1902), *Dánta Sheáin Uí Mhurchadha na Raithíneach* (1907), *Oir-Chiste Fiannaíochta* (1924) and *Filíocht Fiannaíochta* (1933). He published also in collaboration with Fr. P. Dineen and Pearse.

Ó DONABHÁIN ROSA, DIARMUID (O'Donovan Rossa, Jeremiah) (1831–1915). Born in Rosscarbery, Co. Cork, in an area in which Irish was the vernacular, Rossa moved to Skibbereen and opened a thriving business there. He established the Phoenix Society in 1856 a political and literary society, which was to exert a significant influence on his own life and on the political future of the country. In 1858, James Stephens in organising the Fenian movement in Cork found the Phoenix Society to be a willing and valuable nucleus for his revolutionary brotherhood. Ó Donabháin Rosa became manager of the Fenian journal, *The Irish People* and was arrested in 1865 at the offices of the journal with other leaders and sentenced to penal servitude for twenty years. He suffered ignominiously in English prisons where the authorities sought to break his spirit by mean and petty cruelty. On his release in 1871, emigration was mandatory; during his American sojourn he edited *The United Irishman* and published his prison memoirs; *O'Donovan Rossa's Prison Life: Six Years in Six English Prisons* (1874). A larger autobiographical work *Rossa's Recollections* (1838–1898) appeared in 1898. He died in June 1915 and his remains were brought back to a funeral in Dublin on August 1st which was a significant milestone on the road to insurrection. To Pearse, who delivered the graveside oration at Glasnevin, Rossa represented unbreakable courage, to Connolly and Mac Donagh he represented a cause in which the Irish Volunteers and the Irish Citizen Army could unite to salute "the most typical man of the Fenian generation". In 1954, a memorial was unveiled to Rossa in St. Stephen's Green, Dublin, consisting of a granite monolith with a bronze plaque bearing a quotation from Pearse's graveside oration: "Ní dhéanfaidh Gaeil dearmhad ort go brách".

Ó DUINÍN, PÁDRAIG (An tAthair) (1860–1934). Born in Rathmore, Co. Kerry and educated locally and in Jesuit Colleges he entered the Jesuit Order in 1880. He attended university in Dublin and spent some years teaching in Mungret and Clongowes Wood Colleges and was ordained in 1894. In 1900 he left the Jesuits and devoted the rest of his life to scholarship and the Gaelic League; he edited and wrote extensively in Irish and claimed that he was the only person making his living by writing in Irish.

In Gaelic League activities he was a prominent figure in the fields of education and publishing; he was the dominant influence in the Keating Branch, a branch whose members tended to generate considerable controversy and were inclined to be anti-establishment.

His extensive publications include editions of the works of the poets of his native region, Eoin Ruadh Ó Súilleabháin, Aogán Ó Rathaille, Piaras Feirtéir and Tadhg Gaelach Ó Súilleabháin all of which became Gaelic League textbooks; a novel *Cormac Ua Conaill* (1901), some plays on historical topics, and incidental writings on Gaelic League and other topics which appeared in many journals, especially the *Leader*. His outstanding scholarly achievement was the *Irish-English Dictionary* published by the Irish Texts Society in 1904, which will always retain a special position in Irish scholarship. Larger editions were published in 1927 and 1934.

Ó FLANGHAILE, TOMÁS (1846–1916), scholar, poet and writer, was born in Ballinrobe, Co. Mayo, in the famine years and emigrated to Manchester with his entire family in 1853. After attending school in Manchester and London he taught in Hammersmith and in St. Bede's College, Manchester before going permanently to London where he taught from 1876 to 1893 in Kennington and Forest Gate where he lived. From 1894 to his retirement in 1907, he lectured in English and Latin at the City of London Teacher Training College.

During his years in London he was active in the Irish Literary Society Southwark and in its successor, The Irish Literary Society, from which emerged in 1898 a smaller group, The Irish Texts Society. In 1897, the London branch of the Gaelic League was formed and it attracted exiles such as W. P. Ryan, D. P. Moran, Frank Fahy and Ó Flannghaile to its ranks. He was an active member and in 1898 founded the Forest Gate branch which catered for a large local population in east London.

He contributed frequent articles to Irish and English journals, published six or seven volumes of original poetry, translation and criticism; his major works include *De Prosodia Hibernica* (1908), *Laoi Oisín ar Thír na nÓg* (1896) *Duanaire na Macaomh* (1910), *Eachtra Giolla an Amaráin* (1897) and *For the Tongue of the Gael* (1896).

This last volume of essays played a major part in forging a link between the London teacher and Pearse; on being awarded a prize for his performance in his Senior Grade examination in 1896 Pearse selected the recently published book by Ó Flannghaile. In reviewing its second edition in *An Claidheamh Soluis* (1907) Pearse admitted that he had been deeply influenced by the ideas of Ó Flannghaile. During Pearse's editorship, Ó Flannghaile contributed frequent scholarly articles on lexicography and philology and they corresponded extensively.

Ó GAORA, COLM (1887–1954). Born and educated at Rosmuc in the Galway Gaeltacht, Ó Gaora was one of the students whom Pearse examined at Rosmuc in April 1903 for appointment as organisers for the Gaelic League. Pearse encouraged him to write for *An Claidheamh Soluis* and Ó Gaora gathered traditional stories in the Rosmuc area and wrote them in modern idiom; at one stage he was gathering and writing so enthusiastically that Pearse pleaded with him to desist from sending on material lest the other provinces became jealous of the preference being shown to Connacht. *Sgolbglas Mac Riogh 'n Éirinn* (1904) was one such story which Ó Gaora wrote. He also collected poetry and published a collection of such traditional verses in *Fibín* (1905). Ó Gaora's major work was his autobiography *Mise* (1943), the first edition of which carried a copy of the letter Pearse wrote to him in October 1904.

O'GRADY, STANDISH JAMES (1846–1928). Born in Castletownbere, Co. Cork, where his father, Viscount Guillamore, was the local Church of Ireland Rector, he was educated in Tipperary Grammar School and Trinity College, Dublin. He abandoned his career as a lawyer for the combined vocation of editor and creative writer of historical novels; in this capacity he stimulated a wide interest in Ireland's heroic past and has been called by AE "the father of the Irish literary revival".

He edited in turn the Dublin *Daily Express, The Kilkenny Moderator* and the *All-Ireland Review* which he founded in 1900; he also contributed to journals such as *The Irish Peasant* and *The New Age* mainly on social and political issues. His *History of Ireland: Heroic Period* (1878–1880) was a work of major significance. His historical novels include *Red Hugh's Captivity* (1889), *Finn and his Companions* (1892), *The Bog of Stars* (1893), *The Coming of Cúchulainn* (1893), *Lost on Du Corrig* (1894), *The Chain of Gold* (1895), *In the Wake of King James* (1896) and *The Flight of the Eagle* (1897).

He was a cousin of Standish Hayes O'Grady (1832–1915) who in addition to his professional employment as an engineer, compiled and translated an important collection of Irish tales from old manuscripts, *Silva Gadelica* (1892).

Ó GRAMHNAIGH, EOGHAN (Rev. Professor) (1863–1899), was born near Athboy in Co. Meath, and was educated at the local national school and at St. Finian's, Navan, before entering Maynooth in 1882, where he was ordained in 1889. He spent two years teaching in Navan before returning to Maynooth as Professor of Irish in 1891. Earlier in the same year he succeeded Seán Pléimeann in the editorship of *Irisleabhar na Gaeilge*. He was responsible for introducing a new phase in this journal by giving preference to simple Irish prose, modelled on the spoken language. He was instrumental in having Irish included in the course of studies at Maynooth and in giving a new philosophy to a rising generation of Irish clergy.

In 1893, he began publication of his famous *Simple Lessons in Irish* as serialised weekly instalments in the *Weekly Freeman* and in the *Tuam News*; this series exercised a major influence on the language movement for decades offering a graded course to beginners in the League classes. They were published in five parts by the League 1897–1900; Eoin Mac Neill completed the series due to the ill-health of Fr. Ó Gramhnaigh.

Although absent from the inaugural meeting in July 1893, he was one of the founding members of the Gaelic League and with Eoin Mac Neill and Douglas Hyde provided its inspiration and leadership. His health, never robust, deteriorated and in 1894 he went to Arizona and San Francisco to join his former fellow-student, Fr. Peter Yorke. He continued working on the *Simple Lessons* while in America and serialised a version of them in a Chicago paper. He died on 18th October 1899 and his passing was widely mourned in the Gaelic League. In 1903, his body was returned to Ireland and received by the leaders of the League before being buried at Maynooth.

O'HICKEY, MICHEAL (Rev. Dr.) (1861–1916), a noted Gaelic Leaguer and Professor of Irish at Maynooth. Born in Carrickbeg on the Waterford side of the Tipperary town by the Suir, he was educated at the Christian Brothers school there and in St. John's College, Waterford where he was ordained in 1884. Having spent nine years in a Scottish diocese, he returned and spent three years in parochial work and as Diocesan Inspector which gave him an opportunity to promote the Irish language in the schools of a diocese which then contained significant residual Gaeltacht areas. He succeeded Fr. Eoghan Ó Gramhnaigh as Professor of Irish at Maynooth in 1896 and also succeeded him as Vice-President of the Gaelic League. Elected to the League executive in 1898, he was deeply involved in its educational and literary work. In the competition for the editorship of *An Claidheamh Soluis* in 1903 he did not support Pearse and resigned from the executive on his appointment. He was prominent in all of the League's campaigns to reform Irish education and to raise the position of the Irish language within the system. He wielded an able pen in these causes and was most effective as a public orator. In the controversy which arose from the Intermediate Commission of 1899, he replied with vigour to the assertions of Mahaffy, Gwynn and Atkinson of Trinity College: the League published his reply as *The Irish Language and Irish Intermediate Education* (1901).

The major controversy which dominated his life was that concerning the place of Irish in the National University in 1909. The Gaelic League campaigned that Irish be made an essential subject for Matriculation and the Catholic Bishops as a body opposed that stance. In a strong worded paper *An Irish University or Else* – O'Hickey attacked those who opposed the League's policy and thereby incurred the censure of the Bishops. They required him to withdraw; he refused and they dismissed him from his Chair at Maynooth in July 1909. Pearse called the episcopal action "a piece of tyrannical blundering" and supported his former opponent despite being criticised for doing so by elements in Sinn Féin. Dr. O'Hickey was refused permission to seek redress in the secular courts and took his case to the Roman ecclesiastical courts where after years of patient supplication he had exhausted his means without achieving any satisfaction. He died in Waterford and is buried in the Franciscan Abbey at Carrickbeg.

His main works include, *Irish Education and the Irish Language* (1899), *The True National Idea* (1900), *Irish in the Schools* (1900) and *The Nationalisation of Irish Education* (1902).

O'KELLY, J. J. (ÓCeallaigh, Séamas) (Dr.) (1879–1953). A native of Draperstown, Co. Derry, he was educated in Queen's University, Belfast and at University College in Dublin where he graduated B.A. of the Royal University in 1902. Among his student contemporaries in Dublin were Pearse, James Joyce, Con Curran, Tom Kettle and John Marcus O'Sullivan. After completing his Arts degree he enrolled in the Medical Faculty and having qualified in the National University in 1909, he went to Vienna to do postgraduate work in Gynaecology. He maintained an active interest in Celtic Studies and was an authority on the local history, archaeology and place names of Ulster. He was a close friend of Eoin Mac Neill and of Professor E. Hogan S.J. He was also an active member of the Gaelic League with a special interest in its Ulster activities. He was Consultant Physician to Sgoil Éanna.

Ó LAOGHAIRE, PEADAR (An tAthair) (1839–1920). A prominent Gaelic League writer who as parish priest of Castlelyons, Co. Cork, made a significant contribution to modern Irish writing by his use of "caint na ndaoine" and basing his style on the speech

457

forms of the people. Born near Macroom in an Irish-speaking district, he was bilingual from an early age.

His writings included short stories, novels, essays, modern versions of classical tales; his major works were, *Ar nDóthain Araon* (1894), *Séadna* (1898), *Niamh* (1907), *Ag Séideadh agus ag Ithe* (1918), *Seanmóin agus Trí-Fichid* (1909). His autobiography *Mo Sgéal Féin* (1915) and his *Séadna*, a Faustian story, exercised a major influence on succeeding generations.

Ó MUIRGHEASA, ENRÍ (Henry Morris) (1874–1945). A prominent figure in the early days of the Gaelic League from the Farney district of County Monaghan, where he was a teacher at Lisdoonan national school. He was appointed Inspector of National Schools (1921), Divisional Inspector in Sligo (1923) and Deputy Chief Inspector in Dublin (1932). He had a keen active interest in archaeology which he applied in the various districts in which he lived; his major uncompleted work involved a detailed topography of *Táin Bó Cuailgne*. He wrote extensively on Irish literature, music, folklore, history and archaeology and published major works on the Irish poetry and proverbs of Ulster, *Sean-Fhocla Uladh* (1907), *Céad de Cheoltaibh Uladh* (1915), *Dhá Chéad de Cheoltaibh Uladh* (1934).

He was a close associate of Pearse in the various Gaelic League committees and was a strong supporter of his candidature for the editorship of *An Claidheamh Soluis* in 1903. He was a founding member of the Irish Folklore Commission (1927) and was instrumental in his official capacity in promoting the study of local history in the national schools and in the collection and recording of folklore.

Ó NEACHTAIN, EOGHAN, from Spidéal, Co. Galway, was an active Gaelic Leaguer, scholar and writer. He was a frequent contributor to the series of popular booklets published by the League; his works include *I dTaobh na hOibre* (1901), *Dubhaltach Mac Fhirbhísigh* (1902), *Céadtach Mac Fhinn as Éirinn* (1907), and *Stair Cheachta* (1903, 1907). He also edited in association with Pearse, a mediaeval Irish story *Toruigheacht Fiacail Riogh Gréig* (1904) and he translated Mitchel's *Jail Journal.*

When the League in 1902 appointed a full-time editor of *An Claidheamh Soluis,* Ó Neachtain secured the position in succession to Eoin Mac Neill who had edited the paper since its foundation. During the year of Ó Neachtain's editorship Pearse was encouraged by him to write frequently for the paper and in March 1903 Pearse was appointed to succeed Ó Neachtain as editor.

Ó Neachtain was one of the first in the League to realise the importance of providing school textbooks in Irish; his two-volume *Céimseata Euclid* appeared in 1908 and 1913.

O'NEILL, JOSEPH (Seosamh Ó Néill) (1884–1953), was born on Inis Mór, in the Aran Islands, where his father, a member of the R.I.C. was stationed. After his early education in Kilronan and at St. Jarlath's College, Tuam, he attended Queen's College, Galway 1898–1902. He had been a student in the Senior Grade in 1896, the same year as Pearse, in which examination O'Neill received slightly more marks in Irish than Pearse – together they secured first and second place in Ireland. In his visits to the Aran Islands, Pearse made the acquaintance of O'Neill, whom he coached for the matriculation examination in 1898.

After graduation, O'Neill did postgraduate work and some teaching at Manchester and at Freiburg Universities; in Freiburg he formed a lasting friendship with Osborn Bergin and developed his life-long interest in ski-ing. In 1906 he attended the celebrations organised by Kuno Meyer to honour the centenary of the German Celtic Scholar, Zeuss; they were held at Bamberg near Nurnberg and O'Neill delivered a speech in Irish. In 1903, he was appointed Lecturer in Irish at Queen's College, Galway, and in 1907, left Galway to become an Inspector of National Education; two years later he was among the first Inspectors of Secondary Education appointed. In this capacity, accompanied by two other Inspectors, C. E. Wright and E. Ensor, he conducted a general inspection of Sgoil Éanna in May 1910. In the administrative changeover following the Treaty of 1921, O'Neill became a Commissioner of Education and in 1924 on the formation of the Department of Education, he became its Permanent Secretary, a post which he held until 1944. During his long career he held also the positions of Local Appointments Commissioner 1926–1946 and Civil Service Commissioner 1923–1944.

He wrote a number of novels, *Land under England* (1935), *Wind from the North* (1934), *Day of Wrath* (1936) and contributed also to the *Dublin Magazine* and to *Studies*. His wife, the poet Mary Devenport O'Neill, and he, were close friends of AE.

O'REILLY, REV. JOHN MYLES (1863–1941), was born in Louisburgh, County Mayo, and was a contemporary of Fr. Eoin O'Growney and Fr. Peter Yorke at Maynooth, to both of whom he imparted his own vernacular skill in oral Irish. He was an early pre-Gaelic League enthusiast for the revival of the language and contributed to *Irisleabhar na Gaeilge* (The Gaelic Journal) as a student. Although a native of the Tuam Diocese, he was ordained in 1888 in Clonliffe College and spent the next eight years in Australia where he was secretary to Cardinal Moran of Sydney. Returning to Ireland in 1896, he ministered in a succession of remote parishes of the Tuam diocese, among them, Achill and Clare Island. His panegyric at Maynooth for the Requiem of Fr. Eoin O'Growney in 1904 was described by Douglas Hyde as succinct and forthright. Although an active Gaelic Leaguer his practical contribution was limited by the location of his diocesan appointments; he wrote a League pamphlet in 1901, *The Threatening Metémpsychosis of a Nation* and later a trenchant analysis of the role of the native speaker in language revival.

Ó SEARCAIGH, SÉAMAS (1887–1965), writer, scholar and teacher who was born in Donegal, educated there and at Queen's University, Belfast where he studied Celtic Studies. He later lectured in University College, Dublin and Maynooth. He became President of Coláiste Uladh at Cloghaneely, Donegal in his later years.

His major works include *Foghraíocht Ghaeilge ón Tuaiscirt* (1925), *Sgéalta as an tSean-Litríocht* (1945) and a two-language volume on Pearse, *Pádraig Mac Piarais* (1928).

PEARSE, JAMES (1839–1900). Born in London of an artisan family of three sons, James Pearse came to Dublin in the 1860's and set up as a monumental sculptor in Gt. Brunswick St. He married Emily Fox by whom he had two surviving children, James Vincent and Mary Emily. His second wife, Margaret Brady, bore him four children, Margaret, Patrick, William and Mary Brigid. With his first wife he converted to Catholicism in 1870. In his political views he was a radical and was a strong supporter of Michael Davitt and Parnell. In 1886 James Pearse wrote and personally published a pamphlet *England's Duty to Ireland as seen by an Englishman* in reply to one published by Thomas Maguire of Trinity College, *England's Duty to Ireland as Plain to a Loyal Irish Roman Catholic*. Examples of Pearse's ecclesiastical and architectural sculpture may be observed in many Irish churches and in public buildings.

PEARSE, MRS. MARGARET (1857–1932). Mother of the Pearse brothers and second wife of James Pearse whom she married in 1876. Born in Dublin (Margaret Brady) but with a Co. Meath background, she was left a widow in 1900. With the assistance of her eldest son she managed to continue the firm and did so until 1908.

Of a pious and retiring disposition, she was responsible for the domestic arrangements in Sgoil Éanna and was remembered with affection by the students. After the Rising she became more involved in politics and took an active part as a Dáil Deputy in the anti-Treaty side in 1921. She toured America on a number of occasions and succeeded in re-opening Sgoil Éanna at Rathfarnham in 1919. She wished that the Hermitage would be kept as a memorial to her two sons.

PEARSE, MARGARET (1878–1968). Eldest of the second Pearse family, educated in Dublin and France, she opened a junior school in Leeson Park before the family moved to Cullenswood House in 1908 on the founding of Sgoil Éanna; this school was later amalgamated with Sgoil Éanna and she joined the teaching staff where she taught Music and French.

On the re-opening of Sgoil Éanna in 1919 she was active in its management until its closure in 1935. She was a Senator and a member of the National Executive of Fianna Fáil. She resided in the Hermitage for most of her later life and arranged that it be left to the Nation according to the wishes of her mother. In May 1970, the Hermitage was accepted on behalf of the Nation by the President, Éamonn de Valera from the Trustees of the Pearse family, Éamonn de Barra, and John Maher, solicitor.

PEARSE, MARY BRIGID (1884–1947). The youngest of the Pearse family, she was born in Dublin on April 24th, 1884. In delicate health for most of her life, she was unable to participate in any of the activities which enjoyed the attention of her brothers and sister. She was by nature sensitive and had an interest in music and the arts. She wrote *The Home Life of Patrick Pearse* (1935) which included in addition to a version of his autobiographical fragment, some reminiscences by colleagues and former students.

PEARSE, WILLIAM (1881–1916). Though an active member of the Volunteers, who was executed after the Rising, he has been seen as living in the shadow of his brother Patrick. Of a decided artistic temperament, he trained at Dublin School of Art and in Paris, joining his father's firm of monumental sculptors.

He was an assistant teacher in Sgoil Éanna, was an actor of ability and contributed to the management and setting of the many dramatic presentations at Sgoil Éanna.

In the Rising, he was attached to Headquarters Staff at the

461

G.P.O. with the rank of captain; he was sentenced to death and executed at Kilmainham on May 4th. There was a very close bond between Willie Pearse and his brother which was expressed by Patrick in the poem he wrote before his execution, *To My Brother;* it expresses the debt he owed Willie for his generous help in all their joint adventures.

PLUNKETT, JOSEPH MARY (1887–1916). Poet, and revolutionary son of Count Plunkett, he never enjoyed robust health and was forced to spend periods abroad convalescing. He came to Thomas Mac Donagh in Sgoil Éanna to learn Irish; they became close friends and literary associates in the founding of the *Irish Review* and with Martyn in the founding of the Irish Theatre in Hardwicke St. He was active with his friend, Casement in securing German aid for the Rising, became a member of the Military Council of the I.R.B. and despite serious illness took his place in the Post Office in the Rising, and signed the Proclamation. He was executed on May 4th, 1916. He married Grace Gifford on the eve of his execution, whose sister Muriel was the wife of Thomas Mac Donagh.

His poetry includes, *The Circle and the Sword* (1911) and *The Poems of Joseph Mary Plunkett* (1916).

REDMOND, JOHN (1856–1918). Son of William Redmond M.P. for Wexford, educated at Clongowes Wood College and at T.C.D., he was called to the Bar, and elected M.P. in 1881. In the Parnell split he remained faithful to the Chief and became leader of the party on its re-unification in 1900. He secured the Third Home Rule Bill of 1912 and when the Volunteers were formed in 1913, Redmond was anxious to control them; his demand in June 1914 that he be allowed nominate twenty five members of the Volunteer executive was rejected by a minority of nine among whom Pearse and Mac Dermott were the leaders. This resulted in two separate Volunteer organisations, one led by the I.R.B. the other led by Redmond who was encouraging them, on the outbreak of war, to offer their services to England in her struggle for the freedom of small nations. The Rising of 1916 in its impact, seriously demolished his credibility as a political leader and the convention of 1917 held in Dublin was a futile gesture with no hope of success. He died suddenly in March 1918. His younger brother Willie, succeeded his father as M.P. in 1883 for Wexford and later represented Fermanagh and East Clare. He responded to his brother's recruiting drive in 1914 by enlisting in the British army and he was killed in action in June 1917.

RYAN, W. P. (Liam P. Ó Riain) (1867–1942), born in Templemore, he became a journalist in London. He returned to Ireland in 1906 to edit the *Irish Peasant,* published by John Mac Cann at Navan. When the socialist tone of Ryan's editorship displeased Cardinal Logue, he suppressed the paper. Ryan, however, took over the paper and published it in Dublin as *The Peasant* in 1907. Returning to London in 1910, he was deeply involved in socialist and nationalist circles and was active in the Gaelic League. His son, Desmond, was among the first pupils at Sgoil Éanna and became a close friend and confidant of Pearse. In *The Pope's Green Island* (1912), W. P. Ryan pays tribute to the educational work of Pearse in a chapter entitled "The Hero in the College". He wrote extensively in Irish and English; his major works in the history of Irish socialism were *The Labour Revolt and Larkinism* (1913) and *The Irish Labour Movement* (1919). His earlier works included *The Irish Literary Revival* (1894), *Plays for the People* (1904) and *The Heart of Tipperary* (1893).

STARKIE, WILLIAM J. M., was born in Sligo on December 10th, 1860, the fifth son of William Robert Starkie of Cregare Manor, Roscarbery, Co. Cork. After a brief spell at Clongowes Wood College in 1876, he went to Shrewsbury and became the first Catholic head boy in that English public school since the Reformation. He had a brilliant academic career at Cambridge where he won various scholarships at Trinity and took a first class in the Tripos. Proceeding to Trinity College, Dublin, he obtained further distinctions and having won fellowship in 1890, he lectured in the classics. The works of Aristophanes were his special field of interest and he edited in turn, *The Wasps* (1897), *The Archanians* (1909) and *The Clouds* (1911).

In 1897, he was appointed President of Queen's College, Galway and in February 1899 he was invited by the Lord Lieutenant, Lord Cadogan, to accept the position of Resident Commissioner of National Education even though he had not applied for the position. The Belmore Commission (1898) envisaged fundamental reforms in the curriculum and organisation of the national schools and it was felt that the energetic dedication of Starkie was required to implement the new measures.

He promptly applied his unique ability to the problems of the educational system and between 1899 and 1920 his various attempted reforms were informed by a desire to improve the quality and extend the range of Irish education and to promote the concept of popular democratic control of a coordinated system. He was outspoken and dauntless in the analysis which he offered, his two major public statements on Irish education, that to the British Association in Belfast in 1902 and at Queen's University in 1911 promoted widespread controversy. The early speech was instrumental in prompting the Catholic Hierarchy to found the Catholic Clerical Managers Association in 1903, while both speeches outline the policies which were officially pursued in the first two decades of the century.

The period of Starkie's involvement with the educational system was a period of reform, initiative, of Royal Commissions and Educational Bills to improve the position of lay teachers and of public debate of educational issues. His death in July 1920 deprived the educational system of a unique combination of diligence, initiative, frankness and a lack of self-interest. While the national teachers by 1913 had come to distrust him, the secondary teachers had found in him an eternal ally in their quest for fair salary and secure conditions, while the Gaelic League was happy with his constructive and positive attitude to Irish in the curriculum.

WALSH, REV. DR. W. J. (1841–1921), Catholic Archbishop of Dublin from 1885, having been Professor of Theology, Vice-President and President of St. Patrick's College, Maynooth. Born in Dublin he was educated at the Catholic University during Newman's active phase there. From his early Maynooth days he took a special interest in educational developments; he initiated the Catholic Headmasters Association and was a major force in the extension and development of secondary education. He played a prominent part in the extended debate on University education and exercised a determinant influence on the 1908 Act through his friendship with Augustine Birrell. He became the first Chancellor of the National University, was a Commissioner of National and Intermediate Education, chaired the final session and signed the Report of the Belmore Commission (1898) which set out to reform the curriculum and organisation of the National Schools. He was a staunch and active supporter of the Gaelic League, whose policy on Bilingualism he actively advocated. He and Pearse corresponded extensively on Gaelic League and Sgoil Éanna business.

WILSON, ALEX, of Belvoir Park, Belfast, was a prominent chartered accountant who was very active in An Craobh Ruadh branch of the League in Belfast with its headquarters at 27 Queen's St. The Belfast branch attracted members from a wide range of occupational and political backgrounds; it included amongst others, Peadar Mac Fhionnlaoigh, Alex Wilson, Cathal Ó Shannon, Carl Hardebeck, Liam Leydon and Margaret Hutton. Wilson was a

464

staunch advocate of linking industrial and economic development with cultural revival; he contributed an article "The Industrial Movement in Ireland" to An *Craobh Ruadh* in 1913, which was illustrated with the logos which later became so prominent, a large e and the slogan "Déanta in Éirinn".

Wilson's support for Sgoil Éanna revealed itself not only in the generous financial investment which he made but also in the expertise and financial advice which he placed at Pearse's disposal. From 1911 he acted as accountant and adviser to Pearse and drew up the various strategies which enabled Pearse to survive the severe crises in the finances of the school. When in 1911 a limited liability company was formed to manage Sgoil Éanna, Alex Wilson contributed £300 and on the dissolution of the company in 1912, he gave Pearse a further gift of £300 with which to pay the outstanding creditors.

Alex Wilson was one of the speakers invited with W. B. Yeats, Pearse and F. J. Bigger at the Davis Centenary meeting organised by the Gaelic Society of Dublin University in November 1914; this was the meeting which was banned by Mahaffy, the University Vice-Provost, and which was eventually held in the Ancient Concert Rooms on November 17th. The Gaelic Society was suppressed as a College Society by the Board and was not revived until the 1930's.

YEATS, WILLIAM BUTLER (1865–1939). Born in Dublin, the eldest son of John Butler Yeats and Susan Pollexfen, attended school in London and the High School in Dublin on the return of the family in 1880. He studied art at the Metropolitan School and at the R.H.A. Influenced by George Russell. John O'Leary and Standish O'Grady he decided to concentrate on writing and to utilise Irish themes. In London he was prominent among the poets of his day at the Rhymers' Club and in the Irish Literary Society which he founded in 1891. He was a key figure with Lady Gregory and Miss Horniman in the foundation of the Abbey Theatre in 1904. He was a supporter of the Gaelic League and of the educational work of Pearse, whom he compared to his friend, Rabindranath Tagore, in India. He was a frequent visitor to Sgoil Éanna, at the dramatic presentations and on prize days. His earliest works include *The Wanderings of Oisin* (1889), *The Countess Cathleen*, a poetic play (1892), *The Celtic Twilight* (1893) *A Book of Irish Verse* (1895) and *Poems* (1895). His *Cathleen Ni Houlihan* (1902) was written especially for Maud Gonne (Mac Bride). His later poetical and dramatic works include, *The Green Helmet and other Poems* (1910), *Responsibilities* (1914), the four Noh plays for Dancers; *The Wild Swans at Coole* (1919), *Michael Robartes and* the Dancer (1921). *The Tower* (1928) and *The Winding Stair* (1933). His *Collected Poems* were published in 1933 and the *Collected Plays* in 1934. His autobiography appeared in three volumes, *Reveries over Childhood and Youth* (1915), *The Trembling of the Veil* (1922) and *Dramatis Personae*. He is buried in Drumcliffe Churchyard, Co. Sligo. He attributed the origin of the Irish literary revival to Standish James O'Grady, who, according to Yeats, "started us all off".

APPENDIX III

The Gaelic League

The Gaelic League was founded on July 31st, 1893, by a small group among whom Douglas Hyde, Eoin Mac Neill, Fr. E. Ó Growney and T. O'Neill Russell were the prominent personalities. Like its predecessors, the Ossianic Society (1853), the Society for the Preservation of the Irish Language (1877) and the Gaelic Union (1879), the Gaelic League sought to preserve the Irish language as the national language of the country. But unlike the earlier societies, the League emphasised the spoken language and its extension by means of the formal educational system and by the teaching of the language in its own branches. The League also sought to promote the study of the existing literature in Irish and the creation and cultivation of a modern literature in the language. Explicitly, the Gaelic League, envisaged the restoration of the Irish Language as fundamental to the preservation and development of a national identity.

The League was much more than a language revival organisation; it offered Irish cultural separatism a rational, intellectual basis and was a most potent factor in the creation of the new and urgent nationalism which paved the way for political independence.

The organisational unit of the League was the local branch (or craobh), based on either parish or town and sending representatives to a county or district Committee (Coiste Cheantair). The annual Ard-Fheis which was attended by elected representatives of each Coiste Cheantair, decided policy and elected the officers of the National Executive Committee or Coiste Gnótha. This central executive body was the effective nerve-centre of the Gaelic League and created a number of subordinate committees whose functions related to such activities as Education, Publications and the Oireachtas, the annual cultural festival of the League. From its foundation the League had strong links with similar organisations such as the Cymroddorion Society in Wales and An Cumann

467

Gaelach in Scotland; it sent fraternal delegations to the Eisteddfod in Wales and An Mod in Scotland.

Like similar organisations elsewhere in Europe, The Gaelic League placed special emphasis on popular or non-formal education by means of weekly meetings, newspapers and pamphlets. *An Claidheamh Soluis* was the League's celebrated bilingual weekly, which under the editorship of Pearse (1903–1909) became a most influential journal. The League's first president Dr. Douglas Hyde, testifying before the Royal Commission of 1898 on Intermediate Education, described the work of the Gaelic League as "establishing a university for the people". The League's main instructional strategies in that popular university were, its bilingual weekly, the annual cultural festival, in-service courses for teachers, its itinerant teachers and organisers, and the torrent of pamphlets and scholarly publications which its Publications Committee produced.

Its list of authors included such diverse personalities as Professor Eoghan Ó Gramhnaigh of Maynooth, Professor Micheal O'Hickey who succeeded Ó Gramhnaigh in 1896 and was dismissed from the Chair of Irish in Maynooth in 1909 for defending the League's case for essential Irish in the National University, Dr. Douglas Hyde, son of a Church of Ireland Rector and first President of Ireland, An tAthair Peadar Ó Laoghaire, Canon J. O. Hannay, Rector of Westport better known under the pseudonym George A. Birmingham, Eoin Mac Neill, Professor in the National University and Minister of Education in the Free State Cabinet 1922–1925, Dr. W. J. Walsh, Archbishop of Dublin, Peadar Mac Fhionlaoigh and J. J. Doyle of the Excise and Inland Revenue, Edward Martyn, Padraig Ó Siochfhradha, Úna Ní Fhaircheallaigh, Mary Hayden, Pádraig Ó Conaire, Cathal Ó Shannon, Seán Lester, Carl Hardebeck, Michael Mac Ruadhraí (the gardener of Sgoil Éanna), Professor J. Strachan of Manchester University, J. H. Lloyd, Ernest Joynt, Tadhg Ó Donnchadha of University College, Cork, P. H. Pearse, An tAthair P. S. Ó Duinín the noted lexicographer, Fr. John Myles O'Reilly who preached at the O'Growney funeral at Maynooth 1904 and Professor Stanley Lane-Poole of Oxford a self styled Unionist and irreclaimable Tory. In its campaign for Irish in the educational system, the Gaelic League published both the views of its opponents in Ireland as well as those of European scholars who supported its case. Thus while the League offered its pages to Drs. Mahaffy, Atkinson and Bernard of Trinity College, to Fr. Delany S. J. of University College and other opponents of Irish, it also called upon the contrary published evidence of such noted scholars as Stern of Berlin, Windisch of Leipzig, Dottin of Rennes, Zimmer of Greifswald, Pedersen of Copenhagen, York Powell of Oxford and Kuno Meyer of Liverpool. The wide appeal of the Gaelic League is also reflected in the geographical spread of its membership; there were branches in Glasgow, London, Paris, Louvain, Chicago, Boston, New York, Rome and Buenos Aires. In effect the Gaelic League epitomised the cultural and political revival which characterised Irish life in the first decades of this century.

APPENDIX IV

Other Letters—Late Arrivals

To Éamonn Ceannt.

Following his visit to Belgium in 1905, Pearse was convinced of the effectiveness of the Direct Method in language teaching and of the need to provide Irish teachers with pedagogic manuals based upon the method. During 1907–08 he wrote a series of illustrated lessons for *An Claidheamh Soluis* and these he later compiled to form Part 1 of *An Sgoil*, a manual for teachers which was published by Maunsel in January 1913. This volume was the first of a series of textbooks in Irish which he planned for Irish schools; it was possibly the first textbook in Irish to have coloured illustrations. His own *Íosagán* (1907) contained illustrations in colour.

It is most likely that *An Sgoil* is the subject of this postcard to Éamonn Ceannt; the latter had probably complimented Pearse on the reception given to the volume. Pearse seems to have set aside his usual measure of modesty in his claims for his own publication. The reference to a car may concern some means of transport which Ceannt had procured for a school outing, a Gaelic League occasion or the St. Enda's Fete in Croke Park.

Éamonn Ceannt's son, Ronán, was a pupil at St. Enda's from 1913 onwards.

L.(p.c.) 435/P.Ms./G.

11.7.1913.

Thank you very much. It is the only book in Irish of its kind which has coloured illustrations and very few (if any) books in any language, contain as many coloured pictures. It is the most complete and comprehensive written in any language on the Direct Method.

Many thanks in connection with the car.

Your son will be welcome.

Greetings.

P. Mac P.

To Mr. Henehan (Seattle).

The recipient of these two letters from Pearse was an Irish-speaking emigrant from Co. Galway living in Seattle who wished that his son, Kevin, should learn the language. The boy had accompanied his mother on a European holiday, at the end of which his father had enrolled him at St. Enda's. It would appear that towards the end of his first term at school while his mother was preparing to return across the Atlantic, the boy showed signs of homesickness and loneliness. Pearse's appeals to Mr. Henehan in these two letters show a keen understanding of child psychology and a determination to persuade the father to keep the boy at St. Enda's, which latter was as much due to the aim of making him an Irish-speaker as it was with the related critical gain to the finances of his school.

L. 436/U.C.G.

17.10.1910.

Dear Mr. Henehan,

I was about to write to you to say that Kevin has settled down to work very fairly, seems happy and content, and is very satisfactory in his general conduct. Mrs. Henehan, who has just been here, has, however, told me that Kevin has written to you that he feels lonely and homesick, and that you are seriously considering whether it would not be better for him to return home with his mother. This at first surprised and put me out very much, but after talking the matter over with Mrs. Henehan and later with Kevin himself, I see that what has happened is that you and Mrs. Henehan have simply attached too much importance to the natural expressions of homesickness which find a place in every boy's letters – during his first month or two at a boarding school. Kevin is not lonely and not unhappy; he enjoys to the full every moment in the day, and while he is never rude or bold, he is decidedly among the more lively and boisterous spirits in the school. Every boy and master would instinctively rank Kevin Henehan among the half-dozen boys who

471

play, shout and enjoy themselves the most vigorously. At the same time, he has the natural yearning for home which is in every good boy's heart, and it would be a very bad sign in a boy if this were absent. it would show that there was something wrong either with the boy himself or with his home. Believe me, there is nothing in Kevin's case but this very natural and very creditable softness when he thinks of his home. It would be deplorable if you were to think of abandoning your plan of giving him one year at least in an Irish school. Now that he has come 6,000 or 7,000 miles to be taught Irish and Irish history it would be simply disastrous for him to go home before his work is well begun. In after years he would himself bitterly regret the lost opportunity. As well as the disappointment to yourself and us, it would be bad for the boy's own character to allow the softer side of his nature thus, at the first temptation, to gain the mastery over the manlier side. I have just had a long talk with Kevin himself and I think he now sees the matter from this point of view. I beg of you to give us and him a fair chance. I do not promise that he will be an Irish speaker in a year, but I do promise that he will have gained a very fair conversational knowledge of Irish. The opportunity will not recur again; in God's name let him stay now that he is here. By December next, when his mother will have returned from the continent, he will probably have settled down better, and I have no doubt will have made up his mind to remain contentedly till the end of the school year. I will write you again as to how he is getting on.

Believe me, sincerely yours.
P. H. Pearse.

L. 437/U.C.G.

15.11.1910.

Dear Mr. Henehan.

Yours of the 1st. inst. just to hand. I am sorry for your decision. Kevin is losing a tremendous opportunity. In my last letter I said that I could not guarantee that he would be an Irish speaker in June, but that I could guarantee that we would have laid a very good foundation of conversational Irish. I can now go much further. I have since been giving special time and attention to Kevin and I can now promise you that if he remains till June he will be *an Irish speaker* in a very real sense. Is not this something worth sacrificing a little for? I put it to you in the strongest way I can that it is your duty to him to let him remain; that you and he will be proud when he returns in June next *able to converse with you all day in Irish* – as he will. Apart from this, you will do a permanent injury to the

472

boy's character if you do not help him to fight his first temptation. I assure you honestly that he is happy here all the time and that his homesickness is purely due to his knowledge that his mother is near and will soon be returning without him. Once his mother sails he will settle down as contentedly as possible till June, which after all will only be five or six months off. I need not labour the matter further. As I have said, I will make an Irish speaker of him if you leave him till June. Never again will he have such an opportunity. Later on he will be less plastic. I would ask you to write or if necessary cable to say that Kevin may stay till June, *if I succeed (as I think I can) in winning his free consent to stay.*

Sincerely yours,
P. H. Pearse.

To An Cumann Gaedhealach, Harlem, New York.

Following on Pearse's American visit in 1914, various Irish–American organisations raised funds to support St. Enda's; the contribution of one such organisation, The Irish Society, Harlem, New York, is the subject of this letter. It would appear that Pearse had already received $20 from this society during his visit in the spring.

This letter was presented by Mr. Cyril J. Cushing of 506 Michigan Avenue, Ronkonkoma, New York to President de Valera who arranged that it be donated for display in the museum at St. Enda's.

The cryptic short sentence referring to guns, faithfully reflects the heightened political situation obtaining in the summer of 1914, deriving from the impending split in the Volunteers and the approaching European war.

L. 438/O.P.W./G.

16.6.1914.

Dear Friend,

I received today the money which you sent me from The Irish Society, Harlem, to amount $8.50. I wish to tender to you and to the members of the Society my heartfelt gratitude. Please convey my appreciation and gratitude to them and that I wish them prosperity and long life.

I will acknowledge the total received $28.50 from the Irish

Society, Harlem in the *Gaelic American* and other papers within a few weeks. I trust that your Feis is a great success.

The main topic of conversation in Ireland at the moment concerns guns. Please accept my best wishes for the success of the Harlem Irish Society.

      Yours for ever,
          Pádraig Mac Piarais.

To the Rev. Administrator, Marlboro St.

This note was sent by Pearse to the Presbytery of the Pro-Cathedral in Marlboro St. on the first day of the Rising, Easter Monday. A priest of the Pro-Cathedral parish, Fr. Flanagan, responded to Pearse's request and during his visit to the G.P.O. wrote down messages from some of the volunteers for their families. These messages and this note were preserved by Fr. Flanagan.

L. 439/NLI.
24.4.1916.   Army of the Irish Republic
                               (Dublin Command)

To Rev. Administrator or other Priest, Marlboro St.
      Please send a priest to the G.P.O. to remain an hour or two and hear the confessions of some men.
          P. H. Pearse.
          Commandant General.

To Seán Heuston.

This mobilisation order issued by Pearse was part of the initial plans prepared for Easter Sunday afternoon and is similar in wording and detail to that issued to Frank Sheridan of Rathfarnham on the same day and included in this volume as L.413. The order is on a standard Volunteer printed form and the words underlined here were entered in Pearse's hand. Heuston's role in the Rising was strategically important and singularly heroic; he was in charge of a small garrison occupying the Mendicity Institute on the southern banks of the Liffey whose specific task was to hold up the advance of British troops on the Four Courts and the G.P.O. area for a number of hours. Two days after the outbreak of hostilities, his tiny garrison of twenty six was still resisting the onslaught of about four hundred British troops; on Wednesday, April 26th, he reluctantly agreed to surrender and following his court martial on May 4th, he was executed on May 8th in Kilmainham.

L. 440/P.Ms.

20.4.1916.

Irish Volunteers.   COMPANY MOBILISATION ORDER.
DUBLIN BRIGADE.

Your Coy., ...H.Q... Batt., will Mobilise on Easter Sunday

at the hour of ...4... p.m.

Point of Mobilisation ......Beresford Place.......
Full Service Equipment to be worn, including overcoat, haversack, water-bottle, canteen, full arms and ammunition.

Rations for ......eight...... hours to be carried

Cycle Scouts to be mounted, and ALL men having cycles or motor cycles to bring them.
.................P. H. Pearse.................
Captain or Officer Commanding.
Dated this ...20th..... day of ......April...... 1916

To Miss E. Butler.

Having signed the lease of the Hermitage on July 15th 1910, Pearse set about immediately making arrangements for the girls' school Sgoil Íde, which he proposed to open in Cullenswood House on Oakley Road. In his initial discussions it would seem that he considered Miss Louise Gavan Duffy and Miss Eleanor Butler as potential Head mistresses for the new school; both were experienced teachers and would have coincided generally in their views with his own position on cultural and educational questions. His choice eventually favoured Mrs. Gertrude Bloomer, a gifted musician from Derry, who may have met Willie Pearse in the artistic circles of London and who was also a close friend of Thomas Mac Donagh's. Miss Butler's involvement as Headmistress was precluded by the fact that she was an examiner for the Commissioners of Intermediate Education and as such was forbidden to teach in any school whose pupils entered for the Intermediate examinations.

In this letter, Pearse explains with tact and diplomacy how the

475

earlier circular on the school drafted by Miss Butler was superseded by that drafted by Mrs. Bloomer.

L. 441/P.Ms.

21.7.1910.   Gortmore,
                                        Maam Cross,
                                        Co. Galway.

Dear Miss Butler,
   I should have written to you sooner, but it is only within the last few days I have had any thing really definite to report to you. First, I owe you an apology about that draft circular. I laid it on the table in the drawingroom when you gave it to me, but on going to look for it the second next day I found it had disappeared. Some visitors had been entertained in the drawingroom, and the circular had doubtless been swept aside to make room for tea things on the table. However, in the meantime, Mrs. Bloomer had drafted a circular in her and my names; and, as your draft spoke eulogisti-cally of St. Enda's School, it was, under the new arrangement, no longer suitable for inclusion in the circular, since I was to sign the circular and it would hardly do for me to pay warm tributes of admiration to my own work. On your withdrawing from the scheme in the capacity of Head Mistress, we decided on a complete re-arrangement of our plans. I am to be Director and to take the chief responsibility, financial and otherwise. Mrs. Bloomer is to be House Mistress, and we have just engaged Miss Cotter as Assistant Resident Mistress. Miss Maguire is to be a full-time Assistant Mistress, but not resident. I hope we may include your name as another visiting mistress. I am sending advts. to next week's Irish Ireland weeklies and this is how I propose to word them:

     St. Ita's School
   Cullenswood House, Rathmines, Dublin.
   A Boarding and Day School for Catholic Girls
     (in association with St. Enda's School Rathfarnham)
Director – P. H. Pearse, B.A., Barrister-at-Law (Head Master of St. Enda's)
House Mistress – Mrs. Bloomer.
Assistant Resident Mistress – Miss Mary Cotter, B.A.
                            ex. Sch. R.U.I., Teaching Certif. Camb.
Assistant Mistresses – Miss Lena Butler, M.A.
                     Miss Mary Maguire, B.A.

Then will follow a short par. describing the aims of the school. What do you think of this wording and of the way in which your name is introduced? If you have any objection, you might kindly write by return, as I must post the advts. from here on Saturday, if they are to be in time for next week's papers. When you have time you might please let me know how many hours a week you think you could give, what subjects you would like to take, and what your terms would be.

Sincerely yours.

P. H. Pearse.

To Miss E. Butler.

While still in Connemara, Pearse was finalising the publicity arrangements for Scoil Íde and on hearing from Miss Butler indicating her support he feels satisfied that the girls' school would be assured of success.

L. 442/P.Ms.

27.7.1910.

Gortmore,
Maam Cross,
Co. Galway.

Dear Miss Butler,

Very many thanks for your letter of the 22nd., which reached me in excellent time. I duly sent off advt., which should appear in to-morrow's Irish Ireland weeklies. I think we have got a really admirable staff, and that St. Ita's will at any rate deserve to succeed.

Sincerely yours,

P. H. Pearse.

To Canon Arthur Ryan (?).

Although there is no direct indication, yet the internal evidence in this letter would seem to suggest that it was written to Canon Arthur Ryan, Co. Tipperary, a close friend, who wished to have Pearse's pageant on Cúchulainn as part of the Gaelic League annual Feis in his parish in July 1910. Having explained to him why that was not possible due to the long vacation, Pearse discusses his contemplated move to Rathfarnham and the associated financial

477

implications and concludes by inviting Canon Ryan to become a member of the Board of St. Enda's.

The letter is important in two respects; it shows that Pearse in his move to Rathfarnham had assessed the arrangements with a realistic eye to his financial commitments. It is also significant in that it clearly shows that he had plans for an American fund-raising tour in conjunction with Shane Leslie, three years before he actually undertook such a trip. This letter also indicated how the Hermitage satisfied Pearse's criteria for his ideal school environment and it is of interest that he compares it with two of the most prestigious Catholic boarding colleges of the day, Castleknock and Clongowes.

L. 443/P.Ms.

2.5.1910.   Sgoil Éanna,
                                               Rathmines.

A Chara,
Many thanks for your letter. First about the Pageant. You must not have adverted to the fact that our pupils will be scattered to the four ends of Ireland by July 3rd. We break up immediately after the exams., on 23rd. June at latest. There would be no chance of keeping the boys together after that date. Only for this I would gladly have performed the pageant, big and troublesome as the undertaking would have been. The rehearsing at this busy time of the year would have been awkward, but I would cheerfully have faced that and more, first, to oblige you, secondly because it undoubtedly would have been a good advertisement for us, and thirdly because the boys would have enjoyed the adventure. The more I think about it the more disappointed I am that we are not able to do it. But some of the chief actors will be in Connemara, some in Waterford, some in Belfast, and so on. They could not be brought together without considerable expense. I take it that your Committee would scarcely face the expense of bringing even the chief actors up from their homes? But I fear the Pageant would not be a success unless we had *all* our boys. It would need much rehearsing if even the non-speaking parts were to be done by boys on the spot, and how could such rehearsals be arranged? I suppose the date of the Feis is absolutely fixed for July 3rd? If it were before June 13th. or after Sept. 6th. you could count on us.

About the other matter. I have weighed everything, and think it is best to make a move, if I can. This place is already too small. If we grow next year as we have grown this year there will be no room for the boarders. We shall have to rent another house which will be

478

objectionable in many ways, and will make our rent here equal to that of the new place. At present we are paying £125 a year. The new place will mean £175 in addition. But as a set-off against this the land there is worth £100 a year, and by other economies, which will be possible, we can wipe out the odd £75. Thus the net burden will be no heavier. True, we stand to lose most of our day-boys. But against this, I believe that some of our best day-boys will come to us as boarders; that others will be able to cycle or tram out (the place is only ½ mile beyond Rathfarnham); and that we shall get a certain number of new dayboys there. Moreover, we are convinced that we could do far better work if we had more boarders and fewer day-boys. The latter interfere with our work at many points. The school would be more Irish and more efficient generally without, at any rate, the younger day-boys.

I don't think myself that £10,000 will come in, for the present at any rate. But we may get enough to go ahead with. Shane Leslie and I have arranged to go to America in a year or two on a lecturing tour on behalf of the School. We can complete the purchase then. For the present we might rent, with the option of purchasing later. The place is very beautiful, and in many ways extraordinarily suitable. There are woods, a little lake, an old hermitage, a cromlech, an ogham stone, on the land. An ideal place for such a school. We should be on a level with Clongowes or Castleknock as regards housing and surroundings. I feel that if we are to hold our own we must offer boys as beautiful a home, as much room, as much fresh air, as much accommodation for games, as they get in the other places. I would raise the fees a little, but not much, on going to this new place.

Of course, everything must be conditioned by the amount of support I get in answer to this appeal. I may not be able to go on at all. But I should like, at any rate, to have your name in this preliminary appeal as one willing to go on the Board of Governors should the scheme proceed. Please drop me a line giving your consent, if you feel you can do so. I want to print the circular off on Wednesday.

Mise do chara go buan,
Pádraig Mac Piarais.

To Willie Pearse.

This postcard to Willie from New York carried a photograph of the St. Enda's football team; it was one of the set of bilingual postcards

479

which Pearse published, based on the school grounds and on the dramatic and sporting achievements of the pupils. He had sailed from Cobh on February 8th and arrived in New York on the 17th; he had written to his mother from the s.s. *Campania* just prior to sailing and had written to Willie on the 17th as they approached New York. This postcard was written a few days after landing to inform his family of the address in New York which was to be his base during his three months in the States.

L.(p.c.) 444/P.Ms.

20.2.1914.   New York.

> My address is
>   c/o J. McKenna,
>   517 West 144th. Street,
>   New York City,
>   U.S.A.

> Am well. Write.
>   P.

To Mr. Johnston.

The following five letters (i.e. L.445–L.449 inclusive), were written in 1910 to a senior administrator in the Hume St. Office of the Commissioners of Intermediate Education, concerning different aspects of St. Enda's; they were rediscovered recently in the Department of Education. The Editor is very grateful to Mr. John Wilson, T.D., Minister for Education and to Mr. Liam Ó Laidhin, Secretary of the Department for facilitating access to these letters and for permitting their inclusion in this volume.

Mr. Swift Paine Johnston was Assistant Commissioner of Intermediate Education and as such was ultimately responsible for such items of educational administration as the examinations of the Board, the appointment of superintendents and the payment of various grants to schools.

This letter concerns Pearse's application to the Board for an advance of £300 against the grants to which the school was entitled; such advances were frequently sought by secondary schools. He had built a new science laboratory in Cullenswood House in the school year 1909/10 and the advance of £300 was intended to cover the cost of that extension.

25.1.1910.   St. Enda's School,
                                    Cullenswood House,
                                    Rathmines,
                                    Dublin.

Dear Mr. Johnston,

I now enclose Form of Application for Advance with the names of two new sureties who are not examiners to your Board and who will, I feel sure, be entirely acceptable. Both of them have already shown a practical interest in our School and I preferred to ask them to give me their names than to apply to comparative strangers.

As I mentioned to you in conversation, the liability which I want this advance to cover was incurred on the understanding that your Board had funds available for such purposes, and it remains undischarged. The builders expect payment early in March the laboratory furnishers in February, and for this reason I am hoping that you will be able to get the matter completed at your February meeting.

With many thanks for your great courtesy and helpfulness.

      I am, dear Mr. Johnston,
         Yours very truly.
         P. H. Pearse.

To Mr. Johnston.

In this letter, Pearse is supporting the application by Thomas Mac Donagh for appointment as a superintendent at the summer examinations of the Board. Before he came to St. Enda's in 1908 Mac Donagh had been a secondary teacher in St. Colman's College, Fermoy and at Rockwell College, Cashel. He secured the appointment in 1910 and acted as superintendent in Coleraine.

L. 446/P.R.O.

11.4.1910.   St Enda's School,
                                    Cullenswood House,
                                    Rathmines.

Dear Mr. Johnston,

Mr. Thomas Mac Donagh, our Second Master at St. Enda's, is applying for an Intermediate Superintendentship this year. He acted as Superintendent for five years and was re-appointed last year, but as he found he would be otherwise engaged during the examination weeks, he gave notice of inability to act before he was assigned to a centre. he is now applying again for the present year, as he will be able to act, and I hope the Board will re-appoint him. It is not a case of a new man but of one who has already given good service.

> I am, dear Mr. Johnston,
> Yours sincerely,
> P.H.Pearse.

To Mr. Johnston.

It would appear that relations between Johnston and Pearse were cordial; his two requests to the Board were granted. Mac Donagh was studying for his B.A. degree while teaching at St. Enda's; it would appear that the requirements for his course were altered by the changes associated with the 1908 Act establishing the National University of Ireland.

L. 447/P.R.O.

16.4.1910
St. Enda's School,
Cullenswood House,
Rathmines.

Dear Mr. Johnston,

I duly received cheque £300 last night and enclose formal receipt with very many thanks. This advance will smooth things very much for us.

I was much obliged for your reply to my letter about Mr. Mac Donagh and the superintendentship. I hope you will have a chance to nominate him. It is rather hard luck for him. He dropped out last year in order to attend a University examination. Of course he passed the examination, but now finds that the passing of it was unnecessary to his purpose, owing to new conditions brought about by the University Act!

> Again thanking you for your many courtesies,
> Sincerely yours,
> P.H.Pearse.

To Mr. Johnston.

Denis Gwynn was one of Pearse's first pupils and had left Clongowes Wood College in 1908 to come to Cullenswood House. He entered for Senior Grade in 1910 and through some misunderstanding of the rules did not sit for a second subject in the Mathematics division; this deprived him of the exhibition to which his general results and excellence entitled him. His own disappointment and Pearse's chagrin were happily turned to joy when Gwynn was awarded the first open Classical Scholarship in University College Dublin 1910.

This matter is also the subject of Pearse's letter to Mrs. Gwynn of the following day 17.8.1910.

L. 448/P.R.O.

16.8.1910.   St. Enda's School,
                                         Cullenswood House,
                                         Rathmines.

Dear Mr. Johnston,

I enclose a letter re the case of Gwynn, which you might kindly lay before the Board at the *next* meeting – the meeting which decides about exhibitions, prizes etc. I am hoping that there may be some way out of the difficulty, that, in so very special a case, the Board may give the boy and the School credit for their year's work. The winning of an exhibition in Senior Grade in our first year would have made the reputation of the School. Great, however, as is my disappointment on this score I am still more concerned for the poor boy himself and for Mr. and Mrs. Gwynn. Their faith in the school was splendid – they took the boy from Clongowes to send him to us – and after all our hard work, all our expense, we have allowed him to fail on a technicality!

Could an extra exhibition not be given? Or, if this is impossible, could not the boy get the credit of whatever distinctions he has won, even if the exhibition etc. be not paid over? I care nothing about the results fees.

Sincerely yours.
P.H.Pearse.

To Mr. Johnston.

Pearse in this letter shows a determination and a persistence in
483

fighting Gwynn's case with the Board of Intermediate Education; his appeals however were to no avail. While Johnston may have been favourably disposed, the Board was not inclined to create a precedent.

L. 449/P.R.O.

20.8.1910   St. Enda's School,
                                             Cullenswood House,
                                             Rathmines.

Dear Mr. Johnston,

Since I wrote you about young Gwynn's case I have got at the facts. I find that he acted in consultation with one of my assistant-masters and that the rules justify his reading, – viz. that when the Honours course is taken in one mathematical subject a pass may be obtained in Mathematics without taking a second mathematical subject. It is not therefore a case of asking special treatment for Gwynn; he is clearly entitled to a pass, and to whatever distinctions he may have now, inasmuch as he has fulfilled all the conditions laid down by the rules. I am preparing a statement for submission to the Board. I am quite convinced that the rules are open to this interpretation – indeed that it is the natural interpretation – and will, needless to say, fight the case to the last ditch; but I dont think it will be a case of fighting, as the Board must admit the reasonableness of our reading. I may call on you at the office to-morrow, when I hope it will be convenient for you to see me.
                    I am, dear Mr. Johnston,
                         Sincerely Yours,
                         P.H.Pearse.

A Circular.

This letter, signed by Pearse and his friend, Éamonn (Edward) O'Neill, was circulated in the autumn of 1896 prior to the foundation of the New Ireland Literary Society. The Society during the two years of its existence held its meetings in the Star and Garter Hotel. An original copy of this circular is on display in the Museum at St. Enda's.

Star and Garter Hotel,
D'Olier St., Dublin.

Sir,

It is an inexplicable fact that Dublin, which must necessarily contain many young men of ability and culture, should possess fewer literary and debating societies than any city of equal importance in Great Britain. In view of this, it is contemplated to establish a new literary and debating society, of a high-class, yet popular, nature; and we, on behalf of those who have initiated the project, beg to request your presence at a meeting which will be held in the Star and Garter Hotel, D'Olier Street, on Tuesday next, December 1st, at 7.30 p.m.

To dilate on the usefulness of a really good and well managed literary society is needless, as there can be no two opinions respecting it.

It is confidently expected, then, that you will see your way to co-operate; and that the new society will be in full working order in the course of a few weeks.

EDWARD O'NEILL
PATRICK H. PEARSE.

The following letters, (L. 450–L. 457 inclusive), from the W. P. Ryan and D. Ryan papers became available when this volume was in the later stages of production. I am deeply indebted to the Archives Committee of University College, Dublin and to Professor Patrick Lynch for permission to include them in this volume. I wish to thank Professor Dudley Edwards and Mr. S. Helferty for facilitating my access to these papers.

To D. Ryan

L. 450/U.C.D.

11.8.1912.   Sgoil Eanna,
                                    Rath Fearnáin.

A Dheasmhumha na gCarad,
   Bhíos\ag fanacht agus ag fanacht go mbeadh sgéal maith agam le cur chugat, acht fairíor, níl aon sgéal maith agam go fóill. Ní bhfuaireamar an t-airgead úd fós. Níl acht aon seans amháin againn anois .i. go n-aontóchaidh gach éinne a bhfuil airgead aca orainn glacadh le beagán de anois agus bliadhain do thabhairt dúinn leis an gcuid eile d'íoc. Muna féidir an méid sin do shocrughadh taobh istigh de sheachtmhain nó mar sin tá deireadh linn. Cuir t'ainm leis an litir so istigh led' thoil agus seol chugam i le *filleadh an phosta*. Caithfidh gach éinne teacht isteach san socrughadh nó ní bheidh aon bhrígh ann.
   Tabhair mo bheannacht dod' athair agus dod' mhuinntir ar fad. Tá a fhios agam go bhfuil a gcroidhthe liom. Go dtugaidh Dia go dtiocfaimíd slán fós.
        Beir míle beannacht, a chara nár chlis orm riamh.
        Mise,
                Pádraig Mac Piarais.

To W. P. Ryan

L. 451/U.C.D.

15.10.1913   St. Enda's College,
                              Rathfarnham.

A Chara,

I have written a letter, with some enclosures, and addressed them to Mr. Wilfrid Scawen Blunt c/o the Editor, *Daily Herald*, London. I can't find Mr. Blunt's address, but I imagine that the Editor of the *Herald* will know it, or be able to find it, and that he will forward the letter. Perhaps you wouldn't mind mentioning the matter to him and seeing that the letter is sent on with as little delay as possible? It is in a large envelope.

I have another, and somewhat absurd, favour to ask you. If I can at all manage it I will go to America either before or after Christmas to lecture and collect for St. Enda's. It seems the only chance of placing the school on a sound financial basis; and it is only a chance. I am told that it is absolutely necessary to get myself "boomed" in the American and Irish-American papers beforehand, and that they will probably print any well-written matter that is sent on to them about me or about St. Enda's. Well, could you supply a sketch somewhat on the lines of the chapter about St. Enda's in *The Pope's Green Island*. That chapter itself would almost do, but it should not go as an extract from a book, – especially *that* book, for reasons which you will understand. Just a special article – what they call in America a "feature story" – over your name. I could get it typed and sent to two or three papers. I am using one or two of Desmond's articles for a similar purpose. They will gather the impression in America that I am a most interesting character!

We are looking forward to seeing Desmond again next week.

We have at least as many boys as last year, but it is a struggle all the time.

It is cruel to ask one so busy as you to do this article; but on the other hand, there is no use in asking people who are not busy to do anything. And you do this sort of thing well and generously.

Mise do chara go buan,
Pádraig Mac Piarais.

487

To W. P. Ryan
L. 452/U.C.D.

29.10.1913.   St. Enda's College,
                                     Rathfarnham.

A Chara Chroidhe,

It is very good of you to promise to do that article for the American papers. It will be in good time whenever you are a little free. Thanks very much.

Desmond seems to like the work at University College. It will get more congenial as he advances and leaves Latin and Mathematics behind. He will have Latin this first year, but not Mathematics or Natural Philosophy.

Desmond tells me you want me to send on statement of a/c. Starting from Sept. twelve-month, when he came back as a boarder, it is as enclosed. You paid me £30 .. 5s. during the year. That cleared his pension (say £30) and cleared 5/- of his book account for the year (£1 .. 2 .. 2), leaving a balance of 17/2. Then there is the first half of the current year now due, but of course you can pay this how and when you are able – I don't want you to pay it all now; last year your remittances of £5 always came very opportunely. If you think £30 a year above your resources please say so. The other university boys pay £31, but I am under special obligations to Desmond and to you, and I will gladly accept whatever pension you really feel justified in paying.

I don't know when that Anthology will appear in book form. I made a collection of early Irish pieces long ago, but the modern ones I am only selecting from month to month for the *Review*. I think I will publish the modern part first. What I am afraid of is that someone will forestall me, but I have no time to give to it. And I keep drifting more and more to politics and away from books. I feel that we of the Gaelic League generation must be ready for strong political action, leading up to *other* actions within the next few years, whether under Home Rule or in its absence.

In the meantime I have the notion of bringing out as a Christmas booklet a tiny collection of original verse in Irish, not at all political, but mainly personal and subjective!

I hope things go well with you. The "Herald" life must be exciting. The press here is simply vile. It is hard to say what will be the outcome of the labour troubles – whether good or bad for Ireland. I fear the men will suffer.

Sincerely yours,
P.H.Pearse.

To W. P. Ryan

L. 453/U.C.D.

5.8.1914   An Turlach,
Ros Muc,
Co. na Gaillimhe.

A Chara Chroidhe,
    Maith dhom fá nár chuireas an admháil so chugat roimhe so. Bhí mé an-ghnóthach ar fad. Obair mhór ar siubhal againn. Ní raibh sé ar mo chumas dul go dtí an tOireachtas.
    Beir míle buidheachas agus beannacht.
    Mise,
        Pádraig Mac Piarais.

To W. P. Ryan.

L. 454/U.C.D.

18.12.1914   Sgoil Éanna,
Rath Fearnáin.

A Chara Chroidhe,
    Táim fíor-bhuídheach dhíot as ucht do sheice. Tá admháil agam dá cur chugat annso istigh.
    Beannachta na Nodlag chugaibh ar fad.
        Mise do chara go buan.
        Pádraig mac Piarais.

P.S.   Do bhí sé so réidh agam le tabhairt do Dheasmhumhan, acht ní rabhas sa mbaile nuair d'fhág sé an teach.

To W. P. Ryan.

L. 455/U.C.D.

5.3.1915.

St. Enda's College
Rathfarnham.

A Chara,

I am enclosing statement of a/c and shall be very grateful for a cheque when you are able to spare one.

I am sure you are observing the political situation here with interest.

I am keeping myself sane by working a little at intervals at old plays and stories of mine; I am, so to speak, setting my literary affairs in order. Do you think any London publisher would consider translations of three of my plays, – *An Rí*, *Íosagán*, and a third – unpublished – one? I suppose they would hardly be in fashion at the moment.

With kindest regards to all,
Sincerely yours,
P.H.Pearse.

To W. P. Ryan.

L. 456/U.C.D.

18.3.1915.

St. Enda's College,
Rathfarnham.

A Chara Chroidhe,

Very many thanks for chq. duly to hand this morning. I enclose receipt. I know you always do your best, and your chqs. always come in handy.

I feel you are right about London publishers and my plays. I may try America, but it is hard to arrange things at so great a distance. I had not time when I was over there.

Ridiculous as it seems, I have not inquired of the publisher how that book of poems went. I don't imagine there was a large demand for it, as it was a very slender book for a shilling. There is not the same brisk sale for Irish books now that there was some years ago. Gaels are putting their money into guns.

I have a collection of short stories in Irish ready, but can get no one to publish them. Most of them are new; a few appeared in *An Claidheamh*. Some are in the *Íosagan* style and others very different.

Yes, we are having a struggle, but other interests distract my attention from St. Enda's and then it does not seem so bad. St Enda's is now only a part of a bigger thing, and that bigger thing – the Irish movement that you and I have known – is in danger of going out ingloriously; unless something terrific saves it, which may happen. The public situation is more disheartening than ever before in our time, but there is always a germ of hope.

The really difficult time for St. Enda's this year will be from Easter to Summer. Meantime I am too busy to worry much.

> With best wishes to you and yours,
> Mise do chara,
> Pádraig Mac Piarais.

To W. P. Ryan.

L. 457/U.C.D.

30.5.1915.   St. Enda's College,
                                    Rathfarnham.

A Chara Chroidhe,

Beir míle buidheachas ar son do sheice. Is baoghlach liom nár chuireas aon admháil chugat ar an tseic deiridh do chuiris chugam. Táim ag admháil an dá sheic anois mar sin. Táim fíor-bhuidheach dhíot.

Do gabhadh Sheehy Skeffington oidhche aréir mar gheall ar oráideachaibh thug sé uaidh. Táthar ag breith orainn in-ár nduine 's 'n-ár nduine. Sin triúr fear maith gabhtha le coicthighis anuas.

D'éirigh go maith leis na drámannaibh.

> Beir buaidh agus beannacht,
> Mise,
> Pádraig Mac Piarais.

The following letter is published by courtesy of the American Irish Historical Society:

Sgoil Éanna,   St. Enda's College,
Rát Fearnáin.   Rathfarnham.
                                                 12th Aug. 1915

My dear Judge,

The situation of St. Enda's makes it necessary for me to ask Mr. Garvan to fulfil the extra-ordinarily generous promise he made last year, viz., to reduplicate his gift of last year should St. Enda's still be in need this year. At such a moment I hate to intrude the claims of a semi-private concern, but my friend Mr. Plunkett will explain how the matter stands and how I feel about it. I have written Mr. Garvan. If you could see him in my interest, you would be adding one more to many kindnesses.

Give my kindest regards to all your family. Believe me, my dear Judge, Yours very sincerely, P. H. Pearse.

Hon. D. F. Cohalan.

Index to Correspondents

Note: each letter is numbered and the Index refers the reader to this number.

General Index

by letter numbers

497

500

Tagore, Rabindranath, 208, 340, *Post Office*, 208, 340
Tas, Monsignor Alfons, 294
Tawin School, 97
Tempest Press, The, Dundalk, 133, 136
Trinity College, Dublin, 7
"Tórna" (also Ó Donnchadha Tadhg), 26, 28, 40, 44, 47, 71, 81, 118
Tuar Mhic Éide, 114, 116, 376, 382

United Irish League, 100
United Irishmen, 320
University College Dublin, 28, 106, 113, 270

Wallace, Colm, (also de Bhailís, Colm), 82, 83, 128. *Cúirt an tSrutháin Bhuidhe* 82, 85, *Amhrán an Tae*, 82, 85, *An Bás*, 82, 85
War of Austrian Succession, 107
War Bulletin, 1916, 424
Walsh J., 396, 373
Walsh, Most Rev. Dr. W.J., 15, 16, 20, 23, 24, 27, 29, 35, 36, 38, 41, 43, 58, 59, 97, 126, 142, 144, 145, 149, 153, 154, 168, 169, 186, 192, 211, 219, 220, 325, 327, 386, 388. *Bilingual Education*, 23, 36
Westland Row, C.B.S., 3
Whelan, Mr., 166, 167
Whelan, James, 399, 410
White, Peter, 369
Wilde, Oscar, 18
Wilde, William Robert, 18, *Catalogue of the Contents of the Museum*, 18
Wilson Alex 267, 268, 273, 274, 275, 276, 302, 324, 325, 326, 327, 330, 331 383
Wilson W. & Co.. Solrs., 293
Windle, Bertram, 203, 267, 272, 273
Wrenn, 221, 231
Woodbyrne, Henry, 211, 221
Woodbyrne, William, 169, 182, 186, 207, 211, 221, 231, 298, 299, 303, 332

Yeats, W.B., 7, 13, 35, 79, 106, 168, 208, 340, 341. *Countess Cathleen*, 7
Yudson, W.E., 228
Young, Miss Mabel, 157

Zimmer, Prof. Heinrich, 48

An Claideaṁ Soluis.

24 Up. O'Connell Street,
DUBLIN.

24 Sráiꝺ Uaċ uí Conaill,
Baile áta Cliat,

19 = 10 = 1904

a Ċara,

Baó éaꞃꞃ ꝺaṁ (ꞃᵹníoṫuó ꞃ́ᵹaꞃ ꝼao é aᵹ ꞁṁᵱeáiꞃ ꞃꞃꞃ ᵹo ḃḟuaiꞃ ṁé "Sᵹoꞁᵹꞁaꞃ ṁaꞃ ꞃ́uᵹ 'iᵱꞃ́ꞃ", ⁊ ᵹo ᵹꞃꞃꞃ́ó ṁé i ᵹ꞊ꞁó é con ṁoꞃ ꞃ ꞁ́aꞃ ꞃ́ꞃ aᵹam ꝺó. Tá Ꞽꞃꞃꞃoꞃ opm ᵹo ṁꞃꞃ́ꞃ ꞃ́ (ᵹꞃṫam ḃeaᵹ ᵹo ṁꞃꞃ́ꞃ ꞃ́ aꞃ ṁo iṁꞃꞃoꞃ́ é a ꞁuꞃ ꞃ́ꞃeꞃꞃ́, ṁaꞃ ꞃ́ ᵹꞃ ḃoꞃ ꞃe ᵹaꞃoꞁᵹe connꞃꞃ́ᵹ aᵹam. Ꞽꞃ ꞁ́ꞃaꞃ l 'cꞃon na "ᵹᵹaḃo", ⁊ꞁ.), ⁊ ḃeaó na ṁꞃꞃꞃ́ꞃ ᵹ ꞁa hᴜꞁꞃꞃaᵹ aᵹ ꞁꞃꞃꞁ́ꞃ ꞃ́ ᵹꞃꞃꞃꞃꞁꞃ ꞃꞃꞁꞃꞃꞃ ꞃ́ꞃeꞃꞃ́. ṁaꞃꞃꞃ ꞁeᵹ na ꞃꞃꞃꞃꞃꞃꞃaꞃꞃꞃ eꞁó, Ꞽꞃ aᵹ Ꞽᵹꞃꞃó́aꞃó ꞁeaꞃ, aꞃ ꞁ́ꞁ aon íaꞁꞁ aᵹaꞃ ꞃaꞃ a ꞁuꞃ ꞃꞃᵹam ᵹo ᵹꞃꞃꞃꞃeaꞃ "Sᵹoꞁᵹꞁaꞃ" i ꞃ꞊ꞁó, ⁊ ᵹo ᵹꞃꞃoꞃꞃꞃꞃꞃꞃ́ꞃeaꞃ é.

Tá ꞃꞃꞁ aᵹam ᵹo ḃꞼꞃꞁ ꞃꞃꞃ Ꞽꞃꞃꞃ ⁊ ᵹo ꞃꞃꞃꞃꞃꞃꞃ ᵹo ṁaiꞃ.

beiꞃ ḃuaió ⁊ ḃeannaċꞃ
ṁꞃꞃꞃ ᵹo Ċara ᵹo ḃuan
Páꝺꞃaic ṁac Piaꞃaiꞃ.